THE WORLD OF
PROFESSIONAL GOLF

Mark H. McCormack's
Golf Annual 1970

The World of Professional Golf

Mark H. McCormack's
Golf Annual 1970

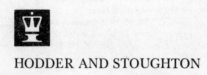

HODDER AND STOUGHTON

Leaḃarlanna Áta Cliaṫ

£ 27026

Aco. 70

Inv.

1247 55/-

Dept...................

Class... 796·352

Copyright © 1970 by International Management, Inc. First printed 1970.
ISBN 0 340 12896 8. All rights reserved. No part of this publication may
be reproduced or transmitted in any form or by any means, electronic or
mechanical including photocopy, recording, or any information storage
and retrieval system, without permission in writing from the publisher.
Typesetting by Print Origination Limited, Liverpool, and printed in Great
Britain for Hodder and Stoughton Limited, St. Paul's House, Warwick
Lane, London, E.C.4 by Compton Printing Limited, London and
Aylesbury.

To
Joseph C. Dey, Jr.
whose appointment as Commissioner
helped to bring stability to the
U. S. Tour in 1969

CONTENTS

APPENDIX

World Money List
World Stroke Averages
Champions and Contenders of 1969
United States Tour
Caribbean Tour
British Tour
European Tour
South African Tour
Far East Tour
Australian Tour
New Zealand Tour
Miscellaneous

ILLUSTRATIONS

First Section

Billy Casper at the Masters, leading the tournament[1]
Billy Casper blowing the tournament[1]
Tom Weiskopf[2]
George Knudson[3]
George Archer, the 1969 Masters champion[2]
Jim Colbert, Monsanto Open[1]
Tom Shaw, Doral Open[1]
Bunky Henry, National Airlines Open[1]
Larry Ziegler, Michigan Golf Classic[1]
Dave Hill, Buik Open[4]
Larry Hinson, Greater New Orleans Open[4]
Frank Beard, the big money winner, at the Westchester Classic[4]
Gene Littler, known as "Gene the Machine"[1]
Orville Moody, winner of U.S. Open[5]
Orville Moody, right on target[1]
Tony Jacklin[5]
Gary Player and Raymond Floyd playing in riot at the PGA Championship[4]
Raymond Floyd wins the PGA Championship[6]
The collapse of the year: Lee Trevino at the Alcan[1]
The weather of the year: Jack Nicklaus at the Crosby[1]
Bob Murphy mops up[7]
A resigned Miller Barber
A corpulent Orville Moody
Miller Barber in a fury[8]
Deane Beman using wood
Orville Moody putting, driving[8] and in tears[4]
View of Royal Birkdale course[9]
The row between Gallacher, Hill and Huggett at the Ryder Cup[10]
A foursome of Birkdale wives[11]
Brian Huggett is consoled by Dai Rees[10]
Arnold Palmer wins the first Heritage Golf Classic[4]
Arnold Palmer holing a putt[4] and missing a putt[4]

ILLUSTRATIONS

Second Section

KEY TO ACKNOWLEDGEMENTS

[1] United Press International Photo
[2] Neil Liefer, Sports Illustrated
[3] Eric Schwekardt
[4] Associated Press Photo
[5] Tony Tomsic
[6] Ira Block
[7] James Drake
[8] Walter Fooss
[9] Jerry Granham
[10] H. W. Neale
[11] Frank Gardner
[12] Mark Shearman
[13] Daily News
[14] The Australian
[15] Carl Roodman, Sports Illustrated
[16] Peter Lin, Sports Illustrated
[17] Allied Pix Services Inc.
[18] Sports Illustrated
[19] Curt Gunther
[20] Sheedy F. Long

1

The Year in Retrospect

A search for a star, and a presence named Palmer

So it is as it was, it concludes as it began, and I am somehow stunned. It is the end of 1969, and every time I pick up a magazine or Sunday newspaper I am confronted with a review of the decade. It is probably a necessary business, this dragging us back to reflect upon what we have wrought, but it is not the most pleasant way to spend the expiring hours of the Sixties. One cannot be much pleased with our achievements or avoid awareness of the erosion of our grand designs. I do not foresee, a decade or two from now, Americans looking back upon the Sixties and shouting, "Those were the days." Wait one moment, though. The decade is sitting here before us like a soggy Christmas pudding upon which the brandy refused to light, but there is one aspect of our human interests that must be ranked as a flaming success. Sport. And especially sport in the United States, where from a meager financial interest in 1960 television has turned on a golden flow that now exceeds $150,000,000 a year, where there is increasing leisure time and a fever to use it, where the enthusiasm and dedication devoted to play is unprecedented. Since this is a sports book, it must assess the Sixties to be the finest of times by far. Since it is a golf book, it must judge in a very specific and self-oriented fashion. Ask me about the Sixties and I must answer that there has never been a time like it; not the era of Mary Queen of Scots or Tom Morris or Walter Hagen or Bobby Jones or Ben Hogan—none of them. This was the decade of Arnold Palmer.

How astonishing it is that the fates, which do not deal much in sentiment, should arrange things so that the pro golf decade ended exactly as it began—with a blaze of Palmer birdies, with the Palmer personality dominating a sport and he and he alone led to riches in the television era. Having just, as I suggested, thrust aside with some annoyance various reviews of the Sixties, I do not myself intend to launch into an extended recapitulation of the ten years just past in golf. And after all, this book is an annual, its purpose being a

summary of the 1969 professional golf season around the world. Still, it is ironical that Palmer should have won the last two tournaments of 1969. Such a caprice demands at least one nostalgic glance back to 1960, for that was the year the Palmer era truly began. In 1960 Palmer won eight U.S. tour tournaments, a feat I doubt will be soon repeated. In one nine-tournament streak he finished first four times and was never worse than fifth. He finished in the top five in 19 of the 29 tournaments he played. This was the year he made famous the Palmer "charge," a heart-attack approach to golf that demanded the situation look hopeless before one really began to play. His last-round 65 which enabled him to come from seven strokes back and win the U.S. Open was the supreme example that the public will never forget, but there were others: he won at Palm Springs with a last-round 65, at Pensacola with a 67, at Hartford with a 66 that got him into a playoff which he won, at Mobile with a 65. Nothing seemed impossible for him, and nothing was. He brought golf to life as a mass spectator sport, and by the year's end he was the world's most famous athlete. Soon he was counting among the people he knew, kings and diplomats, presidents and power merchants. Within three years he would find himself with a family friend, Dwight Eisenhower, who would show up at the Palmer house in Latrobe, Pennsylvania, with a painting he had done that he wanted Palmer to have as a birthday present. The painting hangs in the Palmer living room today, its own testimony of the prestige and esteem that Palmer brought to golf.

So the decade began with Palmer. And it ended with Palmer scoring the only back-to-back win in 1969, the last one coming in the long-remembered fashion—seven strokes behind with just 17 holes to play—as if the clock had been turned back, or perhaps had never moved, and the cry of "charge" was not just a fond memory but a weekly call to arms. The clock has moved, though. There is more than one millionaire golfer now, and more than a few who are willing to look at Palmer at 40 and figure they can take him head to head. "Charge" is a battle cry, but also an echo. And enough of looking back. The Seventies are here.

As the decade drew toward a close, a certain golf phrase began to disappear: the Big Three. The supposition was that the trio of men who had dominated the sport through the mid-Sixties were, for one reason or another, losing their footing at the top. Numerous touring pros had said for years that the three—Palmer, Gary Player and Jack Nicklaus—were not particularly better or worse than any of them.

Regardless of the validity of that notion, upon which I will not comment, the decline of the trio would not cause any tears in competitive circles. Well, just when it seemed safest to suggest that there was not a Big Three any more, the statistics of golf sprung a trap. One thing is certain, a champion golfer's position in the pecking order is established by his performances in major championships. In this regard, Palmer, Player and Nicklaus collectively managed to win only one in 1967, one in 1968 and none in 1969. (1969 was the first year in the Sixties that the trio took none of the championships.) Indeed, by October of 1969, Gary Player was generally out of U.S. sight and mind—he played in only 16 U.S. events all year—Nicklaus was making his galleries blush with some of the worst golf shots of his illustrious career, and Palmer was so pained by both hip and putter that he seemed ready for instant relegation to the ranks of old, beloved television commentators. It was not the Frank Beards and Bill Caspers who had to worry about Palmer now, it was the Byron Nelsons and Cary Middlecoffs. Then, suddenly, Nicklaus won the Sahara, won the Kaiser and ought to have won at Hawaii where a balky putter left him second after an opening 63. Right after that, Palmer won his two. With this, the pair climbed far enough on the World Money List to join Player in the top 20. Meanwhile, Player himself had performed well enough internationally to turn in the world's second best stroke average (70,494 per round). All of which makes one conclude that the Big Three are the Big Three still. The last four years have been the lean years for the trio, but consider how fat the lean was. Here is a selection of ten top golfers with their annual World Stroke Averages and World Money List rankings from 1966 through 1969.

	Stroke Averages				Money List			
	66	67	68	69	66	67	68	69
Nicklaus	1	1	1	15	1	1	4	6
Casper	3	6	2	14	3	3	1	2
Player	19	3	3	2	29	21	8	7
Palmer	2	2	21	13	2	2	9	16
Boros	10	5	5	42	17	5	5	35
Beard	15	17	18	3	12	7	15	1
Archer	30	12	4	40	20	9	3	9
Littler	18	33	17	7	4	32	30	4
Brewer	17	9	36	30	7	4	18	29
Geiberger	21	13	8	44	8	12	16	53

From this I believe an obvious conclusion can be drawn. There is an aristocracy at the top that asserts itself consistently. It is the Big Three plus Casper. And there is no reason to think this situation will not continue for some years to come.

Before examining the performances and prospects of some of the players, there are a few general points worth making. Perhaps the most important is that for the good of golf the top four players need a challenge. Some young, stimulating personalities must begin to catch the public eye. In certain respects, the U.S. tour has never had a more promising future (see Chapter IV) but the lack of new, captivating personalities, ones who not only have flair but can win, is draining the interest in pro golf. It is all very well for we who shouted our lungs into lettuce shreds for Palmer in 1960 to argue that he can be the sustaining hero of the game for another ten years. Perhaps he can. We will grow older with him, and he will always be our hero. But the generation below us is entitled to, and will demand, a star or two of its own or are we to start looking at tour golf as an old foggies' game? Arnold's hair is thinning. Billy is grey at the temples. Gary yearns for the rancher's life. It has been 15 years since Gene was a young lion. The younger golfers are all aware of the opportunity, and aware too that part of what is involved is development of a public personality—doing a thing that catches on. It is not foolishness that has fat Bob Murphy turning up with a watermelon as his insignia or Orville Moody's sometimes tasteless promotors seizing upon the American eagle as an emblem for their sergeant. We live, as the cigarette commercial says, in a you-gotta-have-a-gimmick world. But you have to have a whole lot more as well to attain star status in this business, and year after year nobody seems to manage it. U.S. galleries look at a tournament field: No Palmer? No Nicklaus? No Player? No Casper? Forget it, Martha, we'll stay home and watch the ball game.

That is by way of explanation for the suggestion I will now make that the most important tournament for world golf in 1969 may have been the British Open. The reason was neither the venue, adequate but not earth-shaking Royal Lytham, nor the excitement, the winner played the last nine with victory fairly well in hand, but the age, personality and flair of the victor, Tony Jacklin. Needless to say, being the first British winner of the British Open since Max Faulkner in 1951 will endear Jacklin to his own small island for the next twenty years or so. Nor did it hurt that he was only 25, the son of a lorry driver and enhanced by the company of a most beautiful wife. He is small, and that helps, he has guts, and that helps, and he says what he thinks after thinking about what he is going to say, which helps. Now throw in good looks, a gee-whiz smile, a natural ebullience and an assertive determination to be the best golfer in the business and you begin to get something that draws crowds. And like it or not, professional golf in this day and age has one over-riding rationale—to draw crowds. From that, all manner of manna flows.

Advancing the financial causes of athletes, and especially golfers, is my business. I think that since I began with Arnold Palmer as my first client years ago I have become a fairly good judge of golf techniques, of who has promise and who has not. But I have become, in my own estimation at least, an even better judge of what might be called the star quality of an athlete. It is a characteristic that transcends athletic performance, and it is what sustains sport. I had thought for two years prior to the British Open that Tony Jacklin had this quality. If he could become a fine tour golfer, if he could win a major championship, I could envision the possibility that golf might have another major attraction.

I agreed to represent Tony. At about the same time I said publicly that the first Englishman to win the British Open in this era of celebrity golfers would have a fine chance of making a million dollars. I tried to quell the ever-nagging hope that the two events might quickly be combined. That Jacklin might win the British Open. It was too much to hope for. When he did, I think golf got a boost it could use, and I know Jacklin got one he could use. To date, Jacklin's British Open win has meant well over half a million dollars in contracts for him. The sources of this financial attention are numerous and growing. Dunlop will put out a line of autographed Tony Jacklin golf clubs and has signed Jacklin to a long-term equipment contract for the United Kingdom. Jacklin's golf exhibition fees have increased substantially, and foreign tours to Australia, Sweden and South Africa are being arranged. His publication contracts include a newspaper column, a biography, his story of the British Open and the biggest golf magazine contract ever signed in Great Britain. (Sometimes one thinks quickly, and optimistically, in this line of work.) I arranged for a newspaper series by Jacklin on "How I Won the British Open" before Tony teed off for his last round. It pays to be prepared. And when somebody handed Jacklin a bottle of champagne after his win, I quickly turned it around so that the label—Bollinger—would not show in the photographs. (Sure enough, a champagne company—Bollinger, in fact—approached us about endorsement possibilities.) Clothing contracts have been arranged, exclusive VIP golf days have been scheduled, Pan American World Airways has signed Jacklin to a large contract, British Colgate plans to use him for endorsements and Sea Island, a U.S. resort, has him under contract. Several Jacklin television projects are being prepared for use in the United Kingdom. By year's end Jacklin had received almost every British award for an athlete: Daily Express Sportsman of the Year Award, a BBC award, Golfer of the Year award, and numerous others, including a commendation from Prime Minister Harold Wilson. He was even invited to drive a golf ball across the Thames (George Washington made more impact with his dollar-across-the-Potomac bit). Through all of this Jacklin has remained a very level-headed young man. He is down-to-earth, somewhat in awe of what has happened and not inclined to be swept away by it. He does not think much about the pluses or minuses, but mainly about getting the job done, which is exactly as it should be.

This burst of enthusiasm for the athlete as a folk hero is new to the British golf world, but the pattern is not unfamiliar to me. It was much the same with Palmer, Player and Nicklaus. All had something special to offer, and I can only conclude some six months after Jacklin's win that he has this same touch of the special. Nor is it necessary to point out how worthless any such ephemeral quality is if the essential attribute—superb golf—does not accompany it. Jacklin helped himself no end, for example, by following up his British Open victory with his fantastic play in the Ryder Cup Matches, where a tie against the U.S. made 1969 the finest year British golf followers ever had.

Jacklin is to be set aside, remembered and watched with hope. But set aside nonetheless, for he was not one of 1969's best golfers. Not by a long tee shot. If somebody asked me to pick the golfer of the year, I would probably decline. The U.S. PGA, annually faced with that dilemma, showed the nature of the problem by selecting Orville Moody. I must say that Orville's reaction to this was in keeping with what a lot of other people thought: "Why me?" Certainly Frank Beard, the leading money winner in the U.S., and Dave Hill, the runner-up and winner of three tournaments, had to be asking, why not me? If you insist that I must play the man-of-the-year game, and if you will give me three strokes a side, I would have to vote for Gary Player. He trails Hill by only .071 on the World Stroke Average list and is seventh on the World Money List in spite of his extremely limited play in the golden fairways of the U.S.A. In his 16 U.S. performances he won once and finished in the top five a remarkable ten times. He won the Australian Open for the sixth time, the South African Open for the sixth time and the South African PGA. He is a world golfer, not just a U.S. golfer, and that is always worth a point or two in my book. The more U.S. players who try their hand overseas—and lose—the more we all can appreciate that people outside of the U.S. do play the game, and that it is not easy to win on some one else's turf. Then you turn that reasoning around and Player's performances in the U.S.—hardly his home turf—take on added weight. It is also interesting that Player continues to improve. Yes, I will argue that he was 1969's best.

Not the best were the other three that rule the game with him. Each had a stretch of success, and each had a year that is not going to fill very many pages in his scrapbook. In fact, each of them—Casper, Nicklaus, Palmer—may tear up the whole volume marked 1969. Casper began soundly, a continuation of his fine 1968 showing. By the time the Masters arrived, he was the top figure in the sport, and by the time the Masters was over, he hardly looked better than ordinary. The last day at Augusta must have affected his morale, protestations to the contrary notwithstanding. But after a dreary spell he came back well, and climaxed his year at the Alcan. That was where Lee Trevino came through with the blow-up of '69. A surprised Casper accepted the donation of the $55,000 winner's purse and gratefully moved to second on the World Money List, finally finishing with $170,501.16. Meanwhile Casper continued the policy he set for himself a year ago of trying to compete frequently overseas, and I cannot commend him enough for this. He was in contention in the British Open, but finished 25th after two bad rounds. He was not a factor in the British Dunlop Masters or the Bowmaker, and he did not perform too well in Australia, which reinforces my point about the difficulty of overseas play and suggests that while Casper is a fine golfer, he still may lack the versatility needed to win away from home.

I have tried to explain Nicklaus to myself for some years without success. I have tried to explain Nicklaus to Nicklaus with no success, either. But somewhere, sometime in 1969 a message from somebody must have got through. As fall arrived Jack had contributed to the U.S. tour such finishes as 24th, 25th, 28th, 36th, 47th, 52nd and a couple of missed cuts. He is far too good a golfer for such nonsense, yet over the past two years his game got progressively out of hand. I could not help but think he was losing interest, that though he insisted his dedication and self-discipline was extreme, it was less than that. By last summer Jack found himself getting a taste of something that Arnold has lived with for years, repeated judgments by the press that he was through. Poor Jack, the stories went. He did it all too young, and now he doesn't give a damn. Well, one day or night or morning or dawn Jack Nicklaus must have put his hand on the plump, contented Nicklaus stomach, looked into the round, serene Nicklaus face in the mirror and asked, "What in hell goes on here?" It was the question of the year. One thing that went, dramatically, thanks to a Weight Watchers' diet, was twenty pounds of Nicklaus. In fatter times Nicklaus had jovially told the press that he was not going to diet because "my doctor says I will just lose strength and stamina." He returned to the tour at Sahara lean, hungry and seriously thinking he might still be the year's leading money winner, and he closed out his year very strongly by finishing first, first, second and sixth. That burst put him sixth on the World Money list, silenced his critics and demonstrated to the unvoiced dismay of his fellow professionals that he is still the most menacing figure in pro golf. Nicklaus used to give the impression that some year when he felt like it he might just win them all—sweep the tour. The notion may yet return.

To consider Palmer is to reflect upon what attitude means in sport. Since 1963 there have been spates of publicity about Palmer being over the hill. There were theories that his swing was too hard and was sure to break down when his reflexes could no longer control it. There was the notion that he was the worst wedge player ever to attempt the tour. There was the claim that his attacking style of golf would in itself doom him. Sometimes I felt all the world was waiting for Arnold to vanish—poof! And then, in 1968 and through much of 1969, I began to wonder. Could it be that his hip injury—which was severe at times—would force him off the tour? Or that his putting—the thing that destroyed so many golfing greats—would finally become unbearable for him? I remember standing at the edge of a green during the Hawaiian Open, and by then it was the second week of November, and watching him miss an 18-incher, something I never would have believed a few years before. But even as this was happening—and it may have been the lowest point in his career—I felt there had been a change for the better in Arnold. The change had been coming for a long time. It involved recognition of several things, primary among them the fact that he could not win every tournament he played, that he could not shoot every day's lowest round, that every ball he hit did not have to streak straight for the hole. And with the recognition, and here was the hard part, had to come a return to the pleasure he once had in playing golf. He had fought the game for five years. In a way, I think he had come to hate it, as one must hate a tormentor. But golf will not submit to those who hate it. The game is too personal, and anger is the wrong emotion to bring to it. What Arnold needed, then, was a change in attitude, and I felt, as his detractors increased in 1969, that there were signs of such a change. He did, after all, turn 40, and that is not a statistic an athlete can hide from himself. He learned to pamper his hip when necessary, easing the swing, turning gentle on the follow-through. And the smiles, well, the smiles came more often. Arnold was giving life, and his game, a chance. The rewards came sooner than could have been expected. What was needed was a win, a victory that would give Arnold the conviction that this, too, was a winning way of golf. It came one tournament after Hawaii, in the Heritage at Hilton Head. He won on one of the most difficult courses the tour saw all year. He got in front and he stayed there. The word the press used to describe his last nine holes was "staggering home" as I recall, and I have no desire to amend that. Palmer labored and struggled and worked and worried but in the end he had the win. It was, without doubt, one of the most significant of his entire career, for it opened up the possibility in his own mind that he can continue to dominate the game in the 70s as he did in the 60s. And who is to say he cannot. I think golf is about to see a whole new Palmer, one that may mean as much to the sport, and win as much, as ever before. In fact, I will make a sporting wager: I bet Palmer wins more money in the Seventies than he did in the Sixties.

That is the state of golf's biggest names. And what about its biggest tour, the $6,000,000 extravaganza that the U.S. offers to those with the skill and nerve to take it? There are certain problems. The failure of a young player or two to assert himself is certainly one, as I have mentioned. Another is overexposure. The U.S. PGA, pleased by the fact that sponsors keep coming forward with large bundles of money and pleas for chances to hold golf tournaments is, I fear, lulling the PGA into a false sense of security. As is the case with many U.S. sports, the point of diminishing returns is being reached. Prize money cannot continue to go up. No matter how much prestige a major corporation feels it gets out of sponsoring a golf tournament, there comes a time when the financial involvement exceeds any conceivable return in advertising, product recognition or good will. In addition, television has probably committed something close to its top dollar to tour tournaments (the Masters, the U.S. Open and the PGA Championship are special cases, and TV revenues may increase there), which means the boodle from the networks will not continue to increase in giant leaps. Surely the reservoir of corporations willing to take on golf tournament sponsorship is not endless. It is true that 1970 will set an all-time record for U.S. tour purse money, but if any new minor league tour or set of satellite tournaments is excluded, I do not look for the 1971 money to top that in 1970. Contrary to everything that has happened in U.S. sport in the last ten years, I sense a levelling out in golf. This anti-boom may continue until the next big gold mine in the U.S. sporting sky: pay TV. I do not sense that the top men in American professional golf are much concerned about this. They see only ever-happier days ahead, and I certainly hope they are right. Meanwhile, permit me to wonder if the U.S. tour is not reacting something like a foursome of golfers did last summer at Berry Hill Golf Club near St. Louis, Missouri. They were rather startled as they stood on the ninth tee to see a small private airplane make an emergency landing in the middle of the fairway. After quickly checking to make sure the pilot was safe, the golfers impatiently pulled the plane into the rough and played through to the green. The touring pros see business as usual and boom as usual and are anxious to play through. Far better administration of the PGA tour may make their stance viable for a while yet, but whether the pros like it or not, something is out there in the middle of the fairway.

Meanwhile, it is business as usual, and business went unusually well for two tour regulars, Frank Beard and Dave Hill. Beard led the World Money List, winning $186,993.93, and finally turned in the kind of year that had been expected of him for some time. He is a money player. He was raised in the toughest of golfing fashions, hustling for dimes and quarters. He knows the odds, he figures them, and he plays them, no matter what his emotions might suggest. He evokes memories of Dow Finsterwald in the late Fifties and early Sixties. Dow always felt that second-place money lots of the time was better than first place one week and missing the cut for a month. Day in and day out, Frank Beard gets his share of the money and then some. If the breaks are with him and his putting touch is extra-super instead of its normal routine super, he will win far more than his share. This is what he did in 1969. It has been said so often that Beard himself feels the statement is a bore, but what he lacks is a killer instinct, the ability to polish off a foe or a field in full view of the bloodthirsty throng. I don't know why. Neither does he, for it is a trait that an accomplished assessor of the odds should have. His opponents hope he never gets it, for Frank does too many other things too well.

Dave Hill, who won America's Vardon trophy for the best scoring average on the U.S. tour besides leading the World Stroke Average list, has nothing in common with Beard, even when they both have a golf club in their hands. Tempestuous still at the age of 32, he won three tournaments, finished third on the World Money List, survived a suspension and a stormy Ryder Cup rules brawl and told Frank Beard, who has said the pro golf tour was nothing but hard work, that, in effect, Beard didn't know what real work was and that a man could hardly be better off than by being a successful touring pro. That's Dave. He speaks his mind and always has. Nor should the characteristic necessarily be criticized. At times it is refreshing. Hill played in outbursts, too. His three wins and lots of his money came in one birdie explosion between June 1 and July 20. Seven weeks and years of waiting made Hill a rich man, but in spite of his fine stroke average for the whole year, I do not expect him to improve much on his 1969 showing.

Three familiar names, Gene Littler, Julius Boros and Roberto de Vicenzo, can be considered together even though two of them, reaching into their late forties, finally began the decline long since expected of them. Boros fell from fifth to 35th on the World Money List, and de Vicenzo from 35th to 86th, as unsteady putting strokes undid them. Littler is thought of with them only because he, too, seems to have been so good for so long. Considerably younger, it was not at all surprising for him to come up with another good year, one that included two springtime wins, a victory in the CBS Golf Classic and a loss in the finals of the World Match Play to Bob Charles. Littler's backswing, club control and pace of life suggest that here is another Boros, a man who will take as much as he wants or needs from pro golf for another ten years. Also like Boros, he is a credit to the gracious nature of the game, which makes his probable longevity a true plus for the sport.

The next most interesting group of players is Raymond Floyd, George Archer and Tom Weiskopf. They finished 12th, ninth and rd respectively on the World Money List. Floyd, at the age of 27, at last beginning to realize some of the promise he displayed for years. He is colourful, he hits a long ball and his potential is great. This year he showed more than a hint of it when he won the PGA Championship in a duel with Gary Player and played the finest 72 holes of 1969 in the American Gold Classic at Firestone Country Club, where he won with rounds of 67-68-68-65—268. Firestone is among the most difficult courses that the U.S. pros see. Some touring professionals felt Floyd's record performance there compared with the best 72-hole scores of all time. Unhappily, it was typical of Floyd that after his PGA victory his golf turned routine. His difficulty has always been one of attitude—Raymond enjoys life, and his interest span is short. If and when he decides to truly keep his mind on his game, he could move right to the top echelon of the sport. Archer and Weiskopf both hit the peak of their seasons at the Masters, where they finished first and tied for second respectively. For Archer, winning a major championship was an important hurdle. It was his first, and now he may become more of a factor in similar events. The level of his play makes it something of a surprise that he has not won such a tournament before. This is the third straight year he has been in the top 10 on the World Money List. Weiskopf was less successful, dropping from second on the World Money List in 1968 to 23rd in 1969, but the pattern of his game was upset by a stint of military service and he can be expected to improve in 1970. If his temper steadies, which I am sure it will, he and Floyd must be considered the two youngish U.S. pros most likely to make a major breakthrough. (It is relevant, and says something about the fact that money winnings and prestige do not go hand in hand, to consider that I am suggesting Weiskopf might rise into the upper echelon of golf, when all he did in 1968 was win $172,000.)

Next come Lee Trevino and Orville Moody, who have a lot in common in addition to their remarkable U.S. Open wins in successive years. Both of them came out of nowhere to stagger the tour regulars, and both of them can hit the ball a lick. Trevino, flashing the kind of colour that the tour can stand a dash of, but only a dash, used 1969 to settle once and for all the question of whether he can play this game. He finished eighth on the World Money List, and would have been second, but for some nonsense in a bunker at the Alcan. He was 10th on the World Stroke Averages list. What else is there to say? Moody is not the golfer Trevino is ("I just hope Orville doesn't embarrass himself out there," said Mrs. Moody to the press the evening before her husband teed off in the World Series. He concealed any embarrassment by winning the $50,000 first prize). But Moody is more than adequate, and ought to win handsome amounts of money for some years.

Here is another pair, one to watch and one maybe not to. The quiet man of the year was Tommy Aaron, who finally won his first tournament, the Canadian Open. This is a big hurdle, especially for Aaron, who has been the bridesmaid of the tour for nine years. The win helped his confidence considerably, and his rather unnoticed position in the World Stroke Averages (sixth) suggests he deserves attention in 1970. Miller Barber, on the other hand, may have been shaken badly by his failure in three major championships in which he collapsed after being a strong contender. This kind of thing can have a lasting effect on a golfer's career. His fellow pros still have great respect for Barber's game, and talk of it often, but Miller will have to regroup himself.

Finally some footnotes. Down went some of 1968's rising stars: Bob Murphy, Bob Lunn and Dave Stockton. They only made $61,000 and $92,000. Pity them. With them was Gay Brewer, who has never recovered from winning the 1967 Masters, and behind them at the $37,000 level was Bob Goalby, who has struggled dreadfully since his 1968 Masters win. On the other hand, little Deane Beman did surprisingly well, winning $86,396, which is quite a feat for a man who has to use his fairway woods on holes that others play with a wedge, and so did erratic young Tom Shaw, who won two events and lots of money ($88,332) in a year that saw him miss the cut 15 times in 34 starts. Also missing the cut, to the point that he did not make the list of top 60 money winners on the U.S. tour and must therefore either take up the rabbit's role next year by playing pre-tournament qualifying rounds or try to get by on what special exemptions sponsors will grant him—and many will—is Doug Sanders. It is difficult to explain how a man who ranks seventh on the list of all-time money winners could see his game slip away so fast. As usual, putting troubles are a factor, but that does not account for a decline in two years from sixth on the World Money List to 56th. In the same difficult situation is another familiar U.S. tour figure, Mason Rudolph.

As each year goes by, I become increasingly convinced that professional golf is going to become a true world sport—perhaps the first. And as a result I pay great attention to how foreign golfers are faring with respect to those who compete on the infinitely richer

U.S. tour. They fare exceedingly well. Two foreign golfers rank among the top five money winners on the U.S. tour, Gary Player and Bruce Crampton, though Crampton is virtually an Australian expatriate to the U.S. New Zealand's Bob Charles had a fine year, winning $60,000 and the World Match Play while following very much of an international golf schedule. And Australia's Bruce Devlin made an excellent comeback from a dreadful 1968 to win $78,000 in the U.S. These U.S. money figures are important only because they mean the golfers concerned are in that all-important top-sixty ranking in the U.S. and thus do not face pre-tournament qualification problems. Nor will Jacklin for six months, thanks to his British Open victory. In a way, the opportunity to play on the U.S. tour becomes a vital consideration for a young foreign golfer. As Jacklin said after he won the British Open, the U.S. tour is the golf school where you really learn the game. That is where the lessons about playing under pressure are engraved in the mind for a lifetime. Two fine young foreign players, Peter Townsend and Bobby Cole, are trying to stay afloat on the U.S. tour now, and one can only hope that the struggle does not completely demoralize them before the breakthrough comes—which it surely will. The U.S. PGA is—understandably but unfortunately—not anxious to see large amounts of its purse money drifting away in the hands of foreigners. Over the years efforts have been made to, shall we say, make the problems faced by the foreign golfers as severe as possible. This is changing, but even last year the U.S. PGA lifted Townsend's player's card, along with those of some U.S. pros, when a review of their performances suggested they were not doing well enough. It was a crushing blow to Townsend, and totally unfair because the review considered nothing but his U.S. performances. Townsend, within that year, had won two British tour events, finished second in the Alcan, been the leading money winner on the British tour, won the Western Australian Open, finished second in the Australian Masters and Dunlop International, beaten Nicklaus, Palmer and Player in Australia's largest ever 36 hole pro-am, and been the leading money winner on the Australian tour. In short, his international credentials were substantial. Nor had he played that badly in the U.S., finishing in the money six times in fourteen tries. Numerous young U.S. pros who did not have their cards lifted had done worse. I appealed Townsend's case to U.S. PGA officials, who kindly reconsidered and his card was returned to him. Townsend responded by finishing out the year fairly well and winning $21,000 in the U.S. His immediate U.S. position is far from secure, but I have no doubt that on a world level he is one of the best young players in the game today. He is only 23, and his future is excellent. In the same situation, but with prospects that quake the mind, is South Africa's Bobby Cole. Bobby is now 21. He has no idea how he hits a golf ball or where it is going. But one thing is certain, it is going a long way. He is small, wiry, bubbly, appealing and can draw crowds like a Palmer or Player. I have on several occasions heard U.S. pros who have been paired with Cole say that this is the golfer who might break the game's all-time money marks in the next ten or 15 years. In 1969 his U.S. money total was like Townsend's, $21,000, largely because Cole always had one bad round with his good ones. That will end, and may end soon.

There are some other young golfers whose names must be mentioned so that they will be all the more familiar when they crop up in big type a few years hence. Scotland has Bernard Gallacher, 20, who would have been the toast of the British golf press had he not emerged into prominence the same year Jacklin won the British Open. England has Brian Barnes, 24, who will try the U.S. tour in 1970. And South Africa, which seems to start its pros as children and have them world-wise by their early twenties, has a 16-year-old named Dale Hayes who is setting forth on the path of Bobby Cole and Gary Player. In 1969 Hayes almost won the German Open, reached the semi-finals in the British Amateur, did well in several South African events and hit the ball in a fashion that suggests he has an exceptional future.

So much for the year in general. Aside from the big boom in Britain—which reached immense dimensions in 1970 with the announcement of an astonishing £70,000 tournament at Nottingham in September—it was a trendless year. Financially, everything was a little bit better, aesthetically a little bit worse. It was a year of marking time. The world's unease came to the fairways when Gary Player was attacked by protestors at the U.S. PGA Championship. It was to Player's great credit that he kept cool, and who is to say he may not face more of the same as his country's racial policies increasingly become an international cause. It is fervently to be hoped that dissident groups do not increase their attacks on sports events as a method of getting their various causes before the public. But if that is to be the way of things, it hardly can be prevented. Meanwhile, President Nixon has been giving away autographed golf balls to celebrities and inviting the U.S. Ryder Cup team to the White House, where none of them sank their putts on the Presidential putting green, and telephoning winners in locker rooms. I guess all this is traditional and hardly can be prevented either, but somehow as the Sixties end I find myself wishing not only that protest groups would leave sports alone, but that politicians would keep their hands off for a while, too. While I'm at it, I also wish the Golden Skillett Company of White Plains, New York, had not announced that the latest product for its chain of stores was a special package of cold fried chicken put up for golfers. It is guaranteed to stay tasty for hours in a golf bag. I have this mental picture of aluminium foil and chicken bones strewn around the 10th green and a greasy towel on the ball-washer at 11. I sag ever lower in my chair. Feel free to play through.

This small fit of distemper can be countered by the second annual presentation of the Mark H. McCormack provoker of dispute in club, tavern or pub the world over. Guaranteed to start a golfer's argument anywhere, it is an evaluation system designed to determine the 25 best players in the world today, and in what order they rank. The system provides a method for comparing golfers regardless of their stroke averages or their position on a money list. What it measures is the single most important thing a golfer should be judged on: performance. Two premises are involved. First, no consideration is made for bad luck, injuries, military conscription, wives, laziness and similar vagaries of fortune. It is assumed that all such things balance out. Second, it must be agreed that the position a golfer deserves in his sport today is based to a degree on his performance in previous years. I feel three years is the proper time span, with the year most recently completed the most important one, the previous year next and the third year at least. With these assumptions made, it is now necessary to give a point rating for each tournament or type of tournament, depending on the prestige of the title, the strength of the field and the money at stake. This is the heart of the system and it involves certain arbitrary judgements, but all ones that can be logically defended. What evolves is four categories of tournaments. The first category is made up of the U.S. Open, the Masters and the British Open. Next come the strongest U.S. events. These are determined by how many of the 15 top men on the U.S. money list were entered in the event. The top category had 13 to 15, the next 10 to 12 and the last 9 or fewer. Into each of these three groups were put the foreign events. In general, foreign open championships and events on the British tour were ranked with the middle-class U.S. tour tournaments and other foreign events were ranked with the lowest group of U.S. events. Such tournaments as the World Match Play, World Cup, World Series of Golf, etc., were generally ranked with the top U.S. tour events.

With the categories established, points were assigned to each category. The top ten finishers would get points in a U.S. Open class of tournament, for example, but in a Class 4 event only the top three finishers would get points. And no matter what the event, I decided, the winner of a U.S. tour or international tournament deserved a bonus, which is five points. Broken down in detail, the system looks like this:

FOR 1967

Class 1 Events: Top 10 finishers—15 points for winning, 14 for second, down to 6 for 10th.

Class 2 Events: Top 8 finishers—10 points for winning, 9 for second, down to 3 for 8th.

Class 3 Events: Top 6 finishers—6 points for winning, 5 for second, down to 1 for 6th.

Class 4 Events: Top 3 finishers—3 points for winning, 2 for second, and 1 for 3rd.

FOR 1968

Class 1 Events: Top 10 finishers—20 to 11 points
Class 2 Events: Top 8 finishers—15 to 8 points
Class 3 Events: Top 6 finishers—10 to 5 points
Class 4 Events: Top 3 finishers—5 to 3 points

FOR 1969

Class 1 Events: Top 10 finishers—26 to 16 points
Class 2 Events: Top 8 finishers—20 to 13 points
Class 3 Events: Top 6 finishers—15 to 10 points
Class 4 Events: Top 3 finishers—7 to 5 points

That is the system. And now, who are the top 25 golfers today? Here they are, in order.

1	Jack Nicklaus, *U.S.* ($574,738.70)	164.5	181.5	133.5	479.5
2	Gary Player, *S. Africa* ($339,452.65)	56.5	160	163.5	380
3	Bill Casper, *U.S.* ($560,187.05)	76.5	146.5	129	352
4	Arnold Palmer, *U.S.* ($438,522.87)	162.5	65.5	67	295
5	Bob Charles, *N. Zealand* ($279,589.54)	50.5	118	111.5	280
6	Frank Beard, *U.S.* ($414,375.63)	48	79	125.5	252.5
7	George Archer, *U.S.* ($403,921.81)	53.5	96	102	251.5
8	Lee Trevino, *U.S.* ($315,026.53)	16.5	99.5	132.5	248.5
9	Miller Barber, *U.S.* ($300,488.73)	30	65.5	112.5	208
10	Dan Sikes, *U.S.* ($339,858.56)	50.5	71	70.5	192
11	Brian Huggett, *G. Britain* ($44,108.92)	26.5	67.5	97.5	191.5
12	Julius Boros, *U.S.* ($355,646.53)	77.5	90.5	13	181

13	Kel Nagle, *Australia* ($70,531.96)	39	64.5	75	178.5
14	Bruce Crampton, *Australia* ($278,067.29)	5.5	61	107	173.5
15	Tom Weiskopf, *U.S.* ($305,613.08)	3.5	98.5	71	173
16	Peter Butler, *G. Britain* ($40,262.41)	23.5	79.5	69.5	172.5
T17	Tommy Aaron, *U.S.* ($248,115.64)	19.5	42.5	104	166
	Bruce Devlin, *Australia* ($168,584.41)	15	49.5	101.5	166
	Christie O'Connor, *G. Brit.* ($36,881.57)	17.5	43	105.5	166
20	Bert Yancey, *U.S.* ($238,537.35)	35.5	73	52	160.5
21	Roberto de Vicenzo, *Argen* ($140,244.75)	40.5	60	59.5	160
22	Gene Littler, *U.S.* ($268,549.25)	11	24.5	123.5	159
23	Gay Brewer, *U.S.* ($317,369.80)	60.5	41	56	157.5
24	Neil Coles, *Great Britain* ($30,600.20)	21.5	84	51	156.5
25	Cobie Legrange, *S. Africa* ($44,895.16)	33	54	66.5	153.5

As the first presentation of these ratings showed for the 1968 season, Nicklaus, Player, Casper and Palmer—same four but in slightly different order this time—remain the leading players. But the gap is narrowing.

Gary gained just three rating points for 1967-68-69 over 1966-67-68, yet moved from fourth to second place, as the other three, because of their less successful 1969 seasons, accumulated considerably fewer points this time. Nicklaus had 623.5 points in the first ratings, 479.5 after 1969, but still held first place by almost 100 points.

With the heaviest weighting on the most recent year, Beard, Archer, Trevino and Barber capitalized on their strong 1969 seasons to take positions six through nine behind the consistent Bob Charles. Archer didn't even make the list of 25 after the 1968 campaign. On the other hand, Dave Hill, the No. 2 money-winner on the 1969 U.S. tour, had done so little in the two previous years that he still didn't muster enough points to make the top 25 list. Nor did U.S. Open champion Moody nor PGA champion Floyd.

Crampton, Aaron and Littler of the U.S., Britons Brian Huggett and Peter Butler and Ireland's Christie O'Connor are other newcomers to the ratings, as others such as Peter Thomson, Neil Coles and Sanders dropped out after indifferent-to-poor 1969 seasons. Even the victory in the British Open and its heavy point yield were not enough to offset Jacklin's slow 1969 start in the U.S. and keep him in the rankings. You can expect him back, though. Boros fell from sixth to 12th after his winless 1969 produced just 13 points for the year.

Notice, finally, that 11 of the 25 players in these ratings hail from countries other than the United States, one further evidence of the international growth of the game.

2

The Masters

After one in the water, one for a win

Within hours after it was over one American magazine was dubbing it Dullsville and another was calling it the Giveaway Masters, and I will confess that after watching the last day of play, which probably had more awful golf shots laid cleek to mashie than you could see in the fifth flight of the Royal Muirwick and St. Mary's club championship, the writers had a point. You can watch the contenders in one of the world's most honored golf events hit into just so many pine trees and yank approaches into just so many bunkers before you wish you were out there with a club yourself. You expect, after all, a little dash, a little flair, on the part of any champion that you are about to throw your arm and a green coat around, and on the part of would-be champions, too. But I demur from any deeply pessimistic view of the 1969 Masters Championship. I offer two reasons for enjoying this Masters. One is small, but to me cogent: namely that from the 15th tee on, the true contenders—and there were five of them—hit only two splendid golf shots. Both were struck by the man who won, George Archer, and they came immediately after he had hit bad shots that might well have squelched his hopes and shaken his nerve. Repeatedly, Bill Casper, Tom Weiskopf, Charles Coody and George Knudson had opportunities, and they could not come through. The man who did come through under pressure won, and that is the way the sport should be. The second reason that the 1969 Masters had much to offer is more compelling. The tournament presented, for all who cared to look, an almost frightening portrayal of the philosophy of the conservative, and how so often this availeth a man nought, even when the man is a Mormon preacher. In the eyes of whose who advocate boldness—and many athletes feel no other attitude will win in any sport—Casper was, from the moment he took his first-round lead with an opening 66, a man rolling a boulder up a mountain. The higher he went, the tougher things got, and the more certain his downfall became. So, far from being dull, I found the 1969 Masters absorbing.

I have dealt earlier with what was the basic problem—or excitement—of the year in professional golf, namely that the overall quality of play increased while the performance of the superstars, with the exception of Gary Player, slipped. The result was a formless mishmash of winners, few of whom were particularly stimulating and none of whom was able to take command or seize any significant share of public adulation. That this trend would prevail was clear by the time of the Masters. The first 13 tournaments of the year were won by different golfers. It was not until the week before the Masters that 38 year-old Gene Littler became the first man to win two events. Four of the previous five tournaments, worth a total of $565,000, were taken by such non-celebrities as Tom Shaw, Ken Still, Jim Colbert, and Bunky Henry. What was more, in view of the way most of the famous names in the game were playing, it was difficult to pick a favorite for the Masters.

Looking for winners should not be difficult at Augusta because the field is so small. This year a total of 85 teed off, but if you exercised the wildest stretch of the imagination you would say only 56 of them had the slightest chance to win. People like Gene Sarazen or Henry Picard weren't going to take the $20,000 first prize. The size of the field at Augusta has long been a sore point with touring pros, who are annoyed that so many amateurs are invited (nine this year) and so many foreigners (20). The touring pros argue that at least the top 60 money winners on the U.S. tour should be invited. Bob Jones and Clifford Roberts, the men who founded and run the Masters, say absolutely no, and they are never going to change their minds. "We are always talking with Roberts, trying to get the tour winners and better players into the tournament, but he won't budge. It's a losing battle," said Doug Ford shortly before this year's Masters. It is such a losing battle, in fact, that there were strong rumors that representatives of the players went to Masters representatives last winter and hinted the Masters might be boycotted if the field was not enlarged. Masters officials held a meeting and there was a surprisingly strong sentiment among the club members of Augusta National to drop the tournament completely. At least that's the story I hear. The notion was that professional golf has become so big that the Masters is losing its distinction and charm. If, on top of this, the players were going to be insistent about having too many things their own way, why bother with the Masters at all? After this attitude got whispered back to the players on the tour, there was far less talk about telling Cliff Roberts whom he could invite to his tournament.

I represent, in various capacities, quite a number of young golfers, yet I have long agreed with Roberts that part of the distinction of the Masters is its small field, large foreign representation and inclusion of several amateurs. For the first time, however, I see something that might give traditionalists such as Roberts and myself a moment's pause. Results on the tour in the last two years indicate that as the general level of play increases the era of golf superstars may be vanishing. As a result, it is true that lots of players who could win the Masters do not get into the field. But this is hardly an intolerable situation; it is life. Lots of people who could be corporation presidents don't get that chance either. On the other hand, the rationale behind the Masters invitation list has been that it certainly would include golfers whose quality of play would almost always insure a distinguished champion. The unstated theory was that the average tour player could not handle the combination of the Augusta course and the Masters pressure sufficiently well to make him a possible winner. Thus when he was excluded from the field, a possible champion was not being excluded. The men who won were always championship-level golfers. When this viewpoint is tested by checking the list of Augusta winners, it is almost shocking to find to what degree they were indeed masters of the game. Let's take a look. From 1934, when the tournament began, to 1955 the Masters was won by Smith, Sarazen, Smith, Nelson, Picard, Guldahl, Demaret, Wood, Nelson, Keiser, Demaret, Harmon, Snead, Demaret, Hogan, Snead, Hogan, Snead. Of those, one could raise only the slightest question about the credentials of one—Herman Keiser. Through the next five years the winners were Middlecoff, Burke, Ford, Palmer and Wall. This group may look less distinguished, but Middlecoff, Ford and Wall were all at the very top of the sport in their victory years and Palmer proved later that he certainly belonged in any golf company. Next, from 1960 through 1966, there comes quite a string: Palmer, Player, Palmer, Nicklaus, Palmer, Nicklaus, Nicklaus. No questions there. So in thirty years there were only two champions whose credentials were not superior. But does it mean anything that to this list you now add Brewer, Goalby, Archer? If this kind of thoroughly competent but hardly overwhelming professional can now win the Masters year after year, perhaps a few more spots ought to be opened up for golfers just like them who do not meet one of the ten Qualifications for Invitation that the Masters applies to U.S. professionals. I do not want to see any such change made. I am just saying that the argument is now gathering a trace of validity.

But let us get back to the business at hand. Who could win in 1969? In recent years the first thought had to be Nicklaus, but Jack said it pretty well himself at Jacksonville when he told reporters, "I hit the ball and come up dry." Dry he was, and you could take a bath betting on him. Never had he suffered a worse winter and his preparation plans for Augusta did not stir the imagination, involving as they did a vacation in the Bahamas. But Jack always does things his own way. He told me just before the Masters that he had never come into the tournament feeling better, that "if the weather conditions are right I honestly feel capable of shooting four 66s. I have worked harder than I have since 1965 (the year he set the Masters scoring record of 271)." It was true that Jack had played in as many tournaments as he usually does on the winter tour—seven, compared to six in 1968 and seven in 1967—but even after three practice-round 69s. I would have hesitated to risk the family savings on him winning his third Masters in five years.

However, to look elsewhere meant consultations with specialists; medical specialists. Not since Sherman marched through Georgia had Augusta seen so many walking wounded. Palmer had been forced off the tour for a rest because of his ailing hip. Lee Trevino had a thumb and a half on his left hand, having jammed the digit badly several weeks before. Bruce Devlin was just recovering from pneumonia. Archer had intestinal flu. Casper's hands were swollen because of an allergic reaction to a chemical spray two weeks before. Miller Barber had a left thumb that made Trevino's look like a pinkie, and Barber did not even know what caused it. Add to this the fact that nobody was playing good golf anyway and you could see two things: 1) how Bunky Henry had won the $40,000 first prize in the National Airlines tournament, and 2) that nobody at all could win the Masters.

I shouldn't say nobody. I did have a favorite, Gary Player, who had played in only four U.S. tournaments since the first of the year but seemed to be hitting the ball very well. I lived with Gary and Bob Charles at Augusta, and I was never more confident that Player would have a fine Masters than I was the night before play began. Instead, he played badly, which figures for a Masters that proved to be as perverse as this one.

When you have a sports event such as the Masters, one that is played at the same place with many of the same athletes involved year after year, you tend to pay attention to what your instincts tell you with respect to mood and attitude. It is like being in your own house and hearing an unfamiliar sound, an unexpected twist of the wind that causes some new creak and stops the orderly flow of thoughts within the mind. What is it? Ah? Northeast wind, perhaps. Rain coming. That's all. A stranger would have noticed, filed the information, and reacted with a slight twinge of concern. As I arrived at Augusta National on the morning of the first day of play, I had something of the same sensation. I drove past the boys carrying the signs that said, "I need a ticket"—comforting reminders of golf's success—and began to wonder if this wasn't going to be a different kind of Masters. I had been here a few days now, living with Charles and Player and talking with Jack and Arnold and several of the younger golfers, and there must have been an under-current to what they said—the unexpected shift of wind. Now, as I arrived at the course, the idea came full-blown: the first day was going to be a wild one. All at once, the golfing strategy at Augusta was about to change. The rules in the past, the pattern of play that a man set for himself, was to spend the early days getting into position. This was a holding action, basically conservative and perfectly wise when the field is small and the number of possible winners so limited. A year ago the first three rounds of the Masters had been careful tedium piled on cautious yawn. But when the time came for the men in good positions to move on the last day, *everybody* moved. Player, the third-round leader, shot par and ended up only tied for 7th with four other people. Bruce Devlin and Frank Beard had been in fine shape, but they didn't get close to the green coat with a 69 and 70. All this was because Bob Goalby was shooting a 66, Roberto de Vicenzo was posting what would have been a 65 but for his scoreboard slip (this year, in spite of saying it planned no changes around the 18th green, Masters officials had a de Vicenzo memorial tent where players could assess their scores in privacy, and with help) and Bert Yancey was shooting a 65. This lesson was not lost on the field. Indeed, it reflected what has been happening throughout the U.S. tour. You can't play position golf early in a tournament any more. Not even the Masters. What I had noticed as play began this year was tension. I had never seen this kind of tension early at Augusta. Everybody was determined to start fast.

Let the doubters protest, I say in golf you can feel tension, you can taste it. It was everywhere Thursday morning as I started up on the first fairway much earlier than usual, spurred on by this conviction that things were about to happen. Quickly the pressure showed itself. Bert Yancey needed two to get out of a bunker on the second hole. Art Wall did the same thing at four. Casper birdied the first hole from 12 feet, and then hooked his tee shot on two down past a refreshment stand and into the deep woods. The golfers call that spot The Delta Ticket Counter. They say when you hit the ball down there you call Delta Airlines for reservations, because you sure are going to miss the cut. (Such places don't bother Casper. He chipped out and scrambled to a par 5). Palmer bunkered his second shot on two and exploded across the green into another bunker. Twice in 10 minutes golfers pitched over the third green, and then pitched back completely over it and down a bank coming the other way. All the stops were out—and the nerves too.

If sic-'em-from-the-start golf is going to be played, the course must be receptive to it, and Augusta National was. The fairways were either slightly long or fine, depending on the score of whom you talked to. The weather was perfect, as it was for the entire four days of the tournament. But the key factor was the greens. Augusta has been working to return its greens to the firmness they had in the early post-war years. As the course has aged, the greens have gotten somewhat rich and soft. Too often, balls can be driven right to the flag, with a minimum of finesse involved in keeping the approach shot under control. The U.S. tour has 100 big, strong boys who glory in hanging the ball just that way, yet don't know much about the fine points of the game that makes them rich. But this year, thanks mainly to a new type of brush in the mowers, Augusta had its greens more the way it wants them. They were hard, fast and true as true can be. Putts had to be stroked firmly, yet hitting them firmly was dangerous, just as it should be. Approach shots needed considerable finesse. In short, conditions favored the good golfers, and especially the good putters. (Good putters? Let's see now. How about Casper? Or maybe Archer as a winner?) British writer Pat Ward-Thomas looked over the course and observed with a smile: "They're returning to the proper form of the sport; the way it is played in Scotland."

The combination of the conditions and the new attitude led to the greatest one-day assault on par in the history of the Masters. The red sub-par numbers on the scoreboard took over from the more usual green almost immediately and stayed there for the day as 25 players were under par 72, and seven others matched that figure. The leader was Casper, in with a 66. One stroke back was Archer and Devlin, with Nicklaus at 68.

In addition to the scoring, the day offered some other moments. Each time defending champion Bob Goalby walked onto a green he received a fine ovation, probably the largest of the day at that particular spot. Augusta galleries truly care about their golf, and the feelings of their golfers. Nobody had forgotten the sad scene of a year ago when Goalby found himself a Masters winner, but in a way only half a winner because Roberto de Vicenzo lost his playoff opportunity through his famous scoring error. So now there was a scoring tent, and though it was never mentioned by Masters officials, who usually call all changes to the attention of the press, there also was a new scorecard in use this year. Across the top of the card was a perforated segment. On it the golfer kept his own hole-by-hole score. He could then tear that off and have it to compare with what his playing partner had scored for him. Goalby must have appreciated the applause of the gallery. He had not won a tournament since last year's Masters, and it was good for him to know that he was not considered a tainted champion. Quite the contrary.

There could hardly be such a thing as a Masters that did not take Palmer into consideration, and this one certainly did. A practice round 63 early in the week suggested that Arnold's hip was not bothering him, and it wasn't. Arnold was there, and he was ready to play, but the verve was not there. And because the proper level of excitement would not come, the tension that it always helped balance was greater than ever. As each year passes, Arnold wants to win this championship more. But as you get older, you know what can go wrong, you realize how tough the competition really is, and fear sneaks in around the edges. You can put it into words by saying you can't seem to "get up". This made things doubly difficult for Arnold on an opening day in which the field was dedicated to destroying the Augusta National course. And finally—almost ironically—Palmer was paired with the national amateur champion, Bruce Fleisher, a young, appealing, long-hitting happy youngster who shot a 69 and displayed enough of the traits of the old Palmer to attract his own wiggly gallery of youth. In a single day Augusta bloomed with a Fleisher cult, while Palmer was an elder statesman shooting a 73. Fleisher was fun, but none of the wise ones were surprised when he went on to shoot 75-76-80. Nor was there much shock when Arnold shot 75 on the second day and just made the cut. (Late Friday afternoon Winnie stood in front of the big Masters scoreboard searching for the figures that would show what the cut might be and saying, "I hope we don't miss it two years in a row. That would be just too much.")

Another sight of the first day was Nicklaus with billowing golden hair. Nicklaus could never be accused of being mod—in fact he always rather likes his Ohio State crewcut—but as hair styles changed he let his grow a little. And then at the Doral Open a television announcer commented on Jack Nicklaus walking up the 18th fairway with the tournament winner, youthful Tommy Shaw. "They look enough alike to be father and son," said the announcer. Needless to say, Jack's friends could hardly wait to tell old Jack about his image as an ancient . . . and tell him . . . and tell him. Well, by Masters time Jack's hair was nearing Beatle length, at least by his former standards, and was the subject of a lot of Nicklaus family attention. "He has it fluff-dried," said Barbara Nicklaus. "Can you imagine that? " Jack's golf was the reverse of his hair; first a little flamboyant and then dull. His first two shots of the '69 Masters hit trees, but he survived and was not displeased with his 68. On Friday, however, he offered up one of his most lackluster rounds in years, a 75 that he described as "just awful." He added a 72—76 that hardly mattered to finish tied for 24th on a course where he should never finish out of the top five.

Finally there was Player. Gary was the last of the big names to tee off, not starting until nearly two in the afternoon and finishing when the shadows were strung out across the fairways and the dying sunlight flashed through the sprinklers that had been running for an hour on the earlier holes. Player began his 1969 Masters with a birdie, and from that moment on it was all downhill. I cannot account for his performance and neither can he. Essentially, his putting was frightful, and as can so often happen, poor putting began to affect the rest of his game. The moment I choose to remember is the scene of him on 13 deciding to use an iron to fly over the creek and reach the green in two on this par-5 hole. There was a time when this hole and the 15th, a similar par 5 with a large pond guarding the green, were fine tests of a golfer's nerve. Occasionally you would see a big hitter decide to go for the green after a long drive, but only occasionally. Now going for those greens in two has become routine. Older golfers do it (Snead, Lionel Hebert), middle-aged middle-hitters do it (Littler, January), and young golfers consider it a catastrophe when they can't try for an eagle. Indeed, the last word on going for these greens in two was the sight of mini-hitter Deane

Beman risking it—and with an iron, no less. (He was short.) In five years something has changed in the nature of either the holes, the game, or both, to permit this attacking style. At any rate, Player came into 13 two over par and with a look on his face that suggested the Lord had better stop loafing around Up There and get down here where he was needed. Gary hit a good drive, and you could see his hopes flutter; perhaps he could finish with three birdies for a 69. He looked over his second shot with great care, and then swung into the ball in dreadful fashion, yanking it far to the left. It went over a creek, behind a scoreboard and into a bank blanketed with beautiful four-foot high azalea bushes. The flowers were a deep pink, and in the fading light Gary looked artistically splendid rummaging around in the blooms for his ball.

By all rights we should just leave him there, but Gary eventually emerged, finished with a 74, shot 70 the next day and still wasn't out of it. Then on Saturday he had a 75 that he may never forget. He was paired with George Archer, who shot a 69 to move within a stroke of the leader, Casper. Player hit the ball well, quite well, but on and around the greens, nothing worked. When he missed a two-footer to double bogey 18 he walked straight over to the practice green and there, with furious concentration, stroked two-foot putts for half an hour. That night Gary had no desire to hide his disappointment. "It's a strange game," he said. "A very strange game, I tell you. I had to beat George by 14 strokes today. I hit the ball that much better than he did. You wouldn't believe some of his shots. But you wouldn't believe his putting either. It was fantastic." I always mark this kind of talk. I used to hear it so much about Palmer, how he played so awfully but made all his putts and beat everybody by a ton. Player said something else that night which was to prove very apt the next day. We were discussing Casper, how he had yet to go for one of the back-nine par 5s in two, and how he was playing every shot so safely. Player was terse on the subject. All he said was, "He can't play that way and win. It can't be done."

There have been other days when Augusta National has been mistreated by golfers, and always the reaction has been the same. The course is toughened up by selection of more difficult pin placements, and all at once the tabby is a tiger again. Never was this shown more clearly than in the 1969 Masters. On Thursday night the tournament committee took a long look at the names of those 25 golfers under par and decided to impose some "speed limits" on the course. Often such a process brings cries of protest from the golfers, but I agree with what the Masters does. Look at it this way. You want your course to be a test that presses the ability of the best players to meritorious limits, weeds out the second-best, and yet is not so difficult that it spoils the game and forces everybody to play for bogies. Because of changing grass and weather conditions, the point at which a course is a good test but not unfair can be difficult to determine. The Masters people had made a mistake with their pin placements Thursday morning. The positions were—probably by two or three placements, that's all—too easy. Now Augusta wanted to take those two or three shots back, and it did. Art Wall explained it well to Dick Taylor of *Golf World*. "The tournament committee establishes scoring here," said Wall. "It's up to the players to decide, knowing their games, if they want to challenge the committee's standards of play, as established by the pin placements and tee markers."

I keep wanting to come back to the psychology of aggression, for here we see it again as applied to golf. The players knew that the committee was going to tighten up the course. They knew nothing unfair would be done—and indeed, there was hardly a complaint about Friday's pin positions, just the mournful cry that nobody could ever remember them being more difficult—but they felt they now had to go on the defensive. The situation is something like that of a heavyweight contender who has just busted the champion right on the nose in the first round. He is pleased, but a voice deep inside is wondering if it had been a very smart thing to do. The combination of the new pin positions and the increasing firmness of the greens—they got drier and faster day by day—left the thinking player with no real options. He felt he had to turn conservative, to play for his pars, to try to birdie 13 and 15 by reaching the green in two, and to hope for the best. Nothing else made any sense, for to hit for the pin now was to beg for bogies amid the valleys and humps of Augusta's greens. The result of such defensiveness by a field of golfers is that they usually play a little worse than they should. The lack of aggressiveness with the approach shots translates itself into the rest of the game as well—the five-footers don't drop, the chip shots don't get snug to the pin, and suddenly the man who shot 68 on Thursday and wants a nice safe 71 on Friday ends up with a 75.

That is what happened on the second day at Augusta. Where there had been 11 rounds in the 60s on Thursday, there were only four on Friday, two of those by amateurs who probably didn't know enough to be intimidated by the course. A round that was to have meaning was a 68 by Charles Coody, but the big Texan had opened with a 74 and knew he had to do something constructive to get into the game. Casper did exactly what he wanted to; he shot a 71 for a 137 that left him tied for the lead with Devlin, who had followed his opening 67 with a 70. Of the golfers who were to finish in the top ten, half were over par on this day: Archer, Knudson, January, and Lionel Hebert at 73 and Littler at 75.

Having made its point, Augusta shifted its pins into more amiable locations on Saturday, but the players reacted like a child who had put his hand on a hot stove: they had been burned, and weren't anxious to try again. So, in perfect weather once more, scores stayed comparatively high. One of the highest was a 76 by Devlin, who frankly confessed later that the pressure of being tied for the lead bothered him. Another interesting development was the play of Casper, who was being treated as if he had already won the tournament ("If Casper was out of it we'd have a chance," said Dan Sikes after Saturday's round), but whose play was getting ragged around the edges. Naturally, his opponents had not seen Casper's round, but they might have taken heart if they had. After a routine par on the first hole, Casper drove into the woods on two, but saved his par. He was bunkered on three, over the green on four, off the green on six, and every time he scrambled for a par. He bogied seven and drove into the bunker on eight. A lesser man might easily have been par in for a 41 at this point. But it is a trait of Casper's game that he almost always survives his worst play. Now he suddenly sank a fine putt for a birdie on 9, birdied the difficult 10th and was headed in for a 36–35 – 71 and a one-stroke lead over Archer.

It was Archer who brought in the other meaningful round in this routine day. He was out in 37 and seemed out of the tournament, too, but at 13 he got the kind of lift that Augusta can give you when you go for those par 5s in two. On in two, he picked up a birdie. Then on 15 he went for the green in two, made it, and dropped a 35-footer for an eagle. A birdie at 17 brought him in with a 32 and a total of 209. At 210 was Miller Barber, and at 211 was Coody and Tom Weiskopf, who now had to be given serious consideration because his steady 71-71-69 suggested he was not going to panic. But the basic tone of the tournament had not changed since Casper shot his opening 66 on Thursday: How could you catch Bill?

With so little excitement on the scoreboard, the big talk of the day involved my friend Arnold Palmer. Having started 73–75, Arnold was frustrated and somewhat irritated. He has a special feeling about

Augusta—after all, that is where Arnie's Army began—and he would rather play well before the galleries there than anywhere else. But his last four competitive rounds on the course, which includes his two from 1968, had been 72-79-73-75. Now, on the par-5 second hole, he bunkered his second, hit an explosion shot and when the ball remained in the bunker he swung his wedge through the sand in anger, a motion that was almost a practice-swing duplicate of the shot he had just hit so poorly. Jack Tuthill, the pro tournament director, was on the scene and Palmer was assessed a two-stroke penalty for grounding his club in a bunker. But Arnold was not sure that the penalty was proper, and when he came to the eighth green he asked Frank Hannigan of the USGA, who was posted there, if the ruling could be reviewed. Hannigan said yes, a Masters rules committee meeting was called, and by the time Palmer reached 14 he was informed there was no penalty. His double bogey, which had been posted on the scoreboard, was now changed to a par.

Because Palmer was involved, the ruling created considerable interest among golf followers everywhere. The USGA, as the governing body of amateur golf in the United States, devotes a great deal of time to the problems of rules interpretations and the shaping of new rules when they seem needed. The USGA felt that amateur golfers would like to have the ruling explained, and some time after the Masters it made a public report, in question and answer form, on the Palmer ruling. This is the way the USGA handles innumerable questions of rules interpretations, and I thought you might like to see the report, not so much for the light it throws on the Palmer decision, but as an example of how complex the rules of the game are and how the USGA deals with such matters. This report is signed by P.J. Boatwright, Jr., Executive Director of the USGA, for The Rules of Golf Committee. It reads:

"Q: In the 1969 Masters Tournament Arnold Palmer played a stroke in a bunker which advanced the ball several yards but failed to remove it from the bunker. In disgust and anger, Palmer swung his club and touched the bunker sand at approximately the place from which he played the stroke. The Committee eventually ruled that Palmer had not breached Rule 33-1 and that there was no penalty. Please explain the ruling.

A: Although Rule 33-1 basically prohibits touching the ground in a hazard with a club before the player makes a stroke in the hazard, there are several specific exceptions, including the following:

"After playing a stroke, there is no penalty should the player smooth irregularities in the hazard made by the footprints or the soil displaced by a stroke, provided nothing is done that improves the lie of the ball or assists the player in his subsequent play of the hole." (33-1g)

Palmer's act must be judged by analogy with the above exception. He obviously did not improve the lie of the ball, which lay several yards away. The question then remains whether his practice swing assisted him in his subsequent play of the hole.

Normally, when a player has played a stroke in a bunker he has gained all useful knowledge about the condition of the sand or soil in the hazard (that is one reason why Rule 33-1g permits smoothing irregularities after the stroke, within the limits previously mentioned). The Committee for the Masters Tournament apparently felt there would be no basis for holding that Palmer's act assisted him in his subsequent play. The same ruling was made in an incident involving Bob Goalby in the 1962 United States Open Championship.

Such an action, however, is not proper etiquette and can lay the player open to question whether he has breached the Rule. Any doubt should be resolved against the player. Each case should be considered on its own merits.

It should be noted that subsequent play would be assisted if the player smoothed irregularities at a place from which he again played before extricating the ball from the bunker. This would pertain, for example, to a ball rolling back into the same position or to a ball dropped at the same place after the previous stroke had sent the ball out of bounds."

Stimulating as all this was for the Saturday night cocktail parties in Augusta, it was still merely an appetizer preceding the meat of matters, which was whether or not Casper could continue to pussy-foot his way around Augusta National and win a Masters. The Casper approach to this Masters can be summed up quickly: not once had he gone for the 13th or 15th greens with his second shot, though he was repeatedly in excellent position to do so. There is a gamble involved, and Casper was determined to play this Masters as the ultimate conservative. I have my own feelings about Casper, and they have been borne out over the years even as Bill himself has grown, changed, found deep meaning in religion and put aside—or at least convinced himself he had put aside—the singular pleasures and plenty that come with winning golf. My impression is that Casper can't seize victory. He takes it when it comes his way, which is a far different thing. I criticize him for this, not out of any animosity, but in the way one might criticize an artist—a very successful one—whose work is flawed. And make no mistake that Casper is an artist with golf clubs, one of the best there has ever been. But, to me at least, he is not a winner on a golf course when the chips are down. That he may be a winner in many other ways, non-golf, non-athletic, that his human values and resources may exceed those of many of us, I do not care to dispute. That is not the point.

Casper is probably the most complex, or mystifying, of the big-money men on the tour, and it is helpful to be aware of this when you judge what happened to him at Augusta. I think a *Sports Illustrated* writer, Robert Jones, summed up the man well in a story last summer, as follows:

"William Earl Casper, Jr., is a contradiction. A millionaire on his golf earnings alone, he is so austere in his personal life that by contrast a Franciscan monk looks like a swinger. Phlegmatic to the point of dullness (one acquaintance called him "a walking ad for ennui"), Casper is nonetheless so sensitive to everything from natural gas to apples that he developed agonizing allergies to them. Fanatically committed to learning everything about the few human activities that interest him, he is virtually innocent of book-learning, political opinion, musical or artistic taste. A man whose inner drive and self-discipline would make Vince Lombardi appear a bit of a softie, yet a man who can coo and burble over babies with near-feminine abandon. A saint with the instincts of a savage—or maybe vice versa. In short, a fascinating human being beside whom the simpler psyche of an Arnold Palmer or Jack Nicklaus fade toward cliche. Yet there is no Casper's Army. There isn't even a Casper's Cadre. ....The quintessential Casper is an enigma wrapped in anomaly."

All of which is fascinating, but there is still only one basic question as far as most of us in the game are concerned on any given day—how is he hitting the ball? Casper was hitting the ball very well this spring as usual, but also, as usual, he was having trouble preparing himself for the Masters. For years he had said that he has an allergic reaction to certain chemicals frequently used on southern golf courses and anybody who has ever seen him with his hands and feet swollen, his cheeks puffed and his eyes half closed, is not going to dispute the fact. This has disrupted his preparation for the Masters. He took to skipping the Florida tournaments, but this brought him to Augusta without the competitive sharpness he felt he needed. In any event, he never played the Masters well. This year Casper decided on a different approach. He would risk Florida again. He did, but he had to drop out after the second round of the National Airlines Open in Miami because a pesticide sprayed on the course caused him to suffer an acute reaction. He flew home to San Diego, recovered, and did not fly east again until just before the Masters (having checked with Augusta officials to be sure the course did not have any chemicals on it that might cause an allergic reaction, and choosing a night flight because smoke bothers him, too, and people smoke less on late flights).

One of Casper's problems at Augusta has been a tendency to have bad first rounds. But Bill looked different this year. He had a confident way about him. He was dressed in splendid colors, he looked like he felt extremely well, that he had not a concern in this world or the next, that he was going to have a wonderful time no matter what happened. He smiled a lot, laughed now and then with the gallery, and soon had quite a gathering with him, a crowd that was reacting to his infectious enthusiasm. As I say, it was something of a new Casper for me, and that opening 66 he shot was something new for everybody.

But should it have been a 64? Who knows. Casper had laid up safely on each of the back nine par 5s, showing the game plan he had selected and was determined to stick with. In the next two days he repeated his cautious approach to those holes, once going so far as to use a seven-iron to hit short of the water with his second on 15. He told the press the holes had cost him too dear in the past, that he was convinced they had to be played safely. I doubt that a top golfer in the entire field agreed with him.

That was the background, then, as Casper awoke one Sunday morning with his one-stroke lead over George Archer and the knowledge that he had dominated the 1969 Masters for three of its four days. His tee-off time was not until 1:32, but at 8:30 that morning Casper was conducting a service for a group of Mormons. Later, he told reporters: "If I lose, it's God's will. We should be thankful for our health. All you have to do is visit hospitals and see our veterans without limbs but who have high morale, and then you hear us complaining about missing putts." The sentiments were valid ones, but it struck me as too much dwelling on defeat. And it isn't every day you hear an athlete say that if he loses, God will have to take the rap.

Defeat came with ungodly haste. Casper played the same first nine he had the day before, but this time he did not get away with it. He missed the green on one, but saved himself with a little chip. He hit his tee shot on two down into the Delta Airlines Ticket Counter area again, chipped out and saved a par. On three he salvaged a par with a five-footer. On four he hit over, putted from the fringe all the way across the green and had to chip back to save a bogey. On six he buried his tee shot into the lip of a bunker, took a bogey and was out of the lead. On seven he hit a dreadful slice off the tee, bunkered his second and made bogey. With this, George Archer, who had gone out in 35, moved into a three-stroke lead on the field. Casper parred eight—though in his distraction he hit his second shot on this par-5 hole right over a warning flag and the heads of people who were crossing the fairway in a crosswalk at the time. And then at nine, his Masters presumably over, he yanked an approach shot into a bunker, left his explosion shot in the bunker and then came out and one-putted to salvage his bogey. It was a 40, and as awful as it sounded, "I played like a 14 handicapper," he said later. "My game just fell apart."

It is interesting that once he was out of it, Casper's game returned. He is given all kinds of credit for coming back in the last eight holes and finishing only one stroke behind the winner. But I don't think he wants any credit for that. The pressure was off, for one thing. For another—because, he says, he was so far behind—he went for the 13th and 15th greens in two, made it both times easily and birdied both holes. At any rate, Gary Player was right in the end when he said of Casper, "He can't play that way and win." Casper the conservative would probably insist he can, too. He could surely point out that he came within a stroke in spite of shooting a 40 on the front nine, so his conservative philosophy is not discredited. But neither is it supported.

As for Casper the man, we see him again at the presentation ceremonies minutes after his day of disaster has ended. "About the time you think you have something going you get a reason to be humble. I got a lot of humility out there today . . . But I have a saying—if you can't finish first, it sure is nice to finish second." As far as one could tell, Casper never offered an excuse, never showed a regret. "I'm not really disappointed," he said later. "Years ago I used to get disappointed, but not any more." He may be the hardest man I know. Or the strongest. Or the softest. An enigma wrapped in anomaly.

While Casper was playing the scene out his own way, a lot of mere golfers were on the course, too, and a more rattled bunch of athletes you are never going to see. Miller Barber had been paired with Casper, and Miller had decided, being just two strokes behind Bill when the day began, that he would play Casper head to head. Beat Billy and you win. Isn't that what everybody in the locker room was saying? So Miller went out and matched Casper stroke for awful stroke on that ridiculous front nine. He said later he would never make *that* mistake again. Exit Barber.

Archer took his three-stroke lead into the turn, but bogeyed 10. Coody, playing ahead of Archer, birdied 11 and then spanked a magnificent two iron second shot into 13 and sank a 25-footer for an eagle. With that putt the 31-year-old Texan took the lead, a prospect that had never seriously occurred to him. He was apparently appalled by the thought, for he played 14 dreadfully and bogied it, got a routine birdie on 15 by reaching in two, and then bogied 16 when he picked the wrong club. Shaken by that, he also bogied 17 and 18 to die a dismal and unnoticed death. Meanwhile, young Tom Weiskopf birdied three holes out of four to move into a tie for the lead, and then collapsed just as quickly with a bogey on 17 to move right back out again. When George Knudson played 15 and 16 in birdie, he moved within a stroke of the lead, but never could get closer.

This was all very difficult for the gallery, which hardly knew which way to turn, and every time it turned it saw somebody who had just moved into contention bouncing a ball off a tree limb or into a bunker to move back out again. In the end, those who stuck with Archer saw the pressure shots that worked. He drove into the trees on 17, managed a low four-iron under limbs to within 60 feet of the hole, and sank a grim four-footer for his par. His shot into 18 with a one-stroke lead was a winner all the way, finally stopping 12 feet from the hole. But it was his play at 15 that made Archer a deserving champion in an afternoon of chaos. Archer was playing behind Coody. He had watched from the fairway on 13 as Coody sank his eagle putt to take the lead. He knew Coody had bogeyed 14, but Archer put his own drive into the trees, topped a recovery with an iron, hit a poor chip and could not get his par. This must have disheartened him. When Archer faced his second shot on 15, which Coody had just birdied, there was never any doubt about going for the green. Archer did. He thought he hit an excellent shot, and was astonished when it fell short with a splash that almost echoed off the trees in the hush around the green. "I felt like I was in the water with the ball," Archer said later. One of the problems with playing short at 15 is that the fairway slopes down sharply toward the water, and the green is tabled slightly on the far side. When you hit into the water, you face the same problem from the drop zone—a very tender chip off a downhill lie across a wide pond with the green above you. On this day the pin was very close to the front of the green, making the shot even more dangerous. It had to be hit into the bank and bounce up onto the green. If not executed perfectly the ball would do one of two things; go far past the pin or, worse, be short and come rolling backward down the embankment and into the water again. Archer, knowing the Masters was at stake, struck the shot perfectly. It hit into the bank, skipped up, rolled toward the pin and stopped some 13 feet past the cup. Bob Charles, watching the shot on television in the clubhouse, said "That was a million-dollar chip. The man just hit a million-dollar chip shot." The putt was slick, downhill and toward the water, but you somehow knew Archer and his magic wand would make it, and they did. So call it two superb strokes in a row. They only added up to a par on the scorecard, the kind of thing that would hardly be noticed if you weren't there. But the other golfers noticed, and Archer knew how difficult the one shot was, and how much the pair of them meant.

George Archer made a charming champion as he stood on the putting green in the time-honored Masters ceremony and had last year's champion, Bob Goalby, reach up and put the green coat on him. The coat was the biggest Augusta National could find, for Archer, at 6 feet 6, is the tallest man on the tour. Now 29, Archer has an air of self-depreciation about him, which he need not, considering the fact that he won $276,000 in the previous two years. He told the crowd, "It's pretty hard to say anything because my heart is beating about 39 times a second." And then he got off the line that summarized the furious last nine holes and gave a hint of what goes on when a man who has never won a major championship suddenly faces up to the chance. "I've never been so scared for so long," he said.

A last look at the statistics show that Archer won it where it figures he might—with his putter on the firm and demanding greens. And he also won it, on the par 5s. "I played them in eleven under par," he said. "That was the big difference." It was indeed.

The 1969 Masters had one almost humorous aftermath. Lee Trevino, he of the good nature and immense mouth, made an unparalleled statement a few days after the tournament. "Put in your book, I'll never play that course again," said Trevino. "I can't play there. They can invite me all they want to, but I'm not going to play there anymore." Gary Player, who heard Trevino say this, accused him of kidding, but Lee said he could not be more serious, and soon the quotes, which were overheard by a reporter, were in every newspaper in the country. Turn down an invitation to the Masters? It would be like telling Saint Peter to close the gates, you've decided against the place. Trevino explained himself very carefully at the time. He pointed out that he hits the ball low, and that the Augusta course favors the golfer who gets the ball well up in the air.

Well up in the air, too, apparently, was the establishment of golf. Trevino's comments were construed as a knock on the Masters tournament, though what he said was far more a knock on his own golf game. Pro golfers everywhere began defending Augusta, and telling Trevino if he was a real champion he ought to be able to play anywhere. Commissioner Dey had a brief chat with Trevino, which could probably be summarized as "please, Lee, would you look before you lip," and a rather subdued Trevino said he was sorry if anybody had gotten the wrong idea. He didn't mean to criticize Augusta National. All he was saying was it's no place for his kind of golfer and he wasn't ever going to go back. At least, he did not think he was ever going to go back. He will get a chance to make up his mind next April. As a U.S. Open Champion, his invitation is automatic through 1973. Maybe by next spring he'll think he is hitting his irons a little higher.

3

The U.S. Open

Nobody could outshoot the Sergeant

On the face of it, the tournament golf fan is the boob of sport followers. He spends his money—often a good deal of it, compared to the price of baseball or basketball tickets—and all he gets in return is admission to a stadium that is 150 acres big, offers him no reserved seat, forces him to cover hilly miles on foot, has stern policemen types who herd him here and there, insisting that he keep his mouth shut ere he attract the withering attention of one of his would-be heroes perched over a three-inch putt, and above all makes it a matter of fantastic luck if he happens to be standing in the right place at the right time to see the most dramatic shot of an event unfold before his very eyes. Usually he is looking at Arnold Palmer putt on 14 when Orville Moody hits the tournament-winning chip at 12. Watching a golf tournament is like going to a football game, but knowing you would see only every fourth play. Who'd bother?

But that is just on the face of it, for pro golf offers its fans an unusual reward in return for the inconveniences they suffer. There is no other significant sport in which the paying spectator is permitted to roam the arena, to stand right there on the field as the drama unfolds. He is separated from his sport—both physically and mentally—by only the slightest of margins. He can reach out and almost touch Jack Nicklaus as he swings, hear the grunt of power that goes into a big drive, watch from a mere ten feet away as the face of the athlete in this very personal game reacts to a shot just hit ("Why in the name of heaven did I have to pull the ball on this hole?"). Combined with this astonishing proximity to the action is the fact that the knowing spectator can truly share the effect of what is happening. The fans of other sports almost never know—and thus don't appreciate—the problems confronting the athletes they watch. How can a football rooter really react to what is taking place as John Unitas tries to pass from his own 15 against a hard rush? What does the baseball fan know about the difficulty of hitting a Bob Gibson slider? The golfer, on the other hand, does know because he plays the game. The professional's lament is his own. He, too, has hit the ball into the trees on the final hole and needed a miracle par to save the day. When he sees Bob Rosburg in the same position in the last round of the U.S. Open, his understanding and involvement is complete. The true golf fan gets his money's worth, and then some.

All of this comes to mind in connection with the 1969 U.S. Open, because it struck me that I had never seen an Open gallery so naive as the one at Houston and, therefore, one that was not having the fun it might have. Now, naivete in a gallery is hardly new. I remember standing behind the 11th green at Oakland Hills during the 1961 U.S. Open when a woman noticed Dick Mayer moving up the fairway. "Who's that?" she asked. "Dick Mayer," her escort said. "He's a former U.S. Open Champion." "What's the U.S. Open?" asked the lady. But somehow this Texas gallery seemed particularly out of touch, and one had to idly wonder, "What indeed is the U.S. Open?" or, "What is it coming to?" On the first day I heard a man say, "They're going to have this thing here every year." And a little while later a lady asked who she thought would win, said "Arnold Palmer, because he won in 1966." Well, what they will have on the same course every year is the Houston Champions International, a regular stop on the pro tour like the Texas Open, the Desert Classic and all such things. And that is what Palmer won in 1966. Somebody should have told those people the Houston Champions is not the U.S. Open. On the other hand, by the time the 1969 United States Open Championship was over, I'm not so sure it didn't seem like the Houston Champions after all. Why? Well, there were several reasons. One was the course itself. Another was the way the event was run. And yet another was the winner, Sergt. Orville Moody. Now Orville Moody is a fine man. He is the best cross-handed putter in America. He gets the ball from that mound of grass called the tee into that small hole called the cup with astonishing dispatch, and that is the object of the game. To use a Texas idiom, Orville can whup you. He surely can. But it just doesn't make sense that a man can spend 14 years in the Army, then decide to become a golf pro and right away win the U.S. Open. Does it? No friends, it doesn't. But let's go back now and see if we can throw any light on how it all transpired.

One of the charms of the Open and, incidentally, one of the reasons for its success, is the host club member. The United States Golf Association oversees the Open—in fact, has a representative from its New York office on the grounds six weeks before play begins. But the club members do the work. They are the marshals, the ticket salesmen, the caddie masters, the parking lot attendants. They sell the ads in the program and negotiate contracts with the concessionaires. They are the errand boys—and girls—and the traffic directors. Historically, the members have displayed an awesome loyalty to their clubs; they have wanted *their* Open to be the best ever. And they have contributed much to the success of the Open. But the 1969 U.S. Open was not run by club members. It was administered by a group called the Houston Golf Association, a mixture of members from many clubs in the city—another Texas conglomerate. They were all dressed up in shades of blue, just the way they dress for the Houston Champions International, and they were quite positive that their way of doing things was the right way. Nor, I understand, did they hesitate to so inform the USGA. The result was numerous problems, including crowds that were surprisingly small, inferior marshaling and other factors that diminished the Open aura of the event.

The course itself was a contributing factor. Champions Golf Club has been the site of the Houston International since 1966, and even though it is very long (6,967 yards) and very severe, it is not up to U.S. Open standards. The Open has been held on the great courses of the United States—Oakland Hills, Merion, Oakmont, Olympic—courses with character and history, courses where each hole was memorable. But, sometimes it was difficult to distinguish the holes at Champions. Was that par 3 with the water in front of the green the eighth or the 12th; the 10th and the 11th, now which is which? Certainly the founders of Champions had seen enough courses with character. Champions is the fulfilment of a plan by Jimmy Demaret and Jack Burke, a pair of home-town boys made good. It was built in the late 1950's with two goals in mind. First, it was designed to be financially successful. Second, it was to be a superior course by any standards. Demaret and Burke did not decide five years ago to try to attract the Open, they began to work for it when the course was first conceived.

The partnership of Demaret and Burke may seem strange to those not familiar with the circumstances. Demaret is 10 years older than Burke and they were in their mid-40's and mid-30's, respectively, when the venture began. But their ties are close. Jack is the son of Jack Burke, Sr., a good player of an earlier generation. In 1920 Burke, Sr. shot 296 at Inverness in Toledo, Ohio, and tied for second in the U.S. Open. He moved to Houston from Philadelphia, became a club pro and hired a young Texan to be his shop assistant. The Texan was Demaret. "Jimmy and I talked about this club for 15 years before we did anything about it," Burke recently said of Champions. "Whenever we played a course we looked for its best features, including its clubhouse and mode of operation. When the time came to build Champions, Jimmy and I were agreed on what we wanted to accomplish, and we called in architect Ralph Plummer to achieve it for us."

The result was impressive, for Champions turned out to be the best new golf course in the Southwest. It is frequently referred to as the Augusta National of the Southwest, a comparison nobody in Houston argues against, though part of the basis for it is the fact that—as was true with Bobby Jones at Augusta—this was a case of famous professional golfers starting a club of their own. This is a trend, incidentally, that I expect to see continue. Both Arnold Palmer and Jack Nicklaus have great interest in golf course architecture and I wouldn't be surprised to see them both spend a vast amount of time, if not the great majority of their lives following active play, in the business of designing and building golf courses. Nicklaus is presently working on seven or eight courses in association with Pete Dye and Palmer has three or four under construction at the moment as well.

Burke and Demaret were not without their frustrations. One problem was geography. The land they selected was beautiful, lightly rolling and heavily wooded in pine. The terrain looked more like Maryland than Texas, and was ideally suited for a golf course. But it was north of Houston, and thus on the wrong side of the tracks. There is a lot of money in Houston, big money. It is an oil city, and also the headquarters for the National Aeronautics and Space Administrations Manned Spacecraft Center. But the tycoons and astronauts stick to the south side of town. About the only things north of Houston are a couple of motels, the new airport, and Dallas, 250 miles away. It soon became obvious in Open week that it took an adventurous spirit just to reach Champions Golf Club, some 45 minutes from the city. One result was the scarcity of spectators. In the four days of actual competition the Open drew 48,693, fully 40,000 less than paid to see it at Baltusrol two years earlier.

Champions is a long course. It played at 7,166 yards for the Ryder Cup matches of 1967. While the USGA makes numerous demands of a course, excessive length is not one of them. Consequently, Champions was shortened to 6,967 yards for the 1969 Open. A few miles were taken off the fifth hole, converting it from a par 5 to a 455-yard par 4. The fourth and 12th holes, two formidable par 3's, were cut *down* to 193 and 213 yards, respectively. Par was reduced from 71 to 70, but no matter what the USGA tried to do with the course, in my opinion, Champions never came up to Open standards. I mentioned this later in the year to a high USGA official, and he reluctantly agreed. He intimated, in fact, that it was probably a mistake to take the Open to Champions and added that it was awarded to Demaret and Burke at a time when relations between the USGA and the PGA were not all they might have been. It had seemed like a good public-relations gesture.

The USGA has been running the Open since 1895 when 11 players showed up at the Newport Golf Club in Rhode Island the day after the *real* championship—the National Amateur—had been decided. The field has grown considerably since then. When all the entries for the 69 Open were counted in April, the total was a record 3,400. To cut the field down to the 150 who can tee up on opening day, the USGA has long had a two-echelon qualifying system. About 90 players are exempt from the first qualifying round and about 30 from both the first and second. Those exemptions are earned in a variety of ways. The winners of the last five Opens, for instance, are exempt, and so are winners of the last five PGA championships. The British Open champion is exempt, and so is the U.S. Amateur champion. Everybody who finishes among the top 15 in the previous year's Open and everybody among the top 15 in a special money-winning list compiled by the USGA—it runs from the close of entries for one Open to the close of entries for the next—has a free pass. This year 33 players were exempt from all qualifying. None of which would be worth noting, except that a name of great interest was not on the exempt list: Arnold Palmer. One fact of American professional golf must still be faced: nobody attracts as much interest or excitement as Palmer. The last thing the USGA wanted to do was have a U.S. Open in Houston, Texas, with Arnold Palmer sitting at home in Latrobe watching summer come to western Pennsylvania. Indeed, as things turned out, Palmer was to play a spectacular role at Houston, and in the view of many, provide the highest points that the tournament offered. But should he have been forced to qualify? The question became a heated one in the two months between the Masters and the Open. Until a few years ago, the USGA allowed all former Open champions into the field. But as the number of former champions grew, they began to take up spaces that more properly belonged to active touring professionals, fellows like, well—a Lee Trevino or an Orville Moody. So the USGA limited the former-champion exemption to five years. Palmer had not had a good Open in 1968 at Oak Hill (he finished 58th, remember?), and he was not off to a particularly good start on the 1969 money list. His only chance for an exemption was in the USGA's money-winning category, and there he was beaten out by Frank Beard, who sank a nine-foot putt on the final hole at the Byron Nelson Classic to tie for second place, win $9,250, and top Palmer by $1,291. Beard's total on that special list was $87,503; Palmer's was $86,212. Beard was 15th, Palmer 16th. The USGA could have waived qualifying for Arnold. It had done just that for Ben Hogan in 1966, and certainly Palmer had a better chance of winning the 1969 Open than Hogan did of winning the 1966 Open. Most members of the USGA executive committee, the men who run the Open, were in Augusta for the Masters, and by then they were getting some heat from the press, which in general felt Palmer should not have to qualify and said so loudly. I'm told that the matter never came up for a formal vote by the committee, but a poll was taken and the decision was, I feel, the right one. For the first time since 1959, Palmer would have to qualify. In fact, I think Arnold was probably relieved when the exemption talk ended. It would have mortified him to have been made a special case in these circumstances. The situation was not similar to Hogan's, for Ben was an elder statesman of the game when he was invited to play at Olympic in 1966. Arnold would have much preferred to play his way into the Open, which is exactly what he did.

Palmer teed it up at the Youghiogheny Country Club (say it Yuck-I-Gainy) in McKeesport, Pa., on a raw June morning, and there are some towns on the pro tour that would do well with the galleries that turned out. People began arriving at 5.30 a.m., though Palmer was not due to start until 8. There is usually no admission charged for a qualifying round, but $2 was charged here, with the proceeds going to the caddie scholarship fund of the Western Pennsylvania Golf Association. Fifty-two players were in the qualifying field, with eight places at stake. Except for Tony Jacklin, the competition was minimal, but anything can happen in 36 quick holes. Happily, all that happened was predictable. Palmer shot a comfortable 70 in the morning and followed up with a 68 in the afternoon to lead the qualifying field. You could almost hear the sighs of relief at Champions—and at USGA headquarters.

My first view of Champions Golf Club was on Monday morning of the tournament week. As the car turned into the long drive leading to the modern, bright, and thoroughly air-conditioned clubhouse, I saw a strange sight; a man walking down the road with a golf bag slung over his shoulder, accompanied by a young lady. Could this be the week of the Open? And if so, who was this character? Well, it was Tony Jacklin, and he was walking to the course because it was the only way he could get there. Jacklin was living in a cottage near the club, as were Player, Nicklaus and some of the other top names. Not many players, though, had such pleasant and convenient accommodations. Most had to stay miles away in Houston, and while the Houston Golf Association did well in arranging transportation, not every player had an easy time getting to the course. Bob Shaw, for instance, wound up hitchhiking the morning of his second round. He was picked up by Larry Null, field press secretary of the PGA. Shaw didn't seem to mind; he kept telling Null how it was such an honor to play in the Open he would have walked from the city if that had been the only way to get to the course.

The players had hardly settled in when there began to be some unusual talk about the rough. The USGA has long prided itself on its rough. The U.S. Open traditionally has had the toughest rough of any tournament in America. But not in 1969. In fairness, the USGA tried. But the USGA failed. The reason is that Champions is covered with bermuda, a coarse grass especially suited to hot and humid climates. But bermuda does not begin to grow until the weather is nearly unbearable. Houston's weather did not become unbearable until too late, and the rough the players found when they arrived was far short of what their worst fears had led them to expect. Gary Player dismissed it as insignificant. "I hit into the rough on 18," Player told a group of reporters, "and from 250 yards away I could see the ball sitting there. There's not a spot on this course where Jack Nicklaus can't reach the green." Player had just shot a practice-round 64—which always makes the rough look thin—and was a hot favorite, along with Palmer, Nicklaus, Casper and Lee Trevino, the defending champion.

Player came to Houston with a strong record. Since finishing 16th in the 1968 Open at Oak Hill, he had won his second British Open, the World Series of Golf, the Piccadilly World Matchplay Championship, the Australian Masters, his fourth straight South African Open, and the Tournament of Champions. He had been second in the Colonial Invitation at Fort Worth in May, and third in the Atlanta Classic a week later. The week before the Open he had been fifth in the Western Open. He had played in only 10 tournaments in the United States, but had won nearly $80,000. Casper was a threat, as ever. He had won the Open twice before, and only Nicklaus and Boros of the active players could claim that. Casper had taken the Western Open the previous week, and earlier in the year had won the Bob Hope Desert Classic. But his 1969 record was spotty. At the Colonial, the last tournament he played before the Western, he finished 68th. And he was probably still shaken by his disastrous last round at Augusta.

The greens at Champions were huge, somewhat like Bellerive in St. Louis where Player won the Open in 1965, and as a result there was considerable early talk about Frank Beard's chances. Beard seemed to be on a hot streak as the Open approached, tieing for second in the Byron Nelson Classic and losing the New Orleans Open in a playoff. He was third in the Western and he might have won except for a startling development. He missed two 18-inch putts. When a good putter has this happen he is apt to wonder why. It bothers him, and Frank was probably still fretting during the Open, where is 72-73-73-78 was uninspired, to say the least.

Finally, there was, as always, much discussion of Palmer's chances—how does that old saying go about the wish being father to the deed? And Arnold was getting his normal amount of help from his well-wishers. One large gentleman lay in wait by the path leading into the locker room ready to ambush anybody headed for a door that might lead to Arnie. Finally he spotted a reporter, stopped him and said, "Will you tell Arnie something for me? I've been watching him for a couple of days now and everything he hit goes off to the right. Now I've noticed that he's lining up his feet this way." The man grabbed a golf umbrella, addressed an imaginary ball and placed his feet in a very closed position. "If he would just straighten his feet and set himself up better, I'm sure he'd be all right. Please tell him that for me." The inclination is to laugh when such things happen. But remember what I said earlier about the fan's involvement with the game? This is the ultimate of involvement. You feel free to advise your hero. And who knows, maybe the advice is sound. (In this case, it wasn't.)

Some day I want to digress in one of these annual chapters on the subject of advice. Nobody gets more advice about their profession than golfers, and nobody listens more closely to it if they think the source might possibly be of help. Spend an hour sometime at a tournament practice tee and watch as the clusters of pros, like housewives over coffee, take apart, rebuild, ask about and gossip over golf swings. It is as if they all suffered from a common ailment and were confined to the golf ward of some great athletic hospital where they had nothing to do but compare their symptoms in the hope that somewhere they would find the diagnosis that would save them. This is why nobody ever shoots 63, or leads at the end of three rounds, or wins a tournament without happily confessing that they owe everything that has just happened "to my close friend Harry Whipshaft, who happened to notice on the practice tee last night that I was trying to swing with my wallet in my hip pocket, and this was causing me to . . ."

But for now let's just consider one such case, because it proved to be rather important by the last day of the Open. It was after a practice round at Champions that I happened to notice Carl Lohren, a club pro from Long Island who had qualified for the Open, watching Deane Beman hit some shots. Occasionally Lohren would make a comment and Deane would nod. Lohren and Beman are both from the suburbs of Washington and they were fierce rivals in the late 1950's and early 1960's, just when Beman was winning an international reputation. They had played against each other in high school, played on the same team at the University of Maryland, and there were some around Washington who felt that Lohren was a better golfer than Beman. Lohren turned professional long before Deane, and he became something of a conversation piece during his brief tour career. There was, for example, the time the car Lohren was riding in stopped for a traffic light. Lohren stepped outside to experiment with a new idea about his swing. The driver didn't notice this. When the light turned green the car sped off and Carl was left standing there at the top of his backswing. Well, everybody in golf seems to have a secret. Hogan had a "secret" and sold it to *Life* magazine; Gary Player was cornered in the locker room at Champions and asked if he could explain why he was playing so well. "It's a secret," he said, "and if anybody wants to know what it is he'll have to buy my new book." Gary could hardly control his laughter. Now, it seems, Lohren and Beman had a "secret," and that's what they were discussing on the practice tee. Lohren discovered it, and some months before he had given it to Beman to develop because Beman was playing the tour and could analyze the results better. Beman and Lohren were out there on the tee working on the secret.

On Tuesday night of Open week, the USGA traditionally holds a dinner honoring past champions. The guests are members of USGA committees who are at the site to help out, the press, and officials of other golf associations such as the PGA and R and A. These are not always the most stimulating of occasions, but this year's dinner provided a moment worth recording. Fred McLeod was there, the oldest living champion (he won in 1908), Billy Casper was there, and so were Palmer, Player, Nicklaus, Gene Littler, and Ken Venturi. Hord Hardin, the USGA president, allowed each speaker only a few seconds, but Venturi spoke somewhat longer, and the more he spoke the more subdued became the mood. Venturi won the 1964 Open at Congressional Country Club with a surprising and inspiring performance. He managed his victory in spite of exhausting heat and a swing that no longer resembled the fluid movement he brought to professional golf in 1956. And now he looked back:

"This is my last year of exemption for the Open. How I won it I still don't know. At the end of 1964 I suffered a disease of the hands. I don't know why, but it happened and I can't question it." His voice faltered and he paused. "Unless a miracle happens, my golf days are limited; I may be forced to leave the game I love." Then he looked at the others at the head table. "There's Gary," he said with a slight nod, "a man with fortitude and determination. There's Jack. He had a lot of early success but it didn't spoil him. Gene Littler, one of the greatest talents I've ever seen. He won it with a great swing. And Arnold: articles have been written that maybe have drawn us apart, but I'll always feel privileged to call Arnold a friend, a champion among champions." Venturi turned to his left and looked down at Lee Trevino. "Lee has capitalized financially on his championship, but, Lee, the U.S. Open Championship is more than money. It is something you will cherish forever." Now he looked out at his hushed audience. "There's not much I fear, but I do fear leaving the game I love. I just thank God for the moment of glory He gave me. Whoever wins the Open next Sunday, whether it is an unknown or an established player, whoever wins it, treat it well, because the U.S. Open Championship is the greatest championship in golf." It was a moving speech, and it drew a standing ovation from people who have heard a lot of speeches at athletic banquets. (Venturi shot 76-77—153 to miss the cut by five strokes. He has not survived the Open cut since the year he won.)

A yellow haze settled over Houston the morning of the first round. It was as if somebody has slowly lowered the lid on a cookpot. The humidity was fierce, the temperature in the nineties. To add to the discomfort, rain was threatening. The sensible people were the ones who found nice comfortable chairs in front of the picture windows in the air conditioned clubhouse and there awaited developments. Whether you waited inside or out, the developments came quickly. Each year the first round of the Open introduces us to a little-known player who has a good day, then disappears into the nether regions. Remember Bob Gajda? Or John Felus, who carried with him all the hopes of Gallitzin, Pa.? In Houston there was a young man named Dave Philo, originally from Schenectady and now a club pro in Jacksonville, Fla. Philo was playing along steadily with one bogey on the fourth hole, but then put together a hot streak. On the eighth, ninth and tenth he went birdie, eagle, birdie. There was a stir of interest until he took six on the eleventh, a double bogey. He finished with 71, a commendable score, and had dinner that night with his wife and a member of his home club who kept urging him to go right straight to bed and rest for the tough days ahead. Philo did, and shot a rested 74-78-76 in the next three rounds.

No sooner had Philo taken his double bogey than a string of sub-par numbers went up by Sam Snead's name on the leader board. Snead, of course, has been the most frustrated man in Open history. He shot the second lowest score ever in his first Open in 1937, only to finish second when Ralph Guldahl set a new record. Two years later he took an infamous eight on the last hole at the Philadelphia Country Club when a par 5 would have won and a bogey 6 would have tied. In 1947 he missed a 30-inch putt and lost a playoff to Lew Worsham. By 1969 his devoted fans, none of whom were under 50, had given up. But Snead started their hearts pounding as he began his 1969 Open: par-birdie-birdie-birdie, three under par after four holes. But then heat and age brought back reality as Snead played the next 14 holes in four over par for a 71, added a 77 the next day and was safe once again from the rigors of winning the Open. He eventually shot 292 and finished somewhere south of Rich Bassett, Kermit Zarley, Joe Cambell and Bob E. Smith.

Snead was not the only one with troubles, some of them more embarrassing than going four over par in 14 holes. Tom Weiskopf was cruising along with pars on the first seven holes and was on the par-3 eighth comfortably. As he got down behind his ball to inspect the line of his putt the air was rent with a tearing sound. His pants had split. "Good show!" shouted someone in the gallery. Tom rushed to his golf bag and pulled on a pair of rain pants so that he could continue until his wife returned with another pair. George Knudson lasted a little longer. His pants gave out on the 18th green, and he finished with a sweater around his waist.

Even more chagrined, I'm sure, was Mason Rudolph, a thoroughly experienced touring professional who has played some fine golf in his time and has always been a pretty good putter. On the 11th hole, a strong par 4 of 450 yards, he reached the green with his second but left himself a putt of 60 feet. His first try stopped seven feet short. His next was inches past. He reached across the hole to backhand the ball in, and whiffed it. He missed it completely, stubbing the putter against the ground as he did it. The result was a four-putt green. Waxo Green, who writes golf for the Nashville *Banner*, shook his head in disbelief. "Mase always did have a weak backhand," he muttered. And then two holes later Rudolph four-putted again. He finally staggered off the course with an 82. "I guess I shot out my Vardon average," he said wryly. ."You going to quit, Mase?" someone asked. "No," he answered chuckling. "I think I can do better than 82." He was right. The next day he shot 79. But he would have needed a 66 to stay in the Open because the cut was 148.

All this was secondary, to say the least, in the minds of the gallery. Of the 150 players who teed off, much of the crowd cared only about Arnold Palmer. He had by far the biggest and, as could be expected, the most vocal gallery. Arnold had not won a major tournament since the Masters of 1964, but he usually did well in the Open. He won in 1960; tied for 12th in 1961; tied for first in 1962 and lost a playoff to Nicklaus; tied for first in 1963 and lost a playoff to Julius Boros; tied for fifth in 1964; missed the cut in 1965; tied for first in 1966 and lost a playoff to Bill Casper; finished second to Nicklaus in 1967 and then was 58th in 1968. In all the years the Open has been played, only he and Nicklaus have broken 280 twice. And this year Arnold gave his gallery a thrill right at the start. His approach to the first hole rolled off the right edge of the green—then he chipped into the cup for a birdie. Palmer was paired with Beman and Kel Nagle, the Australian who had lost the 1965 Open Championship to Gary Player in a playoff. Nagle went nowhere this time, but watching Beman and Palmer led to an interesting comparison. Beman does not hit the ball very far—he estimates that his drives average about 230 yards. Yet on a course that was nearly 7,000 yards long, he outscored Palmer in that first round by two strokes, 68-70. To do this Beman used a wood eight times for his second shot on par-4 holes. He also used a wood on one par 3. Here is a comparison of the clubs used by Palmer and Beman for their second shots on par 4 and par 5 holes, and their tee shots on the par 3's:

Hole	Yards	Par	Palmer	Beman
1	435	4	7—iron	4—wood
2	444	4	6—iron	2—iron
3	379	4	wedge	9—iron
4	193	3	3—iron	4—wood
5	451	4	4—wood	3—wood
6	418	4	5—iron	3—iron
7	417	4	2—iron	3—wood
8	180	3	5—iron	4—iron
9	505	5	3—wood	3—wood
10	448	4	5—iron	4—wood
11	450	4	5—iron	4—wood
12	213	3	3—iron	2—iron
13	544	5	3—wood	3—wood
14	430	4	3—iron	4—wood
15	418	4	6—iron	2—iron
16	418	3	5—iron	4—iron
17	436	4	3—iron	3—wood
18	431	4	4—iron	3—wood

The figures are astonishing. Needless to say, Beman hits his woods very straight. He hit 12 greens, as many as Palmer, and the difference in their scores was largely their putting. Palmer used 31 putts, Beman 28. As soon as he finished, Palmer went into the pro shop and replaced the grips on his clubs. Maybe watching Deane shoot 68 made him think he was losing his grip.

Scoring honors for opening day went to Bob Murphy, a pudgy comparative newcomer who is best known on the pro tour for winning $70,000 within three weeks in 1968. Since then his high finish had been a tie for second in the National Airlines Open. He had won only $28,000 for the year, a performance that had disappointed him. And going into the tournament, he was certainly not a logical contender. He had been troubled all year with erratic driving, but had been working on it diligently. (He said he hit 1,000 drives in the weeks before the Open.) He came to Champions with a record of missing the cut in the Masters and then these finishes: 27th, 33rd, missed cut, missed cut, 26th, 26th. In short, he was playing very badly. But Murphy seemed to have everything under control in the intense heat at Champions. Gulping drinks, and shading himself with a huge bath towel to ease the sauna effect on his portly frame, he came up with five birdies. The first birdie was especially inspiring. Murphy needed a 3-iron for his approach to the second hole and dumped it into a bunker. He seemed certain to make a bogey and go over par, but he exploded into the cup and was off to a wonderful start.

There are times when a first-day 66 would give a man a comfortable lead in an Open, but this was no such occasion. Murphy had plenty of close competition. Some of the more interesting scores were:

Bob Murphy	66	Bob Rosburg	70
Miller Barber	67	Arnold Palmer	70
Deane Beman	68	Orville Moody	71
Al Geiberger	68	Gary Player	71
Tom Weiskopf	69	Lee Trevino	74
Dean Refram	69	Jack Nicklaus	74
George Archer	69	Billy Casper	74

Whenever a golfer starts well in a major championship he is certain to be besieged by reporters and photographers during his next round. Murphy was no exception, but unless he learns to accept these conditions, he will have a lot of trouble winning. Photographers dogged Murphy throughout his second round, certainly, and when he finished he complained bitterly. It was never quite clear though, just why he complained. It is true that he was photographed a lot, but even he admitted the photographers did not shoot while he was making a stroke—at least the snap of the camera shutter was not timed so that it disturbed his swing. No, he complained because he was photographed while he walked through the woods, while he took a drink, while he wiped his forehead with his towel. It all seemed childish, not only from him, but also from Casper who backed him up. One suspects that the real reason they complained was because Murphy shot 72 and Casper 73. This was all for Casper; he made the cut but was never in contention. The Open was just another step on Casper's gentle slide downhill after his excellent spring.

Events of the second day brought three golfers to mind—Beman, Nicklaus and Trevino. First Trevino. He had come from some place far on the other side of obscurity in 1967 to finish sixth in the Open at Baltusrol and win enough to finance another year on the tour. Trevino made maximum use of the year, 1968, by winning the Open.

But now it was a new Open, and the defending champion did not get off to a very good start with his 74. The next day he made par on the first two holes, then slipped one stroke on the third. The fourth is a difficult par 3 of 193 yards with a green that is bordered by Cypress Creek, which at this point runs through a steep gorge. Trevino pulled his tee shot onto that treacherous bank. He climbed down to play it, but when he swung his foot slipped and he tumbled down the side of the bank and twisted his knee. He made a double-bogey 5 there and now was three over par for the round and seven over for the tournament. By the time he reached the 18th tee he was eight over and needed a par 4 to make the cut. Trevino has been described as a happy-go-lucky Mexican and he certainly looked the part as he walked confidently up the fairway needing to get down in two from 60 feet for his 4. He even joked with the gallery and showed the length of a putt he missed on an earlier hole. When he reached the green he stroked his putt and left it a good five feet short. So he was in trouble. If he missed, he also missed the cut. And he missed. As his putt curled past the hole he turned away in disappointment, tapped his putter on the green gently a few times, turned back and knocked his ball in. So it was *hasta la vista* for Lee.

Nicklaus also went into the second round with a 74, the same score as Trevino. This was the same Nicklaus who had been struggling all year. He did not know what was wrong, and neither did anybody else. He spent hours on the practice tee at Houston but did not seem to be getting anywhere. Then R.H. Sikes happened to walk up and say, "Jack, you were playing your best when you set yourself up behind the ball, right? Well, try that." Jack did, and his shots improved immediately. So did his scoring, as he stormed in with a 67 on Friday and suddenly seemed a real threat. But Jack himself was not too confident. I saw him that night and he said his game was not right yet; it was coming along, but it wasn't right. He had that feeling we all know when we attempt to repair our swings. "When you're trying something new, every shot is an adventure," he said. "But it should be easier tomorrow." Unfortunately it wasn't easier. I was not surprised to see him shoot 75—73 in the last two rounds.

This was the day—Friday—that Beman took over the lead, and in the process proved the point that he may be short, but he's sharp. He shot 69 for a half-way total of 137, a stroke better than Murphy and Miller Barber. The course did not play nearly as long for Beman in the second round as in the first, for he needed woods to reach only four of the par 4's and, in fact, overshot the first green with a 4 iron.

His accuracy off the tee is worth noting. In the two rounds he hit 24 of 28 fairways on par 4 and par 5 holes, but he hit only 25 of the 36 greens. His putting was his strength, as usual. He needed only 30 putts in his second round.

Friday was, in general, a strange sort of day. By dinner time the second day you can usually sit down and assess the shape a major championship is taking. But this one defied any such mental strictures. Beman was in front by one stroke over Barber and Murphy, but accepting any of the three as the 1969 Open champion was difficult. I found myself looking at the scores and dismissing—for a variety of reasons—Bob Rosburg, Charlie Coody, Al Geiberger, George Knudson, Moody, John Miller, and Bunky Henry. They could win, but why *should* they? Bert Yancey might. He had 71—71 and was five shots behind Beman, but with 36 holes to play there was plenty of time. Palmer was in at 143 after an indifferent 73, but there was no telling what might happen if his putts started to fall. At the low end of the scoring it was a muddled tournament. And at the high end it was simply weird. For example, putting is supposed to be the essence of the game, but consider Jerry Pittman. He used only 56 putts in the first two rounds, 16 less than regulation and fewer than anybody else in the field. Yet he missed the cut by seven strokes with a 74—81. Or how about Littler—having probably his best year—shooting 80 on Friday after an opening 72? Inexplicable. Or Gay Brewer going 75—83? Brewer's 83 included a 9 on the par-3 eighth where he had a bit of an adventure. His tee shot hit the bank of the lake protecting the green and rolled into the water. Brewer dropped out, then hit a second ball into the water. He dropped again, and hit that one into the water. He dropped once more and now—cheers for Gay—got on the green where he two-putted for his 9. But forget that and think about Don January going 76—WD. January was playing in familiar country (his home is Dallas) but he was not doing well at all. His 76 in the first round was discouraging, and on the second day he was considerably worse. Imagine a PGA champion shooting a 46. January did. Then he "got sick." Perhaps January was sick, but it brought to mind the occasion in the 1968 Open when Gardner Dickinson got sick half-way through the third round and stalked off the course. There was every suggestion that Dickinson was only sick of hitting the ball badly. I think the players themselves, through their own Tournament Players Division, which they battled for, should take action against any golfer who claims a questionable ailment just to withdraw from a tournament. There is no room for such petulance in tournament golf, especially among players whose stature is such that they are attractions for the paying spectator.

Now, if Orville Moody had shot 46 and left, nobody would have raised an eyebrow, because who needed moon-faced, pot-bellied, 35 year-old Orville? Draw a crowd? He'd be lucky to draw his relatives. But Moody was not shooting any 46. He was in with a respectable 70—71, and his 141 had him only four strokes off the lead. In two days he had missed only six fairways with his tee shots and eight greens with his approaches. He ranked fourth in the number of greens hit in regulation, but 79th in the number of putts. In short, he was not spectacular, but he was steady. He was driving rather well and his irons were sharp. With luck he might even finish in the top 10, pick up a nice check and be quite proud of himself, since he was hardly pro-tour material. Lots of years ago Moody had won the Oklahoma high school championship and had gone to the University of Oklahoma on a golf scholarship. But he didn't stay long enough to play. He dropped out of school and enlisted in the Army in 1953, spent a year as a rifle instructor at Fort Chaffee, Ark., got transferred around the rest of his time to army golf courses in Japan, Korea, Germany and the United States. He won the Korean Open and the Korean PGA three times each and was runnerup in the Japan Open. Once before during this long chain of golf-oriented service Moody had left the Army in the hope of finding financial backing to try the tour. He played in the 1962 Open at Oakmont, but failed to make the 36-hole cut. He also failed to find anybody with the combination of faith and money. So it was back to the Army. Five years later, Moody found the backers he needed—a lawyer, a retail clothing merchant and a retired Army sergeant named James Blackburn. ("Nobody knows what Blackie does for a living," Moody says. "He's a mystery man, always going off somewhere. Maybe he works for the CIA. I don't know.") Moody qualified through the Approved Tournament Players School and joined the tour.

When he reached Houston only one other player thought Moody had a hope—or at least had the courage to say so out loud. When Lee Trevino was asked who he thought had the best chance of becoming the 1969 United States Open Champion, provided of course he did not win it himself, he answered, "Orville Moody." Everybody snickered and somebody asked, "Why?" "Because," said Trevino, "he's one helluva player." It was Trevino's best shot of the Open.

On the third day the leaders, Beman and Murphy, were paired

together, and watching them was a special form of agony. In three days Murphy had gone from excellent to adequate to awful. After three holes he was four over par. His driving was erratic, and if he missed a green he could not save his par. It must have been more than a little disquieting for Murphy to play this way and watch strokes slip away while Beman, whose shots were not that much better, was saving pars everywhere. The second hole serves as example enough. Both Beman and Murphy put their approach shots into the same greenside bunker. Murphy came out 25 feet from the cup and three-putted for 6. Beman came out three feet away and made his par 4. On the fifth hole Beman went over the green, chipped within three feet and made his par. On the eighth he missed the green again, chipped four feet from the hole and got down for his par. Beman hit only five greens on the front nine, yet was just one over par. Murphy had hit six greens and was four over par. Not even Beman could keep such a show up indefinitely, and eventually he faded to a 73 and a 54-hole total of 210. Asked to describe his round he said, "medium lousy." So were his chances of winning.

While two of the leaders were going gracefully backwards, Orville Moody was quietly shooting himself a 68 to move into second place at 209, and two other scores were attracting great attention. One was Arnold Palmer's. Palmer had come in with a 69 to be at 212—along with a gaggle of people, including Murphy and Al Geiberger. But it was the way Palmer had done his scoring that had his gallery babbling to itself. His scores were:

355 353 434 (35) 353 553 334 (34)

So on his card were nine 3's—half the holes. He had made six birdies, which was worth a roar from anybody's Army, but had frittered them away with five bogies. The other unusual score was that of Bob Rosburg, for Rosburg had suddenly shot himself into fifth place at 211. Having Rosburg, at age 42, a threat in the Open was about like having Jackie Burke himself show up with his clubs and take the lead. Rosburg won the 1959 PGA championship and finished second to Casper in the Open that year, but that was the pinnacle of his career. His game fell off. People close to him, including many of the older players, were very fond of him. He was an "in" person. Rosburg was now a club pro in St. Louis. He played in the PGA's club pros' championship in Florida the past winter and finished second. Returning to the tour, he missed the cut in his first four 1969 tournaments, then in successive weeks tied for 50th, 52nd and

43rd place. The next week he won 80th place outright, and then missed the cut at Pensacola. So it went, a dreary procession of awful finishes that must have hurt a man who once had a glimmer of fame. But suddenly Rosburg turned up at the U.S. Open rock steady. His first three rounds were 70, 69, and 72. He hit 34 of 42 fairways to rank seventh in the field, and hit 41 of the 54 greens to rank fourth. He did not necessarily look good doing it. He has never looked the part of a classic athlete, and now with his stooped shoulders, his stiff-legged walk and his baseball grip wrapped around his driver, you would never mistake him for a Littler or Snead. Or a U.S. Open winner—maybe.

In any event, Rosburg could not be the 1969 U.S. Open champion because another unusual figure on the tour, Miller Barber, often known as Mr. X., had it won. In at 206, Barber had a three-stroke lead with a round to play and not a worry. When he swings a club, Barber makes Rosburg look like a classic Littler. Miller takes the club back as though he were about to drive a railroad spike. But somehow he gets it into position at the top, and when he comes into the ball he is in as good a position as anybody. He is a solid striker of the ball when his timing is good—and when his timing is off, the sky's the limit. "Golf is played in about four feet," Barber has long told anybody who would listen. "It doesn't make any difference how you take the club back. What matters is how you take it through the impact zone." Barber is a 38 year-old bachelor from Sherman, Texas, with strong ties to Arkansas. He went to the University of Arkansas, and there are few more devoted fans of the school's football team. It is hot in the Southwest during football season and lots of games are played Friday or Saturday night. Barber has been known to play a tour tournament round early in the day, hop a plane to see an Arkansas football game, then get back in time to play his next round the following day. He is burly through the chest, narrow in the hips, has a round face and wears prescription sunglasses. ("Take off my glasses and it's 'where'd you go?' ") He is not exactly a Walter Hagen, but he has been known to go on night patrol, though never on tournament nights, he says. "You can't run every night in this business."

At this point, Barber was certainly running on Saturday. His 206 was one stroke off the U.S. Open three-round record, and the way Miller was playing there was no reason to think he would not follow Saturday's 68 with a 58 on Sunday. He was superb. He seemed to be hitting every drive on the screws, and when he connects he is very long. On the fifth hole, for instance, he crushed a drive 283 yards, and that is no estimate. The USGA each year measures drives on two holes of the Open as a check on trends in the game. The holes are measured very accurately and marked unobtrusively so that observers on the site can determine within one yard the distance of a drive. Barber started his Saturday round by dropping an eight-foot putt to save a par on the first, hit a 2-iron tee shot 10 feet from the fourth hole and made a birdie, then holed a 25-footer for another birdie on the eighth. He slipped to a bogey on the 10th, but it didn't bother him. His smile became more confident with each passing hole, for no one else was doing better and his chipping and putting were making up for his few mistakes. The shot of the round was an 8-iron to the 15th that covered the flag all the way. When it came down it looked as if it would drop into the hole on the fly, and even now it is hard to figure how it got directly behind the cup without falling in. So there was Barber, way out in front with one round to go, and only the churlish would shout, "Wait a minute. Haven't we seen Barber have last-round trouble now and then?" Yes, we have. And around the homey clubhouse some smart folks were saying, "Remember Augusta." That's where Barber was two strokes behind Billy Casper going into the last round of the Masters and they were paired together. Casper and Barber *both* shot 74 in that last round. Indeed, Barber was conscious of that final round of the Masters when he finished the third round of the Open. "I'm going to play the course, not the man," he said as he planned his fourth-round strategy. "I got a good taste of that this year at the Masters. I think Casper and I beat ourselves there. We started playing each other and ended up playing like donkeys. I'll never do that again."

When he came to the course Sunday morning, Barber was brimming with confidence. He felt that a round of 70 would win it for him, and as he prepared to go after that 70 he said to Chris Schenkel, the television commentator, "They've got to catch me; I don't have to catch them." But the men immediately behind Barber did not feel their position was hopeless. I know that at least one of them, Palmer, a full six shots back, thought he had a chance. Here is how they stood going into that final round:

Miller Barber	206	Arnold Palmer	212
Orville Moody	209	Bobby Mitchell	212
Deane Beman	210	Bob Murphy	212
Bunky Henry	210	Al Geiberger	212
Bob Rosburg	211	Charles Coody	212

You could almost see the glint in Palmer's eyes as he studied that lineup. Who was there ahead of him he couldn't beat? "If Barber has trouble," he thought, "that leaves Moody, Beman, Henry and Rosburg." If he could just play a little he could beat them. Couldn't he? Anyway, you could see the reason for Arnold's fever. And so could his Army. When Palmer teed off with Coody he took a larger crowd than Barber and Moody, who came along three groups later.

By early Sunday morning it was obvious something had changed at Champions. It was the wind. No longer was Houston like the inside of a cookpot. It was cool. And the wind was blowing from the north. "You know what the odds are against a norther here in June?" Jack Burke asked. "About a million to one. I woke up in the middle of the night and went outside to be sure. Then I came back and woke up my wife. 'There's a norther blowing,' I told her. That's going to change this course. They'll be hitting 3-irons where they were hitting 7-irons yesterday, and they'll be hitting 7-irons where they hit 3-irons. It's going to confuse them." Indeed it did.

The wind did not confuse Palmer on the first hole. For the third time in four days he chipped in for a birdie. Could this be an indication that he was coming on, that for once during the week he would put everything together? The second hole gave the answer, though nobody knew it at the time. He pushed his second shot into a bunker and made a bogey. As soon as the ball left the club I thought of that fan who claimed Arnold was hitting everything to the right because of the way he set himself up. His approach to the third hole went slightly right again, but this time he hit the green and ended up eight feet from the hole, only to miss the birdie putt.

Meanwhile, Moody and Barber started off with standard par 4's on the first hole, and if you were looking for indications that Barber was nervous, you could watch him bouncing the ball off his putter, doing that little juggling act you see the pros do, as Moody looked over a putt. On the second hole Barber hit his approach into the sand and took a bogey 5 after missing a seven-foot putt. But everything seemed still in hand. After the third hole it was not so in hand. There Barber drove into the trees at the bend of the left-to-right dogleg, dumped his second shot into the left greenside bunker, came out 15 feet from the hole and made another bogey. His lead over Moody was down to one stroke.

Palmer now had a chance to get back into the game, but he had bogied the fourth and was one over par, four strokes behind Moody and five behind Barber. It looked, in fact, as though Barber might shoot 100 and still win. Beman had gone four over in five holes. So had Geiberger and Henry. Coody had gone five over in the first six; Mitchell was six over after six. Of the leaders, only Rosburg was under par for the round. He had birdied the second hole and was one under for the round and even for the tournament.

There are those sad times during a golf tournament when you can watch a great golfer losing a championship. I saw it happen now to Palmer. His irons were not sharp. He had put his approach into another bunker at the fifth, but scrambled to a par. He reached the green of the sixth in two and got down in two from 25 feet. But on the seventh it began to look as if Arnold just couldn't make it. His long drive cleared the turn of the dogleg and he hit a beautiful iron that dropped softly onto the green 10 to 12 feet from the hole, decidedly within birdie range. He stroked the putt nicely, then winced as it glided by. No birdie. He missed the green on the par 3 eighth, chipped three feet from the hole and saved his par. Then came the ninth, and a great disappointment. This is perhaps the only let-up hole on the course, a 505-yard par 5 that can be reached in two shots. Palmer laid into a driver, then spanked a wood that looked perfect except that it was a little strong. It rolled just off the edge of the green and left him with a nasty lie. It was close to a bunker and when he took his stance Arnold's right heel overhung the edge of the trap; his right heel was actually off the ground and he did not have a firm stance. He stubbed the chip and instead of a birdie he had a par and made the turn in 36. He had started the round two over, now he was three over.

At the time Palmer was playing his fine shot to the seventh green, Geiberger was on the eighth tee. As Palmer's ball soared toward the green a roar went up, for Geiberger's tee shot rolled toward the hole and just missed being an ace. He holed a birdie putt of about six inches, followed up with birdies at the ninth and 10th, and was tied with Palmer. Even more drama was going on behind Palmer, for Moody was catching up to Barber. Miller had completely lost control of his game and was dropping strokes rapidly. On the eighth hole Barber made his fifth bogey of the round and Moody passed him. They both made birdies on the ninth, which was notable because it was Moody's only birdie of the round. Can you imagine going into the last round of the Open three strokes behind the leader, shooting a 72, coming up with only one birdie, and still winning the championship? I can't.

Up ahead Palmer was still in contention, and with a little luck he could have been a lot closer, for he began to hit fantastic shots that drove his gallery wild. The tournament television broadcast had just started and Arnold must have known it, for he reacted as he used to years ago. Three times in three holes his shot stopped an inch from the cup instead of falling in. He pitched from 30 yards out on the 11th and it stopped an inch away; he came from a bunker on the 12th an inch away; then he almost holed a chip for an eagle on the 13th, only to see it stop an inch away.

At about this time the USGA began to ponder a serious problem. What would happen if four, five, or six players tied? This was certainly possible, because at one point late in the round eight players were within two strokes of the lead. How should the playoff be conducted? Should all six be paired together? Should they be broken into two groups? If they were split wouldn't that give the advantage to the second group? This was just after Palmer played the 13th and got back to two over par. Murphy, Geiberger, Bruce Crampton and Beman were two over also; Rosburg was one over, Moody and Barber were even.

Orville Moody went ahead forever at the 12th. He and Barber both hit their tee shots into the woods to the right, in part out of fear of the lake to the left of the green. Barber had a particularly bad lie on hardpan and his pitch did not clear the lip of the bunker. It fell in the sand, and he needed two putts after a rather difficult recovery shot. Moody also had a bad lie, but his pitch was superb; three feet from the hole, and down it went for a miracle par. Barber was on his way from near-certain victory to a 78 and a sixth place finish. After the round he tore into the clubhouse fuming, almost knocked over a policeman, and instead of apologizing said, "Get out of my way. I just lost the National Open." He had cooled off a little later and when a friend asked if he'd like a drink, he answered, "Hell, yes. I might as well get drunk; I can't play golf."

Moody had shaken off Barber, but he still had others closing in. Geiberger was playing against the advice of his doctors. He had been suffering from an inflammation of the intestines and had not entered a tournament since the Masters. Now, with a chance to win the Open, his approach to the 15th stopped about 12 feet to the left of the hole and he ran it in for the birdie. He was just one over par with three holes to play. Then all kinds of things seemed to happen at once. Palmer was behind Geiberger, still two over par after a routine par 4 at the 14th and he had hooked his drive into the woods on the 15th. He had a sandy lie deep in trouble and only a perfect shot could get him to the green. He would have to hit it low, hook it sharply and hope that it had enough power to run onto the green. The shot could hardly have been better. It streaked out of the trees, took a sharp left turn and kept coming and coming and coming. It looked for an instant as if it might roll into a bunker, skimmed by the edge and caught the green. Arnold's gallery went mad. If Palmer were to make this birdie, it would certainly give him the lift he needed. He was about 40 feet away and hit a good first putt, which just slipped by the right edge of the hole. But it slipped five feet by. Palmer carefully lined up the return putt, stroked it just the way he wanted . . . . and again it slipped by the right edge of the hole. Three putts: bogey 5. He stepped back, took off his cap and stared at the hole. A perfectly hit putt had not fallen in. And that was the end for Arnold. A missed birdie on 17 was mere anti-climax.

Over on 16, Geiberger was ready to hit his tee shot when Palmer's ball rolled onto the green. He could not swing in all that din, so he stepped away. He was ready again when Palmer walked onto the green, but he had to step away when the applause and cheering started once more. Finally he was able to play, hit onto the green, but then three-putted to go two over once more. I can't help but think that those two interruptions upset Geiberger and led to the poor putting. But even this bogey did not mean Geiberger was out of it, for back on the 14th Moody was making a bogey. Now Moody was one over par with four holes to play, tied with Rosburg and a stroke ahead of Geiberger.

Geiberger was the first of the three to play the critical closing holes. After his bogey at the 16th he went over the 17th with his approach, hit a bad chip, then saved himself with a 10-foot putt. Now the 18th and all out for a birdie. He hit a good approach 20 feet or so from the hole and gave the putt a good stroke, but the ball curled away in the last few inches. He finished at 282. Rosburg next. He had saved his par on the 10th with a 10-foot putt, then missed a three-footer at the 11th to go one over. After that he had parred every hole to the 17th. He hit his approach into a bunker there and his recovery left him a putt for his par. Rosburg ran it in to stay even with Moody, and now needed only a par 4 on the finishing hole for 281. In this critical situation Rosburg snapped his drive. The shot hit some trees and dropped down less than 200 yards from the tree. He now needed a massive recovery to reach the green from a poor lie. Using a wood, he hit the shot slightly to the right and into a bunker. Then he played an exceptional recovery three feet from the hole.

When that shot settled close to the cup the crowd of players sprawled in the locker room watching on television roared. Rossy is their man, and golfers like Phil Rodgers and Mike Souchak were rooting him home. There was a non-golfer there, too, Rosburg's teenage son.

What the group saw next, along with a few million people watching national television, was remarkable. It may be unfair to dwell on such things, because only Rosburg could know the truth—and it may be that he can't possibly know, either—but I have to think the discipline, the nerve, the determination that carried Rosburg so far finally gave out with that shot from the bunker on 18. Rosburg, when he thought about it, had to be dumbfounded at having played so well at Champions. He had to have teed off that Sunday morning just hoping he could hold everything together for one more day and finish well—well enough to earn some decent money and get his exemption for next year's Open. And then, as he played steadily along, within himself, the pars kept coming. You could almost imagine him humming away, a little tune about isn't this a pleasant day, and a nice course, too, and even a few people around to watch me and most of all no sweat . . . you used to get yourself all excited, Rossy, but you were a young man then and not so smart . . . what's to get excited about at 42? Eighth place would be nice. Fifth place would be real good. I wonder what they pay for fifth? Let's see, the winner gets . . . Oh my, would you look at that. Poor Miller just made himself another bogey . . .

But by the time Rosburg was on the 17th tee he had to have realized that this was a different game after all. Like it or not, he was in the U.S. Open. He had to stop humming and see what he could find within himself to conquer the last two holes. That is where the explosion shot and par-saving putt came from on 17. They were two courageous shots under the conditions. That is where the duck-hooked tee shot came on 18, a wild lashed-at thing that rattled around in the timber, and then the recovery to the bunker and the knowledge that with Orville behind you shooting pars you had to get the ball down in two. I will now class Rosburg's shot from the bunker on 18 as the gamest shot of 1969. He did not have all that much green to work with, and ask yourself what was there inside of him to work with. Whatever it was, he found it and he used it all. There was a gasp from the crowd when the ball settled down three feet from the hole, just as there had been in the locker room. And then Rosburg did what you might have done, or I might have done, and once again we return to the theme of this chapter—that no sport gets as close to its fans as golf. Rosburg walked up to that little putt and—bang—hit it. He hit it so quickly that the television cameras were hardly focused. If you turned your head away from the television set for a split second you missed the putt completely. There was no lining it up, looking at it from the back side of the hole, studying the grain . . . nothing. Rosburg had decided that his best chance with a three-footer that could win him a U.S. Open at age 42 and change his life forever was to hit it before he could think about it. It is the old story under pressure—if you're going to miss, miss it quick and get to hell out of there. I've done it. You've done it. The moment is so familiar you can almost taste it. There was, it goes without saying, no proper stroke at the ball. The putt was jabbed, and was not struck firmly enough to hold the line. The gallery was shocked. Rosburg looked wan and quickly tapped the ball in. I became something of a Rosburg fan just then. Inside the locker room at that moment there was a sudden hush. Rosburg's son began to cry, and finally Phil Rodgers broke the silence. "He can still make it if the blade comes open on the cross-hander," Rodgers said

No one was more aware of this precise possibility than the cross-handed putter himself, Orville Moody. Now on 17, he needed two pars to win. He had hit his approach on this par 4 hole into the fringe of the green some 30 feet from the cup. As he walked to the green he saw his wife in the gallery, went over to her and said, "Honey, I just can't line up a putt. I'm stroking it all right, but I just can't line it up." She didn't say a word.

So there stood Orville Moody; 35 years old, one third Choctaw Indian or maybe one-quarter, he isn't really sure, resident of Chickasha, Okla., and the last of the great cross-handed putters because to tell the plain, simple truth, he had the yips so bad that he started placing his left hand below the right in the hope his wrists wouldn't "be so flippy." Yes, there stood Orville, who had never had a golf lesson in his life, and who never practiced except to hit a few warm-up balls before a round. This was Orville, who had given up any U.S. Open thoughts after 27 holes of the first qualifying round at Dallas Athletic Club Country Club weeks before. At that point he had to play the last nine holes at two-under par to survive. As he stood on the 10th tee he turned to Bobby Cole, his playing partner, and said, "I don't really mind not qualifying, because I wouldn't have a chance in the Open." "Don't be stupid," Cole answered. "Keep trying." And Moody did, getting the last birdie he needed by exploding out of a bunker and into the cup on the 35th hole. Now on 17, with the U.S. Open nearly his, Orville Moody chipped from 30 feet, got the shot close enough, and held his wrists firm to sink the putt for a par. Meanwhile, Beman had birdied 18 to join Rosburg and Geiberger at 282, so one slip by Moody meant a four-way play-off.

On 18 Moody hit his drive with all the power he could find. There was not an ounce of caution in the stroke. It was not a very pretty swing, but the ball carried dead center of the fairway and Moody had only an 8-iron left. He hit it 14 feet from the hole, started to walk to the green, stopped, picked up his divot, and with the crowd streaking past him toward the green, he went back and carefully put the divot in place. When he reached the green he went to the USGA tent and asked, "What's the best score in?"

"You have two putts for the championship," he was told. He used them both. In fact, he hit the first one so weakly that the second putt was more than a tap-in.

And there you have it—instant U.S. Open winner, a golfer whose biggest previous title was Korean Open champion, a golfer who thought the championship of all of Fort Hood was a pretty big deal. Now he was the U.S. champion with $30,000 in his pocket and a long distance call coming in from President Nixon. Nobody knows for sure what the two talked about. Something was said about a big victory for the middle class and the President said it wasn't often that a man spends 14 years in the Army and then comes out to win the U.S. Open.

"No, sir," said Moody. "It's the first time."

I mentioned, incidentally, that almost everyone was pulling for Palmer. Well, so was President Nixon. He later made another phone call to Houston, this one to Arnold. He told him that while he understood that Moody was a nice guy, he had been rooting for Palmer.

After the call from the President—and a few tears with his wife—Moody went out to receive his trophy and his check. He was all smiles, but he also struck me as a subdued, old-fashioned, very humble kind of athlete. It is possible to put on the country-boy act, but it is not a put-on with Orville Moody. And it is easy to fake humility, but I suspect this is an honest facet of Moody, too. I do know that he is one of a small number of touring pros who meet regularly for informal Bible study. (Babe Hiskey, the leader of the group, called Moody on Sunday morning and suggested a few passages he might read before starting his last round.) When he accepted his trophy Moody said, "I never dreamed I was good enough to win this tournament." Later he was told that his victory meant he would represent the United States in the World Cup matches in Singapore in the fall. "Oh, no," said Orville. "That's for the best golfers this country has. I'm not the best. I was today, but there's lots of people around who can beat me at this game." (Some weeks later, along this same line, television director Frank Chirkinian was asking Orville who he would like to be teamed with in the CBS Golf Classic. Chirkinian arranges the teams. "How about Littler?" Frank asked. "He's having a fine year." "Oh no, Frank," answered Moody. "Gene would never want to play with me. Listen, none of those good golfers would want to play with me." Chirkinian recalls telling Moody, "For heavens sake, Orville, you're the U.S. Open Champion. They'll play with you. Believe me, they'll play with you." "No, Frank," Orville said. "Why there's a sergeant down on the base that can beat me five days out of seven."

As the trophy presentation took place I could not help reflecting on Moody's future. Somebody had told him that being the Open champion would be worth a million dollars to him, and I thought how ridiculous that is. Being an Open champion *can* be worth a million dollars, but you have to be the right champion to start with. You have to have the flair of a Palmer, or the power of a Nicklaus, or the guts of a Gary Player. You really do. When you have this you have something to market, something to build a million-dollar property on. To a degree Casper and Trevino have something special. So does Tony Jacklin. But we tend to forget that there have been lots of U.S. Open winners who are best remembered as old what's-his-name. Orville impresses me as a realist, however. He probably laughed at the million-dollar talk.

So now Orville Moody left Champions and made that long trip back to his hotel in downtown Houston. They had a party for him that night. Orville's manager had a sign put in the lobby of the Hotel America:

RECEPTION FOR ORVILLE MOODY
ROOM 927

A lot of golf fans came, a lot of newspaper reporters came, two of Moody's financial backers came (not Blackburn), some friends from Killeen, Texas, came. And Moody began to get acquainted with the price of fame. Every reporter at the party wanted his own special story and went after it. As an old soldier, Moody knew the value of strategic withdrawal, but along about 1 A.M. he had to turn and make his stand. The reporters had backed him into the bathroom of the suite. There was no further retreat. Eventually Moody and the reporters wore out, and Orville made his exit. He was last seen sitting in a chair in the hallway, still dazed, shaking his head just slightly at the wonder of it all as he waited for an elevator to take him—up or down?

4

The U.S. Tour

There was trouble, but now the Dey is cast

I t is at times difficult to select one event or trend in a sporting year
and say that this single thing was the most significant development
of the past 12 months. But as far as professional golf in the United
States is concerned, there is little doubt that the naming of Joe Dey
as Commissioner of the Tournament Players Division of the PGA is
going to have a greater effect on the sport than anything since the
advent of Arnold Palmer and television's discovery of the game ten
to 15 years before. In due time the appointment of Dey to this new
post will almost surely result in important changes in the structure of
the pro golf tour—some of them changes that golf followers have
long hoped for, and others that certainly seem beneficial.

What has occurred is the fortunate discovery of the right man for
the right job. Rarely is fate so kind. To my mind, the creation of the
job—giving pro golf a commissioner, such as baseball and football
have had in the United States—was probably even more important
than being able to persuade Joe Dey to fill in. Some brief and
unappetizing background is necessary. A long year ago (nothing
becomes ancient history quicker than a settled war) there was a great
deal of shouting, name-calling, law envoking and suit filing over
something that was called the Revolt of the Pros. The touring pros,
with every good reason, were tired of having their tour managed
indifferently by the PGA. They were also, as can be the nature of
things, acquisitive, proud, and pretty disorganized themselves. Their
revolt was successful. They pulled out of the PGA, set up their own
tour and began to schedule tournaments. Defeated in the field, the
PGA retreated to the conference table and instructed its negotiators
to say something like, "We give up, come on back please. Please! "
Of course, the players, who never really wanted to be in the tour
running business, or out of the PGA either, were willing enough to
return on their own terms. They key to the terms was the formation
of something called the Tournament Policy Board. It was made up of

four players, *three* PGA officers, and three millionaire-industrialist types whose interest would clearly be nothing but the good of the sport. These three men were J. Paul Austin, president of the Coca-Cola Company, John Murchison, a Dallas financier and George Love, chairman of the Board of the Consolidated Coal Company. The first serious duty of this 10-man board, which now had full and final authority over the PGA tour, was the selection of a man who would serve—at the board's pleasure—as the commissioner of professional golf. Many names were bandied about, and the presumption always was that the most obvious and desirable candidate, Joseph C. Dey, Jr., the 61-year-old executive director of the United States Golf Association and a USGA official for 34 years, would never leave his post as the dominate figure in amateur golf for the turmoil and disorder of the pro world. The very idea seemed contradictory, an aesthetic impossibility.

The presumption was wrong. In early January certain members of the new Tournament Policy Board came to Dey and asked him if he would both compile a list of names of people he thought might serve as commissioner and offer his thoughts as to what kind of qualifications the commissioner should have. Dey did. It was almost as a parting thought when the matter was next discussed that he was asked if he would ever consider leaving the USGA to take the job himself. Looking back now, one can guess how thoroughly Joe Dey must have thought out the answer to that question. One can almost see him, deep in the comforts of his USGA office, brooding. There he was, revered master of the USGA, surrounded by artifacts of the game; the USGA headquarters is Golf House, a museum for the sport located just off Park Avenue on 38th street in New York City. And any man surrounds himself with the comforts of his life. It is a wrench to leave them. But on January 22 the wrench was made. To the amazement of even the closest insiders—his own aides said he would never consider such a move—Dey left the USGA for the PGA.

Jack Nicklaus summed up the immediate reaction among the players: "Joe's acceptance is fantastic. He will elevate the game." And Hord Hardin, president of the USGA, spoke for others when he said, "Joe Dey is respected by golfers all over the world as the most competent administrator in the game. We cannot think of a better man to take over the affairs of the playing professionals." That is how Joe Dey, not without regrets, stiffly cinched up his USGA necktie (he calls it his "security blanket" and still wears it frequently) and stepped into the world of pro golf.

Billy Casper at the Masters. Leading the tournament in the middle of the third round, Casper is all light and zest and gaiety and charm.

Blowing the tournament in the fourth round, a sombre Casper chips out of the azaleas on the second hole, the place they call the 'Delta Airlines Counter'.

Tom Weiskopf.

Two fellows who got so near, so far, at Augusta.

George Knudson.

And the one who went all the way. George Archer, 1969 Masters champion, under a friendly scoreboard in the final round.

Jim Colbert, Monsanto Open.

Tom Shaw, Doral Open.

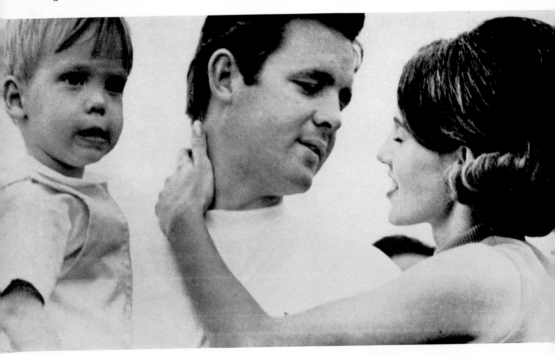

Bunky Henry, National Airlines Open.

The last year of the decade was one of new faces, if not of new superstars, and in the first ten months of the year, whenever the superstars turned their backs, the new men charged right past.

Larry Zeigler, Michigan Golf Classic (for a while, the trophy was Zeigler's only reward – the sponsors could not produce the prize money).

Dave Hill, Buick Open.

Larry Hinson, Greater New Orleans Open.

The big money winner with the big cheque, from the Westchester Classic –
Frank Beard, $50,000, and friends.

'Gene the Machine' they call Littler. His classic swing nailed two winter tournaments and brought him into the Masters as leading money winner.

Tony Jacklin couldn't believe it.

When the World Series, with a first prize of $50,000, came along, Orville was right on target.

Sergeant Orville Moody kept saying he couldn't play a lick, but when the money was big, the sergeant went to war. His first win was the U.S. Open.

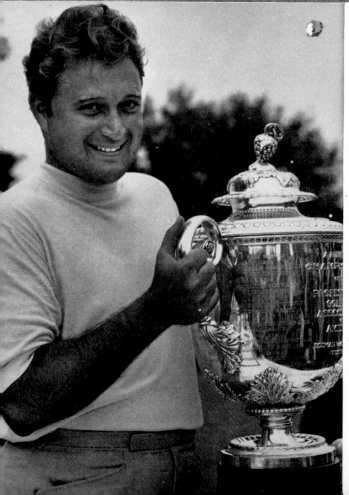

Raymond Floyd and Gary
Player screened by a heavy
police guard after
demonstrators had tried to
attack Gary on the third
day of the PGA
Championship.

Floyd prevailed over Gary's
powerful challenge and
was rewarded with one of
U.S. golf's prime awards –
the PGA Championship.

The collapse of the year award went to Lee Trevino. At the 17th hole of the last round of the Alcan, he failed to get out of sand – note the ball by the lip of the trap – and took three more to get down. And since Casper was busy with four successive birdies at the same time, it all cost Lee a $55,000 first prize.

The weather of the year award went to what is sometimes called sunny California. Jack Nicklaus on the 15th green, Pebble Beach, in the first round of the Crosby.

The U.S. Open, in Texas in June, was something else, something of the fat man's open, in searing heat. Bob Murphy mops up.

Miller Barber is resigned.

Orville Moody is corpulent.

Miller Barber in a fury . . . .

and Deane Beman leaning furiously into a fairway wood shot – little 'Dino' has to, to keep up with the big guys.

Orville Moody, the champion, finger-snaps a putt successfully. Drives one –
in the fairway of course.

And finally, cannot resist the tears when it's all over.

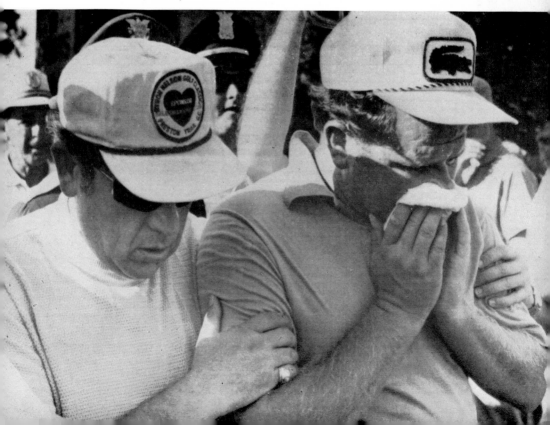

Scrub and sandhills at Royal Birkdale, venue of the 1969 Ryder Cup matches.

The aftermatch of that 7th green squabble when the ancient game was momentarily less than regal. From left, Gallacher (UK), Hill (USA) and Huggett (UK).

A foursome of Birkdale wives. From left, Lorna Townsend, Pat Beard, Vivienne Jacklin and Shirley Casper.

Brian Huggett, choked, in the consoling arms of Dai Rees. The Welshman thought that the birdie putt he had just holed on 18 for a half with Casper had won the entire match for the British.

After slightly more than a year – for Palmer fans a mini-century – Arnold Palmer wins again in the first Heritage Golf Classic.

The old-style Palmer socks it to them with a birdie putt in the same event.

And for one that got away, the equally old-style Palmer glare.

What did Dey bring to the pro game? Why was he the best man to be the first commissioner? There are several answers, but perhaps the most important comes down to something Americans are very conscious of—image. With this one step the image of pro golf, badly tarnished by two years of civil war, received a tremendous boost. Consider one small matter. Overnight the golf tour was being run from a suite of New York City offices instead of the PGA headquarters on a sandspit in Florida. It had been preposterous that for ten years the pro golf tour had not joined other big-time sports and operated from a base where people could be reached and business could be done. Now, as likely as not, the men who have dealings with the commissioner of pro golf might find themselves lunching with Dey at the Union League Club, where the dining rooms and library reflect what 134 years of gentlemanly living at a Park Avenue address ought to reflect. Should this be important? No, but somehow it gets to be if you are a man, say, who is considering putting up a $300,000 purse for the Dow Jones Open. You might be comforted to find yourself talking with people and under conditions that are commensurate with your time and investment. Call it class, call it prestige, even call it a little pretentious if you will; it is something pro golf can use, for golf itself, in my view, has its own sense of class, of prestige, of the right way of doing things. That is all part of the game.

More significant is what the men inside the game thought of the Dey "image", and in this respect Dey brought with him a wealth of plusses. He was probably the one man for whom everybody involved had a great deal of respect. This was most clearly true in the case of the players. Many of them came up through junior golf programs, through college teams, through amateur championships, all of which were administered by the USGA. Eventually they would play in USGA's biggest event, the U.S. Open, which has the fine reputation it does largely because it has run so well for so many years. To the players, Dey was not an outsider. He was a man they felt would appreciate their problems, a man they could talk to. On the other hand, the country club pros, whose numbers constitute the great majority of the PGA membership, make their living off amateur golf, and they knew the USGA had run their sport well under Dey. Finally, sponsors, television people, businessmen, advertising men, indeed all those who had substantial dealings in golf, were likely to look on the Dey appointment with approval. I can put it simply for myself. When it comes to making a decision that is for the good of golf, I trust Joe Dey's judgement above anybody's. Many times I have asked his advice when one of my clients had an opportunity that I was uneasy about—one that I thought could possibly cast either the game or the golfer in a questionable light. If pro golf needs a conscience, Joe Dey's will do just fine.

But respect is one thing, accomplishment another. It is my guess that Dey felt his major task for 1969 had to be development of a genuine reconciliation between the players and the PGA. Before any administrator can propose—gently, here and there—a substantial change, he must have a base of tranquility from which to operate. I think such a reconciliation has been achieved. There will always be a residue of strain between the touring professionals and the club professionals. The one group, after all, sees the other in terms of glamour, prestige and wealth. It is only human that some jealousy arises. But the indications are now that the anti-player sentiment on the part of the club pros is disappearing. There seems to be an understanding that the touring pros are selling the game for everybody. It was meaningful that when Joe Dey went to make a speech before a meeting of PGA members, he received a standing ovation as he was introduced. The relationship between the Tournament Policy Board and the PGA seems to be a constructive one again.

This constructive approach is being applied as well to some long-neglected figures in the game, the tournament sponsors. The basic difficulty with the U.S. pro tour in the Sixties was that it has completely outgrown the administrative capabilities of the PGA officers who were attempting to run it. There was no machinery to operate what had suddenly become a major sport. Sponsors began to invest hundreds of thousands of dollars under conditions that were hardly advantageous to them. Schedules were haphazard, there were last-minute changes, there was no guarantee that an event would not be summarily dropped from the tour, there was no assurance that any big-name golfers would turn up to play in a given event, and there was no help or advice offered by the PGA concerning the staging of a tournament.

There must be changes in these areas, and there almost certainly will be. I am confident we will see some major improvements in the tour in the next few years, all based upon things that are under consideration now by the Tournament Policy Board and Joe Dey. Many of these revisions have been discussed by the PGA in the past, and the need for some of them has long been recognized, but nobody ever got around to actually doing something. Now things are starting to happen.

For example, the PGA's tournament field staff has been adequate—even better than that in the last two years—but now there is a plan to add two advance men to the staff. Their duties will be new. Each of them will be responsible for half of the tour tournaments. They will visit the course and the sponsors for any given tournament six months before the event. They will check on the course quality, offer advice and in general hold the hands of the sponsors. They will come back three months later to see how things are developing—is the course rounding into shape, how are ad sales going in your program, have you solved your parking problem, etc. They will be there to assist, not instruct, but the assistance will have the weight of years of PGA experience behind it. Finally, they will check again ten days before the tournament. The idea is an excellent one. In addition, the PGA will have a full-time agronomist. His job will be to offer ideas or advice to local greens-keepers. Joe Dey has long felt that nothing is 'as important to a tournament as the condition of the golf course. Good courses bring out the best in players, and much enhance the pleasure of everybody. Goat pastures are for goats. Both of these innovations, incidentally, are copies of procedures that the USGA has followed for years. (The USGA advance man for the Open gets there six weeks before the tournament and never leaves.)

Far trickier is the matter of guaranteed fields. It is difficult for a layman to appreciate how much one or two top players mean to the success of a tournament. Like it or not, there are very few true stars in golf, athletes who attract large galleries all by themselves. The average touring pro likes to delude himself into believing that the crowds come out to watch the whole field compete. Sophisticated golf fans might, but there are not that many sophisticates. The big galleries want to see their hero, regardless of his present standings on the money list or how he is playing that week. And how many such stars are there, men whose very presence can all but assure the success of an event? Palmer, above all. Nicklaus and Player. I wish there were more, because golf needs them badly, but there are not. Considerable unhappiness has arisen on the part of sponsors because there is no way of knowing whether or not one of the few stars would appear in the average tour tournament. The key players are wooed, they can't or don't come, sponsors have an inferior event and a whole community is left with a bad taste in its mouth about professional golf. The damage to the sport is considerable, and the problem is acute. The sponsors of one major tournament recently called me to ask if I could insure the appearance of either Palmer or Nicklaus for their event in 1970. They said, quite frankly, that if I could not, they were going to give up on the tournament. They felt they had to have one or the other to break even at the gate. I told them I could not give them that kind of assurance, and they did cancel the event.

The only solution is some form of PGA-enforced appearance guarantee, and this is being given great study by Joe Dey and his staff. Dey himself has worked out two systems, neither of which he is wholly satisfied with. Late last winter he had a questionaire sent to all of the regular touring professionals asking them to indicate where they were likely to play, so that he could assess how some of the fields were shaping up. Within a year or two, I think, some form of an appearance guarantee system will be adopted. I do know this, and can say it flatly. If a system is worked out that appears fair and does not unduly restrict the outside activities or international playing opportunities of the golfers I represent, these golfers will support a guaranteed appearance system. And I think if Palmer, Nicklaus and Player are willing to go along with such a system for the overall benefit of the tour, the rest of the players probably would. It is recognized that touring pros are individual businessmen—and certainly individualists—but I think they are also able to appreciate that they have a responsibility to their sport. Freedom of action is fine, but sometimes it must be limited in the name of common sense and protection of the common good. However, I doubt such a plan would ever be approved were it not that a man with Joe Dey's prestige is now in a position to advocate it, and to find a system that is as fair as possible for all concerned.

The same is true of the other major problem on the U.S. tour. Too many players—rabbits they are called—are attempting to qualify on Mondays and Tuesdays for the few slots that are still open in a tournament that starts on Thursdays. At times, fields of 150 are fighting for ten to fifteen openings, a depressing situation for all concerned. It is harsh to say, and unfair to many young golfers who must have a chance to start somewhere on the tour, but the number of hopefuls trying to get into any tournament must be drastically reduced. What is needed is a minor-league tour. I remember discussing this with Arnold several years ago. He felt, and has said several times since, that the number of major tour tournaments should be reduced to twenty or so, with smaller tournaments being held in the same weeks. This is far more true today than it was five or so years ago. And here again, Dey and the Tournament Policy Board are working on a solution. The structure of the tour cannot be—and should not be—changed overnight. But it can be changed within two years or so to the benefit of everybody, and especially the sport.

Already, Joe Dey has announced the first example of the trend we can expect to see more of. With a minimum of strain or publicity, the PGA announced in mid-December that in the week of March 1, 1970 the Citrus Golf Tournament Fund of Florida would play host to not one PGA event, but two. One would be a familiar tour tournament, the Florida Citrus Invitational. It's purse would be $150,000, which is an increase of $35,000 over last year. In addition, during the same week in another central Florida city, there would be held a $35,000 satellite event known as the Florida Citrus Open Invitational. The first tournament would have a field of only 100 professionals, and they would be invited on the basis of their past and present play. The satellite event would be open to 144 professionals, and it would offer the usual pre-tournament qualifying. In short, here is one form of a Joe Dey plan being tried. "A sort of dual tour is needed to satisfy the interests and needs of the sport," said Dey in announcing the unusual format. "We appreciate the forward looking view of the Citrus Golf Tournament Fund of Florida, which, we believe, is setting a pattern for the future." We believe, too. This is indeed a test for the pattern of the future. Partly for historical reference, it is worth noting how the 100 players for the big-money tournament in this first major-league plus minor-league format are to be selected. The invitees will come from the following categories:

U.S. Open and PGA Champions of the last 10 years;
Current British Open titleholder;
Leading money-winner of each of the last five years;
Members of the 1969 U.S. Ryder Cup Team;
Winners of individual major events in the last year;
Former Citrus Open winners;
1969's top 60 money-winners on the tour;
15 lowest scorers, and those tied for 15th place, in the event which precedes the Invitational, the Doral Open;
20 leading money-winners of 1970;
Head professional at the host club;

Five players to be selected from all former U.S. Open, PGA and British Open Champions, members of the U.S. Ryder Cup team of the last ten years and members of the 1969 British Ryder Cup Team.

The field this invitational system will provide can only be properly judged when we see who tees off in March, but the system looks hard to argue with at this point. The whole thing is a noble experiment.

The benefits of the new PGA organization show in many small ways. For example, I happened to notice the other day that the PGA tournament schedule for the first eight months of 1970 had been mailed to me on the 6th of August 1969. The next time I saw Joe Dey I congratulated him, for such an early schedule certainly showed a new stability and efficiency on the part of the tour. He thanked me, and said his actual goal was to have a complete schedule 18 months to two years in advance. He saw no reason why this could not be done, and felt it would be of great help to both players and sponsors.

Meanwhile, the sport in the United States continues to grow, to a degree that surprises me, in fact. I thought I sensed a downturn in golf interest in 1968, but in 1969 galleries held up well, purses kept increasing and new sponsors flocked in pleading for dates. The eight-month schedule showed that ten tournaments had raised their prize money. By year's end 15 to 20 serious sponsors had been turned down. (Among them were four groups that proposed events worth more than a million dollars. A major factor in their rejection—and certainly a new one by PGA standards— was that Joe Dey did not feel the golf courses to be used were up to the quality that a big-money event merits. As I say, things are changing on the U.S. Tour.)

It would not be proper to move on to the blow-by-blow action on the tour without considering one other aspect of the Commissioner's job. It is a small part of what he does, but one that often looms large in the public mind. This is the matter of disciplining athletes. Men who compete in team sports are accustomed to discipline, but things get out of hand on occasion, commissioners levy fines, and everybody goes back to work aware of—and comforted by—the knowledge that they can get a fair hearing from the man who runs the sport, that Big Daddy is watching them. But, believe me, golfers are different. They are accustomed to thinking they must account only to themselves, though happily they are also aware that their sport has a background of decorum and tradition which they dare not sully. But how would they react to having a commissioner discipline them from above? This is probably a matter that never seriously concerned Joe Dey. But for small turns in his life long ago, Dey might well have become a minister. Indeed, he treats golf as if it were something of a calling for him. As a result, if ever there was a commissioner capable of having a heart-to-heart chat with a mischievous choir boy, Dey is it. "My ideas about this are simple", Joe told me once last year. "These boys are grown men. No one can discipline them. They must discipline themselves. But they will, because they all want their conduct to be a credit to the game."

Right. So along about Jacksonville time Dave Hill, who fears no man and sometimes tells them so in rather intemperate fashion, swore at a PGA official in rather intemperate fashion. Now I swore at PGA officials for years, but I did it in seclusion; in my mind's eye, so to speak, or perhaps in front of my shaving mirror. Dave did it in front of a gallery—women and children and all, one gathers. Anyway, in public. The PGA official called Joe Dey and reported the incident. He was angry and offended, with good reason. That evening Hill received a telephone call from Joe Dey. Would Dave, asked the Commissionner, mind giving his side of the incident? Hill began to explain. No, said Dey, the report should be in writing. Just mail it right away, Dave. Now a man who makes his living with a niblick is not always at ease with a pen. Hill pondered, but about all he could think of to say was that he was wrong. Dey received the explanation, told Hill that weighing the case on its merits it seemed Hill's assessment was accurate. And he fined Hill $150 and suspended him for one tournament. "The players like rules", says Dey. "They know rules are good for them." Hill's reaction suggests this is true. He completely respected Dey's decision.

Interestingly enough, Hill received Joe Dey's attention again, this time at the Ryder Cup Matches when Hill and his partner, Ken Still, were the victims of an unfortunate ruling (see chapter 7). Still and Hill both showed their annoyance, there were remarks passed back and forth with the gallery, and a difficult situation was developing. A hole or so later, who should show up but Joe Dey. He came up to Hill and said something like "Dave, I am the commissioner of golf in the United States and I am going to walk the entire last nine with you to see that you behave." One gathers it was a wonderfully exaggerated statement, put deliberately in pompous tones. Hill caught the humor, said something like, "I am nothing but your humble servant, a mere golf player", and completed his match without incident and in a much better mood.

It all comes back to what Dey says: "I know the players. I respect them. And I trust they will respect me." As other small incidents arose through the year, the kind that always have and always will come up on the golf tour, I noticed one trend. Dey moved immediately whenever something happened that he felt might hurt the image of the game. He got to the source of the trouble quickly, and he resolved it with the least possible fanfare and no pressure. Of course, having to make your explanations to a 61 year-old man in a USGA necktie who for your entire life has been the symbol of rectitude in golf could be considered just the tiniest bit of pressure.

So much for the broad view, and why I am optimistic about this sport again. Now for the details of who did what to whom. As a frame of reference, here are the top ten money winners on the U.S. tour for each of the last two years.

	1968			1969	
1.	Casper	$205,168	1.	Beard	$175,223
2.	Nicklaus	155,285	2.	Hill	156,432
3.	Weiskopf	152,946	3.	Nicklaus	140,167
4.	Archer	150,972	4.	Player	123,897
5.	Boros	148,310	5.	Crampton	118,955
6.	Trevino	132,127	6.	Littler	112,737
7.	Palmer	114,602	7.	Trevino	112,417
8.	Sikes	108,330	8.	Floyd	109,956
9.	Barber	105,845	9.	Palmer	105,128
10.	Murphy	105,595	10.	Casper	104,689

There are six new names in the 1969 list, but as is usually the case, and in spite of the fact that they seemed to dominate the U.S. tour for a brief time, no young golfers have made the top ten. There are no real surprises. Beard and Crampton ranked 12th and 13th on last year's money list. Littler and Player are always on the list or close to it. Hill and Floyd were due for good years. The average years on the tour for 1969's top ten is 10½. All of which suggests that this is one sport in which experience truly pays. If it takes that long to succeed, it must be a sophisticated game. Now here is the U.S. tour; coast-to-coast and Hawaii, too.

Los Angeles Open—$100,000
Winner: Charles Sifford

There are no signs directing the crowds to Rancho Park Municipal golf course for the Los Angeles Open. The promoters apparently feel that anyone interested is a regular habituee—hundreds of thousands play the course each season. "You make your starting time at Rancho from year to year," is the way one Los Angeles pro put it. Yet the course, hacked bare by the public, is traditionally the site of the Tour's opener.

It used to be where Arnold Palmer got cranked up and showed the other pros he was out to collect all $5 million of the purse money being offered on the tour that year. Palmer won at Rancho three times and was runner-up in 1968. But 1969 was not his year right from the beginning, and the Rancho Park tournament went to 46-year old Charlie Sifford. It was the black golfer's second major career victory (his first was the 1967 Hartford Open) and there was a little extra irony, perhaps, in the fact that he beat South Africa's Harold Henning in a sudden-death final. As *Sports Illustrated* phrased it, the tournament was grand old Charlie's from the first day when he "started moving everybody to the back of the bus". Sifford, who was suffering from flu and nearly withdrew before the start of the tournament, played the first nine on Thursday in one-under-par 35, but he had birdied 8 and 9, barely missed two more birdies at 10 and 11 and at 12 began a remarkable stretch, playing six holes in seven under par. He sunk a four-foot birdie putt at 12, wedged in for an eagle at 13 and birdied the next four holes from 10, 3, 10 and 15 feet. He parred 18 and came in with a 63, one stroke off the course record, which is held by Palmer and Phil Rodgers. "I've never had a 63 before," Sifford said. "The course played short, unless I'm getting awfully strong."

Behind Sifford, tied with first-round 66s, were Grier Jones, the 1968 national collegiate champion, and Dave Hill, and in fourth place was Jimmy Walker, another black golfer who began his pro career playing out of a golf school in Harlem. In 1964 he led the New York Metropolitan District qualifying for the U.S. Open and on that occasion registered from Jimmy Taylor's Golf School on 121st Street and 7th Avenue.

"It used to be there was only Charlie Sifford out here," Sifford said of those early days when he was the only non-Caucasian on the tour. "It's a little easier now. There are seven or eight Negro players and that helps. Most of us learned the game as caddies. I started playing because I realized one day that I could hit the ball just as easy as I could hand the club to somebody else."

Sifford had not put in all of his years for nothing and it was he who stayed on top at Los Angeles, while Jimmy Walker faded to finish tied for 34th. Taking a three-stroke lead into the second day Sifford shot a steady par 71 and at nightfall he still was two strokes up on the field. Jones shot 73, and Hill, 74, to drop back and the new challenger was George Archer who had a four under par 67 and a 36-hole total of 136. Through a windy third round, Sifford played the same methodical golf—16 pars, 1 birdie and 1 bogey—and widened his lead once again to three shots. He had established himself already as something of a gallery hero and on the 18th green he was mobbed by autograph seekers, black and white, old and young. It did not seem to bother Sifford when newspaper reporters told him that no pacesetter in the past 13 LA Opens had been able to cling to his lead through the final day. "Whatever is going to happen is going to happen," Sifford said. "I've got confidence. I think I'm going to play well tomorrow and I think I'm going to win."

He began the fourth round well, sinking a four-foot putt for a birdie on the first green. He one-putted for a par at 2 and sunk a 20-foot birdie putt at 3. But then the warm day turned sweater cool. Sifford likes it hot (like that other old golfer, Julius Boros). His game cooled, too, and he bogied 5 and 6. Harold Henning was menacing. He had recovered well from a first round 74, shooting 68-66, and now he was on his way to another 68. When Sifford bogied 12, Henning drew even with him and at 13 Henning passed Sifford with a birdie 3. Sifford fought back, sinking a 20-foot birdie putt on 16, and both men played par into the clubhouse. So now it was back to the 15th for the televised sudden-death playoff. There Henning missed the green, although he recovered to get his par, Sifford had only a four-footer for his birdie, and the win.

"Give that old man a saliva test," fifth-place finisher Dave Hill said and with reason because Sifford's performance was a fine one. Only one golfer in the field hit more fairways for 72 holes, and only three had been able to hit more greens in regulation. Sifford attributed his success, to a considerable degree, to Julius Boros: "He's an old man like me, and an old friend. He told me to do something with my hands that would help me play better as I get older." And so it was the beginning of a year of promise for Charlie Sifford. He hoped to amass enough performance points on the Winter Tour to win an invitation to the Masters at Augusta. No Negro has ever played there—a fact that Sifford is bitterly aware of—and he hoped to be the first.

Alameda County Open—$50,000
Winner: Dick Lotz

Before it made its peace—at last—with the touring pros, the PGA had contracted for a rival season-opening tournament at the Sunol Valley course on San Francisco Bay. The event was designed from the beginning to conflict with the Los Angeles Open, and it never had a chance of outdrawing the more established and prestigious tournament. As things turned out, the most noteworthy performance at Sunol was by bandits. They kidnapped the club manager and robbed him of two-days' gate receipts. Meanwhile, out on the course, Dick Lotz was shooting 72-71-74-73—290, two over par, to win the tournament and $10,000 first prize by one shot from Don Whitt. Lotz had passed up the LA Open, he said, "to play around home." He is from nearby San Lorenzo. The first day leaders with two-under-par 70s were Bill Ogden and Rich Martinez. Two shots back were Lotz, Whitt, Butch Baird and a local professional, Rick Jetter. The second day's play was delayed by rain almost three hours, and then came a PGA first. The Sunol course is equipped with lights and as darkness neared the electricity was turned on. Half the field completed their rounds under artificial light. Tournament supervisor Steve Shabala noted that the lights had been used during the qualifying round and they were adequate. And Bill Ogden thought they were just fine. "Generally a late starter can see every little spike mark and heel print on the greens," he said, "but at night you can't see them." Ogden had shot par and had a one-stroke lead, which explains his sympathetic views. Not so delighted was Deane Beman, ordinarily a superb putter. Deane finished with a 77 and said, "I don't think they should make a hippodrome out of championship golf." The third-round leaders were Dave Ragan and Bob Erickson, who at 39 is a rookie on the tour. Erickson had managed to set the competitive course record of 68, and Ragan had tied him by sinking a 25-foot birdie putt from off the edge at 18. Lotz had never been worse than two-strokes out of the lead, and on the final day, as Ragan and Erickson skied to 78s, Lotz found his 73 was good enough to win. Only 15 sub-par rounds were played in the entire tournament.

Kaiser International Open—$67,500
Winner: Miller Barber

With his blue-tinted glasses, Miller Barber had for years been the mysterious Mr. X of the Tour. When he first started appearing regularly in the players' locker room, the golfers thought he was a bookie—or so the story goes. But in the past two years Barber has been collecting too much money to retain his anonymity. With plodding intensity—he entered 38 of the 42 tournaments played in 1968—and with an indestructible swing he won $111,000 and finished 14th on the world money list. He also earned a place on the 1969 Ryder Cup team and if Miller Barber is still not a household name in mid-America, it really does not bother Miller much these days. To him, it is just bad luck that when he has won tournaments, the newsmen covering the events have been concerned with something else. Take his first victory, which came some years ago in the Cajun Classic. "The big interest in the tournament," Barber says, "was the battle between Nicklaus and Palmer to see who would finish first on the money list. I just remember that I won." Last year Barber took first money in the Byron Nelson Classic, but as one might have suspected, that was more Byron's week than Barber's. It was noted in the press, for instance, that the winner of the tournament had caddied once for Nelson as a boy.

At this year's Kaiser the bad weather took the headlines away from Barber, but it also contributed to his victory. After three days of torrential rains the final 36 holes of the tournament were cancelled and the second-day leader, who happened to be Barber, was declared the event's winner. The golfers received 50% of the announced purse money, which meant $13,500 for the winner instead of $27,000. "I was fortunate to be the leader after two rounds," Barber said. "I know it's disappointing to the other guys, but there is nothing you can do about it. And I'm not really satisfied to win a tournament this way."

The opening round of the Kaiser was on Thursday, as scheduled, but play could not begin until helicopters had been called in to help dry the course. Bob Lunn, who earlier in the month had won the Southern California Open, took the early lead with a 65, seven under par. Close behind was Jacky Cupit, who chipped in from 40 feet on the final green to post a 66. Barber, Lee Trevino and Dave Hill were tied for third with 68s.

Friday also was clear, but the courses (North and South) at the Silverado Country Club were still so sodden that players were permitted to lift and clean balls on fairways and move the ball within a club-length from where it landed. Barber, playing the North Course, had five birdies on the back nine for a 31 and an 18-hole score of 67. This gave him a one-stroke lead over Bruce Devlin and put him two shots ahead of Arnold Palmer. The first-day leader Lunn sunk a 50-foot eagle putt on the 18th to salvage a 73 and fourth place.

And then it began to rain and rain and rain. Saturday. Sunday. Monday. It poured out of the Mayacamus Mountains, drenching this wine-producing community of Napa. Under the PGA contract, the tournament had to end on Tuesday, regardless of how many holes had been played. But the outlook was so bleak on Monday that Jack Tuthill of the PGA decided, "Even if the rain stopped right now we would not be able to play the course tomorrow." The players were paid off and headed south to the Crosby, 175 miles away. Miller Barber packed his money and his drab maroon and navy blue and black slacks. He was thinking, he said, about ordering "all kinds of gold and green and light blue clothes. I'm going to become a little flamboyant." At 37, the bachelor—and golfer—was blooming.

Bing Crosby Pro-Am—$125,000
Winner: George Archer

The pros who played at the Kaiser floated down the freeway to the mudbank that is known as Monterey Peninsula. The Crosby does not have its traditional flavor unless it snows, hails and blows a few golfers out to sea, and this year the weather did its best to make the event a howling success. Thursday it oozed fog, and by mid-morning the 168 pros and their 168 amateur partners were playing in a downpour. Host Bing Crosby was calling it the Jacques Cousteau Open. PGA official Jack Tuthill was saying the rain was worse than at the Kaiser, where water had run waist high in spots between the tees and greens. "This is about the only place in the world, where we could be playing golf in stuff like this, or trying to at least," Tuthill declared. During the afternoon, on the ocean holes, crews of men were taking three-quarters of an hour between foursomes to brush the water off the drenched greens. Finally, officials gave up and stopped the tournament. Harry Toscano, a pro from Pennsylvania, found his sub-par 70 washed away, no mean disappointment since just two years before he had to par in for a 107 in one round of the Crosby. Considerably happier was George Archer who had a 76 blotted out.

On Friday the gallery was filled with fur-coated women and men in waterproof suits. It rained intermittently, and two golfers playing Cypress Point (the players rotate between Cypress, Spyglass and Pebble Beach) scored the best. Terry Wilcox, a club pro who had won a New York metropolitan championship two years before, scored a 68 early in the day and at twilight, when car lights were being turned on to enable the late starters to see the 18th green, Jim Colbert of Kansas City also came in with a 68. "I couldn't see the cup on the last hole, but I hit the ball anyway," he said. At 69 were Steve Spray and Dan Sikes, who had played Spyglass, and Bruce Devlin who had been round the tougher Pebble Beach. In the pro-am competition Bill Casper and British Amateur Champion Michael Bonallack had teamed up for a best ball score of 61. Right behind them were Bob Charles and Sean Connery (formerly James Bond) at 62.

For the second official round the wind was gusting at 40 miles an hour and there was sporadic sun, rain and fog. "I took off two sweaters going down the second fairway," pro Howie Johnson reported, "then put them back on at the next hole. At the fourth I put on my rain suit, then the sun came out. And so it went." After putting out at Pebble Beach (with a 20-footer for a birdie) Arnold Palmer said, "Really there is no way conditions could get any worse, unless you were to ride in a submarine. I'm up to my shoes in mud." The defending champion Johnny Pott had managed a 67 at Spyglass (to go with a first-day 75). The leaders at 140 were George Archer who had a 68, and Dale Douglass and Howie Johnson who had 69s. One of the more peculiar rounds of the day was Bob Dickson's—he made nine birdies, but only came in with a three-under 69, after a triple bogey, a double bogey and a bogey.

That night the power failed in Monterey and many golfers woke up in the morning freezing under non-operating electric blankets. The wind was now gusting up to 80 miles an hour. The Weather Bureau tuned in on its satellite, and continued to get bleak forecasts. The third round was played in hailstorms and sunshine and drizzle. Wind blew down cypress trees. Players were permitted to improve their lies on the soggy fairways—some balls buried four inches into the goo on impact. Dale Douglass, a slim, long-time pro who had never won a tournament, played with a vengeance at Pebble. He had a 19 on one hole there in 1963 ("I finished with all pars for a helluva 92," he recalled) but now he shot a 70 to take the 54-hole lead. Meanwhile Howie Johnson was posting a 71 at Cypress Point. Archer, at Spyglass Hill, got bogged down in sand on the final two holes, made a double and a triple bogey and despite that had a 72. Instead of being three strokes up on the field, he was two shots back of Douglass, but it is a position Archer apparently prefers. "I'd have been scared to death to be in front," he said later. "It's the hardest thing in the world to keep a lead."

On the final day at Pebble Beach Archer contented himself with playing one-under-par golf. "I've played this course about 50 times and I won the California Amateur here one year," he said. "I know you can't ease up, but you can't try too hard either. You have to keep making pars and see what happens." What happened was that Dale Douglass bogied 7, 8 and 9 and had a 74. Howie Johnson turned in a not-good-enough 73. And Bob Dickson, who looked threatening, missed a 10-inch putt at the 11th which cost him a tie with Archer. (Jim Colbert, with rounds of 78-77-77, and Terry Wilcox, with 77-76-76, had drifted out of contention after the first day.)

Dickson, however, won the pro-am championship with Actor Jack Ging, besting Casper and Bonallack, and two other teams, by one shot. Dickson, playing as an amateur, and Casper had finished second in the pro-am in 1968.

Looking out at the soggy Pebble Beach scene, ABC-TV's Jim McKay summed it up well. "They should hold the German army championship here instead of the Crosby," he said. "Achtung! You will play golf! You vill have fun! You vill not slice!"

Andy Williams-San Diego Open—$150,000
Winner: Jack Nicklaus

It was one of the more lackluster winning performances seen on the tour, but Jack Nicklaus took home the City of San Diego's 200th anniversary trophy, the $30,000 first money and hopes that his early-season victory might presage a big year. Torrey Pines Country Club, a municipal layout on the edge of the Pacific, is always tough and was playing especially long after the heavy rains of the preceding weeks. "If we played at a place like this every week, Nicklaus would win 52 tournaments a year," Lee Trevino had said at the start. And

Jack seemed determined to prove Trevino right. On the first day he had four birdies on the front nine and went on to shoot a 68, which gave him a one-stroke lead. Only seven of the 157 golfers broke par that day. Dow Finsterwald, the 1958 PGA champion who is now a club pro in Colorado, had a 69—he used just 27 putts. "I was going real well until I started two-putting some greens near the end," he said.

Larry Ziegler, Dave Eichelberger and Gene Littler were tied with 70s. Finsterwald suspected the scores were so high because the pros had been able to improve their lies in the previous two tournaments. "There's a lot of difference when you can't tee it up," Finsterwald said. And he had a point, for just the year before there had been scores of 64 and 65 in the opening round. On the second day, the wind and mist swept in from the ocean and by afternoon, when Nicklaus played, the greens were crusty and bumpy. Jack four-putted the 4th. His first putt was five feet short; he missed his second by a foot, his third by six inches and finally sank the fourth. He came in with a 72. The new leader was the 29-year-old Ziegler, who had teed off at 7 a.m. and had shot a 69. "The early starters got the break," said Ziegler, "because they had just mowed the greens and they were smooth and fast." Ziegler also attributed his success to a newly purchased $6.50 sand wedge. The prize shot of the day, however, was hit by Miller Barber, who aced the 186-yard 16th with a three-iron and won a Mercury Cougar. Barber has had five hole-in-ones on the tour and they keep him in cars. Two years ago in Dallas he won another Mercury with a hole-in-one.

A hometown hero, Gene Littler, took the lead in the third round. As an amateur in 1954 he had won the San Diego Open, and with his 67 on Saturday it looked like he might be on his way to another victory in the tournament. Littler, who is known as Gene the Machine because of his workmanlike consistency, missed only one fairway and one green and sank six birdie putts, including a 15-footer, a 20-footer and a 25-footer. Nicklaus fell behind on the back nine as Littler got hot. He bogeyed the 10th and 17th and scrambled to a 71, which left him two strokes behind Littler with a round to go.

On Sunday Jack made up one shot on the fourth hole when he sank the first of four important putts, a 10-footer for a par. Littler, who was trapped, had a bogie 5 on the hole. On the next three holes Nicklaus made putts of over 10 feet, two of them for pars, to take the lead. However, he fell back into a tie with Littler at 8 where his second shot was bunkered and he took a double bogey 6. Nicklaus birdied 12 and when Littler bogied 14 and 15, Jack was assured of the title. He came to the final hole with a three-shot lead and took a bogey 6, but his one-over-par 73 was good enough to win by one stroke. His 72-hole total of 284 was 11 strokes higher than Tom Weiskopf's winning performance in 1968. "The scoring was pretty bad this week," Nicklaus conceded. "I can't believe I won the tournament with my score after what we shot here last year. It looked like nobody wanted to win it. But I did manage to get around the course in a minimum number of strokes for the way I was hitting the ball."

Bob Hope Desert Classic—$100,000
Winner: Bill Casper

The golfers live a good and stylish life the week of the Desert Classic. I remember one year Arnold Palmer took his jet from the hotel to the golf course—Palm Springs is that kind of place. No one seems to mind that three times as many amateurs than pros are littering the golf course and that Comedian Danny Thomas shows up to play with the U.S. Open champion dressed in Arab headgear. Trevino shoots a 75, and everyone has a lot of laughs.

Because it has 544 participants—only 136 of them pros—the Desert Classic is played simultaneously on four courses; Bermuda Dunes, Tamarisk, Indian Wells and La Quinta, which is 25 miles outside of Palm Springs. For the first four days each professional is paired with three amateurs. Then on the fifth day the buffoonery stops, the amateurs disappear, and the pros play golf. It was then that Bill Casper shot his best round, a 66, to win the championship and $20,000 purse money by three strokes. Usually Casper is the star of the winter tour, but this year his first victory was a long time coming. He had opened the year with a tie for third at Los Angeles, but never really threatened in subsequent tournaments. At Palm Springs he had a first round 71, hardly noteworthy since four golfers had 67's, seven had 68's, 12 were at 69 and 12 at 70. The leaders were Gene Littler, Marty Fleckman, Lee Trevino and Tom Shaw. Fleckman and Shaw had the best rounds, since they had played Tamarisk, the hardest course. It was ironic that in such a luxury setting Shaw should be a leader, for young Tom had finished 107th on the World Money List last year and earned only $14,000. As a result he was economizing, which included washing his own clothes at Palm Springs.

And it was good he was saving his dollars, for on the second day he shot a 76, while Fleckman fared worse, taking an 80. The new leader was Rod Funseth whose 69-66 gave him a one-stroke edge on Trevino. Lee had a commendable 69, since he had played late in the day and had to contend with rain and stiff winds. Casper had a hole-in-one on the 207-yard 11th at Tamarisk and came in with a 68. Only seven players in the field shot rounds under 70—compared with 23 the first day—which is a good measure of the weather change. At the beginning of the day a message had been scrawled in chalk on the big board in the press tent: "Weather perfect. Temperature 80." It was not long until the notation was erased, the electric heaters in the tent were revved up and the wind was whipping at the flaps of the tent and rocking the lights. It rained, cleared, there was a rainbow, sun and then the deluge began once again.

The third day began black and gloomy, but the weather turned and the skies cleared. Funseth retained his lead with a one-under par 71, and he would have done better (he had three birdies on the first four holes) had he not snap-hooked his tee shot out of bounds on the 17th and taken a double bogey 6. Trevino kept pace with a 71 and remained one stroke behind. At 209 were Frank Beard, Art Wall, Gene Littler and Orville Moody. Relatively unnoticed, five shots back, was Casper, playing a steady game of 71-68-71.

Trevino was optimistic going into the fourth round. He would now play Indian Wells, the easiest course. "I'm not taking the course lightly but it sure gives me an edge to play Indian Wells," he says. It was about this time that Danny Thomas arrived looking like a sheik on the first tee, and a few holes later Trevino had a triple bogey. He shot a 75 and slumped to five back of the leader, who was now Frank Beard. Funseth had also collapsed with a 75 and Beard, shooting a 68, moved out to a two-stroke lead. A 69 by Casper put him in second position along with Art Wall and Jack Montgomery. Casper was particularly pleased with his round. "I felt I was finally swinging at the ball the way I know I can," he said.

On Sunday Casper proved his point getting four birdies and an eagle for a 66. His 90-hole total of 345 was three strokes better than when he won the Bob Hope in 1965. He won easily by three shots over Dave Hill, who matched Casper's six-under-par final round. Beard had closed with a 74, which was good enough for a fifth place tie. The most remarkable performance that final day was Deane Beman's 33-29-62, which set an Indian Wells' course record. Beman had begun Sunday in a tie for 40th and finished in a tie for fifth. If it had been a six-day tournament, he might have caught them all.

Phoenix Open—$100,000
Winner: Gene Littler

Take an average week on the tour and what do you think rounds of 69-69-68-70 might be worth? Pretty good scores, right? Well, at Phoenix they earned Phil Rodgers a tie for 38th and $403. Howie Johnson shot 68-68-68-68 and finished 16th. The winner, Gene Littler, had rounds of 69-66-62-66, which was 21 strokes under par on the Arizona Country Club course. Rod Funseth put it simply: "Every hole here is a birdie hole." On the first day 82 of 150 players broke par, and at the end of the second day only those playing two-under or better made the cut. A 26-year-old certified public accountant found himself shooting a 62, and so it went. The first-day leaders—with 65s—were Larry Ziegler, Lee Elder, Miller Barber, Terry Wilcox, Billy Maxwell, 23-year-old John Jacobs and 58-year-old Dutch Harrison. Of the seven, Wilcox got the most notice because he scored a 154-yard hole-in-one. That gave the newspapermen something special to talk about.

The star of the second day was young Johnny Stevens, the CPA who two years ago decided to live in the red and try out the golf tour. His 29-33 was nine under par and set a course record. It didn't matter that he missed the fairway seven times during the round. He still managed to hit 17 greens and need only 28 putts. The 62 pushed Stevens to within two shots of the leaders, Frank Beard and Billy Maxwell, who had 36-hole totals of 131. For the second successive day there was a hole-in-one at the 154-yard 15th. Jerry McGee hit a 7 iron to the green, saw the ball hit two feet past the cup and spin back into the hole. Littler at this point was 17th, after rounds of 69 and 66, but on Saturday he surged to the front with eight birdies and an eagle, as he matched Stevens' record 62. The 6,389-yard Arizona Country Club course has long been one of Littler's favorites—he won the Phoenix Open in 1955 and 1959 on it, and Gene was playing his best golf in a long time. It had been four years since his last tour win—the 1965 Canadian Open, but he had been second at San Diego and tied for fifth at the Bob Hope. Littler has never pressed his golfing career. "Sure I like to win money," he says, "but there are other things more important. I don't let golf rule my life. I suppose I could have made a bigger name for myself, and won more championships. I just never needed that much money or that much fame. I think a man owes something to his family. So I try to win as much money as I need and then I take off to be with my wife and two children." Littler is the quiet success of the tour—he has won more than 20 professional tournaments and is fifth on the all-time money winning list, behind Palmer, Casper, Nicklaus and Boros, with more than half a million dollars in earnings. Even after his win at Phoenix when he went to the top of the 1969 money list, Littler was hardly mentioned in golfing circles. A photograph in the *New York Times* which showed him putting out on the 18th green for his 62 tells the story of this unflamboyant man. His total gallery was nine people. And this was not a tournament filled with superstars. Palmer, Casper, Nicklaus, Boros and Player all had passed up Phoenix. Contesting with Littler's performance that third day of the tournament were people like Jerry Abbot, Dave Hill and Tommy Jacobs who had 63s, Hugh Royer who shot 65 and Jack Ewing with a 66.

Littler took a one-stroke lead into the final round, and Royer at 198 was all alone in second place. Littler had held the Phoenix Open record (with Bobby Locke) of 268 but before the final 18 he predicted the 1969 winner would break it by four or five strokes: "The course is in great shape and the weather is perfect. You just have to have some low scores."

Nor was Littler going to let up. He had immediate competition from a member of his own threesome, Jack Ewing. Beginning the round two shots back, Ewing birdied the second. Littler matched him. But Ewing then sunk a 40-foot putt for an eagle at 3, and Littler's lead was gone. Ewing went ahead at the 5th when Littler hit a bad approach and bogied the hole. Littler pulled even with a birdie at 7 and went ahead again by sinking a five-footer for a birdie at 8. And that was the end of Jack Ewing. A later challenge came from Miller Barber, but his 64 was simply not good enough. Littler finished with a 66 to break the 72-hole record by five shots with a 263. Don January finished tied for second with Billy Maxwell and Barber; January had played none of his four rounds in worse than 67, but that was poor consolation when they handed the first prize check of $20,000 to Littler.

Tucson Open—$100,000
Winner: Lee Trevino

When Lee Trevino showed up for the first time on the tour he told newspapermen he had learned to play golf in Texas sandstorms wearing goggles. Now you have to think the story is true, for Trevino proved at Tucson that he certainly can bore his long, low tee shots into the wind. Playing in 45 m.p.h. gusts, rain, and sometimes snow, Trevino drilled his way to a seven-stroke victory. The wind was so severe at one point during the third day that play was suspended for 20 minutes. Dale Douglass saw a 25-foot putt that he hit toward the cup blow completely off the green. But throughout the gale, Trevino continued to score astonishingly well. His winning 67, 70, 68, 66—271 was a record 17 under par on the Tucson National course.

For the second straight week Arizona tournament sponsors found themselves with no top-drawing pros. Apparently undiscouraged, they were talking of putting up a minimum purse of $200,000 in 1970. But if Miller Barber had anything to do with the Tucson Open, he'd leave it just like it is. "I never care what players decide to compete," he says. "If Palmer, Casper, Nicklaus and Boros sit out one week, it means I have a better chance to win more money. And that's why I am out here in the first place."

The first day at Tucson Barber looked all set to cash-in on that 100 grand which the big boys had scorned. He had an eagle and five birdies for a seven-under-par 65. He was sinking 10, 12 and 18-footers, and his putting built a two-stroke lead over Trevino and Dale Douglass. But Trevino was putting steadily himself, sinking a 30-footer on 18 for his 67. "Putting," he declared, "is like a wife. Sometimes she'll be good to you." Lee always gives press interviews that have sponsors and reporters smiling. This day he related his experiences on the banquet circuit. As U.S. Open champion he had been invited to scores of dinners. On the Monday before the Tucson tournament he was feted in New York. He flew back to Tucson on Tuesday for a practice round on the course and after the pro-am Wednesday jetted to Los Angeles for a testimonial dinner that night. Though he had only had nine hours' sleep in three days, Trevino was back in Tucson ready to tee off on Thursday morning at 8:56. "My game is suffering from the banquets, and besides that I don't even like the food," he declared.

But when the wind began to blow on the desert, that was to

Trevino's taste. He followed his first-round 67 with a two-under-par 70 and at the halfway point was just two shots back of the new leader, Johnny Pott (70—65). With a par on the 18th Trevino could have had a share of the lead, but he hit his tee shot into a lake and took a double bogey 6. Pott had four birdies in six holes on the back nine and, as he said, "never came close to a bogey." However the next day, with the wind at its fiercest, Pott slumped to a 75 for a 54-hole total of 210. Meanwhile Trevino, with a 68, was moving to a five-stroke lead. He had overtaken Pott and Dale Douglass at the turn and then watched as the wind whittled away at their scores. Douglass finished with a 78, which dropped him from 2nd place to 14th. Explaining his fondness for the wind, Trevino said, "I've made more money in it than when it does not blow." And he said he would continue to attack the course on the final day because Tucson National is the kind of layout where "any one of the pros can shoot a 63 and catch you."

In the final round Trevino did indeed attack. On the front nine he sank birdie putts at 2, 4, 5, 6, and 8. He bogied 10, but came back with two more birdies on 11 and 12. None of the pros could match such a pace. The only other golfer who caused a flutter of excitement that day was a 46-year-old amateur, Dr. Ed Updegraff. A former Walker Cup player, he birdied the first six holes on the back nine. However, he bogeyed 17 and 18. His 280 gave him a tie for fourth with Don Bies and Gene Littler. Unfortunately Updegraff did not sign his scoreboard and was disqualified. As an amateur he would not have collected prize money in any case, so the error was not costly. The runner-up's purse of $11,400 went to Miller Barber. He had now finished second two straight weeks, collecting almost $20,000. It was easy to see why he did not miss having Palmer, Nicklaus and Casper around.

Doral Open—$150,000
Winner: Tom Shaw

When Tom Shaw shot a 65 to take the first-round lead at Doral, the nation's press found a new golf hero. He was exuberant, blond, long-haired and young—the antithesis these days of frowning, harried, hip-hurting Arnold Palmer. Photographs of Shaw on his follow-through showed him, hair flying, with a toothy delighted grin. He whooped as he sunk 55-foot putts and, like a young Palmer, bounced the ball off palm trees but still got down in par. Shaw, at 26, had been on and off the tour since 1963. His first three years he earned a total of $12,000. In 1966, while driving from San Francisco to Palm Springs for the Bob Hope tournament, he broke his back in an auto accident. After a slow recovery he took an assistant pro's job in Golf, Illinois. Shaw tried a comeback in 1968, but his year's earnings were only $14,000. Undaunted, he set out again on the tour in 1969, sharing single motel rooms with two other struggling pros. Their car was borrowed and they washed their clothes in laundromats. One of Shaw's roommates—Joe Carr of Boston—managed to win a satellite event in February, the Hope of Tomorrow tournament in Palm Desert, and along with the check he was given a Dodge Dart to use for a year. So the trio made it to Florida, and Tom Shaw, at least, looks as if he may make it even further.

As a college golfer at the University of Oregon, Shaw often turned in angry, club-throwing performances. But the Doral Open tested his new cool image to the utmost. He survived, for instance, a triple bogey on the 64th hole of the tournament and a double bogey on the 72nd. "My college coach told me to stop club throwing or get off the team," Shaw said. "Now I have fun playing golf. I tried playing the other way but it's too hard."

With his new demeanour Shaw apparently has developed new confidence, for no one expected he would hang on to his early lead throughout 72 holes against very tough competition. Doral marked the return of nearly all the big golfers. Dan Sikes matched Shaw's 65 the first day. Bruce Devlin was at 66 and Palmer at 68 after hitting balls into two lakes. Tom Weiskopf shot 71 on his first day back from a five-month stint with the army and Jack Nicklaus had a par 72. "If you couldn't score today," Palmer said, "there was no excuse. The course was set up about as easy as they could make it." Palmer followed his 68 with a 69, and after 36 holes found himself two shots back of Shaw and Tommy Aaron, who led at 135. Shaw had a 70, going out in par, and his long, straight drives paid off on the back nine. He birdied three holes, one from 30 feet, and declared at the press conference that he would "sell the secret of my swing, if I knew it, to Palmer for a couple of jet planes." Aaron meanwhile had two fine rounds, 67–68. On Friday he missed a birdie try on the par-3 ninth where two years before he took a controversial 7 while leading the tournament. He had been charged with a two-stroke penalty for hitting the water on his backswing as he tried to play a ball out of the hazard. Aaron maintained he had not touched the water, but 'the ruling stood, and he lost the tournament. Although he had often led PGA events and had won a quarter of a million dollars as a golf pro, in his nine years Aaron had never won. "They say its easier to win when you've won one," Aaron said at Doral, "but I don't know how that feels."

Shaw and Aaron remained deadlocked through the third round, both shooting one-under-par 71s. Shaw had arrived at the clubhouse on Saturday morning to find himself paired with Arnold Palmer. "I've never played with him," he said. "I'm glad I didn't know that I would be. I might not have slept last night." Shaw hit into the water at the third hole to take a bogey and three-putted 9 for an outgoing 37. About this time one of the gallery shouted, "Where's that smile, Tommy?" and the incident gave him a lift. He came back to birdie 10, 11 and 14. Palmer, meanwhile, was shooting 73. The big round of the day was a 64 by Jack Nicklaus, which moved him from a tie for 28th after 36 holes into second place, just one stroke behind the leaders. Nicklaus made nine birdie putts, three of them in a row, and said the course had played harder that round than earlier because of a gusty wind. "It was my best 18 of the year," Nicklaus said. "I was able to hook when I wanted to and fade when I wanted to, despite the wind."

But Shaw was apparently unimpressed by the name golfers crowding in on him; Sikes, Jacklin, Brewer, Palmer, Dickinson, Weiskopf, Archer, as well as Nicklaus. He started his final round with a splurge of birdies thanks to deft little shots like 55-foot putts, and he made the turn in 30, six under par. On 10 his approach was buried in mud near a hazard. He took five to reach the green and three-putted for a triple bogey 8. Apparently undismayed that his lead had been cut from four strokes to one, he recovered to birdie 11 with a 15 foot putt. Nor was his bizarre round over yet, for his three-iron approach at 18 hooked into the water. Shaw assessed his position, found he needed only a double bogey to win, since Aaron had gone two-over on both 17 and 18, and he got his 6 on the par 4 hole.

"I still don't believe it but I love it," he said while accepting the winner's $30,000 check. And then he went back to his motel and washed his lucky orange golf shirt to get ready for the next week at Orlando. "My wife gave it to me for Christmas," he explained. "I wore it yesterday and rinsed it out last night so that I could wear it on the final day." At Orlando Shaw missed the cut, but after all the exposure at Doral he and his orange shirt probably needed a rest.

Florida Citrus Open—$115,000
Winner: Ken Still

Ken Still stood on the 18th fairway the final day at Orlando and began to cry. "I knew if I parred it I would win," he explained, and at 34 he had never won a PGA tournament. During those weary years he would periodically quit the tour in disgust. Once he became so dismayed by his unprofessional performances that he became a rug cleaner in Tacoma. A bachelor, he is one of the tour's eccentrics and his performances off the course had been more noteworthy than those on it. One night, at a pro basketball game, he charged on to the court and challenged 7-foot-2 Wilt Chamberlain to a fight. Another time he broke two ribs trying to get into a taxi cab. So goes the saga of Ken Still.

But the Florida Citrus Open began a new chapter. Still's first-round 74 hardly was an optimistic start, as 78 pros had scored better. The leaders at 68 were Rod Funseth and Tom Weiskopf, early starters who missed a late afternoon rain and windstorm. Funseth had five birdies in 7 holes on the back nine. The unlucky golfer of the round was Johnny Pott, who played his final holes in a downpour and 30 m.p.h. gusts. He finished with a double bogey on 18 for a 70. On that hole his drive went into some pines. He hit out across the fairway. His third shot blew back in his face and his fourth finally reached the green. He needed two putts to get down.

The sun shone for the second round and Pott made up the deficit to move into the lead with Tommy Aaron and Bert Yancey. At the 510-yard 15th Pott had an eagle, reaching the green with a four-wood and sinking a 45-foot putt, and he was well on his way to a 66. The tournament record at the pine-lined Rio Pinar C.C. course was equalled by Joe Campbell, who had a 64, including nine birdies—five of them in succession. The lucky shot of the day was a hole-in-one by Homero Blancas on the 184 yard 4th, for with it he just managed to qualify for the final 36 holes. Rod Funseth and Tom Weiskopf dropped three strokes off the pace, both shooting 71s, and a 67 by Still moved him into contention.

With another 67 on Saturday, Still got to within two strokes of the leaders, Pott and Bert Yancey, who were at 206. The late-finishers, of which Pott and Yancey were two, played the final holes in rain and darkness. Bespectacled Tommy Aaron, who had started the day with a share of the lead, stood on the 17th tee and said, "I just can't see." However he decided to play in and bogeyed 18 for a disappointing 73. Yancey, his playing partner, managed the back nine in two under par to finish with a 70. Pott, meanwhile, was playing in-and-out golf, three bogeys and two birdies on the last five holes.

For the first time the PGA had sent the golfers around the course in pairs, to see if this would speed up play. The maximum time needed to complete a round was three hours and forty-one minutes, about an hour less than the pros took when they played the course in threesomes. The experiment was even more of a success than the figures showed, for a number of rulings on the 18th green, where several second shots rolled under a grandstand, had slowed play there.

Sunday was a mad scramble. Gay Brewer, Miller Barber, Pott, Yancey and Still held or shared the lead at one time or another. Pott and Yancey, who began the day one stroke ahead of Dale Douglass, lost their lead to Brewer on the ninth hole. Yancey was skying to a 77 in the blustery wind and Pott was scoring a mediocre 74, even though he had an eagle. Brewer held a one-stroke lead over Still through 11, but at 12, a 165-yard water hole, he double bogeyed when he missed the green, ran his second shot over the green into a bunker and took three to get down from there. Meanwhile Still had birdied 11 to move into the lead. But at 12 he dunked his tee shot into the water and like Brewer, before him, lost the lead. Now it was Miller Barber's turn. He had only three holes to play. He scraped through two of them, blasting out of a bunker on 16 to within four inches of the pin and finding an opening through the woods on 17 to recover a par. At 18, however, he topped his tee shot and the ball bounced into the trees on the left. His second shot ricocheted into trees on the right, and his approach rolled under the bleachers. Yet somehow Barber salvaged a bogey from the debacle. Ken Still, helped by a birdie on 13, now came to 18 needing a par to win. His approach also rolled to the bleachers and like Barber he was given a free drop. Faced with a steep mound, Still rolled the ball within 18 inches of the pin. He made the putt and got his par. So the man whose only victories had been in tournaments like the Cactus Pete and Lilac Opens finally made it on the big time. And Barber for the third time in four weeks had finished second.

Monsanto Open—$100,000
Winner: Jim Colbert

In the pre-Masters competition big national corporations were only too eager to pick up the tab, figuring if Palmer or Nicklaus won they could cash in on all the publicity. But alas, the co-sponsor of the Florida Citrus tournament—Eastern Airlines—found its hero was Ken Still and Monsanto turned up with Jim Colbert. You can just imagine that Board of Directors meeting back in Minneapolis with all those executives walking circles muttering "Jim Colbert . . . Jim Colbert . . . Well, he danced nice on the green when he sunk that final putt, so maybe he is colorful . . . hmmmm. Jim Colbert?" It didn't have to be Colbert. For instance that first day at Pensacola Lee Trevino, Julius Boros, Doug Sanders and Gary Player were all pressing for Monsanto's $20,000 first prize. Trevino was tied for the lead at 67 with Tommy Aaron, Bruce Crampton and Larry Hinson. Boros was at 68, Sanders at 69 and Player, in his first U.S. appearance of the season, had a very respectable 70. Pensacola's course, which had been lengthened 300 yards to 6,523 after being pummelled last year by the pros was playing harder. Par had been dropped to 71.

The second day of the Monsanto Open starred Dick Crawford, long a bit-player on the tour. Crawford had been the national collegiate champion in 1960, but has since become an obscure figure. His best finish as a pro was a second in the 1967 Atlanta Classic. But here he was with rounds of 68—67 leading the tournament by one. Massed together behind him at 136 were Colbert, Ray Floyd, Grier Jones, Ken Still and Lee Trevino. Still had had the best round of the day, a 63, pitching in for an eagle on the third hole and sinking seven birdie putts for a 31—32.

On Saturday Colbert went out in a five-under-par 30 to take the lead. Deane Beman challenged with a string of birdies on the back side and a 63, but Colbert birdied 15 and coasted in with pars to finish with a 64 and a one-stroke lead. The golfers played in a steady rain and 6 more inches were to fall on Sunday and Monday to postpone the finish of the tournament. This was now the wettest tour anybody could remember. Tuesday the winds blew, and the start was delayed as groundkeepers mopped up the course. The favorite because of his penchant for wind was Trevino, who was just two strokes back of Colbert. No one figured that a Jim Colbert could have spent two days in his motel room thinking about his lead and all that money he could win, and survive the final round. But Colbert, it turned out, occupies himself to good avail when cooped up in motels. The week before, after the final round at Orlando he had returned to his room disgusted by his putting and practiced for hours on the rug. He got up the next morning at 3 a.m. and kept putting continuously until he got his feel back.

The intense practice served Colbert well in the final round at Pensacola as he sank long birdie putts on the outgoing nine to move three strokes ahead at 11. He bogied 12 but got that stroke back with another birdie at 16. The most surprising aspect of Colbert's round however was the manner in which he withstood the 35 mile-an-hour winds. He drilled low iron shots and played a game he had first learned when he was nine. As a boy in Kansas he had been buffeted by prairie gusts and had learned to cope with them. While a youngster he had no ambitions to be a pro golfer, hoping instead to become a football star. He quarterbacked the freshman team at Kansas State, but after a shoulder injury gave the game up. Later he became an insurance salesman, and not until 1965, at 25, did he become a golf pro. The second-place finisher at Pensacola was Deane Beman. He birdied the final hole to edge out Lee Trevino, who finished with a 14 under par total of 270. Player tied for fifth, Sanders for eighth and Boros for 12th.

Greater Jacksonville Open—$100,000
Winner: Raymond Floyd

Ray Floyd has long been one of the sports on the tour—a handsome bachelor he has a stable of race horses among other things. But Floyd's golf since his rookie season in 1963 had tailed off. He retained the talent but not the sense of purpose. After the 1967 season, when he finished 42nd on the World Money List, he made a self assessment. "The game has been good to me," he said, "and I intend to start returning something rather than just taking all the time. I've quit drinking, I've lost some weight and I'm practicing more. I mean business." In 1968, though he did not win a tournament, he finished 28th on the World Money List with $66,000 in purses. In 1969 he regained—and then some—his position as one of the tour's solid, front-line golfers. Nor was his performance at Jacksonville the first indication of his return eminence, for Floyd had been playing steadily and well for weeks. Only once did he miss the money.

Floyd started off at Jacksonville with a four-under-par 68, and while it was matched by six other golfers and bettered by Lionel Hebert, who had a 67, Floyd was on his way to another money-winning week. As for Hebert, he hit every green in regulation and was buoyed by the round. "There was a time about a year ago," he said, "when I thought my golfing days might be ended. I had tendonitis in my right arm; then I got it in my left. I couldn't even reach out and raise a glass of milk." The old trumpet player of 41 continued to lead during the second round, though Arnold Palmer, Lee Trevino, Gardner Dickinson, Bobby Cole and Ken Still drew even with him. Palmer shot the best round of the day, a 68, and said he had bogeyed one hole while looking at an alligator. He finished with three birdies in the last five holes and had the crowd at the Deerwood Club roaring "charge," as of yore. Floyd was only a stroke back, shooting a 71 for a 36-hole total of 139.

Floyd moved into the lead on the final hole of the third by sinking an 18-footer for a birdie. He might easily have had a bogey on the hole—his drive was far off line and nearly out of bounds. Using a seven-iron, Floyd hit through tree branches to the fairway. His third shot rolled to the back edge of the green and it was from there that he sunk his birdie putt. "I played well and was very lucky," he said after the round. He had chipped in from 40 feet for one birdie and sunk another birdie putt of 20 feet. Going into the final round Floyd held a one-stroke lead over Gardner Dickinson and DeWitt Weaver, a former Southern Methodist University quarterback who had displayed a fine touch around the bunkers. Weaver had shot a 66 in the third round even though he had found his ball buried in traps on three holes. He salvaged pars twice and the third time extricated himself so well that he got a birdie.

On Sunday Dickinson and Floyd were paired together, and Dickinson immediately drew even with Ray, sinking a birdie putt on the first hole. Gardner moved ahead after four holes, but Floyd evened the match again with birdies at 13 and 14. From there on the leaders played par golf to finish tied at 278. Behind them Lee Trevino seemed to challenge for a while, but then whiffed an iron shot on 14. "My club tickled some branches," he explained after finishing tied for third at 280. "I looked down the fairway but there was no ball in sight. I looked down in the grass and there it was. It hadn't moved an inch. I couldn't believe it." Bobby Cole also played a noteworthy final round, shooting a record—tying 65 to finish with a 281. But again Cole had thrown in the one bad round that consistently ruins his chances. His scores at Jacksonville were 68. 68. 78. 65. "This boy will be a giant when he learns to control his length and his youth," Arnold Palmer, who is twice Cole's age, declared.

Because the tournament was not being televised Floyd and Dickinson began their sudden death playoff on the first hole, a 563-yard par 5 which Dickinson had birdied just four hours before. This time, however, Floyd let go with all his power. His three-wood second shot covered 280 yards and rolled 10 feet into the fringe at the back of the green. Using his putter, Floyd stroked the ball two feet from the hole for an easy birdie and victory. The win pushed Floyd into sixth place on the U.S. money list. (Taking over first place after Jacksonville was steady Miller Barber.) And Floyd was talking about his golf very purposefully. As well as the money, he had picked up 70 Ryder Cup points with his win. "I badly want to make that team," he said. "It would be a great honor to represent the United States." That kind of talk from the happy-go-swinging Floyd made it seem he wanted badly to play good golf, too. At last.

National Airlines Open—$200,000
Winner: Bunky Henry

The sponsors had big things in mind. They jetted all sorts of celebrities into Miami—movie stars like Mickey Rooney, sports heros of the Eddie Arcaro and Mickey Mantle type. They ballyhooed a $5,000 golf bet between football's Joe Namath and TV's Jackie Gleason. And all this was just for the pro-am, a hors d'oeuvre served up before one of the richest tour tournaments of all. But National Air Lines, like those other two corporation sponsors of Florida tournaments, Eastern Airlines and Monsanto, found its top prize and the publicity going to another of those young nonheroes, Bunky Henry, whose best finish in 1969 had been a tie for 41st. Nor did National get much mileage out of the showbiz cast that teed off in the pro-amateur. The event had to be called off after 9 holes when it began to rain heavily. And the tournament lost several star golfers during the week. Lee Trevino jammed his thumb in a door and dropped out with a sprain. Billy Casper, who had been lured to Florida for the first time since 1965 by the big money, developed a rash, which he attributed to an allergy, and withdrew. And Jack

Nicklaus, driving wildly and scoring 73—75, missed the cut. If that didn't ruin the showcase, six striking National Airlines employees did. On the final day they paraded on the 17th green, interrupting play as they waved placards that read "Don't Fly National."

So the heroes of the $200,000 National Airlines Open were people like DeWitt Weaver, Bob Murphy and Bunky Henry. The first day Weaver, one of the longest drivers on the tour, broke the Country Club of Miami course record with a 66, six under par. He hit some noteworthy shots: a three-wood second at the 528-yard 16th that rolled within 12 feet of the flag; a 335-yard drive at the 17th; a 270-yard three-wood to within 10 feet of the pin at the 7th. Weaver managed five birdies and an eagle, and was especially pleased with his short game. "It has been my big worry," he said. "I always used to bust the ball well, ever since I was 13 years old." Right behind Weaver, at 67, was 56-year-old Sam Snead who had finished with three straight birdies and declared "I feel so good I could go out now and shoot 50." The pros were subduing the 6,927 yard course with power. Seven golfers were tied at 68, and 15, including Arnold Palmer and Gary Player, were at 69.

Casper had a 70 in the opening round. When he followed that with a 73, it was obvious his allergy to the petroleum-products used to spray Florida courses was flaring up. Casper's body was covered with a vivid red rash, his eyes were bloodshot and he said his joints were so swollen it was painful to hit a wedge shot. "I feel as if needles are sticking in to me all over," he said. "I am flying home to San Diego."

Nicklaus also disappeared Friday night, after missing the cut by driving a ball out of bounds on one hole, hitting into a pond on another and three-putting here and there. Friday's leader was Bob Murphy, who because of his not-too-solid 216 pounds is sometimes referred to as Murphy the Girth. He equalled Weaver's six-under-par performance, and used only 26 putts. "I made about every putt I looked at," he said. "It reminded me of last summer when I was holing everything up to 20 feet." That was when Murphy put together back-to-back wins at Philadelphia and the Thunderbird and upped his first-year earnings to $106,000. The only pro that could better Murphy's performance around the greens was Dale Douglass, who took just 25 putts and moved into second place with one stroke back. Snead (with 19 putts on *one* nine) and Weaver (with a 73) dropped back.

On Saturday Murphy increased his lead to three shots with a 68. He was playing cautious golf, going with a three-wood instead of a driver at six holes. For all of its flatness, the Country Club of Miami course has character—parallel water hazards and bunkers abound. "The nature of the course doesn't warrant my taking chances," Murphy declared, "and I wasn't driving too well anyway." His putting was something else again; he made five birdie tries. "I feel so strong I don't know what I'll do tomorrow," he said.

Trailing Murphy now was Lionel Hebert, who had a 69 and thought it might have been better. "I was bothered by an airplane flying over the course," he explained. Sponsor, please note. And five strokes back in fifth place was Bunky Henry, who was getting some notice. He had equalled Weaver and Murphy's course record of 66, but the press was not talking about Henry's golf so much as his college career as a football kicking specialist. At Georgia Tech during the 1964-66 seasons he had kicked 50 straight conversion points. His golfing record was not this impressive, although he had won the Southern, Georgia and Canadian championships as an amateur. He turned professional in 1968, and had won only $1,485 in 1969.

From the beginning on Sunday, Henry looked ready to make a name for himself as a pro golfer. He sank putts of 12, 35 and 10 feet on the first three holes and birdied five of the first six to go out in 32. The hot streak was stopped when it began to rain heavily and play was halted. But Murphy, who had started the day three strokes up, was now one stroke behind, and when he hit a spectator at the ninth hole, he apparently lost his concentration. By the time he reached the 13th hole Henry had a three stroke lead. But there, playing it safe with a two-iron second on the 539 yard hole, he hit a not-so-safe slice into a lake. He dropped a ball and knocked that one over the green into another water hazard. He finally got one on the green—in six—and two-putted for a triple bogey. Now his lead had been wiped out, but Henry got it back at 16 when he sank a downhill 12-foot birdie putt. At 17 the striking National Airlines mechanics began their demonstration, marching across the green as Henry and his playing partner, Dale Douglass, waited to putt out. After a scuffle with police, the pickets were removed. Henry got his par, but Murphy, who was waiting to hit his second to the green when the demonstrators appeared, bogied, so Henry took a two-stroke lead to 18. When he three putted Murphy had a chance to tie with a birdie. However, Murphy the Girth failed to sink a 12-footer and Henry won the $40,000 by one shot. He was the fifth unheralded player in 13 weeks to upstage pro golf's Establishment players, and considering the size of the first-place purse his win must have hurt the most.

Greater Greensboro Open—$160,000
Winner: Gene Littler

The crowd at the Sedgefield Country Club was large—29,000 for the final round and a total of 81,000 for the tournament—and unfortunately it was quarrelsome, in part because beer had been sold in abundance on the course. So it is not surprising that there were unfortunate incidents. Charlie Sifford, who had come to Greensboro hoping to score well enough to win a Masters invitation, was heckled and called "nigger". After rounds of 74—71, he left the course angrily, saying, "I'm not saying anything to anybody." Later he said, "I know it's not Greensboro's fault. But why are they picking on me? I'm just trying to make a living and I don't hurt anyone." Another Negro golfer, Lee Elder, said "things got pretty rough out there." Not only the black golfers, but virtually all the golfers in the field were taunted, and nobody could remember such conduct at a tournament before. Four of the most vicious hecklers were evicted from the course by police on Friday. The chairman of the tournament, Bill Hoover, apologised publicly to Sifford, but Greensboro has become known for rowdy crowds and unless preventive measures are taken by the sponsors, lots of golfers are sure to pass up future tournaments there.

The tournament itself was perhaps the most exciting event of the Winter Tour. Gene Littler won a four-way sudden-death playoff. Julius Boros played a streak of eagle-birdie-bogie-eagle golf. And Tom Weiskopf eagled two holes in a row. As well as these fine performances, there was the last-minute scuffle for Masters invitations. The five golfers who amass the most points on the Winter Tour get a trip to Augusta, and the competition was close. Though Sifford, Bob Dickson and Ron Cerrudo failed in this last-tournament attempt, Deane Beman with a tie for 8th made it into the top five, as did R.H. Sikes, who earned his Masters invitation by a fraction of a point. Finally, Gene Littler with his $32,000 first prize and his second victory of the year, moved back to the top of the money-winning list, a place he certainly earned, since he had finished in the top 10 in seven of his nine tournaments.

This consistent, quiet man has a way of making golf shots look unspectacular. He sank a hole-in-one with an eight iron at the 159-yard 8th at Sedgefield and got less applause than Palmer gets when he tees off. Littler's gallery often numbered less than a dozen at Greensboro. Yet he had been playing the finest golf on the tour; and his stroke average was 69.64. Incidentally, here it was only the first week in April and Littler had won $87,000. Palmer took a year to win that much back in 1962, a year in which he was the tour's leading money winner. (It was Littler who was second that year, with $66,200.)

Greensboro's first day leaders were Littler, Gordon Jones and amateur Dale Morey with 66s, and Boros had finished four under on the last four holes for a 67. Seventy players matched or bettered par that day on the 7,034 yard course. On Friday, while Littler lapsed to a 70, former PGA champion Dave Marr shot a 66 and moved two strokes ahead. Heavy rains on Thursday evening had slowed the course and Friday it was playing considerably longer. But the golfers were off and running hard again on Saturday. Billy Maxwell, an early starter, got seven birdies on his way to a 64. He played his golf in spurts at Greensboro, shooting 68-75-64-75. It was on Saturday that Littler made his hole in one and Tom Weiskopf eagled 9 and 10. At nightfall Marr, Beman (68-69-67) and George Archer (67-61-66) were tied for the lead at 204. Gary Player and Littler were at 205 and 23 others were within five strokes of the leaders.

On Sunday Beman staggered to a 73. Player had an efficient 70. Marr and Archer fizzled to 75s. But Littler, who retained his lead with a 69, had company. The 35-year-old ex-Army golfer, Orville Moody, birdied three of the last five holes for a 67 and a tie. Moody was so nervous on 18 that he almost whiffed a 15-foot birdie putt. He left it four feet short and sank that one for a par. Tom Weiskopf hit a hot streak with five birdies in the last eight holes, and he sank a 10-footer for a par and a tie on the final hole. Finally there was Boros, who had been plodding around playing not-too-bad golf—67-71-67. On the final day he eagled the ninth, sinking a 50-footer, and birdied the 12th and 13th holes with putts of 20 and 12 feet. His 69 made it a four-way tie.

The sudden-death playoff began on the 442-yard 15th. Weiskopf missed the green and a 10-footer for a par and was eliminated. Moody, Boros and Littler parred 16, 17 and 18 and returned once again to 15. The second time around only Littler's approach reached the green. Moody bogied. Boros wedged out of a bunker on the right to within four feet and parred the hole, but that was not good enough as Littler closed out the match by sinking a downhill 12-foot birdie putt. "I was just trying to lag it," Littler said of the putt, which was hit in darkness. "If I had charged that putt it might have

gone seven feet by. The light was about the same as when I beat
Nicklaus and Al Geiberger in the 1966 World Series of Golf. Maybe I
play better in the dark."

Magnolia Classic—$35,000
Winner: Larry Mowry

The next week, while the elite of the pro golf world gathered
among the azaleas at Augusta for the Masters, the uninvited went
south to Hattiesburg, Mississippi, where the money was not as good
but the flowers just as pretty. All the blossoms went to 31-year old
Larry Mowry who shot an eight under par 272 on the Hattiesburg CC
course. It is too bad Mowry has never made it to the Masters, because
he gets in winning trim that week. Last year he won the Rebel Yell
Open in Knoxville, which was scheduled opposite Augusta's
championship. Mowry had rounds of 71, 67, 66, 68 this year at
Magnolia to win by one shot from Larry Hinson and a Texas club
pro, Al Odom.

Tournament of Champions—$150,000
Winner: Gary Player

La Costa Country Club is part of a health spa, but the pros were
bruised and weary after a week of coping with the 7,114-yard course.
It was not so much the length, but the heavy rough and narrow
fairways. Only the winner, Gary Player, and runnerup Lee Trevino
finished with sub-par totals for 72 holes. On one day, Jack Nicklaus
shot an 80, and strong-armed Raymond Floyd hacked his way to a
22-over-par 310 for the 72 holes. Someone suggested that they truck
some cows in from George Archer's Gilroy, California ranch to eat
off some of the rough. "They don't have enough cows in Gilroy to
do the job," Trevino said. "They'll have to send to Texas." Bill
Casper said, "You get tired just walking through the tall grass to get
to the fairways."

For purists like Gary Player and Arnold Palmer, however, the
trying conditions (the rough, 113 sand bunkers and water on 11
holes) gave the tournament a desired character. "What difference
does it make if you have a 64 or 74 as long as you're leading the
tournament," Palmer said. "We have been trying for years to get

good golf courses to play our tournaments on and now we've got one. I might shoot an 80 here, but you'll not hear me cry about this good course."

Player put it another way: "Most tour tournaments have become a test of who can hit the ball the longest, whether they are straight or not. You might as well put us out on a driving range and the fellow who hits it the farthest in any direction is the winner."

Of course the golfers who have become used to getting it down for a birdie or par from the rough in tour events did not look on La Costa quite so kindly. After playing the course the first day some described the matted 10-inch rough as well, let's just say, "unfair." And that was to be the day La Costa played the easiest. Thirteen pros broke or equalled par. There were to be only 13 more sub-par rounds for the rest of the tournament. The first day leader was Dick Lotz, who had won his invitation—only tournament victors are invited—with his Alameda County title in January. Lotz had played well at La Costa in the 1967 Haig tournament, and he said he was confident. He went five under par on the first four holes, which dispelled any doubts as to whether he liked La Costa. He sank a 25 footer for a birdie at 1, a 20-footer for an eagle at 2, a 19-incher for a birdie at 3, and a 15 footer for another at 4. Understandably, everything went slightly downhill after that. He drove into water at 5 but salvaged a par. At 12 he had another birdie, and despite a bogey at 17, finished with a 67. At 69, two strokes back were Palmer, Player, Julius Boros, Dave Stockton and Tom Weiskopf.

Lee Trevino recovered from a first-day 74 to move out in front in the second round with George Archer (71—71), as Player bogeyed the last three holes to blow a two-stroke lead. Only Archer, Trevino (68) and Littler (68) had managed to finish with sub-par scores. Speaking of Trevino, Archer said: "He is one of the best drivers on the tour; he never leaves the fairway unless he is answering the phone." As for himself, Archer declared he would rather be in a bunker at La Costa than in the rough. He had bogeys on three holes when he drove off the fairway. It was on the second day that Nicklaus had his 80 and though he now found himself 26th in a field of 27, he could not even go home having missed a cut. In the Tournament of Champions there is no cutoff, and even the last place finisher gets $2000. "I'm washed out. I'm going home after this tournament until I feel like playing golf again," Jack declared.

Player, who had slumped to a 74 in the second round, came back on Saturday with another 69 to tie Trevino at 212. He had the day's low score and hit 15 greens in regulation. He sunk putts of 1, 5 and 12 feet for his birdies. Trevino got a 70 though he bogied 16 when he drove into the rough and 17 when he found himself in both sand and rough. Chi Chi Rodriguez, with rounds of 78-75-76 said he now rated at least a 4-handicap, since he was averaging 76 per round. The most disappointing round probably was Palmer's. He had gone out in 34 to tie for the lead after nine holes but he took a 7 at 10 and another at 17 and finished the day six strokes back of the leaders. Archer, like Palmer, found himself in the water at 17 and had a double bogey for a 74.

On Sunday Player moved out to an early lead with birdies on 3 and 4, but he double-bogeyed 6 to fall back into a tie with Trevino. He birdied 9, but then lost the stroke with a bogey at 10. However, he played the rest of the holes in par and that was good enough when Trevino bogeyed 13 and 14. No one else was playing challenging golf except Nicklaus, who was on his way to a 67, but he had started from too far back. Player finished two strokes up on Trevino and five shots ahead of Dave Stockton and Palmer. And at last the Tournament of Champions had been the decisive test it claimed to be. Four of the top five finishers were past U.S. Open champions—Player, Trevino, Palmer and Littler. It is so refreshing to see good golfers play a testing course.

Azalea Open—$35,000
Winner: Dale Douglass

Thirty-three year old Dale Douglass was overwhelmed by his victory in this small tournament. "This is the biggest thrill of my career," he said, accepting the $5,000 winner's check. It was his first PGA victory after nine years' trying—and it was the start of something big. His nine under par 275 at the Cape Fear Country Club in Wilmington, North Carolina was three shots better than anyone else. Magnolia Classic winner Larry Mowry finished in a tie for second with Jim Langley, Bob Stone and Terry Wilcox. They gave Douglass the Azalea Red Blazer (Wilmington's answer to Augusta's green coat) and he set off once again for the big time. "If good golf is like poor golf," he said, "it may come in good streaks. I sure hope so, because I've just found out there is nothing like winning."

Tallahassee Open—$35,000
Winner: Chuck Courtney

There are so many also-rans on the golf tour these days that one tournament was not enough to keep the lesser pros occupied while the winners played off for the title of Super-champ at La Costa. While some of the tour rabbits feasted on the green stuff being offered at the Azalea Open, another group played for $35,000 at Tallahassee, Florida's Killearn Golf and Country Club. The winner was six-year tour veteran Chuck Courtney, whose 72-69-71-70—282 beat Bob Shaw, Bert Green and Jacky Cupit by a stroke. Shaw missed a tie with Courtney when he failed to sink a two-foot putt on the final green.

Byron Nelson Golf Classic—$100,000
Winner: Bruce Devlin

There were two dramatic considerations at Dallas; one was Bruce Devlin winning the tournament and the other was Arnold Palmer losing 15th place on the U.S. Open qualifying money list. In a career such as Palmer's a money-list problem hardly seems traumatic, but because Arnold dropped out of the top 15 he had to qualify for the U.S. Open for the first time since 1959. Going into the Byron Nelson tournament Palmer was still hanging onto the 15th spot, but Frank Beard in 16th place had a chance to pass Palmer and did when he won $9,250 at Preston Trail to Palmer's $2,825. That settled, attention could focus on Bruce Devlin, who sank an eight-footer for a par on 18 to win first money of $20,000. For Devlin, the win had come laboriously. His last victory in the U.S. had been in 1966, and things were going so badly for him last year that he had to return from Australia to play in the $35,000 Cajun Classic at the end of the season to protect his place on the money list and not be forced in 1969 to qualify on Mondays along with the tour rabbits.

Though 34 of the year's top 50 money winners showed up at Dallas, those that were missing were among the most noteworthy. Masters winner George Archer, Leading Money Winner Gene Littler and Jack Nicklaus had taken the week off. Gary Player was headed back for South Africa after winning the Tournament of Champions. Billy Casper informed Preston Trail officials that an allergist examining their grass spray had told him it might be dangerous for him to compete. Host Byron Nelson was fully prepared when the first round leader of his tournament was one of the tour's young turks. Bert Greene, a 25-year-old from Georgia who has been on the circuit three years, shot a 35-31—66. "There's a real threat to the Old Guard going on," Nelson said. "You are getting a lot higher caliber player in these new boys on the tour. They have already won their spurs at all levels of competition, and they have learned how to cope with pressure. But their games haven't been solidified so that they can play consistently. A veteran's game stays the same, day in and day out. Take Gene Littler, for instance. He has not been a flashy or a streak player. He wins something every week he plays and his game is methodical. The young players don't work enough on their overall games to get this kind of consistency, not like we did. They don't work at learning to finesse the ball. They just go out there and see how far they can hit it. But they are on the putting green for hours and some of them are absolute wizards. They no longer look at the veterans in awe. They say, 'I beat him once, and I can do it again.' "

Greene, who belts the ball great distances, sunk one putt from 40 feet and seemed to prove Nelson's point. Right behind him at the end of the first day were two other youngsters, Chris Blocker and Bob Menne. Also at 67 was Julius Boros, and at 69 were five pros including Palmer. During the round Arnold said he had "the drive of my life—it was about 400 yards." The shot was on the 590-yard third, and Palmer estimated his second as a 190 three-iron. He birdied the hole and was satisfied to end the day a stroke up on Beard.

On Friday, however, the wind blew up and Palmer with it. He soared to a 75 and lost eight strokes to Beard, who came in with a 67. This was giving Beard too great an advantage, and though Palmer finished with rounds of 69—68, it was to no avail. Bert Greene hung in well on the second day, and thanks to a birdie on 18 retained a share of the lead. Tied with him at 137 were Devlin and Beard. In high winds these seasoned pros had turned in fine rounds of 66 and 67. "I told my partners going down the first hole," Green said later, "that a guy would be lucky to shoot 65 on a par 3 course in such wind." Devlin had missed a 65 with a three-putt final green. As for Beard, he was delighted with his round. "I loathe the wind. I hate it with a passion," he said, "but I was bound and determined to play it better today."

Two strokes back were Lee Trevino and Bob Charles and it was they who forged to the front on the third day. Trevino birdied 13, 15 and 16 for a 67 and Charles matched him with a birdie-birdie finish. Beard and Devlin with 70s were still tied but now in second place. On the final day, Trevino began badly, taking four bogeys on the first nine holes, and Charles faded. Devlin played par golf and that was good enough, although he had some tense moments. At 16 he drove his tee shot into the left rough, which must have left Devlin very cold. Under pressure he often snap-hooks and he has been working for some time to weaken his left hand. He had triple-bogeyed this 16th hole in the first round and now he found his ball under a tree. He hit a between-the-legs shot and got up and down with a bogey. Whew. Then on 18 he missed the green and had to sink an eight footer for his par and win. Bruce Crampton missed a 10-footer for a par on 18 that would have tied Devlin and forced an all-Aussie playoff.

Greater New Orleans Open—$100,000
Winner: Larry Hinson

They made the winner's jacket at New Orleans for one of the big men on the tour. That was obvious when lean Larry Hinson put it on and found it was cut for a man of formidable dimensions, say size 50 or 54. Certainly, no one figured on Larry Hinson, just like no one figured on Bunky Shaw or Tom Colbert or whatever all those other winners are called. On the first day Hinson was off the course with a three under par 69 before the spectators had bought their first cup of coffee. And his starting time was so early on the final day that he found himself finished and in the clubhouse with more than an hour to kill before the other leaders came up over the horizon. Like any pro just a year on the tour, Hinson wrung his hands and his towel while he waited. He combed his hair half a dozen times and could not seem to find a secluded place in the locker room where he wouldn't look so obviously nervous. When Frank Beard bogeyed 17, missing a 3-footer, Hinson was in a sudden-death playoff. He bounced shots off trees and sliced around a stand of cypress but the title, in the end, was his.

The first round leaders at six under par 66 were Lee Elder and Kermit Zarley. Elder had putted very well with a borrowed club and was amazed with his round, since he had just returned from an exhibition in Brazil and had been in an airplane for 19 hours. He ordinarily does not putt well on Bermuda grass greens. As for Zarley, he was delighted: "I have been having a pretty rough year," he said. "I don't think I've finished higher than 40th." Zarley believed some of his trouble had developed after he had taken up a weight-lifting program. He had quit it when it began to noticeably affect his putting. That first day at New Orleans he birdied four of the last six holes and seemed to be getting his feel back. Beard was one of 8 golfers just one stroke back of the leaders and Hinson's 69 was only good enough for a tie for 23rd.

On Friday Beard, with his second 67, took over sole possession of the lead and it seemed that the 1966 winner of this tournament might repeat. His putting still was not good, however; he failed to sink anything longer than 10 feet. One shot back was Dave Hill (67—68) and a Texas club pro, Jack Harden, who had gotten into the tournament when George Archer withdrew after burning his hand with a match. Zarley lost some of his touch shooting a 71 and Elder had an even worse round, 73.

Beard retained his lead on Saturday, but was tied by Dave Hill, who had a four-under 68. Hill drew even on the final hole, sinking a 20-foot downhill birdie putt. Three strokes back were Kermit Zarley, Joel Goldstrand and Orville Moody. Hinson was five shots off the lead and tied for 13th after a mediocre 71. That is why his starting time on Sunday was so early. Wide awake, Hinson made the turn in 33, helped by three quick birdies. He got two more on the back nine and retired nervously with his 67. Beard, meanwhile, was playing one under par golf, but he lost a stroke at 17 when he three-putted from 60 feet. "I don't know what it is," he said. "Maybe I choked, but I've never choked in my life and I've been considered a good putter. I guess I'm getting old." He had just celebrated his 30th birthday. When Beard was unable to get a stroke back at the final hole, the tournament went into extra holes. Hinson's performance was remarkable, now that he had a gallery and a few million TV fans watching. At 15, a par 5 hole, he drove into the rough to the right. His second shot bounced off some trees and ended up behind two cypress. He sliced his next shot and ran out from in back of the trees to see it land on the green. Two putts, easy par. At 16, both golfers parred. At 17, Beard missed the green, chipped five feet past the pin and two-putted. Hinson was on the green in regulation and got his par to close out the match.

Beard, the member of the Old Guard, had been runnerup for the second straight week, while the winner once again was one of those handsome laughing youngsters.

Texas Open—$100,000
Winner: Deane Beman

Jack McGowan has been a golf professional for 18 years. Some of them have not been bad years—he earned $27,500 last season, $26,500 the year before. But only once has McGowan won a tournament and that was an obscure event, the 1964 Mountain View Open. At San Antonio, he finally seemed to have the major victory he has sought so long. On the final green McGowan had to sink an 18-inch putt for a par and he would have the Texas Open title and $20,000. But, perhaps hurrying to savour his win, McGowan missed. The given-up gimme dropped him into a tie with Deane Beman, who then sank a 20-foot birdie putt on the first hole of a sudden death playoff to take the trophy.

For Beman who won the British (1959) and U.S. (1960, 1963) Amateurs and was a four-time Walker Cupper, the victory was special. It was his first win since he turned professional two years ago at the advanced age of 29. He had been through lean times proving himself, and proving that a short hitter could sometimes match the scoring punch of golf's new power boys.

After finishing second to Arnold Palmer in the 1968 Bob Hope shortly after his pro debut, Beman developed an ear disorder that affected his equilibrium. Week after week he began to miss the cut. He failed to qualify for several tournaments. After almost a year of disappointment (relative disappointment; he won $35,000) he recovered his health and his golfing form. He finished second at Monsanto and in the 1969 Bob Hope tournament closed from nowhere to tie for fifth with a last-round 62. "It was the most unspectacular spectacular round I've ever seen," his playing partner Tommy Aaron had commented. "Down the middle, on the green, in the hole." That's Beman's brand of golf, and there is the little added thing of a deadly putter. In one round last year at the Haig Open Beman equalled the PGA record of 19 putts in 18 holes. In San Antonio in the final round he needed 11 putts on the front nine. Ho hum.

The first round of the Texas Open was postponed when hail and rain left the course unplayable. The 7,138-yard Pecan Valley Country Club was shortened on Friday when PGA officials moved up the tee markers, and the scoring was good. An early starter, Steve Reid led with a four under par 67, and he said he had been "playing kind of scrappy. I just do not have any confidence in my swing. I was just trying to keep the ball in play and I didn't take any three putts." Reid was hitting close to the pin—his birdies were from 6, 7, 10 and 2 feet. At 68 was South Africa's Bobby Cole (who was to play more consistent rounds than is his wont: 68, 73, 68, 73), and Jess Snead, old Sam's nephew who had given up a minor-league baseball career to try golf. Thirty-one players had shot par or better. Beman and McGowan were one-under with 70s.

The best score the second day was Fred Marti's 66, which moved him into the lead along with Dean Refram, Jacky Cupit, Doug Sanders and Bert Yancey. Marti putted spectacularly, getting four putts in from 12 to 20 feet and a 15-footer for an eagle. McGowan, with a 68, was one stroke back and Beman was two behind the leaders.

On Sunday the golfers played 36 holes. McGowan started strongly and kept a brisk pace with a 67. At the 54-hole mark Beman was four strokes back, and it did not seem that McGowan would falter, for on Sunday afternoon he shot 32 on the front nine. Beman was playing what he calls "seek and find" golf. He one-putted the first three holes of the final round to save pars. Then he began to get birdies—on 4, 6, and 9. He salvaged another par at 10, out of the water and down from 15 feet away. He birdied 11, 12 (from 3 inches) and 13 and finished with a 65, having used 24 putts. Beman was in the clubhouse as McGowan played the closing holes. Jack held a two-stroke lead through 15, but at 16 he missed the green and lost a shot. And then came the disastrous 18th. McGowan's approach was to the right of the green, but he chipped up 18 inches from the cup. Casually he stroked the ball toward the hole—too casually.

On the first extra hole, a par 4, McGowan's second went through the green. Again he chipped well, two feet from the pin, and putted out for his par. But Beman lined up his 20-footer and rammed it in. "I had hoped when I won a tournament I would be playing better," Beman told reporters. It was the eighth PGA tournament of the year with a first-time winner. Jack McGowan could still hope.

Colonial National Invitation—$125,000
Winner: Gardner Dickinson

The Colonial Country Club course in Fort Worth, Texas is Ben Hogan's turf, all 7,175 yards of it. He won five Colonial National Invitations there, a career record second only to his four U.S. Open wins. The tournament is one of the few classics on the American pro tour and the course, built through live oaks and bounded by the muddy Trinity River ranks among the country's premier 18's. "It severly penalizes careless golfers. It is a thinking man's course," is the way Bill Casper puts it. "That is why Hogan has won at Colonial so many times. He is probably the game's greatest thinker." So it was particularly fitting that the pro who has for years modelled himself on Ben Hogan, affecting his mannerisms, his snappishness, and even his white soft cap, should win the 1969 Colonial. On his arrival in Fort Worth, Gardner Dickinson had sought out the old master and received a golf lesson. Taking Hogan's advice, he went out and shot 71-68-73-66, two under par, to win the title. In previous years Dickinson had played poorly at Colonial, once even finishing last. "This course has eaten me alive many a time," he said, "so the win is very rewarding." There was also the $25,000 check as a bonus.

Probably Colonial was not playing as tough as in the past for it had been remodelled after floods had damaged the course. The Trinity was rerouted and Casper, for one, believed the changes made the course two or three strokes easier. The performances on the first day seemed to bear this out. Chuck Courtney, who had won a place in the prestigious field with his victory at Tallahassee just four weeks before, shot a 66. Eight players broke par 70 that day; in the previous 24 years Colonial had never been so humiliated on the opening day of a tournament. Courtney putted sensationally. He was two under after five holes and birdied 12, 13 and 15 on the back nine. Two strokes behind him were Jack Nicklaus, Billy Maxwell and Dick Crawford. Dickinson, with a 71, was tied with 16 other golfers.

On Friday the scoring continued to be excellent as 20 golfers had sub-par rounds. Courtney, however, was not one of them, finishing with a more realistic—for him—74. Taking over the lead was Bert Yancey, who equalled the Colonial Course record held by Hogan and 7 others of 65. "I am proud of this round," the former West Point cadet said solemnly. "It's as rewarding a round as I've ever had, because I still consider this a tough golf course." Yancey had indeed played remarkably, sinking birdie putts from 15, 4, 6, 40, 20 and 6 feet. He nearly birdied the 17th hole when a 20-foot putt hit the hole but bounced out and on three other holes he had birdie putts that missed narrowly. Yancey's four under par total of 136 was two strokes better than his nearest pursuers, who included Nicklaus and Player, and three better than Gardner Dickinson. Player had an erratic round of seven birdies and five bogeys for a 68.

Friday night rains dampened the scoring spree and by Saturday evening only two golfers still had sub-par scores, Billy Maxwell and Bruce Crampton at 208. Yancey had staggered to a 77 and was no longer in contention. Nicklaus had challenged for the lead and then bogeyed four of the last five holes. Seven golfers shot rounds of 80 or better including Arnold Palmer, Tony Jacklin and Raymond Floyd. Palmer's 80 was his highest competitive round since 1967. It included seven bogeys and two double bogeys. Dickinson's moderate 73 left him in a tie for sixth and as he went into the final round he was four strokes in back of the leaders.

Crampton and Maxwell fell apart early on Sunday, skying to five and eight over par. Dickinson, likewise, did not have a good beginning, bogeying the second, but he recovered with birdies on 5 and 8 and at the turn was tied with Player, Don January and the fading Crampton. At 10 Dickinson got a birdie and took the lead. Another at 12 put him two strokes up. Player came back with birdies at 13 and 14 from 20 and 30 feet. But Dickinson sunk a 14-footer for a birdie at 16 and Player whose tee shot was bunkered bogeyed the hole. Again Gardner had a two-stroke advantage and Player was not able to catch him. The names of the top finishers were testimony to the difficulty of Colonial, for they were all tenacious, experienced pros—Dickinson, Player, January, Charles, Nicklaus, Knudson. Eight or so shots back you found the Tommy Shaws and Larry Mowrys and Chuck Courtneys.

But the new generation was making its presence known in another way. At Colonial it took Tommy Shaw more than a quarter of an hour to extricate himself from autograph seekers on the final day. "I don't mind them at all. It's fun really," he said. "I've signed hats, blouses, Bermuda shorts, golf balls, gloves, casts and one girl even held her arm out once. Some ladies have unusual ideas. I autograph a white blouse or shorts, then they embroider the name on the garments."

Times have changed, even at old Colonial. I ask you now, can you see Hogan autographing a shirt-front or a slack-back?

Atlanta Classic—$115,000
Winner: Bert Yancey

On the evening before the Atlanta Classic Arnold Palmer had dinner with Tom Brown, a Georgia executive of the Arnold Palmer Golf Company who has carpeting in his den that simulates a putting green. A standard golf cup is cut in the carpet and Mr. and Mrs. Brown putt-putt-putter around their house. Mrs. Brown, a former state amateur golf champion, decided what her guest needed was an after-dinner lesson. She stroked in 10 straight putts from 10 feet to demonstrate her technique and handed the putter to Arnold. He knocked in 35 in a row from the same distance. Well, it may mean nothing, but the next day at Atlanta Country Club Arnold putted like he was on a living room rug, sinking birdies from 15, 2, 10, 8, 10 and 2 feet for a 68. But on Friday the magic stroke disappeared. After taking 38 putts and shooting a 73 a barefooted Palmer stood in the locker room putting at imaginary holes with his club. "That's the stroke right there," he was saying. "I'm getting that right hand to swing the blade right on through. It's funny, I know what to do, but I can't seem to do it out there on the course." He went out and looked at the IBM board by the 18th green. He was ranked 105th in putting in the field. "How many guys made the cut—77. That shows you how good I'm hitting the ball and just not scoring."

The vignette is worth reporting, for Arnold is losing on the greens and at Atlanta Bert Yancey won on them. He tied Bruce Devlin on the 72nd hole by sinking a 10-footer. And in the sudden death playoff he sank two more 10-foot birdies. "It sure surprised me to make all three of those putts," he said. "That's not the old me. I haven't been making putts like that recently." And Yancey, like Palmer, hadn't been winning.

The tournament drew a strong field, although Bill Casper withdrew because he appeared in a practice round to be allergic to the pesticide spray used on the course. Palmer's first-day 68 was bettered by Jacky Cupit and George Knudson, who finished with five under par 67s. Tied with Palmer were Mason Rudolph and a Tacoma, Washington stevedore, Bob Johnson. For Johnson it was a momentary reprieve—his player's card was to be lifted at the end of the next week because his performances had not been good enough. Sadly, Johnson was to finish the tournament dead last with rounds of 78, 76 and 84 and the one good 18 did him no good at all. The

most bizarre round on Thursday was fashioned by Jack Nicklaus. He
had a 70 despite a quadruple bogey on a par 3 hole. Jack's tee shot
fell into some vines. He slashed away without budging the ball,
finally called it unplayable and ended up with a 7.

That was Nicklaus' finest day, if not his finest hour. On Friday he
had a 77. A lot of other people disappeared out of sight that
day—Tony Jacklin, Doug Sanders and the winners of six 1969
tournaments (Sifford, Shaw, Archer, Trevino, Colbert and
Courtney). Cupit and Knudson shot one under par 71s but Pete
Brown and Bob Shaw, with 66s, forged past the first-day leaders.
Brown now led with a total of 135. He had picked up five strokes
on Cupit and Knudson and he told the press the secret was his
putting. "I'd have to say that I've been putting real well lately,"
Brown said. Shaw, at 136, had six birdies and called his play on the
first two days at Atlanta the best two rounds he had put together
since coming to America from Australia. It was unknown,
26-year-old Bobby Mitchell, who shot Friday's best round, a record
64. He had six birdies in seven holes and vaulted from a first round
75 to just four strokes off the leaders. "Things sort of got out of
hand," was the way Mitchell described his performance. "When
you've got putts rolling like I did it doesn't make much difference
what the greens were like." When Mitchell played, late in the day,
they were at their worst, but he obviously was not going to
complain. Mitchell, like first-day non-hero Johnson, disappeared in
subsequent rounds, with 75—78.

Saturday had a new cast of characters—Bruce Crampton
(69-69-68), Bruce Devlin (71-69-68), Bert Yancey (71-68-69) and
Gary Player (72-70-66). Crampton had seven birdies and five bogeys
to scramble into a two-stroke lead. He was chipping superbly. Brown
had started the day off well, but after making the turn he bogeyed
four of five holes and slipped out of the lead into a tie for fifth. Yet
he was still not out of it, and neither were the nine other pros within
five shots of the leader.

Bert Yancey, who puts himself through stern self examinations,
said at the start of the fourth round, "I think I'm tough enough
inside now to win it." Certainly he was at his coolest and most
confident as he sunk those final putts. But at the turn he was only
one of the pack. Seven golfers still had a chance to win on the closing
nine. If that was not enough to set the players on edge, a 50-minute
delay because of rain did. Devlin, who had won two weeks before,
again looked invincible. He reeled off four birdies, sinking putts of

15, 25, 15 and 30 feet. He bunkered his tee shot on 16 but recovered to within three feet. But he missed his putt for a par, and the tournament suddenly turned around. Yancey had moved within a stroke of Devlin with a birdie on 15. After 16 they were all even. Both players bogeyed 17. Playing 18 first, Yancey sunk the first of his 10-footers for a birdie and a one-stroke lead. Devlin's second barely cleared the water hazard but Bruce extricated himself deftly from a mushy lie, wedging the ball to within 10 feet from the pin. He needed to sink the putt to stay alive, and he did.

The first hole of the playoff was the dogleg 15th. At the corner is a rockpile and a stream where earlier Gary Player had come to grief. Avoiding the danger, Devlin played into the rough on the left. Yancey drove straight and was a good 20 or 30 yards nearer the green. Devlin hit his second six feet from the hole. Yancey's was 10 feet beyond the pin. And both made their birdies. At 16, an uphill par 3, Devlin hit 30 feet from the cup and Yancey was inside him. When Devlin two-putted Yancey had his chance and he got it down from 10 feet to collect the $23,000 first prize. Said Devlin: "I didn't lose the tournament. Bert won it. When you make putts like that, you deserve to win."

MEMPHIS OPEN—$150,000
Winner: Dave Hill

At Memphis Bert Yancey scored a 66 one day and called it "an atrocious round, I was all over the course." The Memphis Open was that kind of tournament. Only four of the 75 pros who played the full 72 holes failed to have a round in the 60s. Steve Reid shot a 61, Bob McCallister a 63 and five players had 64s. The tight Colonial Country Club course is one of the shortest on the tour and the golfers found it burned by a drought and playing like a par-3 layout. The tournament purse, however, was no miniature offering, and the winner, Dave Hill, collected $30,000, or more than $100 for each stroke he hit. Dave Hill is one of the bad boys of the PGA tour. In his career he has been barred from tournaments on numerous occasions after pungently expressing his distaste for PGA rulings. "I've been suspended all together for two months and one week," he said at Memphis. "I keep a separate account of it." His last run-in with golfing authorities was in March at the National Airlines tournament, where he was benched for "conduct unbecoming a PGA member." After an apology, Hill was reinstated. It is fitting that Hill bears a strong resemblance to the late movie actor, James Dean, who often played the role of a bad man, or at least a lost one.

In the first round at Memphis, where he had won in 1967, Hill had a moderate 67, moderate because it was good enough only for a tie for 21st, four strokes back of the leader, Bob McCallister. The 35-year-old McCallister had a memorable round, an eagle, eight birdies and three bogeys. He sunk 25 and 55 putts in a wilting heat. Bunched with 64s we.e Lee Elder, John Lotz, Ronnie Rief and Bert Yancey. The second round was marred by gallery heckling of a fine Negro pro, Lee Elder. On the par 5 13th hole, Elder's tee shot hit a tree and dropped into the left rough. Some young boys raced from the gallery, picked up the ball and hurled it into a hedge. Elder and his playing partner Terry Dill saw what happened and Elder was given permission to drop his ball near where it landed in the rough. The gallery perhaps did not see what had happened or understand the ruling, for children and adults began yelling and heckling Elder. Any golfer would have been upset, but a black man in the South had to be affected deeply in such a circumstance. "It is the first incident I've faced on the tours" Elder said. "It was pretty hot for a while, but then things calmed down. The whole thing lasted about 20 minutes." Elder said he had heard no racial taunts amid the shouting. Despite the upsetting interruption, Elder shot a 67 and moved into the lead at 131 with Bert Yancey. Both had identical scores during the first two rounds 67—67. Meanwhile Thursday's leader Bob McCallister faded to a 75. Hill picked up one stroke with a second-day 66.

The story the third day was completely Steve Reid, who came in with a nine under par 61, one stroke off the PGA competitive record held by Mike Souchak, Ben Hogan and an obscure pro Toby Lyons. With his amazing round (30—31) Reid moved from 38th to third in the Memphis standings. "I felt there was no stopping me," he said. Only the rain threatened him that day. As Reid recounted his 18 to the press, a violent lightning storm moved over the course. Play was suspended and for a while it seemed the young Californian's round might be washed out. Reid had nine birdies and missed four others by inches.

Saturday was the day Yancey came in complaining about his 66, but it was still good enough to maintain his tie for the lead with Elder, who also had a 66 and a much more friendly gallery as well. They were three strokes ahead of six golfers—Hill, Reid, Lou

Graham, Gary Player, Dan Sikes and John Lotz, all deadlocked at 200. On the final day, a blustery wind and an errant driver bothered Yancey, who zoomed to a 76. Elder also bogeyed early, and by the fourth hole Hill, who had had two birdies caught him. Elder, however, was playing a steady round and it was not until the back nine that Hill managed to pass him. Dave birdied 12 and 13 and told his caddie as they were walking down the 14th fairway that he was going to win. Despite a bogey on 15, where he missed the green, Hill continued confidently, sinking two more birdie putts on 16 and 18.

Hill had not won a tournament in three years, but he has been a good money earner (more than $275,000 during his 11-year career). Money was not a worry, nor his gallery ("I can get all my fans on the back of a motor scooter," golf's Jimmy Dean says). It was his weight that concerned Hill. He had dropped from 165 to 140 pounds in five months, and he did not understand why. With the $30,000 at Memphis in his pocket he was off to see a specialist.

WESTERN OPEN—$130,000
Winner: Bill Casper

For Bill Casper it could only have been considered a disappointing season—never mind that he had earned $52,000, he had only one victory. In 1968 he had had four tournament wins by now, and had been beaten out of a fifth title in a sudden death playoff. And then there was the debacle of Augusta, that self-destructive final day when Casper lost the title he had wanted most.

Since Augusta Casper seemed to be playing in fits and starts. He had arrived to play in four tournaments and had withdrawn when one of his allergies flared—at Miami, at New Orleans, at Atlanta, at Memphis. Casper could not seem to get going. He was dispirited when he arrived at the Midlothian Country Club near Chicago for the Western. "I'm just not playing well at all right now," he said. "I don't feel well and my game isn't good. One of these days I expect to wake up and find my whole golf game gone." He talked of his allergies like an old and resigned man: "It's a humbling thing. You go along with everything going right and you don't think how fortunate you are to have good health. Then something like this comes along and you realize how lucky you were. But it can make you a better man. If you were content with what you have, if you didn't have something to strive for, to work for, well, you wouldn't be very much use to yourself or anyone else."

So Casper plodded to the first tee that June morning, and that afternoon came in with a plodding 72 that put him six strokes back of the leaders. After round two he was five strokes out; after round 3, two out. And on Sunday, having persevered religiously, Casper shot a 67 and won the tournament by four strokes. It renewed his faith, his sense of golfing purpose and by Sunday night he was talking confidently of the U.S. Open.

The Western, played two weeks before the national championship, drew a group of anxious and intent golfers hoping to refine their games for the great big open to come. The Western has, as well, considerable stature of its own. It is very old, and there is something nice about history. After all, the National Airlines Open can't list Walter Hagen and Jim Barnes among *its* winners. Palmer did not play—he was resting after the experience of qualifying for the U.S. Open—but Nicklaus, Player, Boros, Trevino and Casper brought enough star quality to satisfy any sponsor or promoter. Nicklaus arrived not knowing quite what to expect. "I haven't played for two weeks," he said. "I really can't tell you how I'm doing." He opened with a 71, but the first-day leader was to be Jack's playing partner, Frank Beard, who was also returning to competition after a two week lay-off. Beard shot a 66 with a fine iron game. He had five birdies, one from 25 feet and the rest inside eight feet. On four occasions he missed birdie putts of six feet or less. Nicklaus said Beard's round could have been "a 62 or 63 easy." Deadlocked at the end of the day with Beard was 39-year old Billy Maxwell, who had scrambled to his 66. He had chipped in for one birdie and had sunk very long putts for pars. Rocky Thompson and Dick Rhyan were tied with 67s and a fivesome, including Player and Bob Murphy, were at 68.

In the second round Gay Brewer putted well to come in with a 67 and a one-stroke lead. Except for two straight Alcan victories, Brewer had not played well since winning the 1967 Masters. He said his putting had been bothering him, but that he had finally realized, after watching home movies, that he was moving his head as he stroked the ball. Beard with a 71 was now one stroke back, along with Thompson and Rhyan. Maxwell had posted a 73. Unnoticed was Casper, who shot a 69 but was still tied for 20th in the standings.

It began to rain heavily on Saturday afternoon and though Frank Beard, who hates playing in bad weather, was caught in the worst of it, he managed to come in one under par and once again moved into the lead. When the rain first started pelting the golfers, Beard was on 7. He bogied the hole, missing the green and an eight foot putt. At nine he saved a par with an eight-footer, and he said later this set him up. He birdied three of the next four holes with putts of 20 and 12 feet and a 30-foot chip shot. Casper, who was completing his round as the rainstorm struck, finished with a 68 which moved him into second, two strokes back of Beard. Brewer, with a 74, dropped into a tie for third.

Heavy rain continued to fall through the evening and on Sunday morning Casper called the golf course twice to make sure the final round really would be played. "I thought the course would be unplayable and even as we teed off I was wondering why it wasn't." The fourth fairway was ankle deep in water. Sand traps had become pools, and some were deemed unplayable. Water was squeezed off the greens. "When it's ruled playable, we play," said Nicklaus, who went out and shot a 73. Beard went around in 74. The wind blew in from Lake Michigan and troubles increased everywhere for everyone, save Casper. He sniffed the air and found it pure and bracing: "The rain cleaned the air and kept the contamination down. That's why I have good results in Great Britain, because they always have this kind of air," he said. After an avacado and buffalo breakfast, he birdied three of the first four holes. No one even got close to him after that. He shot a 67, won by four strokes, and life on the tour was once again a challenge for Casper. He had been battling his allergies with chemical drops—to increase his resistance to pesticide sprays—but now he was back battling par.

KEMPER OPEN—$150,000
Winner: Dale Douglass

Before the Kemper, Dale Douglass told his caddie "I'm going to win one of the next three tournaments." In nine years of slogging around the PGA tour, his game had finally matured. He had won his first tournament, the satellite Azalea Open in April, had then had a string of six straight finishes in the top 10, and now on his return to North Carolina, the scene of his first triumph, he was a confident, assured golfer.

The crowds at the Quail Hollow Country Club in Charlotte were astonishing—4,000 people turned out on Monday to watch the rabbits try to qualify, 8,000 came to the pro-am and the week-long competition was to draw 80,000 people. The first round on Thursday drew 4,000 more people than the opening day of the U.S. Open, played just a week before in Houston. The Open winner, Orville Moody, stepped up to the first tee at Charlotte and thought to himself, "Now I'm the U.S. Open champion. I've got to hit it good." He had a steady par 72. Thursday's leaders were George Archer and Phil Rodgers, who had 67s. Playing in the morning before a stiff wind started to blow across the 7,205-yard course, Archer drove accurately to birdie six holes. "At 13," he said, "I was physically exhausted. I just wanted to tell my caddie go ahead and finish for me." Rodgers, who as a young player had been heralded as a coming champion, now is heralded as a good teacher on the tour instead. However, having trimmed his weight, cut down on his whiskey and armed himself with a new putter, he played a superb round. He went out on the course as the wind whipped up, and despite that managed six birdies. His iron play was excellent as he hit consistently near the cup—all his birdies were from inside 12 feet. Four golfers came in with 68s, and Douglass was one of the six at 69.

It rained on Thursday night and the course played long on Friday as Bob Charles, with a 70, moved to a one-stroke lead. He got hot on the back nine, birdieing three of five holes, one from 40 feet. He sunk another memorable putt—from 80 feet—during the round, but was disturbed by his iron play. Eight players were bunched behind him at 139, including Douglass, Sam Snead and Bruce Devlin. Archer dropped back two strokes with a 73 and Rodgers had had a 74. Douglass made his move on the final holes of the third round. He birdied both 16 and 18 with 10-footers for a 68 and took a one-stroke lead into Sunday. In the humidity (more than 25 spectators fainted) Archer finished with a 68, which he managed thanks to eight one-putt greens, to tie for second with Charles, who had another 70. "I didn't play as well as I did in the first two rounds," Douglass said. "But I got away with it. I didn't feel comfortable. Protect my lead? I don't know how to play safe. I'll just go out tomorrow and play my own game. It either works or doesn't."

Such is the sound philosophy developed in long lackluster years on the tour, and it served Douglass well. As he teed off late, he found that Arnold Palmer, urged on by a gallery of 5,000 had birdied three of the first five holes and four of the first nine. Palmer, who was the defending champion, had begun the day seven strokes back of Douglass and now had made up four of them. Douglass went down the first fairway with a gallery of one thousand and a knot in his stomach. The Palmer cohorts continued to roar as Arnold birdied two more holes and had birdie tries at seven others. "I was scared," Douglass said, and through much of the round he was not sure if Palmer had passed him. He played par golf to the sixth hole where he sank a 15-foot birdie putt. At 10 he hit his drive into the rough but got out well and made another birdie. He knew his competition was Palmer and Charles Coody, but soon word came that Palmer was in the clubhouse with a 66, and eight under would not be good enough to win. Coody then finished at 10 under, after shooting a 65, which gave Dale only a one-stroke margin. But he increased it immediately with birdies at 14 and 15, and the tournament was over. Coody showered and changed before Douglass finished knowing he could expect nothing better now than the second purse of $17,000. Douglass birdied 18 to win by four. If anyone was happier than Douglass it was probably Palmer. The 66 could easily have been a 64, since he rimmed the cup at 17 and missed by one inch at 18. His putting was coming along and he had hit 64 of 72 greens in regulation. Palmer arrived in the locker room grinning broadly, and Phil Rodgers, as usual, had the last word: "Super Underdog is here."

CLEVELAND OPEN—$110,000
Winner: Charles Coody

For Charlie Coody it was a fine fortnight—$17,100 at Charlotte and now $22,000 more at Cleveland. All that money should help soothe his wounds from Augusta. Remember, he lost the Masters championship by bogeying the final three holes. "Finishing like I did was like putting a burr under a horse's saddle," Coody had said. "It doesn't ride good." There had to be times in his career when Coody had to wonder about himself—grim moments of introspection. He became a professional in 1963 after winning 30 amateur tournaments. In his rookie season he won the Dallas Open—and then he did not win again. But as with Dale Douglass, experience seemed to have toughened his game and few doubted that he would eventually win again. Coody carried over his fine finishing form from Charlotte to Cleveland, where he opened on Thursday with a 67. It was matched, late in the day, by Orville Moody and Jerry McGee. Moody birdied five of the last nine holes, sinking an 8-footer on 18 to recover from a poor front nine. The disappointing performance of the day was Arnold Palmer's 74. He had broken the course record with a 64 in the pro-am, but on Thursday lost his concentration and his putting stroke. He had three three-putt greens and on two other occasions needed three strokes to get down from the edge. Jack Nicklaus, who also began poorly had a 68 on the second day and noted, "Things are improving. It may be a week, it may be a month, it may be two months, but it will come around." Meanwhile, the golf world would have to settle for new heroes like Coody and Moody.

Friday was a windy, 90-degree day and Coody had his best round, a record-equalling 64. Playing the back nine of Aurora Country Club first, he had a 30 which included birdie putts from 10 to 35 feet. On the front nine he chipped in to finish with a birdie 3. Coody now had a four-stroke lead and reporters were asking him how it felt. "I learned about nine weeks ago that a tournament isn't over until the last putt drops," he said. "There's a lot of players who still have a good shot at it." Coody lost two of his strokes on Saturday when he double bogeyed the ninth and came in with a one over par 71. He had sprayed his drives and had two three-putt greens. At his heels was Bruce Crampton, who had been scoring well: 69, 66, 69. Crampton would have taken the lead had he not met disaster at the 8th where he hit into some trees, found his ball in a limb and took an unplayable lie and a triple bogey 7. Palmer had a good round, a 66, but Nicklaus slumped to a 74. He had had to play by himself when his partner Laurie Hammer became ill and was hospitalized. "It was the most unenjoyable round of golf I ever played," Nicklaus said later. "It was impossible to concentrate because you have so much free time on your hands. Half the time I felt like going to sleep."

Crampton pursued Coody through the final round. Coody bogeyed the first hole when he hit his drive under a pine tree, but he recovered with two birdies on the front nine and went three up on Crampton. However, at the 11th Crampton got one stroke back and when Coody bogeyed 12 only one shot separated the two players. But Coody played carefully, getting his pars through 17 to preserve his lead and at the 18th his approach was 12 feet from the pin and he got down in one putt for his birdie. So the victory and the money was his. The Masters loss, Coody contributed to this win. On the 16th he explained, he missed a five-foot birdie putt and "That's when I thought about the Masters. Here I was again at the 16th hole, and leading. This time, there was a difference." Crampton, who has been winless since 1965, once again settled for second money. But all those disappointments add up—nicely, if you look at his earnings—$75,000.

Buick Open—$125,000
Winner: Dave Hill

Like Dale Douglass two weeks before, Dave Hill predicted his win. "I'm playing just great," he said as the Buick Open began. "The way I'm putting, I don't have to beat them. They have to beat me." Indeed, it was his Blue Goose mallethead, which he had gotten in a swap, that won him the $25,000 first prize and pushed him into second place (with $99,000) on the year's U.S. money list. It is a measure of how far a golfer can come in one year. In 1968 Hill had ranked 50th on the World Money List. Now he was just $5,000 back of Gene Littler, the leader, and Hill was at the top of the Vardon Trophy standings, which meant he had the lowest scoring average on the U.S. tour. At the end of the 1968 season Hill had a neighbor take away his golf clubs and lock them up. "I was a candidate for a straight jacket," he says. "For the first time in nine years I stopped practicing or playing daily." The layoff improved his outlook and though still an irascible man—he was suspended during the spring by the PGA for using bad language—he does not anger as quickly on the course. "It takes me longer to get mad now," he says, but "when I do get mad, I get three times as mad as I used to."

At Grand Blanc, Michigan, it was not Hill who sounded off but the Buick tournament officials. For the second straight year the PGA scheduled their tournament in the week prior to the British Open, and for the second time Buick had a weak field, as Nicklaus, Casper and the like packed their niblicks for England. At the Tuesday night dinner for past Buick Open champions only one, Mike Souchak, appeared. That grates a little. And how about that pro-am when all those General Motors people expect to play with Palmer instead of Bob Panasiuk? Well all that is something for the PGA to think about—and it better start thinking. The pros who were there just went out and played golf.

Homero Blancas and R.H. Sikes led the field on opening day with record-equalling 65s. Warwick Hills had been shortened to 7,000 yards and 54 golfers bettered par. "They've taken the tiger out of this course," one pro said. "They changed the fourth and fifth holes. Where I formally used a one-iron second on both, I played today with a 9 and a 5." Sikes, who when he joined the tour in 1964 was a superb putter, seemed to regain the stroke that he had lost during the past few years. On the plane flight to Cleveland he had been lectured sternly by wise old Tommy Bolt, and. Sikes thought maybe this helped him mentally. A 65 would make any man optimistic, and the 26 putts buoyed his spirits. "Today was my best putting round since I came on the tour," he said. "My stroke just fell into place. I felt I could knock it in from anywhere. Tomorrow is the big day. If I can break 70 in the second round, I'll feel that I have it back." So Sikes shot 76, and what can you conclude from that? Blancas, for his opening 65, birdied three par-3 holes and eagled the 398-yard 6th when he sank a 130-yard nine-iron approach. He also birdied a hole where he hit out of a bunker using his putter. A fivesome was at 67 and nine golfers were grouped at 68, including Dave Hill.

Hill had another 68 in the second round, which put him a stroke behind Lee Elder. Elder had a 67, with birdies on three of the first six holes but he was saddened by the death of his mentor, Ted Rhodes—"The man who taught me everything I know about the game." Storms had forced a day's delay and the course was heavy but Elder putted well on the soft greens. Hill had a chance to tie Elder, but he bogeyed 15, a hole he has not been able to play in par for four years.

After two 68s Hill was up for the 36-hole final on Sunday. "I figure all I've got to do is to get the ball within 20 feet of the hole, and I'm going to scare it in. I could do it with a broomstick—or a hammer if they'd let me," he said confidently. Both Elder and Hill had 71s on Sunday morning, but in the afternoon Elder bogeyed four of the first six holes and faded from contention. He finished with an 80. Hill, meanwhile, birdied 3 to take the lead and followed it with another birdie at 4. But Blancas, who had begun the day four strokes back, loomed as a threat. He picked up one stroke in the morning round and now drew even with Hill. Blancas in the end could not keep pace, finishing at 17 and 18 with a bogey, double bogey. Hill got the $25,000, an Opel for his wife and a new Buick for each of the next five years. "My man always was a good iron player but now he can chip and putt," said Elijah Moore, Hill's professional caddie for the past year and a half. Yes, bless that Blue Goose mallethead, Elijah.

Minnesota Golf Classic—$100,000
Winner: Frank Beard

Frank Beard was another golfer due for a win. He said this week in Edina, Minnesota that he didn't really feel like playing but he had a family to support and he hadn't won a tournament since 1967. He made it sound as if it was a good thing he wins a few bridge hands now and then. But the second and third money he had been collecting wasn't all that bad. It put Frank third on the 1969 U.S. money earnings list with $95,507. And he won more than $100,000 last year without a victory. At the Braemar Gold Club he told reporters he "was very tired. I haven't wanted to play for the past three weeks. After a while under this kind of mental pressure you become drained."

By Sunday night Beard must have had a lift for he won $20,000 and the Minnesota title by a relaxed seven strokes. His rounds—69, 67, 67, 66—were matchless; and 15 under par. He played in 95 degree temperatures and high humidity and called it "a good summer day in Louisville." Wanting the victory just as badly was Dave Stockton, but with him it was the title, not the money that mattered. "Oh, the money is fine, but I'd rather have $15,000 and have won a tournament. For several years now Stockton has had sufficient silver in his jeans (he ranked seventh in the 1968 World Money List with $135,000) but in 1969 he had not won. "I've been playing badly for a month and a half," he said. "I was putting the worst in my life, but I knew it was just a matter of time before it would come around." He felt ready, and the first day shot a 68 which put him two strokes behind the leaders John Lively Jr. and B.R. McLendon. On Friday Stockton shot a 67 and took over the top spot. But what made him happiest was his nine one-putt greens and birdies from 10, 15 and 30 feet. Beard with rounds of 69 and 67 was tied for second with Hale Irwin and Dan Sikes. A South African golfer, Hugh Inggs, got his first notices on the U.S. tour by shooting a record-equalling 65. The first-day leaders dropped into obscurity, Lively with a 77 and McLendon with a 75. On the third day Beard made his move, and he made it early with a birdie on the first hole. He also birdied four from 15 feet, and had three other birdies on the back nine. Stockton was one stroke back of Beard at the end of the day after shooting a 69, and Irwin was third.

But Beard just kept improving and improving. His last round, a 66, was his finest on the 6,913-yard course. He played monotonously good golf, birdieing 3, 7, 9, 15 and 18 and never going over par. Stockton labored, bogeying three holes to shoot a 73. He scuffed one four wood 80 yards and then three-putted the hole. Beard had a five-stroke lead at the turn. "I felt I had it won then," he said in one of the understatements of the tour year. Beard was not exactly a popular winner in Edina. He had suggested in a radio interview earlier in the week that the course was inadequate—it is a public layout only five years old. The sponsoring Jaycees might also provide some fringe benefits for the players, Beard had said, like courtesy car service and motel accommodations. So in two weeks the pros had angered two sponsors. On to Philadelphia. The tour is such a drudge . . . and we're so tired.

IVB-PHILADEPHIA GOLF CLASSIC—$150,000
Winner: Dave Hill

Dave Hill was enjoying his sudden preeminence on the golf scene just a little. "Boy when they see me leading the money list, why it's just gonna make some of those cats sick," he said after his Philadelphia win. "I can think of about 15 of them who are going to cut their throats. And ol' Dave is on the Ryder Cup team. I might set England back 40 years. They're going to send two special guards along with him just to see I don't get into trouble." So the bad boy of the PGA had triumphed once again, his third win in four starts. He had spread his appearances over two months and this seemed in part to be a secret of his fine performance. After winning at Memphis he took a week off. He then played in the U.S. Open, where he finished 13th. He won the Buick Open, took another week off, and came to Philadelphia where he beat Gay Brewer, Tommy Jacobs and R.H. Sikes in a sudden death playoff. Of his three victories, the one at the Whitemarsh Valley Country Club, which boosted him into first place in the money standings, probably meant least to Hill. "With the way I played," he said, "I thought I should have finished fifth or sixth. The first couple of days I didn't hit the ball good at all. I don't want to be called a scrambler. I didn't win the tournament. The other guys lost it."

From his new lofty position, Hill could afford such reflections. But his analysis is, at the same time, shrewd. He played mediocre first and second rounds, 71s, and yet found himself just three strokes back of the 36-hole leader, Tommy Jacobs. It was too hot for anyone to be swinging very well. The Whitemarsh course is in a suburban lowland that traps and holds the torrid mid-summer heat. On the first day Orville Moody, who hails from sizzling West Texas, collapsed on the 14th hole and an ambulance took him off the course. "The heat is the worst I've endured since I've been playing golf," said Palmer. "You want a sauna bath? Just go out to the 6th green for 10 minutes. It's got to be 210 degrees. There are big trees around the green and a big gallery. So no air comes through. You stand over a putt and its like its raining, the way the perspiration is falling on the ball." On Friday a caddie collapsed on the 12th, and an ambulance took him to the first aid station. Twelve players pulled out of the tournament and women markers were led dazed to the shade by nurses.

Frank Boynton and Bob Dickson, who held the first-round leads, wilted in the second, taking 78 and 79 respectively as Jacobs, with 69—70, moved in front by two. There was a six-way tie for second place and Palmer and Hill were among those another stroke back at 142. Jacobs, despite the heat, continued to lead the third day as he shot a 68. In a slump since he lost the Masters in a playoff in 1966, he had talked of becoming a stockbroker, but now he was saying "the last four months I've been playing better. I think my game's coming along." He had been able to start at Philadelphia only because the sponsor gave him a special exemption. He birdied the first hole Saturday and had another at 9. He followed that with a 15-foot birdie putt at 10, salvaged a par at 11 when his ball ricocheted off a rake into a bunker, and had his final birdie at 17. Playing with Jacobs was young Grier Jones who was four strokes back with nine to play. He closed with a 30, sinking 25 and 30 footers for birdies, and tied Jacobs. Hill bogeyed the final hole on Saturday for a 68 and a 54-hole total of 210, still three back of the leaders. The real loser of the day was the defending champion, Bob Murphy. A thief took two golf bags, balls, shoes and three dozen clubs from his unlocked car. Among the clubs gone was the driver he had used since winning the 1965 U.S. Amateur. "I'd pay $100 a stick just to get them back," he said. "I've got to get them back. I can't play with other clubs. I thought about picking up and leaving, but I figured it wasn't the right thing to do, being the defending champion and all." With a borrowed set, he shot a 73.

Grier Jones dropped from contention on Sunday, but Jacobs tenaciously held to it. Dave Hill made up only one stroke on him in the first nine. Brewer meanwhile was belting out a 66 and Sikes a 67.

They were in the clubhouse at nine under par. Hill drew even with Jacobs when Tommy bogeyed 11 and 12. Two golfers came to 18 with Hill needing a par or Jacobs a birdie to tie the leaders in the clubhouse, Brewer and Sikes. Jacobs drove into the rough, but hit a 175-yard approach to within two feet of the cup for his birdie and his tie. Meanwhile Hill had bunkered his drive *and* his second. But he then wedged five feet from the pin and got the vital par. The four golfers then teed it up in a sudden death playoff. Brewer missed a 12-foot birdie putt, Sikes one from 16 feet and Jacobs two-putted from the fringe. But Dave Hill stroked in his 12-foot birdie try with all the confidence one develops from winning and winning and winning.

Canadian Open—$125,000
Winner: Tommy Aaron

You might know that when Tommy Aaron finally managed to win a tour tournament after nine years of trying, there would be a worm somewhere in the victory—Aaron has that kind of bad luck. The 1969 Canadian Open was declared an unofficial tournament by the U.S. PGA, which was running its own American Golf Classic in Akron the same week, so Aaron still does not have an official PGA win, but Tommy wasn't complaining as he picked up his first trophy in a decade. He had been a fine amateur golfer. In 1958 he finished runnerup to Charlie Coe in the U.S. Amateur, but that was the end of the silverware. Money he had, the result of consistently good performances. As a professional the winless Aaron had collected more than $350,000. But eight times he had finished second, and in a score of other tournaments he had been a leader and then faltered.

But remarkably enough the story of the Canadian Open was not so much the 35 year old Aaron as it was 57 year old Sam Snead, who was out on the golf circuit when Tommy was born. Snead, overcoming the putting yips, led for 70 holes of the tournament and Aaron needed a record-breaking 64 in the final round to tie the old man. The championship was decided in an 18-hole playoff and Sam, more than a little tired, lost by two strokes. Perhaps he had enough victories for any man—131—but the win would have been marvellous. Just think, Snead had won three Canadian Opens, the first of them 31 years earlier in 1938.

In the first round Snead's iron game was superb and he needed only short putts for six birdies and a five-under-par 67. "I just can't remember the last time I played without three-putting," he said jubilantly after his round. An unknown 28 year old Massachusetts pro, Chick Evans, was a stroke back at 68 and Roberto de Vicenzo and Tony Jacklin were among five at 69. Tommy Aaron was back in the bunch at 71 and he was to have two more unspectacular 70s before he zoomed into contention. On Friday Snead said he "played better today than the opener," and came in with a 68, which included five one-putt greens. He was sinking them from 15 to 20 feet, downhill, sidehill, it didn't matter. Another oldtimer with a good putter that day was De Vicenzo who made three 20-footers and shot a 67 for a 36-hole total of 136, just one stroke behind Snead. Evans, meanwhile, had dropped from contention with a 74.

The third day was dampened by rain, but Snead shot a 70 and moved to a five-stroke lead. He had two birdies, including a 25-footer, on the front nine, and three birdies and two bogeys on the back nine. His nearest challenger was now Takaski Kono of Japan, a 140-pound pro who had finished 13th in the U.S. Open. Kono said he was just becoming adjusted to the hilly Pinegrove Country Club layout, but his scores showed he had been playing it well: 72-68-70. Six strokes back of Snead in third place was Tommy Aaron, and as Sam ran his finger down the list at the post-round interview it stopped by Aaron's name. "You know," Snead said, "that guy's got to win a big one some time. In my book he's the one to watch."

Amazingly, Snead continued to play strong golf through the fourth round. He went out in 33, three under par, and Aaron who had an eagle, three birdies and a bogey on the front nine only made up one stroke on him. "I thought I had it," said Snead, and with a five-stroke lead with nine to play it figured that he did. But Sam bogeyed the long 13th and the short 15th, while Aaron birdied the 10th and the 14th to move within a stroke back. At 16 Aaron sunk a 40-footer for a birdie to move into a tie with Snead, and he missed an eagle by inches at 18 but got a birdie to go one up. Now came Snead, who gave his 35-foot putt for an eagle a good try, but it was a foot short. He matched Aaron's birdie and now faced the playoff the next day. "Why did you pick today to set a course record," Snead asked Aaron. "What the hell do you think you're doing, man? I'm tired."

Aaron, though not in his Sunday form, led through most of play. After hitting into a grove of trees on the fifth hole, he sunk a 70-footer for a birdie. Snead also got a birdie on the front nine, but Aaron got another at 9 to take a one-stroke lead again. Then Aaron bogeyed 10, and 11 but extricated himself from trees and sand on 12 for a par. He came back to birdie 13 and 14 and finished with an eagle at 18 to win the playoff 70—72. "He's a wonderful boy," Snead said. "It looks like he was destined to win this tournament." The pros said nine years ago that Aaron's smooth swing would make him a superstar. Destiny had been delayed and now it jumped up to grab old Sam.

American Golf Classic—$125,000
Winner: Ray Floyd

The Chicago Cubs turned out to be among the year's leading losers, but Ray Floyd, or Super Cub as he might well be known, was a big winner in 1969. Floyd makes several appearances during the summer working out in a Cub uniform with the National League baseball team in Wrigley Field. He lives in Chicago just so he can be near the ballpark; and in 1968 he took several weeks off to follow the team around.

But while Floyd got his national championship—the PGA title—the Chicago baseball team collapsed on the 72nd hole.

The Firestone Country Club, site for seven years of the American Golf Classic, has been considered one of the tour's few demanding layouts. Only seven times in the Classic have golfers posted 72-hole scores under 280. But this year was something different. Ray Floyd, playing without the benefit of a practice round, shot four straight rounds in the 60s at Firestone and lowered the tournament record by seven strokes. And eight other golfers finished a 279 or less.

Floyd had been 70 miles away giving a golf clinic in Greenville, Penn. when the rest of the field was playing its practice rounds. He found himself talking earnestly about rhythm and timing to a group of duffers and "Bam," Floyd said, "my eyes lit up. I said to myself, 'you big jerk. You're telling these people about this but you haven't been doing it yourself.' "

He returned to Akron and early on Thursday morning was on the practice tee turning theory into practice. "As soon as I hit the first wedge shot," he said, "I knew I had it back." Before he teed off several people asked Floyd how he was playing. "I said I was playing real good but I don't think they believed me," he said later. Even after a first-day 67 no one noticed him much. The talk that Thursday was of Terry Wilcox and Bobby Mitchell, who had never played at

Firestone before and shot 65s. And Jack Nicklaus coasted in with a 66. Jack figures Ohio is his territory and the Firestone course must be his favorite—he has won $217,850 on it, including two World Series titles. Nicklaus had sprayed his shots, hitting a tree, an electrical tower and a woman's pocketbook, but had putted like a wizard. He needed only 28 putts in his round (Palmer took 22 on *one* nine that same day). "I got a lot of good breaks," Jack said matter-of-factly. Deane Beman was the pro with the bad breaks—a cracked rib suffered in a pickup baseball game with his son. He withdrew from the tournament.

Floyd had another fine round the second day, a 68, and he was very confident: "I don't see how I can shoot higher than that," he said. But Nicklaus was still making headlines as he brought in yet another 66. On the first green he sank a 30-inch putt for a birdie. His drive on 2 careered into a spectator's binoculars, but his second shot on the par 5 hole landed 20 feet from the pin and he got an eagle. At 6 he sank a 25-foot birdie, and so it went until he had lowered the 36-hole tournament record by two shots. However, his 132 was only one better than Bobby Mitchell who had hung in with a fine 68; Wilcox, the co-leader the first day, had dropped to a 74. Firestone took quite a pummelling for a second day—15 more subpar rounds—and that did not include a bizarre performance by Bobby Cole. He shot 42 on the front nine and then took only 12 putts and had five birdies on the back nine. The streak gave him a 30 and a 72 for the day.

Saturday Nicklaus looked as if he was on his way to another spectacular round. He birdied the first two holes to take a five-shot lead, but his putting suddenly soured and he finished with three bogeys and a 71. Floyd meanwhile had gone out in 33, sinking birdies from 20 feet at 3 and 9. He played par golf in and his 68 gave him a share of the lead with Nicklaus and Mitchell. "I've only had four bogeys in three rounds and that's pretty good for me," Floyd told the press, but Nicklaus was still the favorite.

The final round was interrupted by rain and the leaders did not tee off until nearly four o'clock in the afternoon. They were encouraged to play quickly, and Floyd was off and nearly running down the fairway with a birdie at 2. He dropped back into a tie with Nicklaus and Mitchell when he three-putted the fifth, but he put a two iron three feet from the flagstick at 6 and got his second birdie. He got another at 8 from 18 feet and made the turn two strokes ahead. About this time, Nicklaus began to bogey holes—six of eight—and he never was a threat as he finished with a 75. Mitchell also dropped back, but Ray never let up, shooting a 32 on the back nine to finish with a 65. "I've never seen better golf played in my life," said Bobby Nichols of his playing partner. "I've played a lot of rounds with Raymond and the way he played he's deserving of the championship. Indeed, Floyd—all 206 solid pounds of him—looked that day like Super Cub as Golden Bear Nicklaus slunk back in his den.

WESTCHESTER CLASSIC—$250,000
Winner: Frank Beard

Frank Beard is writing a book that has been tentatively titled "I Can't Win Anything But Money," Indeed, he can't seem to win a major championship but knowing Frank, he'll take money over glory any day. With the $50,000 first prize he earned at Westchester he moved solidly into first place on the 1969 tour's money list. Beard's game began gathering momentum in mid-June. In the six tournaments since the U.S. Open he had not shot a round over 72 and had won twice and finished second, fourth, fifth and eighth. His victory at Westchester, where he put together rounds of 69-72-67-67 was his third of the year, and his second in a month. His level-headed theory of golf was paying off, as he always knew it would. "Golf is a business with me," Beard has said. "I try to get my birdies and my pars because they mean money to me. If I'm going to win a tournament, it'll come my way. If I don't, there's always another week and another chance to get my pars and birdies. Consistency is the most important thing in golf."

The Westchester Classic is the richest event on the tour, and 29 of the 30 leading money winners thought it worth their while to play. Only Deane Beman, still sidelined with broken ribs, couldn't make it up to Harrison, N.Y. The tournament is not only a benefit for the pros, but also for local hospitals, which receive about $300,000 from the proceeds. This year it seemed Westchester might extend its charity to the elderly, for Tommy Bolt shot a first-round 66 to lead the tournament. "I just wanted to show those cats I can play a little bit," the PGA senior champion declared. "I'm a senior, baby, but just because you're a senior doesn't mean you have to hang it up." The 52 year old Bolt had a record 30 on the front nine, sinking birdie putts from 45, 10, 13 and 15 feet. His other birdies were from 24 and 30 inches, which is a measure of his fine iron play. The course was wet after heavy rains, and the grass too long. "You had to hit a lot of lob shots," Bolt said. "You couldn't control the ball. You had to hit what we call sailers." Just behind Bolt at 67 were Bruce Devlin and Bert Greene, and seven players were at 68.

On the second day Greene moved into the lead, shooting a 69 to Bolt's 71. Just one year before Greene had finished 50th at Westchester, barely earning his caddie's fee. But his game improved immensely during 1969 and he had earned money in 19 of his previous 21 starts. "It seems like my bad shots were not as bad as they usually are," Bert said after the second round. "I'm more excited about my play right now than thinking about the $50,000 first money." Bolt was bothered by the heavy, uncut fairway grass. "It makes us professionals look like hackers' " he said. Some of the pros indeed were having horrendous problems. Marty Fleckman had a second-day 85 and left for home to "get some rest and straighten out." Tony Jacklin, Orville Moody, Gene Littler and Dave Hill also missed the cut, and for a while tournament officials were anxiously wringing their hands as it looked like Arnold Palmer might also have to retire to Latrobe, Pa. "Goodness, we can't lose him," said one official. Palmer just made it into the final 36 holes with a total of 145, as did the defending champion, Julius Boros.

To the amazement of many, Bert Greene and Tommy Bolt refused to fold. Greene, with a 68, surged to a four-stroke lead at the end of the third round while Bolt, with another 71, clung to a share of second. But now emerging from the pack were people like Frank Beard and Lee Trevino. Both had 67s to be even with Bolt, Harold Henning and Dan Sikes at 208. Unquestionably the strength of Greene's game was in his putting. No one else in the field could match his performance: he had taken 27 putts on each of the first two days and in the third round needed only 26. Beard had taken 30. But Greene had driven erratically, missing four fairways, and he had also missed four greens. Bolt also had a topsy-turvy round. At the fourth his three-iron approach rolled into the cup for an eagle and at 5, he took a double bogey. Beard, meanwhile, was playing his consistent game—five birdies and 13 pars. Trevino started with a flurry of birdies on the first three holes on the way to his 67. "Coming from Texas I like the fairways cut short," he said. "They were long like this last year, too, and I didn't qualify for the last 36 holes. I became a TV commentator and all I was was a free Dr. Pepper."

Things were to be considerably better for Lee at Westchester in

1969, as he finished in a tie for fifth and took home $9,625. But in the final round age caught up with Tommy Bolt, who finished with a 75 for a share of 14th money. And Beard more than caught up with Bert Greene, he passed him on the 72nd hole of the tournament. For a while, however, Dan Sikes figured as the man who would rob Greene of his first pro title. He went out in 32 and at one point took the lead. In the clubhouse, Westchester officials informed the press that if Sikes won, he would have collected over $100,000 at the event in three years. But Sikes bogeyed 13 and three-putted 18 to become a discarded statistic. So the struggle was between Beard and Greene, playing in the final two pairings. The crucial hole was 15, where Greene three-putted to lose his lead and Beard, who was bunkered, salvaged a par with a 15-foot putt. Both golfers played par golf on 16 and 17, but at 18 Beard sunk a birdie putt from three feet and Greene knew he had to match him. He went for the green on the 538-yard hole with a four wood, but bunkered the shot. "A little to the left or a little to the right . . . just five feet over . . . any of those would have done it for me," Greene said later. He came out poorly, some 25 feet from the hole, and his birdie try was long and above the cup. He parred the hole for second money. Beard was asked by a reporter what he felt his claim to fame in the golf world was. He thought for a while and said, "Well, I guess my 84-hole streak in 1967 when I didn't shoot one bogey." Then he went back to work with his ghost writer on the next chapter of "I Can't Win Anything But Money".

Greater Milwaukee Open—$100,000
Winner: Ken Still

Ordinarily, on a Monday the tour rabbits scramble in a qualifying round for 10 or 20 berths in that week's tournament. But so many established players stayed away from Milwaukee that 81 spots were available for the rabbits. It helped a little that Arnold Palmer was there—he was trying to pick up enough points to squeeze onto the Ryder Cup team—and Gary Player was back from South Africa using Milwaukee as a warm-up for the following week's PGA. But the sponsors were understandably angry. The local press dubbed the event the "Rabbit Open". The winner turned out to be a hare, however, for Ken Still loped to a two-stroke victory. Until he won the Florida Citrus Open in March, Still had struggled and often been defeated in those Monday qualifiers. He knows the frustrations of such an existence, and perhaps that made his Milwaukee Open win particularly satisfying—he was now unquestionably a regular, for his win at the North Shore Country Club assured him a place on the U.S. Ryder Cup team.

Still's first round was far from stimulating. A 74 put him seven strokes behind the 22-year-old Peter Townsend. Playing in the best of the blustery weather, Peter had a five-under-par 67. After he came in the wind got unusually strong and gusty. John Miller, a San Francisco rookie who as an amateur finished eighth in the U.S. Open, came in with a 68, and he had also finished early. "At 18 I had a 156-yard approach," he said. "I normally would have used a six or seven iron, but in the wind I went to a four and I still was short." Only Bob Lunn of the afternoon players salvaged a respectable round, a two-under-par 70. Player posted a 73, Palmer a 76 and Dave Stockton a 77.

The name players were nowhere near their best, it seemed, and the second-day leaders were pros like Ed Moehling (winner of $166 in 1969) and Fred Marti (winner of $17,591). Moehling earned his share of the lead by chipping in from 12 feet at the 10th and again at the 16th, a par-5 hole. Marti started poorly, hitting into a lake on the first hole. But he recovered for a 70. Townsend, with a 75, dropped into second place, one stroke back of the leaders. Ken Still, with rounds of 74—71 was another two strokes back. Palmer finished the second day with a 71 to make the cut. He needed to finish fifth or. better at Milwaukee and in the PGA to make the Ryder Cup team, and his third round—68—must have improved his spirits for it put him just four strokes out of the lead. But there were 16 other players in contention as well, as Palmer's irons were too erratic to be counted on. The leaders after 54 holes were Terry Dill, Bob Lunn and Townsend, who came in with a 69. His playing partner Lunn declared, "Peter missed several short putts for bogies he shouldn't have had, and some birdie putts rimmed. It was a pleasure to watch him play. He could have had a 64." Lunn had a fine 68 to talk about, as well. And Still, with a 67, pushed himself within a stroke of the lead. Player also had been slogging around well enough (73-70-71) to figure in the final day's play.

On Sunday Still took the lead with four birdies on the front nine. Player was matching him stroke for stroke until the 16th, but there Gary hit a spectator who had ventured too far into the fairway. "It cost me 90 yards, at least a stroke and maybe the tournament," he said. Player got the stroke back on the final hole—sinking a 40-foot putt and splitting his slacks in the process. He was now tied with Still, but Ken finished with two birdies on the final three holes and the $20,000 first prize was his. "I've never putted like I did today," he said "I only hope it happens again real soon. It sure is great when your putter's hot. It was fantastic—and making the Ryder team, I never dreamed I'd have that honor." As a discouraged rabbit six months before he felt honored whenever he got to play.

PGA Championship—$175,000
Winner: Ray Floyd

It was appropriate that the PGA hold its championship on the National Cash Register course in Dayton, Ohio, now that the PGA tour is ringing up million after million in prize money. But the 1969 PGA Championship was far more than just another six-figure tournament. It was a testy and testing even—one marked by civil rights disturbances, angry golfers and some superb play. The pros played the National Cash Register Company's south course, a hilly and heavily-wooded 6,910 yards that had been designed by Dick Wilson for the company's 15,000 employees. Frank Beard called the layout the "best course for a championship I've ever played." Tom Weiskopf compared it favorably with Augusta and Jack Nicklaus talked of its "split personality. Driving is an important feature. At some holes you can let out. At others you have to place it. You've got to play shots all the way around, but that's the way a good golf course should be." The 18 had no water holes, but more than its share of bunkers and menacing doglegs.

The tournament had not begun when the first fireworks occurred. Dave Hill, the PGA's no. 2 money winner, read in a newspaper where Frank Beard, no. 1 man, had declared there was no place on the tour for funny business—it was all work, work, work. Three-time winner Hill retorted: "Why doesn't Beard quit. I know where he can get a job pumping gas. That's work. What's this man mean complaining about this being work. If you start thinking this is work, go through one of the hospitals and look at all those soldiers. They wouldn't complain this is work." When informed of Hill's outburst, Beard declared that Hill had not yet learned how to handle himself. The PGA told the two golfers to cool it. End of incident.

Other trouble was brewing. The local Chamber of Commerce,

co-sponsor of the championship, had been presented with a list of demands by civil rights organizations in Dayton. The requests were wide, ranging from the general ("to do more for the city's poor") to the specific (to donate 2,000 to 3,000 free tickets to the golf tournament to disadvantaged people—tickets were selling for $8 a day—to support a boycott of California grapes, to declare as a holiday the birthday of assassinated black leader Martin Luther King). The head of the protest threatened "to bring Dayton to its knees in embarrassment" if the C of C did not comply. The first two days of the PGA the only indication of the presence of the group at the course was an orderly picket line at the gate where people carried signs. One read: "Professional Ghetto Association sponsored by the Dayton Chamber of Commerce." Both black and white golfers crossed the picket line and competed. "This is the way I make a living," Lee Elder, the Negro pro, explained. "I intend to play."

Nine players with scores of 69 shared the first day lead. Perhaps it was an omen that the typist compiling the list for newspapers placed Raymond Floyd's name first. Along with him were Al Geiberger, Tom Shaw, Bob Lunn, Johnny Pott, Charles Coody, Bunky Henry, Larry Mowry and Larry Ziegler. Mowry, an early starter, told reporters he doubted his score would stand up. Floyd, who finished late, was to explain why it did: "I expected somebody to shoot 65 or 66 but after playing I can see why the scores weren't any lower. For one thing the golfers were taking five hours to go around and for another, the pin placements were unbelievably hard." One frustrated golfer was Tom Weiskopf, who was coming in with a 68 when he took a double bogey on the final hole. Furious, he refused to grant interviews. "I have no comment," he said. "I'm going home. I don't want to say anything that I might regret later."

The reporters, however, had more than enough to write about. Arnold Palmer had a tortuous round—out in 40, back in 42. The 82 matched his worst performance as a professional (in 1957 in the Kansas City Open), and it was by three strokes the worst round he had ever shot in a major championship. It was immediately apparent when Palmer teed off that he was headed for disaster. On Wednesday, during his final practice round, the bursitis in his right hip had flared once again. It is a chronic condition which developed from an injury in the 1966 New Orleans Open. His wife, Winnie, used to treat it with Ben-Gay, but now neither linaments nor long periods of rest seemed to help much. Palmer was pale and in pain as he met with reporters. "I am and always have been a right side player," he explained. "That's where I get my power. When I really let out on a drive, the pain hits me. When it doesn't hurt I keep thinking about it—afraid that it will. After bogeying the first three holes today, I came to the fourth with a putt of no more than 18 inches for a par. The ball never touched the hole. That is how bad I was." Palmer told of taking out a driver for his second shot on the 535-yard 10th with the idea of going for the green. "Then I said to myself 'That's ridiculous. How can you hit a drive from the fairway when you can't even hit it from the tee?' " Palmer missed another 18-inch putt at 16. He had pulled his drive, trapped his second and failed to get out of the bunker with his third. He said he was so disturbed when he finally put the ball in the hole that "I didn't even know what score I had—I thought I had a 6 until Billy Maxwell (his playing companion) counted them for me." Palmer withdrew from the tournament the next morning. "This is not retirement," he insisted. "I'll be back. But I won't play until this hip heals properly. I have no idea how long that may be. I may take the rest of the year off if the doctors say so. But don't construe this to mean I'm quitting." With that, he cleared out his locker, threw away the good luck notes that were pinned to it, and was gone back to Latrobe in his jet plane.

It rained heavily on Thursday night, which slowed the greens considerably, and the scoring immediately improved. Don Bies managed a 64 despite a double bogey on the opening hole. Gary Player shot a 65, which for a few hours—until Bies came in—was a course record, too, and moved into second place. Player sunk five birdie putts on the last seven holes, and on the 16th hit an exquisite shot out of a trap to within a foot of the pin to save his par. In front by a stroke after 36 holes was Floyd, who had followed his opening 69 with a 66. He was so roiled up the previous evening over the slow play of 54-year-old Jim Ferrier, whom he was paired with, that Floyd had hardly slept at all. "I didn't go to the first tee Friday morning with a good attitude," he said. "I was very irritable." Matters became still worse on Friday when the third golfer in the pairing, Herman Keiser, dropped out of the tournament, and Floyd was left to play by himself with Ferrier. Raymond was in a stormy mood, and not surprisingly he soon had a bogey. He missed the third green and then a three-foot putt. "The key to my round was that bogey," he explained later. "I'd made a very poor pitch. That woke me up. I don't know why, but I was a different player walking off that green than when I walked on. I said to myself, 'Let's go get a birdie.' " With his mind now focused on the task at hand, and not distracted by Ferrier, he got that birdie on 4, sinking a 15-foot putt. He wedged to within two feet at 5 and sunk another. He eagled the 6th from three feet, then birdied 8, 10 and 16. It was only after the round that Floyd let his anger at Ferrier well up. The former PGA champion is a dawdler, but Floyd's remarks were too cruel. "I was playing with a man that I loathe playing with," Raymond said. "There I was in a twosome with him, just me and him, for 18 holes. There couldn't have been four words between us. He's getting old and his nerves are gone, but I don't really feel sorry for him because he shouldn't be out here. He was a great player, but now he's struggling. He studied all his putts laboriously from each side, even though everybody knew he was gonna miss the cut by 10 strokes. He's not a considerate player. If he were a young guy I'd let him know about it." Ferrier missed the cut by four, but he was not about to retire quietly. He demanded an apology and asked Commissioner Joe Dey to make an official investigation. "You want to know something? " Ferrier said. "Eight years ago when Floyd was coming along I was the one who approached the Wilson Sporting Goods people about him. 'He's gonna be good,' I said. 'Take him on.' And they did. At my suggestion they put him on the payroll." On Saturday morning Floyd issued an apology. He "had not intended to damage the character of another professional golfer," he said.

Floyd was not involved in Saturday's melee, which was staged by the civil rights advocates. The first incident came on the fourth tee, and it was a kind of dress rehearsal for the TV cameras that would be focusing on the final holes. As Gary Player addressed his ball, a program was pitched over the heads of the spectators and landed at his feet. Nicklaus, who was Gary's playing partner, grinned and ducked behind his golf bag. The crowd laughed. It seemed, at the time, a humorous, if unfortunate, incident. But at the ninth green, as Nicklaus stood over a birdie putt, someone in the gallery shouted. Jack backed off the putt and again smiled at the disturbance. He missed the putt. It was on the way to the tenth tee that the disturbances became ugly. A spectator threw a cup of ice in Player's face. Obviously shocked, Gary looked at the man and asked, "What have I ever done to you? " The fat young assailant looked confused and then muttered, "Damn racist." He was hustled away by police. At the 10th green, two other demonstrators appeared ready to make an assault on the golfers. Player was approached by a bearded youth and Nicklaus, trying for an eagle, looked up to see a large black man charging through a bunker at him. Both assailants were intercepted but Jack's ball was filched by another man who threw it into the crowd. Amid the chaos, people were arrested. Not surprisingly, Nicklaus missed his eagle but Player sunk a 10 footer for a birdie. The final disruption came at the 13th green when a young girl rolled a plastic golf ball to Player's feet as he prepared to putt. The golfers continued the round, but were constantly expecting more trouble. They had not yet come to the televised holes, and that was where difficulty had been expected. By this time, however, police had arrested 11 demonstrators. There were no further disruptions, but the situation was unsettling. Nicklaus was concerned for his wife and son, who were among the spectators. (On Sunday he insisted they stay in the clubhouse.) Nicklaus came in with a third-round 74 (he took a triple bogey on the 18th) and despite a double bogey at the 9th, Player shot 71. "It is unbelievably tough to play under those conditions," he said. "But the majority of people today were so nice. I don't think you should let lousy things be published. If all those thousands of persons out there are so nice, you can't let five or six drive you in. That's just letting them have their way." In a way, Player's calm gave golf a distinguished moment.

Floyd, playing behind Nicklaus and Player, had not been harassed, and he shot a 67 to take a five-stroke lead, with Player, Bunky Henry and Bert Green deadlocked at 207 for second. Floyd had no bogeys, though he salvaged a par on one hole with a 20-foot putt. At 18 he put an eight iron six inches from the hole for his concluding birdie. "I don't know what my strategy will be tomorrow," Floyd said. "I've never had a five-shot lead going into the last round." But few pros expected Floyd to fold. "He is the best front-runner on the tour," Beard said.

On Sunday Floyd was paired with Player and on the first tee he began thinking about the possibility of disruptions. "I pulled my drive into the trees and after that I really didn't think about the demonstrators," he said. Floyd's game was off. For one thing he was not keyed up "I didn't have butterflies; didn't have the urge—." After two holes Player had picked up two shots on him. Floyd missed possible birdies at 5 and 6, which are par 5 holes. "I'd line up on the flag," Floyd explained later, "but I found myself pushing and pulling shots to the far part of the green. I didn't want to do it—it was just happening." Floyd bogeyed 7, and at the turn his lead was down to three strokes. At 10 he sank a downhill 25-footer for a birdie to dishearten Bert Greene who had drawn to within one stroke. At 12 Player bounced back with a birdie and when Floyd bogeyed 13 after being bunkered Raymond's lead was trimmed to two shots. The 16th was the deciding hole. There Player was trapped but came out well. Floyd, who was 40 feet from the pin read the green cautiously. There was a three-foot break. He rammed the sidehill putt over the humps and in; and Player missed his six-footer. "Ray's was one of the finest birdie putts under pressure that I've ever seen," Player said. "I thought he'd be lucky to get down in two from there." Said Floyd: "If I stood out there with a full practice bag I couldn't make that putt, or the one I sunk at 10, again." Player continued to press Floyd, picking up a birdie at 17. For a moment, on 18, it seemed like Gary would have a chance to win his second PGA championship. Floyd drove into a trap and missed the green with his second, but Player missed the 40-foot birdie he needed and Floyd, with a bogey, won the PGA title by one. "I feel lucky," said the winner. "It's a good thing none of the others had a hot round. I can only remember five or six shots that I was pleased with. After today, I know I'll never play safe again. It's not my game." Floyd's bachelor friends can attest to that. The new champion was asked if the cordon of cops that walked along with him and Player had distracted him. "No," he said, smiling, "I've had a couple of police escorts before, but not on the golf course."

The press conference over, the ebullient Floyd was off to spend some time with his beloved baseball team the Chicago Cubs. In the next few weeks he was seen sitting in their dugout and working out with them before games. "Who's that guy, no. 23," asked an opposing coach, who noticed Floyd on the field in Philadelphia. "Boy is he heavy. Boy, he's really out of shape." Well, the Cubs might have used him during their sad decline in the closing days of the season. They didn't make it to the World Series, but Ray Floyd did. The World Series of Golf, that is.

Avco Classic—$150,000
Winner: Tom Shaw

There were many people who looked upon this year's early season winners, such as Tom Shaw, as the lucky victims of a benign quirk of fate. But now here came Mr. Shaw again just like Ken Still three weeks before victorious once again. A title is a title is a title, and never mind how Tom Shaw got his second. All right, he shot a 77 in the final round, but he earned his $30,000 with some superb golf earlier (68, 68, 67) which gave him a seven-shot lead after 54 holes. Shaw has these roller-coaster performances. He described his performance in the previous week's PGA Championship this way: "I started with a 69, closed with a 69, and had a lot of garbage in between." Since his win at Doral in early March, Shaw missed the cut in 12 of his 21 starts. But never mind all the ups and downs; he had, after all, banked $80,000 in tournament winnings by the end of Avco week.

Avco, like Milwaukee, did not draw an all-star field. The new PGA champion, Ray Floyd promptly withdrew, Arnold Palmer performed in a TV booth, Johnny Pott went off to Mississippi to inspect hurricane damage to his Broadwater Beach home and Lee Trevino, after trying to play a few holes, dropped out with a stiff back. Bill Casper was back after a lay-off caused by "enzyme damage". He said he was healthy, but he shot an unhealthy 81 the first day and missed the cut for the first time in 148 tournaments and five years. Despite the disappointing field, over 100,000 people came during the week to see their matinee idols at Pleasant Valley Country Club in Sutton, Mass. And Tommy Shaw—long haired and blond—is one of the young idols. From the beginning Shaw was his free-wheeling self. He eagled the 530-yard second, bogeyed the third and then settled down to play his best. His four-under-par 68 was excellent on a day of unsettling winds and trickly pin settings, and it gave him a one stroke margin over George Knudson and Monty Kaiser. "That was a great round," Shaw declared grinning. "Now if I can win this one, I'll have only 51 tournaments to go to tie Arnie Palmer." It never hurts a young man to think big. Palmer, at Shaw's age (26) had won only once.

After a second-day 68, the press was talking of Shaw's sun-bleached hair and referring to him as a "sturdy stylist with great poise". He had a five-stroke lead and a spectator looking at the obviously pleased Shaw, declared, "That kid has been grinning since he got here. He may need to take frowning lessons if he ever gets into difficulty." Shaw said he was worried by a sinus infection, but nobody was listening to him. He also said he tired badly on the closing holes, but he bogeyed none of them and added, "I guess I can't complain." Knudson with a 72 remained in second. A third-round 67 increased Shaw's lead to seven strokes. Australian Bob Stanton, who had a 66, must have been discouraged to find he could only pick up one stroke on the leader. Shaw had two eagles and finished his round strongly, three under par on the final two holes.

Even after 63 holes Shaw retained his commanding lead. Stanton picked up one shot by playing the front nine one-under par, but now had to get back six strokes in nine holes, which seemed an unlikely chore. But Shaw bogeyed 10, and 11 and 13, and was only three strokes up with five to play. "I guess when I missed a one-foot putt at 11 it shook me a little," Shaw said later. At 17, 441 yards with water, Shaw pushed a two iron into the right rough. "Let's not kid ourselves," he said. "That was a real shank." His seven-iron second put him on a car path beyond the green. He chipped twice before getting on the green and took two putts for a double-bogey 6. Now Stanton was only one stroke back; on the final green the Australian missed a 10-foot birdie putt, hitting it too hard. Then Shaw, with two good woods, got down for a par. "I guess I won't be known for my strong finishes," he declared. At Doral he had also collapsed, taking 40 on the final nine. Shaw is 51 wins behind Arnie and not worrying about a fast finish yet.

Greater Hartford Open—$100,000
Winner: Bob Lunn

There's a saying in horse racing that a good big horse will beat a good little horse any day. Maybe the same axiom holds true for golf—that a good big pro will beat a good little pro, though Gary Player, for one, would be outraged at the thought. At Hartford Bob Lunn had four inches and 65 pounds on Dave Hill and beat him in a head-to-head playoff. At his best Lunn cannot be considered a Goliath of golf, but he is an adept journeyman and still very young. He is only 24, and in his third year as a professional. Besides the $20,000 first money at Hartford, which boosted Lunn into the top 25 U.S. money winners, he also won a berth in the $55,000-to-the-winner Alcan Golfer of the Year tournament four weeks later. Hoping to lure good golfers to some of its weaker events, the PGA picked Hartford as one of the qualifying sites for the Alcan. The other tournaments were the New Orleans, Western and Philadelphia opens. The lowest scorer in any three of these tournaments was invited to compete in the Alcan at Portland, Ore.

Because of the Labor Day holiday, the Hartford began on Friday and finished Monday. The first-day leaders, at 66, were J.C. Snead, Joel Goldstrand and Bob Murphy, the 1968 rookie of the year who had failed to win in 1969. Murphy was pleased with his round, which he played with new clubs, thieves having never returned his stolen set. Snead's round could have been considerably better, for he missed at least five short putts. Lunn was among eight golfers who shot 67s on the Wethersfield Country Club course, a tight 6,568-yard layout with small greens. The majority of the golfers massed at the top were rabbits, little-known fellows like Jerry Abbot, Roy Pace, and Hal Underwood. On Saturday Lunn added a 68, but he lost his lead to Gay Brewer (a two-time Alcan winner, who was determined to get another invitation). Brewer, with rounds of 68—66, now led by one. He felt he had been playing considerably better and perhaps had recovered from his 1967 Masters win and the resultant commitments that had affected his golf. Brewer bogeyed the first hole, but came back with seven birdies. The first-day leaders had soared out of contention, Murphy with a 73 and Snead and Goldstrand with 74s. That was giving up too much in a tournament that saw dozens of rounds in the 60s. The day's best round was a 65 by Charlie Sifford, who won his first official tournament at Wethersfield in 1967. At the end of the second day 24 golfers were within four strokes of the lead.

Starting with a birdie and an eagle, Lunn forged immediately to the front in the third round and he was never headed thereafter. He made the turn in 32 and birdied 14 and 16 on the back nine. Meanwhile Hill was matching Lunn stroke for stroke and they both came in with 66s. The best 18, however, was played by Howie Johnson, who has been trying to win a PGA tournament for 10 years. He had a 63. Lunn began the final round one stroke ahead of Dave Hill and Johnson. Howie faded almost immediately and ended by shooting a mediocre 70, but Bert Greene, who began five strokes back, suddenly challenged. At the turn Greene shared the lead with Hill and Lunn, but Lunn got two birdies to draw out in front again. At 16 Hill began a final charge. He sank a birdie putt there from 12 feet, at 17 he canned one from 10 feet and at 18 he got his third birdie, from 18 feet. His 66 to Lunn's 67 gave him a tie, but Hill's putting was not nearly so sharp in the playoff. He missed birdie tries on the first three holes—15, 10 and 12 feet—and on the fourth hole of the sudden death, Hill left his 20-footer inches short as Lunn sank a 15-footer and took the title.

Michigan Golf Classic—$100,000 ($50,000)
Winner: Larry Ziegler

There's a group of $100,000 golf tournaments that most people can't keep straight—the Minnesota Classic, the Milwaukee Open, and the Michigan Golf Classic. They are all mid-summer events played out there in the beer belt of America. For the sake of clarity, let us refer hereafter to the Michigan Golf Classic as the Mother·Hubbard Open, for this was where the pros went to collect and found that the cupboard was bare. The sponsors said simply there was no money. For Larry Ziegler, 30, who had hungered a long time for his first win and finally got it that week, the glory was hardly good enough to make up for the $20,000 deficit. The tournament, played at the Shenandoah Country Club in Walled Lane, Mich. drew poorly, both as to golfers and fans. The gallery Thursday and Friday was shocking—less than 500—and for the final two rounds there were only about 4,000 spectators a day. The tournament treasurer, Phil Lackman, claimed the event was "sold out by the PGA. I don't feel an obligation to the PGA whom I feel didn't exert any effort after using me." The foundation of his complaint was plain enough. Only two of the top 20 money earners showed up for the tournament. Lackman described himself as a babe in the woods and declared the tournament was his introduction into golf and he had gotten an education. "I didn't know the golf tour was like vaudeville," he said, "that it sold on names." He certainly must have been an innocent not to realize first off that the tournament conflicted with the World Series of Golf and therefore it had no chance at all to draw the 1969 winners of the Masters, British and U.S. Opens and the PGA. Most of the second echelon of players passed up the event because Tommy Jacobs, who had played an exhibition there in the spring, and Dave Hill, who lives nearby, had told their fellow pros the Shenandoah CC was in poor shape. Joe Dey visited Walled Lake a few months before and was appalled at what he found. He suggested the sponsors move the tournament, and when they refused he asked the greens superintendent from Oakland Hills to try to help patch the place up. Among other problems, half a dozen holes had been ruined by floods on the four-year-old course. The sponsors apparently compounded their difficulties by alienating the local press. The *Detroit News* sent its golf writer to the World Series in Akron, and the other Detroit daily gave the tournament only cursory coverage. In short, it was an unfortunate mess.

The first-day leaders were rookies Bob Menne and Grier Jones who managed to shoot five under par 65s. Their fairways were virtually bare, but 35 pros broke par, an astonishing performance considering the conditions. At 66 was Jack Montgomery, and Al Balding and Bobby Cole had 67s. The next day Cole shot 68, which was good enough to give him a one-stroke lead over Kermit Zarley. Menne and Jones dropped back with 72 and 73 respectively. On Saturday Zarley took over top place with Larry Hinson, but the low rounds of the day were turned in by J.C. Snead and Homero Blancas who had 65s, Ziegler at this point was three strokes off the pace, but he closed on Sunday with a dashing 64—including five straight birdies after a double bogey—to tie Blancas, who had a 65. Ziegler took the playoff by sinking a four-foot birdie putt on the second extra hole. He collected the keys to a new car, courtesy of Chrysler, but that was all. Most of the pros had departed by the time a scribbled message on scratch-pad paper was posted. It read: "Receipts at this time are insufficient to write a check for the prize fund. Payment must be deferred until all our receivables are in. Michigan Golf Classic, Inc."

The PGA immediately declared it would "institute appropriate litigation" to retrieve the players' money. Meanwhile it dipped into its own bank account for $50,000 to give the Michigan Classic pros half of what they had earned.

World Series of Golf—$77,500
Winner: Orville Moody

The National Broadcasting Company says 17 million people watch its annual four-man extravaganza that has the Masters, U.S. Open, British Open and PGA champions playing each other for a first prize of $50,000. Certainly the sponsors of the Michigan Classic (see below) will not squabble with that figure no matter how immense it seems—hardly a mortal in Michigan turned out for their tournament. For one thing, the TV audience is always assured of Arnold Palmer, even if he hasn't managed to win his way to Akron in five years. He acts as an emcee and is surprisingly good performing on the sidelines. However, it was the first time since the World Series began in 1962 that not one of the golf's Big Three—Palmer, Jack Nicklaus or Gary Player was in the starting field.

Everybody in the 1969 field was a World Series rookie, but Ray

Floyd had to be considered the favorite in the 36-hole event since he had won the American Golf Classic on the Firestone Country Club course six weeks before. He was obviously playing his best golf, winning the PGA just four weeks before, and had the best practice round, a 70, on the eve of the tournament. Because of thunderstorms that washed out the traps and flooded several fairways early in the week, the 7,180-yard course could be expected to play long, which also helped Floyd. But Orville Moody was feeling good, and not saying much about it. He had posted a 64 in an exhibition the previous week during a tour in Oklahoma. The governor had proclaimed Orville Moody Day and perhaps Orville was beginning to believe in himself and his success. George Archer was disgusted with his game, "It's just been ridiculous the way I've been playing," he said. "I missed the cut at Hartford. I really didn't play that bad, but I just didn't score good." And to make things worse he had a tennis elbow and an upset stomach. The remaining member of the field, Tony Jacklin had been playing exhibitions, not competitive golf, while moving into a new house. "It's our first house," he told reporters. "It's in the north of England, and it takes a lot of time to get moved in."

Tony showed from the beginning that he was rusty—he three-putted twice in the first round and finished with a 73. "You can't win tournaments playing like that," he said, quite correctly. Archer also had had a poor round, a 74, but so did Orville Moody. The first-day leader was Floyd, with a par 72. But Floyd promptly lost the lead the next day with a bogey on the first hole. Jacklin, however, gave the stroke back with a bogey at 2. In retrospect, the third hole was to be the crucial one. Orville Moody, one stroke out of the lead, hooked his drive onto an adjoining fairway. The third green is guarded by a pond, but Moody elected to go for it. He hit a two iron that flew under some tree limbs and then over the water to end up just 10 feet from the cup. He missed the birdie but he said "it was the best shot I ever hit in my life—one shot in a thousand. I felt from that time on I would take it. I was hitting everything good." Moody birdied 7 and when Jacklin three-putted the 8th Orville had the lead all for his own. Meanwhile, Floyd was going two-over-par. The only competition Moody was to get came from Archer, but George, who is ordinarily such a fine putter, couldn't make any birdie tries drop. By the time they came to 16, Moody had a three-stroke lead. He watched Archer sink a 13-foot birdie there, and apparently unperturbed stood up and stroked in a nine-footer for his par. "His putt fell in the back door," Archer said. "If it hadn't dropped, the difference would have been only one and I was keyed up." But the World Series, to all intents and purposes was over. All the golfers parred in. Orville collected the $50,000 with a one-over par 141 (74–67) Archer, who finished two strokes back collected $15,000 and Floyd and Jacklin earned $6,250 each with 145s. That will buy a few pots and pans for homemaker Jacklin.

In the post-Series Palmer asked Tony, who was headed for England, when he would return to America. "I'll be back in a month," Tony said loudly. "I'll be right here just a month from now playing in the CBS Golf Classic." One could sense the gasp as NBCs television cameras hastily drew back in horror from the scene, while Palmer and Jacklin doubled up in laughter at the faux pas.

ALCAN GOLFER OF THE YEAR—$125,000
Winner: Bill Casper

"Gentlemen, I don't believe it," Bill Casper told the press after his Alcan win. He had made up seven strokes in three holes on Lee Trevino to take the huge $55,000 first prize and he had every reason not to believe it. The situation was reminiscent of the 1966 U.S. Open when Casper made up seven strokes in nine holes on Palmer, "but this was even more fantastic," Casper said. "In San Francisco I could see it coming. Here it was thrown at me blind side. I thought Lee had come and gone with the tournament. I was working hard just to get second place. It wasn't until I holed out on 18 that I realized I had a chance to win." Portland Golf Club, the site of the tournament, must be considered a Casper course. He has won two Portland Opens and has never shot an over-par round there.

The course was playing much longer than its 6,541 yards after a week of heavy rain. As well as a baker's dozen of U.S. pros, the field of 24 included France's Jean Garaialde, Australia's Kel Nagel, Ireland's Christy O'Connor and Britishers Tommy Horton, Brian Barnes, Brian Huggett and Maurice Bembridge. Garaialde was to score the best of the foreigners, finishing in a tie for sixth. The first day leaders were Dan Sikes and Lou Graham with 69s, and Sikes could have had a 65, had he not had a horrendous quadruple bogey on the par-4 13th, where he lost a ball in a fir tree. Neither were winners on the 1969 tour; they, like the other Americans had earned their berths through the qualifying format (golfers with the lowest scores in three-of-four designated tournaments—the Hartford, New Orleans, Philadelphia and Western Opens—were invited). Seven of the Americans were 1969 winners, and if some of the others didn't have much flair, the Alcan people tried to supply the missing quality by hiring charismatic Tom Shaw as a TV interviewer.

Trevino, with rounds of 70—67, became Friday's leader, but the second day was mostly noteworthy because Kel Nagel accidentally put himself down for a 35 on the ninth hole, signed his card and handed it in. His score totalled 105 instead of the 74 he actually shot. Though he had obviously lost all chances to finish anywhere but last, Nagel completed the tournament and his 70-105-73-76 won him $2,000. Casper was one stroke out of the lead after the second round and defending champion Gay Brewer was two back. "In the last two months, I've been playing the best of my life," said the optimistic Brewer. "My putting is good. All I need is a couple of breaks."

Trevino continued along his merry way on Saturday, starting with a 40-foot birdie on the first hole. He had two more birdies and 15 pars for a 69, but complained about his putting. He had missed three birdie tries from inside eight feet on the final five holes. "They could have put this thing out of reach for the other guys," he said, but as it was he had a two stroke margin. His closest challenger, Casper, went out in the pairing ahead of Lee on Sunday and by the time Bill had completed the first nine he was contentedly playing for second money. Trevino's gallery was roaring as he birdied hole after hole—five, in fact, between the 5th and 10th. Trevino collected another birdie on 13, three-putted 14, but came back with an eagle at 15, a 511-yard par 5. Now, though it hardly seemed to matter, Casper got hot. He had been putting poorly but suddenly birdie putts dropped at 15, 16, 17, 18—four holes in a row. Casper was pleased to have nailed down second place, but wait a minute. Back at 16 Trevino pulled his drive and the ball rolled against a tree trunk. He bogeyed the hole. At 17 his caddie handed him a nine iron and against his instincts Trevino used it—his tee shot was short and bunkered. He swung twice before getting the ball out of the sand and then dribbled onto the green thirty feet from the pin; from there he three-putted for a triple bogey. About this time Trevino heard the roar of the gallery at the home green. Casper had sunk a six-foot birdie putt to take the lead.

Trevino could have salvaged a tie had he managed a 15-foot birdie try on 18, but the ball stayed out. This display of the staggers cost Trevino $40,000, the difference between first and second place.

Casper said, "If you figure those last four putts of mine in value per foot, they come up pretty important." Let's see 20 feet, eight feet, seven feet, six feet . . . about $1,000 a foot or $10,000 a putt. Not bad for a man who didn't think the putts mattered.

Robinson Open—$75,000
Winner: Bob Goalby

When all the other tournament sponsors ducked late September and early October dates—baseball playoff and World Series time—plucky little Robinson, Illinois (pop. 8,000) decided to have a big time golf tournament. It was not the town's first venture into professional golf and everybody knew that with a $75,000 purse, the field couldn't be the greatest. In 1962 the sponsors started having small events and by 1967 they were offering a $10,000 purse. In 1968 this was upped to $25,000 and in a flush of community spirit the town decided on a $75,000 Robinson Open in 1969. It took the precaution, however, of insuring the tournament director's life for $150,000—since the whole thing was his idea and he was the one who had to produce. It also managed to get a subsidy of $33,000 from the Alcan corporation which was running a conflicting tournament with an exclusive field. And a lot of free help was arranged. The Robinson Episcopal minister performed as doorman, the local Cadillac dealer as photographer and the firemen as parking lot attendants.

How did it all turn out? Well, Robinson ended up making a profit of $50,000, the pros got their checks (certified) and now there is talk of a $150,000 Robinson Open next year. Possibly this will lure some name players. The tournament only had three this year—Doug Sanders, Dow Finsterwald and Bob Goalby, who lived up to his reputation and won in a sudden death playoff. Since Robinson is 30 minutes from anywhere—anywhere being the nearest motel in Vincennes, Indiana, the pros had a long commute, but there was no grumbling. Robinson is a pleasant place and the course is a fine one, if short. Sadly, for the local ladies, Doug Sanders shot a 75 the first day and withdrew, but Goalby gave them something to talk about, a 10 under par 62. Three strokes behind that first day flash of fire was Richard Martinez. On Friday Goalby slumped to a more human 71 and clung to his lead by only a single stroke. He lost the top spot in the third round when he had his worst round, a 73, and fell into a tie for sixth as Billy Maxwell, who had not won a tournament in seven years, moved in front with rounds of 66-69-67 and Larry Ziegler was second, after bogeying 17 and 18.

Goalby thought he no longer had a chance to win the tournament—he was four strokes back and his putting had become weak and wristy. But he recovered his touch on Sunday morning and once again felt optimistic. He made what he called his best shot in five years on the third hole, coming out of rough from under a tree with a sand wedge to within four feet of the cup. "Houdini couldn't have gotten it any closer," he said. At the turn Goalby moved into a tie with Howie Johnson, Maxwell and Jim Wiechers. By 17 it was a duel between Goalby and Wiechers, and when Goalby missed a four-foot birdie putt on the final hole and later Wiechers made one the tournament went into extra holes. Goalby at the time was being interviewed by the press. He left like Douglas MacArthur, declaring he would return, and he didn't take long. He sank an agonizing 12-foot birdie putt on the first extra hole and had another victory at last. He had not won since the 1968 Masters. It had been a long time, and it hardly mattered that the win had come out in the weeds of southeast Illinois. The Robinson was a sweet tournament for Goalby, and a sweet one for the town, too, which deserved all of the golf fun it got.

Sahara Invitation—$100,000
Winner: Jack Nicklaus

Nicklaus came to Las Vegas ranking 19th on the U.S. money winning list after a poor-for-him-season (one win and seven of 19 times in the top 10). But if there is any place Jack can strike it rich it is in this desert city. He has won the Tournament of Champions twice in Las Vegas and his 1969 victory at Sahara was his fourth triumph in that tournament in seven years. Nicklaus, however, was not counting only on his luck. In the weeks preceding the tournament he had made a stern appraisal of his game. Never in his eight-year professional career had he finished worse than third on the U.S. money list and his dismal 1969 ranking grated. He did not like being back in the pack. Deciding he better shape up, he lost 15 pounds in three weeks by following a Weight Watchers' diet. Next he consulted Gardner Dickinson about his backswing. Dickinson corrected the problem and Jack began to move the club with more rhythm. His swing had not been in a groove all year. "I'm concerned," Nicklaus told reporters on checking in at the Sahara-Nevada Country Club course.

In his first competitive round in six weeks, Nicklaus shot a 69, which put him five strokes and 12 players behind the first-day leader, Doug Sanders. Sanders was also scrambling for money after a poor season—he had earned only $20,000 and was in danger of losing his exemption (the top 60 money winners are excused from qualifying for each week's event). Playing in gusty winds, Sanders had six birdies and 10 threes on his card. He sank some good putts—from 18, 25, 12 and 10 feet—and on the par-3 16th he put his tee shot 18 inches from the cup. His performance was particularly good because the greens were in poor condition, ruined by a mid-summer fungus. Behind Sanders, tied with 66's, were three unknowns—Bob Menne, Ed Merrins and Ted Hayes, Jr. The galleries were having trouble identifying with these pros, and the mass of spectators followed Arnold Palmer who like Nicklaus was making his first appearance after a layoff. Palmer said he was having less trouble with his arthritic hip and his first round 69 looked hopeful.

Palmer's second round was not nearly as bad as his score—75—suggested. He was the victim of over-enthusiasm by his fans. On the 15th hole, a par-5, his second shot rolled out of bounds. Palmer dropped a provisional ball, but he was then told by members of the gallery his original ball was still in bounds. Arnold picked up the provisional and when he got near the green found his first ball was indeed out of bounds. The mix-up cost him a two-stroke penalty and he took a nine on the hole. "It was my fault," he said later. "The player is always responsible for his ball." Billy Casper took an 11 once on the same hole and Bunky Henry hit three shots out of bounds there for a 13—statistics that hardly made Palmer feel better. Doug Sanders, meanwhile, retained his lead through 36 holes with a par 71. His round included three birdies and three bogeys. Grouped one stroke behind him were Defending Champion Chi Chi Rodrigues (69—68), Nicklaus (69—68) and three others.

In Saturday's round Sanders continued his slide with a 73 (he was to finish with a 76 and only earn $493), and the new leader was Frank Beard, who zoomed up from 17th place with a 65. Beard had five birdies on the front nine and one birdie and eight pars on the back side to gain a one-stroke lead over Nicklaus, who had a 70. Beard played his irons well; his longest birdie putt was a 15-footer (others were from 5, 3, 1, 6 and 1 feet). Palmer recovered from his second round with a 68, but was to lapse again in the final 18, fading to a 73.

Nicklaus, however, came back with vengeance. He had been disgusted with his third round, in which he took 20 putts on the last nine, and had given himself a post-round putting lesson. His putting showed immediate improvement on Sunday when he took only 12 strokes on the greens in the first nine holes. He birdied four holes in that stretch, and two more birdies on the back nine gave him a 65 and a four-stroke win over Beard. Jack was exultant. "I played better here than at any time since last year's U.S. Open," he said. "Thanks to a few discoveries about my game, it's a pleasure to be here." With his confidence restored, he set off to reclaim a position of eminence on the money list.

San Francisco Open—$100,000
Winner: Steve Spray

It had been another lean and disheartening year for Steve Spray. About the only time he saw his name in print was when one of the golf writers was making fun of it. Spray was another of the nobodies, winner of $8,175 in a grinding 10 months. After his fifth unsuccessful year on the tour, he could not help but wonder if he should have turned pro. If he'd stayed in Iowa and gone into business he would probably have won the state amateur nine or ten times, and maybe even the National Amateur (as a young golfer he'd gotten to the quarter finals twice). But the San Francisco Open removed, at least for the moment, any doubt of Spray's that he belongs. He went into the final day at the Harding Park course with a three-stroke lead and played solid and sure golf—17 pars and a final birdie—to beat Chi Chi Rodriguez by a stroke. He was the 12th new face to score a victory during 1969.

Spray's first round was a modest 70, and already he seemed hopelessly outdistanced. George Archer, the Masters winner who had not appeared in a regular tournament for two months, shot an eight-under-par 63 that Thursday. It was a remarkable round—he was in the woods three times and fluffed one tee shot so badly that it dribbled only 50 yards. Yet Archer managed 10 birdies and equalled the course record. "I certainly don't have the touch to be a winner," Archer said after his round. "I'm not driving straight enough to last." Harding Park, a municipal course, is a narrow 6,677 yards and many of its fairways are lined with trees. Yet the pros were scoring well. At 64 Jack Montgomery and Dick Mayer, and at 65, Jerry Heard and Bob Lunn. Forty-one golfers did better than Steve Spray in that opening round.

But what a difference a day makes. Friday Spray shot a 63 and forged into a tie for third. He credited professional friends R.H. Sikes and Dale Douglass with the improvement. He said they had straightened out his swing—it was too flat—and his putting—he had been moving his head. "And R.H. has been teaching me to think positively," Spray said, "to think birdies. I've even started to make some." Archer, on the other hand, hardly felt in winning shape. His tennis elbow was throbbing and, as he predicted, he spent much of the second day in the woods. He scraped through with a 67, thanks mainly to one-foot birdie putts on the 5th, 6th and 8th holes, and still had a two-stroke lead. The two pros at his heels after the first round—Montgomery and Mayer—had shot 74s. Only players that had shot par or better for 36 holes made the cut.

As the third round began Archer, Bob Lunn and Miller Barber jostled for the lead. Archer took a double bogey on the sixth hole, once again hitting into the woods, and that was the last of him; he finished with 73—72 and told the press "You ought to nickname me Lumberjack". Spray, meanwhile, birdied the 7th hole from 12 feet and then spurted into the lead with four birdies on five holes on the back nine. He added another birdie at 17 when he sank a 10-foot putt and ended the day three strokes ahead of Miller Barber and Bob Lunn. Chi Chi Rodriguez had been easing himself into contention with rounds of 69-68-67 but he was two strokes back.

Chi Chi won the 1964 Lucky International on the Harding Park course and it evidently is to his liking. Playing ahead of Spray on the last day he immediately began to rack up birdies. By the time he reached the 337-yard 16th he had five of them on his card and now a sixth put him into a tie for the lead with Spray, who had been playing par golf. At 17 Chi Chi missed a 10-foot birdie try ("I must have read it in Spanish and putted in English," he said). He came in with a 66 and sat uneasily at the scorer's table waiting for Spray to finish.

Spray, meanwhile, was extricating himself from tree limbs at the 16th green. His chip was short of the green and he needed, and got, a six-foot putt for his par. He came back to nearly birdie 17 from 25 feet and at 18 found himself with a five-footer to win the tournament. Rodriguez looked away from the putting surface. "I said to myself, 'what are you doing watching? If he makes it the crowd will tell me'," Chi Chi explained. Carol Spray, carrying her two-year-old daughter, also turned her head. "I just couldn't watch him, it meant too much," she said. Steve stood over the ball thinking "hit it firm because you may never have another chance to win." The ball went into the hole. "This is the culmination of our dreams," Carol Spray said later. "For five years we've been struggling out here, always wondering if we were wasting the best years of our lives for nothing." Apparently not; we'll see.

KAISER INTERNATIONAL OPEN (NO.2)—$140,000
Winner: Jack Nicklaus

Tony Lema was the one who first called the lesser pros rabbits. Tony, at the time, was in his salad days and the rabbits, he used to say, "are always hanging around the fringes, nibbling at the lettuce." Until 1969, when autumn came the successful pros would leave what scraps were left in the patch to the small fry and retire from the scene. But the green stuff offered on this year's fall tour was too juicy for anybody to pass up, and crowding into the Silverado Country Club in Napa, California to scrap for $140,000 were people like Jack Nicklaus, Billy Casper, George Archer and Don January. This was the second Kaiser tournament of the year; the first abbreviated by rain, in January, was won by Miller Barber. The sponsors apparently decided holding a tournament in Northern California in the rains and gales of January was not a good risk, and they opted for fall dates.

From his first shot on Thursday Nicklaus played superlative golf. That day he shared the lead with Chuck Courtney and Lou Graham, after the three of them posted six under par 66s on the South Course of Silverado. It is the shorter of the two used in the championship, 6,602 yards to the 6,849-yard North Course. January was right behind the trio with a 67, Casper was at 68 with seven other golfers and Archer was one of 16 at 69. Nicklaus was just as hot in the second round on the North Course. He birdied seven of the last 10 holes that day for a 67 and a two-stroke lead. Lou Graham tried to keep up with Jack, and did well to fire a 69, but Courtney slipped back into the pack after taking a 73. Both Casper and Archer had 69s and remained within striking distance but Nicklaus was buoyantly confident. "If I win here." he said, "that would put me only $1,000 behind Gary Player on the U.S. money list. If I win maybe three in a row, well, I'd be right up there. I don't know whether I'll play in the Danny Thomas tournament in December, but if I'm in a position to improve my standing on the list, maybe take No. 1, I'll sure try to." Nicklaus was now playing as well as he had in two years, and the way he was casually talking of the possibility of winning all those tournaments must have made Frank Beard, the no. 1 man on the earnings list ($174,000 to Jack's $94,000) wince. A lean Jack was down to 190 pounds and hungry.

In the third round it was Archer who starred, shooting a 66 to Nicklaus', Casper's and January's 69. Nicklaus, however, retained his two-shot lead with a 65-hole total of 202. Archer was at 204, Casper at 206 and January at 207. The three challengers had better final rounds than Nicklaus and though they caught him, they could not pass him, as all finished with 72-hole scores of 273. Archer might have won in regulation holes had he not taken a double bogey at the 9th; his ball hit a spectator and bounced behind a tree, then his next

shot went into a creek on the opposite side of the fairway, and when he finally reached the green he three-putted. "It was just a bad break," he said later. "Yesterday I hit a marshal in the head and the ball bounded toward the green and I made a par." Casper finished with birdies on 16 and 17 to win his way into the playoff.

The sudden-death playoff began about 5 p.m. but it was already dusk when the players reached the 16th hole, a 526-yards par 5. January was eliminated there when all he could manage was a par and the other three had birdies—Casper from 18 feet, Nicklaus from 16 and Archer from 14. It was now too dark to continue and the playoff was postponed until morning. It was further delayed by fog on Monday, but after an hour Archer, Casper and Nicklaus teed off at 17, a par 4. Archer was on in two but he left himself a long and nasty downhill putt. Casper bunkered his second and came out poorly. Nicklaus put his approach 14 feet from the pin. Casper took a bogey; Archer missed his birdie try by three feet and Nicklaus rolled his 14-footer straight in, so Jack pocketed first money of $28,000, and headed for Hawaii. He was now just $52,000 behind Frank Beard and his stride was lengthening.

HAWAIIAN OPEN—$125,000
Winner: Bruce Crampton

The man who picks up nine strokes in 18 holes on Nicklaus when
Jack is playing good golf deserves something more than praise, and
Bruce Crampton got his prize, the $25,000 first money at Hawaii. At
the halfway point Nicklaus had a four stroke lead over the field and
looked well on his way to his third win in three starts. But
Crampton, with a 65, stormed to the front Saturday and kept
drawing away over the final 18 to win by four shots. For a man who
has had to settle for the consolation prizes—2nd, 3rd and 4th
money—for more than four years, the victory was sweet. Crampton,
a workmanlike Aussie, plugs away relentlessly on the tour each year,
starting week after week. He earns good money (for the second
straight season his winnings topped $100,000) but be labors for it.
He is a doggedly determined and humorless man and it was good to
see him finally grin in Honolulu.

During the first day's play at Waialae Country Club, gusty trade
winds blew and most of the golfers along with them. Nicklaus' round
was spectacular—many said the best single round of the year—a
course record 63. In fact it was almost unbelievable in the 40-mile
winds. He began the day concentrating grimly; but he became
noticeably affable after birdieing three of the first four holes. He
made the turn in 32 and continued his birdie spree on the back nine.
At the 15th and 16th holes he sank birdie putts of 45 and 50 feet,
and by now was blushing in embarrassment. "Isn't this fun," he said
to his gallery. Nicklaus came up with nine birdies in all; he had not
missed a green nor a putt of less than 15 feet. "This is probably the
best putting round I've ever had," he said. "I can't recall when I
putted this well." His four-stroke lead was the largest first-round
margin of the year. "If he keeps on putting like that," Bill Casper
said, "you just can't beat him." Ken Still, who came in with a 67 to
hold down second place with Dave Stockton, took a considerably
more optimistic view: Nicklaus is on the top of his game right now,"
he said. "But all good things have to come to an end.

But through the second day Nicklaus maintained his four-stroke
edge. Still matched Jack stroke for stroke, both coming in with 71s.
Also in contention was Tom Weiskopf, whose 70—68 gave him a
share of second place with Still, but none of the other golfers seemed
in a position to threaten. Casper and Palmer were in a cluster seven

strokes back of Nicklaus and Crampton seemed to be playing his usual steady (71—71) uninspiring game. Pros like Ray Floyd and Orville Moody missed the cut.

The winds died on Saturday and Nicklaus seemed becalmed. He shot a 74, two over par. Crampton, meanwhile was sinking four birdie putts on the front nine, and then another four on the backside. He had one bogey and finished with a 65, which gave him a one stroke lead at 207. Nicklaus was at 208 and Weiskopf at 209. As Ken Still has prophesied all good things would end—both for himself and Nicklaus. Still double bogeyed the first hole Saturday and that began his downfall. He eventually finished in a tie for 45th.

Crampton started the final round strongly, birdieing the first two holes. He bogeyed 5, but thereafter breezed away from the field with birdies at 9, 13, 14 and 17. Nicklaus, with a 70, never threatened, but the second money of $14,300 that he collected pushed him into third place on the U.S. money list. He now had won almost half his year's earnings in his last three starts. No one paid much attention to Arnold Palmer at Hawaii. He won $818 with rounds of 70-71-72-73. "I'm hitting the ball very, very well," he insisted, when a friend asked him how thing's were. "I just can't put it in the hole." Anyone who had been watching him play would have sensed his frustration. In one depressing round he had half a dozen putts of three feet or less that did not drop. Well, maybe all bad things come to an end, too.

HERITAGE GOLF CLASSIC—$100,000
Winner: Arnold Palmer

It was Thanksgiving weekend—you can put it as simply as that. After 14 months Arnold finally won a tournament. And what made it all the nicer, the victory was on a superb new course that Jack Nicklaus had a hand in designing, the Harbour Town Golf Links on Hilton Head Island, South Carolina. "I think this is one of my most important wins," Palmer said of this 54th career victory. "It is almost like the first one. I wanted to win this one as much as I would a U.S. Open or Masters."

Palmer had been back on the tour for five weeks after a long enforced layoff. He had played well but putted atrociously, and a sports writer at the Hawaiian Open had noted Arnie's Army was dwindling, that some of the deserters were following Nicklaus. That must have grated a little. Palmer came to South Carolina in a determined frame of mind. "I'm going to get my putting sorted out," he said. "I'm going to do it or die trying."

At Harbour Town he could make the most of his strengths—fine tee shots and irons—for it is a course that demands precision placement; the narrow fairways twist through low marshland, giant oaks draped with Spanish moss, brooding pines and thickets of magnolias. There are no fake mounds or elevated greens. The brutal, abrupt character of the course is entirely natural. The final holes wind to the edge of a bay and when the wind blows the finish is reminiscent of Pebble Beach. "We were certainly influenced by Pebble," Nicklaus said, speaking in his new role of golf architect. "There is some Pebble here, but also some Scioto, some Meriod and some Pine Valley." There is even a touch of Scotland in the deep greenside bunkers, some of which are walled with planks and railroad ties. The course was begun only 13 months before and had been opened only three weeks. There was not any rough, but that did not really matter as players were either in the fairway or in the jungle. For all its severity the course was not long, only 6,655 yards and a par 71. "This is the kind of course I really like," Nicklaus said, although it was hardly one he could be expected to play well. "It is the kind that makes you play good golf shots. You have to play to a definite side of the fairway, depending on where the pin is, or you haven't got a shot. You have to play to the side of the green where the pin is or you'll have to use a wedge over a bunker. You've also got the option of going with a driver and, say, and eight-iron to a certain hole, or going with a one-iron and five-iron. This is what golf should be." Lee Trevino called it, "the greatest course I have ever played, and I mean that." Bobby Nichols said, "I wouldn't want to play it every week. I'm not good enough to play it every week." And Jack McGowan declared, "I've never played a course that left me so mentally tired. You don't have to think on every hole. You've got to think on every shot."

If anyone needed further proof of Harbour Town's difficulty, they could look at the scores of Jim Colbert. His two-under 69 put him one stroke out of the lead on opening day. He shot 85 in the second round and missed the cut by three strokes. That Friday there were 26 scores of 80 or higher and the cut of 151 was the highest of the year.

Palmer did 50 situps the night before the tournament and 50 more on Thursday morning. He had been doing such exercises daily, and they helped his ailing hip. He opened with a 34-34—68 and called it "one of the best rounds I've played in a long while. But I'm still not putting. If I'd putted like I have in the past I could have been eight under par after seven holes. It was very possible." He had missed five putts from inside six feet and missed an eagle from eight feet. Still, he had a share of the lead with George Archer, who had come in at three under par despite three bogeys. Behind the front runners were Charlie Sifford, Mac McLendon and the ill-fated Colbert. Nicklaus was at 71.

Friday, in a day-long drizzle and cold weather, Tom Weiskopf rallied with a 65. "I seem to putt better on dark cool days," he said, "when there's moisture on the greens. I can see the line better and the greens are more uniform. This course is so new that the rough areas out of the fairways involve some luck. I got the absolute maximum out of the round today. Considering how tough this course is, this is one of the greatest rounds I've ever played on the tour." Weiskopf moved into a tie with Palmer for the lead, and though Arnold had only come in with a par 71, he was delighted with it. "My bad round is now behind me," he said. "You can't expect to play three sub-par rounds on a course like this. I stole a good score with a bad round." Palmer had not been as accurate as on Thursday, but he balanced his four bogeys with four birdies. A stroke back of the two leaders was Dick Crawford, who had been palying solidly (71-69).

On the closing holes of the third round Palmer moved out in front, largely because various mishaps befell the other contenders. His one under par 70 was good enough to give him a three stroke lead. Nobody could remember when he last had held so big a lead after 54 holes. "I was scrambling well at times and putted pretty well," he said. "I can't say I'm playing any better than I did at Hawaii, or San Francisco, or Napa, or Las Vegas. But I'm putting better." And that was the key. Nicklaus finished bogey, double-bogey for a 71 and was five shots back. "Who laid out this mess," he growled. But there were only three golfers between himself and Palmer, and he must have thought he had a chance. At 212 were Homero Blancas and Dick Crawford, and at 213, Tom Weiskopf.

Opportunity did present itself on Sunday, but no one made any use of it. Nicklaus shot 75. Blancas 76, Weiskopf 77, and only Crawford was left to battle Palmer. Arnold was two over on the front nine on Sunday, but he showed some resolution on 10. He had posted two straight bogeys and now he put his tee shot in the water.

However, he saved his par with a 15-foot putt. He was bunkered at 11 and bogeyed, and looked in real trouble at 13 when Crawford sunk a 30-foot birdie putt. Arnold promptly matched it with a 25-footer of his own. But then at 15 Palmer three-putted. By the 17th hole his lead had dwindled to one stroke. Visibly nervous he hit his shot fat and missed the green. However he managed to get down from 10 feet for his par, and when Crawford bogeyed the hole Palmer went to 18 with a two-stroke cushion. Crawford bogeyed 18 and Palmer won easily. Doing a mock stagger across the green he fell into Jack Nicklaus' arms. The crowd, limited by the sponsors to 5,000 (who paid $32 for a tournament ticket), cheered lustily, but it was too bad there were not more people sharing in the jubilant moment. Television's eye was on football games, so Palmer was back but nobody got to see the return.

DANNY THOMAS—DIPLOMAT CLASSIC—$125,000
Winner: Arnold Palmer

Since his triumph had all but gone unwitnessed, hidden away as it was in a hamlet in South Carolina, Arnold Palmer had to do it again the next week. This time the stage was considerably larger—the Diplomat Hotel and Country Club just north of Miami, and the supporting cast was good—Stan Musial, Mickey Rooney, Don Drysdale, Eddie Arcaro, Whitey Ford, Gordon MacRae, Milton Berle, Bob Hope, Jackie Gleason, Andy Williams and innumerable other show-biz friends of host Danny Thomas. There amid the neon and with all the golf critics present, Palmer put on his act again. And this time he wowed them with some last minute histrionics.

Palmer was still elated by his victory at Heritage when he showed up in Miami. He went out the first day on the flat 6,964 yard Diplomat course and birdied the first four holes. He bogeyed a few, birdied some more and came in with a 68, which put him three strokes back of Gay Brewer, the leader at 65. "I felt fine," Palmer told newsmen. "I swung a couple times like I was sick, but I wasn't." The day had been windless and the pros were calling the course the easiest they had played all year. "Somebody should shoot a 63 out there," R.H. Sikes said after coming in with a 67. Fifty players broke par. Brewer had seven birdies, an eagle and a double bogey at the 15th, where he was bunkered twice. He was putting superbly, sinking a 20 footer at 17 for the eagle. At 67 were Tommy Aaron, Sikes and a rookie, Jim Jamieson, who started out with a bogey but had a 32 on the front nine. "I was choking so badly at the first hole I couldn't stand it," he said. Brewer continued his rapid pace on Friday, shooting 66 and moving four strokes up on the field. Using a large mallet-headed putter, he had seven birdies and 11 one-putt greens. "I was scrambling," he said, "but I was putting so well I was able to hit bad shots and get away with it". Palmer had a 67 and now was deadlocked in second with another rookie, Hal Underwood.

Brewer continued his hot putting (eight one-putt greens) on Saturday. He had taken just 80 strokes in three days on the greens, and now he was an extraordinary 17 under par and had a six-stroke lead on the field. Palmer lost ground, taking a 70 to Brewer's 68, and blamed the lapse on his putting. He missed eight times from within 10 feet. But he also added that the 70 was "possibly the best round" he had played in the tournament. He was all alone in second place.

When Brewer birdied the first hole on Sunday and extended his lead to seven strokes he became overly confident. "I guess I relaxed after that," he said later. "I missed a putt at the fifth that I think started me off to my poor round." It was at the next hole, when Palmer birdied and Brewer bogeyed, that Arnold began to think he had a chance. "You have a feeling, a sixth sense sort of thing when it's going to happen," he explained. Palmer nearly holed his tee shot at 9 and tapped in for a birdie and a 33 going out. Brewer had a 38 so only one stroke separated the golfers. Brewer knew he was seriously threatened. "Go Arnie Go; Go Baby Go," the crowd was hollering. Palmer was now hitching at his pants as he used to in years gone by. The momentum was building and he was relishing every moment. He birdied the 14th from 8 feet, the 15th from 8, the par-5 17th and 18th from 20 feet—four birdies in the last five holes. Brewer was overwhelmed. "Nothing went right," he said.

"This thing, this winning, means everything to me," said the triumphant Palmer. "Getting it going again is probably the thing I wanted most in my life. I knew I was going to play again, but I didn't know how successfully. There were some doubts in my own mind."

So Palmer ended the decade almost as well as he began it—in June, 1960 he had come from seven strokes off the pace in the final round to win that famous U.S. Open at Cherry Hills. And here in December, 1969 he had come from seven back again. Winning still elated him, perhaps more so. Once again Arnold was dancing on the greens.

5

The British Open

A princely show at Royal Lytham

For two important reasons, the British Open of 1969 was the most significant in twenty years. The first is that a British golfer won. The second is that the British golfer was Tony Jacklin. Before I get into the story of Jacklin and the championship itself, I have to recount a little history that is ancient enough to border on the boring, but which forms a rare phenomenon of modern international sport. The fact is that in 18 years, since Max Faulkner at Portrush in 1951, no British golfer had won his own Open Championship. This induced in British golf fans all the doggedness, the patience, the defiance, the stiff-upper-lip-thing that their national character has demonstrated in other directions, but all that, in turn, was merely a mask covering much frustration, a good deal of irritation and perhaps a lot of envy. Ever since World War II they had seen their championship dominated by the likes of Bobby Locke, Peter Thomson, and Gary Player, and the Americans—Sam Snead, Ben Hogan, Arnold Palmer, Tony Lema and Jack Nicklaus. I imagine that in one sense no British golfer was better pleased with Jacklin's win than Max Faulkner, his predecessor. Faulkner had won in 1951 when the championship was at a low ebb. He won against a moderate field at a time when Americans were showing little interest in the event. This should not detract from his achievement. He did win the championship. But when Faulkner said after this year's Open that he was delighted because he had had quite enough of being tagged the "last Briton to win the Open," everyone knew what he meant.

I don't believe that the British failure over the years has been a question of technique or resolution. There have been many talented British players in that period. And every British player desperately wanted to win the championship and turn back the foreigners. It was not a question of not knowing how to play the game. And it was not wholly the fact that American society—and for that matter Australian and South African—is more aggressive and produces more aggressive athletes than does the more tranquil, ordered, British way of things. But what did bear heavily on the matter was the existence and growth of the American tour. In his presentation speech, after they had thrust check, medal and cup into his willing hands, Tony Jacklin made the point that he was convinced that his experiences on the U.S. tour, playing under constant pressure and against fierce competition, had helped him win. He also counselled young British players to give it a try. It is a fact that with the exception of Thomson, all the other non-American winners—Locke, Player, Bob Charles, Roberto de Vicenzo, Kel Nagle—have had wide experience in that testing, stormy nerve-wrenching U.S. school.

But as I said, Jacklin's victory was of double significance. If the Open had been won by one of Britain's older school—the O'Connor-Alliss-Hunt-Coles group—it would not have had the major impact on British golf that I am sure Jacklin's victory will have. For Tony is 25; handsome, joyful, bubbly, smart, determined 25. He has demonstrated to an entire generation of his British contempories that the Americans are not supermen, if indeed they ever were. I suspect a little of this feeling affected play just two months later in the Ryder Cup matches, where the British, with half their team youngsters, put up a spirited battle and earned a tie. Thus Jacklin at Royal Lytham ushered in what I believe will be an entire new era for British golf.

The championship returned to the Royal Lytham and St. Annes Golf Club after six years. Lytham is at the northern end of a marvellous sweep of coastal golfing country that runs 50 miles south from Blackpool to Liverpool. It takes in the St. Annes Old, and then, across the estuary of the Ribble, the Southport courses. It is comparable in every way to Ayrshire in the West of Scotland, or the Lothians shore, which includes Muirfield, Gullane and North Berwick or the Fife coast itself. The British make a tidy grouping of their links. The small resort and dormitory town of Lytham, favored by the merchants of Manchester and the Lancashire mill towns, is near Blackpool, and Blackpool is something else again. Spreading along a fine sand beach for seven or eight miles, it is both Coney Island and Atlantic City, a raucous, hell-for-leather resort town with a resident population of 150,000 that goes over one million at the height of the holiday season. Blackpool makes no pretence to be anything it isn't, and I'd say it has one thing in common with Athens and the Taj Mahal—every man, for better or worse, should see it before he dies. Educational it is. It has one main hotel, the Imperial, which might have been a swinging convention center 50 years ago, and plenty of others of varying quality. Many of the overseas players stayed at the Imperial. In Lytham and St. Annes, adjoining small town now linked to the south end of Blackpool, are the mausoleum-like Majestic and the more intimate Clifton Arms, both of them, of course, fronting on the Irish Sea.

The golf club is pretty much what I have come to expect in Britain—an old, unpretentious clubhouse (this one wonderfully timbered) which by any reasonable judgement would have to be called uncomfortable, and a quite magnificent natural golf course of firm fairways, endless traps brimming with powdery sand, tenacious rough, humps and hollows, and beautiful, velvety greens. In an experience now reaching over half a dozen or more British Opens, I am annually astonished at the quality of the British greens. With their natural grasses, and plenty of moisture in the air even when it doesn't rain, the British don't know how lucky they are.

Royal Lytham was founded in 1886 and it must have been a piece of ready-made land—members playing over it within a week of forming the club. The clubhouse comprised one room in the St. Annes Hotel, and the official handbook records that, "Among its miscellaneous furniture was a bell which, by arrangement with the railway company, rang to signal the advent of a train. This gave the tired golfer time to finish his glass, collect his hat and coat, say goodbye to his friends and reach the platform." At this time Blackpool was little more than a fishing village, but with the opening up of the entire coastline by a railway company, speculative builders moved in. The club decided that its grounds, mostly loaned by local farmers, were none too secure and within a few years it moved to the present site. Just before the end of the century, the present clubhouse and course were ready. The club offered an annual subscription for £2, caddies cost 6d. for 18 holes, lunch was 2/-d. and a good Havana cigar 4d. Port was 3/- a bottle and those, without a doubt, were the days. There is no record of the course being formally planned, but a succession of architects must have changed this and tidied that over the years.

The club prospered, but not until 1926 was it deemed ready for the first of its five Open Championships. It was a case of instant history, for this was where Bobby Jones and Al Watrous fought it out. Going into the last round, Watrous held a two-stroke lead. After 16, they were even. On 17, Watrous was nicely up the fairway but Jones pulled his shot and landed in a bunker in a maze of ground that is still there in the dogleg at the left of the hole. The ball lay cleanly, but Jones could not see the green, which was a good 170 yards away. He had to walk clear across the fairway to judge the shot. Watrous dumped his second on the front of the green. Then Jones, with a mashie, picked his ball clean as a pin out of the trap, carried the jungle and hit the green inside his opponent. Watrous, unnerved, three-putted, then hit into a bunker on 18. Jones won by two strokes, and said in his laconic fashion afterwards, "Well, I played the shot and it came off." A plaque in the bunker records the feat, reading: "R.T. Jones, the Open Championship, 25th June, 1926". The club, a hickory-shafted mashie, is on display in the Lytham clubhouse. In 1952, the next Lytham Open, Bobby Locke won by a stroke from Peter Thomson. In 1958, Thomson won after a play-off with Dave Thomas. In 1963, Bob Charles won after a play-off with Phil Rodgers. And now for the 1969 Open, most of the world's best golfers were on hand. The field included the defending champion, Gary Player, and the previous half-dozen champions— Nagle, Charles, Thomson, Nicklaus, and de Vicenzo. It was a formidable field.

It faced a formidable golf course. Like so many other British links—St. Andrews, Troon, Prestwick, Carnoustie—Lytham is endowed with a railroad track, but even more so. At holes one through three and seven through nine, the railroad is very much in play, marching tightly along the right side of the fairways and positively inviting a slice. At Lytham, as at Carnoustie, trees play no part in the challenge. True, the eleventh green runs up to a little wood and the twelfth tee plays out of the same wood, but it is nothing to influence the flight of a shot. The course was in prime condition, with the rough perhaps not quite so severe as it had been in 1963. The greens were left with heavy collars of rough, particularly at the back, but when the players let it be known, in that special way they have, that they thought this a little too penal, the R. & A. modified the condition somewhat before the action began. The weather throughout the championship was fairly constant, winds from the sea, seldom very boisterous, occasional rain, occasional sun. The weather was never as critical a factor as it so often has been in a British Open, and in my judgement it did not make starting times as significant as usual.

As always the British, without what might be called permanent facilities, organized the championship beautifully. There were massive grandstands at a dozen points on the course, a computerized scoring system that provided up-to-the-minute information and the usual vast tented plaza of cinemas, trade exhibitions, fashion shows, restaurants and press rooms. The BBC had color cameras on nine holes and carried more than 16 hours of Open play, some live and some recorded. The progress of the all-star cast was followed closely.

The defending champion, Player, had performed badly in the Masters, and his Lytham showing was similarly disappointing over the final 36 holes. He opened with rounds of 70, 70, but followed these with a 75, 78, for a 292. Jack Nicklaus broke his favorite driver for about the fourth time, on a pre-Open exhibition tour in Sweden, and came to Lytham with it patched. He was experimenting with his game, which is dangerous before a Championship. PGA Commissioner Joe Dey, a long-time friend of Jack, was to say later that Jack's golf, "for the past two years has been an enigma". He is right. Nicklaus has been such a good British Open player, however, that one expects him to hold his game together and be a factor at the finish. Lee Trevino, the 1968 U.S. Open Champion or Orville Moody, that tournament's 1969 winner, both lacked the necessary experience—of British conditions, and of British Opens—to threaten. Peter Thomson and Roberto de Vicenzo were old hands, but the time is coming when their legs will not stand the four days of a hard championship. Bert Yancey does not seem to take the British Open seriously enough. I thought Gay Brewer a threat, but I can honestly say that I looked to Bob Charles and Jacklin as the men to beat.

Charles had not enjoyed the best year of his career, but he had won the last Open at Lytham and had been going along nicely in his steadfast way. As one of the great putters, and a seasoned British Open player who handles links courses well, I was sure Charles would figure. He had been in a position to win at Carnoustie and blew his chance in the final round. With another year of seasoning on the U.S. tour, Jacklin was, in my opinion, by far the most threatening of the home players, though people like Brian Huggett and Christy O'Connor were having good seasons. Jacklin's progress graph looked right. When you inspect his career in detail, some striking facts emerge. In 1957, when he was 13, he won the Lincolnshire Boys' Championship. It is not a particularly significant tournament, but Jacklin successfully defended his title in 1958 and 1959. At 17, his last year as an amateur, he won the Lincolnshire Open against the pros. In his first year as a touring professional, he played in the Open and finished 30th—at Royal Lytham. In addition, he won Henry Cotton's "Rookie of the Year" prize, worth $100 and total tournament earnings of $343. Jacklin failed to qualify for the 1964 Open in what was his bleak year. He took a tour to South Africa early in 1965 and came home with $35 to show for a $400 investment, but soon he was finishing well in English tournaments. In 1966, he shared a win with Harold Henning in South Africa and thereafter was regularly in the top ten in Britain. He played for England in the Canada Cup in Tokyo. In 1967, he was 16th in the Masters, 12th in the Canadian Open, 7th in the Carling. So he was moving. He won his first tournament in Britain (the Pringle—at Lytham) then the Dunlop Masters at Sandwich, and he took his share of points at the Ryder Cup matches in Houston. The big breakthrough came in 1968 when he won the Jacksonville Open, the first British victory in America for over 40 years. He earned more than $75,000 that year. In early 1969, he was back on the U.S. tour, finishing 8th at Doral and 12th in the National Airlines Open. But in the spring came a slump. He missed the cut in five out of six tournaments, including the Masters, and then flew to England for a couple of weeks' rest. When he went back to the U.S., he finished fifth in the Western Open and the Kemper, and his game seemed strong again in mid-June as he returned to Lytham. The British bookmakers were giving 6—1 on Casper, Nicklaus and Player; 12—1 on Archer, Charles, Devlin and Trevino; 16—1 on Brewer and Yancey; 18—1 on Moody, and 20—1 on Barber, Jacklin and Thomson.

The R. & A. committed some $140,999 to the championship, for the tournament has become a big show, indeed. (Dundee College of Technology did a research study on the 1968 Open at Carnoustie, and its very conservative estimate was that the total attendance of 51,296 fans spent some $360,000.) The R. & A. had seats for 9,326 fans and 438 VIPs in its grandstands. The first day the caterers ordered 300 pounds of beef, 250 pounds of lamb cutlets, 50 turkeys, 50 hams, 12 fresh salmon, 100 pounds of Cheshire cheese, 60 pounds of other cheese, 2,250 pounds of biscuits, 432 gallons of draught beer and 12,000 bottles of beer. In addition, hot-dogs, soft drinks and ice cream were stocked. In all, you could say they were ready at Lytham.

As tournament time neared Jacklin celebrated his 25th birthday with a strict par 71. Roberto de Vicenzo found his regular caddie had been lured away by Lee Trevino and Roberto hired a local lad, 15-year-old Michael Hayworth, of St. Annes. Michael was thrilled, but unabashed. He had been carrying at Lytham for two years in amateur events, he had the course nicely charted, and believed he knew a thing or two about its secrets. Nicklaus was still searching for the right driving technique. George Archer's stomach was acting up and all he could manage was an hour chipping and putting. He went into the championship with only one practice round behind him. And Jacklin might well have been perturbed, for the R. & A. had declared his wedge was illegal. "I have other wedges with me," Jacklin said. "I'll just have to pick out a good-looking one and hope that it works."

The morning the championship began, in an article he wrote for *The Guardian*, Peter Thomson discussed the Open. He made the comment: "There is a 35-yard square of fairway about 250 yards out from the last tee at Lytham. I've been thinking about that piece of fairway for nearly a year, because on July 12 about 4.30 p.m., I may have to hit it with a shot under awful pressure. If I can't do that simple trick, I can't win the championship. In fact, I won't get near to winning it, because straight, pinpoint driving is the key to victory."

On the first day the man who teed off at 10.30, Bob Charles, left a fearsome stamp on Lytham. He opened with two birdies, and from then on there was no stopping him. He birdied 6, 7 and 9 to go out in 31. Charles went over par for the first time at the 12th and then bogeyed 15, but he birdied 16 and came in with a 66. He needed only 28 putts (one competitor said, "That's par for Charles"), and backed this up with brilliant driving. "That's about as good a round of golf as I've ever played," Charles said. "The two opening birdies set me up; I felt as composed as I could be." The fine opening round, tucked away early in the day, shook some of the field—but not quite all. At the end of the day behind Charles came Hedley Muscroft and Jacklin with 68s, Jean Garaiailde of France, Irishman Hugh Jackson and Miller Barber with 69s, David Love, Guy Wolstenholme, Orville Moody, Bill Casper and Bernard Gallacher with 70s and Devlin, Thomson and O'Connor with 71s. So some impressive names had Charles within reach, with three days still to come. Not many people could see Muscroft, Garaialde, Jackson, or Love as Open winners. In the evening, the most philosophical man around—and he had to be—was Roberto de Vicenzo. He was out in 32, but back in 40 for a 72. Said Roberto, "The first nine I played like Sam Snead, the second nine I played like Roberto." It was a pattern that was to plague him. The first round was ominous for two favored golfers, Gary Player (74) and Jack Nicklaus (75). Two holes undermined

Jack. A cheer had greeted him on 13, when a 30-foot putt put him under par for the first time, but at 14 the wind caught a towering drive and dumped it in the rough. Nicklaus could hardly disguise his fury. He had hit 200 practice balls the previous evening, trying to eliminate just that fault. There, three putts gave him a 6. At 18, it happened again. He was caught up in a rose bush and dropped out, taking the penalty. Then he missed the green. Gary fought sternly to hold together a round compromised early by two bad drives. He said afterward that although the greens were in perfect shape he was having trouble reading them. Meanwhile, Jacklin had driven the ball impressively and putted audaciously for his 68. That night, while Verity Charles prescribed remedies for her husband's sore throat, Bob was saying, "It's a little early to talk about pressure, and winning. But there are a few good players in there who have scored in the mid-seventies. The pressure will be on them more than me. They have to make the cut." Trevino, with a 75, was one—he had made bogeys on the five finishing holes.

After 36 holes Charles still led, but this time precariously by one shot over Christy O'Connor. Charles had a 69 for a 135 and O'Connor an incredible 65 for a 136, incredible because of how it was put together. He was out in 32—not exceptional since most of the holes were downwind. At 10 he holed a trap shot for a birdie. At 11 he saved his par with chip and one putt and at 12 he saved another par, coming out of a deep bunker. He birdied 13 from 12 feet. At 16 he drove into the rough, then pitched over the green into more rough and finally made a 30-foot putt for his par. At 17 he pulled his drive into the left rough. From there he hit it two feet from the hole for a birdie. He used only ten putts on the inward nine.

If Bob Charles was a little more nervous than on opening day—and he showed it here and there in the second round—it was not apparent at the first hole. There he hit a 5-iron four feet from the hole for a birdie. From then on, he played one of his most conservative rounds. Hanging in at the end of the day were Jacklin with a comfortable 70 and Casper with a second 70. When asked how he scored, Casper said, "No more, no less." Bob Charles, always a fine front-runner, said the second night, "It's nice to be in front. But the first three rounds the players are just jockeying for position, like in a horse race. When you get right down to it, the last six holes are the ones that count in an Open. I just hope I'm still around when they come round." Up to his old tricks was Roberto de Vicenzo, out in 32, back, this time, in 41. Player (68) and Nicklaus (70) found the low rounds they needed, but closer to Charles, and still in the championship, were Thomson and Moody, six shots back.

Day three is often a day of reckoning in championships, a day when some people drop out of the front-line while others prepare themselves for the final stampede. The wind was now stronger and more troublesome. Roberto de Vicenzo finally tamed the back nine with a masterful round of 66, but it seemed for a while as though the leaders were picking their way through a minefield. Gary Player was mortally wounded at the eighth. He had his round in good control and still had a chance to retain his title when he hit a perfectly safe tee shot. The ball pitched off a fairway divot mark into what was almost an unplayable lie in the left-hand bunker. His eight-iron tee shot at the short ninth, 164 yards, hit on the putting surface but then took a crazy bounce and landed out of bounds. A sloppy, despairing tee shot on 10 put Gary out of the championship. He had posted three successive double bogeys. There is a school of thought that says Lytham is a scrambler's course, and that the winners there—Locke, Thomson, Charles, and for that matter Jacklin—are scramblers. Certainly Lytham's small greens are hard to hit and hard to stay on. In three championships there, Gary has never scored really well. In 1952 he was out of the top twenty. In 1958 he was seventh, five shots behind, and in 1963 seventh, ten shots behind. Casper's game blew up, too, that third day. He made 5 on 15, 5 at 17, then drove into a bunker at 18 and took 6. With 75, he lost his chance. Thomson was stabbed in the eye by a sharp blade of grass when identifying a ball, but held his game together, letting his caddie Jackie Leigh read the greens en route to a 70. O'Connor ran out of heroic recoveries and shot a 74. But Bob Charles did worse. He missed five of the final six fairways and posted a 75. Jacklin, tip-toed through the minefield—and survived. On the 15th tee, Jacklin could look back on a round of confident, controlled golf; he was playing two under par. His drive to 15, a resolute shot, faded slightly and caught an uphill lie in the rough. Still full of spirit, he took a 3-wood to try to get on in two, but hooked the ball and missed the green. His recovery from the rough caught a bunker. But he slashed out of there and made the putt. At 16 he pitched out of the rough to within two feet of the pin for a priceless birdie. At 17 he drove in the rough once again and again hit a greenside bunker, so he recovered and made the putt. At 18 he put his 7-iron approach in a trap on the right. Again he managed to get down in two. A scrambler, did you say? Hmmm. Jacklin's 70 gave him a two-shot lead going into the last day of the Open. It was the kind of Friday evening that many British golfers, young and not so young, have dreamed of. Clearly, the next day would be the most significant in the young life of Tony Jacklin. And it would not be without hazards. Hard on his heels were Charles and O'Connor at 210, Charles the previous Lytham winner and O'Connor vastly experienced in Open, Ryder Cup, Canada Cup and tournament play. At 211 were Roberto de Vicenzo, an Open Champion in almost every country of the world, and Peter Thomson, with a Lytham win among his five British Open titles. And at 213 were Nicklaus and Brian Huggett. Might not Nicklaus, in with a third-round 68, be the most threatening of all?

The Jacklins were sharing a house near the course with Bert Yancey. After supper, Tony watched the television re-run of the day's action, which only made him more nervous. He was sure he would not sleep that night, and was playing Lytham over and over in his mind. So he took a sleeping pill and settled down to watch a late movie. Not many minutes later, Yancey saw Jacklin's eyes close and a cigarette fall from his fingers. He carried Tony upstairs, undressed him and put him to bed. Tony got eight solid hours of sleep. He woke to eat a hearty breakfast of steak and eggs and got to the course none too early for his 1:25 starting time. On the practice tee Jacklin hit nothing but 7-iron shots, for he was bent on establishing and sustaining a rhythm. Much of the hour was spent in fending off well-wishers and potential interviewers, and when the tournament movie crew did get to him on the practice putting green around 1 p.m., he was jumpy as a lynx. He confessed in front of the cameras that he had been "nervous all week. Now I'm just bloody terrified," he said. "But I've decided to try to play my own game, play each shot as it comes, ignore what other people are doing and try to keep my rhythm going. If somebody else is better than me, and beats me, it'll be just too bad." Jacklin wore lavender slacks and sweater, and when Bob Charles appeared in a similar lavender sweater, albeit with black slacks, Tony joshed, "Why didn't you call me and tell me what you were going to wear? " Charles respected Jacklin as an opponent. "Tony has plenty of confidence in his ability, and he has plenty of it," Charles said before the round. "He has been getting it up and down around the greens, and that's the kind of golf that takes you through trouble to good scores, that's the stuff that wins the money. And victory here will guarantee Tony's future as a golf pro."

Until late afternoon it was the greyest day of the week, and a north-westerly wind blew. O'Connor three-putted twice on the first nine and by the 10th hole no longer looked like a winner. De Vicenzo was challenging, going out in 33. But Roberto lost a shot when he was bunkered at 12, and could do no better than fives into the wind at 15 and 17. Nicklaus, like Thomson, played with dogged smoothness, but again like Thomson, he saw three birdie putts hang on the lip of the cup. The breakthrough that each man needed, never came. So the tournament turned into a match-play contest between Charles and Jacklin, with Jacklin leaving the very first green with a handsome three-stroke cushion when Charles landed short, chipped short, putted short and bogeyed. At the 3rd, Jacklin birdied from six feet and at the 4th, from 40 feet. Five strokes up, fourteen to play. He hit over the green at the 5th to lose a stroke and hooked into bushes at the 6th to drop another. But he recovered magnificently with a birdie at the seventh, the monster 553-yard par 5. Tony's drive was to the right in rough and his second, a three-wood, went into a bunker to the left of the green. Charles, who had placed his drive in the fairway, pulled his long-iron second into a fierce tangle of rough near the green and had to pitch 40 yards over broken mounds and a sandtrap. Using a sand wedge, he hit a superb shot four feet from the hole. Jacklin with his third was seven feet away. Tony ran the birdie putt in—and Bob followed him. Jacklin ended up out in 33. Charles had 35, to give Tony a four-stroke lead.

Charles birdied 10 from six feet. At the par-three 12th, Jacklin salvaged a par after being bunkered, but at 13 he lost another stroke when a wedge approach went over the green. He chipped back and missed from about 14 feet. His lead was reduced to two strokes, but at 14 he demonstrated his resiliency, playing the hole perfectly. His long drive was in the center of the fairway, and his five-iron second was on the stick all the way, bouncing 15 feet past it. This same hole had bothered Charles right through the championship, and the final day was no exception. Bob bunkered his approach and this once he didn't wedge close enough. Jacklin's birdie try missed narrowly, and when Charles bogeyed Tony had a three-shot margin with four holes to play. At 15 Tony drove into the left rough and bogeyed. Bob pushed his second into wicked rough to the right of the green and also bogeyed. Jacklin almost birdied 16 from eight feet, Charles almost from 10 feet. Jacklin was now three ahead with two holes to play. He reached the 17th in two, but was 65 feet from the pin and took three-putts. Bob parred that hole. Two up, one hole to play. In this situation pessimists are liable to say, "Well, of course, one could birdie and the other could bogey, and there's the tie." The crowd of more than 10,000 was roaring, confident that at last it had a British champion. But yet to come was the crucial drive that Thomson had written about, that "35-yard square patch of fairway about 250 yards out . . . ."

I suppose every drive on every 72nd hole of every championship course must be terrifying, and many may appear tougher than the one at Lytham. The hole is 389 yards, with a bunker beginning on the left about 170 yards and meandering across the fairway to the right ending about 220 yards from the tee. Farther on, some 250 yards up the right side the scrubby rough is riddled with flat bunkers. And to the left is a cluster of deep, mounded bunkers from which no golfer can reach the green. Charles drove into the rough on the right, but Jacklin, without the slightest flutter or quickening of rhythm, nailed one right down the center of the fairway. As soon as the ball pitched in the fairway, the crowds broke. An armoured regiment could not have stopped them. The players were engulfed by the mob. When Jacklin at last emerged he appeared without a shoe. Even more surprisingly, he went back and found it. Bob Charles hit a magnificent recovery shot, a seven iron 18 feet to the right of the cup. Now Jacklin took out his seven iron and hit a perfect, crisp shot right at the heart of the green. It also was pin high and to the right, but only twelve feet from the hole. When it missed, Jacklin was a sure winner. Tony stepped up and stroked his ball right to the hole. It hung on the edge and stayed out, and Jacklin settled for a par, a 72, a 280 and the title. Grinning broadly, he fished the ball out of the hole and threw it to the crowd. His wife Vivienne and his mother embraced in tears, and there was singing and dancing in the grandstands as the great crowd rejoiced in the triumph of the boy from Scunthorpe. Jacklin had held off the challenge of half a dozen of the toughest competitors in international golf and had won for Britain.

At the presentation ceremony, interrupted by a determined if ill-rehearsed version of "He's a jolly good fellow" and an unexpected training jump by Army parachutists from a transport plane almost overhead, Tony Jacklin took the trophy from Lord Derby, captain of the Royal Lytham club and also President of Britain's PGA. "It was always an ambition of mine to win the British Open," he said, "but I never thought it would come so soon." And there it was. Once again a truly British Open after all these years.

6

The World Match Play

The waving of a magic wand

E ach year since its inception in 1964, the World Match Play Championship has produced some rare thrills and superb golf, and 1969 was no exception to the pattern. It was a year in which, on form, the field looked to be the weakest since the event began; but when you stand near the first tee at Wentworth on an early October morning and hear the starter calling out the qualifications of the players, it would be very difficult to view the golf ahead without great anticipation. The very nature of the event, match play, means that the tension starts at once, that for every golfer the battle is on with the first shot, and that the enemy is right there for him to stare at, stroke after stroke and hour after hour.

The World Match Play begins six months before the event for those of us closely involved in it. Since the defending champion is automatically invited, important matters begin at the Masters, for the Augusta winner gets the first invitation of the year. George Archer, the 1969 Masters winner, was invited almost before he cleared the last green at Augusta, and he quickly accepted. But an unfortunate thing happened with Archer. He has had dreadful luck with his British appearances. When he played the Alcan at Birkdale in 1968, he had to pull out because of illness. He went to Lytham for the 1969 British Open, and quit again because of illness. And toward the end of the summer he wrote to Piccadilly officials and withdrew from the World Match Play because he did not feel he could face the prospect of the 36-hole matches. Archer had been through a trying summer, was not at all well and probably was quite drained of competitive spirit. The case of Orville Moody, the U.S. Open Champion, was somewhat different. He had been invited through his manager, Bucky Woy, and at Lytham during the British Open, Mr. Woy told Philip Wilson, the World Match Play tournament chairman, that the invitation was accepted and Moody would play. Written confirmation of this never came. Instead, a few weeks later Wilson received a letter withdrawing Moody because of a "previous commitment". This seemed strange, and was not appreciated by the British, even though Moody had every right to withdraw. The real point is one I have made before about American pros—they are sometimes too casual about making and breaking agreements overseas. They do not realize that their actions can offend many people; that they are not helping the good name of American golf, or, for that matter, America.

This was the first time in six years that the World Match Play had lacked the U.S. champion and only the second time in six years it had missed the Masters champion. The next man invited was Tony Jacklin, the British Open champion, and he brought some color back to Piccadilly cheeks by saying yes quite simply and without reservation. The field eventually filled out as follows: Gary Player, defending champion; Tony Jacklin; Raymond Floyd, U.S. PGA champion; Tommy Aaron, Canadian Open champion; Maurice Bembridge, British Match Play champion; Jean Garaialde, French German and Spanish Open Champion, plus two men who could not boast of current major championships. And they became the most critical figures of the tournament. One was Bob Charles, second in the British Opens of 1968 and 1969, runner up in the 1968 World Match Play and a former winner of the British, Canadian and New Zealand Opens. The other was Gene Littler, who had a brilliant winter and spring in the U.S. and who has been recognized in America for years as a golfer in the vanishing classic mould.

I suppose the most controversial figure in the field, or more accurately the most controversial selection, was that of Jean Garaialde, the Frenchman. The general philosophy of the World Match Play is that players will be invited on the basis of current championship successes, but overall career achievement is a factor. It could be argued that Garaialde was not up to that requirement. But his achievements in 1969 were creditable. He finished sixth in the Alcan, highest of all non-U.S. players. His European wins were made on good golf courses, but against weak fields. To a degree his selection was a gesture to the growth of European golf, and I am not sure the World Match Play should not have such a figure in its field now and then. The same reasoning applies, to a degree, to Littler; not a current international champion, but a golfer of great merit that English galleries surely would enjoy.

Player, the defending champion, was the first to arrive in London. He had been resting on his farm in South Africa and reached England not having hit a shot in "I-don't-know-how-many-days." Gary has a sharp taste for the dramatic, and Wentworth '69 did nothing to diminish that reputation. On Monday of tournament week, he and Tony Jacklin played a private exhibition at Sunningdale, a couple of miles along the road from Wentworth. He played a Sunningdale practice round with me on the day before and had an effortless 67. He was having no trouble at all with a hook. On Monday he played the exhibition with Jacklin, winning two up with a 68 against Tony's 69, and again hit nothing remotely like a hook. But by Wednesday, when he played a final practice round at Wentworth with Catherine Lacoste, the French girl amateur who may well be the best woman player in the world, Gary was duck-hooking all over the countryside. Miss Lacoste, by the way, playing from the back tees with the small ball, shot Wentworth in 75. Par is 74.

On these international occasions, the British golf press is usually on hand during practice days looking for snippets on which to build fairly substantial tournament preview stories. Player's first contribution to them was the "lost golf bag." When Gary arrived, his London-based bag, a John Letters bag, was not to be found. But when he got to Sunningdale, there was the bag, big as could be, in the bag-rack. When Gary tried to claim it, he was informed that a Sunningdale member had won it in a raffle, and the member wasn't likely to give it back, not for $10,000. So Gary made the papers early. After the Lacoste round, he told the press, "I've never hit the ball so badly in my life. I tried ten different golf swings today." They were a little inclined to believe him when he went straight to the practice area and stayed there until dark. Then Gary came up with the story that he thought he might have cured his problems when a police inspector came by and suggested he turn his left elbow just a fraction. All I can say, reading the papers the next day, is that Gary Player is never going to need a publicity man. In truth, I think Gary was a little concerned about his opening match with Garaialde. The public expected him to thrash Garaialde. Anyone knowing anything about golf can sense that Gary was in an uneasy situation. I suspect all of the talk and complaints about his game were designed by Gary to get himself keyed up.

There has frequently been criticism in Britain about World Match Play draws and the fact that the field is seeded. I have no idea why this protest arises. Wimbledon is seeded quite openly, for example, and every match play event in golf that I have ever heard of is seeded. But this year, instead of seeding four players, which was our

habit in the past (I use "our" because I am the founder and one of
the officials of the World Match Play, something you should know so
that you can look carefully for signs of patronly prejudice in my
account of the event, and perhaps allow me a fond indulgence or
two—I confess it, I am very pleased the tournament has done so well)
it was decided to seed two. These were the defending champion and
the British Open champion—Player and Jacklin. For the rest, an open
draw was arranged at the British PGA's London offices in the
presence of Henry Cotton, Geoffrey Cotton, the chairman of the
PGA's executive Committee, and John Bywaters, PGA secretary. The
draw could not have come out better balanced. It was Player v.
Garaialde, Littler v. Floyd, Bembridge v. Charles and Jacklin v.
Aaron. And in the cards, one would guess, a Player-Jacklin final.
Some guess. Some cards.

The condition of the course was remarkable. It was very dry,
which for Wentworth at this time of year was almost unprecedented.
Wentworth in autumn can be soggy as a bog, and usually is. One year
it was so wet and its 6,997 yards played so long that Bob Charles hit
woods on no fewer than nine second shots in a round. But this year
every hole, except possibly the 555-yard 17th, was within easy range.
This was a consequence of England's long, dry summer, and it
introduced an unexpected peril for the golfers. Said Charles on the
eve of the tournament: "Normally at this time of year at Wentworth
you can be a little off line, either right or left, but as long as you land
on the fairway, you'll stay on it. Not this week. We'll have to drive
the ball dead straight. A little right or left here and the ball kicks off
the fairway."

In practice the greens were thick and a shade bumpy, having been
left uncut until the last possible moment. When they were cut, they
came up as usual at Wentworth, velvety and true. No complaints
there. A very strict par in the windless conditions would have been
70. In fact, during the championship I don't believe anyone reached
the 17th in two, and 18, shaded all along its weather side, was heavy
and demanded two strong shots to reach. No, 70 was not
unreasonable as a true par, although I will refer to the card par
throughout this chapter.

Opening day dawned incredibly beautiful. It was clear, the
temperature headed for the high seventies and it felt like
mid-summer instead of London in October. Gary, first off, stepped
up and rode into a long, impressive drive that bisected the fairway.
All that hook business was consigned to history. He did not play

impressively, with a morning round of 70, but it was enough. Garaialde "held" him, if you could call it that, to the turn, where he was only one down, but Gary won three of the next four holes, and at 18 was five up. Two birdies in the opening four afternoon holes put the thing beyond much consideration, and Gary went on to finish it at the 27th for a 10 and 9 win, the largest margin in the World Match Play so far. But the golf in the other matches more than compensated for this rout. The best was in the struggle between Littler and Floyd. Littler started his first World Match Play with eagle, birdie. It was a fearsome portent of things to come. He played magnificently, and his charm and grace captivated the crowds. Here is one quiet American that the British will welcome back anytime. Littler was out in 33, but only one up to Floyd's 34. Littler then got his putter working even more sharply, holing from 35 feet for an eagle at 12 and from 20 feet on 13. He seemed set for a casual, indolent 65 when he missed from three feet on 17 and blocked his drive into the trees on 18. But it was still a 67 against Floyd's 70, and a three-up margin. Length was no problem to Floyd at Wentworth, but he seemed unable to judge the distances into the greens. After lunch Floyd got two back quickly at 20, where Littler missed the green, and at 21, where he three-putted. But Floyd had to concede 22 after a wild drive into the woods. Littler birdied 24 from three feet, but Floyd looked to have a chance when Littler hooked his tee shot into the forest at the 25th. It was Ray's last chance. Littler chopped the ball out to the front of the two-tier green, and then chipped it up the slope, up the ridge, over the flat, into the hole. Birdie. He also birdied 8, 11 and 12, and it was over. Littler said he had not played better since the early part of the year. He hardly could have. Floyd, in turn, pleased the British press by being quiet, relaxed, modest and informal. He said he enjoyed London—and he seemed to mean it—and he got lots of laughs when he noted, "how kind these Senior Service people have been to me." It was hastily pointed out that the promoters were Piccadilly, not Senior Service, and that the tobacco business in which both companies are engaged is just as ferociously competitive as, say, Ford and General Motors. He said that he did not mind losing to Littler's golf—how could anyone? And he told the story of the American who couldn't stand the British until it occurred to him that half of them were female. All told, Floyd made no secret of the fact that he enjoys the high life, rather like that historic figure of golf who died earlier this very same week, Walter Hagen. And true to his praise of

London. Floyd stayed the whole week, even though his golf was over
So there was now a Player-Littler semi-final at the top of the draw.

And there were fireworks at the bottom. The scoring of Bob Charles
matched that of Littler, in fact went Littler two better on the
morning round. Frankly, Charles destroyed Maurice Bembridge. Bob
opened with a winning eagle, took the third when Bembridge
three-putted and the seventh, where Bembridge hit a wild tee shot.
Charles was out in 33 and two up. But he started back, 2, 4, 4, 3, 2,
4, to go seven up and be nine under for the round. Bembridge had
putted just about as atrociously as Charles had putted brilliantly, but
he is a fighter. He got a couple of holes back on the front nine in the
afternoon to start what looked like a minor rally, but Charles birdied
the short 20th and no man can give Bob Charles an eight-up start
with only 16 holes to go. Charles closed it out, coasting, 6 and 5, and
left Bembridge reflecting, "I can drive it and play it from tee to green
with the best of them. I proved that to myself at the Alcan in
Portland, and to some extent here. But the thing this game is all
about is getting it in the hole. I'm going to spend the next six months
of my life practicing just that, chipping and putting." With that
philosophy branded on his forehead, Bembridge set off to try the
Australian tour.

Finally, there was Jacklin v. Aaron. The American took the second
and third with pars, a suggestion that all was not well with Jacklin,
but Tony birdied the seventh and won 13 when Aaron took three
from the edge of the green. Everything else was halved save 17,
where Jacklin pulled two drives out of bounds on the high left side.
Jacklin took the lead at the 20th, but then the match turned against
him. Aaron won the next three holes, with Jacklin scrambling hard.
Each birdied eight, and then Aaron went off on a streak of golfing
madness. He hit a five-iron second to the 9th (460 yards) and birdied
from eight feet, and when he closed out the match with a birdie at
14 he had played seven consecutive holes in 21. Jacklin could hardly
hope to survive against that kind of scoring. Aaron's tall, upright easy
swing masked a good deal of relentlessness in his afternoon play, but
the fact was that Jacklin never seemed to be charged up for the
event. It had been an eventful season for him and at Wentworth it
looked as though it had been one week too long. "Some of the things
I did were unbelievable," said Jacklin. "I felt like apologizing to
Tommy for them. I was playing badly, but scrambling well. The first
green I hit in regulation was the seventh." The 26th hole, where
Jacklin sank a 20-foot birdie putt only to see Aaron hole right on top

of him for a half, was the turning point. Jacklin said, "No matter what I had done after that, I couldn't have achieved anything. You can only half against birdies, and I needed wins, not halves." He went down 6 and 4, and the bottom semi-final was Charles-Aaron. Never before had the first-day matches at Wentworth been disposed of in such summary fashion. The Jacklin margin was the closest of the four.

For all that, it had been a fascinating opening day, made all the more enjoyable by good crowd behaviour and crowd control. Wentworth is a difficult course to marshall. Some of the fairways, particularly on the back nine, are very tight, and the sponsors had always taken the view that they should defer to the golfers by giving them all possible playing area. Arnold Palmer for five straight years was a vociferous critic of this, saying that the ropes should· be brought in to give the crowd more room. "Narrow the fairways if you have to," he said. "The players won't mind." For the first time, the Piccadilly people took his advice and it was ironic that Arnold was not there to see the effect. The course was roped very well. In addition, for the first time in British golf history, a daily ceiling was placed on attendance and ticket sales were made only in advance. There were no sales at the gate. This was deemed necessary because of surprisingly large crowds in the past. (The Masters has done the same in the U.S. for two or three years, with excellent results.) As a consequence, the crowds could move and watch in perfect comfort, which is something of a triumph in a country where golf fans are apt to believe it is their right to get within six feet of their man when he is making a shot.

On the second day the weather took an unusual turn. There was a heavy morning ground fog and no play was possible until noon. In 1968 the entire tournament had been endangered by torrential rains that washed out one complete day. Now it looked as though the event would be compromised again, and through the long morning, with the mist holding down, there was an endless buzz of possibilities—whether there could be only one round that day, whether play should simply continue until dark, with the balance of the semi-finals finished off next day and the finals pushed forward until Sunday, etc. But thanks to the patience and goodwill of the players, and the public for that matter, things worked out. The players ate before they teed off, agreed to take only a quick bite and a 15 minute break between holes 18 and 19, and both matches were completed that day, just before last light. It was nip and tuck, and it

It is difficult to get across the real quality of play that day. Statistics go part of the way, but only part. The truth is that Wentworth was mauled as it seldom has been before, which is all the more remarkable when the human aspect of match play as against stroke is considered, the contrast and clash of personalities, the tensions that inevitably arise between men all highly equipped technically, so that what holds or tips the balance is the inner quality of moral courage. In the morning round, Gene Littler shot 65, Bob Charles 66, Tommy Aaron 67 and Gary Player 68. Perhaps because of the delay, Player and Littler made a pedestrian start with fives and Littler bogeyed the second. But from the fifth hole to the 11th inclusive, Littler had seven consecutive threes. Only two of these holes were par threes, so he had five birdies in the sequence and was three up. Player, determined as ever, retaliated with an eagle at 12 and a birdie at 14. Littler birdied 16, and they both birdied 17 and 18. Littler two up. But the other match looked even better. Charles birdied the first hole, and obviously still felt marvellously ill. Aaron birdied the first also. Charles birdied the second and the fourth and fifth and the seventh to go out in 31. But he was only two up, because Aaron had a 33. They then halved every other hole in three under par until the 18th, where Charles made a par which, almost needless to say, cost him the hole. Charles shot 66 to Aaron's 67 and was one up.

compressed into six hours some worthwhile golf. Much of it came from Bob Charles, who arrived at the course complaining of headaches and stomach pains that had allowed him no sleep. He was not able to eat breakfast, and for the rest of the tournament lived on soup and crackers. It was a winning diet, and Bob sustained the old adage that sick golfers are the ones to fear.

In the afternoon, or perhaps I should say "early evening," round, Player gave Littler a quick break by three-putting from the edge of the first green, missing from seven feet on the second and missing the fifth green. So Littler was four up, but Player is so relentless at match play that one kept expecting something special from him. It never came. The seventh hole seemed to settle the pattern. There Player pitched up very close to the hole for his birdie, but Littler, well outside him, made a birdie putt for a half. At the ninth and again the 11th, Player putts snuggled close but did not fall, and when you have competitors of this class, you can't play catch-up golf without dropping your putts. From the sixth hole through to the end—by 4 and 3 on the 15th—they halved every hole, being three-under par for the sequence.

In the other semi-final, Charles went Littler one or two better. Aaron was ravaged by the golf Charles threw at him. Once again Charles played the front nine in 31. He managed the 11 holes of afternoon play in four over threes, which is six under par, and that gave him a crushing 9 and 7 to win. Charles, for his 29 holes, averaged 3.55 strokes per hole. Littler, for 33 holes, averaged 3.66 strokes per hole. Small wonder that Pat Ward-Thomas, one of the best of golf writers, waxed lyrical about the winners in *The Guardian* next morning. He wrote, of each:

Littler: "It is splendid that after all these years the almost matchless beauty of his swing and the quiet perfection of his play should be exposed to thousands of British watchers. A more purely orthodox effortless style could not be imagined. I wish that every watcher could study Littler's marvelously relaxed approach to every shot, the gentle half-swings, the stance taken so naturally that he might have been born playing golf. And above all the pace of the takeaway, the completely unhurried start to the downswing and the constancy of arc. Watching him can be almost hypnotic. Beauty is an ephemeral quality; rarely in any golfer has it been more constantly expressed. His match with Player made a rare contrast in method, for while Player's magnificent swing—it is no less—suggests tension and effort, Littler's was the antithesis."

Charles: "Often before, one has written of Charles' unwavering rhythm, implacable concentration and indifference to any kind of disturbance. He ghosts along darkly, impressive, seemingly but not actually taciturn, and to play against him in this mood must seem like an exercise in futile endeavor. Poor Aaron had little chance, but he made an admirable contribution to the occasion with the beauty of his graceful swing and the gentleness of his manner."

So now it was down to Littler vs. Charles. But before they teed off, there was yet again some typical World Match Play excitement intervening. Bob Charles had had no better luck with breakfast than with dinner the night before, and again he was doped up on aspirin and stomach powders. Gene Littler, on his return from the course after his stunning performance against Player, found the sad news that his wife Shirley's mother had died at home in California. So the Littler plans had to be changed. Shirley had to get the first flight out next morning, and the Littlers, with little sleep, passed a somber night. Characteristically, Littler saw no reason to mention this to

Charles, and it was not until the press interview after the final match that Charles heard of it.

Play began, and Littler lost the third hole when he drove into the rough, was short of the green and three-putted. Charles then birdied five and eight to be three up at the turn. Shirley Littler had walked the opening holes, but at the ·fourth, after a rather tearful parting, she hurried off to the airport. Littler, no doubt perturbed in the early going, recovered on the inward half and started a stream of beautiful iron shots at the flags that was to last the rest of the day. Four birdies gave him an inward 34 and brought the match up all square at the lunch break.

Immediately after lunch Charles provided a surprise. It is hard to believe, but he three-putted a Wentworth green. He birdied the 5th to get even again, but then three-putted once more, this time from the lower level of a double-tiered green. That, however, was his last mistake on a green. At the eighth he hit a thin 2-iron into the fairway and an indifferent 4-iron that skittered past the right hand trap and barely made the green. He was 35 feet from the hole with a five-foot break over a ridge and he sank it. At the next hole he made a 30-footer. And at the next he dropped it in the cup from 45 feet. With that one Charles, who I believe has the least emotional temperament in golf, had to raise his head to the sky. Now he was two up. At 13 his driving, the least certain part of his game, let him down and he lost the hole.

All day long Littler had been pumping his approaches into the heart of the greens, yet not quite making his putter work. But at 16, or 34, he at last got a birdie—it was from only six feet—and brought the match back to all square. Littler missed a golden chance on 35, where he hit two fine shots to be just short of the green but needed three more to get down and settle for a half. The 36th hole was one Wentworth galleries won't soon forget. Littler hit two immaculate wood shots to the fringe of the green, but Charles hooked his second into the trees. It came bounding down, about 120 yards from the green. Luckily for Charles, he had a shot, and he pitched out of the woods to exactly 27 feet from the cup. Littler, meantime, ran his approach putt stone dead. So Charles, from 27 feet to save the match—saved the match. He rolled the ball into the hole as though the putt was a two-footer on a practice green. Littler shook his head in amazement, and the match went into extra holes.

On the 37th both players drove into the fairway. From there Charles hit a four iron that ended up 30 inches from the cup. Littler left himself a long putt, missed it, and the new World Match Play champion was Bob Charles. It had been a gutsy performance by Charles, bringing him a remarkable World Match Play record in which in six matches in two years he has beaten Bill Casper and Arnold Palmer, lost to Gary Player by one hole, and beaten Maurice Bembridge, Tommy Aaron and Gene Littler.

There were plenty of rational critics on hand to say that the better man lost, that for at least 27 of the 37 holes, discounting the opening nine, Littler had struck the ball immaculately from tee to green. And he had. But as far as I am concerned, the best man won. Littler said it himself afterwards: "I have to congratulate Bob on his win. He holed more yardage of putts today then anyone else has done in the history of golf. He must be the best putter in the world, including Casper or anyone you care to mention. On the 36th green, I just didn't believe he could go on doing it—but he did." Littler was immediately whisked off by helicopter to make an evening flight from London and therefore missed the trophy presentation, at which Bob, in his dry way, said: "I suppose I have some reputation as a putter, and I think I probably maintained it today."

For the closing 28 holes of the match, Littler was ten under par, Charles eight under par. I have to call this the best of the World Match Play finals. Palmer's finals, against Neil Coles in 1964, the first year of the event (2 and 1) was like his second win, against Peter Thomson in 1967 (2 up). Each was stiff with Palmer dramatics and cliff-hanging, sparkling cut and thrust. Player against Nicklaus in 1966 (6 and 4) produced good shotmaking and scoring. Player against Thomson in 1965 (3 and 2) was dogged and highly professional, and Player against Bob Charles in 1968 (one up) was dour and desperately close. But for quality of play, for quality of scoring, for the fact that almost nothing separated the men in personality and attitude, and for a finish that, for the first time, went past 36 holes, I rank Littler-Charles as the finest final. For two of the quietest men of golf, it was a tigerish climax to a magnificent week, and the pity is that millions of Britons did not see more of it, but fog on Friday killed some of the television coverage and an unfortunate strike blacked out almost all of Saturday's TV. Still, the thousands who thronged Wentworth in sunny autumn weather enjoyed first-class entertainment, and I am old-fashioned enough to think that is what golf tournaments are all about.

7

The British Tour

Youth, thrills and a cup that runneth over

I t has been a long time since one could look back on a British, European tour season with true excitement, but the British Golf fan must feel he had more than his fair share of stimulation this year. There was, after all, not only the small matter of wonderous Tony Jacklin, there was real progress in other directions. The long awaited surge from young golfers may have really begun at last, what with Bernard Gallacher playing so well and attracting attention in his outspoken fashion—perhaps he is more of a type that appeals to Americans than British, but if, as we Colonials like to say it, he puts his golf game where his mouth is, he is going to be quite a celebrity—and Maurice Bembridge winning the PGA Match Play, and John Garner showing well there, too. Also pleasing was the performance of Jean Garaialde on the rising European tour. Nor will one soon forget the Ryder Cup. and there was the Arnold Palmer-Esso affair, which was worth some conversation. In all, I would say it was a vintage year for British golf. One can only hope it will serve as a stepping stone to still more exciting times.

We might begin off the course, with the Arnold Palmer-Esso matter. It offers a perfect illustration of the differences between my country and Britain—different thought processes, different business practices, different logic. And it will let you see some backstage golf business. The issue involved a slightly different marketing process for golf balls than the British were accustomed to. For years Arnold Palmer has had a U.K. contract with Dunlop. In 1967, we tried to get Dunlop to sell an Arnold Palmer autographed ball, or alternatively, to pay him a royalty since he was promoting the sale of their existing ball, the "Dunlop 65". Arnold's current Dunlop contract was nearing termination. Dunlop said no, it did not want to start selling autographed balls, not a Palmer ball or anybody else's. Now you have to realize that the golf ball is the major profit item in golf equipment, perhaps in all sporting goods. We were talking to Dunlop about a matter of only a few thousand pounds, just as we had done with Slazengers a few years earlier when they renewed a Jack Nicklaus contract but would no longer pay him a royalty on their ball, which they had done in a previous contract. This forced us to terminate the golf ball arrangement as a matter of principle, resulting in a ball contract between Jack and Uniroyal. Dunlop dominates the British ball market. They virtually control it, make a considerable profit from this product and there is a feeling in Britain that a strong case might be made for a price reduction. During this same period, I had been keeping my options open by holding meetings with Esso and Uniroyal. The Dunlop people were saying in effect: 'Where can you go. You can't go to Slazengers because we own them. You can't go to Penfold. Uniroyal already has Jack Nicklaus. Why should we do anything for you when you are stymied." We said, more or less, that we would terminate the Dunlop-Palmer golf ball arrangement and seek specialized outlets for sales.

The plan I had in mind was very simple. Esso would sell Arnold Palmer golf balls through its 8,000 filling stations in Britain, with Uniroyal making the ball. There would be no compulsion to buy petrol, and the ball would sell for 5/- as against 5/9d or 5/10d in a pro shop. It should be noted that the vast majority of golf ball sales in the U.K. are through pro shops. Esso and Uniroyal offered to make the ball available to pro shops giving the pro exactly the same mark-up he would get on all other top quality balls. In addition, they offered free promotional and display material on the ball and promised to run a series of television commercials that would feature "available through better pro shops" and the like, at no cost to the pro. But the news of the Palmer-Esso venture provoked a remarkably adverse reaction in the press.

The British PGA responded to the proposal by saying that it saw this as an attempt by the makers of the ball to further their interest in a market that is already well supplied by established makers who have greatly helped British professional golf. The PGA said it did not wish to be associated with any move that might damage the interests of the established manufacturers. All of this was pretty startling. The PGA was virtually saying that nobody should make golf balls but Dunlop, Slazengers and Penfold. It was saying to Uniroyal that it should not further its interest in this market, as if the normal role of a business was anything other than expanding its interests. Not only that, the PGA was saying that it did not want to "damage" Dunlop's interests. At the very least, the PGA was exceeding its brief. The irony of all this was that the pros were ordering the ball quickly and with pleasure. They were ready to sell it, since they were assured of the normal mark-up. Not only that, Spalding promptly cut the price of one ball to meet the challenge. In all, it seemed quite logical that if the consumer was getting the same quality article for a lower price, everyone should have been happy. Perhaps the seller was losing a thick slice of a big profit, but the total volume of golf ball sales might well have increased and covered that, and we were convinced that the entire golf equipment market would have benefitted. In America, where 80 per cent of golf equipment is sold outside professional's shops, Gary Player golf balls have been sold through Kruger supermarket stores by the hundreds of thousands. Millions of Jack Nicklaus balls have been sold through Firestone tire and rubber stores, and Arnold Palmer balls have been sold through Lincoln-Mercury dealers. Ours was a business procedure that I believe should be encouraged, but Arnold certainly had no idea that it would raise such a fuss in Britain. He has always been a pro's man, and he was shocked by the nature and extent of the publicity. It made for a dramatic overture to the year.

When the season—the golf playing season that is—did get started, Guy Wolstenholme and Peter Thomson, both fairly early arrivals, were soon hard at work telling the British pros how to put their affairs in order. Their thoughts in the main were aimed at creating a world circuit that could stand on its own, separate and parallel to the U.S. tour. Their more specific thoughts were to have a ten-week British season and a ten-week continental season ‹centred around the British Open. With Australia and the Far East growing more healthy and increasing their prize money steadily, with South Africa on the mend and with romours of improvement in New Zealand, their notions were worth discussing. They also wanted all British events to have a Sunday finish, which would have solved the problem of the plague of big-money pro-ams in Britain. In fact, they probably overlooked only one thing—it is just as difficult to coordinate schedules and mollify sponsors in Britain as it is anywhere else in the world.

Still painfully absent on the British scene was a rush of sponsors for new PGA tournaments, the absolute reverse of the situation in the U.S. It is now clear that the attitude of the television companies is critical in this respect. Most sponsors want television. It is a premise of their going into golf. But the BBC policy is to televise only the top four or five events, and the commercial television policy is that golf doesn't sell anything. It's a minority sport, who's interested? and so on and on and on. Golf on the Continent, although there are indications of a few public courses being built, remains swank, upper-class, aristocratic. So Europe has its problems. But in the main—thanks in part to that new folk hero, Tony Jacklin—the old.game is looking up.

Penfold Tournament—£4000
Winner: Alex Caygill

Half a dozen or so years ago, you might well have thought of Alex Caygill as the Tony Jacklin of the hour, a golfer just into his twenties, bristling with potential, as strong as need be for a demanding sport and with enough early performance to suggest great things to come. But in 1963 a stomach ulcer laid Alex low. It forced him into a lengthy lay-off and a rigid diet, and it compromised his career substantially.

Thus when he took the opening prize of the season, there was considerable goodwill towards him, not only in the public mind, but inside a game which is sometimes vinegarish in its judgments. Caygill, now a relaxed 28, declared after his win that he was learning to play in a more casual manner and accepting calmly what his play yielded him from day to day. The ulcer had come from tournament tension, nothing else, and he was inclined to avoid that experience again. On the first day, despite a 67 that was good for the lead, he had to be philosophical. He did not make a putt worth mentioning on the round. Pete Matkovitch had led for much of the day with four closing birdies, starting at 15 with a chip-in from 50 feet. Matkovitch is a Rugby-playing South African from Rhodesia of Yugoslav extraction. I wonder who the last Yugoslav pro was? He is also a disciple of Gary Player, including mannerisms, black clothing and all, but he is better than six feet tall and his second day was quite unPlayer-like. He shot 78 and missed the cut.

Another interesting player, Terry Le Brocq, led Caygill and Christie O'Connor by a stroke after 36 holes with a 69, 67. Terry comes from the Channel Islands and plays out of London's Walton Heath. His golf training includes a three-mile run every lunch hour, weight lifting, breathing exercises, etc., supervised by a R.A.F. warrant officer at a nearby remedial center. Though fit and strong, he has some problems of temperament. Caygill (70) was caught in a heavy rain shower that Le Brocq and O'Connor missed. It was a mixed day, because of a sharp rain which slowed the greens. Le Brocq needed an eagle at 18—he holed from 55 feet—to round out his 67. Peter Alliss shot 70—with four three-putt greens. Neil Coles had come out of the winter ten pounds lighter, thanks to a no-sugar, no-potatoes diet, and was only three off the pace. And Dai Rees, who had heard that burglars at his home had cleaned him out of 34 years of golfing trophies, went out to score 69 and make the cut.

Caygill and LeBrocq were paired together on the last day, and that in itself produced some opera buffe. By the tenth tee, they were two holes behind the next group and Caygill was complaining. Caygill took to holing out, marching to the next tee, and waiting there while LeBrocq was still engaged measuring lines and distances. By the 15th LeBrocq had had enough and demanded a ruling.

But in turn, by the time that Arthur Crawley-Boevey had the request and got out to them, they had caught up. His verdict was "No slow play." Perhaps LeBrocq was upset, but he slumped to sixth place with 73-75, while Caygill went 70,71 for a 278 and a two-shot win over O'Connor. Caygill was five ahead with four holes to play, and coasted in for the £750 first prize. The next day, he skipped up to London's Finchley club, won a pro-am there with a three under par 69, and took a further £400 prize, this time for only one round of golf, a purse trend that is irritating to the PGA.

Schweppes Tournament—£5435
Winner: Bernard Gallacher

The pros had a hard time finding the Ashburnham course on the far coast of South Wales. Some of them spent hours driving around looking for the place, and the gag was that it was so far west it should have been a U.S. tournament. When they found Ashburnham they wondered if they should have searched so hard, for it was the toughest course most of them had seen since Carnoustie, '68. A true links laid out on a coast west of Swansea where the game used to be to lure innocent mariners onto the beach with false navigation lights, Ashburnham, with the big ball, high winds and buffeting weather, was a wicked test that saw only four players break par on the first day. One of them was Guy Wolstenholme, who was beginning what might well be his last season in British golf for he plans to live in Melbourne and center his playing life on the booming Australian,

New Zealand and Far East circuit. That decision made, he seems a much more relaxed man, and he went on to play a good season and a very good British Open.

Probably the saddest first-round player at Ashburnham was David Jones, 21, a Belfast boy who led the qualifiers. Jones had left a winter at the Royal Malta club where he had scraped up a few hundred pounds for a win-or-starve season, and arrived at Ashburnham with wife and a Dormobile, a kind of trailer in which they proposed to spend the summer. Young golfers are like youngsters trying to break into show business—they need a lot of bravery, and strong digestive systems. During the eight years of this event, the sponsors had offered a £1000 hole-in-one prize, but since the prize had been won twice in earlier years and the insurance premium doubled, it had been withdrawn. Sure enough, Jones knocked a 6-iron in on the 157-yard 16th. The sponsors did give Jones £100 to blunt his disappointment.

A stiff afternoon wind blew the late starters out to sea, and out of the tournament went such names as Dai Rees, Harry Weetman, Clive Clark and Maurice Bembridge. Wolstenholme, an early starter, ended the day three up on Bernard Gallacher. The most remarkable surge of the day was an inward 32 from Bernard Hunt, with seven one-putt greens and four birdies. And the most remarkable stroke of the day was a tee shot on 18 by Hugh Boyle. Reckoning quite rightly that he needed two to make the cut, he went for the big drive, but hooked it way over the clubhouse, about 350 yards out on the 372-yard hole, downwind, needless to say. It carried everything and landed in a parking lot where it wedged between the bumper and parking light of a Daimler, and proved immovable.

Friday was a long day. The peppery Eric Brown, just named Ryder Cup captain, played behind Patrick Lee and protested that Lee had taken more than five minutes to search for a lost ball. Lee in fact had properly timed himself, had played out and recorded two balls, and had reported it after the round. There was a delay of five hours before a decision was made, in which Lee had to be recalled to the course before he was deemed innocent. For Lee is meant the difference in making and missing the cut. He went on to finish 40th, and win £29.5.

The second of the two Saturday rounds got down to a Wolstenholme-Gallacher battle, Wolstenholme teeing off with a two stroke lead. After six holes they were even. Gallacher's big chance came at the 485-yard eighth when his second, hit blind over sand dunes, found the front of the green. His approach putt from about 35 feet slid 18 inches past—and he missed the little one. For the next half-dozen holes, nothing went right for him. At 9 he had an unplayable lie only 20 yards from the hole and needed four more to get down. At 10 he drove not only into fairway bunker, but into a deep heelmark, too, which should never happen. He three-putted 11, and at the short 12th his tee shot was whisked far over the green by a boisterous wind. He was then five over par and two down to Wolstenholme, but with remarkable cool he decided, "If I can just get it home in par, I still have a chance. Anything can happen on a course like this." It did. Now it was Wolstenholme's turn. He dropped strokes at 15 and 17 and came to the last hole looking for a par to tie. Wolstenholme's pitch was short, his chip was weak and his 14-foot putt died at the hole, giving Gallacher a notable victory. Perhaps Gallacher felt more like the survivor of a shipwreck than a tournament winner, but he had succeeded under pressure. He had one-putted three of the last five holes, and in the morning had held together a potentially weak third round with six one-putt greens on the back nine. Gallacher had won a couple of minor events in East Africa in the spring, on the way back from the South African season, but this was his first major British breakthrough. As far back as anyone could research, he was the youngest player ever to win a British PGA tournament. When Gary Player won the Dunlop in 1956, he was 20 and five months. When Gallacher won the Schweppes he was 20 and three months. And a young man to watch.

Agfacolour Tournament—£4520
Winner: Brian Barnes

One week later, the trend continued—the trend, that is, for new names, new faces and first-time tournament winners. Buckinghamshire's pastoral Stoke Poges course, big ball or no, was a much more sympathetic proposition than Ashburnham, and on opening day something suspiciously like warm sunshine and calm conditions favored the players. Patrick Lee, the man in the lost-ball dispute at Ashburnham, led with 66 and observed, "This is a better way to make the news." He was hotly pursued by Peter Oosterhuis, who had looked impressive for some time. A professional for not quite six months, Oosterhuis was not allowed to win money under the PGA regulations and was putting this one down to experience and Alcan qualification, which the PGA permitted. Since turning pro, he had earned around £1,000 from the South African tour and sundry non-PGA events, and in the British season to date would have won £600 in prize money, had he been eligible. He finished second in the Gor-Ray event (confined to younger players), sixth in the Penfold and fourth in the Schweppes, so he was ready for the action, no matter what. The first day also featured a Peter Alliss offering of 42 front nine, 33 back nine, and a comfortable 71 from Peter Thomson, who was starting his British campaign rather earlier than usual because of the Alcan qualification.

The second day's weather confounded most of the field, Oosterhuis included, when the temperature slumped and a blustering north-easterly wind swept through the Stoke Poges woodlands. But Eric Brown, aged 44, handled it well enough to share the lead with Bryon Hutchinson. Australia's Bobby Tuohy, now a resident of South Africa, and Scot David Webster were challenging.

On Saturday, the day of the final 36 holes, everything turned upside down. For the first time in the season, there was warm weather, no wind, and scoring that salved the pride of the British pros, who had had about enough of indifferent weather, testing courses and that unfamiliar big ball. Brian Barnes, Bernard Gallacher, Dave Thomas and Maurice Bembridge made good moves, riding up to the top with scores in the sixties. Barnes, like Thomas, fashioned a 67. Barnes got an eagle on 15, where he drove the ball 12 feet from the hole on the 320-yard hole, and when he eagled the first hole on the final round (500 yards with a driver, 3-wood and 50 foot putt), he was flying home. But so was Bernard Gallacher, who went 68, 65, with 29 putts in the morning, 30 in the afternoon, which might be described as a hot short game. He was in the clubhouse with a four-under-par 280 posted when Barnes was on the tenth hole, and probably thought well of his chances, since Barnes has had numerous weak finishes in the past three years. But not this time. Barnes was leading coming into 16, a par-three of 192 yards. Not once had he hit this green, but this time he got it with a four iron, front and center, for an easy par. He thereupon birdied 17 and finished seven under par to win his first tournament by the healthy margin of three strokes. Gone, it seemed, was the Barnes of the simmering rage and choking frustration. When it was over, he attributed his first victory to four things, although he had the good grace to apologize in advance that it was "rather corny". He had been reading *The Power of Positive Thinking*, by Norman Vincent Peale—"you know, that book Gary Player is always going on about". He had John Allen, Bill Casper's Scottish caddie, toting the bag for him and keeping him calm. Max Faulkner, his father-in-law, had helped him with his driving, and he prayed on every hole. As Peter Dorereiner said in *The Observer*—"four pretty powerful corner men working for you".

Daks Tournament—£5000
Winner: Brian Huggett

It was nothing if not a season of variety. At the Daks the following week, the poor old and much-loved West course at Wentworth made more the news than the play. After a severe mauling in the rainsodden World Match Play the previous autumn, the course suffered a wet spring. Dead fairways and slow, spongy greens were the result. On top of all this, the rich pockets of North Sea gas that the British are busily tapping caught up with Wentworth in the form of a 30-inch pipeline. A network of these lines is being laid all over the country, and the national plan called for one to slide along the side of Wentworth's tricky par-three 14th hole. The pipeline turned the "fairway" into a mud slide. But this was a meager excuse for the scoring. Some of the prequalifying totals were horrifying, and when the real play began Eddie Pollard found himself with the first-round lead with a 70. At 71 were more ominous pros—Brian Huggett, invariably a good Wentworth player, and Bernard Gallacher, whose name was becoming most familiar. Gallacher opened his second round with two birdies, and when he reached the 36-hole mark he was in with a 68 and 138, three ahead of Huggett and five up on Christie O'Connor.

It was a three-man event for the final 36-holes. Gallacher birdied three of the opening six holes in the morning round, hit the ball remarkable distances in damp, heavy conditions and then closed with four birdies. Huggett, too, knocked off four birdies in a row, but struggled hard to hold together a 71 because of some very erratic driving. He was fortunate to stay in contention, and stomped straight to the practice tee when he had finished. Some noble names, incidentally, missed the cut—erstwhile Open Champions Peter Thomson and Bobby Locke among them. Locke was making his annual sentimental journey to England, during which he unwinds at a few tournaments, but not too seriously. For all that, he still attracts large galleries.

Huggett, from now on. is prepared to agree that father knows best.

George Huggett, the club professional at Limpsfield Chart, a Surrey course, had seen his boy play the closing four holes of the second round, and now told him on the practice tee that he was dipping and swaying a shade too much. Huggett has a habit of raising his head on the backswing and dipping into the downswing. As he worked on the practice tee he seemed to get steadier. By the third hole of the last round, Gallacher had lost his lead. On that hole he hooked a fairway wood into one of Wentworth's prime rhododendron bushes and thrashed after it to such ill effect that he took a seven. Meanwhile, Christie O'Connor was going eagle, par, birdie and taking the tournament lead. Huggett, playing along quietly, made the turn in a par 36, and when O'Connor hooked badly at the eighth—the one thing you must not do, since it stymies the second shot over a lake to the green—and made a double-bogey six, all three were tied with nine to play. O'Connor seemed to run out of steam, and now a strong finish won for Huggett. He birdied both of Wentworth's two closing par fives—one is 555 yards, the other 495 yards—and when Gallacher came unstuck with a 6–5 on the same holes, Huggett had the big check. But again one had to admire Gallacher. Hardly 20, and a pro less than a year, he had finished first, second, second in successive weeks.

Sumrie Tournament—£7500
Winners: Maurice Bembridge and Angel Gallardo

Does it pay to be different? Sumrie, which makes slacks, hopes so, but one has to wonder. This year the company tried a four-ball, better ball tournament, and when you consider that British golf critics have been complaining for years about the monotony of 72-hole stroke play, you would think this event would have been well received. But no—writers complained there were too many balls flying around, play was slow, if it was a romp it might better have been placed at the end of the season instead of in June, what with the serious business of an Open coming up followed by a Ryder Cup, and so forth and so on . . . Which proves again that you can't please all of the people all of the time. The fact is, this was a perfectly good and exciting tournament. It attracted healthy galleries after an opening day of foul weather, it was well covered by the local Yorkshire TV company, and it was played in with a good deal of

Sweet, sweet, sweet are the fruits of victory. Tony and Vivienne Jacklin,
the British Open trophy, and medal.

Question: 'Didn't that train bother you, Bob?' Answer: 'What train?'
Charles and Jacklin at Lytham, final round.

One of many brilliant bunker shots which underpinned Jacklin's Open
triumph.

Last hole, last round and the
joyous Jacklin sequence of success.

Bernard Gallacher, leading money-winner and at 20, the new boy wonder of British professional golf, drives the 17th at Wentworth.

Brian Barnes rejoices in the Agfacolour, his first British tournament win.

Christy O'Connor –
many a long, hard
season under that
tan.

Brian Huggett wins
the Daks
Tournament.

Even Bob Charles has to react in the World Match Play final, when he drops one against Gene Littler – from 45 feet!

Littler's birdie putt on the 34th ties the World Match Play final.

The Gary Player style with a long iron.

Open Champion Tony Jacklin almost in a hazard at Wentworth's 8th.

Bobby Cole of South Africa, with what might be called a full extension.

Player holes the 40-footer from the fringe of the first green at Durban that set him flying to a 64 and a monumental South African Open win.

A highly-coloured Lee Trevino clowning with Tadashi Kitta in the Australian Open Championship.

Gary Player, Australian Open champion yet again.

Celebrations, Oriental-style. Tomio Kamata, airborne above his friends after winning the Singapore Open.

Armed guard, at the Malaysian Open.

Viet Cong smoking pot?
No, just a caddie at
the Hong Kong Open.

The Royal Hong Kong Golf Club – and clubhouse premises which are not exactly cramped.

Hideyo Sugimoto of
Japan, winner of the
Republic of China Open.

Britain's Maurice
Bembridge swinging on the
Far East tour.

Lee Trevino on the way to his individual victory in the World Cup.

Joseph C. Dey, jr.,
the players' man.

'Palmer for Governor'
is the youthful cry
at a Pennsylvania
exhibition match.

One that hurt for Bobby Nicholls. The clubhead followed through round the tree and clunked Nicholls on the head.

The Pacific Ocean, they call it. Storm at Cypress Point.

Three faces of
American golf:
(a) In the desert at
Tucson; (b) The
controversial Spyglass
Hill in California;
and (c) golf in the
islands – Honolulu.

enjoyment by the pros. The sponsors deserve praise for their initiative.

Pannal is a pleasant, rather open moorland course across the valley from Yorkshire's fin-de-siècle spa, Harrogate. Strongly backed in advance were a local favorite, Hedley Muscroft, who is side-whiskered like a Mexican bandit, and his partner, Lionel Platts. They rated 33—1 with a London bookmaker, but no Yorkshire bookmaker would consider anything more than 20—1 on the partnership. After the first day, the Yorkshire bookies looked the wiser, for Muscroft and Platts were tied with Maurice Bembridge and Angel Gallardo from Spain, at 66, a fair score in high winds over a heavy golf course. The trick to this kind of tournament is to dovetail well, to "ham-and-egg it" as we say, each man giving himself birdie chances when his partner doesn't. One special problem is making sure you do not let your concentration sag. The second day brought no change at the top, both pairs shooting 65, but it did move Bernard Hunt and Neil Coles up a couple of shots when they birdied eight of the last nine holes, including a pitch in and three two's for a 29, a 64 and a 133 aggregate. Although some optimists began looking for rounds under 60 before it finished, no team managed to get clear under 64.

Muscroft and Platts got clear of Bembridge and "Angelito" in the third round by two strokes, shooting 64 against 66, and led with 195. Coming on strong at 199 were Martin Roesink, the Dutch bomber, and new pro Ronnie Shade, who was having his first try at the circuit after an Eisenhower Trophy-Walker Cup amateur career. But in the end, the victory went to Bembridge and Gallardo, the Spaniard lighting up Yorkshire with a good deal of Latin animation. He and Bembridge tore into the course, ripping off early birdies to get in front of Muscroft and Platts. As the local favorites reached the last hole they needed a birdie to tie. Each of them had a 15-foot putt for it, but both missed. Later the winners—an unlikely pairing—were reflecting on how they had got together in the first place. Bembridge had met Gallardo in a bus in Bangkok the previous winter, got to talking, and before they got out of the bus they had agreed to be teammates in the Sumrie Tournament. It was a profitable bus ride.

Martini International—£7000
Winner: Alex Caygill and Graham Henning, tied.

Warm, occasionally even hot sunshine, a pleasant, park-like and not-forbiddingly-long course, good crowds and a nip-and-tuck finish, not to mention the fifth tie in nine years of the event, made the Martini look like a golf tournament and spread considerable pleasure among all concerned, played as it was at perhaps the most well-endowed resort in Britain—Bournemouth. The British tour seldom goes to a public course, but when it must, Queen's Park, Bournemouth, is often considered. At 6,487 yards, it poses few problems of distance for the professionals. In good weather all but the ninth hole, 526 yards, was in reach, and the par looked closer to 69 than the card, which was 72. Yet only Peter Butler could better 69 the first time out, shooting a 68. He was closely pursued by Maurice Bembridge, very much in form with a 69, and four men at 70. Butler promptly called the greens "magnificent", but Brian Huggett, out in 36 and apparently set for a low round with three par-3s on the back nine, decided that the pin positions on 14 and 17, both par-3s where he dropped strokes, were poor indeed. Meanwhile, Alex Caygill put together a 41-29 and it was clear that low scoring was possible for the man who could keep the ball in play. Both Caygill and Huggett proved that on the second day. Caygill, using his driver only eight times, reduced Queen's Park to a 66, with Huggett only one stroke worse. Caygill led the field at the end of the day at 136, three ahead of Huggett and five ahead of the next man, Bembridge.

The third round was enlivened by a Brian Barnes disqualification—the usual thing, card total correct but a 3 registered and signed for instead of a 4—and by a remarkable round from Huggett. On the front nine he thrashed around in the woods to such effect that he had an eight and a six, yet hauled himself home in 31 and salvaged a 73. Caygill was less adept at the salvage game. He posted a 77, and suddenly South Africa's Graham Henning, with a steady 73, 69, 68, found himself leading Huggett by two and Caygill by three going into the closing round.

Knowing Huggett's attitude, a reasonable man might have had a few pounds on him but it was Caygill who put all the pieces together. Henning kept his game going smoothly, but with few birdies coming his way. Huggett found the strokes slipping away and

Caygill closed in. When Henning reached the last hole, a par looked good enough to make him the winner. But under the pressure, he drove into trees, chopped out, and could do no better than a bogey. Caygill, playing behind Henning, reached the 18th tee with a birdie to win. His pitch was sweet enough, no more than 15 feet from the pin, but as soon as he hit the putt he grimaced and strode after it. He knew it would be short, and it was. The pair seemed well enough pleased to share the Martini spoils. Caygill was now well on his way to the Ryder Cup spot he wanted badly. And Henning, a winner in South Africa and already sure of an Alcan berth, was getting into the fairly select company of golfers who have proved they can win anywhere in the world.

Carrolls International—£10,000
Winner: Ronnie Shade

R.D.B.M. Shade ("Right Down the Bloody Middle," his amateur chums dubbed him), turned professional on his birthday in October, 1968—his thirtieth birthday. Too old, said the wise ones, too old. But through the winter, Shade picked up enough to pay his bills in local and regional events in Scotland, and here he was, still well inside his first pro year, winning the richest plum on the PGA tour—the £2000 first prize from Carrolls in the clifftop frolic at Bray, a dozen miles from Dublin. Perhaps the point of the tournament was that Shade survived best of all. Woodbrook's 6,666 yards (they somehow fashioned a par 74 out of that, with six holes better than 500 yards long) was lashed by wind and heavy rainstorms to such an extent that the final day's play was all but abandoned. Starting times as much as talent governed the score a man might bring in, and in the entire tournament only Bernard Hunt got a round under 70. Peter Townsend shot an opening 83, declared that he was "fed up to the teeth" and vanished into the Irish countryside in search of fish and peace. But Shade, under last-round pressure from Bernard Gallacher, kept his mechanical swing going and won by a shot. One of the most interesting aspects of the event were some computerized statistics compiled by Carrolls, a first for a British tour event. The average score was 77.41. The first hole, par five at 565 yards produced only 23 birdies, but 101 bogeys and 17 double-bogeys. The ninth hole, 408 yards, produced only ten birdies, but 148 bogeys, which meant eight more bogeys than pars for the tournament. What else need be said about the big ball, sodden conditions and Irish coastal winds.

Bowmaker Tournament—£4000
Winners: Brian Huggett and Tony Grubb

Since 1957, Bowmaker has been doing very nicely with its pro-am as a £3000 event. Now the money has been upped £1000, but I would think the directors of the sponsoring finance house must deem it still cheap at the price. Played on Monday and Tuesday of the week preceding the British Open, the event picks up the early arrivals who want to test themselves under British conditions. This year the star was Billy Casper, who was busy extending his international image. Casper found himself paired with an Air Marshall and a General, which must have worked wonders for his sense of security, but did bring him to the top. He played a couple of relaxed 71d while Brian Huggett and Tony Grubb were putting together two-round totals of 135 on Sunningdale's beautiful Old Course. Casper did have something going for him during the week. He installed his Scottish caddie, John Allen, in a £10-a-day room at London's swank Carlton Tower Hotel—and converted him to the Mormon faith.

Piccadilly Medal—£7000
Winner: Peter Alliss

One week after the Open the British PGA tour picked up again at Prince's Golf Club, Sandwich Bay, which is in that little south-east corner of England that pokes towards France. And again there arose one of those routine controversies that afflict British golf. This time it was the format. Carreras Ltd. who make the Piccadilly brand of cigarette, are rather better-known for their sponsorship of the World Match Play Championship at the end of the season. In former years they have preceeded that event at Wentworth with a 72-hole medal tournament, and more recently with a four-ball tournament. This year Carreras officials decided to move its event out of the Wentworth week—wisely, in my opinion—and at the same time try a different format. In discussions with the PGA, they came up with a knock-out structure based on stroke play. The top 64 players in the order of merit would be invited. They would eliminate each other round by round as in match-play, but on the medal result over the full 18 holes. Every match would go, obviously, to the 18th. This had attractions, and detractions. For example, one man might score a four-over par 76 and win his match, another might be two under par and lose. Yet as Peter Alliss, the eventual winner, pointed out, if one player was within birdie range on one hole while the other had thrashed around in the rough, it still behoved the near man to make the putt and the birdie as insurance for the holes ahead. But the press, as it had with Sumrie, which had also tried something different, was grouchy. What it overlooked was that there was £7000 up for grabs, healthy by current British professional standards. And there was a stellar attraction, Tony Jacklin, the new British Open Champion who brought his Lytham swing with him and cut through to the third round at Prince's. Jacklin played beautifully until he ran into Alliss, who beat him by a stroke with a fine 69, three under par. Alliss took the tournament on the first extra hole of a 36-hole final, and won a place on the cup team, along with Bernard Hunt and Maurice Bembridge. But Will did not make it. Will was suitably chagrined, Alliss suitably pleased. For more than a decade, he has been a Ryder Cup stalwart. And his Piccadilly win was his first victory in a couple of years.

Gallaher Ulster Open—£4000
Winner: Christie O'Connor

At Belfast's Shandon Park course, about an 8-iron shot over 6000 yards with a par of 70, the professionals don't even begin to think of par golf. No Carnoustie, or even Ashburnham, this. The man with the wedge and the putter working effectively, and enough cool to ignore the birdies being flushed from all corners of the course by anyone, is the man to look for in this tournament. And his name is almost always Christie O'Connor, at least it has been three times in the last four years. True, others do flash into a brief orbit. David Carson, 22, an assistant pro who had never hit a shot outside of Ireland, produced a second-round 64. John Garner, not quite unknown, made a first round of 67, and with five second-place finishes to ponder on during the season he much wanted a victory here. O'Connor and Bernard Gallacher led the opening round with 65s while paired together, and come the last round, Garner or no, that's how it still was. O'Connor teed off for the clsoing round knowing that all over Shandon Park they were closing him. But that lazy elegant swing remained unruffled, and he promptly birdied the first hole from 15 feet. From then on, he held the opposition at arms' length—including Gallacher who blew to a 76. His closing 69 gave O'Connor a 271 and a comfortable three-stroke win.

RTV Rentals Open—£5000
Winner: Peter Butler

Down to the other end of Ireland the tour now went, to another short course in a country stiff with hulking and magnificent tests, the 6,271-yard Little Ireland Club at Cork. When Bernard Hunt scored a first-round 63 in balmy weather, world records seemed in peril, but as the event unfolded the weather worsened and the scoring, too. The rough was almost non-existent, the greens in superb condition and holding well, and in spite of the weather, low scoring was the rule. But alas, the public did not respond; galleries were meager in the extreme. Come to think of it, I don't know where they would have come from—Cork not exactly being a metropolis. Hunt had an even-par 71 in the third round, which allowed Peter Butler to catch him. Cobie Le Grange, who had spent the week in slavery on the practice tee, was three behind. Butler and Hunt came to the 14th hole of the last round still tied for the lead, but that neo-Frenchman, Butler—he has a winter job at St. Cloud, Paris—put on a tremendous finish and disposed of Big Ben with birdies at 14 and 16. Butler attributed his victory to rescuing "an old putter I bought in Bombay 12 years ago". It is just a plain wryneck putter, but he has used it off and on for years. His putting had been spotty all season, so Butler went back to the old putter for Cork, and produced his first victory in a year.

Wills Tournament—£7350
Winner: Bernard Gallacher

The story of the Wills Open is substantially the story of Bernard Gallacher, which in a way is almost the story of the British season. This is a bald statement, and it eliminates a lot of good people and interesting happenings, but the remarkable young Scot just could not keep out of the action. This time he broke the back of a tournament with a third-round 63, the season's low score. Gallacher is the young man of whom Gary Player said at Lytham, "A fine player with an excellent short game and one of the worst grips I have ever seen." Moor Park and the Wills tournament showed many of the facets of the gradually-jelling Gallacher image: very aggressive, given to flashes of temperament and the odd public outburst, not afraid of winning, capable of a sudden low score, and when given half a chance to win, ready for the pressure. The boy is only 20 and has a lot of golfing to do, but with a season or two in the hard American school he should make a fine player with some chance of becoming a real champion.

The bigger course of the Moor Park club, which is on the north-west fringe of London, is on the short side and superficially open to low scoring, but it is a course that will yield the score only to careful and accurate play and to a golfer who shows it some respect. The early pacemakers were Dai Rees (65, 69) and Brian Huggett (70, 65), each of whom tied the course record. Gallacher had gone 71, 68 to be five shots off the pace, but his 63 took care of that and left him two ahead of Huggett and four ahead of Christie O'Connor. It was an exceptional round of golf, a nine under par 32-31 that included nine one-putt greens and only 27 putts for the round. Said Gallacher, "I felt I could hole everything. Every time I stood over a putt I was thinking, there is no reason why this shouldn't go in." The card is worth listing: 443, 433, 344—32: 342, 444, 433—31. The round featured some telling work with the 5-wood. "It is a very handy club for a bad two-iron player like me," said Gallacher. If the 63 put Gallacher in a prime position, he needed it. The last day became a scramble by half a dozen players, Gallacher included, to give the tournament away. Gallacher started 14 under par. At various. times Thomas was 11 under, Coles 12 under, O'Connor 12 under and Huggett 13 under. Bembridge made three birdies in the last six holes to reach 11 under. Gallacher rather lost his driving, had to struggle with his round, and was involved in a squabble with a scoreboard carrier when his drive hooked wildly, hit the board and bounded into an awkward lie. Gallacher went over par on the hole, after exchanging hard words with the innocent board man. He dropped another shot at 12, then stopped the rot with a birdie on 13. At 16 he hit the shot that composed him and won the tournament for him, a 6-iron that finished two feet from the stick for a birdie. Thus when he overclubbed 18 he still had the luxury of a careful chip back and two putts to win the tournament from O'Connor by a shot with a 13-under-par 275. By this point in August, Gallacher had won two tournaments and finished second three times. He had claimed a place in the Ryder Cup team, been chosen to play for Scotland in the World Cup, and had qualified for the rich Alcan Golfer of the Year event. His official money was now well past £5000, and as I seem to have said before, he had become one to watch closely.

News of the World PGA Match Play—£5000
Winner: Maurice Bembridge

The 1969 *News of the World* was the last of its kind, at least the last sponsored by the raucous Sunday newspaper. At the time of the championship, in September 1969, that fact in itself seemed to me sad. This was the oldest sustained professional golf tournament in the world, having been in continuous existence since 1903. Some very impressive names must have graced its list of winners. But perhaps I am coming under the influence of that British feeling for history. What happened was last year a young Australian who is big in the publishing business there came to England and bought the paper. As any new proprietor would, he took a close look at the accounts. When he got to "promotions," he decided that one promotion he could do without was the golf tournament.

Sad to say, the tournament did not quite go out in a blaze of glory. Such British stalwarts as Thomas, Will, Weetman, O'Connor and Alliss missed the event. Townsend and Jacklin were in America, O'Connor had a bad shoulder, and Alliss simply forgot to enter. There was a good deal of talk about the pros disliking match play, but I don't believe—particularly among British professionals—that this was the root cause. The problem was that old demon money, or rather a breakdown of the money that has always annoyed the pros. The winner would take £1250, a reasonable sum in itself. But the runner-up was down to £500, a good deal less than 50% and the beaten semi-finalists down to £250 each. For seven or eight rounds in competitive golf in a week, including qualifying, this was scant reward for the fellows who got so near. Maurice Bembridge was explaining before the event that if he reached the quarter-final round, he would earn £100 but would lose money, what with a week of hotels and caddies and his transportation expenses. In addition, the draw seemed unbalanced, with what star names there were bunched in the top, and with Peter Thomson looking particularly solitary and menacing in the bottom. But he lost in the third round. Three up after 12, Thomson was whittled down and eventually out when Bryon Hutchinson, a capable tournament player, holed a wedge shot to eagle the 13th and start a rally that brought him a win at the 21st hole. The semi-finals came out Huggett v. Rees and Bembridge v. Talbot, and produced, if nothing else, the wildest golf shot of the British season. Huggett had Rees nicely beaten at dormie with three holes to go. Then Rees birdied 16 and Huggett made a mess of the par-3 17th. And Rees now won 18 with a million-to-one freak drive. He hooked wildly into the gallery, the ball carrying no more than 150 yards. But it hit a post holding a gallery rope, rebounded back towards the tee and struck Huggett's bag, which was carried by his caddie who quite reasonably thought he was well out of line and range. Golf's Rule 26 2 (b) says quite clearly in this circumstance "loss of hole", and the match was square. Not surprisingly, the bewildered Huggett missed his tee shot at 19 and Rees won with a par. Said Rees, "I feel guilty about being in the final. It made my victory a bit hollow. It was such a rotten way to win." Yet a win it was, and here was old Dai Rees, in his mid-fifties, in another final. In 1967 he was a finalist, 1968 a semi-finalist, and now in 1969 a finalist again. It is quite a feat, considering that he first won the event in 1936. Perhaps Dai was still a little shaken, for when he went out in the afternoon for the 18-hole final against Maurice Bembridge, who was not born when Rees won his first Match Play, the match became a procession. Bembridge opened with a birdie, followed with others at 5, 6 and 9, and eventually closed out the match 6 and 5.

Dunlop Masters—£8500
Winner: Cobie Legrange

In a dull Masters, made more so by the weather, perhaps only Jimmy Hitchcock's putting secret—unlike most of these it stayed secret—and Cobie Legrange's new "stammering swing" would remain memorable. The weather was cold, wet and dreary for most of the four days. Cobie virtually strangled the tournament from beginning to end, and only four British Ryder Cup players scored under par. It seemed ominous at the time, but in kindly hindsight after a marvellous Ryder Cup match, we can say that they were obviously saving themselves for the week ahead at Birkdale. Yet if nothing else, this made it a good year for Cobie, for he had won in South Africa, on the Continent, and now in Britain. Legrange had won this tournament in 1964, when he was 21, and since then had fallen short of making himself a top-level international pro. He had been through two disappointing years in America, and in 1969 was devoted to European golf. One U.S. legacy was his new swing; he brings his backswing to a dead stop after 18 inches or so in an effort to be sure his backswing is inside the line. He explained that he had made this change in an attempt to get more of the distance that he needed on the U.S. tour. Hitchcock, who tied Legrange for the lead on opening day with a 69, had a different story to tell. He said his putting average had come down four or five shots a round since the British Open and a lesson at Lytham from Gay Brewer. Brewer and he also swapped putters, and Hitchcock was still wielding the exchanged weapon, convinced that never again would he have problems on the green. Well, poor Hitchcock was ten strokes worse on the morrow, and finished 17 strokes behind Cobie's seven under par 281. The South African scored 69, 68, 70, 74 for a three-shot win over Peter Butler. On Little Aston's tight, treelined fairways and hard-to-hold greens, this was first-class play, as evidenced by the fact that Bill Casper finished 10th. Incidentally, Jacklin finished third. His last-round 68 was the best 18-hole score of the tournament, and suggested he was ready for the Ryder Cup.

The Ryder Cup Matches
Winner: GB/USA Tie

What is there to say about the 1969 Ryder Cup match? Nothing and everything. There it was, a 12-a-side golf match played between two of the strongest golfing nations in the world on one of the game's most demanding courses during three days, with 32 matches over 18 holes and better than 4,000 golf shots hit in all. Yet it came right down to the last putt on the last hole of the last match on the last day, and ended tied. Sam Snead, the American captain, called it the "greatest match ever played in this country," and it would be hard to disagree with him. When young Clive Clark knocked in a long putt at Baltimore to tie the 1965 Walker Cup match, he set an amateur precedent for the professionals at Royal Birkdale in 1969.

Of course, we are all inclined to believe that our times are the best of times and we do not often look far into the past, but what I can say with some certainty is that the 1969 Ryder Cup match was the most thrilling of the post-war era, even including the 1957 match which the British won, the only time they have been victorious in twenty years. And since the British did not lose at Birkdale, you could almost say that they won. I believe the result, coming a month after the 1969 Walker Cup match in which the British gave the Americans a desperately close battle at Milwaukee, and coming a couple of months after the British at last had won their own Open, is of real significance for the future of British golf.

I am not about to say that the Americans are in trouble, or even that a trend has been reversed—in fact, I believe that in the next match, in the U.S. in 1971, the Americans will once more win handily. The level of competition on the U.S. tour makes the Americans all but invincible on their own ground. The significance of the result lies in the fact that at long last the British are coming to believe that the Americans are no longer supermen. This is particularly true of the young British golfers. They are casting off their inferiority complex. In the past, British teams have been betrayed by being "weak in the tail". They never had enough depth, and could never hold up in tight finishes. In the recent past, British teams had a core of Peter Alliss, Christie O'Connor, Bernard Hunt and Neil Coles, fellows who could be relied on to pick up points here and there, but they also had a few players who were virtually beaten before they started because they were overawed by the occasion and the reputations of the Americans. This was particularly noticeable in 1965 on this same Royal Birkdale course against Bryon Nelson's team, and at Houston in 1967 against Ben Hogan's team. But things have changed somewhat. Tony Jacklin won a U.S. PGA tournament—Jacksonville in 1968. He made strong moves in the Masters and won the British Open. As an anchor man in the Ryder Cup match, he played the maximum six matches and was unbeaten. Peter Townsend played four and won three, has done his beginner's penance on the U.S. tour and is at last beginning to make money and reach up to the higher echelons of the game. After Birkdale, you can be sure there will be more Jacklins and more Townsends giving it a go.

The U.S., not for the first time, produced a Ryder Cup team that was without the reigning Masters or U.S. Open champions. The team was selected by a point system over the preceeding two years, and the system reflected the trend of those years; youngsters or unknown emerged from the pack to win a tournament or tournaments and a lot of the money. "Unknowns" is a phrase that bears some explanation. Most of the U.S. players had been around for a long time. But only now have they started to win. Thus Dave Douglas, Ken Still, Dan Sikes, and Dave Hill were all but unknown to the British. They represented fresh Ryder Cup faces. On the other hand, Snead's team also had Gene Littler, Miller Barber, Bill Casper, Frank Beard, and Jack Nicklaus, which added up to a good deal of seasoning. The British came up with substantially the same mix, but by way of a different method. They decided that six of their twelve would be taken off their tour records, but the other six would be selected by committee. When the time came, Eric Brown, the team captain, Dai Rees and Tom Haliburton went for youth. Thus Tony Jacklin, Peter Townsend, Maurice Bembridge, Brian Barnes, and Bernard Gallacher were available to be thrown at anything the U.S. could offer.

The Americans arrived the preceding weekend and had ample time for practice and preparation on a course in perfect condition. Royal Birkdale was not dry enough to offer fast fairways and firm greens, such as the British are supposed to play well, nor lush enough to make for soggy, holding greens that submit to "dart-board" approaches that the Americans are supposed to favor. Ever with us are misconceptions about golf on the other side of the ocean, and never mind which side of the ocean you stand on. But Birkdale was very green and ripe, actually in perfect condition. The overture to the match was something else. You might have been excused for thinking that a major publicity effort to sell tickets had been deemed necessary three days before play. Eric Brown started it by declaring that his players had been instructed not to look for American balls lost in the rough, on the theory that it would tire them and they might be penalized for accidently treading on a ball. He was able to quote a rule to substantiate his stand, and it took all of a long day to discover that the rule was qualified to say precisely the opposite. That put the writers into a hassle about sportsmanship, and there were many people who took the view that Brown, a hard man with a personal record of four wins in four Ryder Cup singles matches against Lloyd Mangrum, Gary Middlecoff, Tommy Bolt and Jerry Barber, was taking the thing to extremes.

The betting was 5—1 on the U.S. and 3—1 against the British, but Sam Snead said, "Ah don't see it quite like that." Snead announced that he believed the British, after two years of competition with the bigger ball, would hit their pitch shots much better, a department of the game that had supposedly cost them many a match in the past. Snead also spent a good deal of time making the point to his team that the British were improved, and that the match would be tougher than some of them may imagine. "It'll be close," said Snead. Peter Ryde in *The Times* thought that the "U.S. would have no great reserves of morale", and Tony Jacklin announced fairly dramatically that the British putting "can win". With that, the golfers were ready to play.

Next it was the turn of the caddies. Given one-piece coverall uniforms to wear, they threatened a strike because they felt the garments did not fit properly, because since they were made of nylon they would "sweat" and because, let's face it, they were not attractive. This really looked serious until the British PGA suggested that before the caddies got too hysterical about it, why didn't they try them in action? The caddies agreed, and that difficulty dissolved in the autumn air.

Snead kept some experience off of his starting lineup for the first foursomes—Nicklaus and Littler—but Brown had no inhibitions with his young players. He led off with Coles and Huggett, who took care of Barber and Floyd, then paired Gallacher and Bembridge, who beat Trevino and Still handily with some impressive golf. But it was the Jacklin-Townsend partnership which sparked the British this day, and perhaps for the entire three days. They went in against Hill and Tommy Aaron, birdied the three opening holes and finished on the 17th with five birdies, one eagle, and not a single hole over par. A four on the closing hole would have given them 66 over one of Britain's toughest golf courses. The end of the match was dramatic. At the 17th Townsend, set to play the team's second shot, could see Aaron's ball on the front of the green on the 510-yard hole. He rode into a 3-wood, nailed the ball perfectly, and it came up six feet from the hole. Jacklin made the putt and the British were 3—0 with one halved match for the morning. Snead deployed, and the Americans rallied. The day closed with the British 4—3 ahead, with one halved. So the British led in foursome play for the first time in 20 years. That one day's play seemed to set the pattern of the week—the British were better early risers, the Americans strong finishers. Ken Still did not endear himself to many people in his morning match with Trevino against Gallacher and Bembridge. On the 13th tee Bembridge asked him to move out of his line of vision. Still retaliated by moving everyone—players, caddies and officials—away from their usual stance by the tee box. Still then hooked into the rough, and made no secret of his disgust. Trevino's second plugged under the lip of a bunker, and Still's attempted recovery came up and hit him on the shoulder. "It hit you, didn't it?" queried Trevino. There was no reply. Trevino said "Pick it up," and strode on. It was a portent of more trouble to come.

The second day was fourball matches. Casper had injured his wrist in an afternoon match the day before when he and Beard had beaten Townsend and Butler, and was out of the morning action having treatment and massage. This time it was Britain's turn to survive what many people believed would be its most vulnerable day. In the morning, the home team went up 2—1, with one halved. In afternoon play the British lost two, halved two, and brought the entire match to 6—6, with two sets of eight singles to come on the final day. In continuing perfect autumn weather, the schedule went awry and when the last match of the day came to the 18th, they were playing in twilight with the street lights of Southport their backdrop. In the gloom Willie Aitchison, Trevino's caddie, slipped between the 17th green and 18th tee and broke an ankle. But the high drama of the day, leaving a brackish taste all round, had come when the Still-Hill, Huggett-Gallacher match reached the seventh green. He ran his long approach putt to within three feet, then went up and played it into the hole. Still picked up his ball, since he could not improve on Hill's par. Huggett then pointed out to the referee that Hill had played out of turn. The Americans walked off the green. Still later declared that the referee had said, "Loss of hole" (Rule 40 1d is specific that the opponent may require the player to replay the stroke in the correct order WITHOUT penalty). The British were persuaded that the Americans had walked off before getting a ruling. Certainly correct procedures were not carried out, and there was almost total confusion. Going up the eighth fairway, Still, having realised or been told that the ruling was wrong, and not being the most poised or tactful of men, let go with several observations that did not much please the crowd. As ever, there were a few in the crowd bold enough to boo and tell him that if he wanted the Ryder Cup that badly, he should take it and go home. The match went on, tight-lipped.

There was one other match in the long day that was noteworthy. Aaron and Floyd went up on Hunt and Bembridge at the third, which Tommy Aaron birdied. They then halved every hole to the 16th, which Bembridge birdied. The match finished all square, with sixteen halved holes, the better ball score 70 each side, four under the card par, and at least four of the men in all this action well enough pleased. Said Captain Snead in the twilight, "It's a hell of a match up to now." Said Captain Brown, "A little disappointing. But not to go into the last day behind is a great thing."

On the closing Saturday, Brown put Alliss at the top of his team, followed by Townsend, who was beginning to look as though he was running out of steam, and made Jacklin his anchor man at the bottom. Snead did precisely the same, with Trevino and Hill leading off, and Jack Nicklaus at the bottom to face, as it turned out, the British Open champion. Townsend, wilting badly, was slaughtered by an inspired Dave Hill, who was four under par after nine holes. Alliss and Trevino had a tense battle, the margin going to America by virtue 'of Trevino's sharper work on the greens. Neil Coles nipped Tommy Aaron, but Casper beat Barnes on the last green. O'Connor, Bembridge, and Butler defeated, respectively, Beard, Still, and Floyd, and then Jacklin came through like a true champion against Nicklaus. Jack had not been hitting the ball with his usual massive authority, but it was his putting that lost him the match as much as a first-nine 34 by Jacklin. Nicklaus missed no fewer than seven holeable putts ranging from seven feet to 18 inches, and thus could expect no mercy from a player of the quality of Jacklin. But in the afternoon series, the Americans plunged very much into the action, and as the matches moved to the turn, with the wind rising strongly, the British were down in six. The possibility of an anti-climax, after such a valiant week's work, smothered the British gallery like a fog. The British take this match very seriously. Needing only 3½ points for their first outright win in 12 years, they saw that slender margin slipping away in the eight final matches. Peter Butler produced a point, winning handily against rather moderate scoring by Dale Douglass, but it was Bernard Gallacher who led the rally, if rally it was, with a bristling performance against Trevino. Brown had kept him out of the morning play, and young Gallacher looked all the way a fitter, fresher, and of course younger man. His outward half of 33 gave him the edge. O'Connor and Coles went down, exhausted, but the British had two of the points they needed. Could they scramble three halfs out of the four other matches? Barnes and Bembridge, the youngsters, brought nothing.

It was to be left to Huggett and Jacklin, playing against perhaps the two most mature players on the American squad, Casper and Nicklaus. Huggett and Casper had a fine match, nip and tuck all the way, which Huggett squared at 16 when Casper was twice in sand. At 17, Huggett holed from around five feet for a birdie half. As Huggett walked up to a birdie putt on 18 only slightly shorter for a halved match with Casper, he was stopped by an explosion of cheering from 17, where Jacklin and Nicklaus were. Huggett thought the cheers meant Jacklin had won and that his half with Casper would win the Ryder Cup for the British. He rolled his putt into the center of the hole, walked off the green, broke up completely and wept unashamedly in the arms of Eric Brown, his captain. But the noise Huggett had heard from 17 was for Jacklin when he holed a monster putt—later measured at 55 feet—for an eagle to square his match. So the play came to the last green of the last match, with the Ryder Cup hanging on it. With the first touch of evening dew on the green, Jacklin's approach putt pulled up about two feet short of the hole. Nicklaus, noting this, gave his putt from 30 feet every chance, but knocked it four nasty feet past the cup. Now Nicklaus, with the return, had the tying; or losing of the Ryder Cup at the end of his putter. After his fashion, he took a long look, and then holed it. He then picked up Tony's marker and said to him, "I couldn't ask you to putt that one, Tony." Jacklin and Nicklaus walked off the green arm in arm, and in that moment Nicklaus restored to the event the warmth that any great international sporting contest should have. Said Snead, "The greatest golf match I've ever seen. This morning I didn't think we were going to take the cup back." Said Eric Brown, "I'll tell you one thing—the next British team that goes to America will be one helluva team."

AND IN EUROPE

The story of golf in Europe in 1969 is Jean Garaialde, the French pro from La Boulie at Versailles who made an almost unprecedented sweep of Europe's big three titles—the Spanish, the French and the German Opens. I say almost unprecedented because in 1958 Peter Alliss won the Italian, Spanish and Portuguese Open almost in successive weeks and I guess I would rank that as a rough equivalent. Alliss, I might add, was on the verge of quitting tournament golf when he went out to Italy that year, although I hardly believe the same was true of Garaialde when he went to Madrid in the spring of 1969. Garaialde's golfing triple was the playing happening of the year, but there was something else in Europe '69 —the first tangible evidence that the expansion of Continental golf, brewing these past few years, was becoming fact; the first stirrings of what might after all turn out to be the much-anticipated development of a true European tour. Perhaps the World Cup of 1968, played in Rome, spurred things along—an event in which native son Roberto Bernardini finished second in the individual placings and in which the Italian team put up a robust showing. Perhaps it was simply a matter of evolution, but in any event, several new tournaments sneaked almost unheralded onto the scene: Walworth-Aloyco and BP in Italy, the Madrid Open, the Basque Open, which Garaialde also won, and others. These events were not calculated to strike terror into the sponsors of the Rebel Yell Open, much less the Masters or the Westchester, but each of them carried a winning purse of between $2,500 and $5,000—good spending money for European pros. And there were loud murmurings of better things to come.

Jean Garaialde, now in his early thirties, is the son of a pro and the brother of a pro. The family is from the Biarritz region, but for the last dozen or so years the Garaialdes have been teaching at and playing out of La Boulie, a pleasant little course at Versailles, half an hour from Paris. Jean is married to Odile, a charming Parisienne who, as Mlle Semelaigne, won the French Ladies Open three times, was a finalist twice more, and played for France and Europe I don't know how many times. In his big 1969 Jean played a good British Open, he finished sixth—ahead of all the British players—in the Alcan at Portland, and altogether had the year of his life. He attributed his success to added confidence and improved putting. He has always been a solid careful striker of the ball, but he spent much of last winter at work on his putting and evolved a more upright stance, which certainly paid off for him.

The Spanish Open was played for the first time on the course of the "Real Automobil Club de España", the Royal Automobile Club of Spain, 45 minutes out from downtown Madrid. The course, only three years or so old, was built by Bardana, the fine Spanish architect who created El Prat at Barcelona, and whom I would judge to be in the top half dozen architects in the world. It is a fine, big course, on sandy soil and through pine woods, and at full length goes to 7,241 yards with a par of 72. Four holes are better than 500 yards and three of the four par threes top 200 yards. The weather was fine and hot, with some wind on the last day. Coming early in the year, the championship was dominated by Spaniards, six of whom finished close behind Garaialde and most of whom made the early running. Valentin Barrios led the Frenchman by four strokes half way, and by three after three rounds, as did Ramon Sota with a fine third-round 66. But a dramatic last nine turned things around. Garaialde was actually five behind Barrios with nine to play, but played the nine in two under par while Barrios was taking 40. Sota wilted badly on the same nine holes, so Garaialde took it from Barrios by a stroke and from Sota by three. His 283 was five under par for the event.

In July at the French Open at St-Nom-La-Breteche, Garaialde was well aware that there had not been a native win since 1938 when Marcel Dallemagne completed a hat-trick of wins. St-Nom, an hour out of Paris, has two long rather dull courses, with the "red" course going to 7,400 yards on occasion. This was such an occasion. The club is very swank, about ten years old, with a handsome clubhouse, but the courses are laid out along an open, shallow valley, which limits the excitement possibilities. It was the venue of the 1963 Canada Cup, won for the United States by Palmer and Nicklaus. The weather was good, and Garaialde, with the glory of France resting on his strong shoulders, played steadfast golf, scoring 71, 69, 69, 68, which was under par all the way. But he had to finish birdie, birdie to catch Roberto de Vicenzo, the winner of the event in 1960 and 1964. They went into extra holes. At the third hole of the playoff, a par 3, both missed the green. Roberto really missed it—he was under a tree; and chopping out sideways he failed to reach the green in two. Garaialde chipped his second to within two feet of the pin and it was all over, par against bogey. The French were enchanted.

The following week Garaialde did not enter the Dutch Open at Utrecht's Golf Club de Pan. Again the weather was excellent—hot and dry with no wind—as Europe had one of those summers. The tournament was a romp for Guy Wolstenholme, the Englishman now playing out of Melbourne. He led after the first round with a 69, was tied in the second by the UAR's Mohamed Moussa, who shot a course record of 68 that day. Wolstenholme pulled away over the final 36 (68, 69) for an 11-under-par 277 and a five shot win over South Africa's Barry Franklin. Wolstenholme's game has matured in the past few years, and he is not now so prone to hit the occasional destructive shot that used to ruin his scoring.

Next was the German Open. The course at Frankfurt is tight and tree-lined, and was on the dry side. It was the hottest week of the German summer, with temperatures in the high nineties. Jean Garaialde was playing his best game at Frankfurt, and he was especially deadly on the greens. Perhaps he felt obliged to win this one—his wife Odile won the 1969 German Amateur. Dale Hayes, the young South African amateur, had won the German Men's Amateur just prior to the Open and he held his form. He led after the first round with a 65. But Garaialde had an opening 68, which he followed with 66, 67. The last day he coasted to a three-stroke victory over Cobie Legrange with a moderate 71. His 272 was 12 under par. Hayes ended the tournament even better than he had begun, shooting a record 63 on the final day.

Early in September, at Crans-sur-Sierre, a course that is 5,000 feet up a mountain in the Alps, the Swiss Open was played. Roberto Bernardini of Italy won with a fine closing round of 63. Gerhard Koening, a young German pro, and Garaialde were second. But in spite of the second-place finish, Europe's golfing title in 1969 belonged to the Frenchman.

8

The South African Tour

The PGA finds a way, and so does Player

Making prophecies and anticipating trends is as difficult in golf as in anything else, and you might think I have been around the game long enough to limit my forecasting desires. But not so, and once again I have to share with you a strongly-rooted suspicion: better times are coming for professional golf in South Africa. I can't be too tangible about this. It just seems to me that the performances of the top dozen South African players were appreciably better this year, their scoring suddenly much more impressive. And there were signs of improvement in tournament presentation. Part of this improvement may have been provoked by the feelings the players have that at long last their PGA and tournament sponsors are edging their way into the twentieth century. South Africa, of course, has particular problems. Some of them arise because of apartheid—which golfers are allowed to play in which tournaments, which members of the public are allowed to watch—some are created by old laws that limit Sunday play and the taking of admission money on Sundays and many occur because newspapers will not acknowledge in print the name of the company that sponsors a tournament. Thus the "General Motors Open" gets described editorially as the "motors tournament" or some such thing, which is of no great benefit to GM.

Much of the annoyance over such difficulties came to a head a year ago when the 1968 South African Open, the prime event of the season, turned into a shambles. The final 36-holes was scheduled for a Saturday. When one of the rounds was washed out by a rainstorm, the last 18-holes were held over until Monday. Harold Henning, for one, promptly withdrew, and he unleashed a blast that the organization of the Open was "outdated and pathetic". In part because of this the 1969 Open was set up as a four-day event, and sponsors of some other tournaments chose to follow this lead. In general, events were more crisply organized and everyone was a little happier.

Gary Player, in action or not, dominated the season, just as he has been doing for the best part of a decade. He played in four of the seven events, won two, finished fourth in another, and was forced to withdraw early from the fourth because of a wrist injury. It was a record that would be considered passably fair by anyone except those South Africans—there are more than a few of them—who see no reason why Gary should not win every time he starts. But there were also other personalities coloring the season. For example, Bobby Cole produced his long-awaited breakthrough. There was the determination of Trevor Wilkes and the partial eclipse of Cobie Legrange, who is invariably a hard man to beat on his home ground. There was the startling first professional appearance of Britain's Peter Oosterhuis—and there was a lady you should know, Brenda Blumberg.

Maybe Mrs. Blumberg, if anyone can, epitomizes the way ahead for South African golf. As well as being a good player, she is a golf nut. In addition, she is married to the greatest golf nut in Africa. George Blumberg is in the paper bag and container business in Johannesburg, and his business is successful and international enough to permit him and his wife to take an annual round-the world trip in late spring and early summer each year. They usually stop in Australia, then spend some time in the U.S., taking in the U.S. Open, and see the British Open on their way home. Side trips from time to time have taken them to Hong Kong and Japan, the U.S. Masters and most of the various European open championships. More important, many young South African golfers, including Gary Player, Bobby Cole and Dale Hayes, have found a wonderful mentor and counsellor in George Blumberg. And so it could be expected that when Mrs. Blumberg accepted a position on the championship committee of the PGA scheduled for Germiston, she made her presence felt. Her main contribution was developing a multiple-sponsorship concept that proved to be an outstanding success. Eighteen different sponsors took one hole each, and the result was the liveliest event of the year. There were all kinds of prizes for birdies, eagles and holes-in-one. The atmosphere was carnival, with a variety of sponsor signs from hole to hole. The course was the best conditioned of those on the tour. The sun shone, crowds were large, and Gary Player won from Bobby Cole in a tight finish. What else could a South African tournament want? It may not sound like much by more restrained and normal British and American standards, but South African golf needed a way to attract sponsors in the publicity void, and this may be it. The PGA tournament was hardly over before most of the sponsors involved had signed up on the same basis for 1970. In sum, a small, hopeful sign. One of many.

Transvaal Open—R.3,890
Winner: Bobby Verwey

The South African tour began with the Transvaal Open at Kensington, a surburban Johannesburg course which is on the short side, but tight; a parkland circuit with narrow fairways winding through trees. After one of Johannesburg's perennial droughts, the course was short of its best condition and the greens in particular, usually feared as having the worst nap of all Transvaal greens, were more bumpy than nappy. It looked like a course made for a wedge player who could somehow bobble the ball in with the putter. Tienie Britz, the young (22) Southdowns professional, had his hour of glory with an opening 66 that put him two shots in front of Hugh Inggs, but in the second round fortune turned against him. With five threes between the fourth and ninth, he seemed in command, but at the 13th, a wayward second shot went into a tree and did not come down. Unnerved, Britz missed four short putts over the closing holes. At 17, facing an innocent wedge to the green, he dumped it in a trap and had two swings at it before moving it out. At 18 he had his second three feet from the flag and missed. Denis Hutchinson and Graham Henning, each with 68 for 138, made hard runs at Britz and were only a shot behind. And Peter Oosterhuis, playing his first professional tournament, was in third place at 139. If the greens and their infamous nap, which is supposed to devour all non-South African golfers, did not phase Oosterhuis, it upset Cole, one of the more prominent natives. He lamented over 72 putts.

In the third round, golf on the high veldt caught up with Oosterhuis, who needed 77 shots to get in, and it was Bobby Verwey who made a run with a 66 comprised of 14 pars and four birdies; a most polished performance. He and Graham Henning (69) were tied at 207 and in the closing round that afternoon Verwey, as befits a man who was voted a few seasons back as the second best wedge player on the American circuit, took it by a stroke from Graham Henning with a 65 and a 272 total—eight under par. In that final round, Verwey dropped a shot at the first hole, then produced four successive birdies that should have been five, because he missed from only three feet at six. Another birdie at nine put him out in 31, but he still only just squeezed in at the end. Graham Henning, Hutchinson and Inggs all made 66s and Henning's birdie try on the last green from 20 feet to tie barely missed. The weather throughout was hot, but the pros in general did not give the season a blazing start. Only six players broke par, one of them amateur Comrie du Toit. Denis Hutchinson, for one, was surprised at the scores. "Under the conditions," he said, "and on a short course, I expected many to play better than they did." Nine amateurs made the 36-hole cut, and five of them finished "in the money" as it were. There was an explanation for that. The amateurs had played in several tournaments recently while some of the pros had not been in competition for months. And one ironic footnote: that same weekend, for finishing second in the Los Angeles Open, Harold Henning was winning R.8,000—almost as much as he could have won had he played in every South African and Rhodesian tournament and won them all.

Natal Open—R.2,500
Winner: Bobby Cole

No matter where it comes, a man's first professional tournament win is something to remember. Never mind how it's won, or what the challengers failed to do. That first victory means a lot. The Natal Open, in truth, was one of those golf tournaments that nobody wanted to win. Over the final hour or so of play on the Royal Durban course, Bobby Cole, Peter Oosterhuis, Trevor Wilkes, Hugh Inggs and Alan Henning all batted the ball around wildly, like a youngster's croquet game. Cole eventually won with a 282, six under par. Now at the advanced age of 20, it is a measure of his promise that no one was surprised at his victory. Indeed, for the 18 months he has spent as a professional he seemed a long time without a win. He has so much talent and hits the ball so far and with such accuracy—on his good days—that there is no knowing what he will achieve before he finishes with the game. Whatever it is, he will never forget the 1969 Natal Open.

Professional golf takes a good deal of learning, and Cole is still doing just that. He shot a progressively impressive tournament—72, 71, 70, 69—yet the course maintained its record that no tournament has been won there with a score under 280. The Royal Durban is laid out on the infield of the Durban racecourse. It looks easy but is deceptively subtle. On the first nine, out of bounds onto the racecourse is a hazard on six or seven holes. The rough is quite intimidating—a shot in the wrong place means a stroke lost. But the greens were true and despite the hot weather and the usual Durban humidity, good scoring was possible for the man who could keep the ball in play.

Hugh Inggs did just that for 75% of the tournament, tearing off three successive 69s. He, Trevor Wilkes and Alan Henning led after 18 holes, with Peter Oosterhuis one behind at 70. Oosterhuis is the boy who played in the 1967 Walker Cup match for Britain while still a schoolboy at Dulwich College wrestling with exams and barely 18. He follows a British line that includes Jimmy Bruen, John Langley, Peter Townsend and now Michael King of teenaged Walker Cup players. Dubbed "Easter Egg" by his amateur compatriots, he played in the Eisenhower Trophy match in 1968 for the British when they lost by one shot to the Americans in Australia. Later that same year, having decided there was nowhere else to go as an amateur, he turned professional and his venture in South Africa signalled his first public appearance as such. Peter stands 6ft. 4ins., has something of a weight problem, and a huge, sunny water-melon smile. He is a pleasant, attractive, happy personality. But with all this there is a calculating mind that knows where Oosterhuis is going. For example, he keeps a running stroke analysis of his game and can relate his average to tournaments, weeks, months, etc., at the drop of a peaked cap. Like Cole, Oosterhuis was sure to win a pro tournament before too long. In fact, it almost happened right there in Durban.

The second round was a little uneven. Inggs, who to that point had been second 11 times in major tournaments over six years as a professional, played less well but putted soundly to repeat his 69 and take a two-shot lead over Terry Westbrook from Zambia, who had a 67, the low round of the day. The third round was all flurry. Inggs repeated yet again, Brian Henning produced a course record 66, Franklin and Oosterhuis were 67, Trevor Wilkes 68. So as they set off on the final round, Inggs was 207, Wilkes 210 and Cole, Oosterhuis and Westbrook 213.

But that picture changed quickly. Brian Henning made nine on the first hole and Terry Westbrook lost six shots over the first six holes. So they were out of it. Oosterhuis made the turn in 32, three under par, with Cole 33 and Wilkes and Inggs at par 35. It was still anyone's game. Then Inggs made six at the 11th, a short par four, and Wilkes wilted, dropping three shots over the final five holes. Oosterhuis, playing ahead of the leaders, got through 16 holes five under par—and had hit only three fairways from the tee! His was a definitive exhibition of how to make birdies from the rough. He said, "The way I was driving I had no idea where it was going. It caught up with me in the end." At 17, a difficult par four, Peter drove into a trap and made five. At 18, a par five, he needed to hook his drive a little more than he did. The ball broke back into a bunker. From there he tried to play just short of some cross-bunkers and left himself a good 2-iron short of the stick. With that one, he missed the green on the right. A bad chip shot squirted clear over the green onto a concrete path. From there he only just got it on the green and had to settle for a double bogey and a 70. Yet Oosterhuis still managed to walk off the green smiling, an act that endeared him as much to the South Africans as any golf shot he hit during his African trip.

As he stood on the 72nd tee, Oosterhuis thought three men could beat him. As he left the green, he thought the same, and he was even more convinced when Cole birdied 17. Bobby managed to make six on the closing hole, but he still had a winning stroke to spare. By that time, all Oosterhuis could say was "stupid, stupid". Thus it was Cole's week, for the first time, and also a week for the young men. There was another youngster prominent in this tournament, by the way, and I think we had better get the name down right now—Dale Hayes, 16, amateur, who scored 74, 70, 72, 71 for a 287 and sixth place.

Dunlop Masters—R.3,500
Winner: Bobby Cole

Anything a man can do once, he can do twice. At least Bobby Cole must think so, for at Mowbray, Cape Town, there he was again. Mowbray is a big course, par 74, and represents a good test of golf. There were three days of overcast weather with little wind, then a near-gale on the final day. The golfers responded with at least one low, exciting round each day, a new leader or challenger each day, and at the end of it all, a victory for Cole that he could say he really won with a superb final round of golf. After his breakthrough at Durban, Cole was actually favored for the Masters, but his opening 69, or rather his first-round putting, was uneven. He holed his share on the front nine, where he went five under par and seemed set for a very low round, but lost it with the putter on the way back and settled for 69. Barry Franklin made the headlines. His 65 broke an existing Gary Player course record by four shots and gave him a four shot lead on Cole. He required only 12 putts on the front nine and 26 in all, and he played the opening nine in seven under par. Franklin used a set of clubs that came close to being junked the previous August. He came to the end of his affair with them just before the German Open then, but gave them one last chance before switching. You guessed it—he went out and won the German Open with his last-chance clubs, and was still swinging them half-a-year later at Mowbray.

After the second day, Cole looked as though he had recovered from the Durban win. His 68 made up six shots on Franklin, who was no better than even par and carefully tucked behind Cole, 137 to 139. Bobby gave his friends something to ponder with a three-putt green at the first, but he birdied the second and third and was off and running. Meanwhile, Trevor Wilkes, with a 68 second round, improved his first by eight shots. In the third round Wilkes shot a 66. This, coupled with the fact that Cole dropped three shots on the three final holes for a 73, saw them tied at 210. Cole was so annoyed with himself he stormed straight from the final green to the parking lot and swept off before even getting out of his spikes. The newspapers made a big thing of that, but Cole later explained that it was the Oosterhuis car, and "Peter always drives in a cloud of dust". (Oosterhuis proved this later in the year, again with Cole as his passenger, when he had an accident outside of the Lytham club, scene of the British Open. As Cole said, "A tree jumped out in front of us.") Meanwhile, back at the club, Wilkes was describing his front nine (31, six under par, 11 putts) as "the best nine holes I've ever played." He had reason to feel pleased. After the first round, he had been 11 shots off the pace. Now here he was, 48 hours later, tied with Bobby Cole for the lead.

The weather forecast for the final day was for high wind, and with Bob Tuohy two shots behind and Franklin and Oosterhuis one more back at 213, a mauling finish was in prospect. Cole lost a shot on the first hole of the final round, a rather short dog-leg par four that had troubled him all the week. But so too did Wilkes, who went from bad to worse as Cole went from bad to very much better. Bobby eagled two (491 yards) with a drive, 8-iron and 12-foot putt, then birdied five and six. At that moment, Cole had the tournament won. All he had to do was keep it that way. He had two three-putt greens, but the fact that even in this wind he could hit all the par fives in two gave him a tremendous edge. Wilkes was out in 40 and died at the 12th with a seven, including three whacks at his ball under a bush. Cole's final spectacular offering was a 60ft. birdie putt at the 17th and his fine round of 70, played through, or rather under, a hard north-easterly gale, gave him a 280, 16 under par. He said, "I was nervous as I could be. This was much more difficult than the Natal Open. I didn't know how all the other people were doing." Cole's 280 equalled Gary Player's four-round record for the course—perhaps an item of significance for both of them in the future.

Western Province Open—R.3,500
Winner: Cobie Legrange

In the first round of the Western Province Open, over the Royal Cape course, Brian Barnes scored 62. He didn't make a putt of much more than 15 feet. He drove the 11th green (333 yards) and three-putted, and on 18, his birdie putt from about 18 feet went right into the hole and came out again. But he shot 62—and, by the way, did not win the tournament. It was a staggering round of golf. Most of the players could not see how it was possible. On the par 71 course, they could see a man have a good day and make 68, or maybe a man have a specially good day and make 66 or maybe 65. But 62? Said Barnes, "I didn't make the cut at Mowbray last week. Shows what a bit of practice will do!"

Royal Cape was not in its best condition. Always prone to water shortages—all South Africa had suffered yet another drought—Royal Cape had rough as light as could be and fairways patchier than you could imagine. There were fairway areas marked as ground under repair so big that a man would have to cross the whole fairway to get relief. Cedric Amm, at a time when he was debating his entire future in tournament golf, put together a 65 and Cobie Legrange was 68, but for all that, Barnes' 62 was a wonderful round of golf. On the second day, however, Brian rejoined the human race, made 75 and didn't really have his game together for the rest of the tournament.

Cobie Legrange had no problems with his game. A second 68 put him at 136 and a shot ahead of Barnes and Amm. But the big news of round two was the withdrawal of Gary Player. He had come down to the Cape for his first appearance of the season after six straight weeks on his farm in Northern Transvaal, where I don't suppose he hit many golf shots. After a first-round 71, which was none too

distinguished by his standards, Player hurt his wrist at the second
hole of the second round while swinging a 2-iron at a difficult lie. By
the turn, when he withdrew, he was virtually playing one-handed,
and he hurried off to his Johannesburg home to treat the ailing wrist
with an old but proven Player remedy—plunging his hand alternately
into bowls of hot and ice-cold water. He thought he may have
strained the wrist putting in fence poles on his farm. He probably
did—the world's most expensive fence poles.

Cobie's third round 65, virtually flawless, also virtually closed out
the tournament. It left him at 201, four ahead of Brian Barnes, and
allowed him the luxury of a final 71 as he finished three strokes
better than the second man, Peter Oosterhuis. The "Big O"
highlighted the third round with a 64, even though he hit only four
fairways in the first 14 holes. This was the one tournament on the
circuit that Cobie Legrange played consistently well. He had been
having the yips with his putter most of the other events, but on his
own ground, he proved a tremendous competitor.

General Motors Open—R.4,180
Winner: Graham Henning

At the Wedgwood Country Club, in Port Elizabeth, Graham
Henning led from start to finish, to the general pleasure of almost
everyone. It was his first major tournament win anywhere, and it was
all the more rewarding for the fact that although he was chased and
under pressure almost all the way, he was able to hold off the field
and win by two strokes. Residents of Port Elizabeth say they live in
the second windiest city in the world. Ask them what is the windiest,
and they say, "It blew away". It is a lame story, but it is also a very
windy city, the kind of place where Bobby Cole, who still hits an
occasional shot off line, can—and did—make a 9 on a par five hole
with ease. Gary Player tasted the wind, too, and he was not yet back
to his old, familiar, unrelenting game. He finished fourth, six strokes
behind Henning, and at one point was putting with his left hand
below his right. Wedgwood and the wind made a difficult
combination. The start was two long par fours into the wind, then a
par five downwind that was reachable. So one could easily start 444
or 555, a swing of three shots that could make or break a round
before a man had hardly begun his day's work.

The tournament was probably most memorable for two

contrasting happenings, one happy, one less so. First, Denis Hutchinson made a hole in one at the par-3 sixth. Denis is a fellow who has graced the African circuits for several seasons. He has won friends everywhere, but has not won too much else, and has often been close to quitting. As his ball was bouncing toward the hole his playing partner, Clive Clark, heard Denis mumbling, "Go on. Get in. Please get in!" It did, and Denis broke into a Zulu dance, for with the shot came a Chevrolet worth R.5000 (more than the tournament purse), which Denis promptly sold for full price. With that money he bought a share of the professional's shop at Kensington, one of Johannesburg's busiest clubs. It was an investment that should make his tour life easier.

Wedgwood was also the scene of a difficulty with some of the young British pros. The background to this sorry saga is the fact that South Africans are among the most hospitable people in the world. Many young British professionals, escaping from the English winter and having a tentative swing at the South African circuit, can testify to this, for they often receive free accommodation and meals in the private homes of club members, the use of cars, and so on. I suspect that some of them must have gone back home, told their buddies how wonderful it all was, and said, in effect, "You can do the tour for a hundred quid." Some of the buddies, alas, believed them. There is a story of one youngster going out by ship—the cheapest way—selling his clubs, then borrowing another set and bumming his way from tournament to tournament. At Port Elizabeth the situation came to a head when some young players registered at the club and then asked where the cars and accommodation were. Tubby Zaachs, directing the event for General Motors, complained to the PGA captain, who in turn called in George Will, the senior British pro on hand. Will had never heard of some of the young players. Brian Barnes had never heard of them, and still worse, Gerald Micklem, captain of the R. and A., who was having a short holiday in South Africa, had never heard of them either. There was a spate of publicity, which of course found its way back to Britain, and Will made a report to his own PGA when he returned. For lack of very direct evidence, not much could be done, but the British PGA has instituted a system of clearance for its members going to future South African circuits. There is some doubt that all of the offending youngsters were in fact members of the British PGA. It was too bad that this should happen at a time when other British players, such as Will, Barnes, Oosterhuis and Bernard Gallacher were making a colorful and most welcome international addition to the South African tour.

South African Open—R.9,997
Winner: Gary Player

The whole point of the 1969 South African Open was Gary Player. Could he survive the pressure, not only from the others in the field, but from the fact that his own game had not been at its best up to the date of the championship? Could he really tie that extraordinary Bobby Locke record of five successive Open wins? Could he hold off Bobby Cole, who was itching to inherit Gary's crown? And above all could he survive the enormous public pressure that was inclined to demand that he win? He could and he did, setting a course record and tying the Open record. The win was not without travail—one man was seen leaving a Gary Player gallery during the week muttering, "I can't stand watching that man—I have enough worries at my business without coming out here to watch him worrying!" But I think this South African win was one of Gary's meaningful achievements. It is difficult to describe the pressures on Player in his own country. He is so much of an idol that I sometimes wonder how he can stand the strains. Certainly he slaved at the Durban Country Club to get into shape for the championship, not only before it but during the week of play. He spent every possible moment between rounds working on his game.

After an opening 67, the work proved very necessary as the field pounded hard after Player. Denis Hutchinson equalled the course record with an eight-under-par 66 in the second round, in which he passed Gary to lead the field after 36 holes. But in so doing Hutchinson strained a muscle in his back. The pain worsened during the night, and Denis probably never should have started the third round. When he joined his playing partner, Player, on the first tee, he could barely move the club. He made 7 on the first hole and had to quit, seeking out a good club player in the gallery and passing over his clubs, caddie and shoes to him to carry on and mark the score for Player. In stockinged feet, Hutchinson tramped gingerly back to the clubhouse for treatment.

The Durban Country Club's course demands very correct and bold striking and anything like a mishit is costly. To compound the challenge of the course, there was a complete gamut of weather. On the first day, the first hole was into the wind, on the second it was downwind. On the third the wind blew every which way, and on the closing day, early rain gave way to a fair, calm afternoon. Gary led after the first round with his 67. Hutchinson (70, 66) led after the second round and Player (67, 70, 72) after the third, by one stroke over Trevor Wilkes. But Gary almost didn't make the fourth round. When he reached the club, after an hour's fishing in the morning with his children, his neck had stiffened and he went through the now-familiar-hot-and-cold shower routine, gulped seven aspirins and had his neck massaged. He then went out and played a round that had me recalling nothing less than Arnold Palmer's closing 65 in the U.S. Open of 1960. Gary scored 64 to win the South African Open by six shots and tie his own Open record of 273. It was the opening four holes, the killer holes, that crushed the rest of the field and proclaimed beyond the slightest doubt that the party was over. At the first hole, Player hit a fair drive, then a poorish second that finished off the left side of the green, on the fringe. Gary decided he could putt it, and he holed it—a 40 footer. At the second, a par 3, he made par. At the third, he hit two huge wood shots and then holed a long eagle putt. At the fourth, he punched an iron shot five feet from the flag for another birdie, and the Open was closed. That was birdie, par, eagle, birdie. His partner Trevor Wilkes, who finished with a 69, said, "I felt I was hacking it around, compared to Gary." Player had been totally determined to win this one and went on record afterwards by saying he knew he would win after a practice session on Friday evening when he straightened out a final problem he had been having with his irons. Any challenge from Bobby Cole did not materialize. He played well, but not much better than well, although midway through the third round he was hauling Gary back within reach. Then he dropped a stroke at each of five successive holes. So once again it was Gary's Open all the way. It was, incidentally, a much better championship in every respect than in previous years. The 1968 complaint of "too many amateurs" did not apply. This time, in a sense, there were too many pros, or at least too many who were not good enough to be involved in this kind of championship. One of them shot 80, 90. Such is the improvement in South African scoring, as Gary noted at the presentation, that the winning scores when he first played the Open are now no better than the qualifying scores.

PGA Championship—R.6,000
Winner: Gary Player

After the tensions and pressures of the South African Open, the PGA Championship at Germiston Golf Club, near Johannesburg, was stimulating sport, almost a county fair. It began in September, 1968 when Denis Hutchinson suggested to Brenda Blumberg that multi-sponsorship might be worth a try. The blessing of the PGA was quickly obtained, and by January every hole was sold, including the 19th. The sponsor list included Gordon's Gin, Champion Spark Plugs, Coca-Cola, American Express, South African Airways, Lexington cigarettes and, you can be sure, Ysebrand and Co., owned by George Blumberg. Each sponsor decorated his hole. One sponsor actually dyed his green green. There were prizes of appropriate products for birdies, eagles and holes-in-one—liquor, socks, a motor cycle, a car. The weather was perfect and the crowds enormous by South African standards, with as many as 4,000 in the galleries. It was, in short, a swinging event and the players rose to it with some sterling golf and a thrilling final day.

Gary Player and Bobby Cole led off the first day tied at the top with 67s, and they would have been that way again after two rounds, but for a ruling against Cole that was odd, to put it mildly. At the ninth hole, Cole hit a long wayward drive. The ball came to rest sandwiched tightly between a tree and a refreshment tent. The rules committee had classified the tent as a movable obstruction. Cole's best move seemed to be calling the ball unplayable and going back to the tee. Or, had he been more mature, he might have invited the rules committee to move its "movable obstruction". Indeed, he should have received a free drop. Cole ended up trying to play out backwards. He needed two shots to regain the fairway, and scored six on the par-4 hole. Meanwhile, Brian Barnes was in with his second straight 68, and Trevor Wilkes had a 66 to move into contention. Player and Wilkes were paired in the third round, and battled it out hole by hole. Wilkes racked up six birdies and an eagle in a round of 64 and Player had to make a 20-foot birdie putt on the last green for a 68 to tie Wilkes at 201. Barnes scored his third straight 68 and was three shots behind at 204, with Cole one behind him.

The final round was nothing short of feverish. At the turn, Player was 36, Cole 34 and Wilkes had the tournament lead thanks to a 50-foot putt on nine for a one under par 35. And Cobie Legrange

was now in the picture with a 33. A six at the par-4 12th staggered
Wilkes. Cole birdied 11, bogeyed 13, birdied 14—typical Cole form.
Player bogeyed 14, and at that point Player, Cole, Wilkes and
Legrange were even for the tournament. When Wilkes bogeyed 17, he
and Legrange finished with 273s. So it was all up to Player and Cole,
a classic duel for South African golf today. Player birdied 16 with a
bad drive, an even worse second, an approach putt from off the
green and a second putt from 20 feet on the 510-yard hole. But Cole
got the stroke back at 17 when he sank an eight-footer for a birdie.
The final hole is a par 3 of 205 yards. Cole, who had been hitting a
6-iron there all week, this time decided he was all muscle and took a
7-iron. He left it 65 feet short of the stick, and five yards short of the
green, which is just what he deserved. He then chipped short and
missed his putt. Player, 15 feet from the hole with his tee shot, had
to ask the crowd how many he needed to win. They told him "two",
and he took them for a 71, and a 12-under-par 272.

The championship was a welcome financial success. The PGA was
enriched by some R.5,000, a surplus unprecedented in South African
golf and one which should save the PGA Championship for the next
few years. Player had personally sustained the event with donations
in the past, but there was no tournament at all in 1968. Now 1969
has underwritten the future. That, plus the Player-Cole battle, made
an apt conclusion to a good South African season.

And in Rhodesia . . . .

Bobby Cole was off to Miami, and Gary Player was turning his
thoughts westward, but many of the South Africa tour's regulars
moved on as usual for the three tournaments in Rhodesia, and the
results for some were gratifying. Trevor Wilkes, for example, had to
be enthused about his 1,000-mile safari to the Tomango Flame Lily
Tournament at Bulowayo. Wilkes is now substantially a club pro in
South Africa who makes his only tournament appearances "at
home" as it were, but he rounded out his best season for many a year
by romping off with the first of the northern events, beating Cobie
Legrange by six strokes. Wilkes was a first-round front runner,
leading the field at 68, along with Bernard Gallacher from Scotland.
Legrange overtook him in the second, and stayed ahead after three,
but Wilkes came up with a remarkable last round 66 that equalled
the course record, flattened Cobie, and made up eight shots for the

victory. Wilkes had reason to be particularly proud, for not only did he pocket I/650, he mastered a course that goes 7,055 yards and has slow and very nappy greens. Gallacher was another young man very pleased he came. A third place at Bulwayo and a sixth in Salisbury at the Dunlop brought him I/420, or just over $1,000. In Rhodesia, that buys a lot more bread than it will in London or Los Angeles.

The next stop was the country town of Gwelo for the "Bush Babes" event, and this time it was a five stroke win by Tienie Britz, with Hugh Inggs second. No one in Gwelo is going to be distressed if I say their course is not the best in Africa. It features quite a few short par-4s, and none of the par-3s are staggering. Yet it reaches more than 6800 yards, with a par of 71, which made Britz, with all four rounds in the sixties and 11 under par at the end, a deserving winner. In fact, Britz contrived to squander three shots on the 72nd hole and still bring in a 68, and he dominated the tournament from start to finish. Only the Australian Bob Tuohy stayed within reach of him for the first two rounds.

Royal Salisbury Golf Club, the site of the Dunlop tournament, is a very good golf course. It was in excellent condition for the closing event of the tour, and it produced a good tournament. Hugh Inggs and Terry Westbrook opened with 68s, three under par on the 6,723-yard course. Cobie Legrange came through with a course-record 64 in the second round, but it was Graham Henning with 69—66 who had the lead, two ahead of Cobie and three up on Inggs. Only Bobby Verwey was under par in the third round, and they went into the final 18 with a three-way tie—Inggs, Henning and Legrange. It all came down to the 18th, where Inggs prevailed. His 68 for 278 beat Henning by a stroke and Legrange by two. It was Inggs' best showing in a long time, and as was the case in South Africa, the season in Rhodesia closed on an upbeat note.

9

The Far East Tour

No matter where you looked, the Japanese were flying high

Of course, nobody knew it at the time, but the Philippine Open—the oldest, richest and, in the last few years, the most controversial tournament on the circuit—set the trend for the season it was launching in the Far East in 1969. Through its 53-year history, the Philippine Open had been won by Filipinos, Australians, Americans, Chinese. Never, however, by a Japanese golfer. The game of golf came rather late to Japan, an overcrowded empire with little land to spare for golf courses. It began to flourish in the occupation era following World War II and its popularity received great impetus in 1957 when the International Golf Association selected Tokyo as the site for its fifth World Cup (then Canada Cup) Matches.

A defeated people in war thirsting for a place of respectability again in the world of nations drew pride from two men who, until then, were unknown in international circles of golf. Torakichi (Pete) Nakamura and Koichi Ono were selected to represent Japan against the likes of Sam Snead, Jimmy Demaret, Peter Thomson, Gary Player, Peter Alliss and other recognized stars of the game in countries where golf was long established. To the astonishment of the golfing cognoscenti, the two Japanese pros took the play away from all of their more illustrious opponents. Nakamura finished seven strokes in front of Player, Snead and Britain's Dave Thomas in the competition for the individual International Trophy and teamed with Ono to capture the Canada Cup, a convincing nine shots ahead of Snead and Demaret for the United States. The two became instant heroes in Japan and, in the wake of that victory, courses sprang up, many on hillsides where land was more available, and driving ranges, including double and triple-deckers, and miniature courses were squeezed into the more populous areas. Golf had really caught on in Japan. This, in turn, produced a growing group of able professional golfers. The creation in 1962 of the Far East circuit, of which the new Yomiuri Open at the course of the same name near Tokyo became a part, gave them opportunities to show their talents internationally on a much wider scale than the World Cup format permitted.

As was the case with the pros from the other Asian nations, the Japanese played second fiddle to the more experienced Australian and British golfers in the early years. But these seasoned visitors, marveling at the precision short games of the Asian players, knew it wouldn't be long before their monopoly would be broken. A veteran, Tomoo Ishii, scored the breakthrough for Japan in 1964 in the Malaysian Open and at least one member of the big traveling teams from that country picked up a title during the next four seasons. But, during that period, the Chinese players from Formosa were doing better, as Chen Ching Po, Hsieh Yung Yo and Lu Liang Huan became known in world golf circles.

The year 1969, though, was Japan's on the Far East circuit, and Haruo Yasuda got it all started at famous old Wack Wack at Mandaluyong in the Philippines, where he made up a four-stroke deficit on native son Eleuterio Nival in the final round and gave Japan its first Philippine Open championship with a playoff victory.

Tomio Kamata, a lesser-known member of Nippon's 33-man contingent, scored the following week in the Singapore Open in even more difficult fashion, outlasting Australia's David Graham and the much-traveled Briton, Guy Wolstenholme, who now has an Australian address, in a three-hole, sudden death playoff after their 72-hole tie. Takaaki Kono, later to team with Yasuda as Japan's entry in the World Cup Matches, made it a triple for the exuberant Japanese at Kuala Lumpur with an Arnold Palmer finish, coming from six strokes off the lead after 54 holes to win the Malaysian Open by a shot.

The national monopoly ended the fourth week when China's Hsieh Yung Yo, whose circuit record since 1963 qualifies him as the Orient's best player, ran away with the Thailand Open, scoring an eight-stroke victory. Teruo Sugihara broke the brief Japanese win drought in the Hong Kong Open and husky Hideyo Sugimoto, who has been all over the world with his clubs, displaying power unlike most of his smaller countrymen but with little title success outside his country, followed with a victory in the China (Formosa) Open in yet another playoff and first-time victory for a Japanese. The only real disappointment for the Japanese came when, after completing the six long weeks on the road, they yielded their home tournament to Wolstenholme at Yomiuri.

The consistent Yung Yo again was the season's top performer. For the fourth time in six years he collected the $2,000 award for amassing the most points in a system based on position of finish in the seven events. In the last two seasons, the slender Formosan has won three times and finished in the top 10 in 10 of the 14 tournaments. And he has proved his mettle in international circles, too. At Rome and Singapore, he and two different playing partners, Lu Liang Huan in 1968 and Hsu Chi San in 1969, made strong runs at the World Cup team title. They led or were tied for first after 54 holes both years, only to falter each time to finish fourth in Italy and fifth at Singapore. Yung Yo placed third individually in 1969, just two strokes behind winner Lee Trevino.

It seemed an injustice that, under a rather odd qualifying system, Yung Yo did not represent the Far East in the big-money Alcan Golfer of the Year tournament at Portland, Oregon. Aussie Graham did, simply because he happened to play his best golf in three of the four circuit events selected by Alcan officials to determine the single qualifier. Don't get me wrong. David is one of the most promising of the young Australian pros, but his overall record on the 1969 Far East circuit did not approach that of the Formosa veteran.

The aforementioned World Cup meeting, which took the Far East tour competitors back to Singapore Island Country Club's Bukit course for a second time in 1969, brought out several unrelated evidences of the state and nature of world professional golf today. The United States team of Trevino and Orville Moody, the last two winners of the world's biggest championship, the U.S. Open, prevailed in both phases of the competition, but not easily. Conclusions? The United States remains by far the deepest in top-level ability among the golfing nations. Again, I have no intention of demeaning the talents of particular players—I have great respect for any golfer who wins a major championship as Trevino and Moody have done—but they would hardly argue that they are the two best players in America.

The frequently-changing system of the International Golf Association for selection of the U.S. team called for the U.S. Open and PGA champions to play in this year's matches. Thus, Moody gained one spot and accepted the invitation. Of course, Trevino did not win the PGA. Ray Floyd did, was invited—and declined. He was previously committed to participate in the CBS Match Play Classic, a competition filmed for U.S. television that is a lucrative source of income for the participants. When Gary Player, Bob Charles and Tony Jacklin also excused themselves from playing at Singapore, which has equatorial weather and lies halfway around the world from England, where all four were pledged to play in the Piccadilly World Match Play Championship the following week, I came in for some published criticism. The implications were that, as business manager for these four players, I was turning them away from the World Cup, which has only token prize money, to more financially-rewarding events. The facts of the matter were that not only Floyd and Arnold Palmer (who had played in the matches every previous time—seven—he was asked) but also four other Americans not represented by me—Frank Beard, Dave Hill, Gene Littler and George Archer—also declined before Trevino was asked and accepted.

I certainly feel that the World Cup Matches, through their 17 years, have done much for the promotion of international golf—its motto is "Good will through golf"—but, if some of the golfers and their advisors are to be censured for putting money and other playing commitments before country, I think there is a perspective that must also be considered. As one highly respected golf executive pointed out to me recently, the IGA is not without its commercial overtones. Some of our biggest corporations and their executives comprise the board of directors and sponsors of the World Cup. This is fine, yet the IGA is not simply a body, like the USGA or the R. & A., that is amateur and independent in operation and spirit and would seem to have a right to appeal to the patriotism of the players to participate in such an international event.

But, to get away from who wasn't in Singapore and why they weren't and back to the results, it should be further noted that the Chinese team was not alone in demonstrating the increasing strength of professional golf in Asia. While neither Yasuda nor Kono made a serious bid for the International Trophy, they capped Japan's big year by finishing second to the Americans with final-round scores of 67 (Kono) and 69 (Yasuda), and placed seventh and eighth individually. This was almost overshadowed by the totally unexpected showings of the Thailand team, particularly its "Toy Tiger", 26-year-old Sukree Onsham. The little pro and his 22-year-old fellow assistant at Royal Bangkok Sports Club, Suchin Suvannapongse, placed fourth for the country, where two factions only settled a squabble and submitted the country's entry two days before the deadline. Onsham himself put up such a spirited battle against Trevino, Moody and runnerup Roberto de Vicenzo that, after Sukree's bogey on the last hole dropped him into a third-place tie, Orville and Lee lifted the 114-pounder and carried him from the final green in a gesture of admiration for his gutty performance. In a further reflection on the calibre of play of the Asian teams, it should be noted that the Japanese (second), Thais and Chinese (fourth) and Filipinos (sixth) all finished ahead of the teams representing the countries whose golfers used to win the Far East titles—Australia, England, Scotland, Wales, Ireland and South Africa.

A final indication of the expanding state of tournament golf in the Far East was the announcement by the Asia Golf Confederation during the year that the tour was adding the Indian Open and the Korean Open to its 1970 itinerary and would henceforth be called the Asia Golf Circuit. The pros will have an uninterrupted stretch of nine tournaments from February to April and, in 1970, the prize money was to be more than $170,000, not as much as is offered at a few individual U.S. tournaments but still a record amount for the young and ambitious circuit.

Administrative serenity returned to the Philippines Open in 1969 as a new board of directors at Wack Wack reversed a prize-money policy that was, in a word, wacky, and welcomed back the tournament players after the event's one-year stand at Holiday Hills in San Pedro. It was moved there in 1968 by the Philippine Golf Association in sympathy with the pros' protests when, in contrast to normal practices around the world, Wack Wack officials then in charge kept the first prize money in 1966 and 1967 after amateurs won the tournament rather than pass it on to veteran pro Celestino Tugot, the runnerup both years. Obviously, a majority of the Wack Wack members felt the national championship belonged at their club, which had hosted the Philippine Open since 1935, and turned out the "rascals" who had driven it away. They brought the purse back up to $35,000, the biggest on the circuit, and gave up efforts to attract "name" pros from the United States. "The rest of the pros just ran over them anyway," said Wack Wack President Juan J. Carlos, explaining why his organizing committee abandoned past practices of flying in a couple of American stars for the event.

By the end of the first round, Peter Townsend, the young Britisher who was playing in the tournament for the first time, had an explanation why the Yanks had not challenged. Peter had spent five hours under a wilting sun in the throes of a slow-moving, 186-player field in shooting 71 and observed rather tartly: "Now I know why Billy Casper and Gene Littler never did well here. Five hours in that heat is a bit too much. It saps your energy and spoils your concentration." Townsend had waited "half an hour" on the 16th tee and took a triple-bogey six on the 203-yard hole, spoiling a promising start.

Instead, the first day belonged to men well accustomed to the heat of the Philippines—Eleuterio (Caloy) Nival, generally considered the third-ranking playing pro in the country, and Kim Seung Hack, a 22-year-old from Seoul Country Club in South Korea, who had been a pro just nine months at the time. The two were the leaders with four-under-par 68s, as hard-baked Wack Wack, untouched by rain for four months, yeilded an unusual total of 13 sub-par rounds. Tee shots that rolled and rolled shortened Wack Wack's 7,014-yard East course considerably. Townsend and Japan's Sugimoto nearly drove several of the par fours during the tournament.

Lu Liang Huan, the seasoned Chinese star who won the 1965 Philippine Open, had a good shot at the first-round lead. He was five under after holding from a trap for a birdie at the 16th, but bogeyed the last two holes for 69. Four others shot 70, among them Filipino Vic Allin, whose playing career seemed over two years ago when he shattered a leg and pelvic bone in a jeep accident. He still has a limp. The defending champion, Hsu Chi San, virtually shot himself out that first day with a 76 and the eventual winner didn't fare much better. Yasuda was nowhere in sight of the contenders at 74, with 32 players ahead of him.

Nival, the 30-year-old pro at Manila's Muni course, had won three tournaments on the Philippines' own circuit shortly before the Open and his strong start—five birdies, a bogey—was not as surprising as that of Kim, who was holing putts from everywhere, five times from beyond 15 feet. With neither Ben Arda, the country's best known pro in international circles, nor the 53-year-old Tugot, a six-time winner of the tournament, mounting a contending game, the fans began to think of Nival as the seventh Filipino to become Philippine Open champion when he moved into a two-stroke lead in Friday's round.

The stocky, five foot five inch pro, out in 33, worked hard coming in with superb chipping and putting and some softly-muttered prayers between shots—"My God, don't let me fall off now," he was overheard saying once—to score 71 and stand atop an Open field for the first time in his career. Kim stayed close with a 73, but his inexperience began to betray him during the round, when, after driving into the woods, he took three shots getting out and wound up with a triple bogey 8. Japan's Kenji Hosoishi, a standout on the 1968 circuit, birdied three of the last four holes to tie Kim at

141 and Yasuda made his big move with the day's low round—68—to join young Filipino Dick Villalon, Formosa's Chang Chung Fa and the dangerous Hsieh Yung Yo at 142. The spark that headed Yasuda toward the yet-distant title came when he holed a 40-yard wedge shot for an eagle at the 311-yard second hole and followed with a 10-foot eagle putt at the 582-yard fifth.

Nival almost made a runaway of the tournament in the third round. Despite strong winds and some hunger pangs, Caloy moved four shots in front with another 71. He had worked off the heavy meal wife Marcela had fed him before he left for "the office" by the time he took bogeys at the troublesome 16th, after the usual long wait on the tee, and the 18th. Still, at 210, he had the biggest 54-hole margin within memory in the Open and a shot at the Open record of 281 at Wack Wack, posted by 13-time winner Larry Montes in 1953. His only apparent competitors at that point were the four men at 214—Yasuda (72), Lu (70), Chung Fa (72) and Villalon (72)—and Australia's Frank Phillips, the 1960 champion, who reached 215 with a 68.

The week's only sour note dropped Yung Yo from contention. On a protest from playing partner Arda, who directed the woman scorer with the group to keep time, Yung Yo was assessed a two-stroke penalty for waiting too long after his putt hung on the lip at the 12th green. The angry Chinese star said he consumed one minute, the marker's timing was three minutes and the rule permits only "a few seconds". The penalty gave him a 76 and put him at 218.

Nival seemed to have his game and the field in tow until late in the final round when Yasuda, a broad-shouldered, 26-year-old pro from Tokyo's Mutumi Golf Club, turned it into a tense two-man battle when he birdied the 13th, 14th and 15th to close within a stroke. The duel stayed that way to the 18th green, where, as Haruo was parring for 69, Caloy chipped poorly six feet past the cup and left his putt for 72 and victory short of the hole. Some 3,000 partisans groaned.

Yasuda, the winner of the rich Chunichi Crowns tournament in Japan in 1968 after blowing a circuit title earlier that year in the Thailand Open, made certain it didn't happen again. The Nipponese pro, whose travels are financed by a pearl dealer and a printing firm in Tokyo, stuck an 8-iron approach on the 379-yard 15th (the first playoff hole for TV purposes) just five feet from the cup and, after Nival missed from 25 feet, rapped in the birdie putt. The disappointed Nival admitted the $5,000 runnerup prize would still serve an excellent purpose—paying off his new home in nearby Las Pinas. Although he was to make only one other strong bid on the 1969 circuit, Yasuda virtually ensured that he would be the season's leading money-winner with the $10,000 first prize. None of the other tournaments pays more than $2,475 to its champion.

Far down in the final standings at Wack Wack, 15 strokes behind Yasuda, was Tomio Kamata. It was not an unusual position for the 27-year-old Japanese player, who was still trying to apply what he had been learning about the game from his teacher, Pete Nakamura. His best tournament finish had been a 10th in the Japan Open. But Tomio put it all together when the circuit moved to Singapore and the Bukit course at Singapore Island Country Club, where the idea for the Far East tour first germinated.

It was Tomoo, rather than Tomio, who carried the ball for his country the first day. Tomoo Ishii, a regular on the circuit since his history-making win for Japan at Kuala Lumpur in 1964, fashioned a 68 from five birdies and a pair of bogeys for a tenuous one-stroke lead. The 45-year-old pro from Nakayama Country Club, a three-time champion on the circuit, led Australians Alan Murray and Ted Ball as well as Shigeru Uchida by a stroke. Kamata was bunched with three others at 70, Guy Wolstenholme matched par 71 on the 6,584-yard course and on his way out of the tournament was ailing Australian David Graham.

Flu-ridden and feverish, young Graham was on the verge of withdrawing from the torrid scene when he finished the opening round with 78. But, he decided to stick it out and go out via the 36-hole cut. What happened was another case of "watch-out-for-the-ailing-golfer". The 22-year-old from Sydney proceeded to match the Bukit course record of 62 and vault into a tie for the lead at 140 with three other players who were to be the serious contenders for the title the rest of the way. Kamata had another 70, Wolstenholme and Arda, the 1967 Singapore winner, had 69s to forge the deadlock. Graham played a flawless round—nine birdies and nine pars. He used the putter only 24 times, clustering three birdies in the middle of the front nine to go out in 31, then made birdies at the 13th, 15th, 17th and 18th on the back side.

The jockeying for position continued Saturday. Kamata and Wolstenholme forged a stroke ahead of Graham with 68s for 208 and two in front of Arda and Ball, both of whom were to fade Sunday. In fact, Arda had to hole a 35-yard pitch at the 18th for the 210. One of the few Americans on the circuit was heard from that day.

John Felus, an extremely short man who must have felt at home among the small Oriental players, fired the day's best round, picking up $150 for his 67. It reminded those relatively few of us who knew of him of his first-round moments of glory at the U.S. Open 18 months earlier in Rochester, New York. As at Rochester, John wasn't to attract further attention at Singapore Island.

The three eventual playoff participants carried the battle through the tense final round to the 18th, a 478-yard par-5. Kamata finished two holes ahead of Graham and Wolstenholme with a 70 for 278 and watched with his rooting section, the other Japanese pros, as the pair finished. Graham, only 20 yards short of the green in two, pitched to nine feet but missed the putt that would have given him a 68 and the title. Wolstenholme, knowing he needed a birdie to tie, had put his second shot on the fringe. He chipped beautifully within a foot of the cup and joined the Singapore Open's third playoff in four years. Big Guy was eliminated on the first hole when he took three from the edge while his opponents were two-putting for pars. At the par-3 second, Graham was disturbed by clicking cameras and television equipment as he was preparing to putt from some 60 feet. However, he got down in two and stayed alive when Kamata's birdie putt from 12 feet lipped out. It ended at the third. Tomio flipped aside a cigaret and rolled in an 18-foot birdie putt after David had dropped his approach at the 409-yard hole just nine feet from the pin. His effort from there to match the birdie stopped three inches short. The Japanese contingent seized Kamata and his happy teacher, Nakamura, for a traditional and somewhat risky victory celebration. They were "chaired," in the words of a Singapore golf writer, which doesn't seem to describe it at all. Bud Shrake, on hand to do an article for *Sports Illustrated*, did better. Watching them heave Kamata and Nakamura into the air, he called it a blanket toss without a blanket, a game of mob catch. They survived happily and I guess it isn't too tough with men of their small stature. I'd like to see them try it with George Bayer.

There was more of the same the following Sunday at the end of the Malaysian Open. This time, one of the throwers at Singapore was the aerialist—Takaaki Kono, who had just brought off the most sensational finish of the season. The way the tournament had started, it did not seem likely that the Japanese would make it three in a row with a victory at Royal Selangor. Veteran Australian Frank Phillips, who has played all over the world and won at every stop of the Far East circuit except Thailand and Taiwan, took a lead he was to hold for three rounds when he opened with a five-under-par 67 at the 6,793-yard course in Kuala Lumpur. But, more pertinently, Mya Aye, Burma's first touring pro who had an unsuccessful fling on the U.S. tour in 1968, was the only Asian among the next six contenders.

Graham came off his disappointment at Singapore to equal Aye, Walter Godfrey of New Zealand and host pro Mike Kelly at 68. Big Bob Gajda, an aging American pro who heads for tournament competition somewhere when approaching winter weather closes his club in Michigan, and Peter Thomson, nursing an ailing left wrist, turned in 69s. Gajda, incidentally, is another, like Felus, who enjoyed early headlines in the U.S. Open, Bob as the first-round leader at Brookline in 1963.

Phillips, who set the Royal Selangor course record when he won the first Malaysian Open in 1962, remained a stroke in front Friday with a 71 and 138, but the Japanese moved in. Shigeru Uchida had 69, but Kenji Hosoishi made the big advance. The defending champion fired a six-birdie 66 to join Uchida at 139. John Lister, a 22-year-old New Zealander who suffered the great disappointment later in the year of going to the United States to try to qualify for playing privileges on the American tour only to lose in a playoff at the end of the qualifying competition, also mustered a 66 Friday and joined Graham, Kelly, Wolstenholme and a promising Chinese amateur, Ho Ming Chung, at 140. At that point, Kono was at 142. Graham, apparently a young man easily disturbed, complained without naming names of a bit of harassment from fellow pros during the round about his slow-paced play.

A steady, two-under-par 70 Saturday enabled Phillips to improve his position to a two-stroke lead, but he did not shake off a host of pursuers. Two back of his 208 was Lister and three behind were Graham, Uchida and Ho, trying to duplicate the amateur victory of countryman Hsu Sheng San in the Philippine Open in 1967. Ten other players lay between the top and Kono at 214. The talented Nipponese player apparently was oblivious to the progress he was making through the contenders Sunday as he just concentrated on making birdies and pars, 6 and 12 respectively. He learned he had a chance to win at the 18th green as he wrapped up his 66 and waited as the other contenders tried to catch him.

Phillips, Graham and Phillips were still alive. Frank's hopes died when he double bogeyed the 153-yard 17th and neither Graham nor Lister could get the one more birdie each needed to catch Kono. So, it was his teammates who were "catching" Kono. The overjoyed Japanese ambassador to Malaysia dashed up and doused the new champion with champagne. Takaaki, in turn, borrowed the bottle and emptied it on the head of his caddie, who probably appreciated more the $100 check he received for his efforts.

It figured that if the Japanese domination of the circuit was to be broken, Hsieh Yung Yo would be the man who would do it. He did do it and in a most convincing manner, breaking the 18 and 72-hole tournament records at Bangkok's unique, perfectly flat Royal Thai Air Force course at Don Muang in the Thailand Open. Winner of the first Thailand Open in 1965, Yung Yo jumped in front with 66 in the first round and was never headed nor seriously threatened the rest of the hot week. Poor starts, along with the problem at Wack Wack, had led to mediocre showings for him in the first three events. The 66 opener at Royal Thai so buoyed the slender winner of six previous titles on the circuit that he jauntily suggested to the bearer of his $100 prize for the low first round score that he keep it for a day. "I'll pick up tomorrow's as well with it," he said.

His lead was three over American Bob Unger, unknown in our American tournament circles. Unger promptly faded amid high winds and temperatures and slow play to an 80 Friday and Hsieh was not able to fulfill his promise, although holding his lead. His 71 and 137 kept him two strokes in front of Japan's Kosaku Shimada, with Kono, bidding for two victories in a row, at 140.

Hsieh opened a four-stroke advantage in a third day of sweltering heat with a 70 for 207, getting off to an encouraging start when he drove the green on the easy starting hole and sank a nine-foot eagle putt. He did not do anything else spectacular, but did not have to. Countryman Chi San, with 68—69 after his opening 74, moved into second place and only he and two of the lesser-reputed Japanese—Shimada at 212 and Masayuki Imai at 213—had any chance at all going into the final round. Suvannapongse may have clinched his later selection to the World Cup team that day, shooting a 69 that included seven birdies and was the best ever by a Thai golfer in the tournament.

Yung Yo kept his cool in the heat and wind blowing off the adjacent runways of the busy airfield, and those with chances to challenge him wilted. While Hsieh, taking another stroke off par at the easy first with a birdie, was calmly posting a 70 for his record 277, Hsu was struggling to 74 and Shimada and Imai were fading to 77s. As a picture caption in the *Bangkok Post* put it, Hsieh was "winner by a street". It was China's proudest moment of the season as its pros collected $5,256 of the $12,000 purse and $725 of $900 bonus prize money for individual feats and Ho Ming Chung was low amateur for a third straight week.

In contrast to Hsieh's wire-to-wire victory in Thailand, the lead bounced around wildly at the circuit's fifth stop in Hong Kong. In the end, Teruo Sugihara made up for a disappointing near-miss in the 1968 Hong Kong Open, when he had fallen a stroke short of overtaking winner Randall Vines in a head-to-head finish. The Fanling New Course of Royal Hong Kong Golf Club is located in somewhat hilly terrain of the New Territories of the British Crown Colony on the China mainland and requires transportation by water, rail and motor vehicle to reach it from the Island. Persons heading for Royal Hong Kong leave the train one stop before it reaches the border of Communist China. And, despite its official name, Fanling New Course is some 60 years old. In Peter Thomson's opinion, the Fanling course is a better course "for strikers of the ball" and tends to reduce the great chipping-and-putting talents of the Asian players. Nonetheless, at 6,498 yards, it is the shortest on the circuit and the scoring is usually better in the Honk Kong Open than in the other Far East events. This proved true again in 1969, with the Japanese once more winning, just as Yasuda predicted at the start of the week when he said: "This is Japan's year. We are determined to break the Hong Kong jinx. One of us will win."

A return to British soil seemed to have a good effect on Maurice Bembridge. The 24-year-old pro from Birmingham's Little Aston, who was to enjoy his greatest season later in the year back home, was nowhere in sight in the first four tournaments on the circuit. His 13th position at Singapore was his best as he played the circuit for the first time. But, at Fanling he accumulated an eagle and five birdies en route to a course-record 64, six under regulation, and took a three-stroke lead on the field in the opening round. Japan's Shozo Miyamoto was at 67, but the bulk of the strongest players were bunched near or at par.

Things did not go as well for Bembridge in the second round. He lost two strokes to par on the front nine because of shaky putting, then steadied coming in with a pair of birdies and seven pars for a 70. This retained a two-stroke lead at 134, but the Asians were coming again. Two back were Uchida of Japan and Chen Chien Chung and amateur Chang Tung Chan of Formosa. Miyamoto and Fujio Ishii trailed by three and nine other strong players were grouped in the next two score slots.

The picture changed decidedly on Saturday. Bembridge absorbed six bogeys and lost his lead to Spain's Ramon Sota, a sturdy 30-year-old pro from Santander who was making his first round of the Far East after playing rather well just about everywhere else in the world. Even though mentally disturbed about the loss the previous day of a prized watch that was a memento of Spain's runnerup finish in the 1965 World Cup competition, Sota unleashed a 66 that carried him into a three-shot lead at 204, as all of the second-day's leaders except Ishii fell off. Fujio remained three strokes off the lead, but in second place, a shot in front of Bembridge, Sugihara and Ho Ming Chung, who was to be low amateur for the fourth straight time and make his first serious title bid.

Sugihara slipped only once as he shot a final-round 66 to land Japan's first Hong Kong Open title in the 11-year history of the event, which was in operation several years prior to the formation of the Far East circuit. He bogeyed the par-5 10th, but otherwise had things under control as the games of Sota and Ishii came apart early, apparently bothered by greens still wet and unpredictable after an overnight rain. Only Bembridge offered any serious challenge to the 31-year-old pro from Osaka, who, like Bob Charles, never betrays any emotion with his facial expressions. Maurice fought back from his third-round troubles to post a 68 and place second, two strokes behind the poker-faced champion whose only concession to emotion came when he flipped his ball to the gallery after a quick little jump into the air after holing out at the 18th. Sota, who left the circuit for the United States and the Masters from there, was so upset with his closing 75 that he asked reporters to "leave me alone, please . . . No more golf today."

The rest of the circuit riders headed for Taipei and the China Open, where the remarkable domination of the Japanese continued. The players from that country seemed to be passing the titles around and Sugimoto's turn came up. He had been close before but had never won on the circuit, and he arrived at the Taiwan Golf and Country Club, which grew from a three-hole course opened in 1914, with little to attract attention on his 1969 record. He immediately showed signs that his game was on the mend in the pro-amateur with a 65, commenting that he felt he had found his putting touch at Hong Kong, even though he had missed the 54-hole cut.

The powerful 31-year-old pro's self judgement held up in the opening round as he worked a four-under-par 68 out of 6,836-yard Tamsui for a one-stroke lead over two fellow Japanese, Kesahiko

Uchida and Kenji Umino, and two of the host country's best, Hsu and Kuo Chi Hsiung. Yung Yo, shooting for his third straight China Open title, was in good position at 71.

Kuo, a frequent challenger on the circuit the last two years, showed his familiarity with his home course Friday by taking a two-stroke half-way lead in a cold and windy rainstorm that sent scores soaring. Six players dropped out during the round, among them Yasuda. Sugihara had an 80 and Singapore champion Kamata bravely stuck it out and turned in a 91. In fact, Kuo was the only player to break par in the rugged conditions, scoring 71 for 140. Hsu's 73 moved him into second place, a shot in front of Hsieh Min Nan and two ahead of a thoroughly-chilled Sugimoto, who struggled to a 76.

The winds still ripped at the golfers Saturday, but the rain was gone and the scores dropped again. Sugimoto fought back with a 68 and wound up the round in a three-way tie for the lead with Kuo and Hsu at 213. The genial pro from Tokyo now carried all of Japan's hopes for yet another title and the first victory in the four-year-old tournament by any visiting golfer. Between the leaders and the next Japanese player—Uchida at 220—were three other Chinese stars, Min Nan at 215, Yung Yo at par 216 and Chen Ching Po at 218. An unfortunate accident threw the amateur battle wide open when Ho, well on his way to a fifth straight amateur trophy, was struck on the leg by a fellow competitor's club and was forced to withdraw after five holes.

Kuo got the upper hand on the front nine Sunday as the weather calmed and warmed up. He went out in 33 while Sugimoto and Chi San were shooting 36s, Hideyo erratically with three birdies, three bogeys and three pars and Hsu more conventionally with a birdie and a bogey. When Kuo's game failed him in the pressure of the stretch run—he finished with a 73 to place fourth, a stroke behind Min Nan—the battle became a duel between Sugimoto and Chi San. They traced the lead twice, when Sugimoto bogeyed the 10th and when he birdied the 15th, but Hsu canned a short birdie putt on the final green to force the second playoff in the tournament's four-year history. Sugimoto's length helped when they settled it on the dogleg, 410-yard first hole. Hideyo reached the green with his approach. Hsu was trapped, his sand shot left him with a 15-footer and he missed as Sugi was two-putting for a par from 30 feet.

As frequently happens in golf, players often find it particularly difficult to do their best in tournaments at home and this seemed to be the case in the circuit's closing event, the Yomiuri Open, on the hilly 7,052-yard Yomiuri Country Club near Tokyo. After their sensational performances in the six previous events, none of the Japanese players could ever get in front in the Yomiuri, even though the lead changed hands three times over the week end. Korea's Hahn Chang Sang had it first. He birdied four of the first seven holes, finished his opening round with two more and posted a six-under-par 66. Tomoo Ishii began with 68 and five others—Felus, Sugihara, Yung Yo, Hosoishi and Korean World Cupper Lee Il Ahn—had 69s.

New Zealand's Walter Godfrey came out of a pack at 70 to take the half-way lead when he shot 69 under near-perfect weather conditions. Japan's Masaji Kusakabe had the day's best round—67 —to take second place at 140, but generally the scoring was surprisingly high. Only five players broke par, compared to 13 under windier conditions Thursday. Chang Sang was one of the second-day victims, dropping back with a 77.

Not a player broke par when high winds sprang up on Saturday and Godfrey, in a wildly-fluctuating round, managed to cling to a one-stroke lead even though scoring a 76. It appeared that Yung Yo, with the circuit title already clinched, might become the only double winner of 1969. With a 74, he advanced within a stroke of Godfrey at 216. Sugihara also threatened for a second title, resting at 217 with Min Nan, whose par 72 was the best of the day. Wolstenholme, with 71-72-76, trailed Godfrey by four, his position severely damaged by a triple-bogey 8 during the round.

The 38-year-old Wolstenholme, who has played on every circuit in the world since turning pro in the early 1960s, now captured his first Far East crown in strong fashion, making up for several earlier title bids that failed, particularly the one a month earlier at Singapore. He fired a three-under 69, capping the round with a 15-foot birdie putt on the final green to nose out Sugihara by a stroke. Teruo seemed to succumb to the pressure on the last two holes. He had taken a two-stroke lead when he sank a six-foot birdie putt at the 16th, but he missed a three-footer for a bogey at the 17th and took another at the 18th after trapping his drive. Both Godfrey and Yung Yo took 77s and dropped out of contention early with front-nine 39s.

The Indian Open normally has followed the close of the circuit and, despite meager prize money, usually picked up at least a handful of the tour players, pros either on their way home or just looking for more action. In 1969, however, Japan's richest tournament—the $50,000 Chunichi Crowns at Nagoya Golf Club—was scheduled two weeks following the Yomiuri and, quite naturally, the Japanese players stayed home and many of the other circuit pros remained in Japan. Indian Open officials, with their eyes on the promised spot on the 1970 circuit, went ahead anyway, even though Ben Arda was the only foreign pro of any repute who played. Hosoishi, the winner in India in 1967 and 1968, begged off, and Peter Thomson and Wolstenholme sent their regrets. As expected, Arda scored an easy victory at the 6,869-yard Royal Calcutta Golf Club, where the 1970 inaugural on the Asia circuit is scheduled. With rounds of 74, 75, 71, 71 for his one-under-par 291, the stocky, little Filipino won the 1969 championship by seven strokes.

Peter Thomson did play in the Chunichi Crowns the following week, and made up for his lack of success on the 1969 circuit by capturing the $5,540 first prize in a unique playoff. The five-time British Open champion tied Japan's Tadashi Kitta, missing an outright victory when he failed to drop a three-foot putt on the last green after a brilliant 40-yard shot from a bunker. The Chunichi Crowns people had predetermined a three-hole playoff in the event of a tie. Thomson went par-par-birdie to Kitta's bogey-par-par for the decision. With the big purse Chunichi Crowns puts up, I wonder why Asia circuit officials don't work it into the schedule?

I have already commented generally about the World Cup Matches at Singapore, but certainly can't leave it at that. It was, as usual, an interesting and exciting competition that well deserves detailing as the year's concluding event in Asia and one that focused international attention on the Bukit course and the 24-square-mile republic, which was in the midst of its sesquicentennial celebration.

It had been expected that their familiarity with Bukit and their conditioning to the tropical heat of Singapore—one wag commented that he went to a movie there one night and missed winter—would work to the advantage of the Asian players. It obviously did, as the final results illustrated, but not enough to stop Trevino and Moody, who both had some experience with golf in that part of the world while in military service. This was particularly true of Moody, whose most impressive title before his grand achievement earlier in the year in the U.S. Open had been the Korean Open championship. During his long stay in the Far East while in the Army, ex-sergeant Moody learned both Japanese and Korean. When the U.S. was paired with Japan in the second round, Orville frequently talked with Kono and Yasuda in their native tongue, prompting Trevino to remark: "I didn't have anyone to talk to. Everytime I looked at Orville, he was talking to the Japanese. I didn't know who my partner was."

Nonetheless, they made good partners, especially after Trevino settled into a groove following his collapse the preceding Sunday in the Alcan matches in Portland, his long air trip to Singapore and his ill-considered public beef about the absence of drinking water for the players on the sizzling course the first day. Trevino and Moody didn't establish their team superiority until the final day and it took the low-scoring round Lee had been predicting for himself—65—and a 30-foot birdie putt on the 72nd green for Trevino to win the individual championship. His early complaint about the missing water was forgotten amid his constant pleasantries with the fans and other players during the week and his gesture at the victory ceremony of turning over his $2,000 prize money to the Singapore Golf Association for a caddie scholarship fund.

The Americans, with Moody opening with 67 despite a headache and twitching muscles induced late in the round by the extreme heat, and Trevino shooting par, shared the first-round lead with the Chinese. The steady Yung Yo added 13 pars to an eagle and three birdies for 66 and the individual lead while partner Hsu was scoring 72. Onsham, a smiling five foot two inch bantamweight at 114 pounds, and partner Suvannapongse played in obscurity with two Singapore amateurs, who were merely filling out the field. Just for the day, though. Onsham, playing the three back-nine par-5s eagle-birdie-birdie, tied Moody for second place in the individual scoring.

China moved in front and Hsieh stayed there the second day, when Dave Thomas became the biggest money-maker of the week. The Welshman holed a 2-iron shot on the 224-yard 12th hole and was rewarded with $3,333 in cash from the Dunhill tobacco people and a round-the-world plane ticket from Pan-American. Yung Yo's 70 and Hsu's 69 gave the men from Taiwan 277 and a one-stroke lead. A pair of 70s by the Americans put them at 278, a shot in front of Argentina, which advanced on the strength of de Vicenzo's 69—68, and now-noticed Thailand. Suvannapongse was the man Friday. He fired the day's best round—67—with a combination of eight birdies, four bogeys and six pars, a model of inconsistency. In the International Trophy race, the picture was Yung Yo at 136, de Vicenzo and Moody at 137, the Philippines' Arda at 139, Kono at 140 and Trevino at 141.

The Chinese were paired with the U.S. in the third round and proved their competence by adding a stroke to their lead. Trevino began his move with a 69 and a struggling Moody settled for par 71. And there were the Thais at 419, just a shot behind the Americans and three off the lead as Sukree bogeyed the last hole for 67 after Suchin had dropped four strokes on the preceding four holes. Yung Yo's individual lead was two over the little Thai, three on Moody and Arda and five on Trevino.

The team battle for the World Cup turned drastically early in the final round. Trevino and Moody launched a barrage of birdies on the front nine, Lee making three in a row and Orville a pair while avoiding a bogey at the seventh hole after a shot cut open the forehead of a woman spectator. When both Chinese players three-putted the ninth, the U.S. was six strokes in front and well on its way to the winning total of 552—16-under-par. Kono and Yasuda had their best rounds Sunday, 67 and 69, to grab off second place. But the individual battle remained tight to the finish, even though Yung Yo shot himself out of it with a 72. With three early birdies, Sukree took the lead into the final stretch. De Vicenzo, playing in front of the final U.S.-Thai foursome, was 6 under par going to the par-5 15th, missed his birdie there, three-putted the 16th, but birdied the last hole for 65 and 276. Trevino, three behind Sukree going to the 15th, made up one shot with a two-putt birdie there, a second when Sukree three-putted the 16th and another with a 10-foot birdie putt at the 17th. At 18 Trevino topped his second shot on the 478-yard finishing hole and Sukree hooked into the trees. Trevino's 120-yard approach rolled 30 yards past the cup and Onsham's recovery caught a trap at the green. But Lee went to school on partner Moody's putt from the fringe behind him and ran in the birdie for his 65 and individual title with 275. Sukree missed his from 15 feet to drop into a third-place tie with Yung Yo and Moody, who closed with a 69 for his 277.

Thus ended an interesting pro golf season in Asia, one that increased a feeling I have had for the last few years about the prowess of the Asian pros. We will be hearing more and more from them in the wider arena of world golf when (in the near future, I suspect) they venture out in force.

10

The Australian and N.Z. Tours

A big wet, a big brawl, and Bruce juice

Australians have a way with names. I don't know what the talent is, or what its origins might be, but you've got to think the best of a people who have koala bears, kookaburra birds and a golf club called Yarra Yarra. This linguistic knack they carry over into natural events as well, often with descriptive vengence. When the moisture has been falling from the clouds for days an Englishman will say it rains, an American will say it pours, but an Australian will tell you that you've been caught by the big wet. Well, in 1969 the Australian Tour almost drowned in the big wet. And it seems to me when there wasn't a big wet there was a big brawl and a big sick and a big winner—the latter being Bruce Devlin, who overjoyed his countrymen by making off with three of the major events in the face of some esteemed international competition.

Two factors made 1969 the best year ever for the Australian tour. One was increased purse money, the other an improvement in the level of competition. The prize money was a record $245,000—more than Great Britain's, Australian golf officials quickly point out. The figure is especially meaningful when you consider how short the Australian tour has to be and how small the purses have been until very recent years. Partly because of the added money, and partly because many internationally-known pros were in the Far East anyway to play in the World Cup, which was held in Singapore the week before the Australian tour started, an unprecedented number of foreign professionals came to Australia, 38 in all. Among them were four U.S. Open winners, Lee Trevino, Orville Moody, Billy Casper and Gary Player, and the British Open champion, Tony Jacklin. Add to them golfers of the caliber of George Knudson, Peter Thomson and Kel Nagle and you have a field worthy of almost any tournament. It was also a thoroughly international gathering, with the Far East well represented, as well as Great Britain, New Zealand and—yes—Zambia. The evolution of Zambia as a golfing power I cannot explain. As years go on, I'll keep an eye on the Zambians for you.

A summary of the Australian tour is easy enough. Player won the Australian Open—for the fifth time—Knudson won the Wills Masters, with the help of doctors, nurses, oxygen and some missed putts by Peter Thomson, and Devlin won everything else you could think of. It was Devlin's finest season since 1966, and suggests his return to form (in his 20 competitive rounds he was 46 under par and averaged 69.95 strokes per round) is complete. Devlin's comeback is popular in Australia, especially because the other Australian who has been successful on the U.S. tour, Bruce Crampton, will not leave the U.S. long enough to compete in the major Australian events. Crampton is greatly criticized for this in Australia, and while he is right when he says he can win so much more during the same weeks by playing in the U.S., Crampton has earned enough money in recent years to be able to afford the time to play for a month in Australia. Some of Australia's most respected golf figures have not hesitated to tell this in the press.

It is customary when referring to the Australian tour to talk of only one set of tournaments, those played between early October and late November, following which the golfers move on to New Zealand to close out the year. But Australia has two sub-tours that help its pros keep body and alligator shoes together. One runs from January to March, which is late in the Australian summer, and the other, called the Sunshine Tour, is held in the north during the Australian winter. The biggest of the 1969 mini-events was the $10,000 Victorian Open, which was won, as it has been for the past three years, by Kel Nagle. Now 49, the aging Nagle held off two arch rivals, Peter Thomson and Billy Dunk, for his victory. On the last day he was forced to birdie five of the final seven holes and equal Dunk's course record of 66 to insure his victory. The tournament was at heavily wooded Kingston Heath in Melbourne, and the golfers treated the difficult layout like a pitch-and-putt course. Nagle was 17 under par for the tournament, and in the last round the three top golfers came up with 20 birdies and three eagles.

Unfortunately, this was Nagle's last show of form for months. A nagging arthritic condition in his right hand and a serious back injury —legacies of three decades as a touring pro—resulted in his worst year ever. His play during his annual visit to the U.S. was especially weak. He is liked in the U.S., and his playoff loss to Gary Player in the 1965 U.S.Open at St. Louis is well remembered, but he looked like nothing more than a creaking elder statesman this year. It was not until he reached New Zealand late in the season that he showed some of the flash he had displayed at Melbourne in February. His return was an impressive one, however. Meanwhile, the mid-year tournaments in Australia were pretty well dominated by Billy Dunk, with occasional strokes of brilliance from a strong New Zealand pro with tremendous potential, John Lister, and two other young men, David Graham and Tony Mangan.

The significant portion of the Australian tour began with a tournament that was something of an appetizer, the City of Sydney Open. It was a 54-hole event with a $5,000 purse and not the kind of thing that would ordinarily attract top golfers; when was the last time George Knudson and Bruce Devlin played 54 holes for a winner's purse of $900? But a number were willing to try the short Moore Park course, which is just two miles from the center of Sydney and reminds me somewhat of the Indianapolis Speedway layout. One golfer who would not ordinarily have been there—in fact, he had no idea the tournament was being held—was the winner, Devlin. Bruce returned to Australia from the U.S. on the Tuesday of tournament week. As he got off his plane he was met by Bob Wilson, the able tour director of the Australian PGA. Wilson is not above a little aggressive promotion of golf in Australia, and he had taken the liberty of entering Devlin's name in the City of Sydney event. He had not bothered to inform Bruce of this, however, a precaution that may well· have averted a decline from Devlin. Welcomed to his homeland with the news that he was entered, Devlin decided to forego the week off that he had planned and play at Sydney. This was a wise public-relations move, one that was greeted with enthusiasm by Sydney golf followers, and Devlin immediately was ·made the tournament favorite on the strength of his U.S. showing. He had played in 17 tournaments in the U.S. in 1969, won once, lost a playoff to Bert Yancey when Yancey made three straight birdies, and in the end pocketed $82,000. That sounded good enough to make him a winner in the City of Sydney, and it proved to be. But what a struggle it was.

Devlin opened with a six-under-par 65, which gave him a three-stroke lead over Australian Colin McGregor. Bruce was paired with Knudson, who is a very straight driver, and Devlin showed why he was winning more money than in 1968 by hitting the ball off the tee as well as the Canadian. Most of Devlin's ills have been caused by an untrustworthy driver. "It's nice to start back at home with a 65,"

said Devlin after his round, "but I don't think I can keep this up."
He was too modest, however, for his second round was also a 65, and
now he had a three-stroke lead on Japan's Takashi Murakami.

The Japanese have learned a lot about tour golf in the last two
years, enough to make formidable opponents when the going gets
rugged. As the cliché goes, they have learned to win. Devlin came out
on the last day determined merely to protect his lead. This is sensible
strategy, or seems like it should be, but it is always hard to play
defensive golf. Devlin ran his stretch of holes without a bogey to 43,
but the birdies were fewer, and when Murakami, playing ahead of
Devlin, birdied the 16th the tournament was tied. After watching
this, Devlin regained the lead by sinking a six-foot putt for a birdie of
his own. He then missed the 17th green, but saved himself with a
seven-foot putt for a par. A par on 18 gave him the victory. "Boy
were those pressure putts," said Devlin. "My game started to slip, but
I struggled through. Playing a final round when you are in front of
the field is a difficult business. You don't want to be stupid and
gamble too much, yet you must not back off and play safe." Devlin
managed to find the middle ground—just. Knudson found nothing
but 19th place.

A week later the list of familiar names was much longer as
Australia offered its first big event, the $20,000 Wills Masters. The
site was the fine Victoria Golf Club in Melbourne. Billy Casper was
there, determined to improve on his indifferent showings in his last
two Australian trips, and Jacklin and the rest of the top Aussies;
Nagle, Dunk, Thomson and Bob Stanton. A foretaste of what was to
happen came the day before play began when Knudson had seven
birdies during his practice round. He looked more rested than he had
the week before, and said he was delighted with the course. He
added, "I always play well on courses I like. The greens here are fast
and true, the fairways are fine and the atmosphere is delightful." Part
of the atmosphere was 48 straight hours of rain, but that did not
dampen Knudson's enthusiasm. Devlin, meanwhile, was saying in one
of those ghost-written columns that Australian newspapers fancy so,
that "Napolean Bonaparte could well be made to look like a piker as
a general if I get my way in the $20,000 Wills Masters for the next
four days." I've got to ask Bruce just what he had in mind. He did
say the score he had in mind was 276, which would have done nicely.
So would 278.

The first two days were much the same; cold weather, icy winds
and heavy going for all concerned. The man who handled the

conditions best was the 23 year-old Stanton. On the first day he finished his front nine by sinking a 90-foot chip shot and his back nine by dropping a 60-foot chip, two sudden strokes that gave him a 68 and the lead. Casper was out in 33 but "played like a hacker" on the back nine for a 70, too, but missed a three-footer on the last green, and Knudson felt fortunate to salvage a 73. On Friday Stanton held his lead with a 69, but when Knudson went out in 32 it was possible to foresee trouble. While the rest of the golfers did not seem to play as well as they should have on a course that is open to good scoring, Knudson whipped in with a 66 that set a Victoria GC record and brought him to within two strokes of Stanton. Tee-off times may have been a factor in the events of the day. Surely they were for Knudson. He was scheduled to start very late, and by the time he got to the first tee he could see that Stanton—who had three birdies in the first seven holes—was eight under par. George had not come all this way to try and finish safely among the top ten or any such thing, and when he saw how far ahead Stanton had moved he decided there was nothing for him to do but go for broke with every shot. That is what he did, with devastating results. He had six birdies and an eagle, and his card showed ten 3s. His late-in-the-day performance also took some of the string out of a Casper complaint about a late starting time on two straight days. After Stanton at 137 and Knudson at 139, it was three more strokes back to the group tied for third: Devlin, Maurice Bembridge of Great Britain, Lu Liang Huan of China and the pocket-sized golfer who almost won the World Cup for Thailand, Soukree Onchum.

On the first hole Saturday Bob Stanton made a par and lost his two-stroke lead. That seems too sudden to believe, but the hole is a five par that can be reached, and Knudson eagled it before the gallery could even get settled down to its game of follow the leader. Nor did Knudson let up, as he rapped in three birdies on the front nine to post a superb 31. Now he had the tournament completely in his grasp, but as so often happens in golf, just when things seem most secure the fates intrude to restore the delights of uncertainty. I've seen it too often. A golfer running away with a tournament is a golfer in trouble. (Pleasant trouble, to be sure). One thing is certain, George Knudson will remember the 1969 Wills Masters with both a grin and a grimace for the rest of his career.

Knudson's troubles began on the back nine, where the wondrous precision he had shown in the previous 27 holes deserted him. Ragged edges began to appear, an indifferent iron here, a weak chip there, and by the time he reached the 18th tee Knudson was uneasy. He was par in for a 37 and a 68 that would give him a one-stroke lead over Stanton, who had held on quite well through Knudson's searing front nine. Well, George got his par, but on the way he hit four trees. I doubt he has ever managed a par under such conditions before. Perhaps no one has. The details are worthwhile. He cut his drive into the woods on the right. His ball fell in the rough a few yards from a towering gum tree. He tried to slice around the gum tree, but caught it flush in the center of the trunk instead and his ball rocketed back at him, over his head and into the rough behind him. This time Knudson used a three wood—and hit the same gum tree. However, contact was not quite so flush and the ball progressed a way toward the green. His good day's work was fast vanishing as Knudson now took a five iron and tried to reach the green. The ball got up safely, but hit a tree as it neared the green, bounced off the tree onto a hump of fairway, flew off the hump, onto the green and ended up five feet from the hole. Knudson sank the putt, gave the gallery a wan smile and lurched off for the locker room.

Perhaps it was the delight of surviving the 18th hole, perhaps it was the pleasure of being the leader, perhaps it was the merry manners of Melbourne, but Knudson set off to spend a night that was an after-dark version of hitting four trees. Or so, from appearances, it must have been. One report was that a dozen oysters, a bottle of wine and two big steaks at midnight caused the problem. Whatever it was, Knudson found a way to keep the Wills Masters exciting. He arrived at the course two hours before his tee-off time and went straight to the practice area. There, wrapped in a heavy cardigan sweater in spite of the 85-degree temperature, he presented a two-color image to viewers: the black of his sunglasses and the green of his face. A long practice session did not seem to help his composure, so he retreated to the club house and ordered all of the black coffee that could be found. By the time he walked to the first tee and met his playing partners, Devlin and David Graham, he was in a trance. "George played the first nine holes in a dream," says Devlin. "I have never seen a man in a golf tournament so high up in the clouds. Yet he kept hitting greens and making putts. His win was incredible."

Part of Devlin's awe stems from the fact that Knudson not only had Stanton to hold off, he had to contend with two pretty good golfers who had come back into contention with a pair of 67s on the third day. One was Devlin himself, who was only two strokes back of

Knudson, and the other was Peter Thomson, four more back. And Devlin is also somewhat miffed, for he feels under such circumstances he should have won. Instead, just at the point he thought the whole tournament was going to be his, what with George staggering around like a possum in daylight, Devlin did something that should have made *him* sick. He had started with an eagle and a birdie, and when Stanton had lots of trouble on the early holes the battle seemed up to Devlin and Knudson, one of whom was going great and one of whom was coming up the fairways on his knees. Both Devlin and Knudson hit the green on the par-3 fourth hole, with Devlin about 20 feet from the hole for a birdie. Bruce's juices were obviously flowing, and Devlin charged his uphill birdie putt four feed past the cup. The green was exceedingly fast, and there was no mistaking the danger of the downhill putt for the par. Devlin was as careful with it as he could have been, but the ball never touched the cup as it broke two feet past. And then the two-footer would not go in. Devlin had four-putted from 20 feet and shot himself right out of the Masters.

Who knows what Knudson thought as he watched all this, but as soon as he got his own ball down in two he walked slowly over to Tournament Director Wilson and told him he could not continue unless he got help. "I just can't breathe and my heart is pumping like mad," Knudson said. "I can't go on unless you can get me some oxygen and some tranquilizers." Wilson used his walkie-talkie to summon help, and within minutes a doctor and nurse were treating the reeling Knudson. The group was permitted to stop play for a few minutes while a golfing version of a field hospital was set up for Knudson. Off came the heavy sweater and down the Knudson throat went tranquilizers, glucose and salt tablets. Soon Knudson could continue. Later he said his first five holes were the guttiest he had ever played, which may be true, though he showed considerable nerve on the rest of his wobbly round, too. While Knudson had been receiving his treatment, Peter Thomson had made five birdies on the front nine to turn in 32 and take the lead by a stroke. Coming up the sixth fairway Knudson finally grasped the idea that he might lose. His answer was a quick tranquilizer to that kind of fear, a burst of three birdies in five holes. When Thomson missed two three-footers on his way to a 69—a sad ending after such a spirited start—Knudson seemed a sure winner. Thomson was in the clubhouse at 11 under par and Knudson was coming into the par-3 16th with a three-stroke lead. But nothing was to be easy this day. Knudson flew his tee shot over the green into deep trouble and was lucky in the end to escape with a double-bogey. Now he had a one-stroke lead to protect. He parred 17, which brought him to the 18th tee and the sight of that fine Australian gum tree that he could remember so well from the afternoon before. This time was different. Two glorious shots put Knudson on the green and he two-putted for a two-stroke win. Stanton shot a 71 to tie Thomson for second. Amid the usual clubhouse congratulations Knudson had one keen request: "Can somebody please get me a beer." And Peter Thomson—in his role of newspaper columnist—got in something of a last word when he said, "Knudson is, in my opinion, the best golfer we have seen here since Sam Snead played at Royal Melbourne ... The man knows, or at least aims to know, what he is doing, which is not all that common among golfers, even in the top professional flight." So Peter feels he lost to the best. And he seems to be ranking Knudson very high, indeed.

The players next moved north to Sydney where they were joined by more internationalists, including Trevino, Player and Jacklin, for the Australian Open. Early in Open week the flamboyant Trevino won all the headlines. He arrived in Stetson and cowboy boots declaring, "I want to shoot a kangaroo and make myself a kangaroo-skin golf bag," a remark that put the country's conversation-minded citizens in a frenzy. A Sydney sportswriter requested a "serious" interview with Trevino, and it began this way:

Trevino "Okay, baby. Shoot those serious-type questions."

Reporter: "What do you think of your swing? "

Trevino: "Say, isn't it just awful. You know, sometimes I even miss the ball. I've missed it twice in tournaments already this year."

Reporter: "Are you serious? "

Trevino: "Baby, you don't think I'd tell you a lie? "

If the Australians didn't know quite what to make of Trevino, Lee and some of the other foreign golfers were baffled by the chilly reception they received at the host club, Royal Sydney. Signs at the clubhouse door read, "Members and competitors only," and an army of gray uniformed guards stopped golfers' wives, business managers and guests from setting foot in the domain of Australia's aristocracy. Australian PGA officials were also turned away. "I've got to get into the locker room to talk to the players," Tournament Director Wilson explained on one occasion. "Do your business while they are on the course," he was told sternly. Qantas, which was sponsoring the tournament (to the tune of $50,000), also had its officials turned away. Orange-blazered Qantas men had to use the outdoor privys, which were two blackened cans and a length of roof gutter behind the 17th tee. "You'd find better outhouses in the outback," one newsman reported.

"Why is Royal Sydney staging this Australian Open? " Bruce Devlin asked in a by-lined article entitled *Out of Bounds.* "There are more do's and don'ts at this course than a kid would find at his first day in school. I was rather taken aback yesterday to hear of the many restrictions."

He got a stiff-lipped reply to his question from a Royal Sydney member who wrote in a letter to the editor:

"It is with some surprise that one reads in the Press the comments of Mr. B. Devlin, a professional golfer engaged in the Australian Open ... It may be relevant to reflect on the rights of a small group of individuals who have developed great skill at golf, as a living, and to wonder whether this skill, admired and envied as it is by the average golfer, entitles them to demand privileges in the use of their hosts' property and facilities, beyond those necessary to allow them to earn their livelihood .... It is germane to state that without the indulgence and hospitality of the privately owned golf clubs so glibly criticized by Mr. Devlin, he and his fellows would be deprived of the means of earning their living as professional tournament golfers."

Such a smug sense of privilege is not unusual in Australia. Australian golf clubs are exclusive bastions seldom penetrated by outsiders. Many clubs insist that wives of members use a backstairs and women are rarely seen in clubhouse lounges or dining rooms. This Victorian code has hardly changed since 1911 when golf professionals met at Royal Sydney to form the Australian PGA in protest of rules barring them from the clubhouse.

It was in an angry mood that play at Royal Sydney began, and before the halfway point there was considerably more tumult and shouting. The course overlooks Sydney harbor and nestles into the slopes of exclusive Rose Bay. It is one of the country's truly testing layouts. It has almost 200 bunkers and, as Peter Thomson puts it, not a bit of waste sand. Gusty winds whip in from the sea, the rough is demonic and on the first day of the Open pin placements were such that the pros called them "crazy...senseless...sadistic... stupid." At the 230-yard par 3 17th, only one player in the 135 in the field managed to get a birdie.

Then came the last absurdity. Peter Thomson discovered the cups were too small. Thomson used his putter, which has a four and one quarter inch blade (the lawful diameter of a hole), to measure each cup. Not one was the correct size and Thomson, to prove his point, sent his putter to a nearby manufacturing plant to be measured. It was found to be within 1/1,000th of an inch of what he claimed. The next day the cups were cut to the proper size.

Thomson was one of only three players who managed to shoot par or better in the opening round. He and his friend, Guy Wolstenholme, the Britisher who has emigrated to Australia, had 71s and Devlin a 72. Wolstenholme is now 38 and has been living for a year in Melbourne. "I think I'm improving with age, like wine," he says. "Over the past year my game has tightened up and I'm hitting the ball a lot straighter." He won the 1969 Dutch and Yomirui Opens. Wolstenholme bogeyed the 17th at Royal Sydney on opening day, but offset that by sinking a 45-footer at 9 and a 10-footer at 18. Thomson started his day well, with birdies on three of the first eight holes. His play around the greens was superb. In contrast, Bruce Devlin had a frustrating day with his putter. At 14 he began using a cross-handed grip and finally he got a birdie. But he missed four other birdies from inside five feet. Three strokes out of the lead, at 74, was Gary Player, who was seeking his fifth Australian Open win. Only one man, an amateur named Ivo Whitton who played in the hickory shaft days, had won the championship five times and Gary was resolved to do so. His two-over-par 74 may not have looked like much on paper, but he was pleased with it. From tee to green his game was perfect, but by charging his putts he had dropped two shots on the final two holes. "There is a little yellow seed coming through on the greens," he explained, "and it is making the ball bounce. These are the most difficult greens I've ever putted on, and I will guarantee that nobody will break 280 in this tournament. In recent weeks I have been putting well and playing ordinary golf. It was the opposite today. I couldn't hole my putts, but I had more control over my shots than I have had all year." Trevino also was at 74. At 75 was Tony Jacklin, who was thinking more about his wife (at home in Britain awaiting the birth of their first child) than his game.

The second day Jacklin, Trevino and Thomson were grouped together by the Australian amateur golf organization officials running the tournament. The result of this error was that the crowds following the trio were huge, and they nearly stampeded. They became uncontrollable after Trevino started birdie, birdie. "I was pushed, stepped on and shoved down the fairways," Trevino declared with obvious anger after coming in with a 73. "I could not walk in a straight line and I can't count the number of people I trod on. Somebody is going to get seriously hurt out there. It's the worst gallery control I have ever seen. When you hit they just charge right over you. There is no need to take a step. They just carry you along." Thomson agreed, though he had managed a far better score, a 71, to again share the lead. "I was knocked from pillar to post," the Aussie said. "It is 15 years since we have had to put up with this." The head of the Australian Golf Union declared icily that he was satisfied with the marshaling and that no action would be taken by the AGU until some of the professionals protested officially. Qantas, however, took matters into its own hands and order was restored for the final two rounds.

Thomson's second-round 71 was noteworthy, for he had a stretch of five birdies in six holes to offset a triple bogey. Wolstenholme turned in a more level performance while posting a 71, too, but again he bogeyed the 17th. Devlin, still using his cross-handed putting style, had a much better second round, and his 70 put him in a tie with Thomson and Wolstenholme. The best round of the day, however, was a 69 by Player that moved him within one stroke of the leaders. "Golf is an amazing game," he said. "I played better in the first round, but my score was five strokes worse." Player birdied the two toughest holes on the course, 14 and 17, and was pleased. Three strokes farther back were the Australian youngsters, Stanton and Graham, and Japan's slender Tadashi Kitta. Trevino was another stroke back and Jacklin, weakened by the flu, had dropped out of serious contention.

In the third round Player moved in front, shooting a fine 68. Before the round he had spent only a few minutes on the practice tee but more than an hour on the putting green. His putting stroke must have been well grooved, for he went out and sank birdie tries from 14, 12, 45, 25 and 12 feet. But his finest shot was at the 6th hole, where he blasted out of a bunker to within a foot of the pin and got his birdie. Player had one three-putt green in Saturday's round. It came when a Japanese camera crew distracted Gary, and as Player walked off the final green 12 Japanese were there bowing deeply from the waist and apologizing. Wolstenholme, meanwhile, carded his third successive 71 and was just two strokes back. Thomson and Devlin had 74s, and Jacklin a 77 to barely qualify for the final round.

Player looked well on his way to his fifth Australian Open

championship midway through Sunday's round. After nine holes he was three strokes up on Wolstenholme and no one else was threatening. But then a violent summer storm struck the course. Pelting rain whipped across the fairways and winds exceeded 50 miles an hour. Player was at the 12th hole and Wolstenholme was on 15. At the clubhouse the 60-foot by 20-foot scoreboard tumbled down. Lightening flashed and the players scampered for cover. Gradually the rain stopped, but the winds continued. Downwind holes became 80 or 100 yards shorter and those where the golfers had to hit into the gale were impossible to reach. At 13, a 514-yard hole, Player snap-hooked his drive. Trying to slash through the dense rough he only managed to move the ball 20 yards. His next went into a bunker, and suddenly he had lost his lead with a triple-bogey 8. But Wolstenholme was also in trouble. He had no chance of reaching the par-3 17th as the wind whipped into his face at 60 miles an hour. He bogeyed that and then took three strokes to get down from the edge at 18, losing another vital shot. In all, he lost four strokes in the closing seven holes as he finished with a 76 and a one-over-par 289. Meanwhile, Player was two under par with two holes to play. At 17 he smashed into his tee shot, but the winds were so strong that he did not even reach the front line of bunkers and he still needed a full wedge to reach the green. He hit that shot well enough, but then three-putted from 20 feet for a double bogey. Now he needed a par on the 412-yard dogleg 18th for the win. He lashed his drive into a cross wind and the ball landed perilously close to the left rough in the bend of the dogleg. He was left with an eight-iron to the green. The approach shot looked good, but at the last moment the wind carried it to the right some 60 feet from the cup. Walking up 18, Player thought a bogey five would win. But as he neared the green he heard an official tell the crowd, "Player needs a par 4 to win his fifth Open championship." Player raised the five fingers of his right hand to indicate he needed a five, but the official told him no, a 4. "When the loudspeaker announced that I needed a four, my heart fell in my boots," he said later. Player lagged his first putt up to the hole, but it stopped five feet short. He stood over that final putt a long time, but then rapped the ball into the center of the cup. "How I sank that last putt I will never know. Man, I was like jelly. The first thing to go in a man's golf is his nerves and I was frightened my hands wouldn't work as I tried to stroke the putt. I have never known such tension," he said. He had survived with a final round of 77.

Player won not only his fifth Open title, but the $2,500 first prize.

Actually he took home $2,450, because he dropped $50 in a bet with his old friend, Norman von Nida. Player wagered that Von Nida, who is 55, would not break 300 in the tournament. Norman shocked everyone by coming in with impressive rounds of 75, 73, 72, 72 for a four-over-par 292 and a tie for fifth place.

The tour turned south again to Melbourne for the $25,000 Dunlop International, the richest Australian tournament, which was held at Yarra Yarra. "Those cats at Royal Sydney, what a snob mob," Trevino declared while luxuriating in the Melbourne clubhouse. "Every time I got to the 18th green and looked up at those towers I felt like a Mexican bandit about to attack the castle. This is the first clubhouse I've enjoyed in Australia."

Trevino was in a fine mood, in part because he had begun playing well. He had an eight-under-par 65 in a practice round and the bookmakers had made Trevino and Player the favorites at 3 to 1. Player had never lost a tournament at Yarra Yarra and the course had fond memories of him. It was there in 1956 that he won enough money to get married. "It was a $10,000 tournament," he recalled, "and when I won I ran to the phone and called up Vivienne in South Africa and told her I was coming home." In his only other Yarra Yarra appearance, Player won the 1959 Victorian Open.

All of the pros seemed in a better frame of mind at the Dunlop. Jacklin declared, "I am hoping to improve considerably on the display I gave in the Australian Open. I am keen to play well in this event and my practice this week has been encouraging." And Bruce Devlin had found a new putter in the Yarra Yarra pro shop. It was a second-hand home-made mallet-head with 16 holes drilled in it to make it lighter. Devlin called it his "weevil", and after an hour and a half on the putting green he was pleased with his progress. Trevino suggested that Devlin was taking too full a stroke and that a shorter sharper putting motion would help. Bruce took the advice, and four days later it was he who defeated Trevino in a sudden-death playoff.

The field at the Dunlop was even stronger than at the Open. Orville Moody had arrived. There were seven pros from Britain, four each from Japan and Taiwan, 10 New Zealanders and the Zambia pair. For a few hours it seemed that Gary Player might pull out when word came from Johannesburg that his seven year old son had been shot by an air gun while playing with friends. The boy was taken to the hospital and an operation was a success, so Player stayed on.

A drenching rain fell the first two days, but the scores were good. Devlin and Simon Hobday of—you guessed it—Zambia took the first round lead with five-under-par 68s. The course is relatively short and though it has tight fairways and fast greens the par of 73 is generous. Hobday, who was playing in only his ninth tournament as a professional, had a hot and cold round, with eight birdies and three bogeys. He had played before the heavy rains came and considered himself lucky. Devlin was delighted with his round, which included four birdies on the back nine: "It is really good when you can regain your putting touch after a lapse. My whole game became much steadier." But if his "weevil" was working marvels, the worm had turned for Trevino. He took 35 putts on his way to a 70. Moody with a 72 was also complaining about three-putt greens.

The largest gallery followed Player, who was belting his drives 300 yards; he came in with a 70 and could have scored much better if his birdie putts had dropped. Though he still was not content with his putting, Player managed a 68 on the second day, which moved him into the lead with Devlin. "I've three putted five times in two rounds," Player explained. "It is ridiculous." On the 9th hole, a 528-yard par 5, he left himself with a four inch putt for an eagle, and he eagled the 13th from nine feet. Devlin was lucky to come in with a 70, for he was in trouble until the closing holes. But he salvaged a good score with an eagle at 16 and birdies at 17 and 18. "My round did not look as though it was going to be anything for a long while," Devlin said. "The last three holes were like a dream come true." And Bob Stanton equalled the course record with a 67 and said happily, "I'm back in the ball game." Indeed he was, just a stroke back of the leaders at 139.

Stanton has had two full seasons on the U.S. tour and he has benefitted handsomely from the experience. He finished 1969 in the top 60 U.S. money winners and will return to America in 1970. He has talent and unusual perseverance. He never knows when he is beaten. Bracketed with him at 139 was Guy Wolstenholme, again performing consistently (70—69). Though Trevino continued to putt poorly, he had a 71 and was only three strokes out of the lead. The longest putt he had holed in the tournament was a 10-footer. Next came Jacklin, Moody and Malcolm Gregson. Hobday slipped to a 75 and was now tied for ninth.

The weather cleared for the third round and by the end of the day Devlin was alone, two strokes in front. He had five straight birdies on the back nine and seven in 10 holes to finish with a 67. After 45 holes Devlin had been tied with Player (who was celebrating his 34th birthday) but Bruce surged away while Gary three-putted two greens and came in with a 72. The only man to give chase was Stanton, who reeled off four birdies in five holes for a 68. Four shots off the pace was Trevino, whose 68 included an eagle on the final hole. And the Yarra Yarra competitive record was broken by David Graham and Tadashi Kitta, who had 66s. Kitta is a two-time Japanese Open champion and has played in five World Cups.

Early in the final round, Stanton slumped, losing four strokes in the first six holes, and Devlin began protecting his lead by playing par golf. But Player and Trevino were coming on. Gary sunk three birdie putts in the first six holes. He was paired with Stanton and Graham, who were both continually in trouble, and a serious problem arose. The threesome slowed and soon Devlin, Trevino and Moody, playing immediately behind, were waiting on every tee. Tournament Director Wilson warned Player and his partners that they risked a two-stroke penalty for slow play and told them to hurry about their business. Trevino, Devlin and Moody then took a ten-minute break before resuming play at the 6th hole, but by the 7th tee they were again hard on the heels of Player's threesome, which now had three holes open in front of it. Again Wilson approached the lagging group. He told the three that a tournament official would watch the remainder of their round and if they lost any more ground the player or players responsible would be penalized. The warning was a general one, but Player took it personally. "I am three under for seven holes. How can I be playing slowly? " he demanded. He said they were having trouble with their gallery. "If you are going to slap a penalty on us, do it now," he told Wilson, "so that your good friends back there will benefit." Wilson is a friend of Devlin's, and Player's anger is perhaps understandable, though regrettable.

Actually, it was Trevino who was complaining about the slow play, having gotten the rhythm of his game going. By the ninth hole he was even with Devlin, and Player was just one stroke behind, but the slow-play warning had taken the edge off Gary's game and he soon dropped back. The Aussie and American were still all even after the 16th and both bogeyed 17, Devlin by three putting. At 18 Trevino bunkered his approach, while Devlin put his on the back of the green, 40 feet from the pin. Lee came out of the trap very well, leaving himself just five inches from the cup. He got his birdie and so did Devlin. The sudden-death playoff began on the 397-yard 17th, where Trevino's drive hit a spectator but bounded back into the fairway. Devlin's tee shot split the fairway and left him only a seven iron to the green. When Trevino put his approach 75 feet from the pin, Devlin decided to go for the cup. He hit over a bunker and the ball rolled within four feet of the hole. When Devlin made the putt he had his third Dunlop title in five years. He had also upheld the honor of the home country. Player finished two strokes back of Devlin and Trevino, and Jacklin was fourth with a 280. At 281 were Wolstenholme and Maurice Bembridge, who turned in the best round at Yarra Yarra, a 65, on the final day.

The last major event of the Australian circuit was the PGA Championship, which was held in the capital city of Canberra. The U.S. pros had left for home, but it is doubtful any of them could have handled Devlin, who was on his own course and looked invincible. He began by winning the $5,000 Rothman's Celebrity Pro-Am on the eve of the tournament, going around the 7,116 Royal Canberra layout in 68. On a course ranked as one of the most difficult in Australia—7,200 yards through pine trees—he did not have a single bogey, as he won the $1,000 first prize by three shots. Devlin was still experimenting with putters, and he had mulled over his collection of 20 before choosing a small mallet-head for the championship.

In the first round of the championship Devlin shot 67, with five birdies coming in the last 12 holes. "I missed a couple of short ones today, but really I cannot complain," he said. "I am driving well and in spite of the misses I putted well. Give me a good night's rest and a good day on the greens in the second round and I might still be in front." Devlin said he was weary after five hard weeks of competitive golf. But they had been worthwhile weeks. He was now 43 under par for 307 holes of tournament play in Australia. One stroke back was young Clive Clark, who also had been bothered by putting problems. He had apparently been cured by Tony Jacklin, who had given him some advice at Melbourne. Clark had six birdies on the way to his 68 and declared it the finest round he had played in five trips to Australia. He made four straight birdie putts from the 13th to the 16th holes, in spite of the slow, bumpy greens. At 69 was another young Englishman, Peter Oosterhuis, and defending champion Kel Nagel, whose sore hand was still troublesome.

A heavy rain delayed play for 90 minutes in the second round, but Devlin continued his hot pace with another bogey-free round of 69. At the end of the day he found himself with a six-stroke lead. His nearest competition was Hsieh Min Nan of Taiwan, who had a 36-hole total of 142. Four players were grouped at 143—Clark,

Takashi Murkami, Nagle and Stanton. Peter Oosterhuis slumped to a 76 and Nagle's 74 showed he was hurting. For a while the second, ninth and 17th greens were unplayable, but the course, which is only seven years old, drained quickly.

Devlin continued to play unbeatable golf in the third round, shooting a 69 that boosted his lead to eight strokes. Newsmen were writing that the fourth round was a waste of time. "Let's just say I'm playing well," Bruce answered. He certainly was, he had just missed an eagle on the first hole. At the second he took his lone bogey when a spectator's camera distracted him and he missed an 18-inch putt. At the ninth he was stymied by a tree, but saved his par by sinking a 20 footer. By the 18th hole he was so enthused that he rapped an eagle putt far past the hole and needed two to get back for a par 5. Murakami was a distant second at 213, and Peter Thomson, with rounds of 70—75—69, was at 214.

Again relying on his wide lead, Devlin decided to play cautiously on the final day, a tactic he should know by now is dangerous. Murakami made five birdies in the first eight holes and Devlin's eight-stroke lead was suddenly three. Devlin looked in serious trouble at 9 when he drove into the woods. However, Murakami flubbed a downhill chip shot to bogey the hole and Devlin recovered by sinking a 15 footer for a par. Murakami also bogeyed the 10th, and though he came back with two straight birdies it was now too little and too late. Devlin's par 72 gave him a three-stroke victory, and Bruce had finally won the Australian title that long had eluded him. The victory climaxed Devlin's finest season in the Down Under circuit. "I played some bad shots today," he said. "In fact I played three times as many bad shots as I played in my last four rounds. I felt sluggish, perhaps because of my big lead. But this is a nice one to win." Murakami had to be satisfied with second and the fact that his closing 67 was probably the best round of the tournament. He would have scored better had putts that rimmed the cup dropped. On each of the final three holes his ball hit the cup but stayed out.

Not surprisingly, the Australian PGA named Devlin as its Player of the Year. He was an Australian hero, and in bold type the newspapers carried stories of "Devlin's $1.7 Million Project—A Golf Course Fit For A President." It told how Australia's son of a plumber was building Richard Nixon a course on Key Biscayne. Bruce Devlin can tee it up with the best of them.

The PGA was the last prestige event scheduled for the Australian tour, but there was nothing really minor about a new tournament that was to be played the following week, the $10,000 Charities Golf Classic at Sydney. It was to have been a somewhat unusual event, featuring among other things the entry of the U.S. Ladies PGA Champion, Sandra Post, who would be permitted to play against the men while using the front tees. Miss Post received ample pre-tournament publicity and considerable interest was being aroused in the event when along came the big wet again. The pro-am was played in a downpour—and won by Malcolm Gregson with a 66—but that was the end of the action as ten inches of rain fell on Sydney in the next four days. It is always distressing to see a try at a new event fail, and it can only be hoped that the organizers were not too discouraged by what happened.

The Aussie season officially ended the following week as the tour moved north to the resort town of Coffs Harbour, which is near the magnificent Barrier Reef area of Australia. Few of the top golfers made the trip for the $6,200 North Coast Open, and the players who did go had a merciless time of it, partly because of the weather and partly because everybody played so badly that 22 year-old Tony Mangan, who has become a flamboyant figure on the Aussie tour, could shoot 73, 72, 72, 74—291 and still win by three strokes over David Graham. It is almost shocking that nobody broke 70 during the entire tournament. Mangan said of his final round 74 that what it should have been was an 80. Among other things, he missed five fairways with his driver because of a wretched hook. Hook, awful golf and all, the win was worth $1,200 to Mangan in purse money and a considerable private purse as well. Mangan had been listed by bookmakers at 100 to 1 before the tournament started, and one man who thought the wager an attractive one was Mangan. He declined to say how much he bet on himself, only that it was "enough", One aspect of the North Coast Open is worth noting. The tournament started in 1951 with $400 in prize money, and the first winner was Kel Nagle. The course was a ragged nine holes. there were 177 club members and the clubhouse was a weatherboard shed. Now, 19 years later, the event is part of a nine-day "Festival of Golf" at Coffs Harbour. The club has 1,400 members, a fine clubhouse and a good 18-hole course. The game grows everywhere. Australia's best pro tour year to date is testimony to that.

And now it was on to New Zealand, and once again sport stimulated us with the totally unexpected. Kel Nagle had won only one minor event in all of 1969. His hand was hurting and at 49 he must have felt considerably the worse for wear after playing his 23rd season of professional golf. But like another famous figure of the game, Arnold Palmer, Nagle was to bid an astonishing goodby to the decade. What he did was win the first three New Zealand tournaments he entered, an unparalleled feat and one that seems almost unbelievable considering the tendonitis in his right hand and the hurt in his hip.

The other noteworthy figure on the 1969 New Zealand tour was 22 year-old John Lister. Promise you won't forget the name, for it is only a matter of time until he starts showing up at international tournaments. Lister finished second to Nagle in those three November—December events. In his other New Zealand starts he was second to Bob Charles in the Spalding Masters, second in the Travel PGA, fourth in the Watties tournament and winner of the Vonnel International—an impressive performance overall. Lister topped New Zealand's money-winning list with earnings of $7,025 (N.Z.) to Nagle's $6,425 (N.Z.). He has been playing on the Australasian circuit for two years and had hoped to compete in the U.S. in 1970. In October he flew to the States, attended the PGA school and played in the qualifying tournament. There were 12 berths available on the American tour and 181 young men seeking them. Lister was beaten out of the 12th place in a sudden death playoff, but he was apparently undiscouraged, for it was after that that he made strong showing against Nagle and won the Vonnel. Lister's brother Tom is a New Zealand All-Black rugby forward and John seems certain to excel in his profession.

New Zealand golf continued to grow in 1969 and it received an added boost with the appearance of Gary Player in an exhibition series against favorite-son, Bob Charles. Player arrived in early November and though he did not stay on to compete in any tournaments, he played the matches with Charles in the four main cities—Auckland, Christchurch, Wellington and Dunedin—and became a well-known and well-liked individual. The crowds admired his attitude toward golf and liked his frank talk when dealing with South African problems. In fact, Player must rank as the most popular golfer to play in New Zealand for many years, and this is not overlooking Palmer, who came to New Zealand in 1966. The four-match series was promoted by The Dominion and Sunday Times newspapers and was held at the Balmacewan, Shirley, Hutt and Grange courses. Player put together scores of 67-73-67-66—273 to Bob Charles's 71-70-69-70—280. Large galleries followed each around, and although a few demonstrators appeared in the crowds to protest South Africa's apartheid policy, there were no incidents. One other star golfer, Casper, came to New Zealand for exhibitions and he, too, generated good will and enthusiasm for the game. He played two matches in Hamilton and donated a portion of his fee to local Mormon interests.

Early in the year, in the first of the festival tournaments that are played each January in the holiday resort area of the Bay of Plenty, the American woman professional Marilynn Smith made an appearance and created considerable interest. However, Bob Charles dominated the scene, winning the event—the Spalding Masters at Tauranga— by 10 strokes. He fashioned his 260 with rounds of 66-62-69-63, a superlative performance even if it earned him only $800 (N.Z.) The next tournament was the Travel PGA played at Mt. Maunganui. It was won by a local pro, Terry Kendall, but Charles again figures—this time tying for second with John Lister.

When the New Zealand circuit started up again after a 10-month lapse, Charles was not playing as well and the door was open for Nagle became New Zealand Open Champion for the third year in a began with the New Zealand Open, which was sponsored by the BP Oil Company, and was held at the Belmont Club in Wanganui. There NNagle became New Zealand Open Champion for the third year in a row and the seventh time in 13 years. In the opening round England's Maurice Bembridge shot a five-under-par 65, and his birdie putts included a 50 footer, an 18 footer, and a 15 footer. Billy Dunk of Australia had trouble with his approach shots but came in with a 67. Five golfers were at 68, and Nagle was among seven at 69. Bob Charles had a 70, but he followed this with a second-round 67 and at the halfway point found himself only one shot back of Nagle, who was leading (69-67—136). Charles's iron play improved considerably on the second day and he was quietly confident. The final 36 holes was to be played the next day and Charles figured that Nagle, at 49, might no longer be so durable. "Nagle faces the task of conquering the hills, and those within three shots of him have a chance," Charles said before the third round. "If there were 18 holes today and 18 tomorrow he would, I believe, be a much harder man to beat." Bembridge had soared to a 75 and Billy Dunk to a 78, so neither of them appeared to threaten.

The first golfers teed off for the 36-hole final at 6:54 a.m. Nagle continued to play his methodical game and came in at lunch time with a 69. But Charles lost ground, posting a 71. Leading the field after 54 holes were Nagle and Japan's Murakami, with 205s. They were two strokes ahead of John Lister and Randall Vines. To the crowd's disappointment, Murakami faded early in the final round—he came in with a 72 and tied for 4th—but Lister took up the challenge. Nagle was not putting well and Lister, with three straight birdies, moved to a one-stroke lead. The 14th was to be the crucial hole. It is a 511-yard par 5, the kind of hole that makes or breaks a round. Lister bunkered his second shot and then missed a 15 footer for a birdie. Nagle, however, put his second eight feed from the cup and sunk his eagle putt. So the game had turned around, as Nagle picked up two strokes and again was in the lead. Lister, perhaps straining too hard, was bunkered at 18 and lost another stroke to finish two strokes back with a 275. Nagle must be commended for his consistent last-day performance. He had 34 pars, one birdie and an eagle. His putting was poor, and Charles observed that had Nagle been in top form on the greens he could have won by 12 strokes instead of two. Both Charles and Nagle had encouraging words for Lister. "He is going to be a good player," Nagle said. "He is a strong boy and I am sorry he missed getting on the U.S. circuit. I was a bit lucky to get that eagle at the 14th," said Charles, "Lister is the finest tournament golfer among the New Zealand professionals."

The tour moved next to Christchurch for the Garden City Classic at Russley. The course is a flat par 73, and Nagle went out the first day and shot nine under par. The 64 gave him a three-stroke lead over his nearest contenders—Lister and Dunk. It was a hot calm morning when Nagle posted his score and the golfers who played in the afternoon were not so lucky, as they were bothered by wind. Among these were Lister and Dunk. The disappointment of the day for the hometown fans was a lackluster 71 by Charles. "I know what is wrong with my irons but I can't correct it," he said. "I'm bringing the club through from the inside and dragging the ball to the right." (Remember, he is lefthanded). It was Nagle's deft iron play that was enabling him to score so well. He made five birdie putts on the front nine, all within 8 feet. He needed only 26 putts in the entire round.

Nagle's second day performance was as steady as the first, but his putter was not so reliable. On 18 he blew a one-foot tap-in putt when a cameraman moved and distracted him, an incident that allowed Lister to tie him for the lead. Lister had been booming tee shots down the fairways and although they were sometimes off line, there is not that much trouble at Russley. He played his irons well out of the rough and came in with a 67, which included an eagle at 13. The most erratic round of the day was a par 73 by Billy Dunk. He had

tive birdies and five bogeys and raged at his putter. Murakami was also having difficulties on the greens, but they were of his own making. He could have had a 69 had he not tried three tap-ins one-handed. He missed all three.

Nagle took sole possession of the lead in the third round with a fine 66 in a difficult wind. He birdied four of the last five holes to lead Lister by one shot. They were now eight strokes ahead of the other golfers, and it was obvious that no one else in the tournament really mattered. For a while Lister led during the third round—he eagled the 9th and the 13th holes—but he bogeyed 16 when he was bunkered, blasted out across the green and then chipped poorly.

Neither of the leaders played well in the final round, but again Lister eagled 9 and 13, and although he birdied 17 and 18 it was not enough. Nagle came in with a 72 to Lister's 73 and the City of Christchurch title was his by two strokes. His 272 was 20 under par. A 67 by Bob Charles moved him into a tie for third. This fine performance was watched by only 16 people, as thousands followed Lister and Nagle. Charles is New Zealand's golf hero, but as is the case everywhere, and rightly, heroes also have to win. And Lister and Nagle play such contrasting golf that their show is well worth watching. Lister, with the energies of youth, strong-arms the ball. Nagle is a wise, self-confident old pro whose longevity is due to his relaxed game.

The next event was the Caltex tournament at Paraparaumu and again Nagle and Lister starred, but not in the first round. Nagle had a 70 and Lister a 73 that day while a young Australian pro, Kel Garner, set a swift pace with a three-under-par 68. Despite his zestful opener, Garner was talking like a weary man—"I've had a gutful of golf since I turned professional 18 months ago," he told reporters. "After this tournament I'm heading home to Melbourne. Even if I were lucky enough to win here, which is doubtful, I could not be enticed to stay on." Garner, like Charles, is a lefthander. He started brilliantly and was four under after seven holes. But then he had trouble with his putting. At 69 were Billy Dunk and Terry Kendall. Dunk was playing his usual erratic brand of golf, yet the score satisfied him. It was another matter with Lister. "I should not have been allowed on the course, the way I played," the young New Zealand pro said, "I played like a drunk." He had driven out of bounds, been bunkered and three-putted two straight holes. Nagle hit only 11 greens during his round and managed a respectable score only by sinking a 20-foot eagle putt on the final hole. Guy

Wolstenholme also had a disappointing round, so disappointing in fact that he withdrew. He was bothered by the slow play, he said. Through the 16th hole Guy was playing par golf, but at 17 he four putted for a triple bogey and he took a 12 at the 18th hole, where he hit three tee shots out of bounds. "I just have no interest in playing golf at this speed," he muttered after spending four hours and 20 minutes on the course. "I waited on every shot and I've no intention of continuing in this way."

Garner held the lead at the halfway point by shooting a 69. "The fact that I was out in front did not perturb me," the 20 year-old said. "I just kept on as steadily as I could. It was my short game that really kept me going." Bob Charles continued to have difficulty (72-77), but Nagle improved on his first day's score with a 69, one of the best totals of the day. In the strong southerly wind he did have some trouble with his approaches. "You just can't throw it to the stick in these conditions," he said, "and this fact tended to keep the scores high." Nagle was now two strokes out of the lead.

Garner, not surprisingly, blew during the third round and shot an 81. He ended by winning $50 in the tournament. But Nagle maintained a fine pace with a 67, and after 54 holes he led by six strokes. Over the final 18 first Billy Dunk and then John Lister challenged, but Nagle breezed away from the opposition, winning by seven strokes. "It's not the cash. I just love to win," he said grinning. "I did not play really well until today." Altogether Nagle won $6,000 in three weeks. Lister had a strong closing round at Paraparaumu, a 65 which included a course-record 29 on the back nine. He finished the round with a flourish by sinking a 20-foot eagle putt at 18.

Lister carried his hot streak with him to the Watties $5,000 Tournament at Gisbourne. He began with a sizzling 67 which gave him the first round lead, and his second round 71 was good enough to maintain the lead by a stroke. One behind Lister at the halfway point were Charles, Dunk, Alan Murray and George McCully, and Kel Nagle was making everyone uneasy with a 70-70 that left him only two strokes back. On the next day, however, Nagle slumped to a 74 while Charles was shooting a 66, a course record. Somebody else was posting a 66, too, a 20 year-old Melbourne pro named Glen McCully, and it was McCully who went on to win by three shots. McCully said, "I felt pretty good, but I never dreamed of winning." It was his first victory in a 72-hole event, and he had not folded although he had been paired with Billy Dunk and Kel Nagle—no mean company. Like

Lister, he is a big hitter, but he is not as consistent. Charles and Dunk tied for second and Lister, with a final round of 68, was fourth.

At the Vonnel International, a $5,000 36-hole tournament held at the North Shore Golf Club, Lister finally won himself a championship. For awhile it seemed he would not get this satisfaction as four players—Dunk, Terry Kendall, Randall Vines and Lister—finished in a tie and the promoters of the event announced that they would all share the top money, each man receiving $625. But minutes later a voice on the loudspeaker system declared there would be a sudden-death playoff. Dunk, who was about to leave to catch a plane home to Sydney, was furious. And Kendall and Vines showed they were upset by duck hooking their tee shots on the first extra hole. Dunk also pulled his drive, but he was able to power his ball over some tall pines and put it on the front of the green. Lister, not a bit upset, put his drive in the middle of the fairway and his approach 12 feet from the hole. Kendall and Vines bogeyed, but Dunk and Lister parred and went on to the second hole, a 125-yard par 3. Dunk put his tee shot 20 feet from the cup. Lister was well inside, just five feet from the hole. Dunk missed, Lister didn't.

Thus, the New Zealand tour ended with a winner it could call its own. On the 18th green at North Shore that final day the gallery sang Happy Birthday to Kel Nagle after he putted out. Nagle was a little older but a little richer, too, after visiting New Zealand. His parting words were a cheery, "I'll be back." That is a good enough exit line for anybody.

Appendix

WORLD MONEY LIST

This compilation of golf tournament prize money includes figures from all of professional tours in the world, international competitions, major television matches and all non-tour tournaments throughout the world involving four or more professionals on which information could be obtained.

POS.	PLAYER, COUNTRY	MONEY
1	Frank Beard, *U.S.*	$186,993.93
2	Bill Casper, *U.S.*	170,501.16
3	Dave Hill, *U.S.*	163,323.30
4	Gene Littler, *U.S.*	160,092.27
5	Orville Moody, *U.S.*	151,683.27
6	Jack Nicklaus, *U.S.*	143,640.22
7	Gary Player, *South Africa*	140,384.19
8	Lee Trevino, *U.S.*	139,511.31
9	George Archer, *U.S.*	127,945.06
10	Bruce Crampton, *Australia*	124,155.80
11	Tommy Aaron, *U.S.*	122,732.41
12	Ray Floyd, *U.S.*	122,631.43
13	Miller Barber, *U.S.*	112,951.38
14	Dan Sikes, *U.S.*	109,853.68
15	Ken Still, *U.S.*	107,514.21
16	Arnold Palmer, *U.S.*	105,128.42
17	Bruce Devlin, *Australia*	97,379.34
18	Dale Douglass, *U.S.*	96,737.53
19	Bob Lunn, *U.S.*	92,706.17
20	Bert Yancey, *U.S.*	92,156.09
21	Bob Charles, *New Zealand*	89,297.74
22	Tom Shaw, *U.S.*	88,332.01
23	Tom Weiskopf, *U.S.*	87,093.79
24	Deane Beman, *U.S.*	86,396.98
25	Bert Greene, *U.S.*	84,781.47
26	Charles Coody, *U.S.*	84,066.26
27	Dave Stockton, *U.S.*	80,707.43
28	Don January, *U.S.*	71,380.93
29	Gay Brewer, *U.S.*	69,567.80
30	Larry Ziegler, *U.S.*	65,571.12
31	Homero Blancas, *U.S.*	61,854.64
32	Bob Murphy, *U.S.*	61,489.30
33	Tony Jacklin, *Great Britain*	59,545.13
34	Bunky Henry, *U.S.*	58,520.90
35	Julius Boros, *U.S.*	58,098.63

POS.	PLAYER, COUNTRY				MONEY
36	Larry Hinson, *U.S.*	.	.	.	57,167.02
37	Gardner Dickinson, *U.S.*	.	.	.	56,478.97
38	Chi Chi Rodriguez, *U.S.*	.	.	.	56,312.95
39	R. H. Sikes, *U.S.*	.	.	.	54,934.72
40	Lee Elder, *U.S.*	.	.	.	54,178.67
41	Howie Johnson, *U.S.*	.	.	.	53,152.95
42	George Knudson, *Canada*	.	.	.	50,232.05
43	Jim Colbert, *U.S.*	.	.	.	46,668.12
44	Harold Henning, *South Africa*		.	.	44,906.51
45	Dick Crawford, *U.S.*	.	.	.	43,657.56
46	Bobby Nichols, *U.S.*	.	.	.	43,110.93
47	Jim Wiechers, *U.S.*	.	.	.	42,300.90
48	Charles Sifford, *U.S.*	.	.	.	42,139.30
49	Terry Dill, *U.S.*	.	.	.	42,014.87
50	Dick Lotz, *U.S.*	.	.	.	40,710.29
51	Bob Dickson, *U.S.*	.	.	.	40,298.77
52	Grier Jones, *U.S.*	.	.	.	40,293.79
53	Al Geiberger, *U.S.*	.	.	.	40,068.09
54	Bob Stanton, *Australia*	.	.	.	39,242.87
55	Johnny Pott, *U.S.*	.	.	.	38,222.12
56	Doug Sanders, *U.S.*	.	.	.	37,665.92
57	Bob Goalby, *U.S.*	.	.	.	37,196.98
58	Ron Cerrudo, *U.S.*	.	.	.	36,061.25
59	Sam Snead, *U.S.*	.	.	.	35,558.78
60	Tommy Bolt, *U.S.*	.	.	.	35,460.59
61	B. R. McLendon, *U.S.*	.	.	.	35,424.86
62	Don Bies, *U.S.*	.	.	.	35,143.18
63	Fred Marti, *U.S.*	.	.	.	34,945.98
64	Billy Maxwell, *U.S.*	.	.	.	34,549.84
65	Bobby Mitchell, *U.S.*	.	.	.	34,155.31
66	Rod Funseth, *U.S.*	.	.	.	33,295.13
67	Lou Graham, *U.S.*	.	.	.	32,783.92
68	Phil Rodgers, *U.S.*	.	.	.	32,203.43
69	Steve Spray, *U.S.*	.	.	.	31,909.27
70	Steve Reid, *U.S.*	.	.	.	29,634.95
71	Bob Rosburg, *U.S.*	.	.	.	29,086.79
72	Jack McGowan, *U.S.*	.	.	.	28,816.07
73	Peter Townsend, *Great Britain*		.	.	26,736.47
74	Lionel Hebert, *U.S.*	.	.	.	26,603.74
75	Kermit Zarley, *U.S.*	.	.	.	26,531.41
76	Jack Montgomery, *U.S.*	.	.	.	26,409.71
77	Bobby Cole, *South Africa*	.	.	.	26,191.45
78	Jerry Abbott, *U.S.*	.	.	.	25,944.27
79	Terry Wilcox, *U.S.*	.	.	.	25,940.10
80	Jim Wright, *U.S.*	.	.	.	24,547.48
81	Joel Goldstrand, *U.S.*	.	.	.	24,291.60
82	Larry Mowry, *U.S.*	.	.	.	23,881.49
83	Rocky Thompson, *U.S.*	.	.	.	23,540.71

POS.	PLAYER, COUNTRY	MONEY
84 —	Hugh Royer, *U.S.*	23,479.28
85 —	Tommy Jacobs, *U.S.*	23,270.27
86 —	Roberto de Vicenzo, *Argentina*	23,046.98
87 —	Bob Smith, *U.S.*	22,851.19
88 —	Jacky Cupit, *U.S.*	22,389.67
89 —	Maurice Bembridge, *Great Britain*	22,275.41
90 —	Jack Ewing, *U.S.*	21,841.67
91 —	Mason Rudolph, *U.S.*	21,667.71
92 —	Herb Hooper, *U.S.*	21,618.07
93 —	Butch Baird, *U.S.*	21,599.05
94 —	Pete Brown, *U.S.*	21,468.98
95 —	Chuck Courtney, *U.S.*	21,446.62
96 —	J. C. Goosie, *U.S.*	20,540.06
97 —	Johnny Jacobs, *U.S.*	20,520.48
98 —	Al Balding, *Canada*	19,786.71
99 —	Jerry Pittman, *U.S.*	19,706.78
100 —	Dow Finsterwald, *U.S.*	19,515.25
101 —	Peter Thomson, *Australia*	19,385.90
102 —	Hale Irwin, *U.S.*	18,776.48
103 —	John Lotz, *U.S.*	18,568.96
104 —	Dave Marr, *U.S.*	18,144.15
105 —	Bernard Gallacher, *Great Britain*	17,738.20
106 —	Kel Nagle, *Australia*	17,272.32
107 —	Labron Harris, *U.S.*	16,624.42
108 —	Mike Hill, *U.S.*	16,239.09
109 —	Christie O'Connor, *Great Britain*	16,056
110 —	Al Mengert, *U.S.*	16,049.55
111 —	Guy Wolstenholme, *Great Britain*	16,047.85
112 —	Frank Boynton, *U.S.*	15,943.51
113 —	Brian Huggett, *Great Britain*	15,928.27
114 —	Art Wall, *U.S.*	15,206.76
115 —	Bob Cox, *Canada*	15,148.74
116 —	John Schlee, *U.S.*	14,708.17
117 —	Dean Refram, *U.S.*	14,528.45
118 —	Hugh Inggs, *South Africa*	14,464.66
119 —	Takaaki Kono, *Japan*	14,261.01
120 —	Jean Garaialde, *France*	14,231.52
121 —	Jerry McGee, *U.S.*	14,033.04
122 —	Bernard Hunt, *Great Britain*	13,709.45
123 —	Howell Fraser, *U.S.*	13,583.29
124 —	Cobie Legrange, *South Africa*	13,560.88
125 —	Steve Oppermann, *U.S.*	13,474.62
126 —	Haruo Yasuda, *Japan*	13,412.93
127 —	Monty Kaser, *U.S.*	13,123.91
128 —	Wilf Homenuik, *Canada*	12,942.04
129 —	Bill Garrett, *U.S.*	12,773.59
130 —	Jerry Heard, *U.S.*	12,736.71
131 —	Bob Erickson, *U.S.*	12,639.36

POS.	PLAYER, COUNTRY	MONEY
132 —	Paul Harney, *U.S.*	12,461.90
133 —	Roy Pace, *U.S.*	12,389.03
134 —	Bobby Brue, *U.S.*	11,807.97
135 —	Roberto Bernardini, *Italy*	11,750.68
136 —	Bob McCallister, *U.S.*	11,690.62
137 —	Jim Grant, *U.S.*	11,384.13
138 —	Dudley Wysong, *U.S.*	11,286.67
139 —	Dick Rhyan, *U.S.*	11,178.99
140 —	Hal Underwood, *U.S.*	11,167.50
141 —	Jesse Snead, *U.S.*	11,140.28
142 —	Doug Ford, *U.S.*	11,090.62
143 —	Graham Henning, *South Africa*	11,048.18
144 —	Bob Payne, *U.S.*	11,030.28
145 —	Bob Stone, *U.S.*	10,876.51
146 —	Dewitt Weaver, *U.S.*	10,819.37
147 —	John Schroeder, *U.S.*	10,584.30
148 —	Don Whitt, *U.S.*	10,494.13
149 —	Richard Martinez, *U.S.*	10,460.81
150 —	John Lister, *New Zealand*	10,270.05
151 —	Tommy Horton, *Great Britain*	9,992.80
152 —	Johnny Stevens, *U.S.*	9,943.72
153 —	Peter Butler, *Great Britain*	9,872.80
154 —	Jim Jamieson, *U.S.*	9,681.05
155 —	Malcolm Gregson, *Great Britain*	9,598.54
156 —	Don Massengale, *U.S.*	9,586.24
157 —	John Garner, *Great Britain*	9,570.48
158 —	Dave Eichelberger, *U.S.*	9,423.51
159 —	Brian Barnes, *Great Britain*	9,394.80
160 —	John Miller, *U.S.*	9,214.12
161 —	Gordon Jones, *U.S.*	9,196.87
162 —	Cesar Sanudo, *U.S.*	9,092.40
163 —	Bob Shaw, *Australia*	8,949.48
164 —	David Graham, Australia	8,600.87
165 —	Bill Collins, *U.S.*	8,456.01
166 —	Dick Hart, *U.S.*	8,393.12
167 —	Billy Dunk, *Australia*	8,342.88
168 —	Randy Petri, *U.S.*	8,179.07
169 —	Frank Phillips, *Australia*	8,086.33
170 —	Bill Ogden, *U.S.*	8,076.31
171 —	George Will, *Great Britain*	8,074.30
172 —	Randall Vines, *Australia*	8,026.76
173 —	Peter Alliss, *Great Britain*	7,900.61
174 —	Bert Weaver, *U.S.*	7,868.96
175 —	Joe Campbell, *U.S.*	7,764.86
176 —	Rives McBee, *U.S.*	7,726.74
177 —	Ronnie Shade, *Great Britain*	7,705.92
178 —	Jimmy Powell, *U.S.*	7,628.31
179 —	Ken Venturi, *U.S.*	7,626.46

POS.	PLAYER, COUNTRY				MONEY
180	— Takashi Murakami, *Japan*	.	.	.	7,561.58
181	— Bob Panasiuk, *Canada*	.	.	.	7,497.54
182	— Earl Stewart, *U.S.*	.	.	.	7,433.78
183	— Gibby Gilbert, *U.S.*	.	.	.	7,264.30
184	— Bob Menne, *U.S.*	.	.	.	7,238.26
185	— Dave Ragan, *U.S.*	.	.	.	7,138.85
186	— Chris Blocker, *U.S.*	.	.	.	7,033.25
187	— James Black, *U.S.*	.	.	.	7,000
188	— Wayne Vollmer, *Canada*	.	.	.	6,801.32
189	— Neil Coles, *Great Britain*	.	.	.	6,640.80
190	— Alex Caygill, *Great Britain*	.	.	.	6,628.80
191	— Al Besselink, *U.S.*	.	.	.	6,531.25
192	— Wayne Yates, *U.S.*	.	.	.	6,483.76
193	— Trevor Wilkes, *South Africa*	.	.	.	6,472.29
194	— Bob Duden, *U.S.*	.	.	.	6,435.28
195	— Clive Clark, *Great Britain*	.	.	.	6,159.72
196	— Jerry Steelsmith, *U.S.*	.	.	.	6,077.50
197	— Martin Roesink, *Holland*	.	.	.	5,842.93
198	— Peter Oosterhuis, *Great Britain*	.	.	.	5,810
199	— Dutch Harrison, *U.S.*	.	.	.	5,749.44
200	— Hsieh Min Nan, *Formosa*	.	.	.	5,719.24

WORLD STROKE AVERAGES

Another method of evaluating performance in professional golf—and, in the minds of many, a more valid one—is the comparison of stroke averages. This World Stroke Averages list is drawn from the records of all stroke-play tournaments on the established tours of the world and three international stroke-play events. Only players with at least 36 rounds of competition are included.

POS.	PLAYER, COUNTRY	ROUNDS	STROKES	AVERAGE
1 —	Dave Hill, U.S.	104	7,324	70.423
2 —	Gary Player, South Africa	89	6,274	70.494
3 —	Frank Beard, U.S.	126	8,897	70.611
4 —	Trevor Wilkes, South Africa	40	2,825	70.625
5 —	Bob Charles, New Zealand	125	8,833	70.664
6 —	Tommy Aaron, U.S.	119	8,417	70.731
7 —	Gene Littler, U.S.	77	5,449	70.766
8 —	Bruce Devlin, Australia	98	6,946	70.877
9 —	Bruce Crampton, Australia	110	7,801	70.918
10 —	Lee Trevino, U.S.	137	9,720	70.948
11 —	Don January, U.S.	88	6,251	71.034
12 —	Dan Sikes, U.S.	105	7,459	71.038
13 —	Arnold Palmer, U.S.	100	7,104	71.040
14 —	Bill Casper, U.S.	105	7,461	71.057
15 —	Jack Nicklaus, U.S.	93	6,609	71.064
16 —	Deane Beman, U.S.	102	7,261	71.186
17 —	Miller Barber, U.S.	126	8,974	71.222
18 —	Howie Johnson, U.S.	133	9,482	71.293
19 —	Frank Phillips, Australia	77	5,492	71.324
20 —	Cobie Legrange, South Africa	82	5,849	71.329
21 —	Chi Chi Rodriguez, U.S.	107	7,633	71.336
22 —	Dale Douglass, U.S.	136	9,702	71.338
23 —	Roberto de Vicenzo, Argentina	38	2,711	71.342
24 —	Homero Blancas, U.S.	106	7,563	71.349
25 —	Bert Yancey, U.S.	129	9,206	71.364
26 —	George Knudson, Canada	74	5,281	71.364
27 —	Billy Dunk, Australia	61	4,354	71.377
28 —	Hsieh Yung Yo, Formosa	36	2,570	71.388
29 —	Tom Weiskopf, U.S.	102	7,290	71.470
30 —	Gay Brewer, U.S.	101	7,219	71.475
31 —	Tommy Bolt, U.S.	42	3,002	71.476
32 —	Fred Marti, U.S.	111	7,936	71.495
33 —	Orville Moody, U.S.	123	8,795	71.504
34 —	Jim Wiechers, U.S.	115	8,224	71.513

POS.	PLAYER, COUNTRY	ROUNDS	STROKES	AVERAGE
35 —	Terry Dill, *U.S.*	102	7,296	71.529
36 —	Dave Stockton, *U.S.*	116	8,299	71.543
37 —	Bob Lunn, *U.S.*	128	9,159	71.554
38 —	Phil Rodgers, *U.S.*	109	7.801	71.568
39 —	Charles Coody, *U.S.*	109	7,803	71.587
40 —	George Archer, *U.S.*	109	7,806	71.614
41 —	Paul Harney, *U.S.*	53	3,798	71.660
42 —	Julius Boros, *U.S.*	95	6,809	71.674
43 —	R. H. Sikes, *U.S.*	120	8,601	71.675
44 —	Al Geiberger, *U.S.*	60	4,301	71.683
45 —	Bobby Mitchell, *U.S.*	121	8,677	71.710
46 —	Sam Snead, *U.S.*	52	3,729	71.711
47 —	Grier Jones, *U.S.*	122	8,749	71.713
48 —	Ray Floyd, *U.S.*	103	7,387	71.718
49 —	Johnny Pott, *U.S.*	97	6,957	71.721
50 —	Rod Funseth, *U.S.*	119	8,536	71.731

THE CHAMPIONS AND CONTENDERS OF 1969

This listing consolidates the world records of the professionals who won or came close to winning in 1969, totaling their victories and finishes in the top three in all of the events summarized in the appendix of this book.

	WORLD VICTORIES	WORLD 1–2–3 FINISHES
1 — Gary Player, *South Africa*	4	11
2 — Bruce Devlin, *Australia*	4	7
3 — Kel Nagle, *Australia*	4	4
T4 — Dave Hill, *U.S.*	3	8
Cobie Legrange, *South Africa*	3	8
6 — Bill Casper, *U.S.*	3	7
7 — Jack Nicklaus, *U.S.*	3	4
T8 — Ray Floyd, *U.S.*	3	3
Jean Garaialde, *France*	3	3
10 — Lee Trevino, *U.S.*	2	9
11 — Frank Beard, *U.S.*	2	8
12 — Bernard Gallacher, *Great Britain*	2	7
T13 — Bob Charles, *New Zealand*	2	6
Billy Dunk, *Australia*	2	6
T15 — Graham Henning, *South Africa*	2	5
Guy Wolstenholme, *Great Britain*	2	5
Roberto Bernardini, *Italy*	2	5
Maurice Bembridge, *Great Britain*	2	5
T19 — Arnold Palmer, *U.S.*	2	4
Dale Douglass, *U.S.*	2	4
Gene Littler, *U.S.*	2	4
Brian Huggett, *Great Britain*	2	4
Bernard Hunt, *Great Britain*	2	4
Bobby Cole, *South Africa*	2	4
Bert Yancey, *U.S.*	2	4
Orville Moody, *U.S.*	2	4
27 — George Archer, *U.S.*	2	3
T28 — Tom Shaw, *U.S.*	2	2
Ken Still, *U.S.*	2	2
Butch Baird, *U.S.*	2	2
31 — John Lister, *New Zealand*	1	7
T32 — Tommy Aaron, *U.S.*	1	6
Hugh Inggs, *South Africa*	1	6
T34 — Bruce Crampton, *Australia*	1	5
Christie O'Connor, *Great Britain*	1	5
Trevor Wilkes, *South Africa*	1	5

		WORLD VICTORIES	WORLD 1–2–3 FINISHES
T37 —	Peter Thomson, *Australia*	1	4
	Miller Barber, *U.S.*	1	4
	Roberto de Vicenzo, *Argentina*	1	4
T40 —	Deane Beman, *U.S.*	1	3
	Charles Coody, *U.S.*	1	3
	Larry Mowry, *U.S.*	1	3
	Peter Butler, *Great Britain*	1	3
	Frank Phillips, *Australia*	1	3

NON-WINNERS WITH THREE OR MORE FINISHES IN TOP THREE

5 —George Will, *Great Britain*
4 —Dave Stockton, *U.S.*; Tom Weiskopf, *U.S.*; Bob Stanton, *Australia*; John Garner, *Great Britain*; Randall Vines, *Australia*.
3 —Don January, *U.S.*; Dan Sikes, *U.S.*; Bert Greene, *U.S.*; David Graham, *Australia*; Takashi Murakami, *Japan*

NOTE: Thirty-four other professionals won 1969 titles, had no more than one other finish in the top three.

United States Tour

RANCHO PARK GOLF COURSE
Los Angeles, California
January 9–12
Purse...$100,000
Par: 36, 35–71...6,827 yards

	SCORES	TOTAL	MONEY
Charles Sifford	63 71 71 71	276	$20,000
Harold Henning, *South Africa*	74 68 66 68	276	11,400
(Sifford defeated Henning with birdie on first hole of sudden-death playoff.)			
Bill Casper	69 69 72 67	277	5,900
Bruce Devlin, *Australia*	69 72 69 67	277	5,900
Dave Hill	66 73 69 70	278	4,100
Bert Yancey	75 67 71 67	280	3,600
Howell Fraser	72 73 70 66	281	3,200
B. R. McLendon	69 68 77 68	282	2,716.67
Roy Pace	71 69 72 70	282	2,716.67
Tom Shaw	69 68 73 72	282	2,716.66
Ken Ellsworth	70 70 70 73	283	1,900
Howie Johnson	73 70 71 69	283	1,900
Bobby Nichols	74 70 70 69	283	1,900
Mason Rudolph	71 68 71 73	283	1,900
Dave Stockton	70 74 72 67	283	1,900
Larry Ziegler	70 72 72 69	283	1,900
Tommy Aaron	72 67 75 70	284	1,065.46
Terry Dill	67 72 76 69	284	1,065.46
Dale Douglass	70 73 71 70	284	1,065.46
Don January	71 72 72 69	284	1,065.46
Jimmy Powell	73 72 70 69	284	1,065.46
Bruce Crampton, *Australia*	68 70 74 72	284	1,065.45
Dow Finsterwald	72 72 69 71	284	1,065.45
Grier Jones	66 74 73 71	284	1,065.45
Arnold Palmer	72 68 71 73	284	1,065.45
Robert Payne	70 67 72 75	284	1,065.45
Phil Rodgers	70 72 72 70	284	1,065.45
Ray Floyd	71 69 73 72	285	666.67
Jack Montgomery	71 72 70 72	285	666.67
Bob Smith	70 68 74 73	285	666.67
Steve Spray	76 66 73 70	285	666.67
George Archer	69 67 75 74	285	666.66
Wayne Yates	70 72 70 73	285	666.66
Miller Barber	71 70 72 73	286	530
Ray Botts	72 71 73 70	286	530

294

	SCORES				TOTAL	MONEY
Ron Cerrudo	70	69	76	71	286	530
Tony Jacklin, *Great Britain*	74	69	74	69	286	530
George Knudson, *Canada*	71	72	76	67	286	530
James Walker	67	71	73	75	286	530
Chris Blocker	71	73	68	75	287	361.43
Pete Brown	69	73	73	72	287	361.43
Jim Colbert	75	68	74	70	287	361.43
Eddie Merrins	70	74	70	73	287	361.43
Jim Wiechers	73	72	70	72	287	361.43
Johnny Bulla	75	70	72	70	287	361.43
Doug Sanders	71	73	68	75	287	361.42
George Bayer	72	71	72	73	288	220
Bob Duden	69	73	75	71	288	220
Mike Hadlock	72	69	76	71	288	220
Bob McCallister	72	73	72	71	288	220
Peter Townsend, *Great Britain*	73	69	74	72	288	220
Bob Cox	73	72	71	72	288	220
Al Geiberger	73	72	70	74	289	133.34
Jim Grant	72	69	76	72	289	133.34
Laurie Hammer	71	74	73	71	289	133.34
John Lively	72	70	75	72	289	133.34
Johnny Stevens	71	72	75	71	289	133.34
Wayne Vollmer	71	70	74	74	289	133.34
Hale Irwin	73	71	75	71	290	133.34
Jimmy Wright	71	74	74	71	290	133.34
Dave Bollman	71	70	76	73	290	133.34
Paul Bondeson	74	70	74	72	290	133.33
Ken Still	70	73	73	74	290	133.33
Harry Toscano	72	71	74	73	290	133.33
Rex Baxter	70	74	77	70	291	133.33
Gay Brewer	69	76	72	74	291	133.33
Monty Kaser	73	72	72	74	291	133.33
Monte Sanders	71	70	75	75	291	133.33
Dewitt Weaver	70	75	75	71	291	133.33
Les Peterson	72	73	72	74	291	133.33
Bill Garrett	72	71	75	74	292	133.33
Rocky Thompson	70	73	77	72	292	133.33
Bob Goetz	71	74	76	71	292	133.33
Jerry Heard	73	72	78	70	293	133.33
Lee Trevino	72	71	76	74	293	133.33
Jimmy Clark	72	71	76	74	293	133.33
Ed Davis	72	71	75	78	296	133.33
Bill Johnston	72	73	72	81	298	133.33
Ron Drimak	71	72	82	77	302	133.33

ALAMEDA COUNTY OPEN

SUNOL VALLEY COUNTRY CLUB, PALM COURSE
Sunol, California
January 9—12
Purse...$50,000
Par: 36, 36—72...7,408 yards

	SCORES				TOTAL	MONEY
Dick Lotz	72	71	74	73	290	$10,000
Don Whitt	72	77	69	73	291	5,700
Bob Erickson	77	71	68	76	292	3,550
Dave Ragan	75	70	71	78	294	2,350
Bill Ogden	70	72	75	78	295	1,925
Tommy Jacobs	75	76	70	74	295	1,925
Bob Lunn	75	69	73	79	296	1,418.75
John Lotz	74	75	70	77	296	1,418.75
Johnny Jacobs	74	74	76	72	296	1,418.75
Bobby Brue	73	75	72	76	296	1,418.75
Jack Ewing	75	76	75	72	298	1,150
Richard Martinez	70	80	74	75	299	937.50
Scotty McBeath	73	80	70	76	299	937.50
Jimmy Day	74	77	74	74	299	937.50
Rich Bassett	76	74	75	74	299	937.50
Ross Randall	75	78	69	78	300	750
Roberto Bernardini, *Italy*	77	75	73	75	300	750
Buddy Sullivan	75	77	75	73	300	750
Randy Petri	81	72	70	78	301	581.25
Butch Baird	72	76	73	80	301	581.25
Jerry Abbott	75	73	76	77	301	581.25
Ken Towns	75	79	74	73	301	581.25
Jim Bullard	77	73	75	77	302	447
Carl Lohren	73	81	75	73	302	447
Bob Menne	77	77	71	77	302	447
Dick Lundahl	74	80	73	75	302	447
Joe Carr	77	74	76	76	303	387.50
Deane Beman	74	77	74	78	303	387.50
Bill Tindall	73	71	75	85	304	343.75
Jimmy Picard	78	73	77	76	304	343.75
Joe McDermott	75	79	74	76	304	343.75
Dean Refram	74	76	78	76	304	343.75
John Felus	75	75	74	81	305	300
Bill Blanton	79	73	78	75	305	300
Stan Thirsk	76	75	74	80	305	300
Orville Moody	78	75	76	76	305	300
*Forrest Fezler	78	71	75	81	305	
Babe Lichardus	73	74	78	81	306	255
Edward Weck	74	76	76	80	306	255

	SCORES	TOTAL	MONEY
Bill Lively	80 73 76 77	306	255
Rick Jetter	72 78 78 78	306	255
Bill Ezinicki	79 74 74 79	306	255
Maurice Ver Brugge	75 75 78 79	307	166
Harry Taylor	77 78 74 78	307	166
Jim Greer	79 75 77 76	307	166
Denny Lyons	76 73 81 77	307	166
Tom Sanderson	73 78 81 75	307	166
Rolf Deming	74 75 79 80	308	125
Gary Loustalot	76 78 74 80	308	125
*Art McNickle	78 75 76 79	308	
Woody Wright	77 74 78 80	309	107.50
George Hixon	75 78 78 78	309	107.50
Paul Biocini	75 77 77 81	310	100
Lee Davis	79 76 77 79	311	100
Chick Evans	74 75 77 85	311	100
Dave Walters	77 78 77 79	311	100
*Ray Arinno	74 76 78 84	312	
Jim Hardy	75 78 78 81	312	100
Gil Bennett	78 77 76 81	312	100
*Bob Eastwood	77 76 77 82	312	
Joe Mortara Jr.	76 78 81 77	312	100
Dave Eichelberger	81 72 75 85	313	100
Jack Garner	81 74 78 80	313	100
Dino Camonica	78 74 81 80	313	100
William Mitchell	76 79 79 81	315	100
Jack Harden Jr.	78 77 74 87	316	100
Ed Kroll	76 77 78 85	316	100
Dick Crawford	78 77 77 85	317	100
Hal Wells	78 79 81 85	322	100

* Amateur

(First two rounds played 16th and 17th, heavy rain forced postponements the next three days, two-round standings declared final, half of $135,000 purse paid to contestants.)

KAISER INTERNATIONAL OPEN

SILVERADO COUNTRY CLUB
Napa, California
January 16—20
Purse...$67,500
North Course—
Par: 36, 36—72...6,849 yards
South Course—
Par: 35, 37—72...6,602 yards

	SCORES		TOTAL	MONEY
Miller Barber	68	67	135	$13,500
Bruce Devlin, *Australia*	69	67	136	7,700
Arnold Palmer	69	68	137	4,785
Bob Lunn	65	73	138	2,917.25
Charles Coody	70	68	138	2,917.25
Bobby Brue	71	68	139	1,792.82
Jim Colbert	71	68	139	1,792.82
Bob McCallister	69	70	139	1,792.82
Orville Moody	69	70	139	1,792.82
Jacky Cupit	66	73	139	1,792.82
Gene Littler	69	70	139	1,792.82
Lee Trevino	68	71	139	1,792.82
John Lotz	72	67	139	1,792.82
Jimmy Powell	71	69	140	885
Harold Henning, *South Africa*	69	71	140	885
Jerry McGee	70	70	140	885
Howell Fraser	70	70	140	885
Tommy Aaron	71	69	140	885
George Archer	72	68	140	885
Tom Shaw	72	68	140	885
Grier Jones	74	66	140	885
Dave Hill	68	72	140	885
Tony Jacklin, *Great Britain*	69	71	140	885
Bert Yancey	71	69	140	885
Babe Hiskey	71	70	141	414.98
Jim Wiechers	70	71	141	414.97
Frank Beard	73	68	141	414.97
Ron Cerrudo	72	69	141	414.97
Babe Lichardus	73	68	141	414.97
Jim Bullard	72	69	141	414.97
Don Massengale	71	70	141	414.97
Jerry Abbott	71	70	141	414.97
Hugh Royer	71	70	141	414.97
Bill Casper	70	71	141	414.97
Dave Stockton	74	67	141	414.97
Howie Johnson	70	71	141	414.97

	SCORES	TOTAL	MONEY
George Bayer	72 69	141	414.97
Dave Marr	71 70	141	414.97
Don January	72 69	141	414.97
Frank Boynton	71 70	141	414.97
Terry Dill	70 71	141	414.97
Pete Brown	71 71	142	180.80
Deane Beman	71 71	142	180.80
Dale Douglass	72 70	142	180.80
Bob Duden	74 68	142	180.80
Billy Maxwell	70 72	142	180.80
Johnny Stevens	69 73	142	180.80
Ray Floyd	70 72	142	180.80
Marty Fleckman	71 71	142	180.80
Bob Smith	70 72	142	180.80
*John Miller	70 72	142	
Steve Spray	74 68	142	180.80
Ray Botts	70 73	143	65.82
Johnny Pott	72 71	143	65.82
Bob Erickson	71 72	143	65.82
Phil Rodgers	70 73	143	65.82
Doug Sanders	71 72	143	65.82
Scotty McBeath	70 73	143	65.82
Bill Garrett	71 72	143	65.82
Kermit Zarley	70 73	143	65.82
Monty Kaser	70 73	143	65.82
Terry Wilcox	73 70	143	65.82
B. R. McLendon	71 72	143	65.81
Jack Montgomery	69 74	143	65.81
Paul Harney	70 73	143	65.81
Dave Ragan	71 73	144	65.81
Dow Finsterwald	69 75	144	65.81
Gay Brewer	75 69	144	65.81
Bill Ogden	74 70	144	65.81
Don Bies	73 71	144	65.81
Bob Goalby	71 73	144	65.81
Bert Greene	71 73	144	65.81
Al Mengert	70 74	144	65.81
Steve Reid	72 72	144	65.81
Bill Collins	72 72	144	65.81
Rolf Deming	71 73	144	65.81
Mason Rudolph	71 73	144	65.81
Peter Townsend, *Great Britain*	74 70	144	65.81
Bobby Mitchell	74 71	145	65.81
Bobby Nichols	75 70	145	65.81
Gary Loustalot	71 74	145	65.81
Dick Rhyan	74 71	145	65.81
John Lively	78 67	145	65.81
Mike Hill	72 73	145	65.81

	SCORES	TOTAL	MONEY
Rich Bassett	75 70	145	65.81
Ross Coon	71 74	145	65.81
Chris Blocker	74 71	145	65.81
Ken Still	71 74	145	65.81
John Jacobs	73 72	145	65.81
Tommy Jacobs	76 69	145	65.81
Jerry Heard	72 73	145	65.81
Al Geiberger	73 72	145	65.81

* Amateur

BING CROSBY NATIONAL PRO-AMATEUR

Pebble Beach, California
January 23—27
Purse...$125,000 (individual)
          $25,000 (team)
PEBBLE BEACH GOLF LINKS
Par: 36, 36—72...6,747 yards
CYPRESS POINT CLUB
Par: 37, 35—72...6,333 yards
SPYGLASS HILL GOLF CLUB
Par: 36, 36—72...6,972 yards

	SCORES	TOTAL	MONEY
George Archer	72 68 72 71	283	$25,000
Bob Dickson	73 69 74 68	284	9,666.67
Dale Douglass	71 69 70 74	284	9,666.67
Howie Johnson	71 69 71 73	284	9,666.66
John Lotz	71 75 67 72	285	5,125
Jack Nicklaus	71 73 73 70	287	4,500
Lee Elder	71 75 73 69	288	4,000
Bruce Devlin, *Australia*	69 75 78 67	289	2,901.43
Ron Cerrudo	75 72 71 71	289	2,901.43
Don Massengale	72 75 70 72	289	2,901.43
Gene Littler	73 74 70 72	289	2,901.43
Bill Collins	71 73 76 69	289	2,901.43
Jimmy Powell	73 76 68 72	289	2,901.43
Rod Funseth	72 71 73 73	289	2,901.42
Jerry McGee	70 72 72 76	290	1,687.50
Miller Barber	70 73 77 70	290	1,687.50
Gay Brewer	73 72 73 72	290	1,687.50
Bill Casper	70 76 74 70	290	1,687.50
Al Geiberger	71 72 73 74	290	1,687.50
George Knudson, *Canada*	73 73 72 72	290	1,687.50
Johnny Pott	75 67 75 73	290	1,687.50
Bert Yancey	72 73 75 70	290	1,687.50

	SCORES	TOTAL	MONEY
Dow Finsterwald	76 74 72 69	291	992.50
Rocky Thompson	74 72 72 73	291	992.50
Deane Beman	72 71 74 74	291	992.50
Dave Stockton	72 74 73 72	291	992.50
Jim Wiechers	74 72 70 75	291	992.50
Lee Trevino	72 77 70 72	291	992.50
Jerry Abbott	70 73 75 73	291	992.50
Bob Charles, *New Zealand*	70 74 76 71	291	992.50
Doug Sanders	72 72 77 71	292	739.84
Bruce Crampton, *Australia*	73 76 71 72	292	739.84
Bob Goalby	70 72 75 75	292	739.83
Tony Jacklin, *Great Britain*	74 74 71 73	292	739.83
Bob McCallister	71 73 75 73	292	739.83
Hugh Royer	76 72 71 73	292	739.83
Lionel Hebert	74 71 75 73	293	556.72
Paul Harney	73 74 75 71	293	556.72
Dave Marr	75 73 73 72	293	556.72
Arnold Palmer	74 72 74 73	293	556.71
Orville Moody	71 77 72 73	293	556.71
Tom Nieporte	71 72 76 74	293	556.71
Bob Lunn	72 76 73 72	293	556.71
Richard Martinez	73 74 73 74	294	379.67
Pete Brown	73 76 74 71	294	379.67
Dave Eichelberger	71 73 75 75	294	379.66
Harold Henning, *South Africa*	74 73 76 72	295	265.72
Mason Rudolph	71 75 76 73	295	265.72
Roberto Bernardini, *Italy*	71 72 80 72	295	265.72
Billy Maxwell	71 75 72 77	295	265.71
Jack Montgomery	72 76 72 75	295	265.71
Darrell Hickok	74 75 72 75	296	178.58
Harry Toscano	73 72 77 74	296	178.58
Bert Greene	72 76 74 74	296	178.58
Steve Spray	67 77 75 75	296	178.57
Butch Baird	72 73 75 76	296	178.57
Dewitt Weaver	73 74 73 76	296	178.57
Kermit Zarley	75 71 74 76	296	178.57
Bill Ogden	73 76 72 76	297	178.57
Randy Petri	75 75 70 77	297	178.57
Jacky Cupit	74 76 73 74	297	178.57
Doug Ford	74 76 72 75	297	178.57
Terry Wilcox	68 77 76 76	297	178.57
Bobby Brue	74 74 74 75	297	178.57
Grier Jones	71 73 71 83	298	178.57
Ray Floyd	75 76 71 76	298	178.57
Larry Ziegler	74 71 76 78	299	178.57
Jay Dolan	74 70 77 78	299	178.57
Ernie Vossler	76 74 73 76	299	178.57
Bunky Henry	72 79 71 77	299	178.57
Paul Bondeson	72 76 74 77	299	178.57

	SCORES	TOTAL	MONEY
Bob Smith	72 71 80 77	300	178.57
Jim Colbert	68 78 77 77	300	178.57
Ken Ellsworth	70 75 78 78	301	178.57
Bill Blanton	71 76 75 79	301	178.57
Monty Kaser	72 76 75 80	303	178.57
Dick Carpenter	75 74 74 80	303	178.57
Dean Refram	75 75 72 82	304	178.57

PRO—AMATEUR DIVISION

PROFESSIONAL—AMATEUR

	TOTAL	MONEY
Bob Dickson—Jack Ging	257	$3,500
Bill Casper—Mike Bonallack	258	1,725
Tom Nieporte—Richard Remsen	258	1,725
Gene Littler—Dr. John Moler	258	1,725
Tom Shaw—Richard Crane	258	1,725
Jack Nicklaus—Bob Hoag	259	1,100
Al Geiberger—Lew Leis	259	1,100
Frank Beard—Mickey Van Gerbig	259	1,100
Lionel Hebert—Roger Kelly	260	900
Bob McCallister—Guy Madison	260	900
Dale Douglass—Charles De Bretteville	260	900
George Bayer—Morgan Barofsky	261	680
George Knudson—Barry Van Gerbig	261	680
Ron Cerrudo—Harvie Ward	261	680
Grier Jones—John Spencer	261	680
Dan Sikes—Frank Scott	261	680
Phil Rodgers—Jimmy Vickers	261	680
Arnold Palmer—Mark McCormack	262	450
Miller Barber—Lee Corwin	262	450
Johnny Pott—Virgil Sherrill	262	450
John Lotz—Jack Huiskamp	262	450
Dave Ragan—William Hoelle	262	450
Jay Dolan—Lawson Little III	263	330
Lee Trevino—Fr. Len Scannell	264	197.15
Randy Petri—Charles Van Linge	264	197.15
Richard Martinez—Tom Culligan	264	197.14
Jack Montgomery—John Miller	264	197.14
Rod Funseth—Frank Tatum Jr.	264	197.14
George Archer—Bob Roos Jr.	264	197.14
Don Fairfield—James Garner	264	197.14
Paul Bondeson—Glenn Davis	265	125
Rex Baxter—Hobart Manley	265	125
Bert Greene—Fr. John Durkin	266	105
Orville Moody—Robert Haynie	266	105
Harold Henning—Don Schwab	267	50
Howie Johnson—James Walker	267	50

ANDY WILLIAMS—SAN DIEGO OPEN

TORREY PINES GOLF CLUB
La Jolla, California
January 30—February 2
Purse...$150,000
Par: 36, 36—72...6,792 yards

	SCORES				TOTAL	MONEY
Jack Nicklaus	68	72	71	73	284	$30,000
Gene Littler	70	72	67	76	285	17,100
Dave Stockton	74	72	70	70	286	8,850
Tommy Aaron	74	72	70	70	286	8,850
Dow Finsterwald	69	75	72	71	287	6,150
Lee Trevino	75	69	74	70	288	4,875
Larry Ziegler	70	69	76	73	288	4,875
Phil Rodgers	75	72	68	73	288	4,875
Frank Beard	74	72	75	68	289	3,325
Ray Floyd	73	75	69	72	289	3,325
Bruce Devlin, *Australia*	72	72	72	73	289	3,325
Don January	74	73	70	72	289	3,325
Bob Charles, *New Zealand*	74	69	72	74	289	3,325
Dick Lotz	72	71	71	75	289	3,325
Bob Lunn	75	70	76	69	290	2,250
Bob Dickson	72	73	76	69	290	2,250
Harold Henning, *South Africa*	72	72	76	70	290	2,250
Randy Petri	72	76	71	71	290	2,250
Tony Jacklin, *Great Britain*	72	73	71	74	290	2,250
John Lotz	73	73	73	72	291	1,650
George Archer	73	74	69	75	291	1,650
Bob Smith	73	71	70	77	291	1,650
Mike Fetchick	73	74	73	72	292	1,266
John Schlee	73	75	72	72	292	1,266
Paul Harney	73	71	74	74	292	1,266
Jack Montgomery	76	68	74	74	292	1,266
Steve Reid	77	73	69	73	292	1,266
Bert Yancey	73	77	73	70	293	1,000
Bobby Brue	75	74	71	73	293	1,000
Dan Sikes	74	72	74	73	293	1,000
Cesar Sanudo	77	71	71	74	293	1,000
Mason Rudolph	74	74	70	75	293	1,000
Butch Baird	72	73	72	76	293	1,000
Bob McCallister	74	71	78	71	294	740
Dave Eichelberger	70	74	77	73	294	740
Ken Still	74	74	72	74	294	740
Dean Refram	74	71	74	75	294	740
Joel Goldstrand	72	75	72	75	294	740
Tom Shaw	76	74	68	76	294	740
Al Balding, *Canada*	76	71	71	76	294	740

	SCORES	TOTAL	MONEY
Miller Barber	72 74 72 76	294	740
Howie Johnson	72 73 72 77	294	740
Bobby Nichols	74 76 74 71	295	426.43
Bob Goalby	76 74 73 72	295	426.43
Jerry Abbott	71 77 74 73	295	426.43
Dave Ragan	74 75 71 75	295	426.43
Dale Douglass	75 74 70 76	295	426.43
Jack Ewing	72 75 71 77	295	426.43
Jimmy Powell	75 70 72 78	295	426.43
Julius Boros	76 74 73 73	296	235.72
Bill Garrett	75 73 73 75	296	235.72
Lionel Hebert	72 76 73 75	296	235.72
Hugh Royer	71 78 71 76	296	235.71
Jim Wiechers	73 75 76 73	297	214.29
Bruce Crampton, *Australia*	74 76 74 73	297	214.29
Ron Cerrudo	77 69 79 73	298	214.29
Dewitt Weaver	74 75 76 73	298	214.29
Bert Greene	76 74 72 76	298	214.29
Jim Colbert	71 75 74 78	298	214.29
Harry Toscano	73 74 72 79	298	214.29
Bill Blanton	72 77 78 72	299	214.29
Jim Gilbert	72 77 75 75	299	214.29
Kermit Zarley	77 73 75 74	299	214.29
Bill Casper	72 75 76 76	299	214.29
Don Massengale	77 73 73 76	299	214.29
Johnny Pott	72 73 76 78	299	214.29
Everett Vinzant	76 72 76 76	300	214.29
George Johnson	73 77 75 75	300	214.28
Ray Botts	76 74 74 76	300	214.28
Art Wall	79 69 75 77	300	214.28
Charles Coody	74 75 72 79	300	214.28
Ronnie Reif	73 76 76 76	301	214.28
R. H. Sikes	72 77 74 78	301	214.28
Dick Rhyan	76 74 77 76	303	214.28
Paul Runyan	73 74 77 79	303	214.28
Chuck Courtney	74 76 75 78	303	214.28
Bill Collins	75 75 72 81	303	214.28
Martin Roesink, *Holland*	75 75 75 80	305	214.28

BOB HOPE DESERT CLASSIC

February 5—9
Purse...$100,000 (individual)
    $22,000 (team)

INDIAN WELLS COUNTRY CLUB
Palm Desert, California
Par: 36, 36—72...6,711 yards

BERMUDA DUNES COUNTRY CLUB
Bermuda Dunes, California
Par: 36, 36—72...7,010 yards

LA QUINTA COUNTRY CLUB
La Quinta, California
Par: 36, 36—72...6,904 yards

TAMARISK COUNTRY CLUB
Palm Springs, California
Par: 36, 36—72...7,067 yards

	SCORES				TOTAL	MONEY
Bill Casper	71	68	71	69	66	345	$20,000
Dave Hill	69	72	70	71	66	348	11,400
Jack Montgomery	70	68	74	67	70	349	7,100
Art Wall	69	69	71	70	71	350	4,700
Deane Beman	72	77	72	68	62	351	3,175
Bob Charles, *New Zealand*	74	67	69	72	69	351	3,175
Gene Littler	67	74	68	73	69	351	3,175
Orville Moody	72	69	68	72	70	351	3,175
Frank Beard	70	68	71	68	74	351	3,175
George Knudson, *Canada*	72	71	68	69	71	351	3,175
Ray Floyd	69	73	70	72	68	352	2,200
Bobby Nichols	71	70	70	71	70	352	2,200
Tony Jacklin, *Great Britain*	68	72	71	72	70	353	1,800
Bob Murphy	70	72	69	72	70	353	1,800
Lee Trevino	67	69	71	75	71	353	1,800
Bert Yancey	71	72	78	65	68	354	1,350
Larry Ziegler	74	73	71	68	68	354	1,350
Jack Nicklaus	72	71	74	68	69	354	1,350
Gay Brewer	70	71	71	73	69	354	1,350
Tom Shaw	67	76	72	68	71	354	1,350
Rod Funseth	69	66	71	75	73	354	1,350
Bruce Devlin, *Australia*	69	75	72	72	67	355	912.50
Ken Still	68	73	78	70	66	355	912.50
Howie Johnson	70	73	70	73	69	355	912.50
Everett Vinzant	72	72	69	71	71	355	912.50
Tommy Aaron	73	78	66	71	68	356	755
Jim Wiechers	68	74	74	70	70	356	755
Arnold Palmer	72	73	69	72	70	356	755
Malcolm Gregson	70	73	73	69	71	356	755
Bill Johnston	74	70	74	71	68	357	615
Phil Rodgers	75	71	72	70	69	357	615
Johnny Pott	72	70	71	72	72	357	615
Tom Nieporte	69	70	72	74	72	357	615
Charles Coody	69	75	72	68	73	357	615

	SCORES	TOTAL	MONEY
Miller Barber	69 71 72 69 76	357	615
Pete Brown	73 70 75 73 67	358	540
Paul Harney	76 72 69 71 71	359	445.72
Bob Goalby	73 73 73 70 70	359	445.72
Ron Cerrudo	75 76 68 71 69	359	445.72
John Lotz	71 74 73 69 72	359	445.71
Steve Reid	72 70 74 71 72	359	445.71
Bob Duden	69 74 74 73 69	359	445.71
Bob McCallister	73 73 71 75 67	359	445.71
Bob Dickson	73 71 75 70 71	360	271.67
Johnny Jacobs	71 74 74 70 71	360	271.67
Julius Boros	75 72 73 70 70	360	271.67
Billy Maxwell	74 71 72 73 70	360	271.67
Martin Roesink, *Holland*	72 73 73 75 67	360	271.66
Jack Ewing	77 74 72 70 67	360	271.66
Terry Wilcox	72 73 72 71 73	361	173.34
Bobby Brue	69 73 69 77 73	361	173.34
Harry Toscano	70 76 71 72 72	361	173.33
Bob Rosburg	73 76 72 70 70	361	173.33
B. R. McLendon	74 74 74 69 70	361	173.33
Bunky Henry	73 70 70 75 74	362	166.67
Dick Lotz	71 73 73 71 74	362	166.67
Howell Fraser	73 73 72 72 72	362	166.67
Jerry McGee	74 72 75 71 71	363	166.67
Cesar Sanudo	70 78 76 69 70	363	166.67
Jim Ferrier	68 72 73 80 70	363	166.67
Al Balding, *Canada*	77 71 74 71 70	363	166.67
Chuck Courtney	72 72 74 75 71	364	166.67
Dave Marr	72 76 73 72 71	364	166.67
Jack Fleck	71 71 74 73 76	365	166.67
Fred Marti	75 75 68 73 74	365	166.67
Bob Lunn	72 73 77 70 73	365	166.67
Tommy Jacobs	77 71 76 69 72	265	166.67
Dean Refram	73 73 72 74 73	365	166.66
Randy Petri	71 77 71 71 77	367	166.66
Manuel de la Torre	73 70 74 74 76	367	166.66
Ernie Vossler	72 74 73 72 76	367	166.66
Hugh Royer	74 72 71 76 74	367	166.66
Bill Blanton	71 80 70 69 78	368	166.66
Jerry Abbott	72 73 75 72 76	368	166.66

PROFESSIONAL—AMATEUR DIVISION

	TOTAL	MONEY
Frank Beard	242	$2,475
Ernie Vossler	242	2,475
Ron Cerrudo	243	1,540
Jerry Mowlds	243	1,540
Everett Vinzant	244	1,320
Lee Trevino	245	1,155
Orville Moody	245	1,155
Bob Charles	246	693
Hugh Royer	246	693
Bob Ellsworth	246	693
Harold Henning	246	693
George Johnson	246	693
Jack Ewing	246	693
Bobby Nichols	246	693
Tom Shaw	246	693
Steve Spray	246	693
Art Wall	246	693
Tom Nieporte	247	329.93
Paul Harney	247	329.93
Charles Sifford	247	329.93
Bunky Henry	247	329.93
Dudley Wysong	247	329.93
Dave Hill	247	329.93
Manuel de la Torre	247	329.92
Doug Ford	248	189.20
Fred Marti	248	189.20
Jack Fleck	248	189.20
Jay Hebert	248	189.20
Julius Boros	248	189.20
Labron Harris	249	14.05
Bob Rosburg	249	14.05
Bob Duden	249	14.05
Al Mengert	249	14.05
Joel Goldstrand	249	14.05
Charles Coody	249	14.05
Tommy Jacobs	249	14.04
Dow Finsterwald	249	14.04
Cesar Sanudo	249	14.04
Jim Colbert	249	14.04
George Knudson	249	14.04

PHOENIX OPEN

ARIZONA COUNTRY CLUB
Phoenix, Arizona
February 13—16
Purse...$100,000
Par: 35, 36—71...6,389 yards

	SCORES				TOTAL	MONEY
Gene Littler	69	66	62	66	263	$20,000
Miller Barber	65	70	66	64	265	7,733.34
Don January	67	65	67	66	265	7,733.33
Billy Maxwell	65	66	68	66	265	7,733.33
Ray Floyd	69	65	68	65	267	3,633.34
Terry Wilcox	65	69	66	67	267	3,633.33
Jack Ewing	67	66	66	68	267	3,633.33
Larry Ziegler	65	70	70	64	269	2,825
Dave Hill	68	71	63	67	269	2,825
Deane Beman	67	69	67	67	270	2,200
Jim Wiechers	67	67	68	68	270	2,200
Hugh Royer	66	67	65	72	270	2,200
Jerry Abbott	67	69	63	71	270	2,200
Frank Boynton	71	66	67	67	271	1,750
Martin Roesink, *Holland*	67	67	69	68	271	1,750
Ron Cerrudo	71	66	69	66	272	1,450
Grier Jones	69	70	67	66	272	1,450
Howie Johnson	68	68	68	68	272	1,450
Rod Funseth	66	66	69	71	272	1,450
B. R. McLendon	69	70	69	65	273	1,024
Dale Douglass	72	67	68	66	273	1,024
Fred Marti	69	69	67	68	273	1,024
Tommy Aaron	70	66	67	70	273	1,024
Jack Montgomery	69	66	68	70	273	1,024
Harold Henning, *South Africa*	70	70	68	66	274	725
Bruce Crampton, *Australia*	70	65	70	69	274	725
Ross Coon	68	70	67	69	274	725
Mason Rudolph	72	66	67	69	274	725
Labron Harris	67	67	70	70	274	725
Bob Lunn	73	64	67	70	274	725
Johnny Stevens	71	62	71	70	274	725
Jerry Steelsmith	70	67	65	72	274	725
Johnny Jacobs	65	67	74	69	275	570
Sam Carmichael	69	68	68	70	275	570
Orville Moody	68	69	68	70	275	570
Gardner Dickinson	69	69	67	70	275	570
John Lotz	71	68	71	66	276	403
Al Geiberger	74	66	69	67	276	403
Monty Kaser	69	66	72	69	276	403

	SCORES	TOTAL	MONEY
Paul Harney	66 69 72 69	276	403
Roy Pace	68 70 69 69	276	403
Phil Rodgers	69 69 68 70	276	403
Ken Still	70 68 68 70	276	403
Chuck Courtney	70 65 71 70	276	403
Charles Volpone	68 66 70 72	276	403
Dave Eichelberger	69 68 66 73	276	403
Don Bies	68 69 72 68	277	212.58
Lee Elder	65 69 73 70	277	212.57
Al Balding, *Canada*	67 71 67 72	277	212.57
Johnny Pott	71 68 66 72	277	212.57
Jerry McGee	69 69 65 74	277	212.57
Dean Refram	70 70 71 67	278	142.86
Marty Fleckman	69 69 72 68	278	142.86
Terry Dill	73 64 71 70	278	142.86
Kermit Zarley	71 67 67 73	278	142.86
Bill Blanton	68 68 67 75	278	142.86
Frank Beard	66 65 71 76	278	142.86
Bob Rosburg	70 67 66 75	278	142.86
Tommy Jacobs	71 69 63 75	278	142.86
Tony Jacklin, *Great Britain*	68 70 70 71	279	142.86
Bob Murphy	70 68 69 72	279	142.86
George Knudson, *Canada*	67 68 70 75	280	142.86
John Lively	73 67 66 74	280	142.86
Bob McCallister	68 71 69 72	280	142.86
Horace Moore	70 70 70 70	280	142.86
Harry Toscano	71 67 69 73	280	142.86
Dick Turner	72 68 70 70	280	142.86
Bunky Henry	70 69 71 71	281	142.86
Bob Shaw, *Australia*	72 67 71 71	281	142.86
Dutch Harrison	65 69 72 76	282	142.86
Paul Bondeson	71 66 77 69	283	142.85
Mike Hill	68 69 72 74	283	142.85
Steve Reid	71 68 71 73	283	142.85
Jim Ferrier	70 69 71 74	284	142.85
Cesar Sanudo	67 73 71 73	284	142.85
Ed Oldfield	71 68 76 70	285	142.85
Dow Finsterwald	71 69 72 76	288	142.85
Lee Trevino	70 70 71 77	288	142.85

TUCSON OPEN

TUCSON NATIONAL GOLF CLUB
Tucson, Arizona
February 20—23
Purse...$100,000
Par: 36, 36—72...7,200 yards

	SCORES				TOTAL	MONEY
Lee Trevino	67	70	68	66	271	$20,000
Miller Barber	65	72	73	68	278	11,400
Bert Yancey	70	70	70	69	279	7,100
Gene Littler	74	70	68	68	280	4,400
Don Bies	72	67	72	69	280	4,400
Phil Rodgers	69	71	74	67	281	3,600
Dale Douglass	67	69	78	68	282	2,837.50
Ron Cerrudo	68	73	73	68	282	2,837.50
Jimmy Wright	69	69	73	71	282	2,837.50
Johnny Pott	70	65	75	72	282	2,837.50
Frank Beard	72	71	72	68	283	2,200
Jerry McGee	71	71	72	69	283	2,200
Mason Rudolph	71	68	75	70	284	1,850
Bruce Crampton, *Australia*	69	74	70	71	284	1,850
Jim Wiechers	73	71	72	69	285	1,450
Bobby Brue	72	68	74	71	285	1,450
Rod Funseth	68	70	75	72	285	1,450
Orville Moody	72	73	69	71	285	1,450
Al Geiberger	70	72	71	72	285	1,450
Pete Brown	73	69	68	75	285	1,450
Richard Martinez	71	69	76	70	286	1,013.34
Terry Dill	73	69	74	70	286	1,013.33
Tom Shaw	69	72	74	71	286	1,013.33
Grier Jones	69	73	73	72	287	788.34
George Archer	68	71	76	72	287	788.34
Bob Dickson	75	68	73	71	287	788.33
Kermit Zarley	74	70	74	69	287	788.33
Bob Cox, *Canada*	73	71	71	72	287	788.33
Frank Boynton	70	71	71	75	287	788.33
Dave Stockton	70	73	74	71	288	615
Richard Crawford	75	70	72	71	288	615
Larry Ziegler	74	70	72	72	288	615
Steve Reid	71	74	74	69	288	615
Chuck Volpone	69	77	74	68	288	615
Charles Coody	73	67	74	74	288	615
George Knudson, *Canada*	73	70	74	72	289	485
Dick Lotz	71	72	74	72	289	485
Monty Kaser	74	70	76	69	289	485
Jim Mooney	73	73	75	68	289	485
Bob McCallister	73	73	76	67	289	485

	SCORES	TOTAL	MONEY
Johnny Jacobs	71 68 74 76	289	485
Hale Irwin	72 71 74 73	290	286.67
Howie Johnson	72 73 71 74	290	286.67
Paul Harney	71 68 78 73	290	286.67
Bill Ogden	70 72 77 71	290	286.67
Wayne Vollmer, *Canada*	74 71 71 74	290	286.67
Jacky Cupit	73 70 77 70	290	286.67
Harold Henning, *South Africa*	73 73 73 71	290	286.66
Chuck Courtney	71 72 72 75	290	286.66
Jerry Heard	73 73 75 69	290	286.66
Randy Wolfe	71 73 76 71	291	166.67
Everett Vinzant	73 70 73 76	292	166.67
Darrell Hickok	75 70 75 72	292	166.67
Dick Turner	75 71 74 72	292	166.67
Ed Moehling	71 74 72 76	293	166.67
Randy Glover	69 72 77 75	293	166.67
Ken Still	73 72 74 74	293	166.67
Rich Bassett	72 72 76 73	293	166.67
Rocky Thompson	73 73 73 74	293	166.67
Jim Grant	70 71 79 73	293	166.67
Dutch Harrison	74 71 75 73	293	166.67
Bill Johnston	73 73 76 71	293	166.67
Joel Goldstrand	73 72 79 69	293	166.67
Al Balding, *Canada*	72 74 79 69	294	166.67
Wayne Yates	71 74 77 73	295	166.67
Martin Roesink, *Holland*	74 72 74 75	295	166.67
Bob Stone	73 73 77 73	296	166.66
Bob Shaw, *Australia*	74 72 76 75	297	166.66
Jim Jamieson	71 74 77 75	297	166.66
Rick Rhoads	72 72 77 76	297	166.66
Bob Boldt	70 75 75 77	297	166.66
Don Cherry	74 72 78 74	298	166.66
Larry Mancour	74 72 82 72	300	166.66
Joe McDermott	73 72 79 79	303	166.66
*Dr. Ed Updegraff	68 74 71 DQ (Unsigned card)		

* Amateur

DORAL OPEN

DORAL COUNTRY CLUB
Miami, Florida
February 27—March 2
Purse...$150,000
Par: 36, 35—71...7,002 yards

	SCORES				TOTAL	MONEY
Tom Shaw	65	70	71	70	276	$30,000
Tommy Aaron	67	68	71	71	277	17,100
Dan Sikes	65	70	72	71	278	10,650
Homero Blancas	71	68	70	70	279	6,600
Jack Nicklaus	72	71	64	72	279	6,600
Tommy Bolt	69	69	69	73	280	5,400
Gay Brewer	73	68	72	68	281	4,800
Tony Jacklin, *Great Britain*	70	68	72	72	282	4,237.50
Hugh Royer	73	72	69	68	282	4,237.50
Richard Crawford	72	70	73	68	283	3,450
Bobby Nichols	77	67	72	67	283	3,450
Arnold Palmer	68	69	73	73	283	3,450
Miller Barber	75	70	71	68	284	2,625
Pete Brown	72	69	73	70	284	2,625
Dale Douglass	69	71	73	71	284	2,625
Wayne Vollmer, *Canada*	70	73	72	69	284	2,625
George Archer	71	72	69	73	285	2,175
Dave Hill	72	72	71	70	285	2,175
Jerry Abbott	71	74	65	76	286	1,368.75
Bobby Brue	74	71	73	68	286	1,368.75
Al Besselink	74	71	72	69	286	1,368.75
Bobby Cole, *South Africa*	68	78	67	73	286	1,368.75
Bob Dickson	72	71	74	69	286	1,368.75
Paul Harney	71	72	72	71	286	1,368.75
Jerry Heard	74	68	72	72	286	1,368.75
Harold Henning, *South Africa*	67	71	74	74	286	1,368.75
Johnny Jacobs	69	73	77	67	286	1,368.75
Fred Marti	70	72	71	73	286	1,368.75
Jack McGowan	74	72	70	70	286	1,368.75
Tom Weiskopf	71	69	73	73	286	1,368.75
Julius Boros	74	72	72	69	287	872.15
Bruce Devlin, *Australia*	66	75	77	69	287	872.15
Gardner Dickinson	70	71	72	74	287	872.14
Larry Hinson	73	72	72	70	287	872.14
Orville Moody	69	72	75	71	287	872.14
Sam Snead	72	72	72	71	287	872.14
Alvie Thompson, *Canada*	73	70	74	70	287	872.14
Frank Boynton	72	70	75	71	288	672
Billy Maxwell	74	69	76	69	288	672

	SCORES	TOTAL	MONEY
Steve Reid	69 74 73 72	288	672
Charles Sifford	70 74 72 72	288	672
Jimmy Wright	71 71 73 73	288	672
Frank Beard	71 73 74 71	289	442.50
Terry Dill	71 72 73 73	289	442.50
Mike Fetchick	73 71 71 74	289	442.50
Bob McCallister	71 73 72 73	289	442.50
Bob Rosburg	72 73 73 71	289	442.50
Bob Smith	73 71 72 73	289	442.50
Bill Collins	69 67 80 74	290	330
Hale Irwin	71 72 74 74	291	244.61
Don Massengale	72 73 74 72	291	244.61
Chi Chi Rodriguez	75 69 75 72	291	244.61
Bert Yancey	70 76 72 73	291	244.61
Dick Rhyan	70 69 77 75	291	244.60
Bob Goalby	73 70 75 74	292	230.78
Dudley Wysong	74 72 74 72	292	230.78
Rich Bassett	70 72 75 75	292	230.77
Charles Coody	71 74 75 73	293	230.77
Jack Ewing	72 73 76 72	293	230.77
Steve Spray	71 71 73 78	293	230.77
Johnny Stevens	70 74 73 76	293	230.77
Monty Kaser	75 71 71 77	294	230.77
Roy Pace	71 71 75 77	294	230.77
J. C. Goosie	75 71 79 70	295	230.77
Claude Harmon Jr.	74 72 76 73	295	230.77
Bunky Henry	76 69 75 75	295	230.77
Howie Johnson	71 74 72 78	295	230.77
Larry Ziegler	75 71 73 76	295	230.77
Cliff Brown	72 72 75 77	296	230.77
B. R. McLendon	76 70 76 74	296	230.77
Bob Shaw, *Australia*	70 75 75 77	297	230.77
Denny Rouse	72 69 75 82	298	230.77
Bert Greene	73 71 79 76	299	230.77
Dick Lotz	72 74 77 76	299	230.77
Mike Krak	74 72 77 78	301	230.77
Lou Graham	73 73 79 77	302	230.77

FLORIDA CITRUS OPEN

RIO PINAR COUNTRY CLUB
Orlando, Florida
March 6—9
Purse...$115,000
Par: 36, 36—72...6,849 yards

	SCORES	TOTAL	MONEY
Ken Still	74 67 67 70	278	$23,000
Miller Barber	69 68 72 70	279	13,100
Orville Moody	70 70 72 68	280	6,790
Johnny Pott	70 66 70 74	280	6,790
Gay Brewer	70 72 67 72	281	4,720
Lee Trevino	74 70 68 70	282	3,577.50
Tom Weiskopf	68 71 71 72	282	3,577.50
Dave Stockton	72 67 69 74	282	3,577.50
Lee Elder	70 71 67 74	282	3,577.50
Jack Nicklaus	70 71 71 71	283	2,438
Dan Sikes	69 70 70 74	283	2,438
Dean Refram	71 68 69 75	283	2,438
Bert Yancey	70 66 70 77	283	2,438
Dale Douglass	72 67 68 76	283	2,438
Billy Maxwell	73 69 72 70	284	1,840
Charles Sifford	72 70 71 71	284	1,840
Bob Charles, *New Zealand*	70 69 71 74	284	1,840
Jerry McGee	71 73 72 69	285	1,207.78
Paul Harney	73 70 71 71	285	1,207.78
Larry Ziegler	75 70 69 71	285	1,207.78
Jack McGowan	69 73 71 72	285	1,207.78
Bob Dickson	72 69 71 73	285	1,207.78
Joe Campbell	74 64 72 75	285	1,207.78
Bob Murphy	71 71 69 74	285	1,207.78
Frank Beard	71 69 70 75	285	1,207.77
Tommy Aaron	69 67 73 76	285	1,207.77
Harold Henning, *South Africa*	70 73 74 69	286	783.72
Cliff Brown	70 73 71 72	286	783.72
Tommy Bolt	72 70 71 73	286	783.72
Don January	73 71 69 73	286	783.71
R. H. Sikes	71 71 70 74	286	783.71
J. C. Goosie	70 74 68 74	286	783.71
Rod Funseth	68 71 71 76	286	783.71
Ray Floyd	72 70 73 72	287	536.28
Steve Reid	72 69 73 73	287	536.28
Pete Brown	74 69 71 73	287	536.28
Bobby Nichols	70 74 70 73	287	536.27
Ron Cerrudo	72 69 72 74	287	536.27
Bill Ezinicki	73 70 70 74	287	536.27

314

	SCORES	TOTAL	MONEY
Bob Lunn	73 72 68 74	287	536.27
Dave Hill	75 69 69 74	287	536.27
Bob Smith	73 70 69 75	287	536.27
Ken Ellsworth	71 71 70 75	287	536.27
Jerry Abbott	70 70 70 77	287	536.27
Gordon Jones	71 74 74 69	288	266.97
Mike Fetchick	71 72 72 73	288	266.97
Bob Goalby	71 71 73 73	288	266.97
Bill Collins	71 71 73 73	288	266.96
Homero Blancas	74 70 71 73	288	266.96
Charles Coody	72 70 70 76	288	266.96
Hugh Royer	72 72 68 76	288	266.96
Chi Chi Rodriguez	75 69 71 74	289	143.75
Art Wall	71 74 73 71	289	143.75
George Archer	72 72 71 74	289	143.75
Sam Snead	71 71 72 75	289	143.75
Bobby Mitchell	74 70 72 73	289	143.75
Doug Sanders	74 69 70 76	289	143.75
Mason Rudolph	75 70 66 78	289	143.75
Johnny Jacobs	75 70 71 74	290	143.75
Lionel Hebert	71 72 73 74	290	143.75
Johnny Stevens	73 71 73 73	290	143.75
Howell Fraser	73 72 72 73	290	143.75
Wayne Yates	72 72 73 73	290	143.75
Bob McCallister	73 72 73 72	290	143.75
Dudley Wysong	71 71 72 77	291	143.75
Larry Hinson	69 71 74 77	291	143.75
Dick Lotz	71 71 78 71	291	143.75
Howie Johnson	74 70 75 72	291	143.75
Monty Kaser	75 70 71 76	292	143.75
Bob Shaw, *Australia*	71 74 72 75	292	143.75
Richard Martinez	72 73 73 74	292	143.75
Bobby Cole, *South Africa*	72 73 70 78	293	143.75
Tony Jacklin, *Great Britain*	75 70 70 78	293	143.75
Jim Colbert	74 70 72 77	293	143.75
Craig Shankland	72 71 75 75	293	143.75
Alvie Thompson, *Canada*	72 72 74 75	293	143.75
Charles Stock	71 69 75 79	294	143.75
Labron Harris	74 70 72 78	294	143.75
Wayne Vollmer, *Canada*	72 70 79 73	294	143.75
Bert Greene	71 74 74 78	297	143.75
Gardner Dickinson	76 69 74 78	297	143.75
Bob Rosburg	71 71 77 81	300	143.75

MONSANTO OPEN

PENSACOLA COUNTRY CLUB
Pensacola, Florida
March 13—18
Purse...$100,000
Par: 35, 36—71...6,575 yards

	SCORES	TOTAL	MONEY
Jim Colbert	69 67 64 67	267	$20,000
Deane Beman	70 68 63 68	269	11,400
Lee Trevino	67 69 66 68	270	7,100
Ray Floyd	70 66 67 69	272	4,700
Larry Hinson	67 71 69 68	275	3,633.34
Tommy Aaron	67 70 67 71	275	3,633.33
Gary Player, *South Africa*	70 68 65 72	275	3,633.33
Steve Reid	71 72 67 67	277	2,612.50
Doug Sanders	69 69 70 69	277	2,612.50
Bruce Crampton, *Australia*	67 71 70 69	277	2,612.50
Richard Crawford	68 67 69 73	277	2.612.50
Rives McBee	71 67 75 66	279	2,000
Julius Boros	68 71 67 73	279	2,000
R. H. Sikes	68 74 67 71	280	1,700
Hugh Royer	73 67 68 72	280	1,700
Dudley Wysong	69 69 69 73	280	1,700
Bob Lunn	71 71 69 70	281	1,250
Orville Moody	74 65 71 71	281	1,250
Rod Funseth	71 69 70 71	281	1,250
Terry Wilcox	71 71 68 71	281	1,250
Ron Cerrudo	74 66 68 73	281	1,250
Charles Sifford	71 68 69 73	281	1,250
Bob Murphy	72 70 69 71	282	862.50
Bill Collins	71 72 69 70	282	862.50
Al Balding	71 66 71 74	282	862.50
Doug Ford	74 69 71 68	282	862.50
Butch Baird	73 70 68 72	283	681.43
George Johnson	73 69 69 72	283	681.43
Gay Brewer	70 70 70 73	283	681.43
Grier Jones	68 68 73 74	283	681.43
Ken Still	73 63 71 76	283	681.43
Bill Garrett	69 68 69 77	283	681.43
Bobby Cole, *South Africa*	72 66 77 68	283	681.42
Bob Keller	70 72 69 73	284	550
Chris Blocker	69 72 70 73	284	550
Bob Payne	70 71 71 72	284	550
Dick Hart	71 68 73 72	284	550
Chi Chi Rodriguez	71 70 68 76	285	476.67
Gene Ferrell	70 68 70 77	285	476.67

	SCORES	TOTAL	MONEY
Freddie Haas	73 69 71 72	285	476.66
Phil Rodgers	72 71 68 75	286	322.50
Larry Ziegler	72 70 68 76	286	322.50
Dale Douglass	69 69 71 77	286	322.50
Bunky Henry	72 70 66 78	286	322.50
Bobby Mitchell	72 68 71 75	286	322.50
George Archer	72 69 71 74	286	322.50
Howie Johnson	69 71 72 74	286	322.50
Davis Love	73 70 70 73	286	322.50
Bob Dickson	71 70 73 73	287	203.50
Dave Eichelberger	72 71 72 72	287	203.49
Jim Grant	68 74 76 69	287	203.49
Bert Greene	70 70 71 77	288	190.48
Tommy Jacobs	71 71 72 74	288	190.48
Richard Martinez	68 74 72 74	288	190.48
Bob Stanton, *Australia*	69 74 69 76	288	190.48
Wayne Vollmer, *Canada*	70 70 70 78	288	190.48
Wayne Yates	71 72 70 75	288	190.48
Bill Ezinicki	70 72 76 71	289	190.48
John Joseph	70 73 72 74	289	190.48
Dave Stockton	73 68 72 76	289	190.48
Labron Harris	70 73 69 78	290	190.48
Johnny Pott	72 71 72 75	290	190.48
Bob Smith	72 71 73 74	290	190.48
Jerry Abbott	69 73 71 78	291	190.47
Pete Brown	71 71 75 74	291	190.47
Dick Lotz	71 72 74 74	291	190.47
Larry Sears	73 69 76 74	292	190.47
Harry Toscano	74 69 74 75	292	190.47
Malcolm Gregson, *Great Britain*	71 71 71 79	292	190.47
Paul Moran	72 70 78 75	295	190.47
Lee Elder	70 72 76 78	296	190.47

GREATER JACKSONVILLE OPEN

THE DEERWOOD CLUB
Jacksonville, Florida
March 20—23
Purse...$100,000
Par: 36, 36—72...7,221 yards

	SCORES	TOTAL	MONEY
Ray Floyd	68 71 68 71	278	$20,000
Gardner Dickinson	68 70 70 70	278	11,400
(Floyd defeated Dickinson on first hole of sudden-death playoff.)			
Lee Trevino	69 69 72 70	280	5,300

	SCORES	TOTAL	MONEY
Dewitt Weaver	68 74 66 72	280	5,300
Gary Player, *South Africa*	72 69 68 71	280	5,300
Bobby Cole, *South Africa*	69 69 78 75	281	3,400
Arnold Palmer	70 68 72 71	281	3,400
Jim Colbert	72 71 71 68	282	2,612.50
Bob Charles, *New Zealand*	71 72 70 69	282	2,612.50
Bill Casper	71 70 72 69	282	2,612.50
Bob Murphy	71 74 67 70	282	2,612.50
Bob Rosburg	73 67 74 69	283	1,933.34
Al Balding, *Canada*	70 74 69 70	283	1,933.33
Bob Dickson	71 71 68 73	283	1,933.33
Malcolm Gregson, *Great Britain*	71 72 74 67	284	1,450
Frank Boynton	69 73 73 69	284	1,450
Bruce Crampton, *Australia*	69 70 74 71	284	1,450
Frank Beard	69 70 74 71	284	1,450
Lionel Hebert	67 71 72 74	284	1,450
Terry Dill	70 70 70 74	284	1,450
Jim Grant	70 72 73 70	285	902.86
Richard Martinez	72 71 71 71	285	902.86
Bill Collins	74 67 70 74	285	902.86
Rives McBee	72 67 72 74	285	902.86
Tom Weiskopf	69 72 70 74	285	902.86
Bob Lunn	70 70 71 74	285	902.85
Ken Still	69 69 71 76	285	902.85
Orville Moody	73 71 74 68	286	642.50
Chi Chi Rodriguez	70 71 73 72	286	642.50
Dick Hart	69 71 74 72	286	642.50
R. H. Sikes	71 73 70 72	286	642.50
Dave Hill	71 72 71 72	286	642.50
Rich Bassett	71 69 73 73	286	642.50
Jack McGowan	71 68 73 74	286	642.50
Jack Nicklaus	69 72 70 75	286	642.50
Jay Hebert	69 72 75 71	287	540
Wayne Yates	73 71 73 71	288	460
Bob Stanton, *Australia*	73 69 74 72	288	460
Tony Jacklin, *Great Britain*	70 75 71 72	288	460
Ron Cerrudo	73 71 69 75	288	460
Bob Smith	68 71 73 76	288	460
Doug Sanders	71 70 70 77	288	460
Harold Henning, *South Africa*	74 68 79 68	289	273.75
Fred Marti	71 74 73 71	289	273.75
Grier Jones	73 69 75 72	289	273.75
Bill Garrett	73 69 74 73	289	273.75
Dudley Wysong	71 73 72 73	289	273.75
Billy Maxwell	73 70 72 74	289	273.75
Herb Hooper	71 74 69 75	289	273.75
Tom Shaw	73 72 69 75	289	273.75
Dow Finsterwald	70 75 71 74	290	114.29

	SCORES	TOTAL	MONEY
Harold Kneece	73 70 74 73	290	114.29
Bob McCallister	71 71 73 75	290	114.29
Don Bies	74 71 76 70	291	114.29
Homero Blancas	73 68 78 72	291	114.29
Larry Ziegler	74 71 72 74	291	114.29
Lee Elder	74 71 73 73	291	114.29
Dave Stockton	68 74 74 75	291	114.29
Bert Greene	71 72 72 76	291	114.29
Randy Glover	73 72 75 72	292	114.29
Don January	72 71 75 74	292	114.29
David Philo	72 72 74 74	292	114.29
Miller Barber	71 74 73 74	292	114.29
Larry Mowry	68 76 74 74	292	114.29
Terry Wilcox	70 70 77 75	292	114.29
Wilf Homenuik, *Canada*	72 73 73 74	292	114.29
Labron Harris	72 73 71 76	292	114.29
Chris Blocker	70 71 79 73	293	114.29
Paul Moran	72 73 75 73	293	114.29
Dave Ragan	74 69 74 76	293	114.29
Dick Rhyan	72 71 71 79	293	114.28
Gene Ferrell	73 72 75 74	294	114.28
Bobby Mitchell	69 76 72 77	294	114.28
Bert Yancey	71 71 79 74	295	114.28
Jim Ferrier	71 73 75 76	295	114.28
Butch Baird	74 70 74 77	295	114.28
Rod Funseth	71 72 73 79	295	114.28
Bob Goalby	73 72 71 79	295	114.28
John Lotz	73 72 79 72	296	114.28
Jerry Abbott	71 71 75 79	296	114.28
Bunky Henry	73 70 73 80	296	114.28
Fred Haas	70 75 74 79	298	114.28
Davis Love	71 74 76 79	300	114.28
Bob Keller	73 71 81 76	301	114.28
Marty Fleckman	71 74 79 78	302	114.28

NATIONAL AIRLINES OPEN

COUNTRY CLUB OF MIAMI
Miami, Florida
March 27—30
Purse...$200,000
Par: 36, 36—72...6,972 yards

	SCORES	TOTAL	MONEY
Bunky Henry	69 73 66 70	278	$40,000
Bruce Crampton, *Australia*	68 70 75 66	279	13,650

	SCORES	TOTAL	MONEY
Dan Sikes	70 70 71 68	279	13,650
Bob Murphy	69 66 68 76	279	13,650
Dave Stockton	68 72 67 72	279	13,650
Butch Baird	68 69 70 73	280	7,200
Dale Douglass	68 68 73 72	281	6,150
Lionel Hebert	68 69 69 75	281	6,150
Terry Dill	71 67 72 72	282	5,000
Terry Wilcox	69 69 71 73	282	5,000
Deane Beman	69 72 69 72	282	5,000
Julius Boros	73 72 69 69	283	3,428.58
Don Whitt	73 68 71 71	283	3,428.57
Don January	69 73 70 71	283	3,428.57
Tony Jacklin, *Great Britain*	72 70 70 71	283	3,428.57
R. H. Sikes	68 73 70 72	283	3,428.57
Arnold Palmer	69 73 69 72	283	3,428.57
Sam Snead	67 72 71 73	283	3,428.57
Charles Sifford	71 73 70 70	284	2,300
Harold Henning, *South Africa*	73 71 71 69	284	2,300
Gene Littler	74 68 71 71	284	2,300
Bruce Devlin, *Australia*	72 73 67 72	284	2,300
Gary Player, *South Africa*	69 75 72 69	285	1,725
Miller Barber	71 72 72 70	285	1,725
Bobby Cole, *South Africa*	73 69 72 71	285	1,725
Orville Moody	69 71 70 75	285	1,725
Dick Hart	70 72 75 69	286	1,362.86
Bert Greene	72 69 75 70	286	1,362.86
Tommy Aaron	69 71 75 71	286	1,362.86
Howell Fraser	73 70 72 71	286	1,362.86
Fred Marti	73 68 71 74	286	1,362.86
Jack McGowan	73 70 69 74	286	1,362.85
Frank Boynton	71 70 70 75	286	1,362.85
Rod Funseth	70 75 72 70	287	1,037.15
Laurie Hammer	70 72 74 71	287	1,037.15
Dick Rhyan	71 67 74 75	287	1,037.14
Malcolm Gregson, *Great Britain*	73 70 70 74	287	1,037.14
Ken Still	73 68 71 75	287	1,037.14
Hale Irwin	75 68 69 75	287	1,027.14
Gay Brewer	69 69 73 76	287	1,037.14
Herb Hooper	74 71 73 70	288	720
Don Bies	70 74 72 72	288	720
Dewitt Weaver	66 73 76 73	288	720
Howie Johnson	69 70 74 75	288	720
Bob Charles, *New Zealand*	69 73 70 76	288	720
Frank Beard	68 73 76 72	289	480
Dow Finsterwald	69 77 72 71	289	480
Charles Coody	71 74 71 73	289	480
Wilf Homenuik, *Canada*	71 74 71 73	289	480
Grier Jones	70 72 71 76	289	480
George Archer	70 74 77 69	290	363.64

	SCORES	TOTAL	MONEY
Harry Toscano	71 74 73 72	290	363.64
Larry Ziegler	71 73 75 71	290	363.64
Jim Colbert	71 73 73 73	290	363.64
Al Balding, *Canada*	72 72 72 74	290	363.64
Mason Rudolph	74 72 71 74	291	363.64
Don Massengale	73 71 72 76	292	363.64
Jimmy Wright	76 70 76 71	293	363.64
Bob Rosburg	72 72 73 76	293	363.64
Cesar Sanudo	72 74 75 73	294	363.64
Martin Roesink, *Holland*	69 73 75 77	294	363.64
Gene Ferrell	72 74 76 73	295	363.64
Tommy Bolt	69 76 75 75	295	363.64
Larry Hinson	73 73 75 75	296	363.64
Marty Fleckman	73 72 73 78	296	363.63
Bob Stanton, *Australia*	70 74 74 78	296	363.63
Doug Ford	73 73 75 76	297	363.63
Dave Ragan	70 75 77 76	298	363.63
Tom Shaw	71 75 75 77	298	363.63
Jim Grant	74 70 77 80	301	363.63
Chico Miartuz	70 76 79 77	302	363.63
Bobby Mitchell	70 76 80 78	304	363.63

GREATER GREENSBORO OPEN

SEDGEFIELD COUNTRY CLUB
Greensboro, North Carolina
April 3—6
Purse...$160,000
Par: 35, 36—71...7,034 yards

	SCORES	TOTAL	MONEY
Gene Littler	66 70 69 69	274	$32,000
Julius Boros	67 71 67 69	274	12,373.34
Orville Moody	69 70 68 67	274	12,373.33
Tom Weiskopf	67 72 67 68	274	12,373.33

(Littler defeated Boros, Moody and Weiskopf in sudden-death playoff,
Weiskopf eliminated on first extra hole, Boros and Moody on fifth.)

	SCORES	TOTAL	MONEY
Gary Player, *South Africa*	69 68 68 70	275	6,560
Bobby Cole, *South Africa*	70 69 69 68	276	5,440
Chi Chi Rodriguez	69 68 69 70	276	5,440
Deane Beman	68 69 67 73	277	4,520
Ken Still	69 72 68 68	277	4,520
Bruce Crampton, *Australia*	68 69 70 71	278	4,000
George Archer	67 71 66 75	279	3,136
Al Balding, *Canada*	71 69 66 73	279	3,136
Bob Charles, *New Zealand*	70 70 69 70	279	3,136

	SCORES	TOTAL	MONEY
Harold Kneece	69 70 70 70	279	3,136
Dave Marr	68 66 70 75	279	3,136
Dow Finsterwald	73 70 69 68	280	2,400
Dick Lotz	69 68 74 69	280	2,400
Bob Murphy	69 70 70 71	280	2,400
Terry Dill	71 71 67 72	281	1,920
Rod Funseth	67 69 72 73	281	1,920
Don January	71 70 68 72	281	1,920
Frank Boynton	69 69 71 73	282	1,334
Dale Douglass	69 71 69 73	282	1,334
Al Geiberger	69 73 69 71	282	1,334
Tommy Jacobs	69 72 69 72	282	1,334
Grier Jones	69 69 70 74	282	1,334
Billy Maxwell	68 75 64 75	282	1,334
Dan Sikes	72 67 74 69	282	1,334
Sam Snead	69 69 72 72	282	1,334
Tommy Aaron	69 70 69 75	283	819.20
Frank Beard	69 69 76 69	283	819.20
Bob Goalby	72 70 67 74	283	819.20
Jim Grant	68 73 70 72	283	819.20
Malcolm Gregson, *Great Britain*	68 71 69 75	283	819.20
Lionel Hebert	71 72 69 71	283	819.20
Dave Hill	73 70 71 69	283	819.20
Dudley Wysong	71 72 67 73	283	819.20
Bobby Mitchell	70 71 68 74	283	819.20
Tom Nieporte	71 71 69 72	283	819.20
R. H. Sikes	69 72 68 74	283	819.20
Bob Stanton, *Australia*	75 67 71 70	283	819.20
Don Whitt	71 72 67 73	283	819.20
Terry Wilcox	70 70 71 72	283	819.20
Sonny Ridenhour	68 71 74 70	283	819.20
Ray Floyd	70 69 74 71	284	416
Bill Garrett	73 68 69 74	284	416
George Knudson, *Canada*	68 71 70 75	284	416
Martin Roesink, *Holland*	72 69 69 74	284	416
Wilf Homenuik, *Canada*	72 70 69 73	284	416
Mike Hill	72 70 72 71	285	280
Gordon Jones	66 70 73 76	285	280
Jack McGowan	69 72 71 73	285	280
Art Wall	68 69 75 73	285	280
Bob Dickson	70 72 69 75	286	266.67
Laurie Hammer	71 69 72 74	286	266.67
Larry Mowry	68 71 71 76	286	266.67
Mason Rudolph	68 71 77 70	286	266.67
Bob Smith	70 72 74 70	286	266.67
Marty Fleckman	73 70 72 72	287	266.67
Howell Fraser	70 71 71 75	287	266.67
Bunky Henry	68 71 73 75	287	266.67

	SCORES	TOTAL	MONEY
Monty Kaser	72 68 76 71	287	266.67
Dave Stockton	72 71 70 74	287	266.67
Lee Trevino	68 74 72 73	287	266.67
Charles Coody	69 70 73 76	288	266.67
*Dale Morey	66 73 74 75	288	
Dave Ragan	71 70 73 75	289	266.67
Brian Huggett, *Great Britain*	70 72 75 72	289	266.67
Bert Greene	71 69 71 78	289	266.66
Labron Harris	72 70 72 75	289	266.66
*Lanny Wadkins	69 72 74 74	289	
Jim Hardy	72 69 73 75	289	266.66
Hale Irwin	71 71 73 75	290	266.66
Jim Wiechers	72 69 72 77	290	266.66
Larry Ziegler	70 70 76 76	292	266.66
Ed Sneed	70 72 75 76	293	266.66

* Amateur

MASTERS CHAMPIONSHIP

AUGUSTA NATIONAL GOLF CLUB
Augusta, Georgia
April 10—13
Purse...$186,975
Par: 36, 36—72...6,980 yards

	SCORES	TOTAL	MONEY
George Archer	67 73 69 72	281	$20,000
Tom Weiskopf	71 71 69 71	282	12,333.34
George Knudson, *Canada*	70 73 69 70	282	12,333.33
Bill Casper	66 71 71 74	282	12,333.33
Charles Coody	74 68 69 72	283	6,750
Don January	74 73 70 66	283	6,750
Miller Barber	71 71 68 74	284	5,000
Tommy Aaron	71 71 73 70	285	3,600
Lionel Hebert	69 73 70 73	285	3,600
Gene Littler	69 75 70 71	285	3,600
Mason Rudolph	69 73 74 70	286	3,200
Dan Sikes	69 71 73 74	287	3,000
Bruce Crampton, *Australia*	69 73 74 72	288	2,700
Al Geiberger	71 71 74 72	288	2,700
Harold Henning, *South Africa*	73 72 71 72	288	2,700
Takaaki Kono, *Japan*	71 75 68 74	288	2,700
Bert Yancey	69 75 71 73	288	2,700
Dave Stockton	71 71 75 72	289	2,400
Frank Beard	72 74 70 74	290	2,100

	SCORES	TOTAL	MONEY
Deane Beman	74 73 74 69	290	2,100
Bruce Devlin, *Australia*	67 70 76 77	290	2,100
Dale Douglass	73 72 71 74	290	2,100
Lee Trevino	72 74 75 69	290	2,100
Jack Burke	73 72 70 76	291	1,800
Dave Hill	75 73 72 71	291	1,800
Jack Nicklaus	68 75 72 76	291	1,800
Arnold Palmer	73 75 70 74	292	1,450
Johnny Pott	72 72 71 78	293	1,450
Roberto Bernardini, *Italy*	76 71 72 75	294	1,450
Bob Charles, *New Zealand*	70 76 72 76	294	1,450
Gardner Dickinson	73 74 71 76	294	1,450
Bobby Nichols	78 69 74 73	294	1,450
Don Bies	74 70 70 81	295	1,425
Julius Boros	72 73 73 77	295	1,425
Gary Player, *South Africa*	74 70 75 76	295	1,425
Ray Floyd	73 71 78 74	296	1,425
Doug Sanders	72 71 76 77	296	1,425
Ken Still	73 75 71 77	296	1,425
Kermit Zarley	73 73 76 74	296	1,425
Bob Goalby	70 76 76 75	297	1,400
Art Wall	70 77 78 72	297	1,400
Peter Townsend, *Great Britain*	75 71 73 79	298	1,400
Steve Spray	75 72 74 78	299	1,400
*Bruce Fleisher	69 75 73 83	300	
B. R. McLendon	72 75 76 80	303	1,400
*Dick Siderowf	78 69 80 82	309	
Cary Middlecoff	72 76 80 WD		1,000
Herman Keiser	71 77 80 WD		1,000

OUT OF FINAL 36 HOLES

	SCORES	TOTAL
Frank Boynton	76 73	149
Gay Brewer	75 74	149
Marty Fleckman	73 76	149
Rod Funseth	73 76	149
*Vinny Giles	80 69	149
Tony Jacklin, *Great Britain*	73 76	149
Bob Lunn	74 75	149
Jerry Pittman	74 75	149
Roberto de Vicenzo, *Argentina*	75 75	150
Lou Graham	73 77	150
Brian Huggett, *Great Britain*	78 72	150
Bob Murphy	71 79	150
R. H. Sikes	75 75	150
*Rik Massengale	75 76	151

	SCORES	TOTAL
*Allen Miller	77 74	151
Henry Picard	75 76	151
Sam Snead	74 77	151
Tommy Horton, *Great Britain*	74 78	152
Raul Travieso, *Peru*	76 76	152
*Hubert Green	76 77	153
*Jack Lewis	75 78	153
Dave Marr	77 76	153
Peter Thomson, *Australia*	78 75	153
*Bob Barbarossa	75 79	154
Doug Ford	73 81	154
Ramon Sota, *Spain*	75 79	154
*Mike Bonallack, *Great Britain*	76 79	155
Peter Butler, *Great Britain*	77 78	155
*Joe Carr, *Ireland*	79 76	155
Lu Liang Huan, *Formosa*	80 76	156
Gene Sarazen	78 80	158
*John Bohmann	77 82	159
Ralph Guldahl	77 83	160
Ken Venturi	83 77	160
Claude Harmon	WD	

(Each professional who missed cut or withdrew received $1,000.)

* Amateur

MAGNOLIA STATE CLASSIC

HATTIESBURG COUNTRY CLUB
Hattiesburg, Mississippi
April 10—14
Purse...$35,000
Par: 35, 35—70...6,731 yards

	SCORES	TOTAL	MONEY
Larry Mowry	71 67 66 68	272	$5,000
Larry Hinson	68 69 67 69	273	2,900
Alvin Odom	69 68 66 70	273	2,900
Jim Bullard	65 70 67 72	274	1,975
Jerry Abbott	70 63 72 69	274	1,975
Joel Goldstrand	69 70 68 68	275	1,450
Curtis Sifford	71 67 67 70	275	1,450
Bert Greene	72 65 69 69	275	1,450
Rives McBee	66 68 73 68	275	1,450
Johnny Jacobs	71 69 66 70	276	1,200
Jerry Heard	72 68 66 71	277	1,016.67
Bunky Henry	68 72 72 65	277	1,016.67

	SCORES	TOTAL	MONEY
Joe Porter	69 72 69 67	277	1,016.66
Johnny Stevens	71 68 68 71	278	775
Dave Walters	71 68 68 71	278	775
Jerry McGee	68 71 69 70	278	775
Ross Randall	70 68 71 69	278	775
Howell Fraser	68 69 69 72	278	775
Lee Davis	69 68 70 71	278	775
Tom Bailey	68 72 69 70	279	575
Jim Langley	70 68 67 74	279	575
Richard Martinez	71 70 71 68	280	458.34
Jacky Cupit	67 71 70 72	280	458.33
Jack Ewing	69 68 72 71	280	458.33
Martin Roesink, *Holland*	68 72 72 69	281	350
Chuck Courtney	69 71 72 69	281	350
M. C. Fitts	68 74 69 70	281	350
Ed Davis	73 69 70 69	281	350
Bob Erickson	72 70 68 71	281	350
Chick Evans	69 71 69 73	282	237.50
Gene Ferrell	72 71 70 69	282	237.50
Labron Harris	71 71 70 70	282	237.50
Bill Garrett	73 69 69 71	282	237.50
Jim Wiechers	77 66 70 70	283	81.25
Roy Pace	71 71 72 69	283	81.25
Rich Bassett	73 69 74 67	283	81.25
Jimmy Picard	69 72 72 70	283	81.25

TOURNAMENT OF CHAMPIONS

LA COSTA COUNTRY CLUB
Rancho La Costa, California
April 17–20
Purse...$150,000
Par: 36, 36–72...7,114 yards

	SCORES	TOTAL	MONEY
Gary Player, *South Africa*	69 74 69 72	284	$30,000
Lee Trevino	74 68 70 74	286	17,000
Dave Stockton	69 75 75 70	289	10,000
Arnold Palmer	69 74 75 71	289	10,000
Gene Littler	75 68 75 72	290	8,000
George Archer	71 71 74 75	291	7,000
Bob Charles, *New Zealand*	73 73 74 72	292	5,500
Dick Lotz	67 78 70 77	292	5,500
Dan Sikes	73 73 77 70	293	4,116.67
Ron Cerrudo	74 73 75 71	293	4,116.67
Bill Casper	71 76 71 75	293	4,116.66

	SCORES	TOTAL	MONEY
Don January	71 78 73 72	294	3,416.67
Julius Boros	69 74 73 78	294	3,416.67
Steve Reid	71 75 70 78	294	3,416.66
Miller Barber	72 75 78 70	295	3,100
Jack Nicklaus	73 80 76 67	296	2,816.67
Tom Weiskopf	69 78 77 72	296	2,816.67
Ken Still	72 78 74 72	296	2,816.66
Tom Shaw	72 73 75 78	298	2,600
Bob Lunn	75 74 73 77	299	2,500
Roberto de Vicenzo	73 76 77 75	301	2,400
Bob Dickson	77 81 72 73	303	2,350
Charles Sifford	74 76 77 77	304	2,275
Bunky Henry	77 74 76 77	304	2,275
Jim Colbert	73 78 80 75	306	2,175
Chi Chi Rodriguez	78 75 76 77	306	2,175
Bob Murphy	79 72 79 79	309	2,100
Ray Floyd	75 77 80 78	310	2,000

AZALEA OPEN

CAPE FEAR COUNTRY CLUB
Wilmington, North Carolina
April 17—20
Purse...$35,000
Par: 35, 36—71...6,575 yards

	SCORES	TOTAL	MONEY
Dale Douglass	70 70 66 69	275	$5,000
Jim Langley	67 70 70 71	278	2,437.50
Larry Mowry	68 67 73 70	278	2,437.50
Bob Stone	66 70 73 69	278	2,437.50
Terry Wilcox	69 66 72 71	278	2,437.50
Joe Campbell	66 71 70 72	279	1,550
Randy Petri	68 68 68 75	279	1,550
Tommy Bolt	67 71 71 71	280	1,400
Bobby Mitchell	69 71 70 71	281	1,200
B. R. McLendon	69 71 70 71	281	1,200
Bob Duden	70 67 72 72	281	1,200
Al Balding, *Canada*	69 72 71 70	282	950
Sam Snead	70 69 72 71	282	950
Wilf Homenuik, *Canada*	67 72 70 73	282	950
Wes Ellis	70 71 72 70	283	775
Mike Reasor	68 70 72 73	283	775
Howie Johnson	68 71 70 74	283	775
Butch Baird	69 68 71 75	283	775
Rich Bassett	69 71 71 73	284	600
Lee Elder	67 72 69 76	284	600

	SCORES	TOTAL	MONEY
Rocky Thompson	69 70 75 70	284	600
Monty Kaser	73 72 69 71	285	458.34
Jimmy Picard	69 75 72 69	285	458.33
Harold Kneece	70 72 74 69	285	458.33
Chick Evans	67 75 73 71	286	362.50
Gary Bowerman, *Canada*	67 71 74 72	286	362.50
Everett Vinzant	71 71 70 74	286	362.50
Steve Spray	69 73 71 73	286	362.50
Tony Evans	70 71 70 76	287	275
Sonny Ridenhour	74 71 70 72	287	275
John Joseph	67 77 72 71	287	275
Skee Riegel	67 74 73 74	288	150
Bob Batdorff	68 73 77 70	288	150
Jimmy Day	74 71 70 73	288	150
Rolf Deming	70 74 72 72	288	150
Bill Wakeham, *Canada*	71 72 72 73	288	150

TALLAHASSEE OPEN

KILLEARN GOLF AND COUNTRY CLUB
Tallahassee, Florida
April 17—20
Purse...$35,000
Par: 36, 36—72...7,008 yards

	SCORES	TOTAL	MONEY
Chuck Courtney	72 69 71 70	282	$5,000
Jacky Cupit	71 72 73 67	283	2,633.34
Bert Greene	70 72 71 70	283	2,633.33
Bob Shaw, *Australia*	68 74 68 73	283	2,633.33
Jack Ewing	71 72 72 69	284	1,650
Johnny Jacobs	74 70 69 71	284	1,650
Jim Wiechers	76 68 69 71	284	1,650
Larry Hinson	70 64 77 74	285	1,400
Jerry Abbott	73 72 75 66	286	1,300
Grier Jones	74 69 73 71	287	1,062.50
Bob Boldt	77 70 69 71	287	1,062.50
Dick Crawford	71 73 71 72	287	1,062.50
Tommy Aaron	72 71 69 75	287	1,062.50
Pete Brown	71 72 73 72	288	875
Bob Erickson	70 72 73 73	288	875
Randy Wolff	73 72 73 71	289	725
Mike Hill	70 72 74 73	289	725
Cesar Sanudo	71 72 72 74	289	725
Bert Yancey	70 69 74 76	289	725
Bert Weaver	72 74 73 71	290	550
Jerry Heard	75 71 73 71	290	550

	SCORES	TOTAL	MONEY
J. C. Goosie	74 72 71 73	290	550
George Boutell	72 71 77 71	291	387.50
Nathaniel Starks	75 71 73 72	291	387.50
Larry Ziegler	67 72 78 74	291	387.50
Bob Stanton, *Australia*	71 75 71 74	291	387.50
Bill Garrett	69 75 72 75	291	387.50
Steve Oppermann	71 75 69 76	291	387.50
Martin Roesink, *Holland*	73 74 73 72	292	287.50
Orville Moody	70 77 72 73	292	287.50
Richard Martinez	66 76 75 76	293	250
Laurie Hammer	74 73 75 72	294	187.50
Jim Jamieson	72 75 72 75	294	187.50
Charles Houts	72 75 72 75	294	187.50
Dewitt Weaver	76 69 71 78	294	187.50

BYRON NELSON CLASSIC

PRESTON TRAIL GOLF CLUB
Dallas, Texas
April 24—27
Purse...$100,000
Par: 35, 35—70...7,086 yards

	SCORES	TOTAL	MONEY
Bruce Devlin, *Australia*	71 66 70 70	277	$20,000
Frank Beard	70 67 70 71	278	9,250
Bruce Crampton, *Australia*	69 70 70 69	278	9,250
Bob Charles, *New Zealand*	69 70 67 73	279	4,700
Don January	72 72 71 65	280	3,633.34
Bert Greene	66 71 73 70	280	3,633.33
Lee Trevino	69 70 67 74	280	3,633.33
Bob Lunn	69 74 68 71	282	2,825
Arnold Palmer	69 75 69 69	282	2,825
Pete Brown	73 75 69 66	283	2,400
Orville Moody	69 71 71 72	283	2,400
Johnny Pott	73 72 68 71	284	2,100
Julius Boros	67 72 72 74	285	1,750
Dale Douglass	70 73 68 74	285	1,750
Larry Hinson	70 73 75 67	285	1,750
Bob McCallister	74 68 72 71	285	1,750
Charles Coody	71 71 72 72	286	1,350
Dick Crawford	72 73 71 70	286	1,350
Howie Johnson	71 73 73 69	286	1,350
Wilf Homenuik, *Canada*	74 72 70 70	286	1,350
Chris Blocker	67 74 74 72	287	925
Gay Brewer	70 74 70 73	287	925

	SCORES	TOTAL	MONEY
Jacky Cupit	73 69 73 72	287	925
Rocky Thompson	72 69 71 75	287	925
Tom Weiskopf	70 72 74 71	287	925
Bob Shaw, *Australia*	73 70 67 77	287	925
J. C. Goosie	72 72 72 72	288	725
Allan Henning, *South Africa*	72 74 69 73	288	725
R. H. Sikes	72 72 70 74	288	725
Dudley Wysong	71 77 70 70	288	725
Jerry Abbott	72 75 70 72	289	612.50
Terry Dill	74 68 75 72	289	612.50
Fred Marti	73 70 72 74	289	612.50
Rolf Deming	74 72 70 73	289	612.50
Hale Irwin	72 71 73 74	290	508.34
Jerry Edwards	70 75 73 72	290	508.34
Don Bies	74 71 70 75	290	508.33
Homero Blancas	75 73 70 72	290	508.33
Chi Chi Rodriguez	72 72 74 72	290	508.33
Bob Stanton, *Australia*	73 73 73 71	290	508.33
Al Balding, *Canada*	73 75 70 73	291	322.50
Labron Harris	70 78 72 71	291	322.50
Lionel Hebert	72 75 70 74	291	322.50
John Lotz	75 73 70 73	291	322.50
Billy Maxwell	71 75 72 73	291	322.50
Rives McBee	72 73 74 72	291	322.50
Charles Sifford	71 73 73 74	291	322.50
Ross Randall	71 73 78 69	291	322.50
Bobby Cole, *South Africa*	70 74 71 77	292	180
Ken Fulton, *Canada*	73 74 74 71	292	180
Peter Townsend, *Great Britain*	74 70 71 77	292	180
Al Mengert	71 77 71 73	292	180
Bob Menne	67 73 76 76	292	180
Jack Ewing	73 73 76 71	293	160
B. R. McLendon	72 73 74 74	293	160
Jack Montgomery	73 75 73 72	293	160
Kermit Zarley	74 68 72 79	293	160
Doug Sanders	73 73 76 72	294	160
Bert Weaver	73 71 73 77	294	160
Chris Gers	74 74 76 70	294	160
Johnny Jacobs	72 74 75 76	297	160
Bill Martindale	71 77 72 77	297	160
Bob Smith	73 74 73 77	297	160
Bobby Westfall	71 77 73 76	297	160
John Schlee	74 73 75 76	298	160
Jim Wiechers	74 74 77 73	298	160
Lou Graham	72 72 76 79	299	160
Dave Walters	70 78 74 77	299	160
Ken Ellsworth	72 74 80 74	300	160
Bill Garrett	74 73 76 77	300	160

	SCORES	TOTAL	MONEY
Joel Goldstrand	73 75 75 77	300	160
Jerry McGee	77 70 78 76	301	160
Charlie Houts	74 71 81 76	302	160
Steve Oppermann	71 75 77 79	302	160
George Hixon	72 76 76 80	304	160

GREATER NEW ORLEANS OPEN

LAKEWOOD COUNTRY CLUB
New Orleans, Louisiana
May 1—4
Purse...$100,000
Par: 36, 35—71...6,960 yards

	SCORES	TOTAL	MONEY
Larry Hinson	69 68 71 67	275	$20,000
Frank Beard	67 67 69 72	275	11,400
(Hinson defeated Beard on third hole of sudden-death playoff.)			
Joel Goldstrand	70 67 69 70	276	5,300
Dave Hill	67 68 68 73	276	5,300
Bobby Mitchell	70 70 69 67	276	5,300
Johnny Pott	68 68 71 70	277	3,600
Lee Elder	66 73 68 71	278	2,950
Lionel Hebert	68 70 69 71	278	2,950
Herb Hooper	67 70 72 69	278	2,950
Deane Beman	71 70 69 69	279	1,810
Bob Charles, *New Zealand*	73 64 70 72	279	1,810
Bruce Devlin, *Australia*	71 70 69 69	279	1,810
Gardner Dickinson	72 67 71 69	279	1,810
Rod Funseth	69 69 70 71	279	1,810
Labron Harris	72 70 71 66	279	1,810
Johnny Jacobs	68 68 71 72	279	1,810
Grier Jones	68 72 67 72	279	1,810
Dan Sikes	67 72 71 69	279	1,810
Bob Stanton, *Australia*	68 70 72 69	279	1,810
Bill Casper	71 71 69 69	280	1,024
Bobby Cole, *South Africa*	67 71 72 70	280	1,024
Howie Johnson	67 72 70 71	280	1,024
Orville Moody	70 70 66 74	280	1,024
Bob Smith	68 74 69 69	280	1,024
Al Balding, *Canada*	72 68 73 68	281	725
Miller Barber	70 70 68 73	281	725
Harold Henning, *South Africa*	70 71 66 74	281	725
Bob Lunn	72 71 69 69	281	725
Johnny Stevens	68 69 74 70	281	725
Kermit Zarley	66 71 69 75	281	725

	SCORES				TOTAL	MONEY
Larry Ziegler	71	68	76	66	281	725
Jack Harden, Jr.	68	67	74	72	281	725
Ray Floyd	72	68	72	70	282	540
Howell Fraser	71	67	72	72	282	540
Hale Irwin	69	70	72	71	282	540
Bob Murphy	70	70	72	70	282	540
Chi Chi Rodriguez	72	69	69	72	282	540
Lee Trevino	70	72	71	69	282	540
Bert Weaver	69	70	72	71	282	540
Tommy Aaron	71	71	73	68	283	375
Ron Cerrudo	71	68	73	71	283	375
Billy Maxwell	71	70	70	72	283	375
Jack Montgomery	70	71	69	73	283	375
Hugh Royer	69	69	74	71	283	375
Bob Menne	70	70	70	73	283	375
Jack Ewing	68	75	74	67	284	223.81
Bert Greene	72	70	70	72	284	223.81
John Lotz	71	71	71	71	284	223.81
Charles Sifford	67	73	74	70	284	223.81
Jim Wiechers	72	71	72	69	284	223.81
Pete Brown	68	73	68	75	284	223.80
Bill Garrett	69	70	74	72	285	142.86
Lou Graham	72	70	71	72	285	142.86
Dick Rhyan	69	73	72	71	285	142.86
Dave Bollman	70	72	73	70	285	142.86
Bob Dickson	71	72	72	71	286	142.86
Jack McGowan	71	66	72	77	286	142.86
Steve Oppermann	71	69	72	74	286	142.86
John Schlee	69	73	72	72	286	142.86
Frank Boynton	71	70	70	76	287	142.86
Ken Ellsworth	70	73	70	74	287	142.86
Babe Hiskey	70	69	72	76	287	142.86
Earl Stewart	74	69	69	75	287	142.86
George Boutell	71	72	71	74	288	142.86
Peter Townsend, *Great Britain*	74	68	75	71	288	142.86
Dick Crawford	71	71	74	73	289	142.86
Fred Marti	67	76	74	72	289	142.86
Phil Rodgers	71	71	73	74	289	142.86
Dewitt Weaver	71	72	73	73	289	142.86
Don Bies	69	71	74	76	290	142.86
Malcolm Gregson, *Great Britain*	71	71	72	76	290	142.85
Bunky Henry	72	71	74	74	291	142.85
John Lively	71	72	74	74	291	142.85
Jim Hart	72	70	73	76	291	142.85
B. R. McLendon	68	71	74	79	292	142.85
Curtis Sifford	72	71	74	76	293	142.85
Dave Walters	71	72	76	74	293	142.85
Lee Davis	71	72	73	78	294	142.85

TEXAS OPEN

PECAN VALLEY COUNTRY CLUB
San Antonio, Texas
May 8—11
Purse...$100,000
Par: 36, 35—71...7,138 yards

	SCORES	TOTAL	MONEY
Deane Beman	70 69 70 65	274	$20,000
Jack McGowan	70 68 67 69	274	11,400
(Beman defeated McGowan on first hole of sudden-death playoff.)			
Tommy Aaron	71 70 68 68	277	5,300
Lee Trevino	74 68 67 68	277	5,300
Dave Hill	70 68 73 66	277	5,300
Bob Charles, *New Zealand*	70 68 69 71	278	3,400
Steve Reid	67 71 70 70	278	3,400
Doug Sanders	69 68 71 71	279	2,950
Bert Yancey	69 68 71 72	280	2,600
Jacky Cupit	70 67 71 72	280	2,600
Dan Sikes	72 72 67 70	281	2,025
Johnny Stevens	71 69 70 71	281	2,025
Fred Marti	71 66 72 72	281	2,025
Dean Refram	69 68 70 74	281	2,025
Bill Garrett	73 70 70 69	282	1,500
Ron Cerrudo	74 69 68 71	282	1,500
Jerry Hatfield	75 69 70 68	282	1,500
Bob Lunn	71 73 72 66	282	1,500
Bunky Henry	70 71 74 67	282	1,500
Ron Reif	75 68 70 70	283	1,100
Bobby Cole, *South Africa*	68 73 69 73	283	1,100
Dick Crawford	70 71 72 70	283	1,100
Tommy Aycock	71 73 70 70	284	810
Frank Beard	71 72 72 69	284	810
Bob Smith	72 72 68 72	284	810
Chi Chi Rodriguez	74 70 72 68	284	810
Dale Douglass	69 72 75 68	284	810
John Miller	72 68 71 73	284	810
Earl Stewart	71 68 74 71	284	810
Rafe Botts	74 69 72 70	285	626
Homero Blancas	73 71 72 69	285	626
Al Mengert	72 73 71 69	285	626
Bob Stanton, *Australia*	72 73 72 68	285	626
Al Balding, *Canada*	71 70 70 74	285	626
Dick Rhyan	71 72 70 73	286	495.72
Bob McCallister	72 71 71 72	286	495.72
Miller Barber	72 72 71 71	286	495.72
Billy Maxwell	74 71 71 70	286	495.71

	SCORES	TOTAL	MONEY
Steve Oppermann	69 72 73 72	286	495.71
Orville Moody	74 71 71 70	286	495.71
Frank Boynton	72 74 68 72	286	495.71
Dave Eichelberger	71 73 72 71	287	345
Hale Irwin	74 68 73 72	287	345
Terry Wilcox	69 71 76 71	287	345
Dudley Wysong	72 74 73 68	287	345
Bobby Mitchell	73 70 75 70	288	250
Laurie Hammer	73 68 75 72	288	250
J. C. Goosie	71 74 72 71	288	250
Jesse Snead	68 72 74 74	288	250
Jimmy Picard	72 71 71 75	289	160.45
Wayne Yates	69 76 70 74	289	160.45
Bob Erickson	71 70 74 74	289	160.44
Everett Vinzant	71 70 73 75	289	160.44
Jack Montgomery	73 72 73 71	289	160.44
Phil Rodgers	76 69 69 75	289	160.44
Bill Robinson	72 74 72 71	289	160.44
Charles Sifford	73 71 70 76	290	153.85
Ken Ellsworth	74 71 72 73	290	153.85
Rod Funseth	74 72 72 72	290	153.85
Larry Hinson	76 70 73 71	290	153.85
John Schlee	73 73 72 72	290	153.85
Charles Coody	76 69 73 72	290	153.85
Hugh Royer	72 71 74 74	291	153.85
Rod Curl	72 71 73 75	291	153.85
Jay Hebert	74 70 78 69	291	153.85
Kel Nagle, *Australia*	72 74 74 72	292	153.85
Earl Jacobson	74 71 72 76	293	153.84
Malcolm Gregson, *Great Britain*	73 73 76 71	293	153.84
Jim Wiechers	72 72 78 71	293	153.84
Dennie Meyer	71 73 75 74	293	153.84
Don Massengale	76 70 74 74	294	153.84
Gene Ferrell	72 73 74 77	296	153.84
Herb Hooper	74 72 71 79	296	153.84
Ras Allen	76 70 75 75	296	153.84
Bruce Crampton, *Australia*	73 71 78 74	296	153.84
Richard Martinez	77 69 75 78	299	153.84

COLONIAL NATIONAL INVITATION

COLONIAL COUNTRY CLUB
Fort Worth, Texas
May 15—18
Purse...$125,000
Par: 35, 35—70...7,142 yards

	SCORES				TOTAL	MONEY
Gardner Dickinson	71	68	73	66	278	$25,000
Gary Player, *South Africa*	70	68	72	69	279	14,300
Don January	71	70	70	69	280	8.850
Bob Charles, *New Zealand*	69	72	73	68	282	5,487.50
Jack Nicklaus	68	70	73	71	282	5,487.50
Bruce Crampton, *Australia*	70	69	69	75	283	3,890
Dave Hill	74	69	72	68	283	3,890
George Knudson, *Canada*	74	72	71	66	283	3,890
Bob Lunn	72	71	73	67	283	3,890
Frank Beard	73	68	76	67	284	3,125
Chuck Courtney	66	74	72	73	285	2,625
Larry Mowry	71	74	71	69	285	2,625
Johnny Pott	74	71	71	69	285	2,625
Charles Coody	70	69	75	72	286	1,937.50
Dick Crawford	68	74	75	69	286	1,937.50
Bruce Devlin, *Australia*	72	69	75	70	286	1,937.50
Billy Maxwell	68	70	70	78	286	1,937.50
Tom Shaw	70	74	73	69	286	1,937.50
Bert Yancey	71	65	77	73	286	1,937.50
Tommy Aaron	75	69	73	70	287	1,325
Bob Dickson	77	69	71	70	287	1,325
Fred Marti	71	70	73	73	287	1,325
Chi Chi Rodriguez	73	72	71	71	287	1,325
Miller Barber	69	74	74	71	288	985.84
Jack McGowan	73	73	71	71	288	985.84
B. R. McLendon	73	72	71	72	288	985.83
Jack Montgomery	70	68	75	75	288	985.83
Dave Stockton	69	72	73	74	288	985.83
Art Wall	70	73	74	71	288	985.83
Deane Beman	70	72	77	70	289	755.58
Jacky Cupit	72	69	74	74	289	755.57
Dale Douglass	71	71	73	74	289	755.57
Lee Elder	72	74	71	72	289	755.57
Rod Funseth	71	72	75	71	289	755.57
Tommy Jacobs	74	71	74	70	289	755.57
Phil Rodgers	75	69	72	73	289	755.57
Don Bies	70	70	80	70	290	574.50
Tommy Bolt	71	72	72	75	290	574.50
Frank Boynton	70	71	75	74	290	574.50

	SCORES	TOTAL	MONEY
Larry Hinson	75 72 74 69	290	574.50
Howie Johnson	74 71 70 75	290	574.50
Arnold Palmer	73 68 80 69	290	574.50
Gay Brewer	72 71 75 73	291	397.25
Charles Sifford	73 69 75 74	291	397.25
Bob Smith	71 74 74 72	291	397.25
Earl Stewart	72 74 73 72	291	397.25
Julius Boros	72 72 74 74	292	258.34
Lou Graham	73 71 77 71	292	258.34
Bert Greene	76 68 74 74	292	258.33
Grier Jones	74 72 72 74	292	258.33
Gene Littler	73 68 75 76	292	258.33
Dick Lotz	75 72 73 72	292	258.33
Bobby Cole, *South Africa*	71 71 75 76	293	200
Tony Jacklin, *Great Britain*	69 73 81 70	293	200
John Lotz	72 73 75 73	293	200
Mason Rudolph	74 70 73 76	293	200
Doug Sanders	71 72 73 77	293	200
Bob Stanton, *Australia*	72 72 72 77	293	200
Ernie Vossler	74 69 75 75	293	200
George Archer	73 74 72 75	294	200
Harold Henning, *South Africa*	74 71 78 71	294	200
Ken Still	75 69 74 76	294	200
Dudley Wysong	71 75 76 72	294	200
Homero Blancas	72 71 78 74	295	200
Mike Hill	75 72 75 73	295	200
Orville Moody	71 74 70 81	296	200
Kermit Zarley	74 73 75 74	296	200
Bill Casper	71 74 76 76	297	200
R. H. Sikes	72 69 82 74	297	200
Tom Weiskopf	71 76 68 82	297	200
Jim Colbert	71 72 82 73	298	200
Labron Harris	75 72 76 75	298	200
Bobby Mitchell	74 71 76 77	298	200
Jerry Edwards	74 71 73 80	298	200
Al Balding, *Canada*	75 71 80 75	301	200

ATLANTA CLASSIC

ATLANTA COUNTRY CLUB
Atlanta, Georgia
May 22—25
Purse...$115,000
Par: 36, 36—72...7,053 yards

	SCORES	TOTAL	MONEY
Bert Yancey	71 68 69 69	277	$23,000
Bruce Devlin, *Australia*	71 69 68 69	277	13,100
(Yancey defeated Devlin on second hole of sudden-death playoff.)			
Gary Player, *South Africa*	72 70 66 70	278	8,170
Bruce Crampton, *Australia*	69 69 68 73	279	5,410
Pete Brown	69 66 74 71	280	4,180
Grier Jones	71 67 74 68	280	4,180
George Knudson, *Canada*	67 71 71 71	280	4,180
Bob Charles, *New Zealand*	69 70 71 71	281	3,390
Bob Erickson	69 69 71 73	282	2,987.50
Dan Sikes	74 69 72 67	282	2,987.50
Bert Greene	73 71 73 66	283	2,415
Fred Marti	70 70 69 74	283	2,415
Art Wall	69 71 72 71	283	2,415
Dave Marr	72 70 73 69	284	2,012.50
Tom Weiskopf	75 66 72 71	284	2,012.50
Miller Barber	70 75 69 71	285	1,782.50
Jacky Cupit	67 71 71 76	285	1,782.50
Tommy Aaron	72 70 74 70	286	1,285
Lee Elder	74 71 71 70	286	1,285
Ray Floyd	74 73 71 68	286	1,285
Lionel Hebert	72 67 72 75	286	1,285
Harold Henning, *South Africa*	71 72 70 73	286	1,285
Dave Hill	74 72 71 69	286	1,285
Larry Hinson	72 74 71 69	286	1,285
Frank Boynton	71 73 73 70	287	851.15
Gardner Dickinson	75 71 72 69	287	851.15
Arnold Palmer	68 73 74 72	287	851.14
Hugh Royer	70 76 71 70	287	851.14
Mason Rudolph	68 75 72 72	287	851.14
Dave Stockton	74 70 69 74	287	851.14
Bob Shaw, *Australia*	70 66 76 75	287	851.14
Howie Johnson	72 73 69 74	288	690
Jack McGowan	71 71 75 71	288	690
Kel Nagle, *Australia*	72 73 70 73	288	690
Charles Coody	70 74 74 71	289	632.50
J. C. Goosie	73 72 74 70	289	632.50
Dick Crawford	71 75 69 75	290	545
Lou Graham	72 74 70 74	290	545

	SCORES				TOTAL	MONEY
Dick Rhyan	74	71	75	70	290	545
Kermit Zarley	73	70	70	77	290	545
Rod Curl	72	69	75	74	290	545
Labron Harris	73	74	74	70	291	381.80
Jay Hebert	73	72	69	77	291	381.80
Larry Mowry	74	72	70	75	291	381.80
Dean Refram	72	74	73	72	291	381.80
Gibby Gilbert	72	71	70	78	291	381.80
Rod Funseth	74	73	72	73	292	230
Dick Lotz	73	73	74	72	292	230
Bobby Mitchell	75	64	75	78	292	230
Jack Nicklaus	70	77	73	72	292	230
Dave Ragan	75	68	78	71	292	230
Steve Reid	75	71	70	76	292	230
Larry Sears	71	75	73	73	292	230
Doh Bies	73	72	71	77	293	184
Homero Blancas	71	73	74	75	293	184
Dale Douglass	74	73	72	74	293	184
Bob Goalby	74	73	70	76	293	184
Bunky Henry	73	69	77	74	293	184
Jack Montgomery	69	76	73	75	293	184
Ken Still	73	69	75	76	293	184
Chuck Montalbano	74	70	76	73	293	184
Bob Lunn	70	72	71	81	294	184
Ronnie Reif	74	72	73	75	294	184
Dave Eichelberger	72	74	72	77	295	184
Chick Evans	71	70	79	75	295	184
Howell Fraser	71	76	69	79	295	184
Jim Jamieson	74	69	74	78	295	184
B. R. McLendon	75	72	76	72	295	184
Laurie Hammer	72	75	71	78	296	184
Jim Wiechers	74	72	72	78	296	184
R. H. Sikes	73	71	71	82	297	184
Allan Henning, *South Africa*	75	72	73	79	299	184
John Lotz	72	75	76	77	300	184
Steve Oppermann	71	72	77	85	305	184
Bob Johnson	68	78	76	84	306	184

MEMPHIS OPEN

COLONIAL COUNTRY CLUB
Memphis, Tennessee
May 29–June 1
Purse...$150,000
Par: 34, 36–70...6,466 yards

	SCORES	TOTAL	MONEY
Dave Hill	67 67 66 65	265	$30,000
Lee Elder	64 67 66 70	267	17,100
Tommy Aaron	66 69 68 65	268	**8,850**
Charles Coody	66 68 67 67	268	**8,850**
Steve Reid	69 70 61 69	269	6,150
Don January	69 70 64 67	270	5,400
Lee Trevino	65 69 69 68	271	4,425
Lou Graham	65 69 66 71	271	4,425
Dale Douglass	66 66 70 69	271	4,425
Hale Irwin	67 65 72 68	272	3,600
Dan Sikes	66 66 68 72	272	3,600
Bert Greene	70 67 67 69	273	2,812.50
Gene Littler	65 69 69 70	273	2,812.50
Bert Yancey	64 67 66 76	273	2,812.50
Gary Player, *South Africa*	66 67 67 73	273	2,812.50
Grier Jones	69 69 69 67	274	2,325
John Lotz	64 68 68 74	274	2,325
Dean Refram	69 70 70 66	275	1,800
Larry Mowry	69 72 66 68	275	1,800
Jerry Abbott	69 69 68 69	275	1,800
Dave Marr	67 69 69 70	275	1,800
Ken Still	66 69 67 73	275	1,800
Chi Chi Rodriguez	69 68 71 68	276	1,325
Homero Blancas	70 70 67 69	276	1,325
Steve Spray	69 72 66 69	276	1,325
Wayne Vollmer, *Canada*	69 68 72 68	277	1,100
Gardner Dickinson	68 69 71 69	277	1,100
Bob Smith	70 67 71 69	277	1,100
Bobby Mitchell	67 71 69 70	277	1,100
Bob Murphy	68 71 67 71	277	1,100
Ron Reif	64 71 76 67	278	887.50
Howie Johnson	70 68 71 69	278	887.50
B. R. McLendon	65 71 72 70	278	887.50
Dave Eichelberger	69 72 67 70	278	887.50
Steve Oppermann	67 70 70 71	278	887.50
Bob Goalby	70 71 65 72	278	887.50
Rick Rhoads	67 72 72 68	279	711
Hugh Royer	72 69 70 68	279	711
Miller Barber	66 67 74 72	279	711

	SCORES	TOTAL	MONEY
Bobby Cole, *South Africa*	66 73 68 72	279	711
Mike Hill	71 69 66 73	279	711
Jimmy Picard	70 70 71 69	280	540
R. H. Sikes	69 71 70 70	280	540
Peter Townsend, *Great Britain*	72 69 68 71	280	540
Gibby Gilbert	68 68 68 77	281	420
Gay Brewer	69 70 66 76	281	420
John Lively	68 69 67 77	281	420
Pete Brown	70 70 74 68	282	278.58
Rod Funseth	67 72 73 70	282	278.57
Roy Pace	71 70 69 72	282	278.57
Jay Hebert	69 72 69 72	282	278.57
Jerry Edwards	68 69 72 73	282	278.57
Billy Maxwell	67 73 69 73	282	278.57
Marty Fleckman	69 66 72 75	282	278.57
J. C. Goosie	70 71 70 72	283	240
Fred Marti	68 69 70 76	283	240
Jim Grant	66 72 71 75	284	240
Terry Dill	74 67 68 75	284	240
Tommy Jacobs	68 71 71 74	284	240
Charles Montalbano	70 70 71 73	284	240
Art Wall	67 72 72 73	284	240
Herb Hooper	69 67 75 73	284	240
George Boutell	67 73 73 71	284	240
Jerry Heard	70 70 72 73	285	240
Doug Ford	70 69 73 73	285	240
Randy Petri	71 70 72 72	285	240
Phil Rodgers	67 72 74 72	285	240
Mike Reasor	74 66 70 75	285	240
Joe Carr	67 73 76 70	286	240
Bill Parker	72 69 74 71	286	240
Cesar Sanudo	66 74 75 71	286	240
Laurie Hammer	73 68 75 71	287	240
Ken Ellsworth	72 69 70 77	288	240
Jim Ferrier	68 72 77 72	289	240
Gene Dixon	68 73 77 71	289	240

WESTERN OPEN

MIDLOTHIAN COUNTRY CLUB
Midlothian, Illinois
June 5–8
Purse...$130,000
Par: 36, 35–71...6,654 yards

	SCORES				TOTAL	MONEY
Bill Casper	72	69	68	67	276	$26,000
Rocky Thompson	67	70	74	69	280	14,800
Frank Beard	66	71	70	74	281	9,240
Peter Townsend, *Great Britain*	71	72	68	72	283	6,120
Tony Jacklin, *Great Britain*	75	68	72	69	284	4,302
Gary Player, *South Africa*	68	72	72	72	284	4,302
Dick Rhyan	67	70	75	72	284	4,302
Homero Blancas	70	73	67	74	284	4,302
Tom Weiskopf	73	70	67	74	284	4,302
Julius Boros	72	72	69	72	285	2,990
Gay Brewer	69	67	74	75	285	2,990
Ken Still	72	66	72	75	285	2,990
Jack Ewing	68	74	73	71	286	2,340
Bob Lunn	75	65	74	72	286	2,340
Bob Stanton, *Australia*	69	74	68	75	286	2,340
Miller Barber	72	73	70	72	287	2,015
George Archer	74	72	68	73	287	2,015
Bert Greene	69	70	76	73	288	1,406.25
Bert Yancey	74	71	71	72	288	1,406.25
Lee Trevino	72	68	75	73	288	1,406.25
Bob Smith	72	70	73	73	288	1,406.25
Ron Cerrudo	70	72	73	73	288	1,406.25
*Bruce Fleisher	70	71	72	75	288	
Bob Charles, *New Zealand*	71	68	72	77	288	1,406.25
Rod Funseth	72	73	67	76	288	1,406.25
Bobby Brue	70	70	71	77	288	1,406.25
Dale Douglass	71	70	75	73	289	942.84
Hale Irwin	70	70	74	75	289	942.84
Billy Maxwell	66	73	75	75	289	942.83
Hugh Royer	72	73	68	76	289	942.83
Bob Murphy	68	77	68	76	289	942.83
Randy Petri	73	68	71	77	289	942.83
B. R. McLendon	73	72	73	72	290	767
Gibby Gilbert	70	71	75	74	290	767
Fred Haas	73	69	74	74	290	767
Curtis Sifford	71	68	73	78	290	767
Bob Erickson	72	74	74	71	291	663
Jack Nicklaus	71	72	75	73	291	663
Bobby Mitchell	70	72	75	74	291	663

	SCORES	TOTAL	MONEY
Doug Sanders	70 69 77 75	291	663
Bob Goalby	68 76 71 77	292	544.67
Bobby Greenwood	69 70 74 79	292	544.67
Pete Brown	71 75 68 78	292	544.66
Dave Stockton	72 70 79 72	293	369.86
Lionel Hebert	74 72 72 75	293	369.86
John Lotz	72 72 73 76	293	369.86
Charles Sifford	72 72 73 76	293	369.86
Ray Floyd	69 72 75 77	293	369.86
Dean Refram	74 72 69 78	293	369.85
Joel Goldstrand	69 73 71 80	293	369.85
*David Shuster	69 73 80 72	294	
Jacky Cupit	75 71 73 75	294	234.57
Doug Ford	71 74 73 76	294	234.57
Bob Dickson	74 70 73 77	294	234.57
Labron Harris	72 70 73 79	294	234.56
Jim King	76 70 75 74	295	226.09
Chi Chi Rodriguez	69 73 78 75	295	226.09
Howie Johnson	72 67 80 76	295	226.09
Bill Ogden	76 70 73 76	295	226.09
George Boutell	72 72 73 78	295	226.09
Rolf Deming	73 73 70 79	295	226.09
Dewitt Weaver	71 72 77 76	296	226.09
Mike Hill	68 72 78 78	296	226.09
Grier Jones	77 69 73 78	297	226.09
Wayne Vollmer, *Canada*	72 74 74 77	297	226.09
Bobby Cole, *South Africa*	70 69 77 82	298	226.09
Dick Hart	71 74 72 81	298	226.09
Jerry Abbott	70 75 72 82	299	226.09
Rafe Botts	77 69 74 79	299	226.08
Jack Montgomery	71 75 80 73	299	226.08
Al Mengert	75 71 74 81	301	226.08
Bob Eastwood	70 74 75 82	301	226.08
Charles Montalbano	75 70 78 79	302	226.08
Butch Baird	74 71 83 77	305	226.08
Jimmy Picard	74 72 82 81	309	226.08

* Amateur

U.S. OPEN CHAMPIONSHIP

CHAMPIONS GOLF CLUB, CYPRESS CREEK COURSE
Houston, Texas
June 12—15
Purse...$196,900
Par: 35, 35—70...6,967 yards

	SCORES	TOTAL	MONEY
Orville Moody	71 70 68 72	281	$30,000
Deane Beman	68 69 73 72	282	11,000
Al Geiberger	68 72 72 70	282	11,000
Bob Rosburg	70 69 72 71	282	11,000
Bob Murphy	66 72 74 71	283	7,000
Miller Barber	67 71 68 78	284	5,000
Bruce Crampton, *Australia*	73 72 68 71	284	5,000
Arnold Palmer	70 73 69 72	284	5,000
Bunky Henry	70 72 68 75	285	3,500
George Archer	69 74 73 70	286	2,800
Bruce Devlin, *Australia*	73 74 70 69	286	2,800
Dave Marr	75 69 71 71	286	2,800
Julius Boros	71 73 70 73	287	1,888.89
Charles Coody	72 68 72 75	287	1,888.89
Dale Douglass	76 69 70 72	287	1,888.89
Ray Floyd	79 68 68 72	287	1,888.89
Dave Hill	73 74 70 70	287	1,888.89
Dean Refram	69 74 70 74	287	1,888.89
Phil Rodgers	76 70 69 72	287	1,888.89
Kermit Zarley	74 72 70 71	287	1,888.89
Howie Johnson	72 73 72 70	287	1,888.88
Bob Stanton, *Australia*	74 70 71 73	288	1,500
Tom Weiskopf	69 75 71 73	288	1,500
Bert Yancey	71 71 74 72	288	1,500
Dick Crawford	70 75 73 71	289	1,300
Tony Jacklin, *Great Britain*	71 70 73 75	289	1,300
Bobby Mitchell	72 74 66 77	289	1,300
Jack Nicklaus	74 67 75 73	289	1,300
Dave Stockton	75 69 72 73	289	1,300
Joe Campbell	73 74 73 69	289	1,300
Rich Bassett	73 74 69 74	290	1,140
Bobby Cole, *South Africa*	73 72 72 73	290	1,140
Bobby Nichols	74 74 72 70	290	1,140
Bob Smith	76 67 72 75	290	1,140
Jerry Steelsmith	72 72 75 71	290	1,140
Homero Blancas	72 73 69 77	291	1,070
George Knudson, *Canada*	70 70 76 75	291	1,070
Dan Sikes	74 74 72 72	292	1,030
Sam Snead	71 77 70 74	292	1,030

	SCORES				TOTAL	MONEY
Tommy Aaron	71	72	73	77	293	995
Bill Casper	74	73	72	74	293	995
Al Balding, *Canada*	74	73	73	74	294	955
Bert Greene	78	70	74	72	294	955
Bob Lunn	71	72	76	75	294	955
Jack Montgomery	74	73	72	75	294	955
Mike Souchak	72	73	74	75	294	955
John Miller	71	70	80	73	294	955
Don Bies	78	70	70	77	295	915
Gary Player, *South Africa*	71	75	72	77	295	915
Frank Beard	72	73	73	78	296	895
Bob Stone	74	72	75	75	296	895
Bill Collins	75	72	73	77	297	865
Lionel Hebert	74	73	77	73	297	865
Bob Payne	71	74	73	79	297	865
John Schlee	74	74	78	71	297	865
Ken Still	74	74	72	78	298	835
Bill Ogden	76	72	75	75	298	835
Pete Brown	74	74	74	77	299	805
Jack Ewing	70	76	80	73	299	805
Labron Harris	71	75	75	78	299	805
Larry Hinson	73	75	76	75	299	805
Rives McBee	71	77	76	75	299	805
David Philo	71	74	78	76	299	805
Martin Bohen	72	75	74	81	302	800
Dave Eichelberger	76	71	76	80	303	800
Dow Finsterwald	77	71	77	78	303	800
Lee Elder	74	73	79	82	308	800
Chuck Courtney	72	76	80	82	310	800

OUT OF FINAL 36 HOLES

	SCORES		TOTAL
Jim Colbert	74	75	149
Lee Trevino	74	75	149
Johnny Stevens	78	71	149
*Bud Bradley	77	72	149
Tom Nieporte	76	73	149
*Gregory Powers	74	75	149
Jim Hardy	76	74	150
Bob Charles, *New Zealand*	74	76	150
Hugh Royer	76	74	150
R. H. Sikes	73	77	150
Larry Ziegler	76	74	150
Johnny Pott	72	78	150
Harry Toscano	74	77	151
*Bruce Fleisher	75	76	151
Jacky Cupit	78	73	151

	SCORES		TOTAL
Jesse Snead	75	77	152
Chuck Scally	78	74	152
Gordon Jones	74	78	152
Dick Lotz	79	73	152
Gene Littler	72	80	152
*Michael Davis	76	76	152
Bob Verwey, *South Africa*	77	75	152
Jerry Edwards	74	78	152
Dave Ragan	74	78	152
Scotty McBeath	74	79	153
Dick Rhyan	78	75	153
Steve Spray	74	79	153
Ken Venturi	76	77	153
John Lotz	76	77	153
Kel Nagle, *Australia*	80	73	153
Rod Funseth	76	77	153
*James Barker	78	76	154
John Baldwin	78	76	154
Chris Gers	77	77	154
Terry Wilcox	77	77	154
Tom Kochan	72	82	154
Mac Hunter	75	79	154
John Levinson	78	77	155
Bobby Brue	77	78	155
*Terry Small	76	79	155
Jerry Pittman	74	81	155
Skee Riegel	79	76	155
*Ralph Bogart	81	74	155
Don Massengale	79	76	155
Billy Farrell	79	76	155
Carl Lohren	76	79	155
Jose Lopez	81	75	156
Robert Pipkin	79	77	156
John Felus	77	79	156
Robert Bramson	79	78	157
Wayne Yates	80	77	157
Tony Holguin	81	76	157
Rick Rhoads	79	78	157
Larry Campbell	77	80	157
Bob Panasiuk, *Canada*	79	78	157
Andy Borkovich	78	80	158
Bruce Dobie	78	80	158
Les Peterson	76	82	158
Charles Genter	81	77	158
Gay Brewer	75	83	158
*Gregory Trompas	83	75	158
Austin Staub	83	75	158
Al Chandler	81	78	159

	SCORES	TOTAL
Ken Fulton, *Canada*	78 81	159
Bob Duden	83 76	159
Tommy Jacobs	81 79	160
Roy Beattie	81 79	160
Al Besselink	82 78	160
Mason Rudolph	82 79	161
Remo Crovetti	80 81	161
Peter Townsend, *Great Britain*	79 82	161
Joe Cardenas	80 82	162
Henry Johnson	81 82	163
Bob Shaw, *Australia*	84 79	163
*Ed Tutwiler	80 83	163
Pat Rea	85 79	164
*Elliott Phillips	82 82	164
Walter Romans	82 83	165
Norman Rack	85 82	167
*William Carey	85 86	171
Don January	76 WD during second round	
Dan Keefe	WD during first round	

(Each professional who did not complete 72 holes received $500.)

* Amateur

KEMPER OPEN

QUAIL HOLLOW COUNTRY CLUB
Charlotte, North Carolina
June 19—22
Purse...$150,000
Par: 36, 36—72...7,205 yards

	SCORES	TOTAL	MONEY
Dale Douglass	69 70 68 67	274	$30,000
Charles Coody	73 69 71 65	278	17,100
Bruce Crampton, *Australia*	72 68 69 70	279	8,850
Gary Player, *South Africa*	70 73 67 69	279	8,850
George Archer	67 73 68 72	280	5,193.75
Joel Goldstrand	71 72 68 69	280	5,193.75
Tony Jacklin, *Great Britain*	70 69 70 71	280	5,193.75
Arnold Palmer	73 71 70 66	280	5,193.75
Bob Charles, *New Zealand*	68 70 70 73	281	3,750
George Knudson, *Canada*	71 69 70 71	281	3,750
Larry Ziegler	70 73 70 68	281	3,750
Bert Greene	70 71 70 71	282	2,730
Jerry Heard	71 73 72 66	282	2,730

	SCORES	TOTAL	MONEY
Lionel Hebert	70 72 67 73	282	2,730
Dan Sikes	72 67 71 72	282	2,730
Tom Weiskopf	69 71 72 70	282	2,730
Don Bies	70 71 72 70	283	2,025
Bruce Devlin, *Australia*	69 70 72 72	283	2,025
Phil Rodgers	67 74 72 70	283	2,025
Bert Yancey	71 72 69 71	283	2,025
Pete Brown	72 70 71 71	284	1,387.50
Joe Carr	71 72 70 71	284	1,387.50
Jim Colbert	68 73 72 71	284	1,387.50
Billy Maxwell	73 71 70 70	284	1,387.50
Doug Sanders	69 71 73 71	284	1,387.50
Lee Trevino	70 69 71 74	284	1,387.50
Tommy Aaron	70 73 73 69	285	967.50
Tommy Bolt	70 71 74 70	285	967.50
Hale Irwin	70 74 70 71	285	967.50
Jack McGowan	71 71 71 72	285	967.50
B. R. McLendon	72 73 71 69	285	967.50
Jack Montgomery	72 70 73 70	285	967.50
Bob Payne	69 70 73 73	285	967.50
Hugh Royer	73 69 69 74	285	967.50
Sam Snead	70 69 74 72	285	967.50
Rod Curl	74 70 72 69	285	967.50
Julius Boros	71 72 67 76	286	690
Dick Crawford	71 74 72 69	286	690
Howie Johnson	73 72 71 70	286	690
Orville Moody	72 71 73 70	286	690
Bob Murphy	71 71 70 74	286	690
Mason Rudolph	69 70 75 72	286	690
Fred Marti	71 73 74 69	287	387.23
Dewitt Weaver	71 74 73 69	287	387.23
George Boutell	72 70 73 72	287	387.22
Dave Eichelberger	70 73 72 72	287	387.22
Harold Henning, *South Africa*	74 68 73 72	287	387.22
Mike Hill	74 71 71 71	287	387.22
Johnny Pott	71 73 72 71	287	387.22
Bobby Greenwood	70 75 68 74	287	387.22
Bob Shaw, *Australia*	71 73 73 70	287	387.22
Al Balding, *Canada*	70 71 74 73	288	200
Frank Boynton	70 73 71 74	288	200
Bobby Cole, *South Africa*	70 74 72 72	288	200
Rod Funseth	72 73 73 70	288	200
Rocky Thompson	73 70 74 71	288	200
Bob Goalby	68 75 71 75	289	200
Don January	73 70 73 73	289	200
Bradley Anderson	72 71 75 71	289	200
Hugh Inggs, *South Africa*	72 69 72 76	289	200
Ron Cerrudo	74 71 73 72	290	200

	SCORES	TOTAL	MONEY
Bob McCallister	68 75 72 75	290	200
Al Mengert	72 73 70 75	290	200
Marty Fleckman	74 71 74 72	291	200
Jim Grant	72 71 74 74	291	200
Grier Jones	71 72 75 74	292	200
Bob Stone	70 75 73 74	292	200
Clayton Cole	73 70 75 74	292	200
Lee Elder	75 70 74 74	293	200
Gordon Jones	73 71 75 74	293	200
Rick Jetter	71 74 75 73	293	200
R. H. Sikes	73 72 74 75	294	200
John Miller	72 73 73 76	294	200
Butch Baird	71 72 76 77	296	200
Jim Ferrier	72 72 77 75	296	200
J. C. Goosie	73 71 75 77	296	200
Larry Hinson	73 71 76 76	296	200
*David Shuster	74 71 75 76	296	200
Charles Sifford	71 73 74 77	295	200
Jerry Abbott	73 72 74 81	300	200
Chuck Matlack	71 74 75 82	302	200

* Amateur

CLEVELAND OPEN

AURORA COUNTRY CLUB
Aurora, Ohio
June 26—29
Purse...$110,000
Par: 35, 35—70...6,661 yards

	SCORES	TOTAL	MONEY
Charles Coody	67 64 71 69	271	$22,000
Bruce Crampton, *Australia*	69 66 69 69	273	12,500
Bob Murphy	70 71 69 65	275	7,850
Bert Yancey	69 70 72 65	276	4,840
Frank Beard	69 70 71 66	276	4,840
John Schlee	69 66 71 77	277	3,960
John Levinson	73 72 65 68	278	3,382.50
Bob Charles, *New Zealand*	73 67 68 70	278	3,382.50
Harold Henning, *South Africa*	69 70 72 68	279	2,438.34
Gordon Jones	72 71 67 69	279	2,438.34
Terry Dill	69 73 68 69	279	2,438.33
Arnold Palmer	74 69 66 70	279	2,438.33
J. C. Goosie	70 70 68 71	279	2,428.33
Gardner Dickinson	69 70 68 72	279	2,428.33

	SCORES	TOTAL	MONEY
Chi Chi Rodriguez	71 69 71 69	280	1,760
Tommy Aaron	71 67 71 71	280	1,760
Julius Boros	74 70 65 71	280	1,760
Dave Marr	72 69 73 67	281	1,430
Randy Petri	69 76 67 69	281	1,430
Jim Colbert	69 67 75 70	281	1,430
Gene Littler	71 73 71 67	282	1,045
Jacky Cupit	72 70 72 68	282	1,045
Labron Harris	74 70 70 68	282	1,045
Homero Blancas	75 70 68 69	282	1,045
Fred Marti	74 68 69 71	282	1,045
Jerry McGee	67 76 71 69	283	847
Tom Weiskopf	72 73 68 70	283	847
B. R. McLendon	73 68 70 72	283	847
Mike Hill	74 70 72 68	284	704
Dave Bollman	69 74 72 69	284	704
Jim Wiechers	74 71 70 69	284	704
Billy Maxwell	70 73 71 70	284	704
Ron Cerrudo	69 75 69 71	284	704
Phil Rodgers	73 71 69 71	284	704
Bob Stone	68 74 74 69	285	594
Dave Eichelberger	72 72 71 70	285	594
George Hixon	68 70 74 73	285	594
Doug Sanders	70 71 76 69	286	476.67
Bob Erickson	69 72 74 71	286	476.67
Doug Ford	71 74 71 70	286	476.67
Lionel Hebert	72 73 70 71	286	476.67
Bob McCallister	72 70 72 72	286	476.66
Bert Greene	76 67 69 74	286	476.66
John Miller	72 70 74 71	287	310.20
Howie Johnson	69 74 72 72	287	310.20
Howell Fraser	72 70 71 74	287	310.20
Herb Hooper	72 73 69 73	287	310.20
George Boutell	76 68 70 73	287	310.20
Joel Goldstrand	72 72 72 72	288	217.77
Dick Rhyan	74 70 71 73	288	217.77
Al Balding, *Canada*	69 74 74 71	288	217.77
Lee Trevino	71 74 76 68	289	191.31
John Lively	74 70 75 70	289	191.31
Rolf Deming	72 71 76 70	289	191.31
Bob Shaw, *Australia*	73 72 74 70	289	191.31
Richard Martinez	70 73 74 72	289	191.31
George Archer	73 69 75 72	289	191.31
Jim Jamieson	71 71 74 73	289	191.31
Rocky Thompson	71 74 71 73	289	191.31
Jack Nicklaus	73 68 74 74	289	191.31
Steve Reid	71 73 76 70	290	191.31
Tony Jacklin, *Great Britain*	71 72 76 71	290	191.30

	SCORES	TOTAL	MONEY
Bobby Cole, *South Africa*	74 67 77 73	291	191.30
Dave Ragan	70 72 75 74	291	191.30
Jack Montgomery	71 74 77 70	292	191.30
Dave Stockton	70 73 75 74	292	191.30
Orville Moody	67 78 76 72	293	191.30
Vern Novak	76 69 73 75	293	191.30
Dick Lotz	71 73 77 73	294	191.30
Dave Walters	75 70 77 73	295	191.30
Jack McGowan	73 72 75 76	296	191.30
George Bellino	74 71 78 76	299	191.30
Cesar Sanudo	68 76 77 78	299	191.30

BUICK OPEN

WARWICK HILLS COUNTRY CLUB
Grand Blanc, Michigan
July 3—6
Purse...$125,000
Par: 36, 36—72...7001 yards

	SCORES	TOTAL	MONEY
Dave Hill	68 68 71 70	277	$25,000
Frank Beard	70 68 70 71	279	14,300
Homero Blancas	65 73 70 72	280	8,850
Dan Sikes	72 69 69 71	281	5,850
Terry Dill	67 71 73 71	282	5,125
Herb Hooper	69 71 72 72	284	4,061.67
Bobby Nichols	71 69 72 72	284	4,061.67
Julius Boros	69 69 70 76	284	4,061.66
Don Bies	67 71 76 71	285	3,125
R. H. Sikes	65 76 73 71	285	3,125
Jim Wiechers	71 69 77 68	285	3,125
Jacky Cupit	74 69 72 71	286	2,343.75
Bob Dickson	67 71 72 76	286	2,343.75
Lee Elder	68 67 71 80	286	2,343.75
Bert Greene	68 71 76 71	286	2,343.75
Marty Fleckman	69 70 74 74	287	1,812.50
Gene Littler	70 72 70 75	287	1,812.50
Bob Lunn	67 77 73 70	287	1,812.50
Gibby Gilbert	70 72 74 71	287	1,812.50
Deane Beman	67 75 74 72	288	1,147.67
George Boutell	70 71 72 75	288	1,147.67
Mike Hill	69 73 76 70	288	1,147.67
Fred Marti	72 72 74 70	288	1,147.67
Jack Montgomery	72 73 72 71	288	1,147.67
Phil Rodgers	71 73 73 71	288	1,147.67
Dale Douglass	71 70 70 77	288	1,147.66

	SCORES	TOTAL	MONEY
Larry Hinson	70 67 75 76	288	1,147.66
Tom Weiskopf	69 69 78 72	288	1,147.66
Howie Johnson	73 71 75 70	289	831.25
Mason Rudolph	68 78 73 70	289	831.25
Rocky Thompson	72 71 75 71	289	831.25
Larry Ziegler	69 71 74 75	289	831.25
Dow Finsterwald	70 74 73 73	290	737.50
Roy Pace	68 77 73 72	290	737.50
Bruce Crampton, *Australia*	70 76 74 71	291	675
Johnny Jacobs	72 71 75 73	291	675
John Miller	70 70 78 73	291	675
Gordon Jones	71 72 76 73	292	577.75
Jerry McGee	72 72 74 74	292	577.75
Sam Snead	69 75 76 72	292	577.75
Bob Panasiuk, *Canada*	73 72 78 69	292	577.75
Jay Hebert	72 73 72 76	293	358.34
Hugh Royer	72 70 75 76	293	358.34
Claude Harmon Jr.	71 71 75 76	293	358.34
Bob Goalby	74 71 74 74	293	358.33
J. C. Goosie	71 74 73 75	293	358.33
Richard Martinez	68 73 77 75	293	358.33
Bob McCallister	68 70 77 78	293	358.33
Jack McGowan	68 77 73 75	293	358.33
B. R. McLendon	72 73 75 73	293	358.33
Labron Harris	72 74 75 73	294	238.10
Randy Petri	76 69 74 75	294	238.10
Johnny Pott	72 73 73 76	294	238.10
Kermit Zarley	71 71 75 77	294	238.10
Wilf Homenuik, *Canada*	70 70 77 77	294	238.10
Bob Erickson	69 74 75 77	295	238.10
Steve Spray	71 75 71 78	295	238.10
Jerry Abbott	73 72 73 78	296	238.10
Dick Crawford	70 74 75 77	296	238.10
Bob Stone	75 71 75 75	296	238.10
Tom Bailey	74 71 75 76	296	238.10
Bert Weaver	72 74 74 76	296	238.09
Pete Brown .	72 71 77 77	297	238.09
Doug Ford	71 73 79 74	297	238.09
Gary Groh, *Bahamas*	70 73 76 78	297	238.09
Dave Eichelberger	69 75 75 79	298	238.09
Dean Refram	71 73 80 75	299	238.09
Ronnie Reif	74 70 81 75	300	238.09
Dave Bollman	68 76 77 80	301	238.09
Les Peterson	70 76 77 79	302	238.09
Tom Shaw	72 73 80 78	303	238.09

MINNESOTA GOLF CLASSIC

BRAEMAR GOLF CLUB
Edina, Minnesota
July 10—13
Purse...$100,000
Par: 35, 36—71...6,919 yards

	SCORES				TOTAL	MONEY
Frank Beard	69	67	67	66	269	$20,000
Tommy Aaron	70	69	69	68	276	9,250
Hugh Inggs, *South Africa*	72	65	69	70	276	9,250
Labron Harris	70	70	67	70	277	4,400
Dave Stockton	68	67	69	73	277	4,400
Terry Dill	69	71	67	71	278	2,990
Howie Johnson	69	71	69	69	278	2,990
R. H. Sikes	70	68	71	69	278	2,990
Bob Smith	69	71	71	67	278	2,990
Wayne Yates	70	68	70	70	278	2,990
Hale Irwin	69	67	69	74	279	2,200
Dudley Wysong	69	75	68	67	279	2,200
Bob Goalby	69	71	70	70	280	1,800
Mason Rudolph	69	71	73	67	280	1,800
Tom Shaw	69	70	67	74	280	1,800
Frank Boynton	69	72	69	71	281	1,550
Chuck Courtney	68	71	72	70	281	1,550
Homero Blancas	67	73	70	72	282	1,081.25
Joel Goldstrand	70	72	71	69	282	1,081.25
J. C. Goosie	68	70	71	73	282	1,081.25
Dave Gumlia	68	75	70	69	282	1,081.25
Bob McCallister	70	70	71	71	282	1,081.25
Dan Sikes	67	69	75	71	282	1,081.25
Harry Toscano	70	70	69	73	282	1,081.25
Bob Panasiuk, *Canada*	71	71	70	70	282	1,081.25
Pete Brown	72	69	72	70	283	725
Lou Graham	71	68	71	73	283	725
Herb Hooper	69	70	72	72	283	725
Fred Marti	71	72	70	70	283	725
Larry Ziegler	73	69	69	72	283	725
John Miller	69	71	74	69	283	725
George Boutell	77	67	68	72	284	580
Dick Crawford	73	71	69	71	284	580
Bill Garrett	69	74	71	70	284	580
Dean Refram	71	70	73	70	284	580
Ken Still	70	72	70	72	284	580
Don Bies	71	69	73	72	285	403
Ron Cerrudo	69	70	73	73	285	403
Marty Fleckman	70	69	75	71	285	403

	SCORES	TOTAL	MONEY
George Johnson	73 70 71 71	285	403
Rives McBee	71 72 71 71	285	403
Jack McGowan	73 71 70 71	285	403
Johnny Pott	73 71 70 71	285	403
Johnny Stevens	71 73 74 67	285	403
Jim Hardy	70 71 69 75	285	403
Nathaniel Starks	72 71 68 74	285	403
Bunky Henry	72 71 70 73	286	180.41
John Jacobs	71 72 69 74	286	180.41
John Lively	66 77 69 74	286	180.41
Don Massengale	72 71 73 70	286	180.41
Roy Pace	71 68 72 75	286	180.41
Jesse Snead	73 71 66 76	286	180.41
Wilf Homenuik, *Canada*	70 70 71 75	286	180.41
Vern Novak	69 75 69 74	287	114.29
Bob Stanton, *Australia*	73 70 72 72	287	114.29
Bill Ezinicki	70 71 70 76	287	114.29
Dale Douglass	74 70 69 75	288	114.29
Charles Houts	74 70 72 72	288	114.29
Richard Martinez	72 69 73 74	288	114.29
Randy Petri	70 72 74 72	288	114.29
Gene Ferrell	69 73 73 73	288	114.29
Paul Moran	69 72 72 75	288	114.29
Jim Grant	71 71 73 74	289	114.29
Babe Hiskey	74 70 73 72	289	114.29
Gordon Jones	74 70 73 72	289	114.29
Ronnie Reif	71 70 74 74	289	114.29
Rick Rhoads	71 73 72 73	289	114.29
Dave Eichelberger	72 72 74 72	290	114.29
Dow Finsterwald	74 68 76 72	290	114.29
Bob Stone	74 69 73 74	290	114.28
Tom Bailey	74 69 71 76	290	114.28
Don Cherry	75 69 72 74	290	114.28
Jimmy Day	75 69 71 75	290	114.28
Jerry Hatfield	73 71 73 73	290	114.28
Don Parson	72 70 74 74	290	114.28
Les Peterson	71 72 72 75	290	114.28
John Schroeder	71 71 75 73	290	114.28
George Smith	68 72 73 77	290	114.28
Jim King	71 70 73 77	291	114.28
Jerry McGee	72 72 75 72	291	114.28
Jimmy Picard	71 72 74 74	291	114.28
Bob Eastwood	71 72 73 75	291	114.28
Jack Rule	72 72 73 75	292	114.28
Gaylon Simon	71 73 74 76	294	114.28
B. R. McLendon	66 75 78 77	296	114.28

PHILADELPHIA GOLF CLASSIC

WHITEMARSH VALLEY COUNTRY CLUB
Whitemarsh Valley, Pennsylvania
July 17—20
Purse...$150,000
Par: 36, 36—72...6,708 yards

	SCORES	TOTAL	MONEY
Dave Hill	71 71 68 69	279	$30,000
Gay Brewer	71 72 70 66	279	11,600
Tommy Jacobs	69 70 68 72	279	11,600
R. H. Sikes	73 71 68 67	279	11,600

(Hill defeated Brewer, Jacobs and Sikes on first hole of sudden-death playoff.)

	SCORES	TOTAL	MONEY
Frank Beard	72 72 70 66	280	6,150
Deane Beman	69 74 68 70	281	4,485
Bruce Devlin, *Australia*	72 71 73 65	281	4,485
Lou Graham	68 73 70 70	281	4,485
Grier Jones	72 69 66 74	281	4,485
B. R. McLendon	68 74 71 68	281	4,485
Terry Dill	73 74 66 69	282	3,150
Johnny Jacobs	70 77 68 67	282	3,150
Ken Still	75 72 69 66	282	3,150
Dan Sikes	72 71 69 72	284	2,625
Bob Stone	69 73 72 70	284	2,625
George Knudson, *Canada*	74 70 69 72	285	2,175
Chi Chi Rodriguez	71 72 71 71	285	2,175
Doug Sanders	73 72 70 70	285	2,175
Lee Trevino	70 71 75 69	285	2,175
Bill Casper	73 74 71 68	286	1,345.50
Dave Eichelberger	70 75 70 71	286	1,345.50
Herb Hooper	75 69 70 72	286	1,345.50
Hale Irwin	71 73 71 71	286	1,345.50
Bob Lunn	72 75 67 72	286	1,345.50
Arnold Palmer	73 69 73 71	286	1,345.50
Hugh Royer	77 69 71 69	286	1,345.50
Johnny Stevens	72 74 71 69	286	1,345.50
Bert Weaver	72 73 68 73	286	1,345.50
Kermit Zarley	72 75 70 69	286	1,345.50
Butch Baird	74 71 73 69	287	997.50
Labron Harris	72 72 72 71	287	997.50
Charles Coody	72 71 75 70	288	840
Dick Crawford	75 69 74 70	288	840
Gardner Dickinson	73 73 72 70	288	840
Dale Douglass	68 76 70 74	288	840
Don January	71 75 73 69	288	840
Gordon Jones	72 72 76 68	288	840

	SCORES				TOTAL	MONEY
John Schlee	74	72	71	71	288	840
Ray Floyd	69	77	71	72	289	564.38
Joel Goldstrand	69	75	74	71	289	564.38
Charles Sifford	74	71	71	73	289	564.38
Bobby Greenwood	74	68	74	73	289	564.38
Tommy Aaron	72	73	69	75	289	564.37
Ron Cerrudo	72	75	68	74	289	564.37
Larry Mowry	76	69	70	74	289	564.37
Dave Stockton	71	70	73	75	289	564.37
Bob Dickson	67	79	74	70	290	322.16
Jack Ewing	73	72	73	72	290	322.16
George Boutell	71	70	73	76	290	322.15
Steve Oppermann	71	76	71	72	290	322.15
Dudley Wysong	72	74	72	72	290	322.15
Frank Boynton	67	78	73	73	291	230.77
Bill Garrett	70	75	72	74	291	230.77
Fred Marti	71	72	74	74	291	230.77
Miller Barber	76	68	77	71	292	230.77
Bob Charles, *New Zealand*	68	76	71	77	292	230.77
Lionel Hebert	74	73	72	73	292	230.77
Bob Murphy	72	75	73	72	292	230.77
Larry Ziegler	73	74	72	73	292	230.77
Earl Stewart	71	74	72	76	293	230.77
Bert Yancey	76	71	73	73	293	230.77
Jim Colbert	72	73	75	74	294	230.77
Harold Henning, *South Africa*	71	76	69	78	294	230.77
Gene Ferrell	70	76	72	76	294	230.77
Babe Hiskey	69	74	75	77	295	230.77
Jesse Snead	74	73	72	76	295	230.77
Bunky Henry	69	76	75	76	296	230.77
Dean Refram	71	70	78	77	296	230.77
Tom Weiskopf	70	77	76	73	296	230.77
John Schroeder	73	74	76	73	296	230.77
Stan Dudas	75	72	73	77	297	230.77
Al Mengert	71	74	76	77	298	230.77
Art Wall	75	72	73	82	302	230.77
Moon Mullins	72	74	80	77	303	230.77
Wayne Yates	75	71	75	82	303	230.76
Bob Shaw, *Australia*	77	68	73	85	303	230.76

AMERICAN GOLF CLASSIC

FIRESTONE COUNTRY CLUB
Akron, Ohio
July 24—27
Purse...$125,000
Par: 35, 35—70...7,180 yards

	SCORES	TOTAL	MONEY
Ray Floyd	67 68 68 65	268	$25,000
Bobby Nichols	68 70 67 67	272	14,300
Tom Weiskopf	68 73 67 66	274	8,850
Gene Littler	68 69 71 68	276	5,487.50
Bobby Mitchell	65 68 70 73	276	5,487.50
Al Geiberger	68 73 68 69	278	4,250
Jack Nicklaus	66 66 71 75	278	4,250
Frank Beard	68 67 72 72	279	3,530
R. H. Sikes	71 68 74 66	279	3,530
Don Bies	71 69 68 72	280	2,875
Jim Colbert	70 70 71 69	280	2,875
Peter Townsend, *Great Britain*	68 72 68 72	280	2,875
Ron Cerrudo	75 70 68 68	281	2,375
Homero Blancas	72 72 69 69	282	2,062.50
Hale Irwin	71 71 72 68	282	2,062.60
Tommy Jacobs	73 69 66 74	282	2,062.50
Arnold Palmer	75 68 68 71	282	2,062.50
Dave Hill	69 75 69 70	283	1,625
Ken Venturi	71 69 70 73	283	1,625
John Miller	73 68 69 73	283	1,625
Dale Douglass	72 73 70 69	284	1,034.46
Bert Greene	67 72 75 70	284	1,034.46
Don January	69 71 73 71	284	1,034.46
Steve Reid	67 74 74 69	284	1,034.46
Bob Stone	76 69 73 66	284	1,034.46
George Archer	68 70 74 72	284	1,034.45
Tommy Bolt	70 72 70 72	284	1,034.45
Dave Eichelberger	70 70 71 73	284	1,034.45
Lou Graham	69 70 73 72	284	1,034.45
Orville Moody	71 71 67 75	284	1,034.45
John Schlee	71 68 70 75	284	1,034.45
Charles Coody	68 76 68 73	285	725
Dave Marr	70 71 71 73	285	725
Don Massengale	70 70 76 69	285	725
Dan Sikes	70 71 73 71	285	725
Bob Stanton, *Australia*	70 69 75 71	285	725
Julius Boros	71 70 74 71	286	574.50
Gay Brewer	69 70 72 75	286	574.50
Bob Lunn	71 72 72 71	286	574.50
Chi Chi Rodriguez	68 74 73 71	286	574.50

	SCORES	TOTAL	MONEY
Jim Wiechers	73 70 71 72	286	574.50
Terry Wilcox	65 74 71 76	286	574.50
Billy Maxwell	73 71 71 72	287	342.38
Phil Rodgers	69 72 77 69	287	342.38
Dave Stockton	73 71 72 71	287	342.38
Bert Yancey	72 71 73 71	287	342.38
Gardner Dickinson	69 73 72 73	287	342.37
Terry Dill	75 70 69 73	287	342.37
Paul Harney	68 72 72 75	287	342.37
Fred Marti	72 71 71 73	287	342.37
Monty Kaser	69 72 74 73	288	166.67
Dick Rhyan	75 68 72 73	288	166.67
Tom Nieporte	67 74 75 72	288	166.67
Bobby Cole, *South Africa*	69 72 73 75	289	166.67
B. R. McLendon	73 72 70 74	289	166.67
Bob Murphy	71 70 72 76	289	166.67
Johnny Pott	71 73 70 75	289	166.67
Mason Rudolph	71 73 74 71	289	166.67
J. C. Goosie	70 70 75 75	290	166.67
Jack McGowan	70 70 73 77	290	166.67
Dean Refram	72 71 73 74	290	166.67
Butch Baird	72 73 68 78	291	166.67
Howell Fraser	69 73 75 74	291	166.67
Rod Funseth	74 71 72 74	291	166.67
Grier Jones	72 72 70 77	291	166.67
Bob Shaw, *Australia*	72 72 70 77	291	166.67
Miller Barber	71 74 70 77	292	166.67
Frank Boynton	71 72 74 75	292	166.67
Allan Henning, *South Africa*	73 72 74 74	293	166.67
Jerry McGee	71 72 74 76	293	166.67
Paul Bondeson	71 72 75 76	294	166.66
Jay Hebert	70 74 75 75	294	166.66
Steve Oppermann	71 74 77 72	294	166.66
Everett Vinzant	74 70 75 75	294	166.66
Dudley Wysong	75 70 75 74	294	166.66
Ken Still	70 72 74 79	295	166.66
Herman Keiser	70 71 80 74	295	166.66
Bunky Henry	70 75 72 79	296	166.66
*Bill Campbell	73 72 75 77	297	
Marty Fleckman	73 71 74 81	299	166.66
Harry Toscano	70 72 77 81	300	166.66

* Amateur

357

CANADIAN OPEN

PINEGROVE COUNTRY CLUB
St. Luc, Montreal, Canada
July 24—27
Purse...$125,000 (Canadian funds)
Par: 36, 36—72...7,076 yards

	SCORES	TOTAL	MONEY
Tommy Aaron	71 70 70 64	275	$25,000
Sam Snead	67 68 70 70	275	14,300
(Aaron defeated Snead in 18-hole playoff, 70—72.)			
Bill Casper	72 71 70 67	280	8,850
Takaaki Kono, *Japan*	72 68 70 71	281	5,850
Bob Charles, *New Zealand*	71 73 68 70	282	4,812.50
Al Balding, *Canada*	70 70 74 68	282	4,812.50
Johnny Jacobs	74 72 68 69	283	3,546.25
Jack Ewing	72 69 72 70	283	3,546.25
George Knudson, *Canada*	71 72 72 68	283	3,546.25
Bob Rosburg	71 74 72 66	283	3,546.25
Doug Sanders	71 70 75 70	286	2,531.25
Jimmy Day	72 70 71 73	286	2,531.25
Johnny Stevens	71 70 73 72	286	2,531.25
Roberto de Vicenzo, *Argentina*	69 67 78 72	286	2,531.25
Ken Fulton, *Canada*	71 73 69 74	287	2,062.50
Jerry Abbott	70 74 73 70	287	2,062.50
Al Mengert	73 71 69 75	288	1,562.50
Phil Giroux, *Canada*	74 71 72 71	288	1,562.50
Dave Bollman	69 75 70 74	288	1,562.50
Vaughan Trapp, *Canada*	69 70 75 74	288	1,562.50
Jim Jamieson	72 69 76 71	288	1,562.50
Hal Underwood	73 74 72 69	288	1,562.50
Bob Panasiuk, *Canada*	74 71 70 74	289	1,078.75
Jim Grant	69 72 75 73	289	1,078.75
Jerry Barber	71 72 74 72	289	1,078.75
Harold Henning, *South Africa*	74 74 73 68	289	1,078.75
Rolf Deming	73 69 69 79	290	906.25
Babe Hiskey	74 70 71 75	290	906.25
Chick Evans	68 74 74 74	290	906.25
Dutch Harrison	74 74 71 71	290	906.25
Bill Wakeman, *Canada*	76 70 75 70	291	701.56
Cesar Sanudo	73 71 75 72	291	701.56
Dick Rautmann	76 72 72 71	291	701.56
Moe Norman, *Canada*	73 74 72 72	291	701.56
Jimmy Picard	71 73 74 73	291	701.55
Cliff Brown	72 73 70 76	291	701.55
Bill Tindall	73 75 71 72	291	701.55
Bill Lively	74 71 74 72	291	701.55

	SCORES				TOTAL	MONEY
Tony Jacklin, *Great Britain*	69	71	75	77	292	406.10
Larry Sears	76	70	71	75	292	406.10
John Levinson	74	71	71	76	292	406.10
Paul Moran	70	74	74	74	292	406.10
Kel Nagle, *Australia*	73	73	74	72	292	406.10
Les Peterson	70	68	81	73	292	406.10
Vern Novak	72	70	77	73	292	406.10
Gary Bowerman, *Canada*	74	73	72	73	292	406.10
Randy Wolff	72	73	73	74	292	406.10
Ronnie Reif	73	72	75	72	292	406.10
Gibby Gilbert	70	76	75	72	293	193.30
Ross Randall	76	72	70	75	293	193.29
Stan Homenuik, *Canada*	72	74	73	74	293	193.29
Don Cherry	71	75	74	73	293	193.29
Mahlon Moe	70	72	78	73	293	193.29
Hugh Inggs, *South Africa*	75	73	72	73	293	193.29
Jack Bissegger, *Canada*	69	74	75	75	293	193.29
Jerry Hatfield	70	73	76	74	293	193.29
Mike Reasor	75	70	76	73	294	185.19
Bobby Breen, *Canada*	73	73	74	74	294	185.19
Claude Harmon Jr.	73	71	74	76	294	185.19
Nathaniel Starks	71	73	74	76	294	185.19
Wes Ellis	70	76	72	77	295	185.19
Wilf Homenuik, *Canada*	76	72	77	70	295	185.19
Bob Erickson	72	75	73	75	295	185.19
Ernie George	73	72	73	77	295	185.18
George Hixon	73	72	79	72	296	185.18
*Nick Weslock, *Canada*	75	73	74	74	296	
Gary Groh, *Bahamas*	74	74	75	73	296	185.18
Jerry Preuss	72	72	77	75	296	185.18
Larry Mowry	69	76	74	77	296	185.18
Alvie Thompson, *Canada*	75	71	76	75	297	185.18
John Schroeder	72	74	80	71	297	185.18
Dai Rees, *Great Britain*	71	73	74	80	298	185.18
Adrien Bigras, *Canada*	74	72	78	77	301	185.18
Frank Fowler, *Canada*	73	74	78	77	302	185.18
*Mike McCullough	73	75	74	80	302	
Alvin Odom	73	75	77	78	303	185.18
Jerry Barrier	74	73	81	76	304	185.18
Denny Tiziani	72	76	83	80	311	185.18

* Amateur

WESTCHESTER CLASSIC

WESTCHESTER COUNTRY CLUB
Harrison, N.Y.
July 31—August 3
Purse...$250,000
Par: 36, 36—72...6,677 yards

	SCORES	TOTAL	MONEY
Frank Beard	69 72 67 67	275	$50,000
Bert Greene	67 69 68 72	276	28,500
Dan Sikes	71 67 70 69	277	17,750
Harold Henning, *South Africa*	68 72 68 70	278	11,750
Tommy Aaron	70 67 72 70	279	9,625
Lee Trevino	71 70 67 71	279	9.625
Bruce Crampton, *Australia*	68 73 68 71	280	8,000
Dick Lotz	71 71 69 70	281	7,062.50
Jerry Pittman	71 71 69 70	281	7,062.50
Roberto de Vicenzo, *Argentina*	73 70 71 68	282	5,500
Bob Goalby	71 69 71 71	282	5,500
Howie Johnson	75 69 71 67	282	5,500
Al Mengert	70 71 68 73	282	5,500
Dick Crawford	72 72 71 68	283	3,277.28
Terry Dill	68 72 73 70	283	3,277.28
R. H. Sikes	69 74 71 69	283	3,277.28
Tommy Bolt	66 71 71 75	283	3,277.27
Gay Brewer	73 65 72 73	283	3,277.27
Bill Casper	72 71 70 70	283	3,277.27
Ray Floyd	70 73 68 72	283	3,277.27
Paul Harney	68 69 75 71	283	3,277.27
Jack Nicklaus	71 73 69 70	283	3,277.27
Gary Player, *South Africa*	70 74 68 71	283	3,277.27
Tom Weiskopf	69 70 72 72	283	3,277.27
George Archer	73 70 71 70	284	1,887.50
Don Bies	68 69 73 74	284	1,887.50
Ron Cerrudo	71 74 69 70	284	1,887.50
Dave Marr	75 70 68 71	284	1,887.50
Johnny Pott	73 71 72 68	284	1,887.50
Doug Sanders	73 71 68 72	284	1,887.50
Miller Barber	71 72 73 69	285	1,428.13
Homero Blancas	70 71 74 70	285	1,428.13
Rives McBee	72 72 74 67	285	1,428.13
Bobby Nichols	69 72 75 69	285	1,428.13
Bruce Devlin, *Australia*	67 72 76 70	285	1,428.12
Grier Jones	71 71 73 70	285	1,428.12
Jack Montgomery	71 74 70 70	285	1,428.12
Tom Shaw	70 71 71 73	285	1,428.12
Charles Coody	71 72 73 70	286	1,087.50

	SCORES	TOTAL	MONEY
Bob Murphy	73 72 70 71	286	1,087.50
Steve Oppermann	71 74 72 69	286	1,087.50
Bob Smith	72 73 72 69	286	1,087.50
Bob Charles, *New Zealand*	71 73 70 73	287	765
Rod Funseth	74 71 74 68	287	765
Fred Marti	68 77 70 72	287	765
Phil Rodgers	70 73 70 74	287	765
Bert Yancey	71 68 70 78	287	765
Julius Boros	71 74 71 72	288	520.48
Dow Finsterwald	72 72 73 71	288	520.48
Bob Lunn	68 73 74 73	288	520.48
Don Massengale	70 75 73 70	288	520.48
Al Geiberger	70 74 70 74	288	520.47
Larry Hinson	71 74 70 74	289	476.19
Arnold Palmer	71 74 70 74	289	476.19
Steve Reid	73 72 74 70	289	476.19
Sam Snead	75 70 70 74	289	476.19
Jim Wiechers	74 70 76 69	289	476.19
Butch Baird	72 73 72 73	290	476.19
Jim Colbert	69 71 78 72	290	476.19
Tommy Jacobs	73 72 69 76	290	476.19
Don January	70 74 71 75	290	476.19
Randy Wolff	74 68 77 71	290	476.19
Jerry Heard	72 73 72 74	291	476.19
Allan Henning, *South Africa*	70 75 71 75	291	476.19
Bob Stone	70 75 75 72	292	476.19
Frank Boynton	76 68 75 74	293	476.19
Bobby Mitchell	73 72 70 78	293	476.19
Howell Fraser	74 71 72 78	295	476.19
Claude Harmon Jr.	76 69 77 76	298	476.19
Jimmy Picard	71 74 77 77	299	476.19
Mike Fetchick	72 73 79 77	301	476.19

GREATER MILWAUKEE OPEN

NORTH SHORE COUNTRY CLUB
Mequon, Wisconsin
August 7—10
Purse...$100,000
Par: 36, 36—72...7,075 yards

	SCORES	TOTAL	MONEY
Ken Still	74 71 67 65	277	$20,000
Gary Player, *South Africa*	73 70 71 65	279	11,400
Lee Elder	73 73 68 66	280	7,100
Jim Wiechers	70 73 69 69	281	4,700
Bob Lunn	70 73 68 71	282	4,100

	SCORES	TOTAL	MONEY
Larry Ziegler	70 74 70 69	283	3,112.50
Chuck Courtney	72 72 68 71	283	3,112.50
Peter Townsend, *Great Britain*	67 75 69 72	283	3,112.50
Terry Dill	74 71 66 72	283	3,112.50
Ron Cerrudo	76 73 69 66	284	2,120
Kermit Zarley	71 73 72 68	284	2,120
Jerry Abbott	71 72 70 71	284	2,120
Fred Marti	71 70 71 72	284	2,120
Phil Rodgers	72 71 69 72	284	2,120
Allan Henning, *South Africa*	69 73 72 71	285	1,600
R. H. Sikes	76 70 67 72	285	1,600
John Miller	68 74 70 73	285	1,600
Bill Garrett	72 73 73 68	286	1,200
Don Massengale	75 74 69 68	286	1,200
Jim Colbert	73 73 71 69	286	1,200
Steve Oppermann	69 73 73 71	286	1,200
Lou Graham	71 73 72 70	286	1,200
Joel Goldstrand	76 70 74 67	287	910
Arnold Palmer	76 71 68 72	287	910
Bert Greene	75 73 71 69	288	770
George Johnson	73 73 72 70	288	770
Herb Hooper	76 70 71 71	288	770
Bob Smith	73 71 70 74	288	770
Ed Moehling	72 69 72 75	288	770
B. R. McLendon	73 75 74 67	289	626
Bob Goalby	75 70 75 69	289	626
Rick Rhoads	72 75 72 70	289	626
Steve Reid	75 72 71 71	289	626
Jack McGowan	73 72 70 74	289	626
Ross Randall	74 74 73 69	290	530
Les Peterson	72 74 74 70	290	530
Rolf Deming	74 72 73 71	290	530
Chi Chi Rodriguez	72 73 70 75	290	530
Bobby Brue	77 72 76 66	291	420
Dudley Wysong	76 71 75 69	291	420
Howie Johnson	75 73 73 70	291	420
Jack Montgomery	72 76 73 70	291	420
Cliff Brown	78 69 73 71	291	420
Doug Sanders	75 72 77 68	292	282
Curtis Sifford	72 77 72 71	292	282
Jack Harden	75 71 74 72	292	282
Bob Gleason	73 73 74 72	292	282
Rod Curl	76 71 72 73	292	282
*David Shuster	73 74 71 74	292	
Terry Winter	71 76 76 70	293	204
Rod Funseth	75 72 75 71	293	204
Labron Harris	75 74 73 71	293	204
Charles Coody	73 74 73 73	293	204
Mike Nugent	69 78 73 73	293	204

	SCORES	TOTAL	MONEY
Billy Maxwell	75 74 76 70	295	200
Jerry Edwards	76 73 75 71	295	200
Jim Langley	77 72 74 72	295	200
Don Parson	72 75 74 74	295	200
Carl Unis	74 73 78 71	296	200
Babe Hiskey	73 75 71 77	296	200
Nathaniel Starks	73 76 76 72	297	200
Bobby Lockett	76 71 73 77	297	200
John Lively	73 74 75 76	298	200
Mike Hill	74 75 78 72	299	200
Steve Bull	72 76 76 75	299	200
Randy Wolff	75 73 75 76	299	200
Dick Lotz	75 73 79 73	300	200
Gibby Gilbert	71 76 78 75	300	200
Rocky Thompson	72 71 80 77	300	200
John Schroeder	75 74 82 70	301	200
Norm Bernard	74 75 77 78	304	200

* Amateur

PGA CHAMPIONSHIP

NCR COUNTRY CLUB, SOUTH COURSE
Dayton, Ohio
August 14—17
Purse...$175,000
Par: 36, 35—71...6,915 yards

	SCORES	TOTAL	MONEY
Ray Floyd	69 66 67 74	276	$35,000
Gary Player, *South Africa*	71 65 71 70	277	20,000
Bert Greene	71 68 68 71	278	12,400
Jimmy Wright	71 68 69 71	279	8,300
Larry Ziegler	69 71 70 70	280	6,725
Miller Barber	73 75 64 68	280	6,725
Terry Wilcox	72 71 72 66	281	5,143.34
Charles Coody	69 71 72 69	281	5,143.33
Orville Moody	70 68 71 72	281	5,143.33
Frank Beard	70 75 68 69	282	4,375
Jack Nicklaus	70 68 74 71	283	3,543.75
Don Bies	74 64 71 74	283	3,543.75
Bunky Henry	69 68 70 76	283	3,543.75
Larry Mowry	69 71 69 74	283	3,543.75
Dave Hill	74 75 67 68	284	2,712.50
Don January	75 70 70 69	284	2,712.50
Chi Chi Rodriguez	72 72 71 69	284	2,712.50
Bruce Crampton, *Australia*	70 70 72 72	284	2,712.50

	SCORES	TOTAL	MONEY
Johnny Pott	69 75 71 70	285	2,137.50
Howie Johnson	73 68 72 72	285	2,137.50
Tom Shaw	69 75 73 69	286	1,718.75
Bobby Cole, *South Africa*	72 74 71 69	286	1,718.75
Bob Lunn	69 74 73 70	286	1,718.75
Ron Cerrudo	74 66 70 76	286	1,718.75
Gay Brewer	74 71 76 66	287	1,300
Bob Dickson	74 72 70 71	287	1,300
Tony Jacklin, *Great Britain*	73 70 73 71	287	1,300
Julius Boros	72 74 70 71	287	1,300
Fred Marti	73 70 71 73	287	1,300
Dan Sikes	71 74 69 73	287	1,300
George Knudson, *Canada*	70 75 67 75	287	1,300
Al Mengert	74 72 72 70	288	1,055
Butch Baird	71 71 75 71	288	1,055
Bruce Devlin, *Australia*	70 78 69 71	288	1,055
Bob Charles, *New Zealand*	75 73 72 69	289	890
Al Geiberger	69 72 77 71	289	890
Steve Reid	72 75 71 71	289	890
B. R. McLendon	73 68 75 73	289	890
Bill Casper	72 74 70 73	289	890
Dave Stockton	75 67 71 76	289	890
Pete Brown	77 72 70 71	290	686.67
Dick Hart	73 73 72 72	290	686.67
Gardner Dickinson	72 70 72 76	290	686.66
Bobby Nichols	74 71 75 71	291	512.50
Larry Hinson	75 74 70 71	291	512.50
Harold Henning, *South Africa*	74 73 70 74	291	512.50
Tom Weiskopf	70 76 70 75	291	512.50
Dudley Wysong	72 76 73 71	292	289.26
Dale Douglass	73 76 72 71	292	289.26
Gene Littler	73 76 71 72	292	289.26
Bobby Mitchell	73 71 75 73	292	289.25
Bobby Brue	73 71 74 74	292	289.25
Phil Rodgers	70 72 75 75	292	289.25
Dave Marr	78 68 71 75	292	289.25
Dick Lotz	75 73 69 75	292	289.25
Lee Trevino	73 71 72 76	292	289.25
Tommy Aaron	70 72 79 72	293	241.38
Jacky Cupit	70 73 75 75	293	241.38
Mike Souchak	75 73 74 72	294	241.38
Pat Schwab	75 72 73 74	294	241.38
Howell Fraser	72 76 71 75	294	241.38
Kermit Zarley	75 74 69 76	294	241.38
Sam Snead	75 72 71 78	296	241.38
Jay Hebert	75 74 73 74	296	241.38
Bob Murphy	74 71 75 76	296	241.38
Davis Love	73 71 76 76	296	241.38

	SCORES	TOTAL	MONEY
Dick Crawford	73 72 75 76	296	241.38
Billy Maxwell	76 73 75 72	296	241.38
Jack Burke	74 75 74 74	297	241.38
George Archer	75 74 71 77	297	241.38
Jack McGowan	76 73 72 76	297	241.38
Stan Dudas	76 70 76 75	297	241.38
Stan Thirsk	73 75 75 75	298	241.38
Bob Stanton, *Australia*	77 72 73 76	298	241.38
Ed Kroll	72 70 79 77	298	241.38
John Cook	77 69 73 80	299	241.38
Jim Turnesa	74 74 77 74	299	241.38
Dow Finsterwald	75 73 75 76	299	241.37
Ed Merrins	75 70 77 80	302	241.37
Jim Colbert	74 73 WD		

OUT OF FINAL 36 HOLES

	SCORES	TOTAL
Tommy Bolt	74 76	150
Frank Boynton	75 75	150
Manuel de la Torre	77 73	150
Lee Elder	77 73	150
Lou Graham	76 74	150
Lionel Hebert	76 74	150
Joe Jimenez	76 74	150
Mike Krak	74 76	150
Dean Refram	72 78	150
Bob Rosburg	72 78	150
Bob Smith	76 74	150
Roland Stafford	76 74	150
Art Wall	78 72	150
Fred Wampler	77 73	150
Jerry Barber	75 76	151
Johnny Bulla	73 78	151
Chuck Courtney	73 78	151
Eddie Langert	75 76	151
Dick Rhyan	74 77	151
Doug Sanders	72 79	151
George Bellino	79 73	152
Gene Borek	75 77	152
Jerry Mowlds	75 77	152
Earl Stewart	76 76	152
Rocky Thompson	77 75	152
Bert Yancey	76 76	152
Jim Ferrier	74 79	153
Marty Fleckman	75 78	153
Doug Ford	79 74	153
Jimmy Powell	77 76	153

	SCORES	TOTAL	
Ken Still	78 75	153	
Carroll Armstrong	79 75	154	
Bob Goalby	76 78	154	
George McKeown	77 77	154	
Mason Rudolph	74 80	154	
Glenn Stuart	78 76	154	
Joe Cardenas	76 79	155	
Jim O'Hern	81 74	155	
Hampton Auld	78 78	156	
Bill Flynn	77 79	156	
Bob Fry	74 82	156	
Herman Scharlau	78 78	156	
Ernie Vossler	79 77	156	
Chuck Malchaski	78 79	157	
Paul Scodeller	83 74	157	
George Shortridge	79 78	157	
Dan Murphy	79 79	158	
Gary Lockie	82 76	158	
Jimmy Bellizzi	79 80	159	
Merle Backlund	83 76	159	
Mike Podolski	80 79	159	
Doug MacDonald	84 76	160	
Charles Sifford	82 78	160	
Stan Staszowski	86 74	160	
Alan White	86 76	162	
Denny Shute	85 80	165	
Rick Jetter	80 87	167	
Arnold Palmer	82 WD		
Jim Rudolph	DQ	(Unsigned card)	
Herman Keiser	WD during first round		

INDIAN RIDGE OPEN

INDIAN RIDGE COUNTRY CLUB
Andover, Massachusetts
August 14–17
Purse...$37,000
Par: 36, 35–71...6,805 yards

	SCORES				TOTAL	MONEY
Monty Kaser	72	64	69	69	274	$7,400
Steve Oppermann	69	68	69	69	275	4,400
Bert Weaver	69	70	68	69	276	2,200
Mike Hill	69	69	68	70	276	2,200
Joel Goldstrand	71	67	70	69	277	1,300

	SCORES	TOTAL	MONEY
Jack Montgomery	69 71 67 70	277	1,300
Laurie Hammer	72 68 71 67	278	1,100
Ross Coon	68 74 69 68	279	1,050
Peter Townsend, *Great Britain*	67 70 73 70	280	975
Rod Funseth	67 72 70 71	280	975
Hale Irwin	70 74 70 67	281	850
Rolf Deming	69 75 69 68	281	850
Richard Martinez	73 70 65 73	281	850
John Kennedy	68 72 73 69	282	700
Les Peterson	69 72 70 71	282	700
Labron Harris	69 69 70 74	282	700
Dick Hanscom	71 68 75 69	283	516.25
Jerry Barrier	70 73 70 70	283	516.25
Dewitt Weaver	70 74 69 70	283	516.25
Rich Bassett	69 70 73 71	283	516.25
Jerry Hatfield	68 73 70 72	283	516.25
Martin Roesink, *Holland*	71 72 68 72	283	516.25
Jerry McGee	70 72 69 72	283	516.25
Jim Grant	72 69 68 74	283	516.25
Cesar Sanudo	69 75 70 70	284	380
Paul Harney	68 76 69 71	284	380
Babe Hiskey	70 72 70 72	284	380
Jerry Edwards	69 69 74 72	284	380
Terry Winter	69 68 74 73	284	380
J. C. Goosie	69 70 75 71	285	290
Hugh Royer	72 70 70 73	285	290
Paul Barkhouse	75 69 68 73	285	290
Bob Payne	66 65 78 76	285	290
Ras Allen	70 73 73 70	286	230
Don Parson	71 70 74 71	286	230
Butch O'Hearn, *Canada*	66 70 79 72	287	132.15
Steve Spray	69 72 73 73	287	132.15
Denny Lyons	73 69 72 73	287	132.14
Bob Erickson	69 74 70 74	287	132.14
Don Massengale	72 71 69 75	287	132.14
Jim Langley	70 72 70 75	287	132.14
Bob Menne	72 67 71 77	287	132.14
Randy Petri	72 72 73 71	288	62.50
John Miller	74 70 72 72	288	62.50
Harry Toscano	72 72 71 73	288	62.50
Nathaniel Starks	70 72 75 72	289	62.50
Gary Groh, *Bahamas*	71 72 74 72	289	62.50
George Boutell	70 73 73 73	289	62.50
Joe McDermott	69 74 75 72	290	62.50
Jim Browning	74 70 70 77	291	62.50
George Johnson	73 69 77 73	292	62.50
Dave Bollman	69 72 77 75	293	62.50
Bob Gleeson	73 71 74 75	293	62.50

	SCORES	TOTAL	MONEY
Gene Ferrell	73 71 73 76	293	62.50
Vern Novak	74 68 75 78	295	62.50
Dennis Rouse	71 72 80 78	301	62.50

AVCO CLASSIC

PLEASANT VALLEY COUNTRY CLUB
Sutton, Massachusetts
August 21—24
Purse...$150,000
Par: 37, 35—72...7,212 yards

	SCORES	TOTAL	MONEY
Tom Shaw	68 68 67 77	280	$30,000
Bob Stanton, *Australia*	73 71 66 71	281	17,000
Tom Weiskopf	73 75 69 66	283	10,650
Julius Boros	71 74 71 68	284	5,850
George Knudson, *Canada*	69 72 73 70	284	5,850
Fred Marti	75 74 69 66	284	5,850
Bobby Mitchell	72 71 70 71	284	5,850
Larry Ziegler	73 74 71 67	285	4,425
Bruce Crampton, *Australia*	72 71 70 73	286	3,325
Lee Elder	74 74 69 69	286	3,325
Dick Lotz	74 71 71 70	286	3,325
Bob Lunn	75 69 67 75	286	3,325
B. R. McLendon	72 70 74 70	286	3,325
Roy Pace	72 73 73 68	286	3,325
Tommy Aaron	73 75 72 67	287	2,025
Bob Dickson	75 73 68 71	287	2,025
Mike Hill	75 69 70 73	287	2,025
Grier Jones	72 73 73 69	287	2,025
Jack Montgomery	76 68 69 74	287	2,025
Orville Moody	75 73 71 68	287	2,025
Bob Murphy	73 74 70 70	287	2,025
Cesar Sanudo	76 69 74 68	287	2,025
Charles Coody	73 76 69 70	288	1,266
Bill Garrett	76 69 73 70	288	1,266
Dave Stockton	75 72 71 70	288	1,266
Joe Carr	75 74 66 73	288	1,266
Les Peterson	75 72 71 70	288	1,266
Lou Graham	76 73 69 71	289	1,020
Jerry McGee	73 76 68 72	289	1,020
Doug Sanders	72 74 69 74	289	1,020
R. H. Sikes	74 72 73 70	289	1,020
Hal Underwood	71 78 70 70	289	1,020
Pete Brown	76 74 70 70	290	756
Chuck Courtney	71 73 75 71	290	756

	SCORES				TOTAL	MONEY
Joel Goldstrand	73	73	74	70	290	756
Tommy Jacobs	75	73	70	72	290	756
Larry Mowry	76	71	70	73	290	756
Chi Chi Rodriguez	74	72	73	71	290	756
Charles Sifford	72	77	72	69	290	756
Dan Sikes	75	71	75	69	290	756
Bert Yancey	79	66	76	69	290	756
Claude Harmon Jr.	70	73	74	73	290	756
Miller Barber	75	75	69	72	291	476.25
Monty Kaser	69	77	74	71	291	476.25
Rocky Thompson	76	72	72	71	291	476.25
Kermit Zarley	75	73	72	71	291	476.25
Don Bies	74	75	71	72	292	301.43
Al Geiberger	75	75	71	71	292	301.43
Paul Harney	74	72	72	74	292	301.43
Herb Hooper	73	73	73	73	292	301.43
Martin Roesink, *Holland*	74	74	69	75	292	301.43
John Kennedy	74	72	75	71	292	301.43
Bobby Cole, *South Africa*	76	73	73	71	293	214.29
Jack McGowan	76	73	70	74	293	214.29
Peter Townsend, *Great Britain*	72	76	71	74	293	214.29
Rolf Deming	77	71	73	72	293	214.29
Mike Reasor	74	72	72	75	293	214.29
Homero Blancas	72	78	73	71	294	214.29
Rod Funseth	75	74	74	71	294	214.29
Gary Player, *South Africa*	77	73	68	76	294	214.29
Joe Porter	77	73	74	70	294	214.29
George Johnson	76	71	76	72	295	214.29
Bob Payne	75	73	71	76	295	214.29
Steve Reid	78	72	71	74	295	214.29
Mason Rudolph	76	72	75	72	295	214.29
Don Parson	77	71	70	77	296	214.29
Laurie Hammer	76	74	76	70	296	214.28
Rod Curl	75	72	74	75	296	214.28
Bob Erickson	72	76	74	75	297	214.28
Dick Hanscom	74	74	74	75	297	214.28
Dick Mayer	77	73	74	73	297	214.28
Jesse Snead	76	74	75	73	298	214.28
George Archer	76	74	75	74	299	214.28
John Lotz	70	80	75	74	299	214.28
Terry Winter	75	74	74	76	299	214.28
Ken Venturi	70	78	72	80	300	214.28
Earl Stewart	70	71	76	76	302	214.28
Ron Cerrudo	72	76	77	79	304	214.28

GREATER HARTFORD OPEN

WETHERSFEILD COUNTRY CLUB
Wethersfield, Connecticut
August 29—September 1
Purse...$100,000
Par: 35, 36—71...6,568 yards

	SCORES	TOTAL	MONEY
Bob Lunn	67 68 66 67	268	$20,000
Dave Hill	68 68 66 66	268	11,400
(Lunn defeated Hill on fourth hole of sudden-death playoff.)			
Dave Stockton	69 67 67 66	269	7,100
Bert Greene	69 67 70 65	271	4,400
Gay Brewer	68 66 69 68	271	4,400
Howie Johnson	72 67 63 70	272	3,600
Jack Nicklaus	68 68 69 68	273	3,200
Lou Graham	72 67 68 67	274	2,510
Jesse Snead	66 74 66 68	274	2,510
Larry Hinson	69 69 68 68	274	2,510
Deane Beman	70 69 65 70	274	2,510
R. H. Sikes	67 70 67 70	274	2,510
Phil Rodgers	67 68 71 69	275	1,700
Lee Elder	70 71 65 69	275	1,700
Kermit Zarley	69 69 68 69	275	1,700
Lee Trevino	70 67 68 70	275	1,700
Jim Colbert	71 67 67 70	275	1,700
Hale Irwin	68 72 70 66	276	1,350
Bob Murphy	66 73 68 69	276	1,350
Charles Sifford	74 65 73 65	277	964.29
Don Bies	68 71 71 67	277	964.29
Steve Reid	70 68 71 68	277	964.29
Bob Charles, *New Zealand*	68 70 69 70	277	964.29
Les Peterson	68 71 68 70	277	964.28
Dan Sikes	72 68 67 70	277	964.29
Dale Douglass	70 68 68 71	277	964.29
Bill Casper	70 68 70 70	278	725
Dave Eichelberger	70 71 68 69	278	725
Doug Sanders	70 68 70 70	278	725
Hal Underwood	67 71 67 73	278	725
Ross Coon	70 67 72 70	279	612.50
Bobby Mitchell	68 72 70 69	279	612.50
Roy Pace	67 72 69 71	279	612.50
Dick Lotz	72 67 69 71	279	612.50
Ken Still	72 68 72 68	280	495.72
Jerry Abbott	67 71 73 69	280	495.72
Tom Shaw	71 68 72 69	280	495.72
Bruce Crampton, *Australia*	71 70 60 69	280	495.71

370

	SCORES	TOTAL	MONEY
Miller Barber	71 69 70 70	280	495.71
Joel Goldstrand	66 74 67 73	280	495.71
Randy Wolfe	68 69 68 75	280	495.71
Grier Jones	70 72 71 68	281	297.50
Paul Harney	68 73 72 68	281	297.50
Howell Fraser	71 70 71 69	281	297.50
Frank Beard	72 69 71 69	281	297.50
Larry Sears	72 69 71 69	281	297.50
Larry Mowry	70 68 73 70	281	297.50
Cliff Brown	70 70 71 70	281	297.50
Dick Rautmann	71 69 71 70	281	297.50
Jack Montgomery	71 72 71 68	282	165.72
Bob Smith	67 70 75 70	282	165.72
Herb Booper	72 67 73 70	282	165.72
Tommy Jacobs	72 69 71 70	282	165.71
Gardner Dickinson	73 70 69 70	282	165.71
John Miller	72 71 68 71	282	165.71
John Lotz	68 70 72 72	282	165.71
John Kennedy	69 70 74 70	283	160
Bob Stanton, *Australia*	68 73 72 70	283	160
Butch Baird	70 69 71 73	283	160
Labron Harris	71 72 70 71	284	160
Al Balding, *Canada*	69 67 72 76	284	160
Joe Carr	70 69 74 72	285	160
Ron Cerrudo	72 71 71 71	285	160
Dick Stranahan	71 69 73 72	285	160
Frank Boynton	70 70 72 73	285	160
Terry Dill	73 70 69 73	285	160
Mason Rudolph	74 69 75 68	286	160
Billy Maxwell	72 70 74 70	286	160
Claude Harmon Jr.	68 71 76 72	287	160
Jerry McGee	73 68 75 72	288	160
Dave Marr	71 72 72 73	288	160
Bert Yancey	71 70 71 76	288	160
Martin Roesink, *Holland*	67 74 76 75	292	160
Terry Winter	70 73 71 78	292	160
Rafe Botts	76 67 70 80	293	160

MICHIGAN GOLF CLASSIC

SHENANDOAH COUNTRY CLUB
Walled Lake, Michigan
September 4—7
Purse...$100,000
Par: 35, 35—70...6,708 yards

	SCORES	TOTAL	MONEY
Larry Ziegler	72 70 66 64	272	$20,000
Homero Blancas	71 71 65 65	272	11,400

(Ziegler defeated Blancas on second hole of sudden-death playoff.)

	SCORES	TOTAL	MONEY
Phil Rodgers	69 70 67 67	273	5,900
Jesse Snead	71 70 65 67	273	5,900
Grier Jones	65 73 70 66	274	3,462.50
Casmere Jawor	69 70 69 66	274	3,462.50
Mike Hill	68 71 68 67	274	2,462.50
Larry Hinson	69 68 68 69	274	3,462.50
Joel Goldstrand	69 69 69 68	275	2,500
Jerry McGee	68 69 70 68	275	2,500
Kermit Zarley	68 68 69 70	275	2,500
Ed Moehling	70 69 67 70	276	2,100
Wilf Homenuik, *Canada*	69 71 71 66	277	1,700
Bobby Mitchell	72 70 69 66	277	1,700
Jerry Abbott	70 72 68 67	277	1,700
Bob Stanton, *Australia*	70 68 70 69	277	1,700
Bill Garrett	68 71 69 69	277	1,700
Chi Chi Rodriguez	68 72 72 66	278	1,117.15
John Schlee	69 73 68 68	278	1,117.15
John Lotz	70 69 71 68	278	1,117.14
Bob Goalby	68 70 71 69	278	1,117.14
Babe Hiskey	70 69 70 69	278	1,117.14
Deane Beman	70 69 69 70	278	1,117.14
Terry Wilcox	68 72 67 71	278	1,117.14
Jim Wiechers	69 73 70 68	280	755
Johnny Jacobs	69 73 70 68	280	755
Ron Cerrudo	72 69 70 69	280	755
Larry Mowry	72 66 72 70	280	755
Bobby Cole, *South Africa*	67 68 72 73	280	755
Allan Henning, *South Africa*	71 67 69 73	280	755
John Schroeder	74 66 73 68	281	591.67
Al Balding, *Canada*	67 72 73 69	281	591.67
Steve Oppermann	72 69 71 69	281	591.67
Howie Johnson	72 67 71 71	281	591.67
Dick Lotz	72 70 68 71	281	591.66
Dick Rhyan	73 67 69 72	281	591.66
Bob Dickson	72 69 73 68	282	474
Chuck Courtney	71 71 70 70	282	474
Dick Mayer	69 70 72 71	282	474
Denny Lyons	72 69 68 73	282	474
R. H. Sikes	69 69 70 74	282	474
Dave Eichelberger	70 71 72 70	283	332
Dean Refram	69 73 71 70	283	332
Tom Shaw	70 68 74 71	283	332
Rolf Deming	75 65 71 72	283	332
Charles Sifford	69 70 71 73	283	332
Dudley Wysong	69 73 73 69	284	240
John Molenda	70 72 71 71	284	240
Tommy Aycock	69 72 70 73	284	240
John Kennedy	73 70 74 68	285	184.85

	SCORES	TOTAL	MONEY
Ron Aleks	69 71 75 70	285	184.85
Bunky Henry	70 73 71 71	285	184.85
Ed Sneed	70 73 70 72	285	184.85
Steve Reid	69 72 71 73	285	184.85
Jack Harden	69 70 70 76	285	184.85
Frank Boynton	69 72 76 69	286	181.82
Jack Montgomery	66 73 74 73	286	181.82
Rick Rhoads	71 68 74 73	286	181.82
Don Bies	70 71 73 73	287	181.82
Bob Menne	65 72 75 75	287	181.82
Jim Colbert	72 70 70 75	287	181.82
Everett Vinzant	75 67 74 72	288	181.82
Bob Payne	68 75 72 73	288	181.82
Curtis Sifford	68 75 71 74	288	181.82
Bill Lively	69 69 80 71	289	181.82
Labron Harris	71 72 71 75	289	181.82
Dick Crawford	73 69 71 76	289	181.82
Rod Curl	69 71 74 76	290	181.82
Tom Bailey	72 70 74 75	291	181.81
Cesar Sanudo	70 73 71 77	291	181.81
Jim Langley	71 69 74 79	293	181.81
Harold Kneece	74 69 78 75	296	181.81

ALCAN GOLFER OF THE YEAR

PORTLAND GOLF CLUB
Portland, Oregon
September 25—28
Purse...$139,000
Par: 36, 36—72...6,541 yards

	SCORES	TOTAL	MONEY
Bill Casper	70 68 70 66	274	$55,000
Lee Trevino	70 67 69 69	275	15,000
Frank Beard	71 70 69 68	278	7,500
Dan Sikes	69 72 68 70	279	5,800
Lou Graham	69 72 70 69	280	4,500
Jean Garaialde, *France*	71 69 73 68	281	4,100
Gay Brewer	71 68 71 71	281	4,100
Gene Littler	72 68 73 69	282	3,600
Dave Hill	74 72 66 70	282	3,600
Bert Greene	70 68 72 72	282	3,600
Grier Jones	70 72 71 70	283	3,100
Bob Lunn	73 71 69 70	283	3,100
Graham Henning, *South Africa*	73 72 64 75	284	2,800
Deane Beman	70 69 76 70	285	2,600

	SCORES	TOTAL	MONEY
Bob Cox, *Canada*	78 69 71 68	286	2,200
Tommy Horton, *Great Britain*	74 70 69 73	286	2,200
Maurice Bembridge, *Great Britain*	72 70 70 74	286	2,200
Brian Huggett, *Great Britain*	73 71 72 74	290	2,000
Christie O'Connor, *Great Britain*	72 74 72 72	290	2,000
Bernard Gallacher, *Great Britain*	73 72 75 71	291	2,000
Kermit Zarley	74 75 72 73	294	2,000
David Graham, *Australia*	75 74 72 76	297	2,000
Brian Barnes, *Great Britain*	76 73 74 76	299	2,000
Kel Nagle, *Australia*	70 105 73 76	324	2,000

ROBINSON OPEN

CRAWFORD COUNTY COUNTRY CLUB
Robinson, Illinois
September 25—28
Purse...$75,000
Par: 36, 36—72...6,460 yards

	SCORES	TOTAL	MONEY
Bob Goalby	62 71 73 67	273	$15,000
Jim Wiechers	70 68 66 69	273	9,000
(Goalby defeated Wiechers on first hold of sudden-death playoff.)			
Howie Johnson	71 68 70 65	274	5,625
Howell Fraser	68 70 69 68	275	3,275
Bob Payne	72 69 66 68	275	3,275
Billy Maxwell	66 69 67 73	275	3,275
Terry Wilcox	70 66 73 67	276	2,231.25
Bob Stanton, *Australia*	71 64 70 71	276	2,231.25
Bill Garrett	68 68 70 70	276	2,231.25
Richard Martinez	65 69 70 72	276	2,231.25
John Schlee	72 67 71 67	277	1,800
Ted Hayes	70 71 71 66	278	1,525
B. R. McLendon	71 70 68 69	278	1,525
Fred Marti	68 71 69 70	278	1,525
Dave Bollman	69 71 72 67	279	1,275
Hal Underwood	71 70 68 70	279	1,275
Bobby Mitchell	69 70 68 72	279	1,275
Cesar Sanudo	71 72 69 68	280	1,012.50
Jacky Cupit	71 70 70 69	280	1,012.50
J. C. Goosie	71 69 69 71	280	1,012.50
Jim Colbert	68 69 81 72	280	1,012.50
Dewitt Weaver	69 71 73 68	281	669.65
Hale Irwin	71 69 72 69	281	669.64
Ron Cerrudo	72 70 70 69	281	669.64
Monty Kaser	70 69 72 70	281	669.64
Charles Sifford	67 74 69 71	281	669.64
Wilf Homenuik, *Canada*	68 71 69 73	281	669.64

	SCORES	TOTAL	MONEY
Jesse Snead	69 69 67 76	281	669.64
Larry Hinson	72 70 72 68	282	534.38
Chris Blocker	71 69 71 71	282	534.38
Jerry Abbott	70 71 66 75	282	534.38
Larry Ziegler	68 67 68 79	282	534.38
Bob Pipkin	72 71 71 69	283	421.88
Joel Goldstrand	70 73 71 69	283	421.88
Chick Evans	68 72 73 70	283	421.88
Don Parson	68 75 70 70	283	421.88
Pete Fleming	68 72 72 71	283	421.87
Dow Finsterwald	73 68 70 72	283	421.87
Dick Crawford	70 70 70 73	283	421.87
John Kennedy	70 68 70 75	283	421.87
Denny Lyons	70 68 73 73	284	300
Earl Stewart	69 73 69 73	284	300
Mike Hill	68 68 74 74	284	300
Homero Blancas	65 75 75 70	285	182.15
Ed Sneed	69 71 72 73	285	182.15
Dean Refram	73 70 69 73	285	182.14
Tommy Jacobs	71 69 71 74	285	182.14
Bob Menne	71 71 69 74	285	182.14
Dick Rhyan	72 69 69 75	285	182.14
Frank Boynton	71 69 70 76	285	182.14

SAHARA INVITATIONAL

SAHARA-NEVADA COUNTRY CLUB
Las Vegas, Nevada
October 16–19
Purse...$100,000
Par: 36, 35–71...6,751 yards

	SCORES	TOTAL	MONEY
Jack Nicklaus	69 68 70 65	272	$20,000
Frank Beard	69 72 65 70	276	11,400
Dale Douglass	72 68 71 66	277	5,900
Dave Hill	71 67 70 69	277	5,900
Tony Jacklin, *Great Britain*	70 69 70 69	278	3,850
Grier Jones	69 72 69 68	278	3,850
Dick Crawford	70 72 68 69	279	3,200
Steve Spray	67 70 75 68	280	2,172.23
Dave Stockton	71 73 68 68	280	2,172.23
Homero Blancas	72 70 69 69	280	2,172.22
Terry Dill	71 66 74 69	280	2,172.22
Rod Funseth	70 71 69 70	280	2,172.22
Steve Reid	70 68 71 71	280	2,172.22
Chi Chi Rodriguez	69 68 73 70	280	2,172.22

	SCORES	TOTAL	MONEY
Hugh Royer	71 71 68 70	280	2,172.22
Kermit Zarley	68 70 72 70	280	2,172.22
Chuck Courtney	72 69 72 68	281	1,450
Tom Weiskopf	72 71 71 67	281	1,450
Julius Boros	72 72 70 68	282	1,035.72
Jacky Cupit	75 69 70 68	282	1,035.72
Bob Smith	73 67 75 67	282	1,035.72
R. H. Sikes	69 75 70 68	282	1,035.71
Jim Wiechers	70 71 71 70	282	1,035.71
Ted Hayes	66 71 73 72	282	1,035.71
Bob Menne	66 72 70 74	282	1,035.71
Miller Barber	71 70 73 69	283	770
Larry Hinson	71 72 72 68	283	770
Bob Rosburg	68 77 71 67	283	770
Deane Beman	72 72 68 72	284	652
Don January	68 73 68 75	284	652
Jack McGowan	75 70 68 71	284	652
Dewitt Weaver	72 73 70 69	284	652
Dick Mayer	73 71 70 70	284	652
Don Bies	73 71 73 68	285	493.34
Mike Hill	71 74 69 71	285	493.34
Orville Moody	69 72 73 71	285	493.34
Fred Marti	68 72 71 74	285	493.33
Arnold Palmer	69 75 68 73	285	493.33
Doug Sanders	65 71 73 76	285	493.33
Peter Townsend, *Great Britain*	70 71 70 74	285	493.33
Lee Trevino	72 69 71 73	285	493.33
John Levinson	69 72 71 73	285	493.33
Ron Cerrudo	73 72 72 69	286	256.81
Bobby Nichols	74 71 72 69	286	256.81
Jack Ewing	74 70 71 71	286	256.80
Dow Finsterwald	72 69 72 73	286	256.80
Bert Greene	71 70 72 73	286	256.80
Jerry Heard	69 73 73 71	286	256.80
Ed Merrins	66 73 75 72	286	256.80
Paul Moran	71 70 69 76	286	256.80
Jim Ferrier	71 73 68 75	287	121.22
Allan Henning, *South Africa*	73 70 75 69	287	121.22
Dick Lotz	73 68 76 70	287	121.22
Bert Yancey	73 68 76 70	287	121.22
John Schroeder	71 74 71 71	287	121.22
Dick Rhyan	68 75 77 68	288	121.22
Billy Maxwell	70 71 75 72	288	121.21
Charles Sifford	70 75 70 73	288	121.21
Tom Bailey	71 70 77 70	288	121.21
Wilf Homenuik, *Canada*	72 73 72 71	288	121.21
Chris Blocker	71 74 71 73	289	121.21
Jim Colbert	74 70 67 78	289	121.21

	SCORES	TOTAL	MONEY
Gardner Dickinson	74 71 72 72	289	121.21
Hale Irwin	70 72 73 74	289	121.21
Cesar Sanudo	72 73 73 71	289	121.21
Paul Scodeller	74 71 72 72	289	121.21
Pete Brown	72 71 74 73	290	121.21
Tommy Jacobs	69 73 78 70	290	121.21
John Kennedy	70 73 73 74	290	121.21
George Boutell	71 74 74 72	291	121.21
Bert Weaver	72 73 72 74	291	121.21
Bob Goalby	69 73 76 74	292	121.21
Lou Graham	72 71 76 73	292	121.21
Bill Garrett	74 71 70 78	293	121.21
Bobby Mitchell	71 73 70 79	293	121.21
Howell Fraser	67 75 75 77	294	121.21
Joel Goldstrand	72 73 74 75	294	121.21
Jim Bullard	72 73 76 73	294	121.21

SAN FRANCISCO OPEN

HARDING PARK GOLF COURSE
San Francisco, California
October 23—26
Purse...$100,000
Par: 36, 35—71...6,677 yards

	SCORES	TOTAL	MONEY
Steve Spray	70 63 66 70	269	$20,000
Chi Chi Rodriguez	69 68 67 66	270	11,400
Bob Lunn	65 68 69 69	271	7,100
Bob Charles, *New Zealand*	68 69 67 68	272	4,400
Dave Hill	67 69 67 69	272	4,400
Homero Blancas	68 71 67 67	273	3,112.50
Bill Casper	70 68 66 69	273	3,112.50
Jerry Heard	65 69 70 69	273	3,112.50
R. H. Sikes	68 69 66 70	273	3,112.50
Deane Beman	69 69 65 71	274	2,200
Lee Elder	66 68 70 70	274	2,200
Jim Wiechers	70 68 67 69	274	2,200
Bert Yancey	73 67 69 65	274	2,200
George Archer	63 67 73 72	275	1,600
Miller Barber	68 64 70 73	275	1,600
Frank Beard	69 68 69 69	275	1,600
Johnny Pott	69 68 70 68	275	1,600
Phil Rodgers	69 69 67 70	275	1,600
Chris Blocker	68 68 70 70	276	1,006.25
Bob Goalby	67 68 68 73	276	1,006.25
Larry Hinson	72 69 66 69	276	1,006.25

	SCORES	TOTAL	MONEY
B. R. McLendon	75 67 66 68	276	1,006.25
Steve Reid	70 67 71 68	276	1,006.25
Kermit Zarley	71 71 69 65	276	1,006.25
Wilf Homenuik, *Canada*	71 68 71 66	276	1,006.25
Dick Mayer	64 74 71 67	276	1,006.25
Charles Coody	69 70 67 71	277	681.43
Mike Hill	66 74 68 69	277	681.43
Bob Murphy	67 70 70 70	277	681.43
Arnold Palmer	70 67 73 67	277	681.43
Scotty McBeath	75 66 68 68	277	681.43
Al Mengert	68 66 73 70	277	681.43
Fred Marti	69 66 70 72	277	681.42
Hale Irwin	73 65 74 66	278	493.34
Bob Rosburg	72 69 70 67	278	493.34
Bob Menne	68 70 73 67	278	493.34
Tommy Aaron	69 71 69 69	278	493.33
Dale Douglass	67 68 73 70	278	493.33
Jack Ewing	69 71 67 71	278	493.33
Rod Funseth	72 68 70 68	278	493.33
Ken Still	70 69 68 71	278	493.33
John Miller	67 71 72 68	278	493.33
Bert Greene	72 69 70 68	279	256.81
Howie Johnson	71 69 71 68	279	256.81
Don Bies	73 68 69 69	279	256.80
Terry Dill	70 66 69 74	279	256.80
Dow Finsterwald	69 73 67 70	279	256.80
Tommy Jacobs	68 70 72 69	279	256.80
Billy Maxwell	68 71 70 70	279	256.80
Jack Montgomery	64 74 69 72	279	256.80
Tom Weiskopf	69 70 68 72	279	256.80
Dave Eichelberger	71 71 71 67	280	121.22
Bob Smith	68 72 72 68	280	121.22
Dave Stockton	69 69 73 69	280	121.22
Dick Lotz	69 72 72 68	281	121.22
Don January	73 69 67 72	281	121.21
Bobby Mitchell	71 70 70 70	281	121.21
Peter Townsend, *Great Britain*	67 71 73 70	281	121.21
John Schroeder	70 69 70 72	281	121.21
Jim Jamieson	68 71 70 73	282	121.21
Grier Jones	71 68 68 75	282	121.21
Ted Hayes	73 68 71 70	282	121.21
Ken Towns	72 69 75 66	282	121.21
Ron Cerrudo	72 69 69 73	283	121.21
Jim Colbert	71 68 74 70	283	121.21
Bruce Crampton, *Australia*	74 68 71 70	283	121.21
Bill Garrett	71 68 74 70	283	121.21
Dick Rhyan	75 67 71 70	283	121.21
Mason Rudolph	70 71 70 72	283	121.21

	SCORES	TOTAL	MONEY
Charles Sifford	71 70 73 69	283	121.21
Bobby Greenwood	71 71 68 73	283	121.21
Lionel Hebert	72 70 71 71	284	121.21
Brian Barnes, *Great Britain*	72 68 76 68	284	121.21
Tom Gorrell	71 68 72 74	285	121.21
Joel Goldstrand	72 68 73 73	286	121.21
Ed Sneed	71 69 74 72	286	121.21
George Boutell	70 72 75 71	288	121.21
Allan Henning, *South Africa*	69 72 76 71	288	121.21
Jack McGowan	71 70 69 78	288	121.21
Mike Reasor	69 73 71 75	288	121.21
Monty Kaser	70 72 74 74	290	121.21
Jerry Barrier	69 73 73 76	291	121.21
Cesar Sanudo	71 71 74 75	291	121.21

KAISER INTERNATIONAL

SILVERADO COUNTRY CLUB
Napa, California
October 30—November 3
Purse...$140,000
North course—
    Par: 36, 36—72...6,849 yards
South course—
    Par: 35, 37—72...6,602 yards

	SCORES	TOTAL	MONEY
Jack Nicklaus	66 67 69 71	273	$28,000
George Archer	69 69 66 69	273	10,826.67
Bill Casper	68 69 69 67	273	10,826.67
Don January	67 71 69 66	273	10,826.66

(Nicklaus defeated Archer, Casper and January in sudden-death playoff, January eliminated on first extra hole Nov. 2, Archer and Casper on second extra hole Nov. 3 after playoff had been halted by darkness.)

	SCORES	TOTAL	MONEY
Lou Graham	66 69 70 69	274	5,740
Chi Chi Rodriguez	68 68 69 70	275	4,760
Dan Sikes	72 65 71 67	275	4,760
R. H. Sikes	69 72 68 68	277	3,803.34
Arnold Palmer	71 69 68 69	277	3,803.33
Dave Stockton	71 67 66 73	277	3,803.33
Dick Crawford	73 64 70 71	278	3,080
Ed Sneed	67 70 73 68	278	3,080
Don Bies	72 66 68 73	279	2,310
Bob Dickson	69 71 71 68	279	2,310
Bert Greene	75 69 67 68	279	2,310
B. R. McLendon	70 70 70 69	279	2,310

	SCORES	TOTAL	MONEY
Doug Sanders	68 71 69 71	279	2,310
Hal Underwood	71 69 69 70	279	2,310
Chuck Courtney	66 73 73 68	280	1,450
Bruce Crampton, *Australia*	71 69 71 69	280	1,450
Larry Hinson	69 72 72 67	280	1,450
Gene Littler	74 68 69 69	280	1,450
Bob Lunn	72 66 70 72	280	1,450
Kermit Zarley	71 66 71 72	280	1,450
Al Mengert	69 73 68 70	280	1,450
Charles Coody	71 73 67 70	281	1,036
Jacky Cupit	75 69 69 68	281	1,036
Bob Goalby	69 68 68 76	281	1,036
Dick Mayer	71 68 71 71	281	1,036
Wayne Vollmer, *Canada*	73 70 69 69	281	1,036
Frank Beard	68 74 71 69	282	828.34
Homero Blancas	72 68 73 69	282	828.34
Miller Barber	69 74 70 69 ·	282	828.33
Rod Funseth	73 69 70 70	282	828.33
Johnny Jacobs	73 68 70 71	282	828.33
Tommy Jacobs	70 71 70 71	282	828.33
Tommy Aaron	68 70 73 72	283	624
Frank Boynton	72 69 72 70	283	624
Jack McGowan	73 71 68 71	283	624
Steve Reid	68 69 71 75	283	624
Jim Wiechers	70 69 71 73	283	624
Bert Yancey	69 74 69 71	283	624
Don Parsons	73 68 76 66	283	624
Hugh Royer	74 70 72 68	284	380.34
John Miller	68 72 73 71	284	380.34
Jerry Abbott	69 71 70 74	284	380.33
Gay Brewer	69 69 73 73	284	380.33
Al Geiberger	76 67 66 75	284	380.33
Ken Still	69 73 71 71	284	380.33
Bobby Mitchell	70 69 77 69	285	198.34
Dick Rhyan	74 69 71 71	285	198.34
Bob Rosburg	72 71 71 71	285	198.34
Cesar Sanudo	69 73 71 72	285	198.34
John Schroeder	70 71 73 71	285	198.34
Ron Cerrudo	67 69 76 73	285	198.33
Dale Douglass	69 75 69 72	285	198.33
Wilf Homenuik, *Canada*	71 65 73 76	285	198.33
Dewitt Weaver	71 72 70 73	286	186.67
Ken Towns	71 71 74 70	286	186.67
Dow Finsterwald	73 70 70 74	287	186.67
Labron Harris	69 75 71 72	287	186.67
Howie Johnson	72 72 71 72	287	186.67
Rives McBee	70 73 69 75	287	186.67
Jack Ewing	70 70 74 74	288	186.67

	SCORES	TOTAL	MONEY
Jim Ferrier	73 71 72 72	288	186.67
Johnny Pott	71 71 68 78	288	186.67
Mike Reasor	71 73 71 73	288	186.67
Bill Garrett	73 69 70 77	289	186.67
Mason Rudolph	72 72 72 73	289	186.67
Babe Lichardus	73 69 68 79	289	186.67
Chris Blocker	71 68 77 74	290	186.66
Larry Ziegler	72 71 73 74	290	186.66
Ray Floyd	72 72 73 74	291	186.66
Deane Beman	72 71 72 77	292	186.66
Earl Stewart	71 69 76 76	292	186.66
Randy Wolff	72 71 75 74	292	186.66
Jim Colbert	69 73 74 77	293	186.66
Jack Montgomery	71 72 75 75	293	186.66
Lee Elder	70 73 73 80	296	186.66
Billy Maxwell	74 69 79 75	297	186.66

HAWAIIAN INTERNATIONAL OPEN

WAIALAE COUNTRY CLUB
Honolulu, Hawaii
November 6—9
Purse...$100,000
Par: 36, 36—72...7,020 yards

	SCORES	TOTAL	MONEY
Bruce Crampton, *Australia*	71 71 65 67	274	$25,000
Jack Nicklaus	63 71 74 70	278	14,300
John Schroeder	68 72 74 66	280	7,350
Chi Chi Rodriguez	71 71 71 67	280	7,350
Jack McGowan	68 72 71 70	281	4,812.50
Tom Weiskopf	70 68 71 72	281	4,812.50
George Archer	71 71 72 68	282	3,546.25
Gay Brewer	72 72 69 69	282	3,546.25
Bill Casper	73 68 71 70	282	3,546.25
Don Bies	71 73 66 72	282	3,546.25
Jim Colbert	73 75 68 67	283	2,166.67
Bobby Mitchell	74 72 70 67	283	2,166.67
Grier Jones	69 72 73 69	283	2,166.67
Larry Ziegler	69 73 72 69	283	2,166.67
Takaaki Kono, *Japan*	73 69 72 69	283	2,166.67
R. H. Sikes	73 71 69 70	283	2,166.67
B. R. McLendon	71 72 70 70	283	2,166.66
Doug Sanders	71 71 69 72	283	2,166.66
Lee Trevino	74 72 66 71	283	2,166.66
Bob Murphy	74 67 76 67	284	1,325
Dick Crawford	71 71 73 69	284	1,325

	SCORES	TOTAL	MONEY
Dudley Wysong	70 72 71 71	284	1,325
Miller Barber	73 71 68 72	284	1,325
Howie Johnson	70 71 76 68	285	1,026
Dave Stockton	67 75 75 68	285	1,026
Rod Funseth	75 73 68 69	285	1,026
Vern Novak	71 75 69 70	285	1,026
Steve Reid	77 69 71 69	286	817.86
Lee Elder	75 71 70 70	286	817.86
Steve Spray	73 73 70 70	286	817.86
Tom Shaw	72 73 70 71	286	817.86
Herb Hooper	70 70 74 72	286	817.86
Arnold Palmer	70 71 72 73	286	817.85
Al Geiberger	74 69 71 72	286	817.85
Bob Lunn	73 75 70 69	287	687.50
Lou Graham	70 72 72 73	287	687.50
Don Parsons	75 71 71 71	288	538.88
Mike Hill	73 74 70 71	288	538.88
Randy Wolff	69 72 75 72	288	538.88
Jacky Cupit	70 74 71 73	288	538.88
Ken Ellsworth	71 75 69 73	288	538.87
Jack Ewing	72 73 70 73	288	538.87
Dick Rhyan	70 74 72 72	288	538.87
Bert Yancey	73 70 69 76	288	538.87
Tommy Jacobs	75 71 75 68	289	291.67
Terry Dill	75 70 75 69	289	291.67
Joel Goldstrand	75 73 72 69	289	291.67
Peter Townsend, *Great Britain*	74 72 73 70	289	291.67
Bill Johnston	69 72 74 74	289	291.67
Frank Beard	71 72 69 77	289	291.66
Ken Still	67 71 74 77	289	291.66
Al Mengert	74 73 73 70	290	166.67
Ed Merrins	72 75 72 71	290	166.67
Phil Rodgers	70 74 73 73	290	166.67
John Levinson	70 74 73 73	290	166.67
Billy Maxwell	72 72 70 76	290	166.67
Hsieh Yung Yo, *Formosa*	71 76 70 73	290	166.67
Lionel Hebert	72 73 71 74	290	166.67
Kermit Zarley	74 68 72 76	290	166.67
Jack Montgomery	74 73 74 70	291	166.67
Bob Smith	73 75 71 72	291	166.67
Jay Hebert	77 69 72 73	291	166.67
Bobby Cole, *South Africa*	70 73 75 73	291	166.67
Dick Lotz	72 76 70 73	291	166.67
John Jacobs	71 74 73 73	291	166.67
Hideyo Sugimoto, *Japan*	73 75 70 73	291	166.67
Jim Wiechers	73 73 73 73	292	166.67
Rocky Thompson	73 71 71 77	292	166.67
Labron Harris	71 71 80 71	293	166.67

	SCORES	TOTAL	MONEY
Mike Reasor	71 76 74 72	293	166.67
Bob Boldt	72 75 74 72	293	166.66
Homero Blancas	73 75 72 73	293	166.66
Earl Stewart	75 73 71 74	293	166.66
Richard Martinez	73 74 76 71	294	166.66
Chris Blocker	70 77 78 72	297	166.66
Dave Gumlia	70 76 70 81	297	166.66
John Schlee	75 73 74 78	300	166.66
Joe Carr	70 78 77 76	301	166.66
Teruo Sugihara, *Japan*	75 72 78 76	301	166.66
Jim Ferrell	77 70 76 78	301	166.66

HERITAGE CLASSIC

HARBOUR TOWN GOLF LINKS
Hilton Head Island, South Carolina
November 27–30
Purse...$100,000
Par: 36, 35–71...6,655 yards

	SCORES	TOTAL	MONEY
Arnold Palmer	68 71 70 74	283	$20,000
Bert Yancey	76 68 70 72	286	9,250
Dick Crawford	71 69 72 74	286	9,250
Doug Ford	74 68 75 70	287	4,700
Homero Blancas	74 69 69 76	288	4,100
Jack Ewing	75 74 70 70	289	3,250
Jack Nicklaus	71 72 71 75	289	3,250
Earl Stewart	72 73 70 74	289	3,250
Doug Sanders	74 70 75 71	290	2,400
Bob Murphy	73 70 75 72	290	2,400
Dick Hart	72 74 71 73	290	2,400
Tom Weiskopf	74 65 74 77	290	2,400
George Archer	68 73 76 75	292	1,900
Kermit Zarley	71 76 74 72	293	1,650
Julius Boros	73 71 76 73	293	1,650
B. R. McLendon	69 75 74 75	293	1,650
Peter Townsend, *Great Britain*	73 73 70 77	293	1,650
Jack Montgomery	75 74 73 72	294	1,300
Lionel Hebert	75 76 71 72	294	1,300
Dave Ragan	70 72 75 77	294	1,300
Roy Pace	77 74 71 73	295	950
Dow Finsterwald	75 76 70 74	295	950
Lee Trevino	72 78 71 74	295	950
Bobby Nichols	75 75 69 76	295	950
Dan Sikes	73 73 69 80	295	950
Rocky Thompson	72 74 79 71	296	740

	SCORES	TOTAL	MONEY
Bob Dickson	75 75 75 71	296	740
Terry Dill	74 75 75 72	296	740
Steve Spray	74 72 76 74	296	740
Charles Sifford	69 76 74 77	296	740
Gardner Dickinson	72 77 75 73	297	602
Bob Smith	75 76 72 74	297	602
Fred Marti	70 75 77 75	297	602
Paul Moran	74 73 75 75	297	602
Howell Fraser	73 71 73 80	297	602
Tom Bailey	76 74 75 73	298	510
Billy Maxwell	71 77 74 76	298	510
Bobby Brue	73 75 74 76	298	510
Rod Funseth	73 75 71 79	298	510
Davis Love	74 76 76 73	299	405
Hugh Royer	72 76 77 74	299	405
Bobby Mitchell	76 75 73 75	299	405
Don Massengale	77 71 74 77	299	405
Dave Marr	72 77 79 72	300	303.34
Lou Graham	73 75 74 78	300	303.33
Joel Goldstrand	74 69 72 85	300	303.33
Randy Wolff	74 74 78 75	301	220.37
Tommy Aaron	72 77 76 76	301	220.37
Labron Harris	73 77 72 79	301	220.36
Richard Martinez	74 72 75 80	301	220.36
Babe Hiskey	72 79 70 80	301	220.36
Jim Ferree	74 74 77 77	302	181.82
Ken Ellsworth	77 70 76 79	302	181.82
Bert Greene	78 71 73 80	302	181.82
Bob Payne	77 73 72 80	302	181.82
Terry Wilcox	70 75 76 81	302	181.82
Jim Grant	71 76 75 81	303	181.82
R. H. Sikes	76 74 69 84	303	181.82
Larry Hinson	75 74 79 76	304	181.82
Ted Hayes	75 70 80 79	304	181.82
Jim Jamieson	77 71 76 81	305	181.82
Gaylon Simon	77 74 80 75	306	181.82
Al Mengert	76 73 77 80	306	181.82
Lloyd Monroe	71 78 76 81	306	181.82
Grier Jones	70 77 74 85	306	181.82
Randy Glover	76 75 76 80	307	181.82
Jacky Cupit	77 73 83 75	308	181.82
Mason Rudolph	74 76 80 78	308	181.82
Dave Eichelberger	72 75 78 83	308	181.81
Jack McGowan	71 79 80 79	309	181.81
John Schroeder	75 74 81 80	310	181.81
Cesar Sanudo	75 73 78 85	311	181.81

DANNY THOMAS DIPLOMAT CLASSIC

DIPLOMAT PRESIDENTIAL COUNTRY CLUB
Hollywood, Florida
December 4–7
Purse...$125,000
Par: 36, 36–72...6,964 yards

	SCORES				TOTAL	MONEY
Arnold Palmer	68	67	70	65	270	$25,000
Gay Brewer	65	66	68	73	272	14,300
Lee Trevino	70	69	69	66	274	8.850
Larry Hinson	69	69	68	69	275	5,487.50
Hal Underwood	68	67	71	69	275	5,487.50
George Archer	70	75	67	64	276	4,500
Fred Marti	69	70	69	69	277	4,000
Jim Jamieson	67	73	66	72	278	3,530
Sam Sneed	70	67	71	70	278	3,530
Bert Yancey	68	70	69	72	279	2,875
Homero Blancas	68	73	71	67	279	2,875
Gardner Dickinson	70	69	69	71	279	2,875
Tommy Bolt	68	71	73	68	280	2,062.50
Rod Funseth	73	69	70	68	280	2,062.50
Bob Murphy	72	67	74	67	280	2,062.50
Bob Smith	71	70	67	72	280	2,062.50
Mason Rudolph	68	72	69	71	280	2,062.50
Tommy Aaron	67	70	72	71	280	2,062.50
Chi Chi Rodriguez	71	69	69	72	281	1,562.50
Peter Townsend, *Great Britain*	68	73	70	70	281	1,562.50
Jimmy Wright	73	65	72	72	282	1,375
Bob Dickson	71	71	71	70	283	1,141.25
Hugh Royer	68	68	73	74	283	1,141.25
Earl Stewart	70	73	72	68	283	1,141.25
Tom Weiskopf	74	70	69	70	283	1,141.25
Herb Hooper	73	66	73	72	284	925
Deane Beman	69	69	72	74	284	925
Bruce Devlin, *Australia*	72	71	67	74	284	925
Jerry Pittman	68	73	70	73	284	925
John Schroeder	71	73	68	72	284	925
Jim Colbert	76	69	68	72	285	766
Dale Douglass	71	70	71	73	285	766
Jack Ewing	71	71	72	71	285	766
Larry Mowry	72	70	73	70	285	766
Don Massengale	71	72	74	69	286	619.43
Billy Maxwell	73	72	70	71	286	619.43
Bobby Nichols	69	74	71	72	286	619.43
Dick Rhyan	70	72	73	71	286	619.43
John Schlee	73	70	72	71	286	619.43

	SCORES	TOTAL	MONEY
R. H. Sikes	67 74 75 70	286	619.43
B. R. McLendon	72 69 67 78	286	619.42
Paul Moran	71 73 71 72	287	385.72
Bob Payne	76 67 72 72	287	385.72
Dave Ragan	72 70 73 72	287	385.72
Julius Boros	71 67 75 74	287	385.71
Chuck Courtney	71 73 70 73	287	385.71
Chick Evans	74 70 69 74	287	385.71
Bobby Mitchell	73 69 72 73	287	385.71
Frank Beard	70 72 73 73	288	207.28
Ron Cerrudo	72 71 73 72	288	207.28
Dave Hill	70 73 71 74	288	207.28
Jerry McGee	72 71 72 73	288	207.28
Dick Rautmann	74 70 71 73	288	207.28
Kermit Zarley	70 72 75 71	288	207.28
Dave Eichelberger	72 73 69 74	288	207.27
Howell Fraser	72 70 73 74	289	185.19
Richard Martinez	72 73 74 70	289	185.19
Al Mengert	72 70 74 73	289	185.19
Orville Moody	72 73 70 74	289	185.19
Dean Refram	71 72 73 73	289	185.19
Charles Sifford	71 69 78 71	289	185.19
Larry Ziegler	72 73 69 75	289	185.19
Dow Finsterwald	73 72 72 73	290	185.19
Gordon Jones	70 73 74 73	290	185.19
Chris Blocker	73 71 71 75	290	185.18
Hale Irwin	71 69 75 75	290	185.18
Dick Crawford	71 73 75 73	292	185.18
Babe Hiskey	70 73 73 76	292	185.18
Lloyd Monroe	69 74 77 72	292	185.18
Randy Wolff	72 73 75 72	292	185.18
Jack Montgomery	71 74 75 72	292	185.18
John Miller	74 71 70 78	293	185.18
Doug Sanders	72 73 75 73	293	185.18
Cesar Sanudo	73 72 73 75	293	185.18
Jim Awtrey	73 72 79 70	294	185.18
Bob Cox, *Canada*	70 73 77 74	294	185.18
Jesse Snead	70 73 73 81	297	185.18

WEST END CLASSIC

GRAND BAHAMA HOTEL & COUNTRY CLUB
Grand Bahama Island
December 4—7
Purse...$25,000
Par: 36, 36—72...6,836 yards

	SCORES	TOTAL	MONEY
Jim Wiechers	70 65 69 70	274	$5,000
Johnny Pott	64 70 71 74	279	2,437.50

	SCORES	TOTAL	MONEY
Al Besselink	75 66 67 71	279	2,437.50
Mike Reasor	68 69 74 72	283	1,250
Art Silverstrone	70 72 69 73	284	1,075
Bobby Greenwood	70 70 74 71	285	950
Malcolm Gregson, *Great Britain*	72 72 70 72	286	850
Carl Lohren	74 74 67 72	287	681.25
Steve Reid	70 71 73 73	287	681.25
Jerry Abbott	70 74 70 73	287	681.25
Gene Borek	73 69 70 75	287	681.25
Bob Menne	68 76 72 72	288	493.75
Dutch Harrison	73 71 72 72	288	493.75
Jerry Barrier	73 73 70 72	288	493.75
Mike Mitchell	72 71 69 76	288	493.75
Rick Rhoads	74 73 70 72	289	412.50
Jim Ferriell	69 74 71 75	289	412.50
Billy Farrell	73 72 74 71	290	375
Rolf Deming	77 72 72 70	291	337.50
Les Peterson	72 75 72 72	291	337.50
Gary Groh	75 75 71 71	292	275
Joe Carr	77 74 69 72	292	275
Vern Novak	74 70 72 76	292	275
Rex Baxter	73 73 73 74	293	214.59
Tim De Baufre	74 69 74 76	293	214.59
Butch Baird	69 76 71 77	293	214.58
Bob Gleeson	77 72 72 73	294	196.88
Mike Nugent	75 69 73 77	294	196.87
Bob Erickson	73 75 75 72	295	178.13
Rich Bassett	73 73 76 73	295	178.13
Sam Reynolds	73 73 74 75	295	178.12
George Johnson	76 72 72 75	295	178.12
Johnny Jacobs	78 70 76 72	296	159.38
Babe Lichardus	73 73 75 75	296	159.37
Bill Bisdorf	74 73 73 77	297	146.88
Tom Aycock	75 71 73 78	297	146.87
Babe Hart	75 74 75 74	298	134.38
Bob Shave	74 73 76 75	298	134.37
Dave Gumlia	75 75 74 75	299	117.92
Jack Steingraber	75 74 74 76	299	117.92
Jack Connelly	77 72 69 81	299	117.91
Jim Bullard	74 73 77 76	300	95
Dewitt Weaver	75 72 75 78	300	95
Ray Montgomery	75 70 82 74	301	70
John Cutshall	77 74 75 75	301	70
Stan Brion	74 74 76 77	301	70
Jim Terry	77 74 79 72	302	57.50
Bob Gajda	76 74 77 77	304	53.75
Ed Davis	74 73 77 80	304	53.75
Bob Pipkin	76 74 79 79	308	50

The 1969 U.S. Season of the 15 Leading Money-Winners

RANK–PLAYER TOTAL MONEY	Los Angeles	Kaiser (Jan.)	Bing Crosby	Williams–San Diego	Bob Hope	Phoenix	Tucson	Doral	Citrus	Monsanto	Jacksonville	Nat. Airlines	Greensboro	MASTERS	Tournament of Champions	Byron Nelson	New Orleans	Texas	Colonial	Atlanta	Memphis	Western	U.S. OPEN
1—Frank Beard $175,223.93	—	25	MC	9	5	52	11	43	18	—	15	46	30	19	—	2	2	23	10	—	—	3	50
2—Dave Hill $156,423.40	5	14	WD	WD	2	8	—	17	34	—	28	—	30	24	—	DQ	3	3	6	18	1	—	13
3—Jack Nicklaus $140,167.42	—	—	—	MC	18	—	—	4	10	—	82	MC	—	24	—	—	MC	—	4	47	—	36	25
4—Gary Player $123,897.69	—	—	6	1	—	25	—	—	—	5	3	23	5	33	1	—	—	—	2	3	12	5	48
5—Bruce Crampton $118,955.80	17	MC	31	54	5	—	—	—	MC	8	15	2	10	13	—	2	MC	72	4	—	—	—	6
6—Gene Littler $112,737.27	MC	6	8	2	13	1	4	—	6	3	3	19	1	8	5	—	—	—	47	—	12	—	MC
7—Lee Trevino $112,417.51	74	6	23	6	11	77	1	—	34	3	3	—	59	19	2	5	33	3	—	MC	7	18	MC
8—Ray Floyd $109,956.63	28	42	65	9	26	5	—	MC	—	4	1	WD	45	36	28	—	33	—	—	18	WD	43	13
9—Arnold Palmer $105,128.42	19	3	34	—	1	26	—	10	10	—	6	12	—	27	3	8	—	—	37	25	—	—	6
10—Bill Casper $104,689.46	3	25	15	61	—	—	2	2	2	—	8	WD	—	2	9	2	20	—	68	—	—	1	40
11—George Archer $102,707.46	28	14	1	20	MC	20	24	17	52	41	—	51	11	1	6	6	—	—	60	MC	—	16	10
12—Dale Douglass $91,553.53	17	42	2	43	26	20	7	13	10	41	MC	7	22	19	—	13	—	23	30	54	7	26	13
13—Tommy Aaron $91,463.41	17	14	—	3	30	2	—	2	18	5	—	27	30	8	—	—	40	3	20	18	3	—	40
14—Miller Barber $90,107.38	34	1	15	34	—	MC	2	13	2	—	60	23	—	7	15	MC	25	35	24	16	37	16	6
15—Dan Sikes $89,103.68	—	—	MC	28	—	—	—	3	10	—	MC	2	22	12	9	10	10	11	—	9	10	—	38
Number in field	11	12	13	13	11	10	7	10	11	7	12	13	11	15	10	7	10	8	12	12	9	9	15
Number in top 10	2	4	4	6	4	4	4	4	5	5	5	3	3	5	7	4	3	3	5	3	5	3	4

Legend: MC—missed cut, failed to qualify for final round or two rounds
WD—withdrew from tournament after starting.
DQ—disqualified.

Note:
*Douglass also won Azalea Open.
**Aaron won Canadian Open.

388

RANK–PLAYER TOTAL MONEY	Kemper	Cleveland	Buick	Minnesota	Philadelphia	American	Westchester	Milwaukee	PGA	Avco	Hartford	Alcan	Sahara	San Francisco	Kaiser (Oct.)	Hawaiian	Heritage	Danny Thomas	Starts	Victories	Seconds	First 5	First 10
1—Frank Beard $175,223.93	—	4	2	1	5	8	1	—	10	—	42	3	2	14	31	45	—	49	32	2	4	11	15
2—Dave Hill $156,423.30	—	—	1	—	1	18	MC	—	15	—	2	8	3	4	—	—	—	49	28	3	2	10	13
3—Jack Nicklaus $140,167.42	—	52	—	—	—	6	12	—	11	—	7	—	1	—	1	2	6	—	23	3	1	6	11
4—Gary Player $123,897.69	3	—	—	—	—	—	12	2	2	58	—	—	1	—	—	1	—	—	16	1	3	10	10
5—Bruce Crompton $118,955.80	3	2	35	—	—	MC	7	—	15	9	35	—	—	64	19	—	—	—	30	1	3	6	12
6—Gene Littler $112,737.27	—	21	16	—	—	4	MC	—	48	—	—	8	—	—	19	—	21	—	21	2	1	7	11
7—Lee Trevino $112,417.51	21	52	—	—	16	DQ	5	—	48	—	13	2	34	—	—	11	21	3	32	1	2	9	13
8—Ray Floyd $109,956.63	—	WD	—	—	39	1	12	—	1	—	MC	—	MC	MC	73	MC	—	—	29	3	0	5	6
9—Arnold Palmer $105,128.42	5	9	—	—	20	14	53	23	WD	MC	—	—	34	27	8	28	1	1	26	2	0	5	11
10—Bill Casper $104,689.46	—	9	—	—	20	—	12	—	35	73	27	1	—	6	2	7	—	—	22	3	2	6	10
11—George Archer $102,707.46	5	52	—	—	—	21	25	—	69	73	MC	—	—	14	2	7	13	6	28	2	1	4	8
12—Dale Douglass $91,553.53	1	MC	20	57	32	21	MC	—	48	—	20	—	3	34	50	MC	MC	31	36	*1	1	3	7
13—Tommy Aaron $91,462.41	27	15	—	2	39	—	5	—	57	15	—	—	—	34	37	—	47	13	28	**0	2	7	8
14—Miller Barber $90,107.38	—	WD	—	—	55	67	31	—	5	43	35	—	26	14	31	20	—	—	32	1	3	5	7
15—Dan Sikes $89,103.68	12	—	4	18	14	32	3	2	25	33	20	5	—	—	6	—	21	MC	27	0	1	4	10
Number in field	8	11	6	4	11	12	15	2	15	7	11	5	8	10	12	10	7	8					
Number in top 10	5	3	3	2	2	4	55	1	4	1	2	5	4	2	5	4	2	3					

Tournaments included above are those on the main tour schedule only. Satellite events and the Canadian Open are not included because of the absence of virtually all of the 15 leading money-winners from those fields. The numbers in the main body of the chart indicate position of finish. Ties are not noted.

Caribbean Tour
LOS LOGARTOS OPEN

LOS LOGARTOS COUNTRY CLUB
Bogota, Colombia
February 13—16
Purse....$15,500
Par: 36, 36—72

	SCORES				TOTAL	MONEY
Roberto de Vicenzo, *Argentina*	65	71	73	65	274	$3,000
Larry Mowry	71	73	65	68	277	2,000
Rogelio Gonzalez, *Colombia*	70	67	71	71	279	1,500
Alfonso Bohorques, *Colombia*	68	69	70	73	280	975
Dick Hart	71	69	74	66	280	975
Jerry Pittman	70	70	69	71	280	975
Bill Casper	67	67	74	72	280	975
Butch Baird	69	72	68	72	281	650
Julio Hernandez, *Colombia*	69	72	69	71	281	650
Malcolm Gregson, *Great Britain*	73	71	67	72	283	500
Manuel de la Torre	68	69	71	76	284	400
Florentino Molina, *Argentina*	66	71	75	72	284	400
Stan Mosel	69	71	70	74	284	400
Gary Groh, *Bahamas*	71	71	73	70	285	300
Wilf Homenuik, *Canada*	72	74	68	72	286	225
Alberto Rivadeneira, *Colombia*	72	70	75	69	286	225
Heraclio Valenzuela, *Colombia*	76	69	69	72	286	225
Miguel Sala, *Colombia*	73	69	72	73	287	172.50
Juan Pinzon, *Colombia*	73	72	71	71	287	172.50
Bob Benning	69	70	68	81	288	145
Oscar Nari, *Argentina*	73	73	74	68	288	145
Martin Arroyave, *Colimbia*	74	71	67	76	288	145
Bob Ross	74	69	70	76	289	125
Herb Hooper	73	70	76	73	292	73.34
Steve Oppermann	75	72	72	73	292	73.33
Siervo Calderon, *Ecuador*	70	74	73	75	292	73.33

MARACAIBO OPEN

MARACAIBO COUNTRY CLUB
Maracaibo, Venezuela
February 20—23
Purse....$15,500
Par: 36, 36—72

	SCORES				TOTAL	MONEY
Butch Baird	69	67	70	71	277	$3,000
Steve Oppermann	69	67	76	67	279	2,000
Jerry Barrier	73	72	67	68	280	1,500
Art Wall	70	70	68	73	281	1,200
Jerry Pittman	70	69	73	72	284	1,000
Florentino Molina, *Argentian*	73	71	69	72	285	900
Rommy Fonseca	74	71	68	73	286	800
Steve Lyles	68	69	77	73	287	650
Herb Hooper	70	71	69	77	287	650
Jimmy Day	70	74	71	73	288	500
Larry Mowry	74	77	69	69	289	400
Stan Mosel	70	76	70	73	289	400
Gene Borek	71	69	72	77	289	400
Anthony Clecak	70	77	73	71	291	258.34
Juan Pinzon, *Colombia*	75	75	69	72	291	258.33
Gary Groh, *Bahamas*	76	72	70	73	291	258.33
Wayne Etherton	74	73	73	72	292	175
Julio Polania, *Venezuela*	71	72	74	75	292	175
Mike Hadlock	72	67	79	74	292	175
Roberto de Vicenzo, *Argentina*	70	73	75	74	292	175
Malcolm Gregson, *Great Britain*	71	77	75	70	293	125
Alfonso Bohorquez, *Colombia*	70	77	73	73	293	125
Manuel de la Torre	70	72	77	74	293	125
Vicente Fernandez, Argentina	74	71	74	74	293	125
Earl Puckett	75	69	73	76	293	125

PANAMA OPEN

PANAMA GOLF CLUB
Panama City, Republic of Panama
Februay 27—March 2
Purse....$15,500
Par: 36, 36—72

	SCORES	TOTAL	MONEY
Butch Baird	65 71 71 69	276	$3,000
Rogelio Gonzalez, *Colombia*	64 70 70 72	276	1,750
Bob Ross	64 70 70 72	276	1,750

(Baird defeated Gonzalez and Ross in sudden-death playoff, Gonzalez eliminated on second extra hole, Ross on sixth.)

Bob Benning	68 69 70 70	277	1,100
Art Wall	70 72 65 70	277	1,100
Jerry Pittman	69 70 69 70	278	900
Stan Mosel	69 71 72 69	281	800
Gene Borek	69 71 73 69	282	700
Herb Hooper	74 73 71 67	285	516.67
Jerry Barrier	67 70 77 71	285	516.67
Florentino Molina, *Argentina*	68 71 72 74	285	516.66
Gary Groh, *Bahamas*	77 70 73 66	286	400
Bill Erfurth	73 71 74 70	288	325
Alfonso Bohorquez, *Colombia*	72 75 70 71	288	325
Roberto de Vicenzo, *Argentina*	74 72 72 72	290	250
Vicente Fernandez, *Argentina*	74 76 74 67	291	185
Malcolm Gregson, *Great Britain*	72 72 74 73	291	185
Larry Mowry	72 74 75 70	291	185
Earl Puckett	69 75 76 71	291	185
Jeff Voss	74 69 74 74	291	185
Tommy Fonseca	74 78 71 70	293	125
Arthur Paul	77 72 74 70	293	125
Richard Stranahan	69 74 76 74	293	125
Juan Pinzon, *Venezuela*	69 73 75 76	293	125
Joe Conrad	72 74 72 75	293	125

VALLE ARRIBA COUNTRY CLUB
Caracas, Venezuela
November 13–16
Purse....$25,000
Par: 35, 35–70....6,169 yards

	SCORES	TOTAL	MONEY
Peter Townsend, *Great Britain*	72 65 69 70	276	$5,000
Ramon Munoz, *Venezuela*	73 67 66 70	276	3,000
(Townsend defeated Munoz on first hole of sudden-death playoff)			
Bert Weaver	71 70 68 68	277	2,000
Roy Pace	71 68 68 72	279	1,800
Jerry Pittman	67 72 71 70	280	1,325
Jim Grant	67 67 74 72	280	1,325
Al Besselink	66 74 68 72	280	1,325
Herb Hooper	70 64 69 77	280	1,325
Dow Finsterwald	70 67 69 75	281	1,000
Larry Mowry	64 74 71 73	282	900
Butch Baird	70 77 67 69	283	775
Art Wall	76 67 71 69	283	775
Al Mengert	71 70 72 71	284	650
Wes Ellis	70 73 70 71	284	650
Jerry Barrier	69 72 69 74	284	650
Peter Mills, *Venezuela*	67 73 72 73	285	500
Dean Refram	69 72 68 77	286	500
Rocky Thompson	72 73 73 69	287	500
Teobaldo Perez, *Venezuela*	74 72 75 68	289	500
Stan Dudas	75 71 71 75	292	166.67
Monty Kaser	74 75 72 71	292	166.67
Bob Verwey, *South Africa*	72 72 72 76	292	166.66

† Independent of regular Caribbean Tour

British Tour

PENFOLD TOURNAMENT

HILL BARN GOLF CLUB
Worthing, Sussex
May 1−3
Purse...£4,000
Par: 35, 35−70...6,214 yards

	SCORES				TOTAL	MONEY
Alex Caygill	67	70	70	71	278	£731
Christie O'Connor	69	68	75	68	280	487
George Will	70	70	69	72	281	341
Peter Bulter	75	70	69	68	282	263
David Snell	74	71	71	67	283	214
Brian Huggett	73	72	70	69	284	102
Maurice Bembridge	72	71	69	72	284	102
David Talbot	72	70	71	71	284	102
Peter Oosterhuis	72	70	69	73	284	
David Webster	70	71	73	70	284	102
Doug Sewell	69	72	72	71	284	102
Peter Alliss	70	70	74	70	284	102
Neil Coles	71	68	71	74	284	102
Terry le Brocq	69	67	73	75	284	102
Brian Barnes	71	73	71	70	285	63
Dave Thomas	72	72	71	70	285	63
Mike Ingham	71	72	71	71	285	63
William Wilkinson	76	69	71	70	286	47
David Butler	72	73	72	69	286	47
Bill Large	70	74	72	70	286	47
Bernard Hunt	71	72	75	68	286	47
Gordon Cunningham	71	71	72	72	286	47
Richard Gerken	70	71	73	72	286	47
Bill Hector	75	69	70	74	288	34
Tony Grubb	76	67	77	69	289	34
Bernard Gallacher	70	71	75	73	289	63
Dai Rees	76	69	74	71	290	28
Jimmy Martin	76	69	72	73	290	28
David Huish	73	72	73	72	290	28
Alan Ibberson	72	72	72	74	290	28
Robin Davenport	71	73	76	70	290	28
Donald Slicer	72	71	73	74	290	43
Ken Bousfield	75	69	75	72	291	24
Eddie Polland	74	68	75	74	291	24
Hedley Muscroft	73	71	71	77	292	24
Hugh Boyle	76	68	78	71	293	21

	SCORES	TOTAL	MONEY
Cyril Pennington	70 74 77 72	293	21
Alex King	71 72 73 77	293	21
Harry Weetman	71 74 77 72	294	19
Bob Walker	71 74 77 73	295	19
Brian Allen	73 71 76 75	295	19

SCHWEPPES PGA CHAMPIONSHIP

ASHBURNHAM GOLF CLUB
Pembrey, Carmarthenshire
May 15—17
Purse...£5,385
Par: 36, 36—72...6,795 yards

	SCORES	TOTAL	MONEY
Bernard Gallacher	72 72 73 76	293	£1,024
John Garner	75 75 70 74	294	609
Guy Wolstenholme	70 71 74 79	294	609
Peter Oosterhuis	75 74 71 75	295	
Alex Caygill	71 75 75 74	295	292
Bernard Hunt	75 70 74 76	295	292
Brian Huggett	77 74 73 72	296	183
Brian Barnes	74 73 73 76	296	183
Doug Beattie	77 74 74 72	297	131
Paddy Skerritt	73 75 71 78	297	124
Peter Butler	72 76 72 77	297	124
Jimmy Hitchcock	74 73 74 76	297	124
Peter Alliss	76 75 72 75	298	93
Stan Peach, *Australia*	75 74 71 78	298	93
Bill Large	75 74 72 77	298	93
Christie O'Connor	72 80 77 71	300	76
Ronnie Shade	79 73 74 74	300	76
John Panton	74 74 73 79	300	76
Tommy Horton	73 74 75 78	300	76
Vincent Hood	74 78 74 75	301	61
Jimmy Kinsella	79 73 78 71	301	61
Bob Tuohy, *South Africa*	76 76 74 76	302	52
Craig DeFoy	78 71 79 74	302	52
Alan Ibberson	70 77 77 78	302	52
Tony Grubb	77 75 76 75	303	46
Eric Brown	77 74 77 75	303	46
Tony Parcell	76 74 77 76	303	46
David Vaughan	75 72 73 83	303	71
David Snell	75 77 77 75	304	39
Lionel Platts	77 75 74 78	304	39
Cyril Pennington	76 75 75 78	304	39

	SCORES	TOTAL	MONEY
Nick Job	73 77 77 77	304	39
Robin Davenport	76 72 77 79	304	39
David Butler	75 75 77 78	305	34
John Hudson	71 78 75 81	305	34
Jimmy Martin	76 73 75 81	305	34
Hedley Muscroft	74 78 75 79	306	29
Derek Small	75 76 80 75	306	29
Eddie Polland	77 74 76 79	306	29
Patrick Lee	77 74 75 80	306	29
David Webster	75 75 75 81	306	29
George Will	75 77 75 81	308	19
Stuart Levermore	76 74 75 83	308	19
Hugh Jackson	75 75 75 83	308	19
Dave Thomas	73 77 76 82	308	19
Allen Gillies	75 76 79 79	309	19
Michael Murphy	79 71 79 80	309	19
Ernie Jones	75 77 77 81	310	19
Alastair Barr	75 77 79 80	311	19
Michael Gunn	74 78 84 78	314	19
Ian Connelly	74 75 81 84	314	19
Neil Coles	74 74 WD		19

AGFACOLOR FILM TOURNAMENT

STOKE POGES GOLF CLUB
Nr. Slough, Buckinghamshire
May 22—24
Purse...£4,250
Par: 36, 35—71...6,607 yards

	SCORES	TOTAL	MONEY
Brian Barnes	72 71 67 67	277	£731
Bernard Gallacher	73 74 68 65	280	512
Bryon Hutchinson	68 73 72 69	282	336
Dave Thomas	69 78 67 70	284	234
Neil Coles	70 73 72 69	284	234
Peter Butler	71 72 72 70	285	141
Maurice Bembridge	71 71 69 74	285	141
Bernard Hunt	73 73 71 69	286	93
Tony Grubb	70 75 68 73	286	93
Stan Peach, *Australia*	74 71 69 72	286	93
Christie O'Connor	72 70 71 73	286	93
John Hudson	74 73 68 72	287	65
George Will	74 72 69 72	287	65
Peter Alliss	75 70 70 72	287	65
Tommy Horton	71 72 75 69	287	65
Peter Thomson, *Australia*	71 71 73 72	287	65

	SCORES	TOTAL	MONEY
Eric Brown	70 71 72 74	287	65
Guy Hunt	74 71 70 73	288	56
Brian Huggett	72 73 71 73	289	55
Cyril Pennington	74 73 72 71	290	52
Richard Davis	71 75 73 71	290	52
David Bulter	73 72 72 73	290	52
Robin Davenport	69 75 71 75	290	52
Gordon Cunningham	72 75 72 72	291	49
Hedley Muscroft	69 75 72 75	291	49
Peter Oosterhuis	67 76 76 72	291	
Alex Caygill	75 71 75 71	292	47
Bill Large	75 69 75 73	292	47
Doug Beattie	74 75 70 74	293	42
Guy Wolstenholme	74 75 71 73	293	42
Doug Sewell	71 77 72 73	293	42
Roger Fidler	73 74 74 72	293	42
David Huish	74 72 73 74	293	42
Marshall Douglas	70 74 75 74	293	42
Patrick Lee	66 77 74 76	293	42
Bob Tuohy, *South Africa*	71 71 74 77	293	42
Clive Clark	73 76 77 68	294	37
David Webster	68 74 78 74	294	37
Manuel Ballesteros, *Spain*	71 77 76 71	295	50
Ian Richardson	72 74 71 78	295	36
John Panton	73 76 75 73	297	22
Lionel Platts	74 74 73 76	297	22
David Jones	73 76 74 75	298	10
Eddie Polland	69 76 76 78	299	10
Peter Jones	75 74 75 78	302	10
Stuart Murray	74 74 78 76	302	10

DAKS TOURNAMENT

WENTWORTH GOLF CLUB—WEST COURSE
Virginia Water, Surrey
May 29—31
Purse...£5,000
Par: 36, 38—74...6,997 yards

	SCORES	TOTAL	MONEY
Brian Huggett	71 71 75 72	289	£975
Bernard Gallacher	71 68 75 77	291	653
George Will	73 76 71 72	292	439
Richard Davies	75 76 68 74	293	292
Christie O'Connor	71 73 74 75	293	292
John Garner	72 75 73 75	295	183
Neil Coles	74 72 75 74	295	183

397

	SCORES	TOTAL	MONEY
Tony Grubb	72 75 74 76	297	122
Jimmy Hitchcock	72 75 76 74	297	122
Ken Bousfield	74 72 76 75	297	122
Hugh Jackson	76 75 75 73	299	90
Ronnie Shade	72 75 77 75	299	90
David Snell	75 72 76 77	300	83
Clive Clark	74 77 76 74	301	76
Guy Hunt	74 75 75 77	301	76
Maurice Bembridge	82 70 79 72	303	63
Bernard Hunt	79 72 77 75	303	63
Craig Defoy	79 72 71 81	303	63
Bill Hector	76 76 76 76	304	50
Graham Henning, *South Africa*	74 78 77 75	304	50
Nick Job	71 75 77 81	304	65
Guy Wolstenholme	74 77 79 75	305	45
Valentin Barrios, *Spain*	76 75 74 80	305	45
Bill Large	77 71 79 78	305	45
John Panton	72 75 81 77	305	45
Patrick Lee	76 75 76 79	306	42
Richard Emery	73 77 78 78	306	42
Dai Rees	76 72 78 80	306	42
Bob Tuohy, *South Africa*	74 77 79 77	307	38
Jimmy Kinsella	73 77 76 81	307	38
Marshall Douglas	74 74 78 81	307	38
John Larrad	72 73 81 81	307	38
Stan Peach, *Australia*	75 77 79 77	308	35
David Butler	74 78 78 78	308	35
David Jones	74 76 78 80	308	35
Basil Proudfoot	74 75 78 82	309	33
Terry le Brocq	73 76 86 74	309	33
Eddie Polland	70 76 86 80	312	31

SUMRIE TOURNAMENT

PANNAL GOLF CLUB
Harrogate, Yorkshire
June 4—7
Purse...£7,500
Par: 36, 37—73...6,738 yards

	SCORES	TOTAL	MONEY
Maurice Bembridge	66 65 66 66	263	£975
Angel Gallardo, *Spain*			975
Hedley Muscroft	66 65 64 69	264	487
Lionel Platts			487
Martin Roesink, *Holland*	69 65 65 68	267	252
Ronnie Shade			252

398

	SCORES	TOTAL	MONEY
Malcolm Gregson	68 70 61 68	267	252
Brian Huggett			252
Bernard Hunt	69 64 65 69	267	252
Neil Coles			252
Peter Butler	71 66 67 65	269	158
Clive Clark			158
Peter Alliss	75 65 64 65	269	158
Dave Thomas			158
Guy Hunt	67 68 72 63	270	117
Vincent Hood			117
Graham Henning, *South Africa*	72 65 65 68	270	117
Cobie Legrange, *South Africa*			117
Hugh Jackson	71 68 65 69	273	97
Bobby Walker			97
Brian Barnes	68 67 70 69	274	85
Bill Large			85
Valentin Barrios, *Spain*	68 69 68 69	274	85
Gordon Cunningham			85
Bryon Hutchinson	70 68 70 67	275	67
David Talbot			67
Peter Matkovich, *South Africa*	72 68 68 67	275	67
Stan Peach, *Australia*			67
Brian Allen	72 67 67 69	275	67
Robin Davenport			67
Richard Emery	67 69 68 71	275	67
Sean Hunt			67
Harry Weetman	68 70 71 67	276	47
George Will			47
Hugh Boyle	70 68 70 68	276	47
Tony Grubb			47
Christie O'Connor	70 70 68 68	276	47
Jimmy Kinsella			47
Ian Clark	70 69 68 69	276	47
Eddie Polland			47
Bob Tuohy, *South Africa*	72 67 69 69	277	41
John Cockin			41
Craig DeFoy	70 70 68 69	277	41
Nick Job			41
Jimmy Hume	72 67 70 73	282	40
George Parton			40
Nick Lynch	70 70 73 72	285	39
Paddy Skerrit			39

MARTINI INTERNATIONAL TOURNAMENT

QUEEN'S PARK GOLF CLUB
Bournemouth, Hampshire
June 12—14
Purse...£7,000
Par: 37, 35—72...6,487 yards

	SCORES				TOTAL	MONEY
Graham Henning, *South Africa*	73	69	68	72	282	£1,075
Alex Caygill	70	66	77	69	282	1,075
John Garner	70	74	73	67	284	650
Brian Huggett	72	67	73	73	285	500
Bob Tuohy	73	75	69	69	286	375
Neil Coles	72	73	71	71	287	250
Bernard Hunt	71	72	70	74	287	250
Denis Hutchinson	76	74	71	67	288	175
Tony Grubb	73	73	69	73	288	175
Vincent Hood	72	72	70	74	288	175
Angel Gallardo	72	70	73	73	288	175
Guy Wolstenholme	75	73	71	70	289	140
Doug Sewell	75	71	69	74	289	140
Bernard Gallacher	72	73	72	72	289	140
Peter Thomson, *Australia*	74	72	72	72	290	115
Peter Butler	68	74	73	75	290	115
Hugh Jackson	79	70	70	72	291	90
Hedley Muscroft	71	74	72	74	291	90
Maurice Bembridge	69	72	75	75	291	90
Barry Franklin, *South Africa*	70	77	71	74	292	68
Ken Bousfield	73	73	73	73	292	68
Nick Job	72	73	73	74	292	68
Bill Large	78	70	71	74	293	61
Guy Hunt	76	71	76	70	293	61
Cobie Legrange, *South Africa*	72	75	71	75	293	61
Gordon Cunningham	74	73	75	71	293	61
Christie O'Connor	70	80	71	73	294	53
George Will	77	73	73	71	294	53
Peter Oosterhuis	77	72	70	75	294	53
Dave Thomas	74	75	73	72	294	53
John Panton	75	75	71	74	295	48
Jimmy Martin	73	69	78	75	295	48
Alfonso Angelini, *Italy*	74	76	70	76	296	46
David Snell	71	76	75	74	296	46
Jimmy Kinsella	72	78	75	74	299	43
Harry Bannerman	71	77	75	76	299	43
David Bulter	71	76	74	78	299	43
Bryon Hutchinson	74	73	75	77	299	43
Peter Alliss	75	74	75	76	300	41

	SCORES	TOTAL	MONEY
Ronnie Shade	76 74 74 77	301	30
Tommy Horton	76 71 81 73	301	30
Fred Boobyer	73 76 77 76	302	20
Cyril Pennington	77 68 80 77	302	20
Stan Peach, *Australia*	73 77 73 80	303	20
Brian Barnes	74 74 DQ		20

CARROLLS INTERNATIONAL TOURNAMENT

WOODBROOK GOLF CLUB
Woodbrook, Dublin
June 20—22
Purse...£10,000
Par: 38, 36—74...6,666 yards

	SCORES	TOTAL	MONEY
Ronnie Shade	73 73 72 71	289	£1,999
Bernard Gallacher	75 71 70 74	290	1,462
Brian Huggett	73 73 74 73	293	829
Christie O'Connor	74 70 76 73	293	829
Maurice Bembridge	75 71 74 74	294	439
Bernard Hunt	76 69 73 76	294	439
Hugh Jackson	72 78 74 71	295	341
Mike Ingram	74 78 70 75	297	244
Clive Clark	75 72 74 76	297	244
Tony Grubb	71 73 78 75	297	130
Peter Butler	75 77 73 73	298	130
Brian Barnes	75 76 72 75	298	130
Martin Roesink, *Holland*	74 73 74 77	298	97
Christy Greene	76 76 72 75	299	97
Dave Thomas	73 76 73 77	299	97
Bill Large	75 74 78 72	299	97
Craig DeFoy	73 76 74 76	299	97
Alex Caygill	74 72 77 76	299	97
Neil Coles	78 74 75 73	300	89
Bryon Hutchinson	72 78 77 73	300	89
David Talbot	77 75 72 77	301	81
Kel Nagle, *Australia*	75 77 73 76	301	81
David Snell	72 78 76 75	301	81
Stan Peach, *Australia*	76 74 77 74	301	81
Jimmy Kinsella	72 78 78 73	301	81
Graham Everett	76 74 74 77	301	93
Guy Hunt	74 78 74 76	302	73
Norman Drew	75 74 77 76	302	73
Bob Tuohy, *South Africa*	74 78 74 77	303	68
Michael Murphy	75 74 75 79	303	68
George Will	71 77 77 78	303	68

	SCORES				TOTAL	MONEY
*Paddy Caul	77	75	76	75	303	
Harry Bannerman	75	74	80	75	304	64
John Garner	74	76	77	79	306	61
Gordon Gray	76	74	73	83	306	61
Marshall Douglas	76	76	76	79	307	56
Ken Bousfield	74	77	80	76	307	56
David Webster	74	77	75	81	307	56
Ernie Jones	74	74	82	77	307	56
Cyril Pennington	75	74	81	78	308	50
Ralph Moffitt	73	76	81	78	308	50

* Amateur

BOWMAKER TOURNAMENT

SUNNINGDALE GOLF CLUB, OLD COURSE
Sunningdale, Berkshire
June 30–July 1
Purse...£3,000
Par: 35, 35–70...6,348 yards

	SCORES		TOTAL	MONEY
Brian Huggett	68	67	135	£489
Tony Grubb	67	68	135	489
Peter Butler	67	69	136	195
George Will	66	70	136	195
Maurice Bembridge	67	70	137	96
Bernard Hunt	70	67	137	96
Neil Coles	67	70	137	96
Bill Large	70	67	137	96
Guy Hunt	68	70	138	68
Peter Thomson, *Australia*	70	69	139	59
Doug Sewell	67	73	140	10
Cyril Pennington	71	69	140	10
Eric Brown	72	69	141	10
John Panton	69	72	141	10
Tommy Horton	71	70	141	10
Peter Alliss	73	68	141	10
Malcolm Gregson	72	69	141	10
Gordon Cunningham	73	68	141	10
Bryon Hutchinson	69	72	141	10
Norman Von Nida, *Australia*	69	73	142	10
Bill Casper, *U.S.*	71	71	142	10
Clive Clark	70	72	142	10
David Snell	70	72	142	10
David Talbot	71	72	143	10
Graham Henning, *South Africa*	74	70	144	10

	SCORES	TOTAL	MONEY
Jimmy Hitchcock	70 74	144	10
Vincent Hood	71 73	144	10
Jimmy Martin	75 69	144	10
Guy Wolstenholme	71 73	144	10
Fred Boobyer	75 69	144	10
Hedley Muscroft	72 73	145	10
Richard Emery	77 68	145	10
Peter Ackerley	72 73	145	10
Bob Tuohy, *South Africa*	74 71	145	10
Dave Thomas	74 72	146	10
Dai Rees	74 72	146	10
Bobby Locke, *South Africa*	72 74	146	10
Arthur Lees	74 72	146	10
Lionel Platts	76 70	146	10
Hugh Jackson	76 71	147	10
Stan Peach, *Australia*	75 72	147	10
Harry Bannerman	72 76	148	10
David Webster	74 74	148	10
Craig DeFoy	73 75	148	10
Denis Hutchinson, *South Africa*	72 77	149	10
Martin Roesink, *Holland*	73 76	149	10
Nick Lynch	73 77	150	10
Eddie Polland	77 75	152	10
Patrick Lee	83 73	156	10
John Ince, *Zambia*	86 85	171	10

BRITISH OPEN CHAMPIONSHIP

ROYAL LYTHAM & ST. ANNES GOLF CLUB
St. Annes-on-Sea, Lancashire
July 9—12
Purse...£30,335
Par: 35, 36—71...6,848 yards

	SCORES	TOTAL	MONEY
Tony Jacklin	68 70 70 72	280	£4,250
Bob Charles, *New Zealand*	66 69 75 72	282	3,000
Peter Thomson, *Australia*	71 70 70 72	283	2,125
Roberto de Vicenzo, *Argentina*	72 73 66 72	283	2,125
Christie O'Connor	71 65 74 74	284	1,750
Davis Love, *U.S.*	70 73 71 71	285	1,375
Jack Nicklaus, *U.S.*	75 70 68 72	285	1,375
Peter Alliss	73 74 73 66	286	1,100
Kel Nagle, *Australia*	74 71 72 70	287	1,000
Miller Barber, *U.S.*	69 75 75 69	288	900
Neil Coles	75 76 70 68	289	657
Cobie Legrange, *South Africa*	79 70 71 69	289	657

	SCORES	TOTAL	MONEY
Guy Wolstenholme	70 71 76 72	289	657
Tommy Horton	71 76 70 72	289	657
Gay Brewer, *U.S.*	76 71 68 75	290	480
Peter Townsend	73 70 76 72	291	327
Harold Henning, *South Africa*	72 71 75 73	291	327
Eric Brown	73 76 69 73	291	327
Brian Huggett	72 72 69 78	291	327
Bruce Devlin, *Australia*	71 73 75 72	291	327
Orville Moody, *U.S.*	71 70 74 76	291	327
Bert Yancey, *U.S.*	72 71 71 77	291	327
Bernard Hunt	73 71 75 73	292	225
Gary Player, *South Africa*	74 68 76 74	292	225
Fred Boobyer	74 70 76 73	293	202
Alex Caygill	71 67 79 76	293	202
Bill Casper, *U.S.*	70 70 75 78	293	202
Hedley Muscroft	68 77 73 76	294	190
*Peter Tupling	73 71 78 72	294	
Donald Swaelens, *Belgium*	72 73 76 74	295	177
Jean Garaialde, *France*	69 77 76 73	295	177
Mike Ingham	73 73 74 75	295	177
Max Faulkner	71 74 76 74	295	177
Brian Waites	73 75 74 74	296	152
Vincent Hood	75 71 74 76	296	152
John Garner	72 71 76 77	296	152
Gordon Cunningham	74 72 71 79	296	152
Ray Floyd, *U.S.*	74 70 76 76	296	152
Lee Trevino, *U.S.*	75 72 71 78	296	152
Brian Barnes	73 73 76 75	297	132
Jimmy Hitchcock	74 74 73 76	297	132
Peter Wilcock	73 74 74 77	298	125
Angel Gallardo, *Spain*	72 76 73 77	298	125
*Mike Bonallack	74 72 73 79	298	
John Panton	73 69 76 82	300	125
Hugh Jackson	69 78 75 79	301	125

OUT OF FINAL 18 HOLES

	SCORES	TOTAL
Jimmy Martin	72 79 72	223
Craig DeFoy	72 76 75	223
Bernard Gallacher	70 78 75	223
Antonio Garrido, *Spain*	79 71 73	223
*Jimmy Buckley	73 75 75	223
*Bruce Fleisher, *U.S.*	74 73 76	223
Dai Rees	75 75 74	224
Maurice Bembridge	73 76 75	224
Tony Fisher	75 73 76	224

	SCORES	TOTAL
Martin Roesink, *Holland*	76 75 74	225
Robin Davenport	75 76 74	225
David Snell	75 74 76	225
Richard Livingston	75 74 76	225
Tony Grubb	73 74 78	225
Bobby Walker	73 74 78	225
Hugh Lewis	75 72 78	225
*William Humphreys	76 74 75	225
Paddy Skerritt	79 72 75	226
Malcolm Gregson	77 74 75	226
David Huish	77 74 75	226
Jimmy Hume	72 76 78	226
Ronnie Shade	73 74 79	226
Gardner Dickinson, *U.S.*	76 74 76	226
Nick Job	72 79 76	227
Valentin Barrios, *Spain*	73 75 79	227
Dave Thomas	76 75 77	228
John McGuirk	76 74 78	228

OUT OF FINAL 36 HOLES

	SCORES	TOTAL
Barry Franklin, *South Africa*	74 78	152
Nick Lynch	76 76	152
Bobby Cole, *South Africa*	78 74	152
David Butler	78 74	152
David Talbot	77 75	152
Jack Wilkshire	76 76	152
Michael Murphy	83 69	152
Rich Bassett, *U.S.*	78 75	153
Brian Allen	78 75	153
Sean Hunt	74 79	153
Lionel Platts	83 70	153
Ross Whitehead	82 71	153
*Rodney Foster	74 79	153
Harry Bannerman	75 79	154
Peter Oosterhuis	74 80	154
Ernie Jones	78 76	154
Bill Large	75 79	154
Allen Gillies	77 77	154
Mike Hoyle	77 77	154
Bud Edmundson	77 77	154
Guy Hunt	76 79	155
David Parsonage	80 75	155
George Evans	79 76	155
Roger Livesey	76 79	155
Manuel Ballesteros, *Spain*	80 75	155
Norman Drew	78 77	155
*Dale Hayes, *South Africa*	80 75	155

	SCORES	TOTAL
Pat McGuirk	79 77	156
George Tomlinson	77 79	156
Donald Gammon, *South Africa*	75 81	156
Richard Anderson	72 85	157
Peter Butler	80 77	157
David Ridley	79 78	157
Abdul Halim, *Egypt*	80 77	157
Jimmy Kinsella	78 80	158
*John Kippax	78 80	158
Jock Burns	81 78	159
William Ferguson	79 80	159
Hugh Boyle	76 83	159
*Michael King	81 78	159
Mick Notley	79 81	160
Ken Morrison	83 77	160
George Will	81 79	160
Roy Williamson	80 80	160
Bill McHardy	77 84	161
Maurice Moir	81 81	162
Bill Hector	77 85	162
*Reg Glading	82 80	162
Richard Emery	77 86	163
Alan Hall	82 82	164
Mario Napoleoni, *Italy*	84 80	164
Sandy Wilson	82 83	165
Aldo Casera, *Italy*	77 89	166
Howard Bennett	85 84	169
Dudley Millensted	78 WD	
Stuart Brown	79 DQ	
George Archer, *U.S.*	79 WD	

* Amateur

PICCADILLY MEDAL

PRINCE'S GOLF CLUB
Sandwich Bay, Kent
July 16—19
Purse...£7,000
Par: 35, 37—72...6,974 yards

FIRST ROUND
Hugh Jackson defeated Maurice Bembridge, 71—80.
Doug Beattie defeated Richard Davies, 72—79.
Neil Coles defeated Bill Large, 72—76.
Guy Hunt defeated Jimmy Martin, 72—74.

Peter Alliss defeated Vincent Hood, 71—75.
Fred Boobyer defeated Hugh Boyle, 72—80.
Robin Davenport defeated Ken Bousfield, 73—76.
Tony Jacklin defeated Cyril Pennington, 70—75.
Terry le Brocq defeated Richard Emery, 76—82.
Bernard Gallacher defeated Lionel Platts, 72—75.
Tony Grubb defeated Ronnie Shade, 73—76.
Craig DeFoy defeated David Snell, 74—75.
Christie O'Connor defeated David Butler, 75—76.
Peter Oosterhuis defeated Alan Ibberson, 75—79.
Jimmy Hitchcock defeated Malcolm Gregson, 75—77.
John Panton defeated Nick Lynch, 78—81.
Jimmy Kinsella defeated Mike Ingham, 77—80.
Sean Hunt defeated Alex Caygill, 80—81.
Bob Tuohy (South Africa) defeated Harry Bannerman, 73—79.
Gordon Cunningham defeated Dave Thomas, 72—79.
George Will defeated Nick Job, 70—73.
Tommy Horton defeated Hedley Muscroft, 72—78.
Bryon Hutchinson defeated Dai Rees, 74—77.
Brian Barnes defeated Bobby Walker, 76—78.
Patrick Lee defeated Max Faulkner, 80—81.
Brian Huggett defeated David Talbot, 68—78.
Harry Weetman defeated Bill Hector, 76—79.
Doug Sewell defeated Allen Gillies, 74—75.
Eric Brown defeated Roger Fidler, 73—79.
John Garner defeated David Webster, 76—76, 20th hole.
Eddie Polland defeated Bernard Hunt, 74—80.
Clive Clark defeated Paddy Skerritt, 74—75.

(Each defeated player received £25.)

SECOND ROUND

Kinsella defeated Sean Hunt, 72—73.
Cunningham defeated Tuohy, 73—75.
Will defeated Horton, 69—73.
Barnes defeated Hutchinson by default.
Huggett defeated Lee, 73—73, 20th hole.
Garner defeated Weetman, 74—75.
Sewell defeated Brown, 78—82.
Clark defeated Polland, 75—75, 19th hole.
Jackson defeated Beattie, 74—77.
Guy Hunt defeated Coles, 76—81.
Alliss defeated Boobyer, 74—76.
Jacklin defeated Davenport, 71—72.
Gallacher defeated le Brocq, 73—73, 21st hole.
Grubb defeated DeFoy, 73—74.
O'Connor defeated Oosterhuis, 73—76.
Panton defeated Hitchcock, 74—77

(Each dcfeated player received £50.)

THIRD ROUND

Cunningham defeated Kinsella, 75—78.
Will defeated Barnes, 73—74.
Huggett defeated Garner, 73—76.
Sewell defeated Clark, 73—78.
Jackson defeated Guy Hunt, 70—83.
Alliss defeated Jacklin, 69—71.
Gallacher defeated Grubb, 72—73.
Panton defeated O'Connor, 72—73.

(Each defeated player received £125.)

FOURTH ROUND

Alliss defeated Jackson, 78—78, 22nd hole.
Panton defeated Gallacher, 72—72, 20th hole.
Will defeated Cunningham, 71—79.
Huggett defeated Sewell, 73—74.

(Each defeated player received £225.)

SEMI-FINALS

Will defeated Huggett, 73—73, 20th hole.
Alliss defeated Panton, 74—76.

(Huggett and Panton received £500.)

FINALS

Alliss defeated Will, 76—73—149 to 74—75—149, 37th hole.

(Alliss received £1,500; Will £1,000.)

GALLAHER ULSTER OPEN

SHANDON PARK GOLF CLUB
Belfast, Ireland
July 31—August 2
Purse...£4,000
Par: 34, 36—70...6,100 yards

	SCORES	TOTAL	MONEY
Christie O'Connor	65 69 68 69	271	£683
Malcolm Gregson	70 69 67 68	274	299
Bernard Hunt	72 65 71 66	274	299
Jimmy Martin	70 65 69 70	274	299
Norman Drew	71 69 65 69	274	299
Peter Butler	73 68 67 67	275	156
Alex Caygill	71 69 68 68	276	111
Tommy Horton	71 68 68 69	276	111
Tony Grubb	70 67 72 67	276	111
David Webster	72 68 66 71	277	91

	SCORES	TOTAL	MONEY
Bryon Hutchinson	71 68 71 67	277	91
Terry le Brocq	68 71 69 69	277	91
Eddie Polland	71 71 66 70	278	62
Neil Coles	71 69 69 69	278	62
Robert Anderson	69 70 70 69	278	62
John Garner	67 71 72 68	278	62
Maurice Bembridge	68 69 69 72	278	62
Harry Bannerman	71 69 69 70	279	52
Hedley Muscroft	69 70 71 69	279	52
Bobby Walker	72 65 73 69	279	52
Gordon Cunningham	66 70 70 73	279	52
Bernard Gallacher	65 70 68 76	279	52
Hugh Boyle	74 68 70 68	280	49
Jimmy Hitchcock	70 70 70 70	280	49
David Snell	69 73 71 68	281	41
David Butler	71 70 69 71	281	41
Norman Wood	71 69 69 72	281	41
Peter Matkovich, *South Africa*	73 67 72 69	281	41
Cyril Pennington	73 67 73 68	281	41
Michael Murphy	72 70 68 72	282	35
Derek Small	68 72 69 73	282	35
David Talbot	69 70 72 71	282	35
Paddy Skerritt	69 68 76 69	282	35
Frank Rennie	72 70 71 70	283	33
David Vaughan	70 72 69 72	283	33
Nick Lynch	69 73 68 73	283	33
Denis Hutchinson, *South Africa*	71 68 71 74	284	29
Christy Greene	69 70 74 71	284	29
Jimmy Kinsella	72 66 73 73	284	29
Robin Davenport	69 72 69 75	285	4
David Carson	70 64 76 75	285	4
Cobie Legrange, *South Africa*	70 72 74 70	286	4
Ernie Jones	70 70 75 71	286	4
Pat McGuirk	71 71 73 72	287	4
Graham Burroughs	74 68 74 72	288	4
Alan Ibberson	68 74 73 73	288	4
Bill Large	72 70 77 77	296	4

RTV RENTALS INTERNATIONAL TOURNAMENT

CORK GOLF CLUB
Little Island, Cork
August 8—10
Purse...£5,000
Par: 36, 35—71...6,271 yards

	SCORES	TOTAL	MONEY
Peter Butler	67 67 68 71	273	£975
Cobie Legrange, *South Africa*	69 68 68 71	276	536
Bernard Hunt	63 68 71 74	276	536
Tommy Horton	66 67 73 71	277	341
Bryon Hutchinson	69 71 69 70	279	292
Gordon Cunningham	74 66 69 71	280	219
Cyril Pennington	71 70 69 71	281	154
Clive Clark	70 71 67 73	281	154
Brian Huggett	66 74 71 70	281	154
George Will	74 67 70 71	282	81
David Butler	72 69 69 72	282	81
Jimmy Kinsella	70 70 68 74	282	81
John Panton	70 69 71 72	282	81
Neil Coles	67 69 74 72	282	81
Harry Bannerman	73 69 71 70	283	54
Hugh Jackson	70 72 71 70	283	54
Maurice Bembridge	70 71 71 71	283	54
David Webster	72 70 72 69	283	54
Christie O'Connor	69 69 71 74	283	54
David Talbot	68 71 73 72	284	47
Guy Hunt	71 72 72 70	285	44
Nick Job	72 70 69 74	285	44
Terry le Brocq	71 70 70 74	285	44
Jimmy Hitchcock	68 71 71 75	285	44
Malcolm Gregson	67 72 70 76	285	44
Marshall Douglas	71 71 69 75	286	39
Bob Tuohy, *South Africa*	72 69 73 72	286	39
Dai Rees	65 73 74 74	286	39
Hedley Muscroft	68 69 74 75	286	39
Jimmy Martin	71 71 73 72	287	37
Bernard Gallacher	72 70 73 72	287	37
Lionel Platts	70 73 72 73	288	34
Gordon Gray	71 72 73 72	288	34
Jimmy Kinsella	70 68 78 72	288	34
Tony Grubb	71 66 72 79	288	34
Dave Thomas	68 72 73 76	289	31
Robin Davenport	69 69 75 76	289	31
*T. Egan	73 69 73 75	290	
Michael Murphy	69 73 75 74	291	29

410

	SCORES	TOTAL	MONEY
Peter Wilcock	72 71 76 73	292	29
Norman Wood	73 70 76 76	295	29
Denis Hutchinson, *South Africa*	70 70 79 76	295	29
Nick Lynch	71 71 74 81	297	29
*E. Higgins	70 73 74 82	299	
Donald Ross	71 72 76 82	301	29
Peter Matkovich, *South Africa*	69 71 76 85	301	29

* Amateur

WILLS TOURNAMENT

MOOR PARK GOLF CLUB, HIGH COURSE
Rickmansworth, Hertfordshire
August 13—16
Purse...£7,350
Par: 37, 35—72...6,652 yards

	SCORES	TOTAL	MONEY
Bernard Gallacher	71 68 63 73	275	£1,258
Christie O'Connor	69 69 68 70	276	877
Maurice Bembridge	69 72 68 68	277	539
Brian Huggett	70 65 69 73	277	539
Dave Thomas	71 66 71 70	278	366
Peter Oosterhuis	68 69 71 71	279	253
Neil Coles	71 68 68 72	279	253
Tommy Horton	72 71 65 72	280	200
Malcolm Gregson	72 68 72 69	281	163
Brian Barnes	70 71 69 71	281	163
Tony Grubb	73 69 70 70	282	132
John Garner	67 71 72 72	282	132
Cobie Legrange, *South Africa*	69 71 71 72	283	119
Peter Gill	70 72 69 72	283	119
John Panton	72 70 72 70	284	110
Harry Weetman	71 68 72 73	284	110
Peter Thomson, *Australia*	72 71 71 71	285	95
Craig DeFoy	69 70 72 74	285	95
Bernard Hunt	71 66 72 76	285	95
Dai Rees	65 69 75 76	285	95
Guy Hunt	72 70 72 72	286	84
Peter Alliss	72 70 71 73	286	84
Jimmy Hitchcock	67 70 76 73	286	84
Doug Sewell	72 68 72 75	287	80
Bill Large	71 71 75 71	288	77
Gordon Cunningham	70 71 75 72	288	77
Lionel Platts	70 73 71 75	289	74
Doug Beattie	71 72 75 72	290	69

	SCORES	TOTAL	MONEY
Michael Murphy	71 73 74 72	290	69
Hedley Muscroft	73 70 74 73	290	69
Roger Fidler	69 72 74 75	290	69
George Low	71 71 74 75	291	63
Sean Hunt	70 74 72 75	291	63
Nick Job	70 73 76 73	292	75
James Hulme	73 71 75 73	292	58
Christopher Baker	73 68 77 74	292	92
Peter Matkovich, *South Africa*	75 68 75 74	292	58
David Vaughan	72 70 75 75	292	58
David Snell	71 73 76 73	293	51
Mike Ingham	71 73 78 72	294	37
Keith MacDonald	72 71 77 74	294	37
Roger Janes	73 69 77 76	295	24
Derek Nash	72 72 77 77	298	49

PGA MATCH PLAY CHAMPIONSHIP
(News of the World)

WALTON HEATH GOLF CLUB
Tadworth, Surrey
September 2—7
Purse...£5,020
Par: 35, 38—73...7,157 yards

FIRST ROUND
Neil Coles defeated Peter Wilcock, 2 and 1.
John Garner defeated Doug Beattie, 1 up.
Ronnie Shade defeated Eddie Polland, 3 and 1.
Tommy Horton defeated Bobby Walker, 5 and 4.
Lionel Platts defeated Eric Stillwell, 7 and 5.
Sean Hunt defeated Peter Blaze, 7 and 5.
Derek Small defeated Bernard Firkins, 2 and 1.
Brian Huggett defeated Terry le Brocq, 5 and 4.
Dai Rees defeated Jimmy Martin, 1 up, 19 holes.
Robert Richards defeated John Little, 4 and 3.
Guy Hunt defeated Geoffrey Norton, 2 and 1.
Peter Oosterhuis defeated David Vaughan, 3 and 2.
Hugh Jackson defeated Malcolm Gregson, 1 up.
Reg Hill defeated Marshall Douglas, 1 up.
Cyril Pennington defeated Stuart Murray, 1 up.
Jimmy Hitchcock defeated Clive Clark, 4 and 3.
William Wilkinson defeated Bernard Hunt, 4 and 3.
Ian Mac Donald defeated Eddie Cogle, 4 and 3.
Leslie Hooker defeated Leslie Jones, 7 and 5.
Alex King defeated George Johnson, 3 and 2.
David Talbot defeated Stuart Levermore, 2 and 1.

Tony Fisher defeated John Ellis, 1 up.

Bryon Hutchinson defeated Geoffrey Pook, 1 up.

Peter Thomson (Australia) defeated David Snell, 7 and 6.

David Webster defeated Peter Gill, 1 up.

Brian Bamford defeated Denis Scanlan, 3 and 2.

Maurice Bembridge defeated Richard Emery, 6 and 4.

Roger Fidler defeated John Hudson, 1 up, 19 holes.

Brian Waites defeated Nicholas Underwood, 5 and 4.

Tony Grubb defeated Bill Large, 1 up.

Robin Page defeated Jack Wiltshire, 2 and 1.

Ken Bousfield defeated Peter Butler, 2 up.

(Each defeated player received £24.7)

SECOND ROUND

Coles defeated Garner, 5 and 4.

Shade defeated Horton, 5 and 4.

Sean Hunt defeated Platts, 3 and 1.

Huggett defeated Small, 2 up.

Rees defeated Richards, 6 and 4.

Oosterhuis defeated Guy Hunt, 3 and 1.

Jackson defeated Hill, 1 up.

Hitchcock defeated Pennington, 4 and 3.

MacDonald defeated Wilkinson, 2 and 1.

Hooker defeated King, 1 up.

Talbot defeated Fisher, 4 and 3.

Hutchinson defeated Thomson, 1 up, 21 holes.

Webster defeated Fidler, 7 and 6.

Bembridge defeated Bamford, 7 and 6.

Waites defeated Grubb, 1 up.

Bousfield defeated Page, 4 and 3.

(Each defeated player received £39)

THIRD ROUND

Coles defeated Shade, 7 and 6.

Huggett defeated Hunt, 5 and 4.

Rees defeated Oosterhuis, 1 up.

Jackson defeated Hitchcock, 2 and 1.

Hooker defeated MacDonald, 1 up, 21 holes.

Talbot defeated Hutchinson, 3 and 2.

Bembridge defeated Webster, 4 and 2.

Waites defeated Bousfield, 2 up.

(Each defeated player received £58.10)

FOURTH ROUND

Huggett defeated Coles, 4 and 2.

Rees defeated Jackson, 4 and 2.

Talbot defeated Hooker, 2 and 1.

Bembridge defeated Waites, 4 and 2.

(Each defeated player received £97.10)

Rees defeated Huggett, 1 up, 19 holes.
Bembridge defeated Talbot, 2 and 1.
            (Huggett and Talbot received £243.15)

FINALS
Bembridge defeated Rees, 6 and 5.
            (Bembridge received £1,218.15; Rees £487.10)

DUNLOP MASTERS

LITTLE ASTON GOLF CLUB
Streetly, Staffordshire
September 10—13
Purse...£8,500
Par: 35, 38—73...6,689 yards

	SCORES	TOTAL	MONEY
Cobie Legrange, *South Africa*	69 68 70 74	281	£1,463
Peter Butler	73 70 70 71	284	975
Tony Jacklin	72 72 73 68	285	489
Christie O'Connor	73 70 71 71	285	489
Tommy Horton	70 72 75 70	287	293
Neil Coles	75 71 70 72	288	244
Maurice Bembridge	74 73 72 70	289	195
Peter Townsend	75 73 71 70	289	195
Bernard Hunt	74 72 71 72	289	195
Bill Casper, *U.S.*	73 74 72 71	290	141
David Snell	71 70 73 76	290	141
Peter Thomson, *Australia*	73 72 74 72	291	127
Max Faulkner	71 73 74 73	291	127
Malcolm Gregson	71 75 71 74	291	127
Peter Alliss	71 78 72 71	292	117
Ronnie Shade	77 75 69 72	293	112
Peter Oosterhuis	78 71 73 72	294	100
Eric Brown	73 72 76 73	294	100
Bryon Hutchinson	74 71 75 74	294	100
George Will	73 74 72 75	294	100
Gordon Cunningham	75 72 73 75	295	88
Clive Clark	75 72 71 77	295	88
Brian Barnes	80 71 73 72	296	88
Cyril Pennington	71 74 74 77	296	88
Brian Huggett	74 75 75 73	297	85
Jimmy Kinsella	76 71 75 75	297	85
Alex Caygill	70 75 76 76	297	85
Jimmy Hitchcock	69 79 76 74	298	83

	SCORES	TOTAL	MONEY
David Webster	78 70 76 74	298	83
David Talbot	73 75 75 75	298	83
John Panton	75 76 74 74	299	78
Bernard Gallacher	74 75 73 77	299	78
Nick Job	76 72 76 76	300	76
Angel Gallardo, *Spain*	77 74 73 76	300	76
Dave Thomas	79 71 74 76	300	76
Doug Sewell	77 73 72 78	300	76
Lionel Platts	78 75 75 73	301	68
Dai Rees	74 73 76 78	301	68
Hugh Jackson	74 74 76 78	302	68
Bob Tuohy	81 75 74 73	303	61
John Garner	78 72 77 76	303	61
Craig DeFoy	74 78 75 76	303	61
Hugh Inggs, *South Africa*	78 70 78 77	303	61
Richard Emery	79 71 77 77	304	55
Bill Large	76 76 75 77	304	55
Tony Grubb	76 79 72 77	304	55
Michael Murphy	76 77 74 78	305	49
Hedley Muscroft	78 75 71 81	305	49
Graham Henning, *South Africa*	77 72 83 74	306	49
Guy Hunt	77 73 78 78	306	49
Eddie Polland	74 75 77 80	306	49
Terry le Brocq	77 75 77 78	307	49
David Butler	77 78 70 82	307	49
Fred Boobyer	76 76 78 78	308	49
Jimmy Martin	78 79 80 76	313	49
Ernie Bauer, *Switzerland*	85 83 73 77	318	49

PICCADILLY WORLD MATCH PLAY CHAMPIONSHIP

WENTWORTH GOLF CLUB—WEST COURSE
Virginia Water, Surrey
October 9—11
Purse....£18,400
Par: 534 534 444—36; 345 435 455—38—74
6,997 yards

QUARTER-FINALS

Gary Player (South Africa) defeated Jean Garaialde (France), 10 and 9.

PLAYER	Out: 435 424 445—35	In: 244 435 445—35—70
GARAIALDE	Out: 445 444 444—37	In: 354 525 555—39—76

Player 5 up

PLAYER	Out: 524 434 444—34
GARAIALDE	Out: 535 534 554—39

Gene Littler (U.S.) defeated Ray Floyd (U.S.), 6 and 5.

LITTLER	Out:	324 533 454—33	In:	343 334 455—34—67
FLOYD	Out:	434 424 445—34	In:	344 434 455—36—70

Littler 3 up

LITTLER	Out:	545 433 334—34	In:	334 4
FLOYD	Out:	534 633 444—36	In:	345 4

Bob Charles (New Zealand) defeated Maurice Bembridge, 6 and 5.

BEMBRIDGE	Out:	435 434 534—35	In:	345 435 454—37—72
CHARLES	Out:	334 434 444—33	In:	244 324 454—32—65

Charles 7 up

BEMBRIDGE	Out:	444 423 545—35	In:	443 4
CHARLES	Out:	425 434 444—34	In:	445 4

Tommy Aaron (U.S.) defeated Tony Jacklin, 6 and 4.

JACKLIN	Out:	446 534 344—37	In:	344 434 4C4—X—X
AARON	Out:	435 534 444—36	In:	344 534 4W4—X—X

Aaron 1 up

JACKLIN	Out:	434 544 434—35	In:	344 43
AARON	Out:	543 434 433—33	In:	334 32

SEMI-FINALS

Littler defeated Player, 4 and 3.

PLAYER	Out:	534 534 434—35	In:	343 424 544—33—68
LITTLER	Out:	544 533 333—33	In:	334 434 344—32—65

Littler 2 up

PLAYER	Out:	534 544 344—36	In:	344 434
LITTLER	Out:	434 534 344—34	In:	344 434

Charles defeated Aaron, 9 and 7.

CHARLES	Out:	424 433 344—31	In:	344 434 445—35—66
AARON	Out:	435 424 344—33	In:	344 434 444—34—67

Charles 1 up

CHARLES	Out:	434 424 334—31	In:	33
AARON	Out:	535 534 445—38	In:	34

FINALS

Charles defeated Littler, 1 up, 37 holes.

LITTLER	Out:	436 534 445—38	In:	344 434 444—34—72
CHARLES	Out:	435 524 435—35	In:	344 544 445—37—72

Match even

LITTLER	Out:	434 534 444—35	In:	344 434 354—34—69
CHARLES	Out:	534 524 533—34	In:	244 534 454—35—69

Match even

37th Hole: Charles 3, Littler 4.

Charles received £5,750; Littler £3,450; Player and Aaron £2,300; Garaialde, Floyd, Bembridge, Jacklin £1,150.

LEGEND: W—won hole; C—conceded hole to opponent; X—no total score.

European Tour

ALGARVE OPEN

PENINA GOLF COURSE
Algarve, Portugal
March 20—23
Purse....$14,056
Par: 36, 38—73...7,100 yards

	SCORES	TOTAL	MONEY
Bernard Hunt, *Great Britain*	74 72 71 75	292	$2,470.56
John Garner, *Great Britain*	79 71 73 72	295	1,588.32
Harry Bannerman, *Great Britain*	78 71 72 74	295	1,588.32
Jaime Benito, *Spain*	75 79 71 71	296	1,235.28
Ronnie Shade, *Great Britain*	76 74 74 73	297	1,058.88
Stan Mosel, *U.S.*	77 72 76 76	301	617.64
David Webster, *Great Britain*	75 73 77 76	301	617.64
Peter Jones, *Great Britain*	76 75 73 77	301	617.64
Valentin Barrios, *Spain*	74 75 74 78	301	617.64
Peter Wilcock, *Great Britain*	78 74 75 76	303	211.68
Jaime Gallardo, *Spain*	80 72 75 76	303	211.68
Bob Watson, *U.S.*	78 78 70 77	303	211.68
Nick Job, *Great Britain*	76 77 75 76	304	88.32
Donald Ross, *Great Britain*	82 79 73 71	305	88.32
Jack Wilkshire, *Great Britain*	80 76 77 72	305	88.32
Craig DeFoy, *Great Britain*	74 77 79 75	305	88.32
Tony Grubb, *Great Britain*	78 78 74 75	305	88.32
Juan Cruz, *Spain*	77 78 75 76	306	88.32
Bob Benning, *U.S.*	78 80 78 71	307	88.32
Norman Wood, *Great Britain*	81 79 73 75	308	88.32
Ron Letellier, *U.S.*	80 76 79 74	309	88.32
Manuel Cabrera, *Spain*	80 78 75 76	309	88.32
S. P. Zorilla, *Spain*	81 78 73 77	309	88.32
Bill Hector, *Great Britain*	80 75 76 78	309	88.32
Keith Ashdown, *Great Britain*	77 73 79 80	309	88.32
Antonio Garrido, *Spain*	78 73 77 81	309	88.32
Ian Richardson, *Great Britain*	78 77 78 78	311	88.32
J. L. Alonso, *Spain*	83 76 78 75	312	88.32
M. Ribeiro	81 79 76 76	312	88.32
J. M. Roca, *Spain*	78 78 76 81	313	88.32
Brian Bamford, *Great Britain*	78 72 81 82	313	88.32

BP OPEN

OLGIATA GOLF CLUB
Rome, Italy
March 29—31
Purse...$6,452
Par: 36, 36—72...6,879 yards

	SCORES				TOTAL	MONEY
Bernard Hunt, *Great Britain*	72	68	71	71	282	$2,419.44
Roberto Bernardini	73	71	70	70	284	1,128.96
Dave Thomas, *Great Britain*	69	78	68	75	290	645.12
Luciano Grappasonni	71	72	72	76	291	483.84
Bruno Ghezzo	72	71	74	76	293	322.56
Harry Bannerman, *Great Britain*	75	73	71	75	294	241.92
David Butler, *Great Britain*	69	76	76	74	295	161.28
Abdul Halim, *Egypt*	71	71	74	80	296	80.64
Hedley Muscroft, *Great Britain*	74	73	72	77	296	80.64
John Garner, *Great Britain*	70	77	74	75	296	80.64
Alfonso Angelini	78	73	73	72	296	80.64
Valentin Barrios, *Spain*	71	74	78	74	297	80.64
Manuel Ballesteros, *Spain*	72	76	76	74	298	80.64
Peter Alliss, *Great Britain*	73	75	77	74	299	80.64
Patrick Cros, *France*	79	71	77	73	300	80.64
Robert Campagnoli	75	74	77	76	302	80.64
Allan Henning, *South Africa*	77	74	71	81	303	80.64
Alberto Croce	73	75	79	76	303	80.64
Clive Clark, *Great Britain*	74	76	77	76	303	80.64
Craig DeFoy, *Great Britain*	76	75	77	77	305	80.64

WALWORTH-ALOYCO INTERNATIONAL

ROME GOLF CLUB
Rome, Italy
April 3—5
Purse...$16,129
Par: 36, 35—71...6,458 yards

	SCORES				TOTAL	MONEY
Roberto Bernardini	73	70	70	69	282	$4,838.88
Bill Large, *Great Britain*	67	70	72	82	291	1,774.32
Manuel Ballesteros, *Spain*	72	71	74	74	291	1,774.32
John Garner, *Great Britain*	73	72	73	73	291	1,774.32
Hedley Muscroft, *Great Britain*	73	75	72	73	293	967.68
Alberto Croce	73	74	73	73	293	967.68
David Butler, *Great Britain*	69	72	74	78	293	967.68
Bernard Hunt, *Great Britain*	78	73	74	69	294	483.84

	SCORES	TOTAL	MONEY
Alfonso Angelini	73 72 75 74	294	483.84
Barry Franklin, *South Africa*	72 69 79 74	294	483.84
Antonio Garrido, *Spain*	72 76 72 75	295	234
Luciano Grappasonni	76 72 69 78	295	234
Valentin Barrios, *Spain*	75 74 74 73	296	193.44
Augusto Croce	73 76 71 76	296	193.44
Ronnie Shade, *Great Britain*	72 71 77 76	296	193.44
Harry Bannerman, *Great Britain*	74 75 70 78	297	120.96
Alan Ibberson, *Great Britain*	76 77 71 73	297	120.96
Robert Campagnoli	74 76 69 78	297	120.96
Giorgio Delfino	77 76 69 75	297	120.96
Ugo Grappasonni	75 74 78 71	298	40.32
Bruno Ghezzo	73 75 78 72	298	40.32
Jaime Benito, *Spain*	76 72 70 82	300	
Graham Henning, *South Africa*	73 78 71 78	300	
Patrick Cros, *France*	71 79 75 75	300	
Olivio Bolognesi	72 75 76 78	301	
David Snell, *Great Britain*	73 73 78 77	301	

SPANISH OPEN

ROYAL AUTOMOBILE CLUB OF SPAIN
Madrid
April 17—19
Purse...$10,108.77
Par: 36, 36—72...7,241 yards

	SCORES	TOTAL	MONEY
Jean Garaialde, *France*	72 73 68 70	283	$2,888.16
Valentin Barrios	72 69 69 74	284	2,021.76
Ramon Sota	73 72 66 75	286	1,444.08
Sebastian Miguel	72 76 73 67	288	938.64
Manuel Ballesteros	71 72 70 76	289	649.92
Tomas Lopez	70 70 73 77	290	433.23
Antonio Garrido	71 71 73 75	290	433.23
Peter Alliss, *Great Britain*	70 73 73 75	291	259.97
Jaime Gallardo	77 70 71 73	291	259.97
Stan Peach, *Australia*	76 70 69 77	292	202.18
Dave Thomas, *Great Britain*	74 70 75 74	293	173.28
Hugh Boyle, *Great Britain*	74 75 73 72	294	122.75
Jaime Roqueni	76 71 68 79	294	122.75
Jose Alvarez	75 72 76 72	295	79.43
Angel Gallardo	75 71 76 73	295	79.43
Patrick Cros, *France*	73 77 72 74	296	
German Garrido	75 75 74 72	296	
Rogelio Echevarria	75 76 75 71	297	
Barry Franklin, *South Africa*	72 73 74 80	299	

419

	SCORES	TOTAL	MONEY
Jose Canizares	74 73 75 77	299	
Jose Ceba	73 75 74 78	300	
Bill Large, *Great Britain*	76 75 71 78	300	
Ubaldo Nogal	73 72 78 78	301	
Hedley Muscroft, *Great Britain*	71 73 76 81	301	
Antonio Hernandez	71 80 73 78	302	
Diego San Roman	76 73 75 79	303	
*Jose Ganceda	74 74 78 78	304	
Francisco Lopez	75 75 76 78	304	

*Amateur

FRENCH OPEN

ST.-NOM-LA-BRETECHE
July 15—17
Purse...$6,080
Par: 36, 36—72...6,825 yards

	SCORES	TOTAL	MONEY
Jean Garaialde	71 69 69 68	277	$2,000
Roberto de Vicenzo, *Argentina*	69 70 68 70	277	1,400
(Garaialde defeated de Vicenzo on third hole of sudden-death playoff.)			
Roberto Bernardini, *Italy*	68 71 71 71	281	800
Sebastian Miguel, *Spain*	72 71 71 70	284	500
Donald Swaelens, *Belgium*	70 70 72 72	284	500
Tienie Britz, *South Africa*	71 69 71 74	285	180
Peter Butler, *Great Britain*	70 74 71 70	285	180
Denis Hutchinson, *South Africa*	69 78 70 70	287	120
Graham Henning, *South Africa*	70 71 75 72	288	90
Angel Gallardo, *Spain*	75 71 70 72	288	90
Patrick Cros	68 76 74 71	289	46.67
Antonio Garrido, *Spain*	69 69 75 76	289	46.67
Cobie Legrange, *South Africa*	72 74 70 73	289	46.67
Jose Gallardo, *Spain*	71 72 75 72	290	40
Valentin Barrios, *Spain*	71 72 73 75	291	20
Rich Bassett *U.S.*	73 70 73 75	391	20
Ramon Sota, *Spain*	72 74 74 72	292	
Alberto Croce, *Italy*	73 72 72 75	292	
*Jack Newton, *Australia*	75 68 74 75	292	
Barry Franklin, *South Africa*	74 69 72 79	294	
*Herve Frayssineau	73 71 78 72	294	
Peter Green, *Great Britain*	67 78 78 71	294	
Alain Niederlitz, *U.S.*	75 71 71 78	295	
Simon Hobday, *South Africa*	73 71 77 74	295	
Abdul Halim, *Egypt*	74 74 71 76	295	

	SCORES	TOTAL	MONEY
*Gaetan Mourgue d'Alque	70 71 75 79	295	
Hans Henrik Lund, *Denmark*	72 70 76 78	296	
David Mills, *Great Britain*	72 77 74 73	296	
Manuel Ballesteros, *Spain*	73 78 74 72	297	
*Bob Sweeny, *U.S.*	76 72 75 74	297	

*Amateur

DUTCH OPEN

GOLF CLUB DE PAN
Utrecht
July 19—21
Purse...$4,025
Par: 36, 36—72...6,717 yards

	SCORES	TOTAL	MONEY
Guy Wolstenholme, *Great Britain*	69 71 68 69	277	$1,000
Barry Franklin, *South Africa*	71 73 69 69	282	600
Denis Hutchinson, *South Africa*	71 69 71 74	285	450
Mohamed Moussa, *Egypt*	72 68 69 78	287	350
Cobie Legrange, *South Africa*	75 71 72 71	289	300
Abdul Halim, *Egypt*	74 72 73 71	290	210
Graham Henning, *South Africa*	72 71 74 73	290	210
Donald Swaelens, *Belgium*	73 72 68 77	290	210
Tienie Britz, *South Africa*	74 71 74 73	292	130
Hans Janzen	76 74 68 74	292	130
Patrick Cros, *France*	70 70 78 75	293	75
Donald Gammon, *South Africa*	78 70 71 74	293	75
George Keyes, *U.S.*	75 72 72 74	293	75
Mike Hollywood, *U.S.*	72 72 73 76	293	75
Rich Bassett, *U.S.*	75 77 70 73	295	45
André van Pinxten	70 70 77 78	295	45
Jean Delgado, *France*	76 75 73 71	295	45
Jan Ouderdorp	75 75 75 71	296	
Gerhard Hoenig, *Germany*	74 75 74 75	298	
Jan Dorrestein	76 73 77 72	298	
Roberto Bernardini, *Italy*	76 75 72 75	298	
M. D. Melville, *Great Britain*	73 80 75 71	299	
Jean Michel Larretche, *France*	75 76 71 78	300	
Herbert Becker	73 74 75 78	300	
Cees Dorrestein	74 74 77 76	301	
Tony Finlayson, *South Africa*	78 71 75 78	302	
John Morgan, *Great Britain*	78 74 72 79	303	
David Midgley, *Great Britain*	78 72 78 75	303	
Alan Ibberson, *Great Britain*	74 79 74 76	303	

	SCORES	TOTAL	MONEY
Michael Evans, *U.S.*	79 74 74 77	304	
Peter Matkovich, *South Africa*	75 77 75 77	304	
James Hopper, *Great Britain*	75 75 75 79	304	

GERMAN OPEN

FRANKFURTER GOLF CLUB
Frankfurt
July 25—27
Purse...$7,580
Par: 35, 36—71...6,770 yards

	SCORES	TOTAL	MONEY
Jean Garaialde, *France*	68 66 67 61	272	$1,768.32
Cobie Legrange, *South Africa*	69 71 67 68	275	1,515.60
*Dale Hayes, *South Africa*	65 72 76 63	276	
Bernard Hunt, *Great Britain*	67 70 70 71	278	1,263.12
Donald Gammon, *South Africa*	70 66 68 75	279	884.16
Angel Gallardo, *Spain*	70 68 70 72	280	631.68
Donald Swaelens, *Belgium*	71 70 75 67	283	315.84
Flory Van Donck, *Belgium*	72 71 72 68	283	315.84
Guy Wolstenholme, *Great Britain*	70 70 73 71	284	252.72
Roberto Bernardini, *Italy*	69 73 72 71	285	164.16
Denis Hutchinson, *South Africa*	72 69 77 67	285	164.16
Simon Hobday, *South Africa*	73 69 71 73	286	101.04
Luciano Gappasonni, *Italy*	73 72 70 72	287	75.84
Graham Henning, *South Africa*	70 74 68 75	287	75.84
*R. Issit, *Great Britain*	68 74 71 75	288	
Gerhard Doenig	72 69 74 73	288	50.40
K. Gogele	72 70 73 74	289	50.40
Randy Glover, *U.S.*	74 72 69 75	290	50.40
Hans Heiser	73 73 72 74	292	37.92
Barry Franklin, *South Africa*	72 72 73 75	292	37.92
*Jack Newton, *Australia*	75 68 69 81	293	
*Robin Hunter, *Great Britain*	70 68 76 79	293	
Peter Matkovich, *South Africa*	72 70 74 77	293	25.20
Toni Kugelmuller	77 72 71 73	293	25.20
Mike Hollywood, *U.S.*	75 73 69 76	293	25.20
*H. Giesen	71 76 69 78	294	
R. Krause	72 74 72 76	294	25.20

*Amateur

SWISS OPEN

CRANS GOLF CLUB
Crans-sur-Sierre
September 1—4
Purse...$7,600
Par: 37, 36—73...6,880 yards

	SCORES	TOTAL	MONEY
Roberto Bernardini, *Italy*	68 71 71 67	277	$2,352.96
Gerhard Koenig, *Germany*	70 71 68 70	279	1,529.28
Graham Henning, *South Africa*	72 72 67 70	281	941.28
Donald Swaelens, *Belgium*	67 73 76 66	282	470.64
Alberto Croce, *Italy*	76 67 72 69	284	290.24
Angel Gallardo, *Spain*	67 69 76 72	284	290.24
Jean Garaialde, *France*	73 72 65 74	284	290.24
Denis Hutchinson, *South Africa*	72 74 72 67	285	147.06
Lazaro Rodriguez, *Spain*	74 70 72 69	285	147.06
Jurgen Harder, *Germany*	71 71 71 72	285	147.06
Gonzales Barrios, *Spain*	74 72 66 73	285	147.06
Carlo Grappasonni, *Italy*	72 72 71 71	286	94.08
Tony Coop, *Great Britain*	71 74 73 70	288	52.80
Duro Contreras, *Spain*	73 71 72 72	288	52.80
Roger Cotton, *France*	70 73 72 72	288	52.80
Mario Napoleoni, *Italy*	72 71 69 76	288	52.80
Patrick Cros, *France*	74 71 73 71	289	23.52
Hedley Muscroft, *Great Britain*	72 71 74 72	289	23.52
Peter Kugelmuller, *Germany*	75 70 69 75	289	23.52
Peter Matkovich, *South Africa*	73 69 72 75	289	23.52
Syd Scott, *Great Britain*	69 73 71 76	289	23.52
Flory Van Donck, *Belgium*	73 70 75 72	290	23.52
Jan Dorrestein, *Holland*	69 74 75 72	290	23.52
Cobie Legrange, *South Africa*	73 73 71 74	291	23.52
Olivio Bolognese, *Italy*	76 69 73 74	292	23.52
*Antoine Matti	74 76 75 68	293	
Luciano Grappasonni, *Italy*	78 68 74 73	293	23.52
Emmanuele Canessa, *Italy*	73 71 73 76	293	23.52
Santiago Perez, *Spain*	73 74 77 70	294	23.52
Luciano Bernardini, *Italy*	73 75 75 71	294	23.52
Thomas Lopez, *Spain*	75 71 76 72	294	23.52
Siegfried Vollrath, *Germany*	74 72 76 72	294	23.52
Mike Lopez, *Spain*	73 74 73 74	294	23.52
Jean Charpenel, *France*	76 71 71 76	294	23.52

*Amateur

South African Tour

TRANSVAAL OPEN

KENSINGTON GOLF CLUB
Johannesburg
January 9—11
Purse....R3,890
Par: 35, 35—70...6,774 yards

	SCORE				TOTAL	MONEY
Bob Verwey	71	70	66	65	272	R800
Graham Henning	70	68	69	66	273	525
Denis Hutchinson	70	68	71	66	275	400
Hugh Inggs	68	73	70	66	277	315
*Comrie du Toit	70	70	71	67	278	
Benny Brews	70	69	70	70	279	260
Tienie Britz	66	71	73	70	280	210
*Selwyn Schewitz	76	68	68	68	280	
*Dave Symons	71	72	71	67	281	
Cobie Legrange	71	71	72	67	281	160
*Rob Williams	70	72	68	71	281	
Bob Tuohy	70	71	72	68	281	160
Roger Manning	69	71	68	73	281	160
*John Fourie	72	72	68	70	282	
Trevor Wilkes	70	73	70	69	282	140
Brian Barnes, *Great Britain*	69	71	71	71	282	130
Barry Franklin	71	73	71	68	283	120
Gert Van Biljon	74	69	70	70	283	110
Bobby Cole	71	71	73	68	283	100
Marshall Douglas, *Great Britain*	71	72	70	71	284	90
Allan Henning	71	71	72	70	284	80
Terry Westbrook, *Zambia*	73·	69	67	75	284	70
Tony Rice, *Zambia*	75	70	70	70	285	60
Jimmy Hitchcock, *Great Britain*	71	71	73	70	285	
John Bland	74	71	71	70	286	
Roy Van Wezel	73	69	75	69	286	
Peter Oosterhuis, *Great Britain*	71	68	77	71	287	
Peter Beames, *Great Britain*	72	72	73	71	288	
*Johan Murray	75	69	72	72	288	
*Alan Hofmann	73	71	74	70	288	
Bobby Locke	70	72	75	71	288	

+ 1 rand = $1.40
* Amateur

NATAL OPEN

ROYAL DURBAN GOLF CLUB
Durban
January 17—19
Purse...R2,500
Par: 35, 37—72...6,554 yards

	SCORE				TOTAL	MONEY
Bobby Cole	72	71	70	69	282	R750
Peter Oosterhuis, *Great Britain*	70	76	67	70	283	450
Hugh Inggs	69	69	69	77	284	275
Trevor Wilkes	69	73	68	74	284	275
Allan Henning	69	73	75	68	285	150
*Dale Hayes	74	70	72	71	287	
Denis Hutchinson	72	75	71	70	288	130
Bob Verwey	79	70	70	69	288	130
Terry Westbrook, *Zambia*	73	67	73	76	289	90
Barry Franklin	75	72	67	75	289	90
Cobie Legrange	75	68	71	76	290	60
Graham Henning	73	73	71	73	290	60
Bob Tuohy	75	71	72	74	292	40
Brian Barnes, *Great Britain*	71	71	73	78	293	
Luciani Castignani, *Zambia*	70	74	76	73	293	
Brian Wilkes	77	71	72	74	294	
Hugh Jackson, *Great Britain*	76	73	72	73	294	
Bernard Gallacher, *Great Britain*	74	74	73	73	294	
Donald Gammon	75	73	72	74	294	
Brain Henning	71	78	66	82	297	
Jimmy Falconer	70	74	77	77	298	
Roger Manning	75	77	74	73	299	
Tienie Britz	73	78	74	75	300	
Cyril Pennington, *Great Britain*	71	76	75	79	301	
Jimmy Hitchcock, *Great Britain*	72	76	76	78	302	
Gert Van Biljon	73	75	77	77	302	
Tony Rice, *Zambia*	76	73	79	74	302	
Geoffrey Lyons, *Great Britain*	71	74	80	77	302	
John Bland	79	70	71	83	303	
Hector Zerbst	76	76	74	78	304	
Graham Roebert	74	77	76	79	306	
Tertius Claasens	76	76	74	82	308	

* Amateur

DUNLOP MASTERS

MOWBRAY GOLF CLUB
Cape Town
January 23—25
Purse...R3,500
Par: 37, 37—74...6,850 yards

	SCORE				TOTAL	MONEY
Bobby Cole	69	68	73	70	280	R750
Bob Tuohy	70	72	70	74	286	475
Tienie Britz	72	71	72	71	286	475
Trevor Wilkes	76	68	66	77	287	325
Bob Verwey	73	71	71	73	288	255
Peter Oosterhuis, *Great Britain*	71	70	72	76	289	200
Barry Franklin	65	74	74	77	290	150
George Will, *Great Britain*	73	72	73	72	290	150
John Bland	74	71	70	75	290	150
Graham Henning	76	68	73	73	290	150
Cedric Amm	72	74	70	76	292	105
Cobie Legrange	74	73	74	71	292	105
Allan Henning	71	70	77	75	293	80
*Jeremy Stokoe	72	73	70	78	293	
Eric Moore	70	74	76	76	296	65
Martin Le Roux	73	73	72	78	296	65
Hugh Inggs	72	74	73	78	297	
Terry Westbrook, *Zambia*	73	74	74	76	297	
*Simon Hobday, *Zambia*	71	75	75	77	298	
Denis Hutchinson	76	72	73	77	298	
Bobby Locke	77	74	74	73	298	
Jimmy Hitchcock, *Great Britain*	80	70	75	73	298	
Brian Henning	76	70	75	77	298	
Donald Ross, *Great Britain*	72	77	74	76	299	
Marshall Douglas, *Great Britain*	77	69	74	80	300	
*Dave Liddell	73	72	75	82	302	
*Henry Green	73	73	73	84	303	
Guy Hunt, *Great Britain*	76	74	77	76	303	
Bobby Walker, *Great Britain*	71	74	78	81	304	
Donald Gammon	71	76	74	83	304	
Leon Evans	76	75	76	77	304	
Clive Clark, *Great Britain*	77	72	78	77	304	

* Amateur

WESTERN PROVINCE OPEN

ROYAL CAPE GOLF CLUB
Cape Town
January 30—February 1
Purse...R3,500
Par: 36, 36—72...6,750 yards

	SCORE				TOTAL	MONEY
Cobie Legrange	68	68	65	71	272	R750
Peter Oosterhuis, *Great Britain*	71	71	64	69	275	525
Hugh Inggs	73	68	68	69	278	425
Bobby Cole	71	70	71	67	279	325
Bob Tuohy	69	70	69	72	280	245
Cedric Amm	65	72	72	72	281	190
Hugh Jackson, *Great Britain*	70	71	68	82	281	190
Brian Barnes, *Great Britain*	62	75	68	77	282	160
Harry Bannerman, *Great Britain*	74	72	69	69	284	140
George Will, *Great Britain*	72	69	70	74	285	130
Trevor Wilkes	71	74	72	68	286	105
Bob Verwey	69	73	71	73	286	105
Tony Rice, *Zambia*	72	73	73	69	287	70
Geoffrey Lyons, *Great Britain*	74	69	71	73	287	70
Bernard Gallacher, *Great Britain*	69	71	73	74	287	70
Denis Hutchinson	72	74	71	71	288	
John Bland	74	73	67	74	288	
Tertius Claasens	69	72	73	74	288	
Allan Henning	73	71	70	74	288	
Pierre Oosthuizen	73	73	72	71	289	
Cyril Pennington, *Great Britain*	72	73	69	75	289	
Graham Henning	69	74	73	74	290	
Marshall Douglas, *Great Britain*	73	71	73	73	290	
Brian Henning	76	73	69	73	291	
Donald Gammon	74	75	71	71	291	
Tienie Britz	71	75	76	69	291	
Peter Matkovich	75	71	72	73	291	
Eric Moore	70	78	72	73	293	
Roger Manning	71	71	78	74	294	
Jimmy Hitchcock, *Great Britain*	72	74	72	76	294	
Gert Van Biljon	71	75	71	77	294	
Bobby Walker, *Great Britain*	72	76	73	73	294	

GENERAL MOTORS OPEN

WEDGEWOOD PARK GOLF CLUB
Port Elizabeth
February 6—8
Purse...R4,180
Par: 36, 35—71...6,457 yards

	SCORE	TOTAL	MONEY
Graham Henning	67 68 72 72	279	R950
Hugh Inggs	70 72 70 69	281	712.50
George Will, *Great Britain*	70 70 71 72	283	522.50
Gary Player	69 72 72 72	285	427.50
Denis Hutchinson	71 73 73 69	286	332.50
Bob Verwey	70 71 75 71	287	237.50
Bobby Cole	70 77 69 72	288	190
Brian Barnes, *Great Britain*	72 75 71 71	289	166.85
Bob Tuohy	71 71 74 74	290	110.45
Jimmy Hitchcock, *Great Britain*	73 72 71 74	290	110.45
Cobie Legrange	73 74 71 72	290	110.45
Trevor Wilkes	75 74 73 68	290	110.45
Tienie Britz	69 74 76 72	291	76
Cyril Pennington, *Great Britain*	76 70 73 73	292	66.50
Clive Clark, *Great Britain*	74 74 70 75	293	19
John Bland	71 75 75 72	293	19
Hugh Jackson, *Great Britain*	74 72 73 74	293	19
Sean Hunt, *Great Britain*	75 74 76 71	296	
Peter Oosterhuis, *Great Britain*	74 74 75 74	297	
Peter Matkovich	71 74 75 79	299	
Mike Ness	77 78 67 77	299	
Terry Westbrook, *Zambia*	79 73 78 72	302	
Bernard Gallacher, *Great Britain*	74 76 76 77	303	
Gert Van Biljon	72 79 75 78	304	
Wally Hyam	71 77 76 81	305	
John Hopper, *Great Britain*	72 73 81 80	306	
David Jacobs, *Great Britain*	77 75 75 79	306	
Leon Evans	76 73 82 75	306	
Geoffrey Lyons, *Great Britain*	76 73 81 76	306	
Barry Dutton	78 74 76 79	307	

SOUTH AFRICAN OPEN

DURBAN COUNTRY CLUB
Durban
February 12—15
Purse...R9,997
Par: 36, 36—72...6,570 yards

	SCORE				TOTAL	MONEY
Gary Player	67	70	72	64	273	R2,000
Trevor Wilkes	69	68	73	69	279	1,500
Jimmy Hitchcock, *Great Britain*	70	67	78	70	285	1,100
Bobby Cole	69	72	74	70	285	1,100
Bobby Walker, *Great Britain*	70	68	74	74	286	800
Bob Tuohy	72	72	75	68	287	575
Hugh Inggs	71	72	77	67	287	575
Terry Westbrook, *Zambia*	75	68	72	74	289	313
Brian Barnes, *Great Britain*	72	72	71	74	289	313
Bob Verwey	77	70	73	69	289	313
Harry Bannerman, *Great Britain*	71	72	73	74	290	190
Graham Henning	75	72	73	73	293	150
Allan Henning	70	75	76	72	293	150
Eric Moore	72	75	74	72	293	150
Bernard Gallacher, *Great Britain*	77	70	76	71	294	110
George Will, *Great Britain*	73	74	75	72	294	110
Peter Oosterhuis, *Great Britain*	73	74	75	72	294	110
Clive Clark, *Great Britain*	72	75	75	75	297	90
Cobie Legrange	70	74	80	74	298	80
Peter Beames, *Great Britain*	70	76	77	76	299	56
Donald Ross, *Great Britain*	71	74	78	76	299	56
Cedric Amm	75	68	80	76	299	56
David Proctor	68	78	75	79	300	50
Sean Hunt, *Great Britain*	71	77	78	76	302	50
Tony Rice, *Zambia*	76	73	82	73	304	
Sandy Guthrie	71	77	77	85	310	
Warwick Monk	74	75	79	83	311	

PGA CHAMPIONSHIP

GERMISTON GOLF CLUB
Germiston
February 19—22
Purse...R6,000
Par: 36, 35—71...6,980 yards

	SCORE	TOTAL	MONEY
Gary Player	67 68 66 71	272	R1,100
Cobie Legrange	71 68 67 67	273	633.33
Trevor Wilkes	71 66 64 72	273	633.33
Bobby Cole	67 70 68 68	273	633.32
Brian Barnes, *Great Britain*	68 68 68 71	275	425
Bob Tuohy	71 71 70 68	280	350
Barry Franklin	69 71 67 73	280	350
Hugh Inggs	73 73 69 66	281	250
Cedric Amm	71 73 71 66	281	250
Tienie Britz	72 70 68 81	281	250
Terry Westbrook, *Zambia*	73 70 71 68	282	200
Tony Rice, *Zambia*	78 71 66 70	285	162.50
Allan Henning	72 69 73 71	285	162.50
Bernard Gallacher, *Great Britain*	70 76 69 72	287	125
Denis Hutchinson	72 72 73 71	288	93.33
Graham Henning	72 73 71 72	288	93.33
Wally Hyam	75 71 66 76	288	93.33
John Bland	73 71 73 72	289	39
Jimmy Hitchcock, *Great Britain*	73 70 73 73	289	39
Bob Verwey	73 72 71 73	289	39
Leon Evans	75 72 71 71	289	39
Peter Oosterhuis, *Great Britain*	70 71 77 71	289	39
Bobby Walker, *Great Britain*	71 72 75 72	290	
Marshall Douglas, *Great Britain*	73 74 71 72	290	
Eric Moore	71 72 75 72	290	
Brian Lundie	73 75 73 71	292	
Peter Beames, *Great Britain*	72 71 74 76	293	
Gert Van Biljon	75 69 73 76	293	
Mike Ness	69 70 75 80	294	
Hugh Jackson	73 73 76 73	295	
Roger Manning	68 74 80 73	295	
Benny Brews	71 78 72 74	295	

430

RHODESIA

FLAME LILY TOURNAMENT

BULAWAYO GOLF CLUB
Bulawayo, Rhodesia
February 28—March 2
Purse...£2,500 +
Par: 36, 36—72...7,055 yards

	SCORE	TOTAL	MONEY
Trevor Wilkes, *South Africa*	68 72 69 66	275	£650
Cobie Legrange, *South Africa*	71 68 68 74	281	450
Bernard Gallacher, *Great Britain*	68 75 72 68	283	325
Denis Hutchinson, *South Africa*	71 71 71 71	284	230
Clive Clark, *Great Britain*	70 74 70 70	284	230
Tienie Britz, *South Africa*	69 74 72 70	285	124
Graham Henning, *South Africa*	73 71 69 72	285	124
John Bland, *South Africa*	71 71 73 70	285	124
Marshall Douglas, *Great Britain*	70 71 72 73	286	80
Bob Verwey, *South Africa*	71 74 73 69	287	60
Donald Ross, *Great Britain*	71 73 73 70	287	60
Bob Tuohy, *South Africa*	75 72 73 68	288	22.10
Sean Hunt, *Great Britain*	73 71 72 72	288	22.10

+ 1 pound = $2.40

BUSH BABES OPEN

GWELO GOLF CLUB
Gwelo, Rhodesia
March 7—9
Purse...£1,500
Par: 35, 36—71...6,862 yards

	SCORE	TOTAL	MONEY
Tienie Britz, *South Africa*	68 68 69 68	273	£350
Hugh Inggs, *South Africa*	69 70 71 68	278	275
Terry Westbrook, *Zambia*	70 70 73 70	283	200
Trevor Wilkes, *South Africa*	73 66 72 72	283	200
Bob Tuohy, *South Africa*	69 69 76 70	284	125
Barry Franklin, *South Africa*	70 71 69 74	284	125
Graham Henning, *South Africa*	75 71 72 67	285	55
Stan Peach, *Australia*	70 71 73 71	285	55
Cobie Legrange, *South Africa*	69 70 75 71	285	55
Sean Hunt, *Great Britain*	72 69 73 72	286	30
Donald Gammon	71 75 68 74	288	15
Leon Evans, *South Africa*	67 71 74 76	288	15

431

DUNLOP TOURNAMENT

ROYAL SALISBURY GOLF CLUB
Salisbury, Rhodesia
March 14—16
Purse...£1,500
Par: 36, 35—71...6,723 yards

	SCORE				TOTAL	MONEY
Hugh Inggs, *South Africa*	68	70	72	68	278	£350
Graham Henning, *South Africa*	69	66	75	69	279	275
Cobie Legrange, *South Africa*	73	64	73	70	280	225
Bob Verwey, *South Africa*	70	73	69	72	284	155
Terry Westbrook, *Zambia*	68	74	73	69	284	155
John Bland, *South Africa*	71	70	73	71	285	95
Bernard Gallacher, *Great Britain*	72	67	74	72	285	95
Denis Hutchinson, *South Africa*	70	71	73	72	286	45
Trevor Wilkes, *South Africa*	71	71	73	71	286	45
Cedric Amm, *South Africa*	71	75	72	69	287	30
Tienie Britz, *South Africa*	74	70	73	71	288	15
Donald Gammon	75	70	71	72	288	15

Far East Tour

PHILIPPINES OPEN

WACK WACK GOLF AND COUNTRY CLUB
Mandaluyong, Rizal
February 27—March 2
Purse...$35,000
Par: 36, 36—72...7,014 yards

	SCORE	TOTAL	MONEY
Haruo Yasuda, *Japan*	74 68 72 69	283	$10,000
Eleuterio Nival	68 71 71 73	283	5,000
(Yasuda defeated Nival on first hole of sudden-death playoff.)			
Frank Phillips, *Australia*	75 72 68 71	286	2,500
Chang Chung Fa, *Formosa*	72 70 72 73	287	1,187.50
Kenji Hosoishi, *Japan*	72 69 76 70	287	1,187.50
Lu Liang Huan, *Formosa*	69 75 70 75	289	875
Randall Vines, *Australia*	74 73 70 72	289	875
Alex Sutton, *U.S.*	74 70 77 68	289	875
Ramon Sota, *Spain*	76 73 75 66	290	454.17
Ben Arda	73 71 75 71	290	454.17
Kuo Chi Hsiung, *Formosa*	72 73 73 72	290	454.17
Guy Wolstenholme, *Great Britain*	72 76 70 72	290	454.17
Vic Allin	70 75 71 74	290	454.17
Dick Villalon	72 70 72 76	290	454.17
Takaaki Kono, *Japan*	76 74 71 70	291	337.50
Kosaku Shimada, *Japan*	74 74 73 71	292	287.50
Pacifico Villa	71 74 73 74	292	287.50
Hsieh Yung Yo, *Formosa*	71 71 76 74	292	287.50
Takashi Murakami, *Japan*	74 73 76 70	293	214.60
Isao Aoki, *Japan*	78 71 71 73	293	214.60
Ted Ball, *Australia*	75 73 73 72	293	214.60
Alan Murray, *Australia*	74 72 73 74	293	214.60
Shigeru Uchida, *Japan*	72 74 71 76	293	214.60
John Felus, *U.S.*	74 75 69 75	293	214.60
Mitsutaka Kono, *Japan*	73 72 72 77	294	131.25
Torakichi Nakamura, *Japan*	79 71 73 71	294	131.25
Frankie Racho	71 72 77 74	294	131.25
Teruo Suzumura, *Japan*	76 74 72 72	294	131.25
Hideyo Sugimoto, *Japan*	75 72 73 74	294	131.25
Celestino Tugot	73 73 75 73	294	131.25
*Luis Silverio	76 74 69 76	295	
Hsu Chi San, *Formosa*	76 70 77 73	296	54.18
Ireneo Legaspi	70 81 72 73	296	54.18
David Graham, *Australia*	73 74 73 76	296	54.18

	SCORES	TOTAL	MONEY
Peter Townsend, *Great Britain*	71 74 76 75	296	54.18
Tomoo Ishii, *Japan*	73 74 74 75	296	54.18
Jose Arosa Jr.	74 72 74 76	296	54.18

* Amateur

SINGAPORE OPEN

SINGAPORE ISLAND COUNTRY CLUB, BUKIT COURSE
Singapore
March 6—9
Purse... $14,000
Par: 35, 36—71...6,584 yards

	SCORE	TOTAL	MONEY
Tomio Kamata, *Japan*	70 70 68 70	278	$1,766.67
David Graham, *Australia*	78 62 69 69	278	1,133.33
Guy Wolstenholme, *Great Britain*	71 69 68 70	278	733.33
(Kamata defeated Graham and Wolstenholme in sudden-death playoff, Wolstenholme eliminated on first extra hole, Graham on third.)			
Ben Arda, *Philippines*	71 69 71 72	283	633.33
Hsieh Jung Yo, *Formosa*	73 74 70 69	286	473.33
Kuo Chi Hsiung, *Formosa*	74 69 73 70	286	473.33
Shiro Matsuda, *Japan*	73 72 71 70	286	473.33
Shigeru Uchida, *Japan*	69 72 74 71	286	473.33
Ted Ball, *Australia*	69 72 70 75	286	473.33
Chen Chien Chung, *Formosa*	74 72 71 70	287	339
Hsieh Min Nan, *Formosa*	74 73 69 71	287	339
Ramon Sota, *Spain*	72 75 69 71	287	339
Hideyo Sugimoto, *Japan*	75 75 70 68	288	268.67
Maurice Bembridge, *Great Britain*	73 72 73 70	288	268.67
Shozo Miyamoto, *Japan*	76 70 72 70	288	268.67
Eleuterio Nival, *Philippines*	72 70 73 73	288	268.67
Hahn Chang Sang, *Korea*	73 73 70 72	288	268.67
*Ho Ming Chung, *Formosa*	77 69 72 70	288	
Takaaki Kono, *Japan*	78 72 71 68	289	206.67
Lee Il Ahn, *Korea*	75 71 74 69	289	206.67
Kenji Umino, *Japan*	76 71 70 72	289	206.67
John Felus, *U.S.*	76 72 67 74	289	206.67
Isao Aoki, *Japan*	73 75 72 70	290	180
Haruo Yasuda, *Japan*	72 74 74 70	290	180
Takuo Terajima, *Japan*	75 73 70 72	290	180
Randall Vines, *Australia*	74 73 74 70	291	135
Alan Murray, *Australia*	69 78 73 71	291	135

434

	SCORES	TOTAL	MONEY
Fujio Ishii, *Japan*	68 75 76 72	291	135
Tomoo Ishii, *Japan*	68 75 76 72	291	135
Kenji Hosoishi, *Japan*	75 72 72 72	291	135
Mya Aye, *Burma*	73 74 72 72	291	135
Graham Marsh, *Australia*	73 74 74 71	292	95
Lu Liang Huan, *Formosa*	72 74 72 74	292	95
Tadashi Kitta, *Japan*	71 79 71 72	293	66.67
Angel Gallardo, *Spain*	73 72 76 72	293	66.67
John Lister, *New Zealand*	70 75 75 73	293	66.67
Kosaku Shimada, *Japan*	72 73 73 75	293	66.67
Hsu Sheng San, *Formosa*	73 73 70 77	293	66.67
Akihiro Teramoto, *Japan*	72 78 68 76	294	41
Celestino Tugot, *Philippines*	75 73 73 73	294	41
Kenji Umino, *Japan*	76 71 70 77	294	41
Sukree Onsham, *Thailand*	78 70 73 74	295	18.33
Tim Woolbank, *Australia*	77 69 74 75	295	18.33

* Amateur

MALAYSIAN OPEN

ROYAL SELANGOR GOLF CLUB
Kuala Lumpur
March 13—16
Purse....$16,666.67
Par: 36, 36—72...6,793 yards

	SCORE	TOTAL	MONEY
Takaaki Kono, *Japan*	72 70 72 66	280	$2,166.67
John Lister, *New Zealand*	74 66 70 71	281	1,183.33
David Graham, *Australia*	68 72 71 70	281	1,183.33
Haruo Yasuda, *Japan*	72 70 72 68	282	763.33
Masayuki Imai, *Japan*	71 71 73 67	282	763.33
Hahn Chang Sang, *Korea*	70 72 70 71	283	629.16
Kuo Chi Hsiung, *Formosa*	75 69 69 70	283	629.16
Frank Phillips, *Australia*	67 71 70 76	284	515
Ramon Sota, *Spain*	72 69 71 72	284	515
Hsieh Yung Yo, *Formosa*	74 72 69 69	284	515
Takashi Murakami, *Japan*	70 76 66 73	285	394.17
Kenji Hosoishi, *Japan*	73 66 73 73	285	394.17
Guy Wolstenholme, *Great Britain*	71 69 72 73	285	394.17
Ben Arda, *Philippines*	70 72 72 71	285	394.17
Hsu Chi San, *Formosa*	74 72 69 71	286	325
Tadashi Kitta, *Japan*	73 71 71 71	286	325
*Ho Ming Chung, *Formosa*	70 70 71 75	286	
Celestino Tugot, *Philippines*	73 69 75 69	286	325

	SCORES	TOTAL	MONEY
Namio Takasu, *Japan*	73 76 66 72	287	272.50
Fujio Ishii, *Japan*	71 72 70 74	287	272.50
Sukree Onsham, *Thailand*	70 73 71 73	287	272.50
Tomio Kamata, *Japan*	77 68 71 71	287	272.50
*Zanial Abidin	73 72 72 71	288	
Peter Thomson, *Australia*	69 73 74 72	288	216.67
Bob Unger, *U.S.*	70 72 75 71	288	216.67
Shozo Miyamoto, *Japan*	70 71 71 76	288	216.67
Walter Godfrey, *New Zealand*	68 74 70 76	288	216.67
Mike Kelly	68 72 75 74	289	178.81
David Clark	71 74 71 73	289	178.81
Ireneo Legaspi, *Philippines*	75 72 71 71	289	178.81
Mitsutaka Kono, *Japan*	76 71 71 71	289	178.81
Shigeru Uchida, *Japan*	70 69 72 78	289	178.81
Terry Kendall, *New Zealand*	72 75 72 70	289	178.81
Hsieh Min Nan, *Formosa*	72 70 78 69	289	178.81
Angel Gallardo, *Spain*	74 71 69 76	290	159.44
Torakichi Nakamura, *Japan*	70 72 71 77	290	159.44
Hideyo Sugimoto, *Japan*	75 70 75 70	290	159.44
Tomoo Ishii, *Japan*	74 71 70 76	291	150.56
Shiro Matsuda, *Japan*	76 72 72 71	291	150.56
Tim Woolbank, *Australia*	71 73 75 72	291	150.56
Isao Aoki, *Japan*	75 72 75 70	292	70
Paul Hart, *Australia*	75 69 75 73	292	70
Graham Marsh, *Australia*	73 71 74 74	292	70
Takuo Terajima, *Japan*	75 72 74 71	292	70

* Amateur

THAILAND OPEN

ROYAL THAI AFB GOLF CLUB
Don Muang, Bangkok
March 20—23
Purse...$12,000
Par: 36, 36—72...7,127 yards

	SCORE	TOTAL	MONEY
Hsieh Yung Yo, *Formosa*	66 71 70 70	277	$2,000
Hsu Chi San, *Formosa*	74 68 69 74	285	1,200
Takashi Murakami, *Japan*	72 71 74 70	287	1,000
Kosaku Shimada, *Japan*	70 69 73 77	289	850
Chang Chang Fa, *Formosa*	74 75 71 69	289	850
Hsieh Min Nan, *Formosa*	71 72 74 73	290	650
Masayuki Imai, *Japan*	70 71 72 77	290	650
Takaaki Kono, *Japan*	71 69 76 74	290	650

	SCORES	TOTAL	MONEY
Ireneo Legaspi, *Philippines*	76 71 71 73	291	450
Ben Arda, *Philippines*	72 71 74 74	291	450
Lu Liang Huan, *Formosa*	74 76 69 72	291	450
Frank Phillips, *Australia*	71 73 72 75	291	450
Suchin Suvannapongse	77 75 69 71	292	275
Akio Toyoda, *Japan*	72 76 70 74	292	275
*Ho Ming Chung, *Formosa*	75 76 71 70	292	
John Lister, *New Zealand*	77 73 72 71	293	158
Uthai Thabvibul	70 77 75 71	293	158
Angel Gallardo, *Spain*	72 76 72 73	293	158
*Luis Silverio, *Philippines*	74 76 74 69	293	
Mitsutaka Kono, *Japan*	73 75 72 74	294	106
Peter Thomson, *Australia*	73 75 73 73	294	106
Kuo Chi Hsiung, *Formosa*	74 74 73 73	294	106
Paul Hart, *Australia*	73 75 72 74	294	106
Alan Murray, *Australia*	73 71 79 72	295	100
Ramon Sota, *Spain*	73 77 72 73	295	100
Mya Aye, *Burma*	75 74 73 73	295	100
Sukree Onsham	74 71 73 77	295	100
Kenji Umino, *Japan*	73 75 71 76	295	100
Randall Vines, *Australia*	76 72 74 74	296	100
Margerito Arda, *Philippines*	76 70 76 74	296	100
Maurice Bembridge, *Great Britain*	75 76 70 75	296	100
Eleuterio Nival, *Philippines*	73 73 75 75	296	100

* Amateur

HONG KONG OPEN

ROYAL HONG KONG GOLF CLUB, FANLING COURSE
Kowloon, Hong Kong
March 27–30
Purse...$12,706
Par: 34, 36—70...6,498 yards

	SCORE	TOTAL	MONEY
Teruo Sugihara, *Japan*	71 68 69 66	274	$2,475.25
Maurice Bembridge, *Great Britain*	64 70 74 68	276	1,650.17
*Ho Ming Chung, *Formosa*	70 68 70 70	278	
Chen Chien Chung, *Formosa*	69 67 74 68	278	1,237.62
Ramon Sota, *Spain*	68 70 66 75	279	990.10
*Luis Silverio, *Philippines*	74 67 70 69	280	
Fujio Ishii, *Japan*	68 69 70 73	280	742.57
Ireneo Legaspi, *Philippines*	71 67 72 70	280	742.57
Chang Chung Fa, *Formosa*	68 71 72 70	281	325.08
Chen Ching Po, *Formosa*	70 70 70 71	281	325.08

	SCORES	TOTAL	MONEY
Hsu Chi San, *Formosa*	69 71 70 71	281	325.08
Lee Il Ahn, *Korea*	69 69 72 71	281	325.08
Shelby Futch, *U.S.*	72 68 69 72	281	325.08
Teruo Suzumura, *Japan*	70 72 72 68	282	198.85
Frank Phillips, *Australia*	71 70 72 69	282	198.85
John Lister, *New Zealand*	74 69 69 70	282	198.85
Hahn Chang Sang, *Korea*	71 70 70 71	282	198.85
David Graham, *Australia*	69 69 73 71	282	198.85
Graham Marsh, *Australia*	72 72 68 71	283	152.64
Hsieh Yung Yo, *Formosa*	69 72 70 72	283	152.64
Torakichi Nakamura, *Japan*	68 72 70 73	283	152.64
Kosaku Shimada, *Japan*	72 69 68 75	284	140.26
Hsieh Min Nan, *Formosa*	72 72 70 71	285	125.83
Bob Unger, *U.S.*	74 72 67 72	285	125.83
Tomoo Ishii, *Japan*	71 68 72 74	285	125.83
Shozo Miyamoto, *Japan*	67 70 73 75	285	125.83
Randall Vines, *Australia*	73 70 66 76	285	125.83
Peter Thomson, *Australia*	72 69 68 76	285	125.83
Haruo Yasuda, *Japan*	70 72 72 72	286	101.60
Dennis Clark, *New Zealand*	69 71 74 72	286	101.60
Tomio Kamata, *Japan*	75 72 66 73	286	101.60
Kenji Hosoishi, *Japan*	71 70 72 73	286	101.60
Akihiro Teramoto, *Japan*	72 68 70 76	286	101.60
Eleuterio Nival, *Philippines*	72 68 69 77	286	101.60
Ted Ball, *Australia*	69 70 70 77	286	101.60
Kuo Chi Hsiung, *Formosa*	73 73 69 72	287	92
Alan Murray, *Australia*	74 68 73 72	287	92

* Amateur

CHINA (FORMOSA) OPEN

TAIWAN GOLF AND COUNTRY CLUB
Tamsui, Taiwan
April 3—6
Purse...$9,000
Par: 36, 36—72...6,838 yards

	SCORE	TOTAL	MONEY
Hideyo Sugimoto, *Japan*	68 76 69 71	284	$2,000
Hsu Chi San	69 73 71 71	284	1,250
(Sugimoto defeated Hsu on first hole of sudden-death playoff.)			
Hsieh Min Nan	71 72 72 70	285	750
Kuo Chi Hsiung	69 71 73 73	286	500
Hsieh Yung Yo	71 75 70 72	288	400
Chen Ching Po	72 74 72 75	293	350
Shay Yi Shiong	72 74 74 74	294	287.50

	SCORES	TOTAL	MONEY
David Graham, *Australia*	73 74 74 73	294	287.50
Shigeru Uchida, *Japan*	74 72 74 74	294	287.50
Hahn Chang Sang, *Korea*	72 77 72 73	294	287.50
Paul Hart, *Australia*	73 79 72 71	295	218.75
Jerry Stolhand, *U.S.*	72 73 74 76	295	218.75
Cheri Kien Chung	71 78 76 71	296	193.75
Fujio Ishii, *Japan*	74 75 73 74	296	193.75
Kosaku Shimada, *Japan*	72 76 78 71	297	162.50
Eleuterio Nival, *Philippines*	71 79 76 71	297	162.50
Chang Chung Fa	74 74 79 73	300	118.75
Tomoo Ishii, *Japan*	72 75 74 79	300	118.75
Teruo Sugihara, *Japan*	72 80 77 71	300	118.75
Namio Takasu, *Japan*	79 75 74 72	300	118.75
Teruo Suzumura, *Japan*	71 80 75 75	301	100
Kenji Umino, *Japan*	69 77 78 77	301	100
Ireneo Legaspi, *Philippines*	71 78 79 73	301	100
Bob Unger, *U.S.*	71 82 72 76	301	100
Masaharu Kusakabe, *Japan*	75 78 73 76	302	100
Takashi Murakami, *Japan*	72 78 75 77	302	100
*Cehn Chien Chi	76 74 75 78	303	
Hsu Sheng San	73 79 74 77	303	100
Margarito Arda, *Philippines*	72 82 76 73	303	100
*Lee Chen Hsiung	70 79 77 78	304	
Chen Chien Chin	71 78 80 75	304	43.75
Graham Marsh, *Australia*	74 75 77 78	304	43.75
Kikuo Arai, *Japan*	76 73 75 80	304	43.75
Masayuki Imai, *Japan*	77 72 81 74	304	43.75

* Amateur

YOMIURI OPEN

YOMIURI COUNTRY CLUB
Tokyo, Japan
April 10—13
Purse...$15,000
Par: 36, 36—72...7,052 yards

	SCORE	TOTAL	MONEY
Guy Wolstenholme, *Great Britain*	71 72 76 69	288	$2,000
Teruo Sugihara	69 74 74 72	289	1,500
Takuo Terashima	70 73 75 72	290	1,000
Kenji Hosoishi	69 74 75 73	291	900
Walter Godfrey, *New Zealand*	70 69 76 77	292	800
*Ginjiro Nakabe	72 73 76 72	293	
Hsieh Yung Yo, *Formosa*	69 73 74 77	293	700
Bob Unger, *U.S.*	73 71 76 74	294	554

	SCORES	TOTAL	MONEY
Hahn Chang Sang, *Korea*	66 77 76 75	294	554
Hsieh Min Nan, *Formosa*	74 71 72 77	294	554
Kesahiko Uchida	75 75 73 71	294	554
Hideyo Sugimoto	74 73 76 71	294	554
Haruo Yasuda	73 75 74 73	295	410
Tomoo Ishii	68 74 78 75	295	410
Masaji Kusakabe	73 67 79 76	295	410
Frank Phillips, *Australia*	74 73 76 73	296	330
Tadashi Kitta	74 75 76 71	296	330
Seiichi Sato	71 73 81 71	296	330
Hsu Chin San, *Formosa*	72 72 78 75	297	290
Torakichi Nakamura	74 72 76 76	298	256.25
Masayuki Imai	77 71 74 76	298	256.25
Alan Murray, *Australia*	75 74 77 72	298	256.25
Takashi Murakami	74 75 78 71	298	256.25
Shozo Miyamoto	75 71 75 78	299	227.14
Akihiro Teramoto	75 73 75 76	299	227.14
Fujio Ishii	76 74 74 75	299	227.14
Hisashi Morioka	74 73 77 75	299	227.14
Kuo Chi Hsiung, *Formosa*	75 74 76 74	299	227.14
Norifumi Mizuno	76 75 76 72	299	227.14
Yukihiro Kudo	75 73 79 72	299	227.14
Namio Takasu	77 72 73 78	300	31.42
Shigeru Uchida	75 73 76 76	300	31.42
Chen Chien Chin, *Formosa*	74 77 74 75	300	31.42
Takao Hara	74 76 75 75	300	31.42
Katsushi Yanagida	73 74 78 75	300	31.42
Kikuo Arai	73 75 78 74	300	31.42
Ireneo Legaspi, *Philippines*	71 76 80 73	300	31.42

* Amateur

INDIAN OPEN

ROYAL CALCUTTA GOLF CLUB
Calcutta
April 17—20
Purse...$5,400
Par: 38, 35—73...6,869 yards

	SCORE				TOTAL	MONEY
Ben Arda, *Philippines*	74	75	71	71	291	$1,500
Shadi Lal	75	79	73	71	298	750
*R. K. Pitamber	78	75	73	72	298	
Shohei Nishida, *Japan*	77	74	80	72	303	625
Ruda Valji	78	79	74	74	305	500
Jolu	79	77	76	75	307	400
Lal Chand	76	77	81	74	308	350
*A. S. Malik	72	78	81	77	308	
*P. G. Sethi	81	76	77	78	312	
*Ashok Mehra	83	79	79	72	313	
Hyder Khan	74	83	80	76	313	300
Tsunehiko Matsuki, *Japan*	80	81	77	75	313	250
J. A. Hardwick	82	83	73	76	314	200
Jamshed	81	81	78	76	316	125
*Madhu Misra	79	76	82	79	316	
Amar Singh	76	84	77	79	316	110
Pritam Singh	77	80	84	76	317	80
Nabi Rasul Ansari	83	75	81	78	317	80
S. N. Padugale	79	78	79	81	317	80
*Major S. Chaudhri	77	86	80	76	319	
Md. Hussain	81	82	79	77	319	50

* Amateur

Australian Tour

BRISBANE WATERS OPEN

WOY WOY GOLF CLUB, NSW
Par: 67
THE ENTRANCE GOLF CLUB, NSW
Par: 69
January 16—19
Purse: $A4,000†

TEGGERAH GOLF CLUB, NSW
Par: 69
EVERGLADES GOLF CLUB, NSW
Par: 69

	SCORES	TOTAL	MONEY
Billy Dunk	68 69 67 69	273	$A800
Alan Murray	66 72 65 71	274	400
Maurice Bembridge, *Great Britain*	63 73 65 73	274	400
Frank Phillips	69 68 68 69	274	400
Vic Bennetts	70 68 67 71	276	225
Peter Harvey	67 67 70 72	276	225
Colin Johnston	64 70 73 71	278	150
*Jeff Watts	66 71 70 71	278	
Ted Ball	65 71 70 73	279	116
Tom Linskey	66 68 72 73	279	116
Peter Jackson	63 67 71 78	279	116
Tony Mangan	67 72 71 70	280	105
Ian Richardson, *Great Britain*	69 67 73 71	280	105
Stan Peach	68 68 71 73	280	105
*Barry Burgess	67 70 67 76	280	
Walter Godfrey, *New Zealand*	67 68 72 74	281	90
Alex Mercer	69 72 68 73	282	75
David Graham	67 68 69 78	282	75
*Des Turner	66 73 73 71	283	
John Sullivan	67 73 69 74	283	55
Bob Shaw	66 72 70 75	283	55
Len Woodward	69 72 67 75	283	55
Bob Richards	71 66 73 74	284	46.66
Brian Moran	70 70 69 75	284	46.66
Paul Hart	64 70 75 75	284	46.66
Chris Tickner	69 70 75 71	285	40
Barry Bent	72 67 75 71	285	40
Tim Woolbank	70 71 71 74	286	30
Tim Ireland	69 71 70 76	286	30

† One Australian dollar = $1.12 US.
*Amateur

TASMANIAN OPEN

RIVERSIDE GOLF CLUB
Launceston, Tasmania
January 31—February 2
Purse...$A3,000
Par: 72

	SCORES	TOTAL	MONEY
Alan Murray	69 68 68 75	280	$A750
Randall Vines	68 71 70 72	281	420
Tim Woolbank	70 71 73 68	282	250
Barry Coxon	73 70 67 73	283	190
Paul Hart	70 73 69 72	284	150
Clive Johnston	72 71 69 72	284	150
Maurice Bembridge, *Great Britain*	69 71 74 71	285	120
Ted Ball	76 68 74 69	287	90
Tony Mangan	71 72 74 70	287	90
Walter Godfrey, *New Zealand*	75 69 74 70	288	75
John Lister, *New Zealand*	72 72 72 72	288	75
Bruce Hodson	73 72 70 74	289	75
Brian Boys, *New Zealand*	73 72 74 71	290	67.50
Terry Kendall, *New Zealand*	73 68 73 76	290	67.50
George Kramer	77 72 73 70	292	60
Alan Campbell	71 74 71 76	292	60
Bill Watson	78 74 73 69	294	60
Dick Flood	76 73 76 70	295	30
Ted Stirling	71 72 75 77	295	30

VICTORIAN OPEN

KINGSTON HEATH GOLF CLUB
Melbourne, Victoria
February 6—9
Purse...$A10,000
Par: 74

	SCORES	TOTAL	MONEY
Kel Nagle	71 73 69 66	279	$A2,000
Billy Dunk	71 75 70 66	282	1,200
Peter Thomson	68 75 71 68	282	1,200
Frank Phillips	74 72 69 69	284	750
Maurice Bembridge, *Great Britain*	71 70 73 72	286	500
Walter Godfrey, *New Zealand*	69 70 73 74	286	500
Stan Peach	72 74 69 71	286	500
Glen McCully	71 71 71 74	287	280
Wally Gale	74 71 70 72	287	280

	SCORES	TOTAL	MONEY
David Graham	74 70 70 73	287	280
Bruce Hodson	70 78 72 67	287	280
John Sullivan	72 75 67 74	288	200
Alan Murray	71 77 70 71	289	190
Col Harrington	70 74 73 73	290	180
Colin Johnston	75 71 72 73	291	170
*Roger Cowan	74 74 70 73	291	
John Davis	67 79 71 75	292	160
*Jack Newton	73 77 69 73	292	
Stewart Ginn	74 71 72 76	293	173.50
Dennis Clark, New Zealand	71 74 77 71	293	137.50
Alan Heil	74 73 76 70	293	137.50
Peter Harvey	80 69 72 73	294	130
*Kevin Hartley	72 80 70 72	294	
*Don Reiter	73 75 73 73	294	
Terry Kendall, New Zealand	69 74 75 77	295	100
John Lister, New Zealand	74 75 74 72	295	100
Peter Jackson	74 75 74 72	295	100
Geoff Donald	76 74 74 71	295	100
Peter Clutton	76 77 73 69	295	100
Ian Stanley	72 74 80 70	296	37.14
George Bell	74 74 75 73	296	37.14
Jack Daugherty, U.S.	72 70 76 78	296	37.14
Bob Mesnil	71 76 71 79	297	37.14
Guy Wolstenholme, Great Britain	73 76 73 75	297	37.14
Jack Westmore	73 77 73 74	297	37.14
Paul Hart	73 77 72 75	297	37.14

*Amateur

QUEENSLAND OPEN

BRISBANE GOLF CLUB
Brisbane, Queensland
July 24—27
Purse...$A5,000
Par: 73

	SCORES	TOTAL	MONEY
Tim Woolbank	72 66 68 72	278	$A1,000
Graham Marsh	75 72 67 67	281	600
Randall Vines	70 69 71 73	283	500
John Lister, New Zealand	71 74 70 69	284	350
Jerry Stolhand, U.S.	75 70 71 68	284	350
Les Wilson	70 71 73 71	285	213.33
Alan Murray	71 69 72 73	285	213.33

	SCORES	TOTAL	MONEY
Brian Boys, *New Zealand*	71 71 70 73	285	213.33
Vic Bennetts	70 74 70 72	286	180
Tony Mangan	72 72 74 70	288	150
John Donald	73 75 71 70	289	104
John Sullivan	71 73 72 73	289	104
David Graham	69 74 74 72	289	104
Billy Dunk	74 70 72 73	289	104
Frank Phillips	70 72 72 75	289	104
Colin Johnston	70 69 80 72	291	80
John Klatt	74 77 73 68	292	66.67
John Dyer	72 67 79 74	292	66.67
Brian Moran	74 66 78 74	292	66.67
Alex Mercer	75 70 72 75	292	66.67
Paul Hart	72 73 72 75	292	66.67
Terry Kendall, *New Zealand*	68 78 72 74	292	66.67
*Jerry Kay	72 71 70 79	292	
Barry Bent	73 75 74 73	295	50
Robert Gibson	75 78 73 70	296	50
Bob Richards	73 73 73 77	296	50
*Ron Hertich	77 76 69 75	297	
Dennis Clark, *New Zealand*	74 73 76 74	297	40

*Amateur

AERON OPEN

KOGARAH GOLF CLUB
Sydney, NSW
February 13—15
Purse...$A3,000
Par: 71

	SCORES	TOTAL	MONEY
Frank Phillips	66 71 70 70	277	$A600
Darrel Welch	74 70 66 69	279	400
Walter Godfrey, *New Zealand*	69 71 71 70	281	300
Peter Harvey	72 71 71 69	283	220
Wally Gale	70 73 74 67	284	156.66
Ted Ball	72 71 68 73	284	156.66
Guy Wolstenholme, *Great Britain*	72 70 71 71	284	156.66
Randall Vines	71 68 75 71	285	110
†Vic Bennetts	70 74 71 70	285	
Billy Dunk	69 70 73 74	286	100
Maurice Bembridge, *Great Britain*	73 74 68 72	287	71.66
Tony Mangan	75 70 71 71	287	71.66
John Sullivan	72 71 70 74	287	71.66

	SCORES	TOTAL	MONEY
Alan Murray	71 72 74 70	287	71.66
Paul Hart	71 72 71 73	287	71.66
Bob Richards	73 69 70 75	287	71.66
John Lister, *New Zealand*	75 67 72 74	288	45
Terry Kendall, *New Zealand*	69 72 74 73	288	45
Ian Richardson, *Great Britain*	69 76 70 74	289	20
Dennis Clark, *New Zealand*	72 72 71 74	289	20
Kel Nagle	70 72 73 74	289	20
Colin Johnston	71 68 73 77	289	20
Ian Brander	72 69 74 74	289	20

† probationary professional, ineligible for prize money.

NEW SOUTH WALES PGA CHAMPIONSHIP

CASTLE HILL GOLF CLUB
Sydney, NSW
September 4—7
Purse...$A3,500
Par: 72

	SCORES	TOTAL	MONEY
Billy Dunk	73 70 70 70	284	$A700
John Sullivan	72 69 73 71	285	460
Barry Coxon	71 75 73 68	287	350
Randall Vines	71 73 74 70	288	290
Terry Kendall, *New Zealand*	73 75 71 72	291	185
Brian Boys, *New Zealand*	73 71 79 68	291	185
David Graham	75 74 69 74	292	130
Walter Godfrey, *New Zealand*	70 76 71 75	292	130
Guy Wolstenholme, *Great Britain*	71 74 74 74	293	110
Clive Johnston	76 74 71 73	294	105
Colin Johnston	76 74 71 73	294	105
Jerry Stolhand, *U.S.*	71 74 75 75	295	90
Malcolm Willis	73 75 73 74	295	90
Kel Nagle	77 71 76 73	297	75
Barry Bent	77 73 71 76	297	75
Alan Murray	75 77 74 72	298	60
Colin McGregor	76 75 72 75	298	60
Darrel Welch	72 76 77 73	298	60
Paul Hart	79 74 73 74	300	25
Tom Linskey	76 72 76 76	300	25
Malcolm Moulds	76 77 72 75	300	25
Graham Watson	76 75 73 76	300	25
Tim Woolbank	78 71 79 74	302	20
Peter Clutton	77 73 77 76	303	20

	SCORES	TOTAL	MONEY
Ray Wilson	79 74 76 75	304	
Barry Eves	74 75 77 79	305	
Don Gray	78 77 75 75	305	

CITY OF SYDNEY OPEN

MOORE PARK GOLF CLUB
Sydney, NSW
October 9—12
Purse...$A5,000
Par: 71...6,676 yards

	SCORES	TOTAL	MONEY
Bruce Devlin	65 65 70	200	$A1,000
Takashi Murakami, *Japan*	67 66 68	201	600
Colin McGregor	68 67 68	203	500
David Graham	69 69 66	204	400
Hsieh Min Nan, *Formosa*	65 69 71	205	250
Tim Woolbank	68 68 69	205	250
Bob Stanton	69 67 69	205	250
John Sullivan	67 71 69	207	176.67
Barry Coxon	71 67 69	207	176.67
Vic Bennetts	71 67 69	207	176.67
Graham Marsh	71 69 68	208	120
Bob Shaw	73 67 68	208	120
Darrel Welch	68 71 70	209	90
Paul Hart	70 74 65	209	90
Kel Nagle	68 72 69	209	90
Colin Johnston	69 69 71	209	90
Frank Phillips	70 71 69	210	80
Guy Wolstenholme, *Great Britain*	74 70 67	211	70
Billy Dunk	72 71 68	211	70
*Mick O'Connor	70 72 69	211	
George Knudson, *Canada*	70 71 70	211	70
Randall Vines	70 71 70	211	70
*Bill Wright	71 71 70	212	
*Trevor Woods	67 73 72	212	
Eric Cremin	70 70 72	212	60
Alan Murray	72 66 74	212	60
Mike Kelly	74 70 69	213	50
Hsu Chi San, *Formosa*	67 73 73	213	50
David Mercer	70 69 74	213	50
Wally Gale	71 73 70	214	20
Alister Palmer, *New Zealand*	72 72 70	214	20

*Amateur

WILLS MASTERS

VICTORIA GOLF CLUB
Melbourne, Victoria
October 16—19
Purse...$A20,000
Par: 73

	SCORES	TOTAL	MONEY
George Knudson, *Canada*	73 66 68 72	279	$A3,300
Peter Thomson	72 73 67 69	281	2,200
Bob Stanton	68 69 71 73	281	2,200
Billy Dunk	72 71 71 69	283	1,500
Randall Vines	72 73 74 66	285	1,200
Barry Coxon	70 73 72 71	286	850
Bruce Devlin	71 71 67 77	286	850
Lu Liang Huan, *Formosa*	70 72 74 72	288	700
Bill Casper, *U.S.*	70 76 72 71	289	600
Takashi Murakami, *Japan*	72 72 72 73	289	600
Sukree Onsham, *Thailand*	73 69 74 73	289	600
Tim Woolbank	70 75 72 72	289	600
Hsieh Min Nan, *Formosa*	71 74 71 74	290	450
Alan Heil	75 72 75 69	291	400
Kuo Chi Hsiung, *Formosa*	75 73 72 72	292	300
Graham Marsh	71 74 73 74	292	300
Peter Oosterhuis, *Great Britain*	72 72 75 73	292	300
David Graham	76 69 68 80	293	195
John Sullivan	75 73 74 71	293	195
Brian Boys, *New Zealand*	77 72 75 70	294	175
Alan Murray	73 72 77 72	294	175
Geoff Donald	69 76 73 77	295	153.33
Simon Hobday, *South Africa*	71 73 78 73	295	153.33
Bob Shaw	74 73 74 74	295	153.33
Peter Harvey	75 75 70 76	296	142.50
Brian Moran	76 75 74 71	296	142.50
Kel Nagle	73 78 72 73	296	142.50
Guy Wolstenholme, *Great Britain*	76 75 72 73	296	142.50
Maurice Bembridge, *Great Britain*	70 72 77 78	297	122.85
Barry Bent	75 72 76 74	297	122.85
Walter Godfrey, *New Zealand*	75 74 75 73	297	122.85
Bruce Green	74 79 71 73	297	122.85
Hsu Chi San, *Formosa*	74 76 72 75	297	122.85
Stuart Vernon, *New Zealand*	79 73 72 73	297	122.85
Les Wilson	73 81 72 71	297	122.85
Clive Clark, *Great Britain*	77 78 71 72	298	105
Malcolm Gregson, *Great Britain*	75 75 73 75	298	105
Paul Hart	74 79 70 75	298	105
Ray Jennings	77 71 74 76	298	105

	SCORES	TOTAL	MONEY
Tom Linskey	73 72 76 78	299	33.33
Geoff Parslow	79 74 73 73	299	33.33
Malcolm Willis	74 75 76 74	299	33.33

AUSTRALIAN OPEN

ROYAL SYDNEY GOLF CLUB
Sydney, NSW
October 23–26
Purse...$A15,000
Par: 72...6,722 yards

	SCORES	TOTAL	MONEY
Gary Player, *South Africa*	74 69 68 77	288	$A2,500
Guy Wolstenholme, *Great Britain*	71 71 71 76	289	1,800
Bob Stanton	73 73 73 71	290	1,150
Tadashi Kitta, *Japan*	75 71 71 73	290	1,150
Norman Von Nida	75 73 72 72	292	750
Kel Nagle	76 72 71 73	292	750
Bruce Devlin	72 70 74 76	292	750
Takashi Murakami, *Japan*	77 72 74 70	293	575
Peter Thomson	71 71 74 77	293	575
Lee Trevino, *U.S.*	74 73 72 76	295	450
Randall Vines	76 73 74 72	295	450
Haruo Suzumura, *Japan*	74 74 72 75	295	450
Ted Ball	74 79 71 72	296	325
Walter Godfrey, *New Zealand*	76 77 72 71	296	325
Simon Hobday, *South Africa*	73 77 74 73	297	250
Tony Mangan	75 72 79 72	298	200
Frank Phillips	76 74 75 74	299	175
Malcolm Gregson, *Great Britain*	76 73 75 75	299	175
*Jeff Watts	78 72 78 72	300	
*Tony Gresham	75 76 74 75	300	
Hsieh Min Nan, *Formosa*	77 73 74 76	300	155
David Graham	77 69 81 73	300	155
John Sullivan	73 79 77 72	301	140
Hsu Chi San, *Formosa*	73 79 77 72	301	140
David Fearns	74 73 75 79	301	140
Tim Woolbank	73 74 75 79	301	140
Maurice Bembridge, *Great Britain*	74 76 76 75	301	140
Billy Dunk	76 75 75 75	301	140
Wally Gale	73 75 78 75	301	140
*Barry Burgess	77 72 75 78	302	
Barry Coxon	75 78 74 75	302	130
Brian Boys, *New Zealand*	76 73 82 71	302	120
*Tom Crow	81 71 74 77	303	

	SCORES	TOTAL	MONEY
Graham Marsh	74 73 80 77	304	120
Tony Jacklin, *Great Britain*	75 76 77 77	305	90
Sukree Onsham, *Thailand*	73 76 80 76	305	90
Barry Bent	80 74 77 74	305	90
Eric Cremin	79 74 76 76	305	90
Chris Porter	73 81 75 76	305	90
Stan Peach	78 73 77 77	305	90

*Amateur

DUNLOP INTERNATIONAL

YARRA YARRA GOLF CLUB
Melbourne, Victoria
October 30—November 2
Purse...$A25,000
Par: 73

	SCORES	TOTAL	MONEY
Bruce Devlin	68 70 67 71	276	$A4,000
Lee Trevino, *U.S.*	70 71 68 67	276	3,000
(Devlin defeated Trevino on first hole of sudden-death playoff.)			
Gary Player, *South Africa*	70 68 72 68	278	2,400
Tony Jacklin, *Great Britain*	70 72 71 67	280	1,900
Maurice Bembridge, *Great Britain*	70 73 73 65	281	1,300
Guy Wolstenholme, *Great Britain*	70 69 75 67	281	1,300
Bob Stanton	72 67 68 76	283	950
Orville Moody, *U.S.*	72 70 69 73	284	850
Graham Marsh	75 70 71 69	285	775
Hsieh Min Nan, *Formosa*	72 71 70 72	285	775
Clive Clark, *Great Britain*	74 71 69 72	286	675
Geoff Parslow	73 72 69 72	286	675
Alan Heil	72 72 68 75	287	600
Simon Hobday, *South Africa*	68 75 72 73	288	550
Malcolm Gregson, *Great Britain*	69 72 76 72	289	450
Ted Ball	72 72 72 73	289	450
Glen McCully	69 77 71 72	289	450
David Graham	74 72 66 78	290	340
Tadashi Kitta, *Japan*	73 79 66 73	291	267.50
Takashi Murakami, *Japan*	71 73 72 75	291	267.50
John Sullivan	73 74 74 70	291	267.50
Peter Thomson	74 71 73 73	291	267.50
Kel Nagle	74 71 72 75	292	185
Lu Liang Huan, *Formosa*	73 72 73 74	292	185
Hsu Chi San, *Formosa*	73 74 71 75	293	157.50
Brian Boys, *New Zealand*	74 73 76 70	293	157.50

	SCORES	TOTAL	MONEY
Vic Bennetts	73 74 73 73	293	157.50
Tim Woolbank	74 72 74 73	293	157.50
Paul Hart	76 71 71 76	294	143.33
Geoff Donald	75 74 70 75	294	143.33
Errol Hartvigsen	76 74 69 75	294	143.33
Peter-Oosterhuis, *Great Britain*	75 74 71 75	295	140
Bob Shaw	75 73 72 76	296	130
Brian Smith	74 73 71 79	297	115
Billy Dunk	80 72 71 74	297	115
Paul Connell	72 73 75 76	297	115
Terry Kendall, *New Zealand*	75 72 73 77	297	115
Mike Kelly	77 72 72 77	298	100
Darrel Welch	77 72 73 77	299	20
Sukree Onsham, *Thailand*	75 76 70 78	299	20
Tom Linskey	73 75 73 78	299	20
Colin Johnston	74 76 73 76	299	20
Barry Bent	74 74 75 76	299	20

AUSTRALIAN PGA CHAMPIONSHIP

ROYAL CANBERRA GOLF CLUB
Canberra, ACT
November 6—9
Purse...$A10,000
Par: 72

	SCORES	TOTAL	MONEY
Bruce Devlin	67 69 69 72	277	$A2,000
Takashi Murakami, *Japan*	71 72 70 67	280	1,400
Bob Stanton	73 70 73 68	284	1,000
Hsieh Min Nan, *Formosa*	71 71 75 70	287	562.50
Peter Oosterhuis, *Great Britain*	69 76 70 72	287	562.50
Peter Thomson	70 75 69 73	287	562.50
Guy Wolstenholme, *Great Britain*	74 72 70 71	287	562.50
Haruo Suzumura, *Japan*	76 75 69 69	289	350
Billy Dunk	72 77 69 72	290	300
Frank Phillips	75 76 72 68	291	208
Brian Boys, *New Zealand*	74 72 75 70	291	208
Malcolm Gregson, *Great Britain*	71 76 73 71	291	208
Geoff Parslow	73 75 72 71	291	208
Clive Clark, *Great Britain*	68 75 74 74	291	208
Lu Liang Huan, *Formosa*	77 73 71 71	292	160
Vic Bennetts	73 74 70 75	292	160
Graham Marsh	72 75 70 75	292	160
Darrel Welch	74 74 75 70	293	130
Stan Peach	72 75 72 74	293	130

	SCORES	TOTAL	MONEY
Maurice Bembridge, *Great Britain*	74 71 71 77	293	130
Kel Nagle	69 74 77 74	294	95
Alan Murray	72 73 75 74	294	95
Colin McGregor	72 76 72 74	294	95
David Graham	73 76 71 74	294	95
Randall Vines	75 77 73 70	295	73.33
Bob Shaw	73 77 74 71	295	73.33
Ted Ball	76 72 73 74	295	73.33
Ian Alexander	72 78 74 72	296	70
Barry Bent	72 77 75 73	297	20
Len Woodward	74 75 73 75	297	20
Tadashi Kitta, *Japan*	73 75 75 74	297	20
Paul Murray	75 74 73 75	297	20
Clive Johnston	74 75 74 74	297	20
Kuo Chi Hsiung, *Formosa*	76 74 71 76	297	20

NORTH COAST OPEN

COFFS HARBOUR GOLF CLUB
Coffs Harbour, NSW
November 20—23
Purse...$A6,000
Par: 72

	SCORES	TOTAL	MONEY
Tony Mangan	73 72 72 74	291	$A1,200
David Graham	75 71 71 77	294	800
Eric Cremin	73 76 73 73	295	512.50
Clive Clark, *Great Britain*	70 76 75 74	295	512.50
*Keith Drage	73 75 75 72	295	
Barry Coxon	71 74 76 75	296	300
Vic Bennetts	71 75 74 76	296	300
Randall Vines	72 76 72 76	296	300
David Fearns	71 76 78 73	298	200
Chris Tickner	76 71 78 74	299	180
George Kramer	73 78 71 77	299	180
*Barry See Hoe	74 71 76 79	300	
Ted Ball	74 77 78 72	301	140
John Lister, *New Zealand*	76 75 77 73	301	140
Bob Richards	76 75 75 76	302	120
Frank Phillips	72 83 74 74	303	100
*Jack Newton	72 76 79 76	303	
Simon Hobday, *South Africa*	71 78 76 78	303	100
Tom Linskey	76 73 80 74	303	100
Rob Taylor	79 77 74 74	304	78
Bruce Hodson	73 76 80 75	304	78

	SCORES				TOTAL	MONEY
Tim Woolbank	72	76	79	77	304	78
Paul Hart	74	74	75	81	304	78
Alan Murray	70	82	76	76	304	78
Fred Belle	74	78	73	80	305	70
Vic Richardson	75	77	74	80	306	60
Geoff Donald	75	77	81	74	307	60
*Noel Ratcliffe	76	80	75	76	307	
Frank Conallin	78	74	77	78	307	60
Reg Want	78	76	77	77	308	50
Graham Bell	74	75	80	79	308	50
Barry Deitz	72	78	78	80	308	50
*Don Sharp	76	77	77	78	308	

*Amateur

New Zealand Tour

SPALDING MASTERS

TAURANGA
January 3—5
Purse...$NZ4,000†
Par: 71...6,025 yards

	SCORES	TOTAL	MONEY
Bob Charles	66 62 69 63	260	$NZ800
John Lister	69 67 68 66	270	600
Bob Shaw, *Australia*	68 65 72 66	271	316.66
Brian Boys	70 65 72 64	271	316.66
Paul Hart, *Australia*	69 69 62 71	271	316.66
*Stuart Jones	69 65 68 71	273	
Ted Ball, *Australia*	67 68 68 71	274	220
Guy Wolstenholme, *Great Britain*	67 70 70 68	275	173.33
Bob Stanton, *Australia*	69 67 69 70	275	173.33
Jerry Stolhand, *U.S.*	68 71 66 70	275	173.33
Frank Malloy	70 66 68 72	276	133.33
Walter Godfrey	70 68 66 72	276	133.33
Maurice Bembridge, *Great Britain*	69 69 72 66	276	133.33
Jess Vaughn, *U.S.*	70 69 72 67	278	110
*Ross Murray	69 69 73 68	279	
Stan Peach, *Australia*	68 71 70 70	279	90
John Sullivan, *Australia*	72 67 68 72	279	90
Frank Buckler	69 71 71 68	279	90
Alan Murray, *Australia*	68 69 74 69	280	70
Terry Kendall	68 72 72 70	282	60

† 1 New Zealand Dollar = $1.12
* Amateur

STARS TRAVEL PGA

MOUNT MAUNGANUI
January 6—8
Purse...$NZ5,000
Par: 73...6,575 yards

	SCORES	TOTAL	MONEY
Terry Kendall	69 63 70 72	274	$NZ750
Bob Charles	68 67 71 69	275	575
John Lister	70 67 69 69	275	575

	SCORES	TOTAL	MONEY
Bob Stanton, *Australia*	74 67 73 67	281	485
*Bruce Rafferty	77 69 70 67	283	
Maurice Bembridge, *Great Britain*	73 71 69 72	285	410
Walter Godfrey	73 72 68 73	286	310
Guy Wolstenholme, *Great Britain*	74 70 71 71	286	310
Bob Shaw, *Australia*	77 72 68 70	287	203.33
Tim Woolbank, *Australia*	72 72 73 70	287	203.33
John Sullivan, *Australia*	71 73 72 71	287	203.33
*Stuart Jones	71 73 72 71	287	
Brian Boys	71 74 72 71	288	150
Stan Peach, *Australia*	73 68 70 78	289	130
Frank Malloy	73 67 73 76	289	130
Alan Murray, *Australia*	74 67 76 73	290	110
Ted Ball, *Australia*	72 76 70 73	291	86.66
Frank Buckler	74 73 71 73	291	86.66
Dennis Clark	74 66 77 74	291	86.66
*Ross Murray	72 75 74 71	292	
*P. Shadlock	76 73 71 72	292	
Paul Hart, *Australia*	68 77 69 79	293	65
Stuart Vernon	75 72 71 75	293	65
Barry Bent, *Australia*	74 77 73 69	293	65

* Amateur

NEW ZEALAND OPEN

WANGANUI
November 27—29
Purse...$NZ12,500
Par: 70...6,466 yards

	SCORES	TOTAL	MONEY
Kel Nagle, *Australia*	69 67 69 68	273	$NZ2,500
John Lister	68 70 69 68	275	2,000
Randall Vines, *Australia*	69 69 69 69	276	1,500
Takashi Murakami, *Japan*	68 70 67 72	277	833.33
Frank Phillips, *Australia*	69 69 70 69	277	833.33
Maurice Bembridge, *Great Britain*	65 75 70 67	277	833.33
Bob Charles	70 67 71 72	280	475
Guy Wolstenholme, *Great Britain*	73 67 72 68	280	475
Vic Bennetts, *Australia*	73 68 69 70	280	475
Frank Buckler	68 74 69 70	281	350
Brian Boys	69 74 67 72	282	300
Graham Marsh, *Australia*	72 73 64 74	283	262.50
David Graham, *Australia*	69 69 72 73	283	262.50
Clive Clark, *Great Britain*	76 69 69 70	284	175
John Croskery	71 72 70 71	284	175

	SCORES	TOTAL	MONEY
L. Brown	71 71 70 72	284	175
Peter Harvey, *Australia*	71 70 72 71	284	175
Frank Malloy	68 71 73 72	284	175
Barry Coxon, *Australia*	71 68 75 72	286	95
Glen McCully, *Australia*	69 74 68 75	286	95
*Jack Lacy	72 74 69 71	286	
Alan Murray, *Australia*	71 70 73 73	287	85
Billy Dunk, *Australia*	67 78 69 74	288	70
Terry Kendall	73 74 70 71	288	70
*Stuart Jones	70 69 74 75	288	
*Ted McDougall	76 70 75 67	288	
Geoff Donald, *Australia*	70 72 73 74	289	27.50
Walter Godfrey	72 72 69 76	289	27.50
Barry Bent, *Australia*	72 74 70 73	289	27.50
Stuart Vernon	74 73 66 76	289	27.50

* Amateur

GARDEN CITY CLASSIC

RUSSLEY
Christchurch
December 4—7
Purse...$NZ15,000
Par: 73

	SCORES	TOTAL	MONEY
Kel Nagle, *Australia*	64 70 66 72	272	$NZ2,500
John Lister	67 67 67 73	274	1,900
Bob Charles	71 70 70 67	278	1,250
Tony Mangan, *Australia*	69 69 71 69	278	1,250
Graham Marsh, *Australia*	70 70 70 69	279	900
Billy Dunk, *Australia*	67 73 71 73	284	750
Takashi Murakami, *Japan*	72 72 71 71	286	625
Guy Wolstenholme, *Great Britain*	69 71 71 75	286	625
Glen McCully, *Australia*	72 73 73 69	287	525
Peter Oosterhuis, *Great Britain*	73 72 71 71	287	525
Brian Boys	73 70 70 75	288	450
Walter Godfrey	70 74 73 72	289	350
Alan Murray, *Australia*	71 71 74 73	289	350
Randall Vines, *Australia*	72 71 69 77	289	350
Clive Clark, *Great Britain*	74 72 69 75	290	225
R. Metherell, *Australia*	71 75 73 71	290	225
Barry Coxon, *Australia*	72 76 72 72	292	150
Frank Phillips, *Australia*	68 75 73 77	293	135
Dennis Sullivan	70 74 78 71	293	135

	SCORES	TOTAL	MONEY
Vic Bennetts, *Australia*	70 72 77 75	294	115
Keith Garner, *Australia*	74 73 73 74	294	115
*P. R. Adams	74 71 74 74	294	
Tim Woolbank, *Australia*	77 70 74 74	295	100
David Graham, *Australia*	73 70 75 77	295	100
Maurice Bembridge, *Great Britain*	74 77 71 73	295	100
Richard Slee	71 74 75 76	296	90
Barry Bent, *Australia*	76 72 76 72	296	90
Paul Hart, *Australia*	73 74 72 78	297	80
Jerry Stolhand, *U.S.*	71 75 80 73	299	80
Geoff Donald, *Australia*	78 72 79 71	300	53.33
Frank Malloy	74 69 80 77	300	53.33
Colin Caldwell	75 75 76 74	300	53.33
*R. H. Bradley	74 72 74 80	300	

* Amateur

CALTEX

PARAPARAUMU
December 11—13
Purse...$NZ5,000
Par: 71...6,552 yards

	SCORES	TOTAL	MONEY
Kel Nagle, *Australia*	70 69 67 69	275	$NZ1,000
John Lister	73 74 70 65	282	550
Billy Dunk, *Australia*	69 73 70 70	282	550
Graham Marsh, *Australia*	71 74 70 68	283	316.66
Jerry Stolhand, *U.S.*	71 74 68 70	283	316.66
Tim Woolbank, *Australia*	72 71 71 69	283	316.66
Barry Coxon, *Australia*	70 73 71 71	285	200
Alan Murray, *Australia*	73 74 71 68	286	165
Frank Malloy	73 69 72 72	286	165
Randall Vines, *Australia*	72 76 72 67	287	110
Tony Mangan, *Australia*	74 72 68 73	287	110
Terry Kendall	69 79 73 67	288	90
Vic Bennetts, *Australia*	72 74 69 73	288	90
Ted Ball, *Australia*	73 71 69 75	288	90
Peter Harvey, *Australia*	70 72 71 75	288	90
Lindsay Sharp, *Australia*	72 71 72 74	289	80
Glen McCully, *Australia*	71 75 73 71	290	65
Clive Clark, *Great Britain*	71 72 74 73	290	65
David Graham, *Australia*	70 72 77 71	290	65
Frank Phillips, *Australia*	72 77 70 71	290	65
Walter Godfrey	77 69 72 73	291	50
Maurice Bembridge, *Great Britain*	77 71 73 71	292	50

	SCORES	TOTAL	MONEY
R. Metherell, *Australia*	76 71 70 75	292	50
Brian Boys	76 75 70 71	292	50
Keith Garner, *Australia*	68 69 81 74	292	50
Peter Oosterhuis, *Great Britain*	77 73 72 72	294	
Bob Charles	72 77 75 70	294	
*John Durry	76 77 72 70	295	
*Jack Lacy	76 76 70 73	295	
*Jack Daugherty, *U.S.*	75 74 75 71	295	

* Amateur

WATTIES

GISBORNE
December 16—18
Purse...$NZ5,000

	SCORES	TOTAL	MONEY
Glen McCully, *Australia*	70 69 66 69	274	$NZ1,000
Bob Charles	68 71 66 72	277	550
Billy Dunk, *Australia*	71 68 67 71	277	550
John Lister	67 71 72 68	278	400
Graham Marsh, *Australia*	70 73 70 70	283	275
Kel Nagle, *Australia*	70 70 74 69	283	275
Randall Vines, *Australia*	71 72 72 69	284	190
Peter Harvey, *Australia*	69 73 69 73	284	190
Dennis Clark	70 74 68 74	286	135
Peter Oosterhuis, *Great Britain*	68 72 73 73	286	135
Maurice Bembridge, *Great Britain*	71 75 72 69	287	100
Barry Coxon, *Australia*	73 73 73 68	287	100
Brian Boys	68 77 72 71	288	86.66
Ted Ball, *Australia*	73 76 68 71	288	86.66
Clive Clark, *Great Britain*	72 73 73 70	288	86.66
Alan Murray, *Australia*	70 69 74 76	289	75
Lindsay Sharp, *Australia*	72 72 73 72	289	75
*Allan Snape	70 73 69 77	289	
David Graham, *Australia*	74 70 74 73	291	70
*M. J. Fisher	75 74 74 69	292	
*Stuart Jones	73 76 74 69	292	
Jerry Stolhand, *U.S.*	73 72 77 71	293	60
Vic Bennetts, *Australia*	75 76 68 75	294	60
Frank Phillips, *Australia*	75 72 74 74	295	50
Geoff Donald, *Australia*	70 73 77 76	296	50
Frank Malloy	69 77 74 76	296	50
*W. Neill	74 74 75 73	296	
John Croskery	75 75 76 71	297	50

458

	SCORES	TOTAL	MONEY
Walter Godfrey	73 74 75 76	298	16.66
Paul Hart, *Australia*	73 74 76 75	298	16.66
Alistair Palmer	77 72 75 74	298	16.66
*W. L. Hill	73 76 74 75	298	

* Amateur

VONNEL INTERNATIONAL

NORTH SHORE GOLF CLUB
Auckland
December 20—21
Purse...$NZ5,000

	SCORES	TOTAL	MONEY
John Lister	70 70	140	$NZ1,000
Billy Dunk, *Australia*	71 69	140	500
Terry Kendall	71 69	140	500
Randall Vines, *Australia*	69 71	140	500
(Lister won sudden-death playoff on second hole.)			
Walter Godfrey	71 70	141	300
Jerry Stolhand, *U.S.*	69 73	142	250
Lindsay Sharp, *Australia*	70 73	143	150
Kel Nagle, *Australia*	70 73	143	150
Frank Phillips, *Australia*	70 73	143	150
Alan Murray, *Australia*	75 68	143	150
Ted Ball, *Australia*	73 70	143	150
Barry Coxon, *Australia*	73 71	144	93.33
David Graham, *Australia*	73 71	144	93.33
Tim Woolbank, *Australia*	74 70	144	93.33
*Ted McDougall	71 73	144	
*B. Day	73 72	145	
Guy Wolstenholme, *Great Britain*	73 72	145	67.14
Charles Pettit, *Australia*	74 71	145	67.14
Frank Buckler, *Australia*	72 73	145	67.14
Brian Boys	72 73	145	67.14
Dennis Clark	73 72	145	67.14
Glen McCully, *Australia*	74 71	145	67.14
Tony Mangan, *Australia*	74 71	145	67.14
Peter Harvey, *Australia*	74 72	146	40
Graham Marsh, *Australia*	72 74	146	40
R. Metherell, *Australia*	72 74	146	40
Peter Oosterhuis, *Great Britain*	77 69	146	40
N. D. Hayden	71 75	146	40
*P. Shadlock	73 73	146	

* Amateur

Miscellaneous

RYDER CUP MATCHES

ROYAL BIRKDALE GOLF CLUB
Southport, England
September 18—20
Par: 35, 38—73...7,037 yards

FINAL STANDINGS: U.S. 16, Great Britain 16.

FOURSOMES
Morning

Tony Jacklin and Peter Townsend (Great Britain) defeated Dave Hill and Tommy Aaron, 3 and 1.

Neil Coles and Brian Huggett (Great Britain) defeated Miller Barber and Ray Floyd, 3 and 2.

Bernard Gallacher and Maurice Bembridge (Great Britain) defeated Lee Trevino and Ken Still, 2 and 1.

Bill Casper and Frank Beard (U.S.) halved with Christie O'Connor and Peter Alliss (Great Britain).

Afternoon

Jack Nicklaus and Dan Sikes (U.S.) defeated Bernard Hunt and Peter Butler, 1 up.

Gene Littler and Trevino (U.S.) defeated Gallacher and Bembridge, 2 up.

Jacklin and Townsend (Great Britain) defeated Casper and Beard, 2 up.

Hill and Aaron (U.S.) defeated Coles and Huggett, 1 up.

(Great Britain leads, 4 1/2 to 3 1/2)

FOUR BALL
Morning

Jacklin and Coles (Great Britain) defeated Nicklaus and Sikes, 1 up.

O'Connor and Townsend (Great Britain) defeated Hill and Dale Douglass, 1 up.

Huggett and Alex Caygill (Great Britain) halved with Floyd and Barber (U.S.)

Trevino and Littler (U.S.) defeated Alliss and Brian Barnes, 1 up.

Afternoon

Casper and Beard (U.S.) defeated Townsend and Butler, 2 up.

Hill and Still (U.S.) defeated Huggett and Gallacher, 2 and 1.

Bembridge and Hunt (Great Britain) halved with Aaron and Floyd (U.S.)

Trevino and Barber (U.S.) halved with Jacklin and Coles (Great Britain).

(U.S. 8, Great Britain 8)

SINGLES
Morning
Trevino (U.S.) defeated Alliss, 2 and 1.
Hill (U.S.) defeated Townsend, 5 and 4.
Coles (Great Britain) defeated Aaron, 1 up.
Casper (U.S.) defeated Barnes, 1 up.
O'Connor (Great Britain) defeated Beard, 5 and 4.
Bembridge (Great Britain) defeated Still, 1 up.
Butler (Great Britain) defeated Floyd, 1 up.
Jacklin (Great Britain) defeated Nicklaus, 4 and 3.

Afternoon
Hill (U.S.) defeated Barnes, 4 and 2.
Gallacher (Great Britain) defeated Trevino, 4 and 3.
Barber (U.S.) defeated Bembridge, 7 and 6.
Butler (Great Britain) defeated Douglass, 3 and 2.
Littler (U.S.) defeated O'Connor, 2 and 1.
Huggett (Great Britain) halved with Casper (U.S.)
Sikes (U.S.) defeated Coles, 4 and 3.
Jacklin (Great Britain) halved with Nicklaus (U.S.)

WORLD CUP AND INTERNATIONAL TROPHY CHAMPIONSHIP

SINGAPORE ISLAND COUNTRY CLUB—BUKIT COURSE
Singapore
October 2—5
Par: 35, 36—71...6,584 yards

TEAM COMPETITION

	SCORE				TOTAL
United States	138	140	140	134	552
Japan	142	140	142	136	560
Argentina	141	138	145	137	561
Thailand	139	140	140	143	562
Formosa	138	139	139	146	562
Philippines	140	144	136	144	564
Spain	144	140	144	140	568
Belgium	149	145	141	138	573
Australia	144	139	148	143	574
Colombia	143	144	143	145	575
Wales	149	140	144	143	576
South Africa	142	149	145	141	577
Canada	143	146	144	145	578
England	149	145	146	139	579
Italy	145	144	147	143	579

Brazil	149	143	147	141	580
Mexico	140	145	146	150	581
Egypt	150	144	144	144	582
New Zealand	148	147	144	146	585
Scotland	153	143	146	144	586
Korea	146	148	147	145	586
France	147	150	149	143	589
Germany	150	147	149	145	591
Austria	155	141	147	149	592
Singapore	150	145	146	152	593
Holland	148	150	150	147	595
Chile	149	151	151	145	596
Puerto Rico	153	149	146	148	596
Malaysia	151	148	152	147	598
Peru	152	146	157	147	602
Denmark	153	148	151	150	602
Ireland	151	149	154	153	607
India	150	152	158	149	609
Hawaii	156	151	152	151	610
Indonesia	154	156	152	150	612
Greece	155	147	153	158	613
Burma	154	151	155	155	615
Switzerland	154	149	154	158	615
Venezuela	151	155	155	156	617
Portugal	154	152	151	160	617
Uruguay	157	154	153	154	618
Czechoslovakia	151	157	156	163	627
Sweden	162	156	157	154	629
Morocco	168	161	155	166	650
Rumania	170	172	167	175	684

(PRIZE MONEY: United States—$1,000 each; Japan—$500 each; Argentina—$400 each; Thailand, Formosa—$100 each.)

INDIVIDUAL COMPETITION

	SCORE				TOTAL
Lee Trevino, *U.S.*	71	70	69	65	275
Roberto de Vicenzo, *Argentina*	69	68	74	65	276
Hsieh Yung Yo, *Formosa*	66	70	69	72	277
Sukree Onsham, *Thailand*	67	73	67	70	277
Orville Moody, *U.S.*	67	70	71	69	277
Ben Arda, *Philippines*	70	69	69	70	278
Takaaki Kono, *Japan*	72	68	72	67	279
Haruo Yasuda, *Japan*	70	72	70	69	281
Martin Roesink, *Holland*	71	72	69	71	283
Ramon Sota, *Spain*	71	71	72	69	283
Roberto Bernardini, *Italy*	73	71	71	70	285
Angel Gallardo, *Spain*	73	69	72	71	285

	SCORES				TOTAL
Leopoldo Ruiz, *Argentina*	72	70	71	72	285
Suchin Suvannapongse, *Thailand*	72	67	73	73	285
Hsu Chi San, *Formosa*	72	69	70	74	285
Flory Van Donck, *Belgium*	74	72	71	69	286
Eleuterio Nival, *Philippines*	70	75	67	74	286
Rogelio Gonzalez, *Colombia*	71	70	72	74	287
Bill Dunk, *Australia*	71	71	74	71	287
Peter Thomson, *Australia*	73	68	74	72	287
Donald Swaelens, *Belgium*	75	73	70	69	287
Alfonso Bohorquez, *Colombia*	72	74	71	71	288
Ramon Cruz, *Mexico*	69	72	70	77	288
Brian Huggett, *Wales*	73	71	72	72	288
Dave Thomas, *Wales*	76	69	72	71	288
Mya Aye, *Burma*	73	71	72	72	288
Peter Townsend, *England*	73	72	74	69	288
Mohamed Said Moussa, *Egypt*	75	73	68	72	288
John Lister, *New Zealand*	72	73	71	72	288
Al Balding, *Canada*	72	72	70	74	288
Bobby Cole, *South Africa*	70	76	71	71	288
George Will, *Scotland*	76	71	73	69	289
*Klaus Nierlich, *Austria*	75	69	72	73	289
Luiz Carlos Pinto, *Brazil*	76	72	72	69	289
Lee Il An, *Korea*	72	74	72	71	289
Graham Henning, *South Africa*	72	73	74	70	289
Francisco Cerda, *Chile*	73	75	74	67	289
Hans Heiser, *Germany*	73	74	73	70	290
George Knudson, *Canada*	71	74	74	71	290
Peter Butler, *England*	76	73	72	70	291
Umberto Rocha, *Brazil*	73	71	75	72	291
Bernabe Fajardo, *Peru*	70	70	77	75	292
Roger Cotton, *France*	74	73	73	72	292
Juan Neri, *Mexico*	71	73	76	73	293
Phua Thin Kiay, *Singapore*	74	69	76	74	293
Herluf Hansen, *Denmark*	72	74	73	74	293
*Choo Kwan Choong, *Malaysia*	70	70	78	75	293
Alfonso Angelini, *Italy*	72	73	76	73	294
Abdel Halim M. *Egypt*	75	71	76	72	294
*Allan Yamamoto, *Hawaii*	75	75	72	73	295
Bernard Gallacher, *Scotland*	77	72	73	75	297
Kim Sung Yun, *Korea*	74	74	75	74	297
Terry Kendall, *New Zealand*	76	74	73	74	297
Patrick Cros, *France*	73	77	76	71	297
Juan Gonzalez, *Puerto Rico*	77	73	72	75	297
Christie O'Connor, *Ireland*	72	73	75	78	298
Jesus Rodriguez, *Puerto Rico*	76	76	74	73	299
Alvin Liau, *Singapore*	76	76	70	78	300
Toni Kugelmuller, *Germany*	77	73	76	75	301
Salim B. Denin, *Indonesia*	75	75	75	76	301

	SCORES			TOTAL
John Sotiropoulos, *Greece*	79	73	75	75	302
Ossi Gartenmaier, *Austria*	80	72	75	76	303
Juan Sereda, *Uruguay*	81	73	75	75	304
Shadi Lal, *India*	76	76	79	73	304
Manuel Ribeiro, *Portugal*	74	74	77	79	304
Ruda Valji, *India*	74	76	79	76	305
*Jalal Deran, *Malaysia*	81	78	74	72	305
Angel Sanchez, *Venezuela*	77	77	75	78	307
Bernhard Cordonier, *Switzerland*	76	74	78	79	307
Manuel Morales, *Chile*	76	76	77	78	307
Jacky Bonvin, *Switzerland*	78	75	76	79	308
Ake Bergkvist, *Sweden*	77	75	81	76	309
James Kinsella, *Ireland*	79	76	79	75	309
Henning Kristensen, *Denmark*	81	74	78	76	309
Cruz Garcia, *Venezuela*	74	78	80	78	310
Hugo Nari, *Peru*	82	76	80	72	310
Azis Narwi, *Indonesia*	79	81	77	74	311
*Stefano Vafiadis, *Greece*	76	74	78	83	311
Bertus Van Mook, *Holland*	77	78	81	76	312
*Jan Kunsta, *Czechoslovakia*	76	75	79	83	313
Joaquim Rodriguez, *Portugal*	80	78	74	81	313
*Jiri Dvorak, *Czechoslovakia*	75	82	77	80	314
Pascual Viola, *Uruguay*	76	81	78	79	314
Jerry Johnston, *Hawaii*	81	76	80	78	315
Paul Tomita, *Rumania*	77	81	79	80	317
Tony Lidholm, *Sweden*	85	81	76	78	320
Meskine Hajjaj, *Morocco*	82	80	78	83	323
Malouki M'Bark, *Morocco*	86	81	77	83	327
*Kyaw Nyunt, *Burma*	81	80	83	83	327
Dumitru Munteanu, *Rumania*	93	91	88	95	367

* Amateur

(PRIZE MONEY: Trevino—$1,000; de Vicenzo—$500; Hsieh Yung Yo, Onchum and Moody—$200 each.)

WORLD SERIES OF GOLF

FIRESTONE COUNTRY CLUB
Akron, Ohio
September 6—7
Purse...$77,500
Par: 35, 35—70...7,180 yards

	SCORE		TOTAL	MONEY
Orville Moody	74	67	141	$50,000
George Archer	74	69	143	15,000
Ray Floyd	72	73	145	6,250
Tony Jacklin, *Great Britain*	73	72	145	6,250

THE END

Quality for People
Pooras Street Branch
Tel No 772708